MORS BRITANNICA

Mors Britannica

Lifestyle and Death-Style in Britain Today

DOUGLAS J. DAVIES

OXFORD

UNIVERSITY PRESS

OXFORD

UNIVERSITY PRESS

Great Clarendon Street, Oxford, OX2 6DP,
United Kingdom

Oxford University Press is a department of the University of Oxford.
It furthers the University's objective of excellence in research, scholarship,
and education by publishing worldwide. Oxford is a registered trade mark of
Oxford University Press in the UK and in certain other countries

Published in the United States of America by Oxford University Press
198 Madison Avenue, New York, NY 10016, United States of America

British Library Cataloguing in Publication Data

Data available

Library of Congress Control Number: 2015940143

ISBN 978-0-19-964497-1

Printed and bound by
CPI Group (UK) Ltd, Croydon, CR0 4YY

Links to third party websites are provided by Oxford in good faith and
for information only. Oxford disclaims any responsibility for the materials
contained in any third party website referenced in this work.

Acknowledgements

Many networked relationships with funeral professionals and academics engaged in what is now often called Death Studies underlie this volume. The British Cremation Society and International Cremation Federation, represented by their recently retired general secretary Mr Roger Arber, have long supported my research, allowing the Archives of the British Cremation Society to be lodged at Durham University's Library—accessible to all researchers—and in funding that helped create *The Encyclopedia of Cremation* (Davies and Mates 2005). The occasion of the Archive's hand-over when the Society's President, Richard—the late Sixth Earl Grey—and Roger Arber shared a most convivial dinner at St Chad's College here in Durham is entirely memorable.

As for natural burial, I thank Mr Ken West MA (Hon. Dunelm), MBE, for his help and insight as the prime mover of this funeral innovation in Britain, not least his participation in the launch event of *Natural Burial* (Davies and Rumble 2012). That study was the developed outcome of an Arts and Humanities and Economic and Social Research Council collaborative doctoral award that enabled Dr Hannah Rumble to work on the Arbory Trust Natural Burial site of Barton Glebe near Cambridge. I especially acknowledge Hannah's work, scholarship, and friendship over some years, not least her initiative for the film *Natural Burial and the Church of England* (2012) undertaken by ethnographic film maker Sarah Thomas, and from which I draw material in this present volume. Members of the Arbory Trust were very supportive of that venture, not least Dr Matthew Lavis and the late Right Revd Professor Stephen Sykes, a key ecclesiastic behind the Barton Glebe site when Bishop of Ely. As a colleague at Durham's Theology and Religion Department and Principal of St John's College he was always supportive of our work. His funeral in Durham Cathedral in October 2014 witnessed, probably for the first time, a noted Anglican dignitary owning a wickerwork coffin prepared for subsequent interment at Barton Glebe. At Durham I also thank Michael Sadgrove as Dean, and his Canon Colleagues, especially the Revd Dr Rosalind Brown, for supporting a study of prayer requests made at this great Cathedral. I also thank Mr David Childs RN (rtd.), CBE, an inspirational and most creative individual for his direct knowledge as the founding figure behind the National Memorial Arboretum.

The Leverhulme Trust was generous in supporting the *Cremation in Scotland Project* whose Research Fellows engaged in this venture through Durham University's Centre for Death and Life Study, and have, for some years, added much to my grasp of death's interdisciplinary possibilities, notably, architectural historian Professor Hilary Granger, the Revd Dr Peter Jupp with his historical, sociological, and theological knowledge, Dr Gordon Raeburn and his theological research and, not least, Mr Stephen White whose knowledge of cremation law is exemplary. More recently Dr Bosco Bae has cheerfully and carefully assisted with various elements of the present volume.

I thank Professor Richard Dawkins, not simply for an enjoyable conversation during a perambulation of the Barton Glebe site during the production of a television programme on death but, more particularly here, for permission to use survey material generated by the Richard Dawkins Foundation (Tables 2.1, 8.1). Similar thanks for survey material is due to the Theos Think Tank for Table 2.2, and the YouGov organization for Tables 2.4–2.9. For information contained in Tables 3.1 and 3.2 I acknowledge the help and support of The Cremation Society of Great Britain and its official journal *Pharos International*.

Finally, I acknowledge Durham University, my Departmental and Centre colleagues, and Hatfield College for recently appointing me a Research Fellow and supporting research ventures. During the gestation period of this book I valued a Visiting Research Fellowship at Helsinki University's Institute of Advanced Studies and, during part of 2014 when this book took marked shape, I benefited greatly from a Visiting Fellowship at Harris Manchester College, Oxford for which I warmly thank its Principal, the Revd. Dr Ralph Waller, and other Fellows—that College's new tower being a timely catalyst of endeavour.

Durham 2015

Contents

List of Tables

Introduction

Lifestyle and Death-Style in Britain Today

Life runs rampant in the relatively thin biosphere clothing the surface of the Earth, its cells empowered by chloroplasts converting sunshine into energy in plants and mitochondria achieving energy production in animals. The intricate complexities of DNA and its interplay with challenging environments becomes this force of nature that we abstractly describe as 'life', whose myriad forms include humans and our evolution. Life as a whole fostered human social life, whose own 'force' will be invoked throughout this volume as the social dynamics through which cultures adapt to both natural and social environments.

Death is, similarly, all-pervasive, and integral to plant, animal, and other forms of life, with its living processes of decay enriching environments with nutrients for growth. In domains of conscious awareness, possibly in some animals, and certainly in the self-awareness of human beings, death prompts both positive and negative emotional values, with cultural interpretations of death frequently transforming negative feeling into positive by positing post-mortal environments of survival. Whether or not there is some evolutionary advantage associated with afterlife beliefs in that they help to produce a stable frame around the human proclivity for meaning-making is a question of its own, part of which I pursued in a previous study when arguing that death became a part of the biocultural environment to which humans have adapted, largely through religious beliefs in an afterlife.[1] In this volume my intention is less speculative, taking the different direction of asking how the lifestyles of particular groups correlate with what we identify as their death-styles.[2]

To adopt these lifestyle and death-style motifs is, then, to take organic life energy not only into its general manifestation of social force but into the

---

[1] Douglas J. Davies (1997: 1–7).
[2] Douglas J. Davies (2005: 129); Davies and Rumble (2012: 121–4). Convention insists that I write of death-style and not deathstyle to parallel lifestyle.

particular manifestation or style of social force adopted by cultural groups. We will address this in a variety of ways, not least by invoking the notion of the Establishment, focused on in chapter 3, as a concept influencing 'style', including aspects of media-carried funerary rites in the UK in general: other societies will, doubtless, possess their own equivalent categories.[3] Another idiomatic image that will complement that of 'style' concerns the 'windows' opened onto British society by different forms of dying and death. Moreover, two major social institutions covering British death in the twentieth century were those of the Church of England and the National Health Service (NHS). Indeed, both the Church of England, along with some allied denominations, and the British NHS, along with the way the latter has in some ways taken over from the former, will appear at many points in this volume when death is being considered. It is certainly the case that, as far as death is concerned, no study of religion in contemporary Britain can ignore the interplay between two of the largest social institutions of the land.

While the Church has long engaged in the theme of salvation and eternal wellbeing, the modern NHS has increasingly dealt with health and temporal wellbeing for the majority of the public. Over roughly the same period since the 1950s and 1960s the decline of Church influence in society has occupied intense secularization debates. The rise of the Welfare State and its flagship institutions of regional hospitals and local general practitioners, however, is largely beyond dispute as far as public welfare is concerned. Various religion-linked notions of spirituality have also emerged during this period and it is important yet curious to note that the NHS has, more recently, also developed its own interest in spirituality quite apart from religious settings. This has generated what might be called a therapeutic form of 'new secularization' and a 'new spirituality'. Since dying and death have largely been the preserve of the Church for centuries, but have, increasingly, been approached through the NHS since the middle of the twentieth century, it is understandable that the relationship between Church and Hospital—if I might be allowed that short-hand expression—should interplay in a volume on religion in contemporary Britain, and not only as far as death is concerned. Other hopes and aspirations of personal, family, and community life have also been vested in the NHS.

Subsequent chapters will not, however, single out only the NHS but, following the fact that religion has tended to be the major vehicle for dealing with death—especially funerals—in Great Britain, they will ask how the evolution of funeral forms may reflect the changing role of religion. This will help contribute towards an understanding of the sociology of religion, with following chapters considering the British adoption of cremation from the 1880s; the development of personalized ritual with cremated remains,

---

[3] Throughout this volume synonymous references are made to the Establishment, 'Establish-ment', establishment, or 'establishment' as context requires.

especially from the 1970s; and the emergence of woodland or ecological burial from the 1990s. Issues of assisted dying and euthanasia also highlight a renewed engagement with mortality and give a general sense that 'talking about death' is more generally accepted—a view reinforced by extensive news coverage of celebrity deaths, natural disasters, terrorism, suicide bombers, civil wars, and forms of genocide. Nevertheless, despite such constant listing of deaths and the desire of some groups to foster death-talk in the population at large, there remains a strong cultural reticence over our mortality which peaks over suicide. Ironically, however, that embarrassed silence that suicide prompts amongst the chattering classes is accompanied by a boldness in advocating assisted suicide or doctor-assisted dying, perhaps in a fashion that echoes a previous generation's debates on the adoption of abortion. Here the themes of mortality and vitality stand in contest to one another, with the desire for life extending into a desire to control death.

It is precisely such complexity that raises the theme of world view or life view,[4] which will appear frequently in this volume, of the dynamic interplay of a people's lifestyle and death-style. For those interested in some of the underlying theoretical drivers of this volume I mention at the outset the lead advocated by André Droogers and Anton Harskamp in their attempt to set 'religious studies' in a wider frame of 'worldview studies', one that valuably contextualizes some of the potentially unhelpful discussions over 'religion', 'spirituality', and 'secularization'.[5] Another theoretical catalyst underlying the eclecticism evident in this volume echoes Dan Miller's 'extremist' anthropological challenge 'to our common-sense opposition between the person and the thing, the animate and inanimate, the subject and the object', while seeking to 'demonstrate the consequences of the universal for the particular and of the particular for the universal by equal devotion to the empathetic understanding and encompassment of both', and overall seeking 'understanding and insight' while trying 'to avoid reductionism'.[6] In bridging these divides I draw upon my previous work on emotions and identity in religious communities;[7] on numerous aspects of my death-studies research that will appear in due course; and on other theorists whose perspectives will also emerge as this volume on the interplay of lifestyle and death-style in Britain proceeds.

The interaction of these elements, critically observed for their proximity or distance, will serve as its own index of contemporary Britain where cultural changes involve distinctions between traditional religion, secularization, and emergent forms of spirituality, all of which involve emotions as fear, longing,

---

[4] Adler and Farndon (1999: 65), refer to 'context of situation' for Malinowski, 'language games' for Wittgenstein, 'worldview' for Humboldt, and Whorf's linguistic context of language.

[5] Droogers and Harskamp (2014).

[6] Miller (2010: 5, 10, 154). I have long shared his secret 'affection for functionalism' (2010: 147).

[7] Douglas J. Davies (2011).

and a sense of loss, rising in waves when death marks the contemporary embodiment of our humanity. These world orientations, expressed in old and new ritual practices, frequently engage death in the hopeful desire that loving and other relationships, community, and identity be not rendered meaningless; still, they do so through emotions and rituals revealing a certain uneasiness with death's slippery framing of the early twenty-first century.

To gain some purchase on this social complexity, the following chapters draw from a largely anthropological–sociological perspective complemented by historical, literary, philosophical, psychological, and theological insights. More abstract, academic, theories will engage with ordinary knowledge as scholarly 'papers' partner newspapers in opening windows on life in death's presence, spotlighting in the process contemporary life's profound irony, viz. that while many individual lives are relatively untouched by death until their maturity, their media news and viewing leisure time is entirely death-pervaded. Whether in world news where real corpses so easily litter alien streets that television blanks the scene lest people be upset or offended, or in popular entertainment where 'fictional' murder customarily demands an autopsy scene with cosmetically created corpses, death becomes only strangely familiar. This duplicity poses the poignant question of 'death' as an identifiable category; it also raises the shifting backdrop of life orientations captured in terms of traditional religion, modern spirituality, and the secular, or the cultural mixing of the three.

RELIGION, SPIRITUALITY, AND THE SECULAR

All these concerns are important for this volume, presented as its own form of social scientific account of religion in Britain. However, instead of following classical works in spending much time defining terms and establishing sharp classifications, I seek descriptions of humanity's meaning-making as it integrates ideas and emotions in the forging of individual and group identities under the framing influence of distinctive narratives, all enhanced by a provision of some sense of destiny.[8] Religious studies have gone some way in showing how the well-established religions of the world develop distinctive patterns of meaning along historical pathways of ritual and doctrine, bringing a sense of destiny to people at the emotional and intellectual level in alliance with political–economic, philosophical, hierarchical, and geographical factors.[9] As for the idea of spirituality, it also reflects an emotional and

---

[8] See Douglas J. Davies (1984: 61–76), which includes Wilhelm Dupré's notion of religion as an 'intensive quality of the process of symbolization in general' (1975: 139).

[9] See Weber ([1922]1965: 171) for the felt emotional unity of knowledge and volitional mood.

intellectual stream of making sense of life and conferring a quality of depth to existence whether approached within the corporate structures of major traditions—religious or secular—or as a more personal dimension beyond institutional control.[10] In this sense spirituality can be religious or secular, or, in the reality of complex societies, a combination of elements derived from either or from wider cultural fields. The secular frame is one that can also vary from an outlook that expressly rejects religious accounts of 'reality' to one of simple disregard of religious life views. So, whether concerned with world religions, the UK's NHS, local authority provision of personal care, or individuals and their private practice of life-meaning, this volume may need to consider the several concerns of formal religious doctrines and liturgical rites, psychologically driven notions of 'mindfulness' as espoused in some healthcare contexts, and secular motifs and their ritual expression in funerals.

And it is with funerals and emotional notions of grief that these contested ideas of religion, spirituality, and secularity find their place in the following chapters. Indeed, dying, death, afterlife beliefs, and the role of grief and memory in human experience all highlight the issues often raised in definitions of religion, spirituality, and secularism.[11] Still, as already intimated, this volume is less concerned with the fine-tuning of definitions than with the fact that abstract notions of religion, spirituality, or secularism, are often far from distinct in everyday life, especially where people define themselves as spiritual but not religious, or as secular and spiritual, or as Christian but not denominationally tagged. Indeed, it may even be that particular contexts trigger one orientation more than another.

Such loose labels are reminders that words capture cultural shifts of emotional expression and shifting preferences for one mood base over another, especially when core values are concerned as with assisted dying in chapter 8. This volume takes these emotional bases seriously by aligning life's meaning in relation to death with the general notion of social force that influences emotions and social values. This approach to social force is much like that 'field of power' underlying Pierre Bourdieu's outlook that extends 'from the economic field, at one end, to the field of cultural production' at the other, albeit with greater emphasis on the role of emotion death and grief.[12] This perspective on people surrounded by influences that take distinctive form comes to cultural expression through ritual–symbolic events surrounding dying, death, and bereavement. These moments provide occasion to deploy the notion of the sacred, an almost archaic idea that is, however, of

---

[10] Tarlow's comment on a 'considerable resistance to the study of emotion and experience in the academic world' largely vanished with the turn of the twenty-first century (1991: 31), cf. Prinz (2004: vii–ix).

[11] See Thate (2013: 195–245) for memory and memory theory's considerable literature.

[12] See Wacquant (1996: xi), and Bourdieu ([1989] 1996).

surprisingly contemporary significance in framing life's qualitative depths for people who describe themselves, variously, as traditionally religious, spiritual but not religious, or secular, or as some mix of these descriptors.

SOCIAL FORCE

As human beings, then, we live and die in fields of social force where tradition, community, family, and peer pressures forge cultural expectations and where fashion helps filter these dynamic influences. Concurrently, symbols and ritual expressing core values tend to be framed as religious or spiritual in nature and contribute to our sense of identity. Even to speak of such events as 'traditional' is to invest them with a status similar to those of the 'religious' or 'spiritual'. This force-field pervades our entire social world, from international politics to private dreams, and it resonates psychologically while fluctuating in intensity moment by moment throughout our life course. In cultural terms, it inheres in Britain's civic, legal, military, and educational culture; it sparkles in sporting and entertainment celebrities; endures in historical, mythical, and divine figures; and in an overarching sense also engenders a vibrant territory of urban, rural, public, domestic, occupational, and employment domains, in the media and consumerism and in aspects of private life. The following chapters also assume that this social force exerts significant influence in and through the British 'Establishment' at large and, by social imitation, in numerous other institutions. This force also links dead and living kin, for one of its sources lies in each individual's sense of awareness of others that, in itself, is grounded in people's networks of relationships.

Such a preoccupation with 'force' could lead this volume into numerous well-known theoretical analyses of force and power, a temptation avoided so as to keep this volume open to general interests whilst also pursuing some less-followed scholarly paths. One such is the Dutch sociologist-philosopher Anton Zijderveld's classical sociological approach to 'force' focused on religion as a meaning-making process and on the institutions of modern society that increasingly replaced religion's role. His argument on the relationship between individuals and the bureaucratic institutions of modern society viewed 'modern bureaucracy as the general coercive force in pluralistic society that keeps this society together as a functionally integrated whole', and stated that 'force in pluralistic society has taken over from religion its integrative function'.[13]

This approach to force embraces its capacity to enhance or deplete our sense of identity, especially when emotion-flowing domains encounter death,

---

[13] Anton C. Zijderveld, born 1937 ([1970] 1972: 132).

with bereavement framing the disruption we characterize as grief. Funerals and patterns of mourning all mark this dynamic interplay of psychological, social, and environmental factors that forges the bond between individual and society and helps assuage fear. And fear will reappear throughout this volume as a part of human life with which 'religions' have much engaged as they highlight and manage selected emotions. Not to be ignored in such grief-shifting force-fields are the memory-carrying moments, words, and objects left behind by those who die and that enter into the reformulated lives of their surviving relatives and friends. One theoretical perspective reflecting past and ongoing links with the dead, and which underlies many emotions and patterns of social force is that of reciprocity or gift theory, whose significance will surface in numerous chapters, not least as a key aspect in notions of identity.

THE MORTALITY WINDOW

Identity interplaying with the theme of social force in the life-challenge of meaning-making in the environment of death will, then, integrate a variety of foundational ideas derived from anthropology and sociology to create its own account of religion in Britain. As indicated, death-related events become windows opening upon a social world of forces that make, remake, remove, and transform people's selves. Though it might be tempting to describe this volume as primarily a sociology of religion approached through death, that would limit its scope and yield to one discipline more insight than it intrinsically commands. Accordingly, this volume also adopts historical and theological lenses alongside psychological and literary insights in an eclectic approach that reflects the complexity of human existence and acknowledges the problematic single-method academic tendency to bring unwarranted order to life situations, including contexts of order-defying anxiety and fear. In my understanding both sociology and anthropology are deeply interlinked in the approach to social life,[14] while the inclusion of psychological, historical, and philosophical ideas also reflects my concern with the broad fields of what we frequently identify as the history and phenomenology of religion as elements substantiating the domain of Religious Studies.

Still, some valuable direction will be given to the following chapters if we allow these various disciplines to influence them through a set of paired themes, viz. (i) vitality–mortality; (ii) meaning-making and narrative; (iii) cultural intensification and identity; (iv) embodiment and sense of presence;

---

[14] I take the Durkheimian theme of the individual–society bond and the Weberian concern with thought and action as firm complements in dealing with individual and group identity, orientation to the world, and to the place of emotion and ideology in it.

(v) dual sovereignty and social force; and (vi) the mysteriously uncanny. Explained in detail in chapter 1, these topics generate their own—albeit limited—form of social theory, linking the motifs of lifestyle and death-style as constituent elements of an overarching cultural wisdom focused largely upon Great Britain over recent decades.

CULTURAL WISDOM AND MEANING

Together, these processes allow an approach to life and death that is applicable to traditional religion, to secularism, and to other configurations described in terms of spirituality. They ensure that all life views are seen not simply as rational, philosophical, or doctrinal entities but as more complex, emotion-pervaded perspectives that combine in 'cultural wisdom', itself a cumulative pattern of understanding generating the 'sense of things' that emerge over time within any society.[15] Indeed, this very notion of the 'sense of things' encapsulates the intimate conjoining of thought and feeling captured in, for example, the notion of 'presence' that so often underlies human embodiment. Cultural wisdom and the periodic intensification of the sense of things will be shown to embrace traditional forms of church, denominational, and sect-like belief and practice, as well as popular spirituality, secularism, and civic ceremony. The way a society frames its knowledge of the world reveals its wisdom. For long durations in Europe this cultural knowledge has been framed and managed by 'religion' and today the notion of 'spirituality' has arisen to do the same. Alongside these, however, we also find competing cultural explanations vying with the religion–spirituality forms of life explanation, as in science or political activism. Brief comment will be made on the science element, though politics will lie largely, though not entirely, beyond our scope. The aim of this volume, then, is to provide a distinctive anthropological–sociological account of contemporary British religion through a perspective derived from cultural concerns with death, dying, mourning, and the dead. This focus avoids the tendency of many discipline-constrained scholars to either ignore death in their wider historical or socio-logical accounts of British life, or to focus relatively exclusively upon dying, death, and funerals, to the loss of some other social factors.

So, the unremarkable theoretical assumption underlying this account of death in Britain is that meaning-making comprises the prime human

---

[15] Many definitions of 'wisdom' are feasible, from 'the fear of the Lord' as 'the beginning of wisdom' (Psalm 111: 10), to Cicero's 'Wisdom is the knowledge of good and evil and of the things that are neither good nor evil' (1972: 207). I take it to mean a community's shared insight into life.

project,[16] with 'religion' and 'spirituality' being its subsets, just as science, politics, or philosophy could be pursued as their own framed subsets of meaning-making. Secularization, too, offers its own form of meaning-making, whether pursued separately from traditional religion or in negative response to it: meaning-making is the constant human factor while 'religion', 'spirituality', or the 'secular' are its culturally variable forms of expression.

To say this is not to engage in the simple redundancy in which 'meaning' means nothing because it means everything, but is to show that the human drive for meaning takes up available resources and deploys them in a great variety of ways in a creative response to cultural time and place. Some involve extensive theologies and philosophies extended to embrace the whole of the cosmos and beyond, while others focus upon life in this world, or even upon a single family or individual life. Embedded within the notion of 'meaning-making' is the understanding that emotional and cognitive elements intimately combine in the 'meaning' that arises from our human engagement with each other and the world around us, not least in coping with fear in its many forms. For many religious devotees, belief in and a sensed relationship with a supernatural domain heighten the sense of meaning. Towler's insightful study, to which we return in chapter 9, expressed this well in arguing that 'one of the most striking features of the supernatural is that it introduced more order than there would be without it:' for him, 'order on a cosmic scale' is just what 'religious certainty' engenders.[17]

So, while this mortality window will often disclose complex sets of behaviour popularly identified as religious, it will also reveal other aspects of life that frequently self-identify in terms of spirituality, or even as secular ventures. Such a death-driven account of meaning-making allows us to see how, at different times and amongst different groups of people, 'meaning-making' becomes an intensified process, rooted in sacred or other texts and ritual or driven by the meaning-making route of politics or science. Here 'fundamentalism' appears as one form of energetic intensification focused on traditional texts or customs, while 'liberalism' tends to focus on human freedom and individual wellbeing. For some scholars 'religion' is too problematic a term; they see it as a notion driven by many hidden assumptions and agendas and prefer to abandon the word.[18] I will retain it, however, because it remains important for many wider contemporary concerns because of its interplay with such notions as 'fundamentalism', 'spirituality', and atheism, and because, in the British context, the cultural history of death has frequently been embedded within ecclesiastical thought, rites, and places.

---

[16] Towler (1984: 1–18) summarizes sociological theories of religion and 'meaning'.
[17] Towler (1984: 103–4).
[18] Wilfred Cantwell Smith (1963); McCutcheon (1997); Fitzgerald (2000); Beyer (2006).

Theoretically speaking, this 'religion' issue has been an ongoing question in my own mind since the later 1970s when, following issues of the sociology of knowledge, I began to wonder how the general human desire to make meaning in the world resulted in ideas of world religions whilst largely ignoring the life-worlds of local traditions.[19] More recently I have asked how emotions engage with 'religious' phenomena to provide an identity intensified through a sense of destiny.[20] Accordingly, some of this present volume on death will deal with the much debated but practically irresistible word, 'religion', while also discussing the pluriform notion of 'spirituality'.

What we so readily call 'religion' has frequently possessed dying, death, funerary rites, and afterlife beliefs as key features of its ideology and ritual. Indeed, major 'world religion' traditions pay dying, death, and death rites considerable due, while concerns with wider issues of spirituality also frequently apply to dying, death, and funerals. This makes it all the more strange that numerous sociological studies that devote much analysis to the nature of religion, spirituality, and secularization in Western societies often reveal a relative absence of concern over mortality. To some degree, death's sequestration by a vibrant and interdisciplinary domain of 'death studies' offsets this sociological isolation and is currently generating an exciting cluster of studies ranging from archaeology and art, through history and theology, to the ethics of mortality and the increasingly significant sphere of palliative and end-of-life care. This is exemplified in Britain by the Association for the Study of Death and Society, formed in 2009, preceded by its allied journal—*Mortality*—launched in 1996, and the international 'Death, Dying, and Disposal' conferences whose eleventh biennial event was held in 2013.

This academic interest parallels growing public concern over assisted suicide or doctor-administered death; issues highlighting the complexity and social paradoxes typified by the competing notions of sanctity of life, medical ethics, justice, and human dignity. No account of religion or spirituality in Britain can ignore the complex interplay of theological, ideological, ethical, and common-sense drivers behind these life and death matters that flood the media and touch the lives of the population at large. For our purposes, then, the labels of 'religion' and 'spirituality', and the same can be said for humanism or atheism, will serve as qualifying frames for the intrinsic pictures of feeling and thinking that combine to give a person the 'sense of things' in life as embedded in 'cultural wisdom'. This creative accumulation of knowing how to frame and respond to life circumstances might also be captured in the notion of 'tradition', whether emanating from the British Establishment in its several professional modes, or from family and local community life.

---

[19] Douglas J. Davies (1984).   [20] Douglas J. Davies (2011).

Meaning in Time

While it is entirely unsurprising for this social scientifically driven study of human activity to be rooted in meaning-making, this becomes poignantly obvious when dealing with death and the fact that during the course of a day, week, month, year, or lifetime, the graph of 'meaning' rises or falls as a sense of life's significance is intensified or depleted. In that process the complex interplay of emotional and rational elements of 'meaning' does not restrict 'meaning' only to theological, philosophical, or rational forms of intelligibility.

Personalia

All readers, and myself as author, come to this volume with our own experiences or anticipated experiences of dying, death, and mourning, and their consequences for that sense of meaning in life. Many will have experienced peak moments of stabbing grief, depressed moods of mourning, and moments of both regret-tinged and of fond memory, as well as those sparks of hope and renewed appetite for tomorrow and its outcomes. Some will frame such awareness in traditional religious perspectives; others in notions of family or network support sustained by poetic, philosophical, or common-sense values, whether or not framed as a form of 'spirituality'. Many will also find support from family and friendship networks, as well as from health service provision in hospital, home, or hospice care, and from the professional services of funeral directors, clergy, and civil or secular celebrants.

This volume works from such contexts to build its own complex picture of British religion, drawing heavily from some anthropological and sociological ideas but avoiding sharp divides between traditional disciplines, and welcoming psychological, theological, historical, and literary sources in accounting for the variety of social attitudes on dying, death, mourning, and memorializing the dead. This eclecticism is needed to bring mortality from a periphery occupied by a very small number of 'death-studies' sociologists, historians, and theologians, to a centre-stage position already occupied by health-care professionals and by both established and more recently innovative ritual practitioners. This enormous task will, inevitably, be accomplished only in part.

Human animals living and dying

The following chapters seek not to lose sight of ourselves as human animals in social dress—folk whose engagement with the world engenders cultural life in ways that belie any causal flow from act to thought or thought to act. Our sense of identity and the myriad acts that creatively express it reveal a vitality empowering our imagination whilst being simultaneously powered by it. This 'vitality' will focus within personal life the much-rehearsed notion of 'power' that frequents analyses of social status, gender, politics, and economics. Moreover, the pairing of vitality with mortality as a primal and primary bonding in our existence facilitates an explicit analysis of emotion—something of real importance for any study of death. It will also, for example, open ways of thinking about military death, sacrifice, and wellbeing related to the NHS. Still, 'power', as an inescapable secondary concern, will be addressed through the anthropologist Rodney Needham's model of 'dual sovereignty' with its dynamic bonding of mystical and jural forms of 'authority'.[21] As also intimated above, the other inclusion of a power motif will come from Ernesto de Martino's theory of 'presence', and also from other long-established theoretical influences derived from Max Weber, Robert Hertz, Emile Durkheim, with Mary Douglas and more recent scholars such as Tim Ingold and Daniel Miller also playing significant parts.

FUNERALS AS 'RELIGIOUS' BEHAVIOUR

Turning to the specific theme of this volume we find that early twenty-first century British funerals are conducted not only by clergy of the mainstream Christian or other major religions but by members of the British Humanist Association, independently trained civil celebrants, occasionally by funeral directors, and, sometimes, by family members themselves. This diversity reflects social change and could mean that, if we defined 'religion' in sociological terms that included the performance of funerary ritual, the British Humanist Association, for example, would seem to become 'religious'—much against their will. Until recent decades Church of England clergy and those of allied denominations have, indeed, monopolized death rites, but times are changing. While it would seem fair, and easily understood by many, to describe new and alternative ritual leaders as 'secular', and propose that their ceremonies be taken as a significant index of secularization in Britain, others would strongly object and insist on introducing the idea of 'spirituality' into the debate. This interplay of belief, changed attitudes, and diversity of ritualizing of death is played out today against an intense culture history in which dying, death, and funerary liturgy occupied a central role amongst the British populace and its ecclesiastical personnel, from medieval times, through the English Reformation, and into our contemporary experiences of

---

[21] Needham takes precedence over Foucault because his work was driven more by social research and less by philosophical–literary–historical speculation. See also Weber ([c.1910] 1991: 159–79).

attitudinal and behavioural diversity. Some of these complex issues of trad-itional Christian spirituality set alongside themes of indifference towards religion in secular worlds where it is also seen as irrelevant are specifically addressed in chapter 4.

Accordingly, these concepts—religion, secularization, spirituality—will all play significant parts in this volume, signposting past practice and new social trends. They mark social changes that touch the emotional–ideological lives of Britons and invite an account of the interplay of lifestyle and death-style. Death rites and dying's emotional environs become windows upon patterns of British cultural life; indeed, 'cultural life' is the abiding concept that frames all others. For religion, secularization, and spirituality are only modes of culture as that creative complexity of meaning-making which humans create as an environment of security and flourishing.

As one of these complex terms, 'religion' can refer to so many things that some have wished to do away with it altogether. The problem is not simply one of definition but of recognition that definitions need to embrace different times, places, forms of social life, and the process of individual appropriation of tradition.[22] Max Weber offers an excellent recognition of this issue at the very outset of his *Sociology of Religion*,[23] by saying that 'to define "religion" is not possible at the start of a presentation such as this. Definition can be attempted, if at all, only at the conclusion of the study.' His preference was to highlight 'the conditions and effects of a particular type of social behaviour'.[24]

ECLECTIC COHESION

While following Weber in more ways than one, this volume will engage with numerous other scholars and with ideas from popular culture in a theoretical eclecticism that is risky given standard academic preferences for either the specificity of a diligently pursued theory or for some contemporary theoretical innovation. In opting for a breadth of description and interpretation I reflect both my previous academic interdisciplinary collaborations and my long-term liaison with non-academic service providers of funerals in Britain and beyond.

Such varied resources highlight the fact that numerous sociological accounts focused on British religion have tended to ignore death. Much as the religious theme faded from sociological concern by the mid twentieth century to become a sector interest of some sociologists of religion, so, as mentioned, the

---

[22] W. C. Smith (1963: 186) wished to replace 'religion' with both 'faith' (marking individual experience) and 'cumulative tradition' (marking cultural histories).

[23] Fischoff (1966: x).

[24] Weber ([1922] 1966: 1). Mauss had similar theoretical problems of definition over 'prayer'.

emergence of an interest in the sociology of death found its home in the emergent generic domain of 'death studies' in that century's closing decades. With the emergence of the twenty-first century, however, the importance of death within clinical, medical, and counselling professions has been a significant catalyst for death studies at large in ways that have not been so influential in most other arts and humanities, or even many social science disciplines. In approaching the theme of contemporary British death it is inevitable that those clinical domains will be influential, but so too is the social–historical framing of culture. It is now more obvious than ever that the issue of when history 'ends' and sociology 'begins' is artificial and increasingly redundant as historians, theologians, and others embrace social–psychological ideas within their own formal studies. Sociologist David Martin's assertion that 'so much sociology is over-organised history' is certainly true, while Evans-Pritchard's much earlier essay makes a similar point for history and anthropology.[25] Complexity is, inevitably, the order of the day, granting most scholars great wisdom after the fact but little predictive power.[26] Manuel Castells, for example, describes his sociological work as avoiding 'speculation and social forecasting, building theory from observation, within the limits of my knowledge and competence'; similarly, 'I will not be prescriptive or prophetic, but, rather, I will elaborate on the provisional results of my observation of social movements and political processes.' In practical terms the scribe triumphs over the prophet, and it will be much the same in this volume.

In terms of the complexity of interplay between history and sociology it is also worth adding a note on a different kind of complexity prompted by the notions of 'culture' and 'nature'. Even to use these words in a sentence that implies some radical difference between the two is problematic, for in this volume I regard 'culture' as perfectly 'natural'. Our cultural life, including our attitudes and ritual performance related to death, is 'natural' to us. Culture grows out of and into nature with our naturally cultured selves being both restricted and enhanced by inner and outer environmental factors.[27] One application of this approach is to human emotions understood as biocultural phenomena developing as an interplay of somatic, psychological, and social factors.[28] Such interplay becomes especially important, for example, in the case of grief and of anxiety and fear surrounding death. It is worth emphasizing this deep interplay of dimensions of life given that some approaches can easily reinforce the impression of a gulf existing between 'nature' on the one hand and 'culture' on the other. A slightly analogous polarity has also haunted some

[25] David Martin (2013: 128); Evans-Pritchard (1962).
[26] Castells (2010: xxxviii, 422).
[27] Partly, included in the sociological and philosophical notion of 'projection'.
[28] See 'moral–somatics' Douglas J. Davies (2011: 186–91), and chapter 2.

theology, as when the Christian tradition of revelation is offset against all-too-human 'culture'.[29]

Social Complexity

A historical sense is important for this volume on death in Britain, bearing in mind the late eighteenth- and nineteenth-century industrialization and accompanying intellectual and engineering creativity, and the major wars of the twentieth century and their accompanying social-class and generational shifts. To this must be added the communication-driven world of the twenty-first century where consumerism and apparent cultural safety encounter trust fragmentation in the pillars of society as well as fears of terrorism at its margins. A second look at this time-span reveals social changes grounded in late eighteenth- and nineteenth-century urban slums and what was, in effect, little short of industrial slavery in mine and factory. Religious doubt pervaded small circles of thinkers, with previous scepticism or simple inattention being reinforced or newly focused through social reform, evolutionary thought, and theological–philosophical criticism. Spasmodic religious revivalism produced an urban evangelicalism in denominations that sparkled with sect-like ardour for long periods, whilst newly awakened clergy and some bishops sought to serve increasingly impossible numbers of people. Centuries of urban and market-town parish ministries and churchyards for the dead were ill-prepared for the numbers game of industrial Britain and its slums. The mid-nineteenth-century building of civic cemeteries and, later, the advocacy and introduction of cremation were but two death-focused outcomes of planners and free thinkers adapting to overcrowding which would have consequences for traditional religion. From the mid to late twentieth century, immigration brought Sikh, Hindu, and Muslim groups into the UK and into public prominence. The very late twentieth century then added the innovation of woodland or ecological burial as an available resource, initially preferred by middle-class Britons.

Era-wise, it is ironic that Darwin's evolutionary insights on the survival of the fittest should have been a cultural prelude to the twentieth century's watershed for the British Empire and the clash of actual or erstwhile Christian cultures, not least those of Germany and Russia. The war-widowed and war-orphaned, alongside thousands of their dead in Continental war graves, furnished a strange foundation for a European Economic Community, let alone a European Union in the second half of the twentieth century, albeit

---

[29] As in Helmut Richard Niebuhr (1894–1962), brother of theologian-ethicist Reinhold (1892–1971), who approached culture as 'the artificial, secondary environment' (1951: 32).

one whose identity is increasingly problematic even as its membership grows in the twenty-first century's first decades.

As the later twentieth century progressed, earlier outlier wars and 'troubles' simmered or erupted, whether in the Balkans or Northern Ireland, while heartland Europe, allied with the USA, took notice of emergent Islamic influences in the Middle East and triggered new battles there. Islam not only attracted political–military attention 'abroad' but also in the homelands of the UK and USA, as terrorism disturbed the easy peace of the 1980s–2000s and its otherwise increasingly safe society. Amongst those born post-1945, death assumed an exceptional cultural presence as war memory was gently aroused by small numbers of military deaths in Middle Eastern conflicts, and in a more insistent profile in disease, shadowed by the largely unwelcome anticipation of old age. Cancer, the hospice, and the old people's home, came to symbolize these cultural quagmires where autonomy and an acquired taste for control of one's life slowly submerged. This slow form of decline offered a strange complement to the fast destruction associated with the early upsurge of HIV/AIDS in the last third of the twentieth century.

Then, as might be expected in the new celebrity-culture world of the later twentieth and early twenty-first century, the death of high-profiled figures could focus these diverse worries into massed public expression as with the death of Diana, Princess of Wales, or the intensely covered funeral of Margaret Thatcher. One feature of such events lay in the challenge faced by the media, and also by many academic commentators, in how to explain public emotions. What was very largely missed was the increase in public applause—both metaphorical and in the literal applause of hand-clapping—for celebrities in the such spheres as pop music and sports. Television and massive entertainment venues provided arenas for the increasingly adopted mass applause response of large crowds in public. The innovation in the Diana funeral, inasmuch as there was one, lay in a simple transfer of the accepted though appropriately moderated behaviour of celebrity welcome to a celebrity farewell—a factor noticed in the very public funeral of Lady Thatcher in April 2013. We will return to this in chapter 6, but here that event poses its own question on the relationship between emotion and religion as part of the general approach of a society in which religion has taken primacy of place in dealing with death.

Emotional Variations

Diana's death was glossed time and again by the media in the phrase 'outpouring of grief'. This expression not only offered an immediate refuge for media commentators and journalists alike but also seemed to explain things. One explanation for this lies in Britain's cultural shift in the second half of the twentieth century. The control of emotional display that a class-based, industrial society had exercised had been extensive, necessitated in large measure through the frequency of occasionally disastrous events in warfare, mine, factory, and at sea. The relative luxury of public grief was ill-affordable, with millions suffering in many unrecorded ways as the social value of duty and service subsumed the notion of sacrifice. In terms of Britain's Christian culture-history this was grounded in the devotional sense of Christ's sacrifice of moral duty and its motivation in love. Nowhere was this more evident than in the 'greater love' motif expressly stated on war memorials across the UK after the First and Second World Wars.[30] Men and boys volunteered for military service against public and family backgrounds of duty, shadowed by the possible fear of accusations of cowardice. Mothers, sisters, wives, and wives-to-be mirrored their men folk's actions, with millions eventually suffering their own loss through bereavement, often without the relative comfort of corpse, coffin, and grave.[31] Economic hardship and distress affected many. It was no wonder that the notion of a 'stiff upper lip' could be taken to typify a cultural emotion of class-controlled society in which the Church of England played a major public role, not least in annual memorials of the Wars. Death, memorial, and religion united in a strong preference for controlled emotion.

The religious–cultural preference for emotional control in the face of death easily found ritual expression in the three-hour devotional service of Good Friday which the Church of England developed from some post-Reformation Catholic practice. Here the focus lay in the controlled obedience of Christ to the necessity of self-sacrifice for the purpose of mankind's salvation. The hymns, prayers, and biblical readings reflect this sense of Christ's betrayal, passion, judgement, and death. 'Not my will, but thine be done' being one keystone text of the entire liturgical edifice.[32] The role of silence in these ritual–liturgical events serves as its own commentary on emotional control. The Church of England's own tone of liturgy, grounded in hierarchical leadership and individually controlled response, found it easy to develop these features of sacrificial remembrance. The absence of purgatory-like after-life beliefs, combined with its strong incarnational focus, made it relatively easy to accommodate the 'greater love' motif attributed to the military dead, even if they had been ever so un-churched.

---

[30] 'Greater love hath no man than this, that a man lay down his life for his friends' (John 15:13). Jon Davies (1995) sees this sacrificial motif as engendering a form of 'Euro-Christianity'.

[31] Designed by a Briton, though not in the UK, the Anzac war memorial in Sydney depicts women holding above their heads a dead soldier in a crucifixion-style pose.

[32] Luke 22: 42.

The NHS

Then, from roughly 1945 to 1965, the emotional scene changed, partly through the rise of the post-war generation, and partly through political–economic social reform in the creation of the Welfare State with its educational restructuring and the innovative NHS of 1948. This health-care provision became an enormously significant dimension in British life, growing with the twentieth and into the twenty-first century. In the following chapters its significance—as an institution that has come to embrace practically all aspects of family life, from birth, through life-crisis illnesses, to death—will be hard to exaggerate. Indeed, one major presupposition of this volume is that the NHS, in becoming its own form of life-care system, came to mirror or even supplant the role of the Church of England. The phrase, 'from cradle to the grave', has often been used to describe the role of major churches, notably the Church of England with its baptism and funeral rites, but it is also applicable to the NHS, from pregnancy to end-of-life care and death. Though there are many differences between the nature and provision of the Church and the NHS, it is with the similarities focused on core cultural values that I am most concerned, and to which we will return. At this stage it can simply be said that no account of religion in contemporary Britain can ignore the rise of the NHS as the one background institution framing popular life.

Musical Generations

One other major social change regarding generational identities and shifts in taste concerns the mass-entertainment market of popular music, with its special appeal to the newly emergent domain of 'teenagers'. Given that music is a crucial cultural expression of emotion, the development of skiffle in the 1950s, and then of rock and roll and allied dance forms, made the decades of the 1960s onwards a new era of emotion: music and emotion that subtly superseded the regimented marching of martial music. While dancing was changing from traditional ballroom to rock and roll—with associated shifts in emotional dynamics, including the rise in sound levels of musical production—many churches were attempting to maintain young people's interest, with the resulting image of the guitar-playing curate almost becoming a caricature of the Church of England seeking relevance to a potentially lost generation. By the later 1960s, however, the churches, especially Protestant groups, were creating their own innovations, which would divide ongoing streams of thought into both conservative and liberal directions. The conservatives included what came to be called the charismatic movement with its theological emphasis on the Holy Spirit and the spiritual gifts typified by speaking in tongues and receiving what was believed to be revelations or messages from God. At the time it was fashionable to say that charismatics had no 'theology', but that soon changed. Within a relatively short period charismatics within different denominations felt a stronger alliance between themselves than had, it might be argued, been produced by the more committee-based form of fellowship planning evident in the ecumenical movement with its roots in the early decades of the twentieth century. The mood base of ecumenical and charismatic routes was different with the latter felt more keenly by many more people, especially lay people. Popular music was increasingly evident inside and outside churches, with songbooks and hymnbooks developed to include guitar-friendly material. While organs continued to play, other 'keyboards', drums, and available instruments joined guitars in charismatic flows that grew in significance even if they did not drown out more traditional services in most of the churches. Evangelicalism was both stimulated and partially divided by the charismatic turn, not least perhaps because its longer-established and preferred emotional pattern of controlled joy remained embedded in the sacrificial atonement of Christ. There remained a degree of stiff upper lip in the often middle-class groups of evangelicals. 'Thy will, not mine, be done' remained the basis of ethical life, while biblically focused expository teaching continued to play a vital spiritual role for these groups. The Cross constrained the kind of exhuberance that the Spirit encouraged.

The charismatic turn involved a relative shift of theological perspective that paralleled an emotional shift in spirituality. The Holy Spirit emerged more from the liturgical wings either to partner Jesus as the Divine Son or partially to replace him. The emotions shifted from less to more sound. The quietness of the typical Anglican service of Holy Communion, Matins, or Evensong, or even of the traditional evangelical prayer meeting came to include periods of 'praise'. 'Praise' included formal singing, music, and prayers, but had its signature in the formally unscripted arrival of speaking or singing in tongues by individuals. The standing still of previous hymn singing often moved to swaying, hands held aloft, with eyes closed in a devotional sense of the nearness of the Holy Spirit. The traditional evangelical mood tone of memory of Christ's sacrificial substitutionary atonement easily passed into the sense of immediacy of presence of the Holy Spirit.

As for the more liberal stream of post-1960s thinking, this was deeply influenced by philosophical and systematic theologies becoming more generally available to lay members of the mainstream churches, and, through the media, including the television, to the thinking public at large as through John Robinson, a Cambridge biblical scholar who popularized the existential theology of Paul Tillich.[33] As Bishop of Woolwich, his books, notably *Honest to*

---

[33] John Robinson 1919–83, Bishop of Woolwich 1959–69. See Robinson (1963).

God of 1963; various television appearances; and his supportive contribution to the 1960 trial of D. H. Lawrence's *Lady Chatterley's Lover*, gave high profile to a more public liberal theology in the Church of England, yet, despite some considerable response to his work, analysed by Robert Towler, he did not develop a following as such.[34] By contrast, another Cambridge theologian, albeit a philosopher of religion, Don Cupitt, born in 1934, found that his publications and broadcast on deeply liberal views of Christianity engendered the Sea of Faith movement that will be discussed in chapter 5 in direct connection with death beliefs.

As the twentieth century passed into the twenty-first, further developments took place across all these devotional modes, 'teenagers' aged and new generations arrived, and formal developments influenced liturgical change in the churches, including the ordination of women to the priesthood and as bishops in the Church of England. One significant shift was reflected in what some have called post-evangelicalism, a stream of religiosity in which many who formerly identified themselves as evangelicals (sometimes having also experienced a charismatic period) now repositioned themselves as relatively non-dogmatic, relatively liberal, seekers after authenticity of identity in and through exploratory forms of worship and group activity. If music systems and guitars had facilitated 1960s Christians, the 1990s took to elaborate light and sound systems to engage in visual–auditory flights of exploratory imagination in worship. Whether in conjunction with charismatic-like mood music fostering reflective heightened sensitivities or not, this style also fostered a reflective mood of wonder, amazement, and possibility. The relative shift in sensory impact from the aural to the visual would, itself, merit exploration.

The first two decades of the twenty-first century have, in the UK, been characterized by a vocal secularism and atheism, perhaps in response to a rise in British evangelicalism—and, more covertly, Catholicism, felt more in London and some other cities than in the country at large—and in response to the much more high-profile world of politics in the USA, not least in terms of flagship notions such as creationism. The media has frequently reported such moves with individuals such as the biologist Richard Dawkins being taken as embodiments of this domain. He, too, however, would affirm the value of aesthetic appreciation of the world and its artistic products when challenged over issues of depth in human life.[35] To reflect this period, chapter 2 will focus on some results of social surveys which deal with religious and other beliefs, and also with death and afterlife, including a pole sponsored by the Richard Dawkins Foundation for Reason and Science.

---

[34] See Towler (1984) for analysis of responses to Robinson's work. See chapter 9 in this volume for description of Towler's 'cognitive styles' of UK religion.
[35] Personal conversation for a television programme.

Death Intrusion

Behind these cultural shifts lies another transformation that influenced British society in many ways and which frames much of the rest of this volume. It concerns the changing prevalence of death, and is best pinpointed in the observation that at the very beginning of the twentieth century infants in their first year accounted for some 25 per cent of all deaths, while by the end of the century mortality affected less than 1 per cent. Then, in terms of older people, the century began with 12 per cent of deaths being of those aged 75 or older, and it ended with a figure of over 59 per cent for that age group.[36] The demography of the dead had changed.

Cultural Betrayal

In the public domain, the new decades of twenty-first century Britain have also witnessed an increasing significance of emotion-grounded values, albeit in the form of rapid decrease of trust in politicians, economic leaders, the press, and some church leaders. The rare but much publicized malpractice of some medical and care professionals has also attracted doubts, embodied in the case of the infamous Dr Harold Shipman, reckoned to have killed over two hundred of his elderly patients while in general practice.[37] One response to this kind of cultural betrayal—for such it seems to be—lies in an increased desire for personal control over one's life wherever this is economically and socially possible, with rising debates over assisted suicide and accounts of the terminally ill seeking to take control of the time and nature of their death. Such concerns frequently display a fear of powerlessness of self in an uncaring society, or in the hands of professionals whose ethical concerns may be at variance with one's own.

This brings into question the bond between individual and society, itself sociology's prime concern. Who may be trusted with my hopes? This has rapidly become an increasingly poignant question within a welfare state whose capacities shift in parallel with economic crisis or stability, and in a social world where long-term couple-companionate bonds at the core of nuclear and extended families are subject to relatively high rates of divorce or separation. Trust becomes an aspirational hope whose shattering is sufficiently frequent in personal experience as to question its widespread dependability. There is a sense in which trust is, to some degree, framed with fear, or at least with anxiety, and this may affect a wide band of social life, especially during periods of social change. This can affect different segments of society in different ways,

---

[36] Halsey and Webb (2000: 98–9).   [37] Whittle and Richie (2005).

as, for example, with the military as we see in chapter 7, but it can also apply to doctors, as with Shipman, and to priests and public celebrities such as the late television celebrity Jimmy Savile, as chapter 5 shows. The decades around the 2000 millennium witnessed numerous examples of cultural betrayal in terrorism and political anxieties of national and international life–death issues, as well as the near collapse of the world financial and banking system. That kind of 'background' anxiety can itself intensify the immediate crises of families in their grief, as an underlying meaningfulness of the world is challenged. This highlights the importance of, for example, funeral directors and the way the vast majority of people allow them to care for their dead. In more technical terms, we might say that the sociology of hope involves the trust placed in this kind of professional agency, not least at a time of crisis.

THEORETICAL POINTERS

Having touched on the variety of cultural forms in their emotional relation to death, we can now consider techniques in the literature that have been applied to this subject. To speak of trust, hope, and betrayal on the wide canvas of society is to identify and highlight the role of emotional aspects of life that inevitably encompass bereavement and the hard fact of coping with corpses at the private and family level. Here the anthropology of ritual and the psychology of grief come into their own as complementary modes of analysing the notion of embodiment—itself a significant theoretical notion for approaching human identity and emotions, as we will see in subsequent case studies and social surveys. A series of life cameos and paradigmatic scenes will also facilitate this complex task of accounting for death in Britain today. Indeed, to give an account of any social context involves an awareness of complexity that temptingly invites intellectual paralysis[38]—a temptation that is all the stronger when our human engagement with death is concerned.

Mortality Perspectives

So, this entire volume assumes that death-related phenomena offer a window into a people's lives.[39] In patterns of bereavement, forms of funerals, in varieties of memorials and memories of the dead, as in cultural idioms over

---

[38] Berlin (1997: 434) notes contradictions between rational desires and 'the forces of unreason'.
[39] The 'window' image resembles Seremetakis's (1991: 14) 'the optic of death' as a theoretical focus. Hyunchul Kim (2011: 31–3) drew my attention to this notion.

bad and good deaths, we access both the foundational link between individual and society and that complex internal domain of individual self-reflection. While acknowledging an element of veracity in the popular assumption that death rites are amongst the most enduringly conservative of behaviours, this volume shows how rapidly they may actually alter in response to changing social conditions. Not least significant is the way death serves as a medium for politics, whether in the explicit military context of wars or its semi-hidden form of illness and health care.

To strain the fenestration analogy yet further, we should not forget that windows come in many forms, offering crystal clarity, to blandly distorted opacity through frosting, to the dogmatic narrative of stained glass. Or again, we might contrast open windows with sealed double glazing, to distinguish between advocates of an emotional pro-activity towards the corpse and funeral arrangement and others who passively prefer to be recipients of funeral management. These positions reflect the debate as to whether death is more open or hidden in early twenty-first century Britain; an argument replete with issues of social class, ethnicity, NHS policies, gender, and identity. Then, more technically, we also need to ponder the complex fact that rituals and their constituent symbols sometimes conceal as much as they reveal: here 'broken windows' as well as 'mirrors' of all sorts have a part to play in the shifting places of death, grief, and mourning in Britain today.

Ritual, emotions, and identity

To speak of these funerary themes is to highlight the emotional dynamics of the dying and the bereaved, whether in close family circles or in wider groups of family, work associates, and friends. To do justice to these human depths of feeling this volume will often focus on emotions and their symbolic mediation in the rituals surrounding mortality. While no account of British religion approached through death, dying, and disposal would be feasible without some detailed consideration of ritual, that is not as easy a task as might first appear because 'ritual' belongs to the category of deutero-truth concepts.[40] Such second-order ideas serve as slightly abstract labels that allow a group to speak of such things as 'God', 'love', 'democracy', and perhaps of 'family' or even 'death' in a way that conveys a sense that everyone knows what the idea means. Or at least they do until called upon to define it in some detail, when the easy reference now becomes problematic. Moreover, when one group tries to communicate with another, all may seem well until some such definitions are sought. Ritual is one such deutero-truth. In archaeology, for example, ritual is often deployed when a carry-all term is needed for an excavated site

---

[40] Rappaport (1999).

that seems to be of a more than domestic or utilitarian purpose. In theology, 'ritual' is often viewed as the content of liturgy, though some Protestant traditions would place a disclaimer against their own organized behaviour and see 'ritual' as something that other traditions practise, probably with the connotation that such 'ritual' reflects a less sincere and more 'mechanical' approach to the divine. Further, in some psychological domains, 'ritualization' can carry pathological overtones of ordinary behaviours carried to compulsive excess. These important issues will be explored in chapter 3.

Whether in a hands-on or hands-off preference, it is through ritual activity that both the corpse and its attendant kith and kin are socially managed and expression is given to people's self- and world views. Within Britain, funerary ritual has to be set, historically, against narratives of Christian pastoral care, liturgy, and funeral practice, all played out through centuries of changing polity and life circumstances. From the time of popular ritualism of death in medieval Britain, for example, its varied transformation was fired by the English Reformation, the Industrial Revolution with its subsequent urbanization, social-class shifts, the emergence of civic cemeteries, the high Victorian performance of death, and the innovation of cremation. Two World Wars and numerous war-like 'troubles' later, Britain witnessed the further popularization of cremation and the subsequent inventiveness associated with cremated remains, especially from the 1970s on. As the decades passed from the 1990s to the 2010s, new woodland or natural burials made an appearance and showed an initially rapid growth, while yet other disposal methods of freezing, dissolving, and composting corpses were being entrepreneurially advocated. Britain's emergent multiculturalism from the second half of the twentieth century also added demands for a variety of funerary forms.

To engage with the complexities of such changes, this volume will also have to consider the major background themes of social change, secularization, multiculturalism, and the pro-activity and responsiveness both of small, death-related protest and support groups on one hand and of major institutions such as mainstream religious, health care, and political bodies on the other. Between these lie the professional commercial groups of funeral directors and insurance agents. All are surrounded by the media sources of radio, television, film, and newspaper and magazine press, and by the online and cell-phone webs of social networking.

Words Against Death

Behind my approach to all these issues lies previous work that discussed both anthropologically and theologically constructed 'words against death', a motif in a phrase describing many cultured forms of human response to the challenge death brings to our sense of survival.[41] The emergence of language and of that self-consciousness which fosters the capacity to imagine the liveliness of others also drives the impact effected by the death of others. Indeed, the human capacity of and for imagination, and of that 'theory of mind' that senses that others also have the sense of living that I have myself, frames this volume, where 'imagination' captures the drive for meaning expressed through cultural opportunity. This human capacity to create meaningful patterns, even amongst random arrangements in a visual field, makes the stillness of a corpse paradoxical, and seems to be one phenomenon that prompts a demand for meaning where, in a biological and naturalistic sense, it does not exist.

Death Avoidance: Life Control

At the outset we face the cultural options of denial, avoidance, marginalization, or acceptance of death. One popular British outlook seems to be that many live as though they will not die, and when, at the personal level, death is encountered it is often described in terms of tragedy rather than as natural. However, to speak of life devoid of death, almost as a functional fiction, is to raise some important themes. Since most will generally regard death in a strongly negative light, it is perfectly understandable that they will not wish to dwell upon it any more than is deemed absolutely necessary. This could apply to any emotionally or physically painful event or experience. Sociologist Zygmunt Bauman argued that any extensive dwelling upon death might render the living less engaged with life. Such a death-induced depression would, doubtless, be disadvantageous to any social group, yet there are some who regard death avoidance as its own form of immaturity, and who would prefer to think and reflect upon life as bounded by death.

   This polarity between death-deflection and death-reflection is highly instructive of the way daily life is experienced. It comes to sharp focus in the way many experience bereavement. Here I am thinking of the way our everyday life-world is constituted during 'normal' times outside of bereavement and grief. We are caught up in domestic, occupational, and leisure activities that demand and absorb our energies as we engage with others caught up in the same kinds of life-effort normality where 'normality' is typified by its degree of vitality. For many, such normality and its energizing vitality is characterized by a degree of control over life events, an issue to which we will return in chapter 1 when we develop it alongside the complementary notion of 'presence'.

   'Normality', however, is not for all of us all of the time. Life control is constrained by many things, not least by illness, when the ongoing flow of

---

[41]   Douglas J. Davies (1997; 2008). At least one doctoral dissertation has utilized this perspective in relation to funeral attendance in the UK; Tara Bailey (2012).

life—its vitality and allied 'sense of presence'—is interrupted. Similar inter-
ruptions follow unemployment or divorce and, quintessentially, bereavement.
The confusion over this normal lifestyle comes, for example, when a successful
businessman tries to consult his diary to see when a medical operation may be
fitted into his hectic programme, or when a completely unexpected death is
visited upon his immediate family and planned events have to vanish under
the inevitability of grief and funeral planning. Priorities, indeed competing
realities, become confused as the appreciation dawns that 'normality' must
now give way to unanticipated necessities. He is no longer in control of affairs.
The functional fiction of life that deflects mortality is reversed as mortality
becomes the pragmatic reality that potentially or actually eclipses vitality and
drives events. Here the social force of funeral management interplays with the
strong psychological dynamics of grief.

Many who live in the otherwise safe society enclaves of contemporary
Western states experience something of a shock through the life-disruptive
events of personal betrayal, divorce, abuse, unemployment, sickness, or bereavement, and here the issue of suicide often assumes enormous significance.
This is all the more problematic when such disruptions impact upon a
relatively closed circle of kin while the rest of the world continues in its
uninterrupted cycles of activity. To approach the theme of death in this way
is instructive if, for example, we want to understand the way some depict the
scene of an acquaintance avoiding a bereaved person because they 'do not
know what to say'. Though such a scene is often interpreted in terms of death
avoidance and a kind of emotional incompetence towards the bereaved, it is
also possible to see these people, just then, as living in different 'worlds'. Their
respective 'universes of meaning' and their functional fictions of survival
operate in different ways, which make it hard for one to engage with the other.

Lifestyle, Death-Style, and Emotional Transformers

Amidst such an interaction much will depend upon what can be called the
relationship between the lifestyle and the death-style of such individuals and
the group(s) of which they are a part. These expressions offer very handy
terms for summarizing an individual's or a group's outlook on the world. We
can speak of lifestyle and death-style integration when attitudes towards death
find a relatively easy place within the ongoing experience of everyday living,
when death is, as it were, 'normal'. By contrast, we can speak of lifestyle and
death-style incoherence when the fact of death seems abnormal, out of place,
or somehow unacceptable to people. We will explore this issue throughout the
following chapters, notably in chapter 3 on woodland burial and in chapter 9
through a series of funeral forms.

Underlying any portrayal of lifestyle or death-style are the many outlooks and experiences of bereaved people. To help shape our theoretical grasp of this emotion-filled domain I use the term 'emotional transformers' to describe the emotional history of an individual and the way that biographical history filters, interprets, and transforms new experiences and events. Take any two of us facing any life context, say that of an allotment, art gallery, car-boot sale, cathedral, crematorium, boutique hotel, kitchen, the national lottery sign, or a corpse: what do we see, if it even registers with us at all? Whatever the sense perception is, it is certain that some emotional transformer will influence what each person 'sees'. Memories are evoked, values stirred, and sense is made through a complex interplay of rational and emotional, conscious and unconscious, factors, though it is the emotional centre of gravity that I highlight here. Psychologists sometimes speak of the 'halo effect' that influences our view of certain other people, and this seems to express something of the 'emotional transformer' that I pinpoint here in the form of grief. It is perfectly likely, for example, that a man who has been more recently bereaved is much less likely to cross the street when approaching another recently bereaved person. The individual's emotional transformer renders the sight of, say, an approaching widower into a scene of sympathy, not avoidance. He will have some sense of how to approach, or of 'what to say' or not to say. The role of emotional transformers becomes especially important in distinctive cultural groups and increasingly problematic across different groups whose diverse cultural values and traditions shape their configuration.

In alluding to an encounter in a street or, for that matter, in hospital, school, church, crematorium, woodland burial site, or simply at home, we highlight the places in and through which our relationships develop and experiences accumulate. Space and its implications for thinking about ourselves and our dead will be addressed in chapter 2, alongside Tim Ingold's anthropological insights on time, place, and movement in terms of 'being alive' and of gaining knowledge in life.[42] For now, however, I simply mark the importance of the notions both of 'tradition' and 'establishment' as background factors to British life, and to some of the key places aligned with them.

TRADITION, ESTABLISHMENT, CELEBRITY

It is obvious that in any society, or, indeed, during the course of any one life, there will be variation between those individuals whose 'sense of things' depends upon extensive participation in 'religious' activities and institutions

---

[42] Ingold (2011: 241). I share his theoretical conviction over anthropology 'as an inquisitive mode of inhabiting the world'.

and those who depend upon other activities and institutions concerning family, employment, or recreation. Such variation influences death practices, with the broad context of 'tradition' as an inclusive concept expressing familiarity with and a degree of sharing in overlapping world views. British 'tradition' is a complex phenomenon arising from the interplay of monarchy, social class, and democratic movements, worked out through the checks and balances of religion, law, the military, education, and employment—all in relation to geographical, architectural, and historical factors. One aspect of 'tradition' lies precisely in 'the Establishment'—a concept that captures an essential feature of British life. It includes social class relations and is manifest in practically every aspect of life, from diversity in sporting and cultural interests to availability of school and university places, and even the naming of children. While, historically speaking, this Establishment has a major focus in the Church of England—by definition established—its social role has long been played out in relation both to the many streams of religious dissent (especially from the eighteenth to the twentieth century), and to new influences from non-Christian traditions from the later twentieth century.[43]

Britain differs from many societies in its long-term cohesion as an identifiably evolving polity sustained throughout the dramatic shifts of religious Reformation, Civil War, Industrial Revolution, and World Wars, despite eras of imperial expansion and contraction and, currently, of post-colonial realignment amidst European Union debates and multicultural contexts. Death has played a significant role in carrying a variety of cultural meanings for each of these, whether in terms of martyrdom, regicide, industrial deaths, military mortality, or terrorist assault, and has always involved a certain pull exerted by the social force-field of history evident in memorial buildings, and by the ongoing military power behind the government, all under the symbolically powerful headship of the monarch. In these contexts, Britain is notable for its ritual–ceremonial expression of national identity and cultural values, most often with senior ecclesiastical figures taking part. In terms of social change it is worth noting how increasing numbers of events provide a stage shared by both traditional-establishment and celebrity figures. Change is, however, a simple word which covers complex aspects of the force-field of society and the diverse forms of social and cultural capital sustaining it. Celebrity culture also carries with it the potential for a form of cultural betrayal, as we will see in the cases of 'Sir' Jimmy Savile, the popular entertainer posthumously accused of multiple sexual abuse of children, and Rolf Harris, convicted and imprisoned in 2014 for similar abuse.

While in this volume it will only be possible to sketch occasional aspects of the complex interplay of tradition, establishment, and celebrity in British

---

[43] E. P. Thompson ([1963] 1991: 40, 99, 386, etc.) documented the interplay of dissent and establishment for numerous working-class groups in the early-modern and modern periods.

religion, it is important to note its significance as a backdrop for cultural life within the British Isles. One journalist, Terence Blacker, for example, began an article facilitated by material gained through persevering with the Freedom of Information Act, saying that, 'Now and then it is possible to catch a glimpse of how the British establishment works'. His focus was on those who had refused awards from the British honours 'system'.[44] He obtained a list in which some 2 per cent of those included had rejected honours, among them Lucien Freud, Philip Larkin, F. R. Leavis, C. S. Lewis, Henry Moore, and J. B. Priestly. These may be compared with some of the 98 per cent accepting awards, including Mick Jagger, Elton John, Helen Mirren, and John Prescott—all described by the journalist as 'respected, eminent men and women', albeit now 'reduced' and whose 'voices are muffled by ermine'.[45] Two directions of flow are discernible in these responses: one integrative and the other differentiating the individual and their 'preferred' group.

The former direction of flow highlights the identification a person has with their local community, or professional, artistic, sporting, or other body. Sir Elton John, for example, is a popular entertainer with an extensive fan-base, with his new title resonating positively with his public lifestyle, including his famed 'Candle in the Wind' song at Westminster Abbey's funeral of Diana—a remarkable moment in which a kind of popular light music cameo was set amidst formal Anglican liturgy, thus bringing into the 'Establishment' world something of the other radically significant British social fact; that of celebrity. Title coheres with fame and fans, especially in the twentieth–twenty-first century realm of 'celebrity', a category that helps sustain the worldwide entertainment industry, itself symbolic of globalization. British 'tradition' unites both, as the opening ceremony of London's 2012 Olympic Games made dramatically obvious.

One feature that occasionally finds expression in celebrity, though less so in establishment contexts, is a kind of submissive deference, which I have de-scribed elsewhere as 'the humility response', and which appears as a sense of passive gratitude for having been praised by one's main reference group.[46] When an individual speaks of his or her 'award' or 'honour', their vocal tone differs from the assertiveness often associated with that person or a person of that individual's status. A sense of worthiness accorded by others prompts this grateful submissiveness. It is here that the power of society over an individual—its social force—becomes clearly apparent, and marks people who work with and for others in collaborations that underlie a great deal of their sense of identity; of who they are, not least in military contexts where an honoured individual may well speak of receiving his award 'for all his fellow

---

[44] Blacker (2012: 25).
[45] Ermine being the symbolic fur decorating the formal robes of their noble office.
[46] Douglas J. Davies (2011: 158).

soldiers'. In such cases, the excellence of performance, endurance, or the like, is noted: a prized social value is identified with its embodiment. Such humility is life-enhancing and the lifestyle generating it commended.

The differentiation model, however, including the context where an honour is refused, marks individuals whose lifestyle is frequently highly 'individual-ized', almost as a necessity of and for their activity. Writers, artists, and critics, for example, often see themselves as 'individualists'. They often spend a great deal of their time not as 'team players', as do soldiers or entertainers, but in isolated work. Their 'creative task' is to write, sculpt, think, or bring to being entities different from prevailing patterns. Their pleasure is self-generated and their 'work' its own reward. These are life-engaged people who would not wish to allow the Establishment to temper their opinions.

CONCLUSION

So it is that, while human life may but thinly veneer the Earth's surface, its evolution into complex cultural forms has generated dense patterns of behav-iour that create and sustain human identities. Yet, despite the power of such identities, and whatever prestige and honours are bestowed, biological death still remains. But it remains in a curious fashion, for its own organic decease is seldom matched by the cultural decease of the dead person. Though the death of 'life' may be as rapid as it takes each body's organs to cease functioning, the death of identity takes as long or as short a time as its cultural world wishes. This makes death a shifting concept in changing times, especially in multicul-tural contexts where, for example, theological uncertainties of more liberal Christianity contrast with more religiously conservative Islam, while agnostic, 'spiritual', and secular world views help frame death as a 'waiting to be understood' phenomenon. Meanwhile, a largely conservative domain of fu-neral directors, harried by small 'existential elites' with their own views of death, manages the dead through purpose-made funerals. It is precisely the nature of this cultural understanding, and the management of the dead and of their identity, that preoccupies this volume through the interplaying motifs of lifestyle and death-style.

1

Life Forces

Theoretical Perspectives

The Introduction considered the sensed value of life and that cultural wisdom aligned with human meaning-making expressed in traditional religion, secularity, spirituality, or some mix of world views. It also pinpointed a cluster of paired concepts that furnish a theoretical foundation for our ongoing consideration of life, death, and funerals. One background feature to this clustering of the sensed significance of life concerns 'value', both in the economic and existential sense of worth, and though the monetary dimension will scarcely appear in this chapter it must not be forgotten as a medium in and through which 'life forces' often take cultural shape, not least in the context of health and wellbeing and their provision through the NHS. In modern, developed societies individuals have to pay or be paid for both time and space, with the very notion of lifestyle carrying its own economic cost, not least in terms of taxation. But death-style too bears a charge, and the interplay of economic and moral–social costs and values will often be implicit in this and following chapters; at times, it will also be made explicitly clear.

Having made that point we now move to an elaboration of our conceptual cluster of paired themes, beginning with vitality–mortality and elaborating the part each pairing will play in this volume, whose eclecticism will include philosophical, theological, literary, and historical material within our more social-scientific arena. This is amply reflected in this chapter in Thomas Hobbes, George Herbert, Jeremy Taylor, and Sir Thomas Browne with whose famed though not necessarily widely read study of forms of funeral this chapter will lead to a final conclusion.

VITALITY–MORTALITY

Vitality and mortality set the scene for this volume on death within the reality of life at large, by emphasizing the 'sense of' life and the 'sense of' death.

Vitality expresses the energy and dynamic activity that characterizes the force-field in which we live; it differentiates the living from the dead and takes its essential meaning in opposition to mortality.[1] As for 'dynamism', it appears more intense in some individuals than in others; they are more 'lively' and 'animated', and possess more 'life in them'. Contrariwise, others are 'lifeless', 'morose', like 'death warmed up'. The dynamic and lively person fosters hope; the 'deadly' person sucks away hope. While many aspects of life can be portrayed on this vitality–mortality spectrum it is peculiarly appropriate for the life-course. Vitality accompanies joy at the birth of a child, expressing hope for a new generation; love in maturity marks the power of attachment, while sickness and death herald mortality and emotional chords of fear. From the sense of tragedy in infant and early death, through a grateful reflection on full lives lived, to a longing for the end by the terminally ill or life-weary, we all catch glimpses of our shared existence and ponder our own end. Poets, priests, funeral directors, theologians, historical and social scientists, parents and children: we all have our own interpretative view of the rise and fall of our lives and those of others. As the idea of hope already indicates, there are strong emotional energies embedded within the notion of vitality as a life force underlying our sense of identity that grows as we grow in our social worlds. Likewise, mortality alludes to the cessation of such powers, with grief as a complex response to the cessation of life in another and their slow withdrawal of influence in our ongoing lives. Yet in all this a social force of obligation and expectation frames and pervades the individual's life. In contemporary Britain much of this 'vitality' factor is framed in and through the NHS, from pregnancy, through infancy, adulthood, old age, and end-of-life care.[2]

The Body, Physical and Social

Vitality and mortality provide the essential dynamics of the symbolic capacity of the body, a concept underlying this entire volume. 'Vitality', indicates an emotionally patterned impetus that transforms mere statements—bare cognitive signs—about the 'body' into energized symbols. So it is that ideas, when pervaded by emotion, are transformed into values, and such values themselves assume the status of beliefs when they help forge a person's sense of identity.[3] This is all the more evident when that sense of identity entails a sense of

---

[1] Mortality is the 'imaginary' of vitality: each defined in terms of the other.

[2] In this NHS contextualizing of vitality in life and death the UK differs fundamentally from the USA, a factor of considerable importance for comparative studies on the sociology of religion.

[3] Douglas J. Davies (2011: 13–36), see Zijderveld ([1970] 1972: 143): 'Rationalized emotions are usually called ideologies.'

ultimacy or destiny. In chapter 2 I describe a similar progression from abstraction of idea to individual identity for the theme of grief. Before that, however, we consider the way that religion may be understood in terms of accessing and utilizing a 'power' that drives life, with 'vitality' being one mode of such 'power'; a 'power' that is itself energized through people's experience of bereavement. In other words, vitality, as a sense of power that drives life, is open to many changes in intensity, both within an individual's and a group's lifetime. Death, experienced as bereavement, is notable for its capacity to generate phases in life that encapsulate depletion and a potential for a corresponding resurgent intensification of life.[4] To phrase this in terms of Bloch and Parry's well-known book title, 'death and the regeneration of life' describes how strong emotions engage, highlight each other's difference, and complement each other during periods of dying, death, grief, and beyond.[5] In other words, mortality and vitality are true 'imaginary' partners in the philosophical–linguistic sense of a pairing of concepts in which one concept is ultimately unintelligible without the other.[6]

It is, then, precisely this human body—its dying and death, and their consequences within British society—that appears here as the profoundest of all symbols. From its fertilization, its gestation and birth, through its maturation, reproduction, periods of flourishing and sickness, to old age and its decline into death, the body is our central symbol. Even then, through its undergoing preparation for a funeral and the way it is materially or mentally remembered, the body continues to influence the ongoing identity of others, be it at the immediate level of family and friends, or in the larger arena of a particular society, or even of the world itself. In chapter 3 we explore further the role of the body both as a biological entity and as a social fact participating both in vitality and mortality, but, at that chapter's outset, we stress the way vitality and mortality cohere in the weaving of the cultural tapestries that tell the tale of life and death underlying individual and corporate identities in the class-organized, ethnic, and belief-patchworked society of Great Britain. The following chapters describe varied cultural flows of vitality and mortality that negate any universal world view yet attest to the deeply shared fact of having to deal with the dead and then continue living through the pragmatic necessities of funerals. Such necessity forges its own form of social unity as people from widely differing traditions acknowledge the need to deal with the dead in ritualized behaviour and with due attention to the emotional dynamics of grief. It is this material form of funeral rites, rather than any specific content, that offers a binding tie across classes and communities.

---

[4] In some individual contexts grief may endure in ways involving no resurgence, only a general hopelessness.

[5] Bloch and Parry (1982).   [6] Douglas J. Davies (2008: 151–3).

Style, habitus, and force

In approaching human emotions, especially those surrounding death, Durkheim's long-established notion of *Homo duplex* remains profoundly important in marking the way a person is constituted by a physical nature pervaded by socially derived ideas, as Anton Zijderveld appreciated decades ago.[7] Whether in Durkheim or in numerous subsequent theorists, this perspective takes a person to be a combination of individual and society. Just how these apparently polar opposite concepts relate, complement, or oppose each other within any particular person is an immense issue that lies beyond the scope of this volume. Suffice it to say that we need some model to cope with the biological and conscious basis of our bodily life, to accompany our socially derived sense of ourselves acquired through language, through the default setting of our cultural classifications, and through our daily interpersonal relationships. In classical antiquity, for example, Plato had the sense that rulers ought not even to engage with actors; those who 'be clever at acting a ... disgraceful part on the stage for fear of catching the infection in real life'. Similarly, schoolboy dramatic recitation should not be 'prolonged into adult life' lest it 'establish habits of physical, poise, intonation and thought which become second nature'.[8]

Such insights on the interplay of forms of social life are apt reminders of the idea of lifestyle and associated death-style presented in the Introduction as an easy way of describing ourselves as social animals engaged practically with life through our world views. This *Homo duplex* approach has an established complement in another way of describing the embodiment of cultural values; that of *habitus*. As a classical Latin word denoting bodily deportment, state, or appearance, and, by derivation, certain forms of costume, as in the habit of monks, this term developed distinctive meaning within theology in terms of aptitudes that are naturally implicit, or that may be acquired, or even given by divine influence. Because this approach to human nature raised fundamental issues, both over human capabilities (or lack of them) and over divine grace, it became controversial during the Reformation.[9] As one of those words with shared ancestry but which subsequently develop prominence in different fields, *habitus* passed into sociology and was, for example, used by Max Weber to pinpoint a 'pattern of life' adopted by certain groups.[10] It is, however, more often associated with Pierre Bourdieu's theoretical approach to cultural 'dispositions' that 'generate', inform, and direct modes of behaviour or cultural 'practice'.[11] With a slightly different theoretical provenance,

---

[7] Zijderveld ([1970] 1972: xii).

[8] Plato, *The Republic* Book III. 395, d. (1974: 153–4). See also Aristotle on fear of death (Warrington, 1963: 127–8).

[9] McFarland (2011: 205).   [10] Weber ([1922] 1966: 161).

[11] Bourdieu ([1972] 1977: 72–87).

ideas of embodiment can also be traced both from Marcel Mauss's anthropological notion of techniques of the body,[12] and from his fellow theoretician
Emile Durkheim's work on the sociological theory of knowledge which argued
that the basic categories of human thought are entirely derived values.[13]
A generation later, and from a slightly different sociological perspective,
Raymond Williams captured something of the community-informing 'structure of feeling' when depicting

> ... a particular sense of life, a particular community of experience hardly needing
> expression, through which the characteristics of our way of life ... are in some
> way passed, giving them a particular and characteristic colour ... a particular and
> native style ... it is as firm as 'structure' suggests, yet it operates in the most
> delicate and least tangible parts of our activity. In one sense this structure of
> feeling is the culture of a period ... and it is in this respect that the arts of a
> period ... are of major importance.[14]

At much the same time, but from a more explicitly anthropological perspective, Mary Douglas, influenced by Durkheim's work, developed significant
ideas on the interplay between social influences upon members of society and
the corresponding views individuals might have of themselves. Though her
perspective has been much debated its enduring significance here lies in how
she saw human bodily behaviour and thought of it as assuming different
patterns depending on the relative strength of social control exerted over an
individual and on how that individual, in turn, exerted control over himself. In
alluding to her work here and in chapters 2 and 6, I adapt this control model of
her 'purity rule' to interpreting death, memorials, and grief. Another theorist
writing in the 1960s, albeit from the different field of history, E. P. Thompson
spoke several times of 'psychic energy' when discussing motivations of religious behaviour. Referring to the historical–sociological accounts of Tawney
and Weber on Puritanism's contribution to middle-class ideas of being 'called'
or 'elected' by God when engaged in 'acquisitive pursuits', he highlights
'psychic energy and social coherence'. He also describes the 'psychic processes
of counter-revolution' associated with Methodism in the late eighteenth and
early nineteenth centuries, and looks at Joanna Southcott's 'psychic blackmail'
exacted 'upon the credulous' and their 'hysterical intensity' in 'the desire for
personal salvation', in what was a 'cult of the poor'.[15] Thompson's use of
'psychic' factors when discussing social influences over behaviour in general,
and on the dynamics of emotions in explicitly religious groups in particular,
is but one of many potential perspectives on this hard-to-define zone of

---

[12] Mauss ([1936] 1979).
[13] Douglas J. Davies (2011: 27–31) relates *Homo duplex* to ideas of emotion.
[14] Raymond Williams (1961: 64). Idea presented earlier in R. Williams and M. Oram (1954).
I am indebted to my former doctoral student Maeve Blackman for this connection.
[15] E. P. Thompson ([1963] 1991: 391, 419, 424).

individual and corporate feelings on one hand and social invitation and directive on the other.[16]

Even so, this complexity is fundamental to our approach to death, set as it is within a power that frames the whole of human life, from international politics, through the national, local, family levels, and encompasses our employment, educational, and leisure lives. Colloquially, we often speak of feeling 'under pressure', of 'being pressurized', or of sensing an obligation to someone, or of 'feeling responsible' for something. Sometimes, these sensations carry an emotional name and sometimes simply a vague sense of having to behave in a particular way.[17] All such experiences reflect our nature as social animals whose very identity is grounded in networks of alliance and the power driving them. As Isaiah Berlin, with his characteristically informed fortitude, put it, 'the discovery that politics is the play of power—that political relationships between and within independent communities involve the use of force and fraud, and are unrelated to the principles professed by the players. That knowledge is as old as conscious thought about politics—certainly as old as Thucydides and Plato.'[18] Subsequent chapters will only occasionally involve international and national dimensions of power, for more relevant to this volume is the more immediately experienced force of closer social circles, not least at times of death.[19]

I have highlighted this 'force' from different sources as a preliminary exercise before focusing it on the sense of embodiment framed by bereavement. To think of 'force' in this way is not simply to think in terms of power or authority, but of the impetus arising in an individual as a member of a group. To speak simply of 'obligation' is to highlight a too-formal level of need to act. Social force, in the sense identified here, is not simply a rational or even legal obligation of one person to react to another, but indicates a degree of mutuality between them. In this sense 'force' belongs to the same logical type as *habitus*, and *Homo duplex*; one in which personal and interpersonal emotions attract a response more than they compel one. Just how individuals manage to experience and influence the 'force' of their day, whether in community, family, or their interior life, belongs to the complexity of social life in its changing economic–political and general ideological–religious outlook lying beyond any single theoretical interpretation.[20] Sometimes it is noted in

---

[16] Horlick-Jones (2012) notes Thompson falling out of fashion with later sociologists.

[17] John Ruskin's 'numinous experience' explicitly noted the absence of names for some experiences. See Rudolph Otto ([1917] 1924: 221).

[18] Berlin (1997: 319).

[19] Otto ([1917] 1924: 121) identified 'the strange idea of "power"' along with ritual purity, and the influence of the dead as helping to form 'the vestibule of religion' in the evolution of religion.

[20] Charles Taylor (2007: 391–3) plays with the notion of 'impersonal force in the universe', and its cultural shadow evident in his 'British social imaginary' and the role of monarchy, Protestantism, 'decency', and 'civilization' as times change.

passing by thinkers, sometimes scholars set out to evaluate it in terms of eras. In the 1880s, for example, W. R. Inge, intellectual and churchman whose life (1860–1954) spanned that most crucial era in modern cultural and religious history, retrospectively spoke of becoming aware in the 1880s that 'the centre of gravity in religion' had shifted in his day away 'from authority and experience'.[21]

Excitement–depression

In addition to vitality and power, one further factor will allow us to appreciate the ambiguities and ambivalences associated with death, viz. the interplay of excitement and depression. Behaviour surrounding death is often exciting in the physiological sense that it intensifies the emotional dynamics of individuals and their communities, even if that excitement is prompted in people circling those who are immediately bereaved and in the opposite state of depression. A social group often comes alive as one of its members dies. In the ensuing death rites, opportunities are created for another kind of intensification, viz. of the core values of the group, along with its hopes for the future. Death as a biological necessity fosters the sense of social existence which, in its turn, is the community basis for the ongoing biological nature of humanity. Were one to speak in the language of 'the selfish gene', death would be one of the creative social tricks played upon organic necessity of material decline whereby negative necessities are transformed into positive possibilities: but that argument, in those terms at least, is not a line followed in this volume.

MEANING-MAKING AND NARRATIVE

Just as vitality and mortality weave the meaning-making that drives everyday stories about individual and group experience, they also drive the abstract theories constructed to explain the nature of bodily and cultural existence. In a qualitative sense, the positive aspects of meaning-making embedded within individual, family, and wider social narratives should not ignore negative dynamics, as in the contemporary British concern over assisted dying. For at a time when government policies on such things as education and health care emphasize personal choice in a form of market economy there remains a clear lack of choice over assisted dying. As for social and scientific theories, these also replicate the human proclivity for narrative, albeit at a more abstract and technical level depicting human identity emerging within a social world and

---

[21] W. R. Inge (1934: 34).

physical environment. These issues of narrative-embedded aspects of death, especially as focused in grief, will be developed in chapter 6. Underlying the entire process of narrative meaning-making over death lies the basic fact of orality—of speaking about death, or, indeed, of not speaking about death, in an intentional way, and especially of speaking to or about the dead. When de Certeau and Giard describe orality as framed by a 'social exchange' that correlates 'gestures and bodies . . . marks of breathing and passion, . . . nuances added by intonation, facial movements', they offer us a valuable way of approaching social life, death, and the nature of sympathy.[22]

It has been argued that 'meaning is a community of understanding, so that for the time being you and I think in the same terms'.[23] While that general-ization pushes narrative to the surface of social life as a major vehicle of social cohesion, it also highlights periods of bereavement when death stands as its own form of radical constraint upon human meaning-making. At such times, the role of narrative plays an enormous part in cultural histories of grief. Indeed, in the most basic way, the many forms of memorial created for the dead are, in themselves, an expression of the narrative drive behind human meaning-making. Long before the notion of 'continuing bonds' appeared on the agenda of grief counselling, stories of the dead and their relation with the living, and of allied ritual, all played a significant role within religious tradi-tions, as later chapters will show. But, at the outset, it is worth highlighting the overarching vitality–mortality narrative evident within Western cultural his-tory and in the ongoing life of millions of people the world over—the story of the person of Jesus. Biblical accounts of his life, death, and resurrection, along with the complex multiplicity of art, architecture, ethics, music, liturgy, the-ology, and popular belief, have related personal, family, and community life to this interplay of excitement and depression over life and death for centuries. We explore this in focused ways when considering forms of funeral in chapter 3, and celebrity, sporting, and military issues in chapter 7.

Concealing–Revealing

Another dimension of force influencing meaning-making appears in the theme of disclosure and concealment of mortality in contemporary society. This double function of exhibiting or inhibiting death touches the double-sidedness of vitality's mortality and reflects the shadow side of meaning-making. It frames the social face of identity and privacy's complementary opacity; the sense of presence and absence in embodiment occasioned by a corpse, and is invaluable when considering the uncanny. In other words, the

---

[22] De Certeau, Giard, and Mayol ([1994] 1998: 253), and see chapter 6 here.
[23] Mario Pei (1964: 110).

very nature of individual and social life is not always obvious as religious, philosophical, and other modes of life appraisal acknowledge. Anthropological studies of ritual symbolism, for example, have often spoken of the 'latent' and 'hidden' meaning of symbols,[24] of how some rituals may 'bring into the open the secret and even unconscious' dimensions of existence,[25] and of the potential of different theoretical approaches for identifying the revelatory capacity of ritual symbolism.[26]

Sacrifice: Culture's Nature in Battlefield and Household

One familiar image that helps us approach this cultural framing of vitality and mortality, one that embraces themes of power and excitement, is that of sacrifice. Here Christianity's interpretation of the life and death of Jesus set in terms of sacrifice is foundational. This has been enacted for over a millennium in the sacrifice-like ritual of the Mass and a half-millennium in Protestant versions of the Eucharist and preaching on the atoning death of Jesus. To exist within a Christianly informed British history involved identity factors informed by sacrificial motifs rooted in Christ's exemplary death that offered a ready model of and for human actions, notably death in battle, that demand high levels of validation in a developing democracy, or in forms of devoted service to a cause or family surrounded by hardship. To say that a person sacrificed a career for a family or, indeed, a family for a career would attract positive valuation. Chapter 4 will raise this notion of sacrifice within the context of martyrdom before the theme is taken further, in chapter 7 on military deaths and in chapter 8 in a consideration of children's fiction.

CULTURAL INTENSIFICATION AND IDENTITY

Sacrifice provides a good example of another of our key conceptual clusters, that of cultural intensification and identity which, for example, sets religion in narratives that influence the sense of identity developed within devotees by intensifying these narratives through ritual acts, when emotions pervade religious 'ideas' and turn them not only into 'values' but, under the influence of conferring a sense of destiny upon people, also into beliefs.[27] Following this

---

[24] Victor and Edith Turner (1978: 246).
[25] Victor Turner (1975: 231–2). Cf. Victor Turner (1987: 25).
[26] Lawson and McCauley (1990: 184).
[27] See Douglas J. Davies (2008a) for 'cultural intensification', and (2011) for the rationale of idea, idea plus emotion yielding a value, and value plus destiny generating religious identity.

developmental process from ideas to beliefs, I argue that the more a sense of
destiny comes to frame some emotion-laden idea, the more we may expect
local 'religious' processes to be evoked and utilized in response.[28] Closely
related themes include the way dead relatives live on in the developing identity
of their surviving kin with memories energized by contemporary emotional–
ritual contexts, and as potential fear is assuaged.

The question of identity is, indeed, integral to understanding the interplay
of religion and death within any particular community, and, while the
process of 'meaning-making on the basis of a cultural attribute' is where
one might expect a sociologist such as Manuel Castells to begin, it is not
where a fuller understanding of human life should end.[29] For, despite the
fact that Castells is expressly concerned with *The Power of Identity,* and with
the way 'meaning is organized around a primary identity', he offers very
little opportunity for explaining just how 'power' comes to be expressed
in 'identity'.[30] The missing factor involves what may best be captured
by combining notions of emotion and vitality, factors that will play a
significant part in ensuing chapters. The relative absence of such factors is,
perhaps, understandable in Castells' case, for his sociological focus is primarily 'collective, rather than individual, identity', and in his 'network
society . . . meaning is organized around a primary identity'.[31] The level at
which a theoretical account is pitched inevitably affects the concepts that can
be explored or exploited, and, while it is true that Castells does list a host of
factors that enter into the construction of identity, including 'building
materials from history . . . geography . . . biology . . . collective memory and
from personal fantasies . . . power apparatuses, and religious revelations',
these all remain beyond the more immediate embodied dynamism of individual men and women.[32] My preference lies with a lower level of social
scientific engagement and with an approach to identity 'viewed as a negotiated sense of self developed over time through the emotions and moods that
characterize feelings people have of themselves in relation to core values
of their group'.[33] One influential theorist with much to contribute to this
analysis, and who will recur in later chapters, is Hans Mol, who presents the
argument that phenomena that help contribute to our sense of identity are,
in turn, ascribed with attributes that approximate to ideas of the sacred.[34]

---

[28] Acknowledging Hans Mol's (1976) theoretical influence on ideas of identity and sacrality.
See also Davies and Powell (2015).
[29] Castells (2010: 6, 7).
[30] Castells (2010: 7). *The Power of Identity* is the title for the second volume of his trilogy, *The
Information Age.*
[31] Castells (2010: 9–10).   [32] Castells (2010: 7).
[33] Douglas J. Davies (2011: 5).   [34] Mol (1976).

The Sacred

The rise and fall of fashionable ideas in successive academic generations offers its own index of social change and, indeed, of intellectual interest. This is the case with 'the sacred', a notion that played a central role from later nineteenth-century approaches to the study of religion, but which went out of fashion in the later twentieth century—but which now seems to be making something of a welcome comeback.

In terms of the more recent history of religious ideas, the theologian, and Hebrew and Arabic scholar, William Robertson Smith, generated considerable interest in conceptual categories through his study of Semitic religion.[35] Driven by evolutionary theory and the rise of textual biblical scholarship, he focused on sacrificial rites understood in terms of the difference between the 'holy' and the 'common'. This distinction was adopted by Emile Durkheim, albeit rephrased in terms of the 'sacred' and the 'profane', as one basis for his enduring yet much-debated sociology of religion in which socially binding ritual circles around 'sacred things' that otherwise tend to be 'set apart and forbidden'.[36] Both these scholarly interests preceded the First World War, which, as we show in chapter 7, prompted several crucial studies of the sacred and pivotal religious experience within theology. As the twentieth century progressed, 'the sacred' tended to disappear within theological discourse, only to find representation within the history and phenomenology of religion, with 'religious studies' emerging as a new form of engagement with religion. So it was that Mircea Eliade, for example, deployed 'the sacred' as an invaluable and non-theological category. Eschewing more speculative evolutionary views of human religiosity, he located the sacred as 'an element of the structure of consciousness and not a moment in the history of consciousness'.[37] This allowed him to explore a wide variety of religious phenomena as an outworking of human nature in and through natural and cultural environments. Ninian Smart, the British scholar who did more than anyone else to establish Religious Studies as a discipline in Great Britain in the 1960s, similarly discussed religious phenomena in ways that opened up 'the sacred' to religions at large.[38] And that laid the foundation for its own form of existential approach to life as religious, or indeed, as 'spiritual', with numerous accounts of 'spirituality' following from the 1960s into the 1970s and on into the twenty-first century.[39] There were some, however, who called for 'the sacred', especially given its theological provenance, to be abandoned 'as a generic term' unless local contexts demanded its use.[40]

---

[35] William Robertson Smith (1889).   [36] Durkheim (1912).
[37] Eliade (1978: 313).   [38] Smart (1996).
[39] Heelas (1996).   [40] Terence Thomas (2004: 65).

That theological origin problem is easily overcome when we take the key to 'the sacred' to be the motivating force-field and emotional dynamics that foster a cultural intensification of identity. Such a background helps us understand how 'the sacred' can reappear today as a religion-free, and even 'spirituality'-free, category accounting for the highly valued meaningfulness and depth of life. The sacred, once rooted in and gaining its cultural significance from religion, now becomes freed up for general use. So, the 'sacred' need not appear as a noun pinpointing divinity, nor as some antique phase of human cultural development, but as a term acknowledged as carrying an emotional intensity aligned with life concerns that underpin identity.[41] The sacred becomes one cultural resource allowing people to negotiate their sense of self in the face of their particular life circumstances.

Indeed, at the core of this volume lies the intriguing task of attempting some critical reflection on our own ways of life in relation to death, and on how notions like or carrying the same emotional dynamic effect as 'the sacred' may be active around that interface. This is not easy, given that on the one hand a characteristic feature of daily life is that we operate on implicit assumptions, on the taken-for-granted nature of the way things are while, on the one other hand the underlying approach of a volume like this lies in the critical analysis of those assumptions of daily life. This will become very obvious, for example, in chapter 6 when we question the popular assumption of the uniqueness of grief for each of us. Indeed, grief stands out at this point as it raises the crucial question of the similarity or difference of emotional experience between that of the people of today and those of the distant past. The study of emotions now occupies a significant place within a variety of academic disciplines and poses afresh the much debated nature–nurture issue of cultural influence over 'basic' human experience, a debate that parallels the longstanding concern over cultural and historical relativism as frames for all the human sciences. This is especially germane given the intellectual fashion to classify distinctive kinds of 'self' generated by traditional, modern, and postmodern societies, let alone by class, gender, or healthy–pathological divides within those groups.

The position adopted in this volume assumes that human beings are more alike than we are different across time and place. I assume that more things link the first thinking and feeling hominids with us today than divide us, and that this is also the case across contemporary cultures. While developmental and cultural variations that shape the expression of emotions are frequently deep, I am not persuaded that some postmodern 'self' possessed of the attribute of a 'liquid' identity is so unlike some traditional, kindred, and place-embedded self that, for example, their experience of grief is likely to be different. To say this is, naturally, to be aware that grief responses may vary

---

[41] Heelas (2000: 237–54).

greatly within any single group along a continuum from slight to pathological expressions. Similarly, both face-to–face traditional societies and social-media-framed hi-tech populations are equally open to emotionally charged experiences of bullying and social ostracism. But the shared response to loss is far from being as multi-faceted as a certain form of postmodernity might assume. Though many will reject this view as naïve in preference for a model of cultural complexity, I will err on the side of human similarity when it comes to matters of mortality and vitality in the emotional dynamics of humanity engaging with identity and destiny. So it is that this volume can empathize with Homer as he begins his *Iliad* with a command 'to sing . . . the accursed anger which brought uncounted anguish' to heroes in the mingled lives of gods and humanity, all in a tale that ends with the cremation of Hector and the collecting of his bones by mourners with 'heavy tears' falling from their cheeks, who place those bones in a golden box, bury it, and gather for a feast.[42]

EMBODIMENT AND SENSE OF PRESENCE

Another way of analysing such an emotion-suffused identity is through the conceptual notions of embodiment and 'sense of presence'. This is especially evident in those bereaved people who sense the presence of their dead, or of some force coming from those sustaining them in their grief. Whether in dreams, passing thoughts, or an awareness that a dead person is, just now, nearby, our own sense of embodiment brings them close once more: such is the force of others within our own sense of self. So it is, too, with that of shared possession; things once owned by the dead that carry their distinctive influence over us, reminding us that embodiment is always embedded in time and place. In some traditional anthropological perspectives this theme of embodiment weds the individual to society and sees the individual as a kind of microcosm of society.

'Body-Force' and Power

That bond of individual and society is, in practical life, experienced as a force or power, whether expressed as a sense of necessity, tradition, or expectation. Radcliffe-Brown offered his anthropological judgement on 'a power which we may speak of as a spiritual or moral power' in terms of 'a sense of dependence

---

[42] Homer, *Iliad* (1987, 1:1–5, 24: 780–804), and Homer, *Odyssey* ([1946] 1991: 159–78).

on a power outside ourselves' in his general approach to religion, albeit in a way not directly related to the notion of embodiment.[43] There is no indication that his social-scientific sense of 'dependence' owed anything to the classic theological advocacy of Schleiermacher, for whom the very basis of piety was rooted in 'the consciousness of being absolutely dependent, or, which is the same thing, of being in relation to God'.[44] In this volume there will be no attempt to describe the long theological traditions preceding and following Schleiermacher in which a sense of dependence upon God is deemed the very basis of faith, nor of the liturgical bases of worship engaging with that sense. I have, elsewhere, considered some of these issues in terms of 'otherness' and human emotion.[45] It suffices to say that both theology and anthropology have found it necessary to describe human life in terms of sensed relationships, whether with God, ancestors, kinsfolk, or 'society' at large.

In this chapter our theoretical perspective on 'power' turns on the expression of 'vitality' and on how this is located in the body itself.[46] The eminent phenomenologist of religion Gerardus van der Leeuw developed an entire classification of the religious world in terms of a phenomenology of power, and there is much to be learned from him and his understanding of 'power' as part of a human demand 'to find some meaning in life'.[47] More-recent thinkers have added their own depictions of different types of power that influence the form a society takes, but Durkheim's train of thought remains helpful even though my intention is to try and be more narrowly focused and to speak of vitality as a sense of positive power. Two advantages spring from this. The first is that the idea of mortality can be taken as the negative mirror image of vitality: mortality involves a 'sense of' death, just as 'vitality' involves a 'sense of' life. It is also inevitable that we allude here to Freud's positive and negative aspects of life force, expressed in his *eros* and *thanatos* principles; the former revealed in a creative force for life, with the latter doing the same for a movement towards death. The second advantage lies in being able to correlate this sense of vitality with the notion of 'force' or 'social force' that is embedded in the early Durkheimian tradition of the relation between individual and society and which appears in two somewhat different forms in Marcel Mauss's treatment of 'the gift' in his powerful theory of reciprocity, and in Rodney Needham's engagement with the notion of dual sovereignty. Both of these now need some brief introductory description.

---

[43] Radcliffe-Brown (1952: 157).   [44] Schleiermacher ([1821–2] 1928: 12).
[45] Douglas J. Davies (2011).
[46] It lies beyond this volume to analyse 'power' and identity for different times and places. A comparison of Colin Wilson's *The Outsider* (1956) and Michael Foley's *The Age of Absurdity* (2010) would reveal a shift in focus from philosophical to social scientific cum humanitarian trends during a half-century that increasingly understood 'embodiment' as demanding attention.
[47] Van der Leeuw ([1933] 1967: 679).

RECIPROCITY: INDIVIDUAL AND SOCIETY

Marcel Mauss gave some clear shape to what he saw as a very widespread aspect of human behaviour rooted in mutual give and take that helped forge the very nature of social life, most especially of traditional societies prior to the emergence of an all-embracing capitalist and market economy. Despite later criticism and elaboration by others,[48] his classification still remains useful for many aspects of group life, not least within families and smaller-scale networks in which personal relationships are of the essence. For him 'gifts' could take very many forms, from physical objects to patterns of formal behaviour, and were classified in terms of being alienable or inalienable. The former were evaluated in terms of market value and playing a part in an ongoing process of reciprocity in which the person who receives such a gift becomes obliged to make a return gift in the future while bearing in mind the appropriate value that needs a 'return'. The inalienable 'gift' and its significance, by contrast, exists independently of market value and belongs to the weight given to phenomena bearing strong sentimental and emotional values aligned with such things as kinship bonds across generations. Such entities might include pieces of jewellery, furniture, or property, or even 'family traditions' whose worth is not to be counted in financial terms as they contribute to a person's very sense of identity and personal worth.

Working from Mauss, many have appreciated his distinction between the threefold obligation to give, to receive, and to make a return gift at some future time, but his 'fourth obligation' to give 'to the gods' or to engage in some way in the core values of a group whether religiously or secularly conceived should not be ignored. The threefold obligation tends to deploy goods of market value and hence their alienability, whilst the fourth obligation deals with the inalienable—objects or entities beyond mere price whose significance is referred to as their 'sentimental value'. Death is of special relevance in that it activates issues of reciprocity of both alienable and inalienable gifts at the same time as it activates their underlying kinship relationships and the professional services involved in funeral management.

In all of this, Mauss's reference is to the 'force' inherent in alienable gifts which prompts a recipient to make that return gift at some future time. It is, however, also worth considering the force inherent in inalienable gifts, a force rooted in the emotional nexus of kinship and other personal forms of alliance. The alienable 'force' is best understood in both Mauss and Durkheim's theoretical world as characteristic of the very nature of society as a moral community of interactive obligation; but the inalienable 'force' also needs inclusion, to cover the intricate nature of identity between generations of

---

[48] Cheal (1988); Godbout with Caillé (1998); James and Allen (1998); Karen Sykes (2005).

individuals. This inalienable version is also evident in Mauss and the collective 'forces' operating in domains of magic.[49] This broad perspective takes our social nature to be embedded in a sensed obligation to participate with others in an orderly group life framing a meaningful individual existence. Non-participation on the part of many would yield social chaos, sensed personally as anomie. It is no accident that this line of thinking on anomie in connection with suicide was developed, Durkheim being the first sociologist to do so, and it is a theme we will take up in chapter 8. From that same theoretical tradition, as we will see in chapter 7, the germinal work of Robert Hertz also continues to generate value, especially his idea of the way society incarnates itself in the individual, allowing us to speak of the individual as a microcosm of society, that is particularly significant in terms of death; a theoretical perspective that Mary Douglas took much further in general terms, and which Christine Valentine has developed in interesting ways for the complex identity of mourners and the 'presence' of the dead within their personal experience, as chapter 3 will show.[50]

Overall, then, this approach of reciprocity not only expresses something of the relationship between individual and society, but, quite properly, also between living and dead members of society. This inevitably involves the nature of the bonds between the living and the dead and offers its own way of framing theories of grief that are, in their more psychological way, also an account of interpersonal relationships between the living and the dead, as will become obvious in subsequent chapters dealing with funerals and ongoing patterns of linkage between life and death. Reciprocity of both kinds remains significant in twenty-first-century Britain, as we will see in association with various forms of funeral.

DUAL SOVEREIGNTY IN LIFE AND DEATH

Another dimension of the bond between individual and society and which is deeply significant in terms of death can be depicted through the concept of dual sovereignty; a notion identifying the subtle distinction between the jural–legal process of society on one hand and its 'mystical' capacity on the other. The dynamic experience of living—something that makes mortality a distant prospect for the young—ensures that social values are encountered as pervaded by emotion. Indeed, the interplay of emotion with social values comprises the arena in which the individual–society bond is forged, for ideas underlying social values do not come to a person as abstractions devoid of

---

[49] Mauss ([1902] 2001: 150–73).
[50] Hertz ([1905–6] 1960); Douglas (1966); Valentine (2008).

emotion (which would be a logical error born of an over-philosophical approach to knowledge), but are encountered as already emotion-framed. Here the work of two scholars, Guénon and Needham, will prove helpful as they discuss the interplay of different kinds of power which, together, seem to me to help constitute the 'force' of society. To their work I will then add both my own concept of moral–somatic relationships to help explain the bond of individual and society, and also the notion of the uncanny, which adds its own dimension to the complexity of cultural awareness of force.

The theme of an interplay between 'spiritual and temporal power' was high on the 1920s agenda of historian of religion René Guénon, who, though his thought was primarily focused on ancient Indian religion, thought that 'the opposition between the spiritual and temporal powers is found in one form or another among almost all peoples'.[51] Later, the anthropologist Rodney Needham took up the same general theme under the heading of dual sovereignty.[52] This category offers a slightly more useful framing of the idea of the two differing kinds of authority—one jural or legal, and the other mystical—and of their interaction. Though not initially deployed in terms of death, this conceptual pairing scheme is valuable for analysing the vitality–mortality polarity within human social organization, and especially for interpreting religion in general and death rites in particular, not least in terms of suicide and capital punishment, as we see in chapter 8. While Rodney Needham saw in dual sovereignty a means of interpreting human society, he did not elaborate upon his insight: it will be one venture of this present volume to do so. Human societies exist because they manage to attain some degree of organization, maintained through forms of recognized authority and, in this theoretical position, by an appropriate balance between jural–legal and mystical forms of authority. This concept also allows us one nuanced model for approaching the notion of social force that is important in this volume.

Jural Forms

In jural or legal forms of authority we encounter the conventions of rules of law administered by appropriate officers whose force of arms through police or the military maintains codes of justice. Practical aspects of life in its economic and political dealings, its mercantile transactions over goods and property, all require legal control. In Great Britain the rule of law is embodied iconographically in the statue of justice, depicted as a blindfolded figure holding the scales and sword of justice. Parliament passes laws that are upheld by the judicial system and by the police. Behind the courts and Parliament

---

[51] Guénon ([1929] 2001: 15).   [52] Needham (1980).

stands the ultimate deterrent of military force, seen within the country in its ceremonial dress and behaviour, but abroad transformed into an active fighting force. The success of the British form of democratic society lies in the very absence of military action within its own social world; deep problems are caused if ever it has to intrude into the civil realm, as during the Northern Ireland 'Troubles'. It exists for defence of the realm, with martial law only occurring in periods of failure of democracy by courts and police. It is the force of last resort within a democracy, but of first resort in totalitarian regimes where naked power can overrule recognized and acceptable authority.

Mystical Forms

Mystical authority takes us into the rather different realm of the quality of interpersonal relationships and human flourishing. It acknowledges those aspects of life that reflect the goodwill a person may have of another person. In the terms of Hocart, an anthropologist of a previous generation, mystical authority concerns things that 'foster life' amidst the enormously complex and diverse human 'quest for life'.[53] This entails and embraces many aspects of emotional life and human identity, not least those dealing with destiny and the unknown and risky aspects of existence. In general terms we may see mystical authority as the enhancement of personhood. Though the very word 'mystical' is, of course, problematic because of its association with explicitly religious ideas of supernatural invocation or transcendent awe and with implicit emotions both within and beyond traditional 'religious' domains. While such domains may well be part of the phenomena that are recognized as fostering human flourishing, it is this volume's intention to take the 'mystical' as a description of just those reported phenomena rather than accepting any supernatural source for them. These issues will be pursued much more fully in chapter 5. At this stage I can simply emphasize the importance of such a fostering of life. It was a point extremely well made in Raymond Williams' magisterial study, *Culture and Society 1780–1950*, when he insisted on speaking of culture in terms of the 'the social reality' of 'tending' aspects of life: 'any culture, in its whole process, is a selection, an emphasis, a particular tending'. Without using the terms, he unites 'nature' and 'nurture' in a shared discourse on 'natural growth' and 'tending', as 'parts of a mutual process'.[54] Behind his outlook is the sense that a particular human group possesses a natural affinity—that 'selection' and 'emphasis'—with certain choices of life-ways; this is a concept appearing throughout this volume in terms of lifestyle and death-style, and we return to it in chapter 9.

---

[53] Hocart (1933: 137).   [54] Raymond Williams ([1958] 1961: 323).

THE MORAL–SOMATIC

One further theoretical idea that also brings within its purview an integrating factor is that of 'moral–somatic' relationships, a term I introduced to indicate the interplay of social identity and the emotional dynamics of individuals within the embodiment of individuals.[55] This term pinpoints the fact that, theoretically speaking, a person serves as the nexus of the social or moral world on one hand and the bodily world on the other. While we are very used to the idea of psycho-somatic relationships, this notion of moral–somatics simply extends the link to the social world in which the psycho-somatic individual has its place. In psycho-somatic terms even the memory of some past social situation can trigger a current emotional response: we blush at the thought of some past embarrassment, or are saddened by the memory of some bereavement. The moral–somatic domain brings responses triggered by 'external' stimuli, as when a person is grief-stricken at the news of a death, sickened when hearing of a particularly inhuman attack on an innocent victim, or expressing a sense of being humbled when accorded a social honour or public recognition. We will encounter such cases in subsequent chapters and find this concept of some significance when linked with behaviours interpreted in terms of ritual purity and impurity.

CAPTURING EXPERIENCE: THE HOLY
AND THE UNCANNY

One final phenomenon relating to the above paired concepts concerns that awe, mystery, hiddenness, unknowingness, or uncanny awareness of things encountered in life in general, and often in association with death and bereavement. This phenomenon of the uncanny can be encountered as comforting or fearful, and, as far as death is concerned, reflects the degree of intimacy and distance between lifestyle and death-style in a society. Though a difficult concept to introduce within an essentially social-scientific volume, whose primary stress lies on rational explanation and interpretative theories, the uncanny is valuable for enabling scientific description to do justice to certain more elusive elements of human awareness.[56] At the outset it needs to be made clear that this notion straddles numerous disciplines, but is most evident in theological studies, for the self-evident reason that theologians, reflective devotees that they are, frequently feel the need to describe the

---

[55] Douglas J. Davies (2011: 186–91). First used in an address to the Scandinavian Sociological Association (2004).
[56] Some might set it within the general scope of phenomenological hermeneutics.

deity as ineffable and, in so doing reveal their own difficulty in 'spelling out' their own experience. So it is that God remains beyond words, with some notion of mystery invoked to cover the condition of not knowing. It is precisely in alignment with this sense of 'not knowing' that 'mystery' emerges, not only or simply as a philosophical marker of the existence of that 'unknown', but also as a sensed awareness of that which lies behind the unknown. Rudolph Otto, theologian, philosopher, and historian of religion, is the scholar most strongly identified with this phenomenon in his *The Idea of the Holy* in which he speaks of the amazingly attractive power of mystery that underlies individual religious experience and is sometimes associated with ritual actions.[57] Something similar lies behind William James and his accounts of *The Varieties of Religious Experience* with its numerous accounts of conversion experiences. But many sources could be rehearsed to make the point that the human drive for meaning encounters constraints that are often creatively framed rather than accepted as contradictions. The divine mystery, in particular, lies beyond cavil, and simply fosters greater devotion.[58] Similar issues of mystery are aligned with concepts of sacred space and with influences of 'power' that are frequently interpreted as contact with supernatural forces.[59] In chapter 8 I will also include some material on the fictional but enormously popular Harry Potter books, given their uncanny framing of death, loss, and grief.

While I have considered 'mysterious' issues elsewhere,[60] this theme of the uncanny remains significant given its deployment, for example, the two quite different domains of robotic engineering and townscape architecture. Each concerns the way human awareness is influenced by its environment, one focused on the way robots possess certain human-like features capable of triggering uncanny experience in our 'relations' with them, and the other derived from the influence of older buildings on new developments in urban contexts. The robotic or android case we leave for our discussion on grief in chapter 6, while the issue of townscape is relevant here and will be taken up again in chapters 2 (relating to places to die and remember), and 7 (relating to military memorials).

In terms of the uncanny and urban contexts I take my lead from Michel de Certeau and Luce Giard whose 'Ghosts in the City' depicts transformed urban landscapes and the way certain buildings seem to stand as 'resistances' to town planners' desire to create new cityscapes; such edifices 'seduce the nostalgia attached to a world on its way to disappearing'. They described an uncanniness in the way these older buildings not only stand out against development

---

[57] Famously captured in Otto's (1924) *Mysterium Tremendum et Fascinans*.
[58] Typically expressed biblically in Romans 11: 33–6.
[59] As with van der Leeuw ([1933] 1967).
[60] Douglas J. Davies (2011: 261–70).

but may also benefit developers 'in periods of recession' when a 'protectionist economy' is influential.[61]

These architectural issues contribute to our study of death in that they manifest the human experience of moving from the past to the future, a process embedded in the environmental framing of human embodiment. The architectural basis of the 'uncanniness' of, for example, a certain building that 'lurks there, in the everyday life of the city', and which is 'a ghost that henceforth haunts urban planning', so easily resembles the memory and remaining goods of the dead in the everyday life of the living.[62] But this comparison is not simply a fortuitous analogy; it is grounded in daily materiality, as the world in which our memory and emotion interplay as we live in the present and direct activity towards the future. The issue is one of entailment of relationships with things and places, and while this relates most especially to the home, it can also relate to many other locations of personal engagement, as we will see in the next chapter with the placement of cremated remains. The uncanny touches a part of existence with deep resonances at the personal level as well at the level of public awareness. It is essentially experiential, concerning experiences prompted by place as event; that is to say, the uncanny is prompted by our engagement with a place in such a way that the experienced moment becomes an event. It is an idea that covers a variety of life circumstances. One person unexpectedly and unusually meets another in the street and says 'that's funny . . .' (or even, 'that's strange . . .') ' . . . I was just talking about you to someone'. Or, again, two individuals who have not been in touch with each other for some years, and with no obvious prompting, reason, or occasion, send emails to each other from quite different time zones in different parts of the world at the same time, such that one has not received the other before sending his own: 'that's strange!' Even in the better-known moment of déjà-vu experience, or in reaction to some dream, a sense of the strange or uncanny nature of things may arise. Such things may consist in 'opening a certain depth within the present', and de Certeau and Giard speak of such uncanny things and places serving as 'wild objects' and as the 'equivalent of what the gods of antiquity were, the "spirits" of the place'.[63] We will take up this theme of the uncanny numerous times in this volume, not least in chapter 7's consideration of the proliferation of British war memorials. For the moment, however, one of the most obvious applications of this idea of the uncanny relates not only to our sense of others or of place but also to our sense of self. While this will be immediately obvious when we return to the idea in chapter 6 in relation to the idea of grief, it is something that can apply

---

[61] De Certeau, Giard, and Mayol ([1994] 1998: 133).
[62] Ibid. Cf. Otto ([1917] 1924: 133) for empty-house uncanniness.
[63] Ibid., 135.

to people at many times and periods of their life. It becomes clearer, for example, when we explore the issue of identity.

BEING A PERSON

Just what it is that makes us who we are is something that contemporary life easily ignores, despite often laying claim to a sophisticated self-awareness typified in such liberal–intellectual notions as that of irony. This is especially the case as human identity is kaleidoscopically lived out within a field of influencing factors. Not only do the poles of birth and death have their own cultural frame of tradition and destiny that shift through the influence of developments such as that of pregnancy scans or the freezing of sperm for potential future use, but each individual has to negotiate his or her own sense of self between the forces of private awareness and acceptability to peers, family, and wider society.

There is very little available by way of formal teaching on life and identity in contemporary Britain, let alone on life and death. In terms of cultural values, numerous traditional religious groups exist in some degree of stand-off tension with scientific ideas of genetics, evolutionary biology, and cognitive science, while relatively small numbers of dedicated adherents populate diverse fundamentalisms.[64] Many people live through a kind of situational bricolage, mustering ideas as circumstances demand without any necessary commitment to their ongoing value. While social class, ethnic background, idiosyncrasy, and the educational aspirations or irrelevances that pervade all of these energize these differences between people, all inhabit a shared world of politics, law, and public services to some degree. It may well be that the general cultural absence of direct dealing with ideas of identity and death lies precisely in the fact that death dumfounds the liberal consumerism of the free market within generally secularized Western contexts. This is one reason why suicide is so problematic, as chapter 8 will show, while it is also, paradoxically, evident in more conservative forms of early twenty-first-century militant Islam whose own force in the dialectic of terrorism highlights the desirability of death as a portal to Paradise.

Twenty-Several Men

As for the nature of personhood, one excellent background source can be found in George Herbert's poem 'Giddiness' which begins with the well-known—'Oh, what a thing is man!'—a rhetorical utterance that finds

---

[64] E.g. Jeeves (ed.) (2011), a multidisciplinary attempt at *Rethinking Human Nature*, from a relatively conservative Christian perspective.

development in his understanding of human complexity and diversity of identity, even within a single individual. 'He is some twenty several men at least/Each several hour.' Then, in a moment of stark realism, he reminds us of what we do not see in each other's complexity: 'Surely if each one saw another's heart, There would be no commerce, No sale or bargain pass: all would disperse, And live apart.'[65] From Herbert's seventeenth-century perception of spirituality and human relations to Robert Louis Stevenson's *Jekyll and Hyde* of 1886, there is a wide literary span depicting human character and identity, yet few literary works have become as well known as Stevenson's invention. Repeated in film and narrative versions, it dwells upon human nature and its moral possibilities. It has of course been argued that 'Calvinism marked Stevenson's personality and imagination unequivocally',[66] and this would go some way to help us see why he builds into his fable the explicit account of 'a profound duplicity of life' that led to his eponymous hero's forensic self-description of 'a degradation in my faults, that . . . severed in me those provinces of good and evil which divide and compound man's dual nature'. In being such a 'double-dealer' he had, as Jekyll expressed it, been 'driven to reflect deeply and inveterately on that hard law of life which lies at the root of religion', viz. 'the perennial war among my members'.[67] Such a consideration of multiple motivations benefits from being set in a nineteenth-century Britain that was already creating an 'increasingly regulated world', whether in terms of factory production, education, or in 'football and sports at large'.[68]

The Jekyll–Hyde dichotomy deriving from biblical religion, and Herbert's diversity from observation of life, aptly represent a widespread human sense of the complexity of self. Just how this is portrayed culture by culture is a perennial issue for cultural anthropology and the constitution of the self. Historically–philosophically it is evident in the Platonic body–soul divide and psychologically in Freud's tripartite vision of a person. As already discussed, it appears in Durkheim's sociology as *Homo duplex*, a person whose dual composition comes from self and society in interaction. Such a complex self will also stand as an interesting backcloth for our own account of British identities in relation to death. But there is one aspect of individuality that cannot be ignored within historical, literary, or theological studies, and that is the narrative frame of the single individual, whether heroic or demonic, who embodies the ideas, beliefs, and the aspirations or fears, carried by the masses. It is precisely that 'individual' who is frequently lost in social-scientific analyses of trends, ideal types, or interpretations of social structures or processes. And this is why some accounts of life are deemed to be 'merely academic': in their abstraction they fail to activate those inbuilt human systems of cognition

---

[65] Herbert (1994: 110).   [66] Calder (1979: 8).
[67] Stevenson ([1886] 1979: 81–2). Cf. Epistle to the Romans 7: 14–25.
[68] Walvin (1986: 110).

that respond emotionally to the life of another. Ivory towers are 'things', and so are many sociological and theological theories; stories, myths, and many literary forms are 'personal'. One commentator portrayed this issue thus.

> It is an unfair truth about human nature that we are only properly interested in single maverick figures. We understand about crowds; we train ourselves to value statistical and cumulative events. But all that can gain the interest of most of us is the exceptional individual.... We... understand the world through people who may be very unlike the rest of humanity. Institutions, movements, communal excellence rest on the individual.[69]

That theoretical cameo, albeit from a journalist and not a sociologist, will prove fruitful in what follows as we seek to balance some understanding of individual and society in relation to death. Meanwhile, we acknowledge the vital social frame for individual and communal living and dying, a perspective that lay at the foundation of both Thomas Hobbes' account of the nature of England as an ecclesiastical and civil commonwealth and Jeremy Taylor's Anglican spirituality on life and death, with both writing in the mid-seventeenth century. For Hobbes, the 'passions', or what we would now call emotions, suffuse much of his analysis of human existence, with considerable space devoted to religious beliefs about immortality and the afterlife.[70] One editor depicts Hobbes' view of man as 'a creature civilized by the fear of death', observing that 'Hobbes, no less than others of his time—Montaigne and Pascal for example—felt the impact of this fear', with Hobbes dying 'in mortal fear of hell-fire'.[71] Taylor, by contrast, sought to foster a destiny of confidence in believers who organized their lives aright even amidst the perilous political–religious period of the English Reformation, the Commonwealth, and beyond.[72] With Taylor, as so often in theological work, it is often in prayers and liturgies that a theology's influence most readily appears, and this is evident in one of Taylor's prayers for a dying person. It asks of God that,

> when it shall please thee that his soul goes out from the prison of his body, it may be received by angels, and preserved from the surprise of evil spirits, and from the horrors and amazements of strange and new regions, and be laid up in the bosom of our Lord, till at the day of thy second coming it shall be reunited to the body... forever to live, and to behold the face of God in the glories of the Lord Jesus.[73]

---

[69] Hensher (2012: 15).
[70] Thomas Hobbes, 1588–1679 ([1651] n.d., pp. 291–459). Contemporary of Anglican divine Jeremy Taylor, 1613–67, Hobbes saw earliest Christianity decline as 'hierarchical structures' took over, a radically mistaken interpretation according to the Jesuit Gerald O'Collins (2011: 266).
[71] Oakeshott (n.d., pp. xxxvi, and lxiv, respectively).
[72] His *Holy Living* and *Holy Dying* followed each other in 1650 and 1651, respectively.
[73] Jeremy Taylor ([1650] 1830: 339).

Taylor, writing amidst Reformation antagonisms, places the transit of the disembodied soul in the care of angels as it moves to being 'laid up in the bosom of the Lord', much reflecting the characteristic Protestant notion of 'soul sleep', until the time of its resurrection and re-embodiment.[74] But it is interesting to see him seek divine preservation of the departing soul 'from the surprise of evil spirits, and from the horrors and amazements of strange and new regions'. This could easily be heard by the faithful of his day as an anodyne against the centuries-old Catholic notion of purgatory. Writing at the time of Oliver Cromwell's ravages of the Church of England, when variations of Puritan and Protestant theologies were dominant, it is also interesting to see Taylor advocate the 'great truth' of 'twelve signs of grace and predestination'. He is bold enough to argue that any one of those having his listed 'signs' 'does as certainly belong to God and is his son, as surely as he is his creature'.[75] So, having dealt with potential Catholic-inspired fears, he now dispels the extreme Protestant-induced fear of whether one was or was not among God's elect; an issue that fired the sociological imagination of Max Weber and his 'Protestant Ethic and the Spirit of Capitalism' thesis nearly four hundred years later. For Taylor, the well-ordered Christian life, set within the Anglican Church's sacraments, given to charitable living, and being 'just in his dealing and diligent in his calling', was surety enough for avoiding yet another form of post-mortem fear.

POSTMODERNITY

The British nation state, in its provision of welfare through educational, health, and policing, maintains a relatively stable society while economic necessities of home, food, and work are catered for through the immense commercial venture of banks, building societies, and supermarket and domestically targeted consumerism. The media, as they self-serve to maintain their own existence through journalistic comment and advertising concerning these social dynamics, all alongside sporting events, catalyse the sense of a unified society. The media presence in each home has, increasingly, been complemented by a pervasive electronic presence within each individual's consciousness of self, as technology has relocated millions within personal spheres of entertainment and social-network fields.

---

[74] John Calvin, reformer par excellence, set his first publication on 'soul sleep', objecting to the idea and asserting that the soul 'remains fully alive as it is taken up in the Lord' (G. E. Tavard 2000: 1).
[75] Jeremy Taylor ([1650] 1830: xi–xii).

The much-heralded domain of postmodernity, itself an output of text- and narrative-dependent critics emphasizing what they perceive as an absent meta-narrative of life's meaning, has been rapidly subverted, not so much by ideological replacements, as in human rights, world ecology, or even by ideas of 'liquid' identities,[76] but by the ritual forms of mobile communication in which thumbs have assumed a new power in enabling meaningful behaviour in fostering or manufacturing social networks with their expanse of 'friends'. As social animals on the edge of potential social isolation, or fearful of alienation from centres of social power, an adaptive response has emerged in populations through the pragmatics of manipulation. Although these marketed tools of this communication revolution have only been possible through complex electronic engineering, their power lies, quite literally, 'in the hands of' their consumerist owners. For millions, especially those of younger generations, it would seem that a sense of identity in public is aligned with owning, carrying, and using mobile equipment whose capacity for information generation is enormous. Many speak as though their life would be seriously affected if they were not a lively presence to their electronic peers, kin, and beyond. Yet the scene is one in which the complexity of electronic communication runs alongside the relative simplicity of human emotions of belonging and fear of loneliness. This is typified in the acronym FOMO or 'fear of missing out', where the rise of social media parallels the long-embedded social and status-seeking nature of human beings. Here cultural intensification faces off against cultural fragmentation.

Theoretical Limitation and Strength

These brief comments on pragmatism and social theory highlight the relative paucity of persuasive social theory to explain human life on the broad scale, just as it is often partial within daily existence. C. P. Snow said of Lloyd George that he was 'one of the cleverest of men' possessing 'great social insight', but that 'his social passions never got organized into an intellectual framework'.[77] While that may well be a formula for political success by retaining a certain openness to events, it is also a sensible theoretical approach to the emergent complexities of social life. This is not to say that a politician may possess a clear formulation of social policy that may be implemented for a period of time, but that events will, sooner or later, prove seriously hazardous for formulaic interpretation. And social scientists are in much the same situation. The first decades of the twenty-first century serve as their own example of the fact that politicians and social theorists are often wise after the social event but

---

[76] Bauman (2011).   [77] Snow (1969: 110).

largely ignorant in advance of major cultural shifts prompted by economic, political, or other triggers. Events, accidents, conglomerations of trends, and radical disjunctions all play a part in the utter complexity of human society as a global phenomenon.

Let one example hint at many others. *The Times* newspaper made its 'Person of the Year Award' of 2011 to Mohamed Bouazizi, the twenty-six-year-old street merchant from Tunis who burned himself in protest at disrespectful treatment from a 'female municipal agent' who is alleged to have slapped his face when he protested at having goods improperly confiscated from his street-seller's stall in December 2010. His death in hospital was declared on 4 January 2011. This 'barrow-boy . . . changed the world' when 'his dramatic protest struck a chord across the Arab world'.[78] From the seven-hundred or so who protested the very night of his self-immolation to the thousands who protested against perceived despotic leadership of President Mubarak in Egypt or Colonel Gaddafi in Libya emerged the 'Arab Spring', which another journalist described as 'astounding' and something not to be dismissed as 2011 drew to a close: he reckoned that 'it has been a year to match 1989 and the fall of Communism'.[79] The hopes entailed in this 'Arab Spring' were, however, frustrated, and even dashed, so that by the dawn of 2014 the parallel with the fall of communism was impossible to sustain.

The drive for meaning that typifies the human species is, inevitably, also a driver of political–sociological theory and often takes the form of classifications of modernity and its modulations as post-, late high, modernity and so on. While such nomenclature possesses some limited descriptive power of society, and often gains a reified currency amongst academic elites generating social theory, its more ultimate applicability as explanation is limited.[80] Indeed, the distinction between description and interpretation is crucial within the humanities and much of social science, and although the debate as to whether any particular social science may have predictive value analogous to some of the harder sciences is now largely outdated, it remains as a cautionary signpost in the history of theory.

What does remain important is the power of description as its own form of explanation. This is one reason why many now invoke the notions of phenomenology and ethnography in numerous social studies. In terms of anthropological and sociological theory, for example, the classic work of someone like Evans-Pritchard took its power from detailed ethnography, while much of Weber's work on religion lies in detailed description derived from historical material.[81] In the latter case, his development of the

---

[78] Bone (2011).   [79] Fletcher (2011).
[80] Horlick-Jones (2012: 1223) for a theorist becoming 'unfashionable in sociological circles so quickly'.
[81] Max Weber ([1915b] 1991).

classifications of things, not least utilizing the notion of ideal types, is but a formalizing of description. The endeavour of the present volume lies precisely in attempting descriptive accounts of limited contexts. For this reason there will be very sparing use of such terminology in the following chapters, and where it does occur I will seek to note the limited context of its interpretative significance. When it comes to thinking about broad-scale explanation it is wise to bear in mind something of that classical account of physicists when reckoning that fuller accounts of 'light' sometimes require a particle and sometimes a wave-theory approach in order to do justice to material evidence. Even such a crude analogy might well aid sociological thinking when we sometimes need a 'great man' and sometimes a 'social process' theory to cope with events and their outcomes.

Social Change and Invented Tradition

Britain has undergone major transformations in the social organization of power, belief, and philosophical–scientific thought during its developing history of national identity, not least through what are conventionally described as periods of Reformation, Enlightenment, and scientific, industrial, and welfare revolutions, all amidst a relatively establishment-influenced, traditionalist, society.[82] As far as death is concerned, for much of the nineteenth and twentieth centuries the British often led the world in implementing changes associated with coping with death, a fact that reinforces the value of seeing death as a viable cultural access point to social change within British life.[83] Cases in point are those of cremation, ash dispersal, woodland burial, and the prospect of the innovatory process of resomation. These exemplify cultural creativity in the invention of tradition and express something of an interplay between religious and secular meaning.

SPIRITUALITY, RELIGION, AND RITUAL

As for 'spirituality', this notion will be accorded suitable importance when handling these 'religious' and 'secular' perspectives, recognizing that death presents an access point for issues of humanist and secularist world views as well as the fact that 'spirituality' is now of increasing practical importance within the health-care concerns of the NHS, itself a potential complement to

---

[82] Owen Jones ([2014] 2015: xviii): 'We live in a time of Establishment triumphalism.'
[83] See, for example, Jindra and Noret (2011: 16–40) for an African comparison.

or even replacement of religious institutional provision, as chapter 5 will show. Moving beyond its longstanding use of hospital chaplains, such a medical spirituality can be interpreted either as a valuable bridging device between the traditionally religious and the secular or as a dissolution–transformation of it. The practical needs of hospital patients, as of others, rapidly contextualizes such an abstract notion as 'spirituality', within therapeutic and ritualized contexts.

Because this role of ritual, understood from a social-scientific perspective, and of liturgy, as a theologically understood form of ritual, will recur throughout this volume, we will, in chapter 3, account for its distinctive features in the context of considering ecclesial and secular–humanist types of formalized funerary behaviour. Changes in church rites and the emergence of secular ceremonial, though germinal in the later nineteenth century, burgeoned during the second half of the twentieth century, and are especially important as a form of competition for public usage. The theme of an increased ritualization of aspects of British life, from citizenship ceremonies to stereotyped television contests, will also be noted as an aspect of cultural change, raising at times the useful notion of the invention of tradition,[84] not least in association with crematoria and cremated remains, woodland burial, humanist funerals, and military memorials.

EMOTIONS, GRIEF, AND IDENTITY

The social force evident in cultural innovation will, quite appropriately, be allied in the following chapters with the theme of emotions, and of ritual as the scene for the intensification of emotion. This may help contribute to an integrated approach to the sociology of religion in Britain reached through death, grief, and mourning. This will inevitably raise the issue of individualism as emphasis upon consumerism is balanced by lives framed by family, workmates, colleagues, and leisure friends, the death of whom affects these networks of identity. Pre-planned funeral music and words, location of the body or of cremated remains, and style of memorials all reflect this interplay as expressions of a religion–secularization spectrum explicitly offered by funeral directors as commercial entrepreneurs alert to a decreasing popular familiarity with established religious ceremonies. One significant element that will also touch these issues will concern gender, and the increasing role of women in death-related ritual in Britain.

---

[84] See Hobsbawm and Ranger ([1983] 2005).

ELECTIVE AFFINITY AND PARADIGMATIC SCENES

Two further theoretical concepts that will be of considerable value in this volume are those of elective affinity and paradigmatic scenes, each with its own sense of social force expressing the draw felt towards funeral phenomena of abstract ideas, concrete images, objects, persons, or place.[85] The notion of elective affinity has a conceptual provenance running back from Max Weber's sociology through Goethe's literary work, notably his novel *Elective Affinities* which, itself, transformed a previous notion of the Swedish chemist Torbern Olof Bergmann[86] concerning chemical attraction into one of human interpersonal emotional sensitivity where previously existing partners break their bonds and realign with other available partners.[87] For our purposes we will see how such an affinity has existed, in turn, with traditional burial, cremation and private use of ashes, and now with woodland burial.

Then, in paradigmatic scenes we see how such attractive ideas are revealed in social images with which people become deeply accustomed. I have discussed the nature and role of paradigmatic scenes elsewhere in terms of their use in classical antiquity, biblical studies, and modern anthropology, have shown how they relate to such ideas as 'cultural scenario', and have demonstrated their value for capturing and enshrining the preferred emotional tones of a group and framing them in narrative formats.[88] The notion of paradigm is also valuable because it allows for a sense of both proximity to and an appropriation of core values. It should not be taken as a blueprint to which social life must conform in some rigid way, but as an indicative approximation.[89] A closely similar idea is very familiar to anthropologists, from Claude Lévi-Strauss's treatment of the idea of 'totemism' when he argued that certain phenomena are 'good to think',[90] to the slightly less well-known application in Goldschmidt's notion of things being 'good to feel'.[91] This expresses the fact that human beings often think in terms of analogy between things, with the degree of indirectness involved actually aiding and not hindering comprehension of what are, sometimes, rather complex notions. One clear example applicable in this volume, and to which we return in chapter 9, is expressed in the biblical account of humanity as 'dust': 'dust thou art and unto dust shalt

---

[85] Similar to Otto's 'law of the association of feelings' (1924: 43–51) and not unlike the more psychological 'association of ideas'.

[86] Bergman (1785), *De attractionibus electivis*. German translation *Wahlverwandschaft*.

[87] Goethe ([1809] 1971: 51–6). A century later, Herman Hesse ([1905] 1973: 61) speaks of a 'horde of boys' in the 'first few weeks of community life' as resembling 'a chemical mixture in which clouds and flakes in suspension come together, separate again, form other compounds until it results in a number of chemical compositions'.

[88] Douglas J. Davies (2011: 42–60).

[89] Even Plato's use of 'paradigm' in *The Republic* (Book V. 472, 1, e) suggests approximation (1974: 262, 266).

[90] Lévi-Strauss (1962: 89). Cf. Bloch (1988).   [91] Douglas J. Davies (2011: 61).

thou return'.[92] In this context 'dust' is 'good to think'; it provides a means of self-reflection that is hard to find in some direct act of non-referential logical analysis. Such a process resembles the concept of projection, which has its own long philosophical and psychological history in assumptions about how people think. Things that are 'good to think' or 'good to feel', just like 'paradigmatic scenes', are of fundamental significance when considering life-style and, not least, death-style.

SIR THOMAS BROWNE'S *HYDRIOTAPHIA*

This reference to biblical dust and paradigmatic scenes, following our wider account of theoretical perspectives, brings us to Sir Thomas Browne, an individual whose work offers its own window on life and death in the history of Britain. This man's medical training included study in Padua, along with his medical degree received in the equally famous university of Leiden; Pembroke was his Cambridge College. Browne's account of funeral rites stands out in early-modern British cultural history, published as *Hydriotaphia or Urne-Burial* in 1658. It is part of an extensive encyclopedia-like *Works* that embraces natural history, a real engagement with religion, and an early form of anthropology.[93] *Urne-Burial* is a reminder both of the impact of death-related issues on an individual in his own day and of the importance of historically embedded studies for our own. Prompted by the discovery of what we now see as Bronze Age burial urns at 'old Walsingham', he sets out on a sketch of funeral practices which moves from biblical times to classical Greece and Rome and, indeed, to Britain with Bede. This considers funeral culture amongst the Chinese, Egyptians, Jewish Nation, Muslims (*Musselman*), Parsees, Gauls, and numerous ancient British and Scandinavian groups. Its panorama includes cremation, burial, exposure and containment of bodies, the posture of corpses, the use of music 'to quiet the affectations', the transmigration of the soul, the resurrection of the body, and the nature of grave goods; in all this, such distant times and places as those listed pass into accounts of British contexts such as Buxton and Yarmouth.

Some of his notes still carry resonance in Britain today, where woodland burial echoes his mention of pine trees planted at graves by some Chinese (102), or the ancient custom elsewhere of not cremating children 'before their teeth appeared as apprehending their bodies too tender a morsel for fire, and that their gristly bones would scarce leave separable reliques after the pyral combustion' (129), an issue still of concern in the cremation of neo-natal

---

[92] Genesis 3: 19 (King James Version).
[93] Thomas Browne ([1658] 1927, three volumes) *Urne-Burial*, Vol. III: 97–144.

deaths with the potential for there being nothing left for the parents afterwards.[94] Alongside his comparative study, in which he is some two-and-a-half
centuries in advance of the collector of world customs, Sir James Frazer of
Trinity College, Cambridge, Sir Thomas adds his own evaluation of peoples'
attitudes. He is all too alert to the fact that 'men have lost their reason in
nothing so much as their Religion. Wherein stones and clouts make Martyrs;
and since the Religion of one seems madness unto another.' In another
famous work on religion and doctors he rejects the accusation of atheism
heard in the 'common speech (but only amongst the unlearn'd sort)' that
where there are three doctors there are two atheists, an accusation also
levelled at 'Philosophers in general' and those seeking to understand 'Nature'
(original italics).[95] The significance of this scholar, born in 1605 and dying
in 1682, and who spent much of his later life as a doctor in Norwich, is that
he lived in times of extreme opinions battled out between Protestant and
Catholic views in the emergent Church of England and during the English
Civil War of 1642–51. For him 'Life is a pure flame, and we live by an
invisible Sun within us'[96]. Some long for tombs and an enduring memorial
but others realize that we live on in the memory of others but for a
generation. Mummies are futile since they were now sold as medicine;
'Mummie is become Merchandise, Mizraim cures wounds, and Pharoa is
sold for balsoms.'[97] There lingers in his language a certain ambiguity that
might later in this volume appear now as traditional Christian faith, now as
a spirituality of nature, or even as rational agnosticism—if not that atheism,
to which he seemingly objects. He alludes to the persuasive power of
experience that is a 'handsome anticipation of heaven', but does so in a
strongly poetic, and mystic-like passage describing, 'Christian annihilation,
exstasis, exolution, liquefaction, transformation, the kisse of the Spouse,
gustation of God, and ingression of the divine shadow'. Such people 'have
already had an handsome anticipation of heaven; the glory of the world is
surely over, and the earth in ashes unto them'. For him 'the Metaphysics of
true belief' bypasses 'lasting Monuments', 'Ready to be anything, in the
exstasie of being ever, and as content with six foot as the Moles of Adrianus'.
In terms of the integrated lifestyle and death-style of this volume we leave
his very human, and perhaps unsystematic yet heartfelt, reflections with part
of one of his concluding sentences: 'To live indeed is to be again ourselves,
which being not only an hope but an evidence in noble beleevers.'[98]

---

[94] Ibid., 102, 129.
[95] Browne (Religio Medici [1927] Vol. I: xiv), 'Ubi tres Medici, duo Athei.'
[96] Browne ([1658] 1927, three volumes) Urne-Burial, Vol. III: 142.   [97] Ibid., 141.
[98] Ibid., 144 (sic), 'Moles of Adrianus' referring to 'a stately Mausoleum built by Adrianus in
Rome'.

CONCLUSION

Unlike in Sir Thomas or in Lévi-Strauss's idiom, 'death' is not generally regarded as 'good to think' in contemporary Britain, for it exists at some distance from 'life'. Drawing from popularized interpretation of grief theories it is partly understood as loss and partly as the stilling or distancing of a voice whose family-based identity is increasingly curtailed. Death and bereavement combine in mixed clusters of popular experience that require a combination of theoretical perspectives for anything like adequate interpretation. For here we have to ponder death at many levels and deaths of many sorts. Just as the death of parents may rupture lives while helping to mature their adult offspring, so may the demise of some political leaders frustrate or enhance social change and the ongoing transformation of society. More than a few families have been glad to see the death of someone; so too when it comes to political institutions or regimes in which despots reign or the much more benign situation where formal retirement is unknown.[99] Cultural values and beliefs influence the way these outcomes are voiced, kept silent, or even thought at all, and in the next chapter we take up some of these issues in considering profiles of religious identity in Britain, in terms of both social surveys and cultures of memory.

---

[99] Several UK news items on 4 August 2014 commented on the House of Lords having too many members for its physical facilities. Given that the Lords have no retirement date, at least one newscaster alluded to death as one solution to overcrowding. *The Times*, August 2012 p. 2.

2

Beliefs and Valued Memorials

Knowledge of personal and cultural attitudes gained through social surveys combines in this chapter with selected theoretical and case-study approaches to death, afterlife, and memorials to the dead, as well as to phenomena that help create individual identity. This combination will help provide a perspective for mainstream religious and non-religious outlooks present in Great Britain in the twenty-first-century's initial decades.

SURVEYS

Of the many existing surveys, the National Census of 2011, along with surveys sponsored by specific organizations and some by the present author have been brought together to map British religion and to pinpoint more particular issues of death.[1]

Census (2011)

The key descriptive social survey of religion in Britain must lie with the National Census of 2011 whose survey of 56,075,912 individuals revealed the following picture of traditionally religious groupings. In rank order it showed 59.3% identified as Christian, 4.8% Muslim, 1.5% Hindu, 0.8% Sikh, 0.5% Jewish, and 0.4% Buddhist. Although Jains did not gain percentage recognition nationally, they did possess demographic pockets as in London's Boroughs of Barnet (0.6%), Brent (0.8%), and Harrow (2.2%), and were also present in smaller percentages in areas of Leicestershire and Northamptonshire. Similarly, Rastafarians at the 0.1% level were, apart from Bristol City,

---

[1] Spencer and Weldon (2012) sketch numerous UK surveys. Considerable variation is found in the nature of questions posed.

located largely in London areas of Hackney, Haringey, Lambeth, Lewisham, Southall, Brent, and Waltham Forest.

A great variety of further stated religions also revealed zero percentage nationally, but this time without demographic pockets indicative of ethnic or national origin; these included Animism, Chinese Religion, Confucianism, Druid, Druze, Eckankar, Heathen, Mysticism, New Age, and Native American Religion, Occult, and Pantheism. This suggests that particular caution is merited when using those terms within a contemporary British context.

As for Paganism, that gained 0.1% nationally, with a fairly regular incidence across England and Wales. However, three of Derbyshire's eight districts showed 0.2%, and so too did Southend-on-Sea, North-west Leicestershire, Lincoln, four of Norfolk's seven districts, one of Suffolk's seven districts, ten of Inner London's fourteen districts, Brighton and Hove, the Isle of Wight, East Sussex, and Devon, Dorset, and Somerset in the South West. Then Cornwall made 0.3%, as did Ceredigion in Wales, while Mendip in Somerset topped the table at 0.4%.

Spiritualism, presumably understood in terms of spiritualist churches, was marked by a 0.1% range in general, including the whole of inner London, barring Lewisham, and approximately half of outer London areas. The 0.2% range was evident, for example, in Bournemouth, Stevenage, the Isle of Wight, Torbay, Christchurch (Dorset), and Merthyr Tydfil.

The Census also took account of humanist, agnostic, and atheist positions. Both agnosticism and atheism were reflected at 0.1%, largely in urban areas, but both made 0.2% in Brighton and Hove, Cambridge, and Oxford. As for the humanist category, this did not achieve 0.1% nationally but was evident at that level in a spread of towns in England and Wales.

Apart from these very low-level occurrences of what might be taken as identifiable secular categories, especially given the highly vocal and publicity-engendering secularism associated with them, is the further category of 'no religion', not least because practically a quarter of respondents (24.7%) were identified with it. Quite unlike the fairly equal incidence of humanism and atheism, the 'no religion' category possessed considerable variation as this selection of areas from higher to lower incidence reveals: Norwich (41.5%), Brighton and Hove (41%), Blaenau Gwent (40.8%), Caerphilly (40.5%), Rhondda Cynon Taff (40.4%), Merthyr Tydfil (40.4%), Bristol (37.4%), Exeter (34%), Cambridge (36.9%), Hull, Nottingham, and Portsmouth (all 34%), Oxford and the City of London (both 33%), Lincoln (32%), and Newcastle upon Tyne (27.8%). At the other end of the continuum, by contrast, we have Blackburn (13.6%), Copeland (Cumbria) (14.1%), Slough (11.9%), Borough of Brent (10.4%), and Harrow (9.3%).

One comparative comment that should be made on these results is that this Christianity level of 59.3% of the public was a reduction from 71.7% obtained in the Census of 2001. This suggests a significant shift in public opinion over a relatively short period of time and is something to which we will pay more detailed attention later in this chapter in respect of secularization and of death.

British Social Attitudes (2008)

The British Social Attitudes survey of 2008, involving a sample of 2,229 individuals, posed a number of religion-related questions.[2] One that is especially germane for this volume was the question concerning how 'spiritual' people considered themselves to be. The approximate results were as follows: Very 8%, Moderately 27%, Slightly 25%, Not at all 41%. It is, of course, an open issue as to just how respondents might have understood 'spiritual', but that must be left open. That result for the total sample can, however, be compared with respondents who reported themselves as having 'no religion'. Their approximate responses to the 'spirituality' question were as follows: Very 4%, Moderately 12%, Slightly 19%, Not at all 66%. This suggests that the 'spirituality' designation resonates to some degree with about 60% of the population at large and with some 44% of those of 'no religion'. This implies that it is an idea of some significance for Britons at large in that even in the 'no religion' group there is some alignment with being 'spiritual'.

As for belief in 'life after death', this survey recorded the following for the total sample and for the 'no religion' group (whose response is marked here in brackets). Yes, definitely 22% (11%), Yes, probably 30% (23%), No, probably not 26% (30%), and No, definitely not 22% (36%). Taking a relatively critical reading of these results, it would seem to indicate that even those with 'no religion'—some 34% or so—(adding the 'definites' (11%) and 'probables' (23%) together) had an inclination towards belief in an afterlife.

One additional question of relevance for this volume, which might serve as a complement to this afterlife perspective and relates to a later discussion on sensing the presence of the dead, asked 'Do you believe in the supernatural powers of deceased ancestors?'. Again, comparing the total sample and the 'no religion' group, the following approximate results were reported:. Yes, definitely 6% (4%), Yes, probably 17% (16%), No, probably not 33% (31%), and No, definitely not 45% (49%). There is relatively little difference between these groups, which suggests that the influence of ordinary life experience operates across the population. We return to this issue below in terms of experiencing the presence of the dead.

[2] *British Social Attitudes* 2008.

Richard Dawkins Foundation–Ipsos MORI (2011–12)

With sample sizes relatively similar to those of the British Social Attitudes survey, but much smaller than those for the Census, we can now continue with more focused issues of ideas related to death. First we take a group of 1,136 individuals drawn from a sampled group of 2,107 surveyed by Ipsos MORI during 1–7 April 2011 for the Richard Dawkins Foundation for Reason and Science, and published in February 2012. Dawkins, already mentioned in the Introduction as highly critical on matters of religion and belief, sought to foster 'reason and science', with this survey presumably aimed to further that cause. The survey focused on a subset of 1,136 persons (54% of its original 2,107) 'who say they were recorded as Christian in the 2011 Census, or would have recorded themselves as Christian'. Factors behind this self-identification were: having being baptized (72%), having parents in this tradition (38%), having gone to a Sunday school (37%), believing the teachings (28%), having gone to a church school (21%), having attended ordinary services (19%) or currently attending ordinary services (19%), having a partner in this tradition (13%), and having a child at a church school (7%). When asked how they might best identify themselves, some 30% opted for having 'strong beliefs' as a Christian, a very similar number (29%) not having strong beliefs but still thinking of themselves as Christian, and a further 19% also not having strong beliefs but having been 'brought up to think of myself as Christian'.

These are important figures for understanding the cultural Christianity of Britain and not simply for definitions of 'Christian' preferred by ecclesiastic figures or religiously motivated sociologists of religion for whom dedicated commitment is signalled by frequent church attendance. In a wide-ranging exploration of themes, including that of 'being a good person' (to which we return in chapter 5), people were also asked specific questions on issues of destiny, afterlife, and the supernatural in general. The results are pinpointed in Table 2.1.

Ideas of heaven seemed firm for over a third (36%), while another 27% held in 'to some extent', thus reflecting a core notion of a heavenly afterlife of 63%; almost two-thirds of those with some church connection.[3] That hell should attract support of around 18% in a firm way and another 23% 'to some extent' is interesting in an age when many mainstream denominations might be thought to place little emphasis upon it.[4] The issue of 'fate' with its 22% (complete) and 42% acceptance to some extent is difficult to interpret, apart from indicating some ultimate intention lying behind events. It may be that

---

[3] In comparison, the *British Social Attitudes Survey* (2008) with a sample of 2,229 found belief in heaven: Definitely 20%, Probably 28%, Probably not 26%, Definitely not 26%.

[4] In comparison, the *British Social Attitudes Survey* (2008) with a sample of 2,229 found belief in hell: Definitely 13%, Probably 19%, Probably not 33%, Definitely not 34%.

Table 2.1. 'Different people believe in different things. To what extent do YOU PERSONALLY believe in the following?'

	Completely	To some extent	Not sure	Not really	Not at all	Don't know	Not saying
Heaven	36	27	16	9	11	1	1
Hell	18	23	18	15	25	1	—
Astrology	7	20	15	19	37	1	1
The power of prayer	26	37	14	9	12	1	1
Ghosts	15	22	17	14	31	1	—
Reincarnation	8	19	21	15	34	2	1
Fate	22	42	13	11	12	1	1

Note: Approximate values, shown in %.
Source: Ipsos MORI for Richard Dawkins Foundation 2011–12, questions 12–18.

'fate' captures the theme of concealment and disclosure that will occur later in this volume in terms of the nature of symbols. In other words, 'fate' acknowledges a 'meaning' to life even though we do not know its outcome until it arrives. In comparative terms this is reminiscent of Maurice Bloch's depiction of a Madagascan Zafimaniry notion expressing a 'destiny which is neither reward nor punishment, simply a state of affairs which affects you and which you cannot resist'.[5]

Looking at a different category it is, perhaps, intelligible that ghosts are acknowledged amongst perhaps 37% when we bear in mind, as shown later, the frequency in the bereaved sensing the presence of the dead. It is telling that roughly the same profile of 'belief' was reflected over astrology and reincarnation.

Within this same sample, some 52% spoke of their 'personal view of God' in terms of relationship, while some 40% entertained ideas of some 'laws of nature', 'supernatural intelligence', or 'whatever caused the universe'.[6] Again, staying with this Christian-related group, we find two significant questions related to Jesus and his identity within people's beliefs. One asked people to describe their belief about the resurrection; some 39% described Jesus as having come 'back to life spiritually but not physically after being dead'. Another sizeable minority (32%) reckoned that 'Jesus came back to life physically from the dead', while a further 18% did not believe in the resurrection. While these responses indicate a sizeable majority for whom 'resurrection' caries a strong significance whether in a 'physical' (32%) or 'spiritual' (39%) sense as far as Jesus was concerned, this does not necessarily imply that they retain the same image of their own future since they were not asked that question.

[5] Bloch (1995: 67).   [6] Question 19.

Theos survey (2009)—funeral choice

In another survey, conducted for the Theos Think Tank in April 2009,[7] people were asked a variety of questions relating to mortality. So, when asked about the sort of funeral they would like some 37% said they would like a Christian funeral, compared with 17% saying a non-religious one, and 4% wanting a religious but not Christian ceremony. There was a growing trend in people wanting a Christian funeral by age group, from young adults through to old people: 20% (18–24 year olds) rising to 28% (25–34), 31% (35–44), 35% (45–54), 44% (55–64), and 53% (65+). Strikingly, although the smallest proportion of people wanting a Christian funeral was within the 18–24 age group (20% compared with a national average of 37%) this group also contained the highest proportion of people wanting a religious but not Christian funeral (9% compared with an overall average of 4%). In terms of a funeral that has no reference to God in it, the 18–24 year olds totalled 12%, while the middle generations were higher at 23% (25–34), 22% (35–44), and 20% (45–54), with older groups at 16% (55–64), and 11% (65+). In terms of social class and Christian funeral the pattern was, AB (senior, middle, management, professionals, 39%), C1 (junior management, clerical, administrative, 33%), C2 (skilled manual, 43%), and DE (semi-skilled workers, pensioners, unemployed, 32%). In terms of those who at this stage in their life would opt for a non-religious service with no mention of God, the AB group marked 21%, the C1 16%, the C2 14%, and the DE 19%. This profile will become relevant later when discussing civic and non-religious celebrants leading increasing numbers of funerals.

The question of dead bodies was raised in this survey, revealing that two-thirds (66%) had seen a dead body. This broke down into over half (55%) of all the 18–24 year olds not having seen one themselves, compared with 16% of people aged 65 who had not done so. If we assume, as is reasonable, that non-surveyed people under 18 were even less likely to have seen a real as opposed to some online virtual corpse, then it means that over half of this young section of society is unfamiliar with the emotions of death associated with being in the presence of a dead body. Perhaps it is even more noteworthy that 16% of those over the age of 65 had not seen a body. This must be amongst the first generational set in the history of mankind when death has been alien to such a proportion of a population and is highly significant in terms of the lifestyle and death-style interface. If we take the corpse to be a symbol of death then this social fact of seeing or not seeing a dead person speaks of the hidden–revealed symbolic nature of death in Britain, a theme that will recur throughout this volume.

---

[7] ComRes survey interviewing 1018 adults online between 24 and 26 April 2009 for Theos Think Tank on religious in public life, data weighted to be representative demographically of all UK adults.

Table 2.2. 'I have made my peace with my God.'

	Men	Women
Yes	16	27
No	28	25
Don't know	14	13
Not applicable	34	27
Refuse to answer	8	8

Note: Values shown in %.
Source: Theos Think Tank.

As for those who stated that their religious faith helped them to deal with the death of a loved one and prepare for their own death, this was the case for 42% of people aged 65 and over, compared with 23% of 18–24 year olds. Regarding making arrangements for their own funerals only 7% of the population had done so, 16% had not given it any thought, and 13% of people said they would let their family or friends decide. Still, some 41% had taken out life insurance, and 42% had made a will. This overall profile also indicates something of a marginalizing of death within life-concerns. However, this Theos poll also touched on an unusual question for a British social survey, even for a survey on an religion, viz. the theme of personal peace, a topic posed in the form, 'I have made my peace with my God'. To cite the question in its given format allows us not only to emphasize the double personalization of 'my peace' with 'my God' but also because it provides a focused sense of personalized spirituality within something of a traditional frame. Table 2.2 shows the responses.

These results are especially important because they mark the gender factor, one that is vital for matters of mortality and religion and yet is not always evident in the presentation or interpretation of data.[8] But here its spotlight does fall, showing some 27% of women and 16% of men reckoned to have made their peace with their God. We may suppose that even to recognize the question in the first place reflects something of a traditional grasp of Christian discourse. Once that potential hurdle is overcome we then need to consider not only those answering in the affirmative, but also those in the 'no' category. For we may, I think, assume that they also have some grasp of the fact that this question is intelligible to them, but that they do sense within themselves some life issues that are not resolved. When we move to a potentially different group, to the 34% of men and 27% of women who thought that the question was not applicable to them, we probably encounter people whose style of self-identity simply does not relate to some significant divine 'other', and who probably express a kind of secularity in terms of traditional religiosity. Just how to interpret the 'don't know' category is difficult: the people involved

---

[8] Trzebiatowska and Bruce (2012) offer general thoughts on women and religion.

Table 2.3. 'Do you believe in life after death?'

		1950[1]	1963[2]	1991[3]	2004[4]
Men	Yes	39	41	38	29
	No	28	26	37	44
	Don't know	33	33	25	27
Women	Yes	56	55	60	57
	No	14	16	17	19
	Don't know	30	29	23	24

[1] Gorer (1965: 166) from Gorer (1955).
[2] Gorer (1965: 166).
[3] Douglas J. Davies (1997).
[4] YouGov Survey for ITV 'This Morning' programme, fieldwork 8–11 October 2004.
Note: Values shown in %.

could well recognize God and acknowledge some sense of relation with deity but remain unsure of how the complexities of life may be managed in terms of 'making peace'. These may include folk who straddle religious and secular modes of framing life, but they could, equally well, be folk for whom the notion is simply outside their normal discourse.

Further Surveys

To add a slightly more extensive range to these very contemporary surveys we will now create a composite historical sketch from a variety of surveys from 1950 to 2004 that allows access to both afterlife beliefs and gender variation. Table 2.3 presents the data.

What is very clear in the above statistics is that men and women differ a great deal on these matters, with a major shift evident; women retain a relatively constant profile, while the men move rapidly into disbelief in an afterlife.

YouGov Survey (2004)

This gender division also applies to other factors that were taken further in a YouGov survey (also cited in the table above for the 2004 column) with a sample size of 2,116, conducted for the ITV 'This Morning' programme in 2004, where we find division evident on beliefs concerning ghosts, angels, and mediums. But before considering those factors it is worth reproducing its results on the question of seeking help at times of distress because this brings a sense of pragmatic realism to the subsequent questions on mediums and angels. Table 2.4 presents the data.

Table 2.4. 'If distressed, which would you be most likely to seek help from?'

	Total	Men	Women
Family and friends	79	78	81
Medical profession	11	13	9
Religious figure	2	3	2
Psychic medium	2	0	4
Angel	1	0	1
Don't know	4	6	3

Note: Approximate values, shown in %.
Source: YouGov Survey for ITV 'This Morning' programme, fieldwork 8–11 October 2004.

Table 2.5. 'Do you believe in ghosts (and have you personally seen a ghost)?'

	Total	Men	Women
Yes	41 (13)	28 (8)	52 (18)
No	37 (73)	52 (81)	24 (66)
Don't know	22 (14)	20 (12)	24 (16)

Note: Approximate values, shown in %.
Source: YouGov Survey for ITV 'This Morning' programme, fieldwork 8–11 October 2004.

Here the gender divide is of relative insignificance, with women and men reckoning on the importance of their family and friends and, to a certain degree on the NHS, a factor germane to the prominence accorded to the NHS in subsequent chapters. The fact that religious figures appear more or less alongside psychic mediums (astrologers were also included in that question) indicates something of the potential perspective held on them by the general public.

Moving from this relatively pragmatic question of help to a more speculative set of questions on factors mysterious or supernatural we find, first, material on those who reckoned to 'believe in' and those reporting actually having seen a ghost (figures in brackets). Table 2.5 presents the data.

Comparing Table 2.5 with Table 2.4 we see a similarity of ghost belief with afterlife belief both in overall range of response and for gender difference. The intriguing element in this table lies in the difference between a general 'belief in' ghosts and in actually reckoning to have 'seen' one which indicates a distinction on issues of cultural ideas in relation to personal experience as such.[9] These aspects of life were extended in further questions concerning mediums, angels, and psychics which we now take in turn.

[9] See Finucane (1982).

Table 2.6. 'Can mediums make contact with the dead?'

	Total	Men	Women
Yes	33	19	47
No	45	62	29
Don't know	22	19	24

Note: Values shown in %.
Source: YouGov Survey for ITV 'This Morning' programme, field-work 8–11 October 2004.

Table 2.7. 'Do you believe in angels?' ('Have you ever felt you have been helped by an angel?')

	Total	Men	Women
Yes	31 (17)	18 (9)	43 (24)
No	42 (61)	57 (72)	29 (51)
Don't know	26 (22)	25 (19)	28 (25)

Note: Approximate values, shown in %.
Source: YouGov Survey for ITV 'This Morning' programme, fieldwork 8–11 October 2004.

Table 2.8. 'Have you ever consulted a psychic or medium?'

	Total	Men	Women
No, never	76	90	64
Yes but only for fun	12	6	17
Once or more and not just for fun	12	4	19

Note: Values shown in %.
Source: YouGov Survey for ITV 'This Morning' programme, fieldwork 8–11 October 2004.

The fact that approximately a third of this sample thought mediums really could contact the dead, with a significant minority being unsure, reinforces the broad belief in an afterlife, albeit on a more restricted basis of contact (Table 2.6). Again the gender divide is enormous, and so it is when we come to expressions of beliefs in angels, as Table 2.7 indicates both for 'belief in angels' and, in brackets, for a sense of 'having been helped by angels'.

This level of reported belief in angels, especially if we take the 31% and count in the 26% of 'don't knows', is remarkable. Setting it alongside (as we do in brackets) those who reckon to have felt helped by an angel, albeit a response at practically half the 'belief' range, we are, once more, met with a strong gender divide. This perspective can be aligned with the widespread use of the 'angel' motif in the case of the death of children and of the written memorials and cards for them that frequently speak of 'my little angel' or of being with angels. We can add to this the response to a further question on whether people had actually consulted a psychic or medium (Table 2.8).

Table 2.9. 'Do you believe in reincarnation?'

	Total	Men	Women
Yes	29	18	39
No	41	55	28
Don't know	30	27	32

Note: Approximate values, shown in %.

Source: YouGov Survey for ITV 'This Morning' programme, fieldwork 8–11 October 2004.

The 19% of women who had used a medium seriously had done so, as further information in the survey revealed, either once or twice (9%) or more than twice (10%). Many of these are likely to have done so in connection with a family bereavement and with a desire to ensure that things are 'all right' with their lost kin. The domain between the living and dead is not simply reflected in mediums and the 'spirit world' as schematized, for example, by spiritualist churches, but also in the notion that is captured in the idea of reincarnation, one that needs some care in its analysis (Table 2.9).

The gender difference is marked in this question on reincarnation, a topic presented in terms of 'people with past lives being born again', not necessarily the clearest of expressions. It is also notable that the 'don't know' category consists of a significant minority as is also the case for afterlife and ghost beliefs. This illustrates aspects of human life over which many have uncertainties and which touch quite complex experiences that are not easily labelled. Indeed, labelling of reincarnation and ghosts offers broad brushstrokes that may touch experiences that do not, in any strict sense, possess anything like a clearly identifiable cultural classification. But since Britain, unlike India for example, has no culture of reincarnation beliefs, it might be surprising to find the results in the above table; that over a third of the women recognized the notion, however vague it may appear, is remarkable.

Davies and Shaw (1994–5)

This reincarnation element now takes us to another survey, conducted by Douglas Davies and Alister Shaw for some eighty or more UK local authorities, and concerned with burial law reform regarding the potential re-use of old graves in overfilled cemeteries. The research was conducted between October 1994 and January 1995 by Public Attitudes Survey (PAS) Ltd, surveyed some 1,603 persons in their own homes, and focused on funerary matters.[10]

---

[10] Davies and Shaw (1995).

Table 2.10. 'Which, if any, of the views on this card accord with your own attitude towards life after death?'

Option	Number	Percentage of 1,603
Our soul passes on to another world	546	34.1%
Nothing happens; we come to the end of life	461	28.8%
Trust in God; all is in God's hands	348	21.7%
We come back as someone or something else	195	12.1%
Our bodies await resurrection	126	7.9%
Don't know	145	9%
Some other option	23	1.4%

Source: Davies and Shaw (1995).

As far as 'reincarnation' was concerned, this survey did not use that word but, on the basis that not all might know what it meant, adopted the form that 'we come back as something or someone else'. The overall results showed that the public at large had a 12.2% option for this, with those who self-identified with the Church of England having a slightly higher (14%) and Roman Catholics a slightly lower (11%) agreement that we might 'come back as something or someone else'. As for Methodists and members of the Church of Scotland, they registered a lower 6% each.[11]

This 1995 Davies and Shaw survey is valuable for showing something of the dynamic complexity of afterlife beliefs, with people being offered a series of questions covering a range of possibilities. People could choose as many of the following beliefs as they wished, but the majority opted for one. Table 2.10 shows both numbers of respondents opting for each view, with that number rendered as a percentage of the total 1,603 in the survey. People were offered a card containing the following questions (given in full in the table) and were asked which of the questions matched most closely to their view.

Note that the total number of responses amounts to 1,844 which reflects some multiple choices amongst the 1,603 interviewed, choices that are detailed below. So, in terms of this table, 546 of the 1,603 individuals, or 34% of those interviewed opted for the 'soul passing on'. In both historical and cross-cultural terms this reflects the most widespread form of explanation of an afterlife, albeit a form framed in different ways across cultures. Within Christianity, 'soul' language has a long and complex tradition, not least in terms of how it relates to 'body' language and to the complex notion of resurrection, themes I have discussed at length elsewhere both in terms of formal theologies and of popular attitudes.[12]

Something of that complexity is evident in that the 1,844 responses from 1,603 individuals reflects some 354 persons who opted for more than one

[11] Davies and Shaw (1995: 93).   [12] Douglas J. Davies (2008).

Table 2.11. Choice of two afterlife beliefs (numbers of individuals; not percentages)

Soul passes AND trust in God	54
Soul passes AND come back as someone or something else	26
Soul passes AND bodies await resurrection	21
Bodies await resurrection AND trust in God	11
Life is the end AND coming back as something or someone else	8

Source: Davies and Shaw (1995).

choice. When that happened most went for two options, as Table 2.11 shows for actual numbers of individuals responding.

Yet smaller groups opted for the following combinations:

Soul passes AND resurrection AND trust in God = 42 people.

Soul passes AND come back AND trust in God = 8 people.

A small number of five individuals combined four afterlife views; 1 person took all five.

These variations are included to show something of the diversity and complexity of afterlife beliefs and to take the edge off the earlier tables that too easily imply a simple 'yes'/'no'/'don't know' to afterlife beliefs. Still, tabular large-scale surveys do offer a significant view of social patterns as in this final element of the Davies and Shaw survey that once more engages gender but this time in terms of the question, 'Have you ever felt a sense of the presence of someone you know after they have died?'[13] People were offered options of 'yes, often'; 'yes, occasionally'; 'yes, rarely'; and 'yes, just once'. The results show a marked difference between men and women (Table 2.12).

The most notable factor is, then, the much higher incidence of women having such experiences. Most often these experiences are of a positive, encouraging, or supportive nature.[14] Other authors have also noted this kind of experience.[15] The power of such experiences in forging an intuitive sense of self and of what a person 'is' cannot be overestimated. For many, a sense of seeing, hearing the voice of, sensing the presence in the same room of, smelling, or being touched by the deceased can be enormous. Though never or seldom a topic of conversation, such phenomena help make sense of the general idea of a 'soul' and can provide an intuitive basis for approaching ideas of Jesus and his post-mortem existence. This is probably also the reason why ideas of the 'soul passing on' make such good sense and supplant ideas of resurrection in the minds of many self-identified Christians, notably women. In terms of the

[13] Davies and Shaw (1995: 96–8, 123).
[14] Davies, Watkins, and Winter (1991: 261).   [15] Hay (1990: 84).

Table 2.12. 'Have you ever felt a sense of the presence of someone you know after they have died?'

Sensed presence	Number	Men %	Women%	Total %
Often	136	17	83	100
Occasionally	218	34	66	100
Rarely	95	35	65	100
Once only	117	33	67	100
Never	1,011	55	45	100

Source: Douglas Davies (1997: 139), adapted from Davies and Shaw survey data (1995).

sociology of theology one wonders whether it is male theologians who may never have had such experiences who tend to be more philosophical over 'souls' and opt for a more programmatic view of resurrection.

IDENTITY, VALUES, AND BELIEFS

So, whether in formal theological, sociological, or in more popular terms, just what constitutes a 'person' and their identity in life or in a posited afterlife remains a complex issue, one that can be usefully analysed through the notion of 'deutero-truth' as pursued in anthropologist Roy Rappaport's magisterial study of ritual. Deutero- or second-order truth pinpoints shared ideas that everyone understands until asked for a close definition; as with family, democracy, marriage, love, prophet, God, and many others. Such words carry a shared understanding allied with appropriate emotional tones within a speech community, not least within Christian churches as each denomination and their sub-groups speak of 'soul', 'spirit', 'body and soul', 'resurrection', 'the Lord', 'heaven' and 'hell', and 'God'. Within distinctive communities deutero-truths enable people to communicate and bond over ideas rather than be divided by them, though, at times of social and cultural change, as in the sixteenth-century Reformation, increased precision over formal meaning and emotional significance mean division can occur. Similarly, the decades following the late 1960s brought the notion of the Holy Spirit into focused debate as the emotional experiences of being 'Spirit-filled' advocated by the emergent charismatic movement came into contention with established views aligning 'Spirit' with tradition and rituals. The relatively peripheral world of spiritualist churches also exemplifies some quite different meanings of 'spirit' among religious groups. This affects bereaved people as and when a small number take recourse to spiritualist churches following recent loss and are told of their relatives now being 'in spirit'. In contemporary, multicultural Britain, there are, then, many 'speech communities' in terms of world view, whose terms may as easily divide as bind and who indicate the value of deutero-truths, not least in contexts of interfaith activities. It may well be that it is precisely the deutero-truth nature of ideas such as 'spirituality', and perhaps of 'Spirit' and 'God', that allows those elite groups given to interfaith ventures to sense a unity of purpose amongst themselves. As we will see in due course, in terms of this volume it is the very word 'grief' that suggests itself as a deutero-truth, albeit one of a distinctive nature in that many use the word but for those whose life experience has or has not as yet encountered close personal loss it is likely to carry quite different loads of emotional–existential significance. In other words, 'grief' can be as easily socially divisive as binding.

DEUTERO-MEMORIALS

This analytical idea of deutero-truth also provides a valuable theoretical basis when moving from the integrative or divisive common words of a community to a consideration of the more concretely material world evident in memorials to the dead that abound in the social spaces shared by speech communities of quite diverse world views on human identity and the afterlife. In the sharing of physical space marked by centuries-old memorials to the dead as well as by more recent memorials to the war dead, diverse groups bring their own significance to communal monuments, and to the deutero-truths often in-scribed upon them. Such monuments might be described in this context as deutero-memorials, whose second-order capacity of uniting a diversity of people differs from the primary or first-order memorials that an individual establishes for their close kin, whether in a headstone at a grave or, more directly, in the location of cremated remains in the home, garden, or place of couple-companionate choice.

Whether in first-order or second-order terms of personal emotional truth, memorials capture something of death's slippery transition between vitality and mortality. Identity's source in the imagination-driven memory flows from individual recollections through the intimacies of relation with family or peer group to the realm of public institutions, not least those of hospitals and funeral directors. Such memorials and institutions highlight death as one relatively uniting feature of human experience in a complex society otherwise divided by social class, wealth, education, employment, gender, religiosity, and ethnicities. Grief, despite its complexity, also affords a degree of empathy between society's highest and lowest, and engages experience of memorial times, places, and events.[16] This helps explain how tradition sustains identity

---

[16] Belshaw and Purvey (2009: 42–9), for nineteenth-century British Columbia.

and creates its own force-field of social expectation in which emotional intensification fosters memory. To share memories is to share experiences recognized as having taken shape in particular contexts—times and places of enduring significance related to specific individuals who, though dead, may be retained in a sense of presence. For example, the artist Maggi Hambling offers her approach to deceased friends: 'It is a habit of mine to go on making portraits of them, because if you have loved someone, the person goes on being alive inside us all. It is where artists are lucky, because they have a positive way of grieving. It is ironic, of course, because you are trying to make a portrait with as much life as possible of someone who is dead.'[17]

The interplay of memory, identity, and relationships is notably important at times of bereavement, as autobiography, community narratives, commemorative eulogies, established literary masterpieces, and obituaries show.[18] Within the media-pervaded nature of contemporary British society the nature of remembrance has found extensive opportunity for publicity. The anniversaries of particular deaths, notably of media and political celebrities, are frequently marked with commemorative television and radio programmes. And this is even more evident when the commemoration is of some death-grounded disaster, for tragic death has an appeal that goes beyond death in old age. Our media age, with many hours of on-air time to fill, finds apt opportunity to attract an emotionally alerted audience in the commemoration of tragic events, most especially events that strike at a society's wellbeing. The period of 2014–18, in particular, is already gaining high media visibility in engaging with the centenary of the Great War of 1914–18.[19]

Life Course and Scene

Such recollection is inevitable given the way human experience is fashioned by recall of the past whilst anticipating eventualities and being engaged in current social and private life. The life course is, itself, constructed of successive memories whose sedimented foundations allow adult life to be construed.[20] While young adults are frequently full of life but low in informative memories, the old have more memories than can be creatively activated by their relatively

---

[17] Dico (2015: 32). [18] Tarlow (1999).

[19] Some First World War medals are inscribed with 'Great War for Civilization'.

[20] Homer's *Odyssey*, one classic of world mythology, originating perhaps in the eighth century BC, allows Odysseus in his adventurous travels, including a visit to Hades, to encounter amidst the 'multitude of souls' that 'flutter to and fro' some of the famous dead, including his mother, when his 'eyes filled tears' and he was 'stirred to compassion' (Book 11: 40, 85). It portrays life as a destiny-framed journey pervaded by deep emotions triggered by intimate and hostile relationships.

lower level of immediate vitality. These states can make both young and old boring to those in their prime whose interplay of memory and contemporary life-interest is at its height. Indeed, one might even define life's 'prime' as lying at the optimal balance of informative memory and moderating vitality, probably occurring when experience is mustered for the challenges lying ahead. But, and this is a significant cautionary qualification, that 'prime' almost certainly requires some touch of mortality to bridle unfettered optimism. When cultures take an individualist turn, and when experience of mortality is relatively rare or even absent from many adults until later in their life, then a sense of the past easily becomes narrowly focused on the self instead of taking a broader perspective. However, when death-linked events strike many people, as in a natural disaster or terrorist strike, then communal interest burgeons, not least as the mass media come into their own, as we show later in this chapter.

While this kind of dynamic view of individual and social identity, death, and memorialization can be framed in many ways, one helpful approach comes through Tim Ingold's anthropology of human existence, notably his argument that 'wayfaring is our most fundamental mode of being in the world'. As chapters 6 and 8 show, this motif offers fruitful insight for our discussion of death in contemporary Britain. I welcome both his general argument 'against space', which considers the 'modern oxymoron of "space and place"' as unhelpful, and his discussion of the '*meshwork* of wayfaring' (original italics) by which human beings, as 'wayfarers' exist and acquire knowledge.[21]

While a great deal could be said about ancient British wayfarers constructing funerary monuments, making death and ancestral links a deep substratum of cultural wisdom, our concern begins only from the middle of the nineteenth century with its image of the newly instituted civic cemeteries, often taking the form of a zoned necropolis of richer and poorer graves, extending the long-standing British cultural motif of a graveyard surrounding a parish church inside which tombs of local worthies were often located. Christianity's long acceptance of, and often its desire for, the corpse to be aligned with places of worship, reflected its sense of a field of sacred power. Buried facing east, often with their parish priest buried facing west to greet them, they awaited resurrection; this eastward line manifested its own theological–historical force-field. The doctrinal idea of the Communion of Saints also made spatial sense as the living worshipped in juxtaposition with their dead. The English Reformation may have had its sixteenth-century qualms over prayers and rites for the dead, and these remained well into the twentieth century, but parishioners still entered and left church through the memorials of their deceased kith and

---

[21] Ingold (2011: 147, 151).

kin. Such memorials hint at the social force of the past in framing acts of contemporary memory and fostering its allied emotions. Just as ideas of 'home', 'friendship', or Christmas carry an emotional rooting, so too do memorials and the remembrance of our dead. It is, then, all the more surprising that by the mid 1960s a predominant shift from burial to cremation had taken place, and by the 1970s increasing numbers of people were taking cremated remains away from crematoria for private placing in sites of individual significance.[22] By the twenty-first century this personal deposition is practically normative even if some religious groups, such as the Anglican Church in Wales, seek to insist on their 'traditional' and formal burial. If the late nineteenth century witnessed a plethora of funerary monuments in public cemeteries, themselves an extension of previous memorials in churchyards, and, for 'establishment' figures, also within churches, the late twentieth century witnessed an increasing social invisibility of the dead as cremation rendered them to ashes for private deposition. That, however, should not mean their existential presence in the memory of the living is ignored: the 'emotional memorial' continues and will reappear in later chapters.

Ritual Purity–Impurity

Memorials of all sorts, whether in private or public realms, foster ritual, ceremony, or, in ecclesiastical terms, liturgy, with one theoretical concept useful for understanding such activity being that of ritual purity. This complex anthropological idea can be simplified for our purposes in two ways, one focusing on the intrinsic value of a phenomenon and the other on behaviour surrounding it. The first describes the inhering value of some cultural object such as the monarch's crown, court of law, church altar, or one's mother's cremated remains. These are treated with respect because they enshrine key cultural values, underpin a group's sense of identity, and are frequently allied with positive emotions; as powerful symbols they participate in what they represent. In this sense ritual purity describes entities fostering the very survival of social groups. The second application of ritual purity describes the qualifying status of those designated to manipulate these culturally dominant symbols, usually in the controlled formality of ritual activity and often in designated ritual arenas.[23]

---

[22] Davies and Guest (1999: 26–30).

[23] Duschinsky and Lampitt briefly describe ritual purity in Douglas, and Bourdieu's stress on power hidden behind notions of purity. Their 'new theory of purity and impurity' concerns 'the adjudication of phenomena in terms of their relative identity with or divergence from their imputed essence' (2012: 1204). They make no reference to Bernstein's significant influence on Douglas—an area which may prove useful for future death studies.

Mary Douglas's fruitful approach to this topic, summarized in her albeit oddly named 'purity rule', proposed that the degree of authority exercised by a society over an individual is reflected in the degree of control that person exercises over his or her own body. Her basic argument spoke of degrees of control over thought and over behaviour with options for high and low levels in each case. Her general proposition is that the degree of control over speech, and over the physical presentation of the body, its dress, and deportment is highest when engaged with prime cultural symbols, and it seems fair to take cultural images of life and death as just such prime symbols.[24] It is precisely this control of appropriate behaviour in funerary and memorial contexts that makes her approach valuable for this volume. Other issues of her retraction of some earlier ideas on cultural classification, anomalies, and abominations are not applicable to our concerns.

A clear example of prime symbols and their treatment occurs on Remembrance Day, when London's Cenotaph becomes the arena for engaging with the prime cultural values of life and death expressed through patriotism and the idea of self-sacrifice for the social good, all within a democratic monarchy.[25] Death now ceases to be a slippery concept, as cultural time and place assert self-sacrifice for the communal good when a nation is set against evil. Though given detail in chapter 7 this scene applies here in terms of ritual behaviour. The normal social movement of citizen, tourist, and traffic-filled street is transformed into the formal slow walking and marching of designated persons. The mundane sound of traffic is replaced by silence, and military and religious music. The space around the monument is clear and first approached by the monarch who, as head of state, lays the first wreath, stands in silence, bows her head, and moves backwards before turning to leave. These are the very acts her subjects observe towards her when meeting or, especially, when receiving some honour. Wreath-laying exemplifies ritual purity. The cultural values of the nation's war dead and living monarch combine in the measured approach, wreath-laying, and withdrawal of the monarch.

Similar behaviour occurs in sacrament-focused churches when priests approach altars and worshippers receive sacramental elements of bread and wine, for things that matter become subject to behaviour expressing the fact that they matter. Action becomes as important as the central 'objects' of concern. 'Purity' captures this sense of propriety, and should not be understood in the normal sense of moral righteousness or some sort of 'inner' sanctity of the moral core of a person, even though such inner sanctity may also be associated with the ritual specialist in some contexts. Practitioners need

---

[24] Prime symbols, notably when they participate in the notion of life or vitality, could equate with Bourdieu's 'authentic essence' ([1976] 1993: 74).

[25] Wolffe (1999: 294), noted the 'unexplored and significant linkages between the study of death and the study of patriotism and nationalism'.

to be properly qualified, whether as monarch, priest, church member, or the like, and need to behave in the prescribed way, in order that the cultural value be expressed in full fashion. Another classic example lies in the rite of coronation when the crown is placed upon the monarch's head and allied symbolic objects of state are placed in their hand, all after the anointing of the monarch's very physical body. Enthronement-seat, and physical body and the body of state—the monarch's 'two bodies'—are all subject to ecclesiastical rite at the hands of the Archbishop of Canterbury. But all this behaviour, and more besides, is highly controlled and tradition-led, as will be the funeral of the monarch when, in tradition-embedded custom, it will be said in Great Britain in the twenty-first century: 'the Queen is dead, long live the King'.

In the following chapters' consideration of royalty, it is the mortuary element rather than coronation that stands out, and we will encounter royal deaths alongside those of celebrities and of ordinary families. In all of these, the ritual purity motif will help us understand the nature of links between public and private memorials, and the way high-profile funerals and memorials relate to private grief and family memorials. This will aid our study of death and society given that some core cultural values and beliefs are embodied or materialized in people, things, events, times, and places, as in war memorials—'physical places connected with the fundamental values of society',[26] that 'help to sustain the spiritual origins of a society'.[27]

In the different theoretical terms of reciprocity theory, already outlined in chapter 1 and which will recur throughout this volume, such memorials, as well as the material culture of family photographs and objects, serve as inalienable gifts that enhance the flow of cultural inheritance from past to present to future. Boundaries of space, time, and action set around certain key memorials help mark them out as places for value-laden behaviour. For example, one family whose infant daughter had been lost, presumed abducted, while on holiday continued to hold a kind of anniversary commemoration for her. The seventh such gathering, albeit low-key and attended by closer friends and neighbours in 2014, was held at the war memorial in their village of Rothley in Leicestershire, at which photographs and flowers were placed.[28]

Abomination

With this in mind we could adapt Mary Douglas's ideas that an 'abomination' is something that radically subverts ritually pure behaviour, breaks conventional boundaries, or straddles disparate classes of things. It is when domains

---

[26] Barber (1949: 65).   [27] Mayo (1988: 75).

[28] Myers (2014: 15). This was the family of Gerry and Kate McCann and their lost daughter Madeleine.

that do not belong together are starkly linked that our moral–somatic response is triggered and disgust ensues; an emotion that takes us back to the Latin '*gustus*' or 'taste' and to that bad feeling of something that makes us feel sick.

Such was the case of a British student who urinated on a British war memorial in Sheffield in November 2009 and who was given some 250 hours of community service rather than, as many indicated in the press, a jail sentence. His act of ritual impurity lay in a bodily behaviour directly contradicting appropriate social behaviour at a war memorial and its com-memorative wreaths. Use of terms such as 'revulsion' and 'outrage' expressed the social–emotional response to 'abominable' behaviour contradicting all social propriety in the presence of symbols of core cultural values. The fact that the individual was taking part in a student drinking event and reckoned himself to have been so drunk that he could not remember his own behaviour did not prevent the judge and many online sources holding him responsible for his actions.[29] While youth and student drinking has long constituted a world of its own, it seldom attracts the idea of repulsion; it was its direct transgression into the public realm and space of cherished cultural values that attracted opprobrium.

Such an incident is all the more objectionable given the multiplicity of war memorials, not only in public contexts, but many also in semi-public contexts, as when related to particular institutions such as the Post Office, or the commercial Co-operative Society in the UK.[30] Many schools across the coun-try similarly mark their dead. This multiple existence of concrete memorials fosters the symbolic interplay of one with another, and this makes national, focal, celebrations all the more powerful, as we indicate later in this chapter. These memorials' subliminal status for much of the year may help reinforce their significance on days that are ritually marked. They are in a sense uncanny because of their capacity to rise as prime foci from an obscure cultural background. Tony Walter, for example, has drawn attention to the way in which some British supermarkets espouse a period of silence for Armistice day, noting how life's bustle is stilled and the sense of 'common humanity' fostered.[31]

Titanic responses

A different form of memorial occurs when some unexpected event, likely to be described as a tragedy, is embraced by long-established ritual context and practice. Such was the case in April 2012 when a boat sailed for the spot at which the *Titanic* sank in April 1912. As well as the inevitable media reporters, it contained relatives of people who had perished in that epoch-marking

---

[29] Wainwright (2009).   [30] Coss (2012).   [31] Walter (200: 503).

disaster in which an iceberg combined with human error to destroy that 'mighty modern ship' that had 'out of the docks of Southampton sailed on her maiden trip': a vessel that was a symbol of the Industrial Revolution's achievement within the British Empire.[32] The Belfast area of that ship's birth remains as the Titanic Quarter, reminiscent of the pride of its production and of that city's identity in shipbuilding. Another vessel that travelled to the point of shipwreck came from Nova Scotia, in memory of the role played by its seafaring folk in recovery and burial of some who had drowned in 1912. Most of the 1,500 were however, lost at sea.

This centenary memorial rite offers its own window into British society, irrespective of its falling in a decade almost obsessed by anniversaries and summarized histories of many cultural topics which furnish the media with easy material.[33] This titanic event gains immediate intelligibility through the considerable popularity of the film *Titanic*; it exemplifies massed British response to large-scale loss of life. W. R. Inge, while in the second of his twenty-two years as Dean of St Paul's Cathedral, told how a 'great service was held for the victims of the Titanic' and how 'thousands were unable to get in' (and St Paul's is London's largest church). Ten months later, at a 'Memorial service for Captain Scott of the Antarctic and his four companions', who now have their memorial in the Crypt at St Paul's, we are told that 'the mob broke through the cordon of police into the reserved part of the cathedral'. It is telling that, both in the case of the *Titanic* and of Captain Scott, their places of loss, the Atlantic and Antarctic, become subsumed by their nation's capital memorialization. During the First World War, when Lord Roberts was buried in the Cathedral in November 1914, we hear of an immense crowd in attendance. He had died of pneumonia after inspecting troops: 'They have no coats, why should I have one?'[34] He took his place amongst many other, and greater, heroes in that Crypt, not least the Duke of Wellington. There is something about the Crypt that serves as its own national location that, in the context of British culture and reformed religion, cannot be called a shrine, but serves as a centre of historical culture in which the emotions of patriotism extend into a sense of future confidence. And all this in a capital city that intensifies the capacity of many other cities and towns to attract crowds at times of emotional flows focusing sorrow or joy as aspects of community identity; issues that align with the 'uncanny'—a sentiment that undergirds both the great Cathedral and the city itself, and which we discuss in chapter 6.

[32] This poem—'The Titanic'—fell easily from my own mother's memory, learned as a girl in elementary school: 'Not a soul on board had dread or fear of meeting an ocean grave!'

[33] As seen in the 'History Channel' on television providing a constant recycling of old film footage, and with radio channels also re-airing innumerable series that probably speak to the nostalgic memories of an ageing audience.

[34] W. R. Inge (n.d., pp. 15, 18, 32).

Place, Value, and Allure

Here, however, we explore another aspect of the memorial nature of certain places, not through the uncanny but through their 'allure'—a concept that captures emotional awareness and integrates it with culturally designated phenomena. The allure or avoidance of certain places in which to live, die, and be memorialized marks out the cultural values of every society and is a reminder of Tim Ingold's anthropological argument 'against the notion of space', on the basis that it is 'the most abstract, empty and detached . . . of all the terms we use to describe the world we inhabit'.[35] Allure is one concept that is enormously useful in connection with the transformation of 'space' into 'place'. Allure is a remarkable concept that integrates excitement, risk, hope, and anticipation in a specific place. It can do much the same in terms of attitudes towards a person and, in that case, 'allure' resembles the positive elements in the notion of 'charisma'. Allure echoes Otto's idea of the 'holy',[36] a dynamic mystery that fascinates us in relation to the divine. Allure can be identified in many other thinkers, times, and places including the eighteenth-century notion of the 'sublime', which indicated something of an allure found in spectacular places in nature, or in Lindsay Jones's twentieth-century approach to sacred architecture.[37] But what of allure in terms of death: is there an allure of mortality? I think there is. Regarding the 'holy' Otto noted the two emotional responses of 'disgust and startled fright' and thought they became subsumed in a 'dread' or 'awe' of *sui generis* nature.[38] This can be seen in a less philosophical light; many corpses both attract and repel, something anthropologist Bronislaw Malinowski highlighted in the 'double-edged sword of hope and fear which sets in always in the face of death'.[39] This theme is often evident in the film genre of the living dead, the undead, ghosts, and revenants at large. In other words we are drawn to certain images whilst yet being repelled by them. It is because there is a potential for experiencing an approach-avoidance factor in the human experience of the human dead that a similar sense can be projected on to the imagined living dead. The fear induced by films that lie in the realm of mythological or religious fiction plays upon this aspect of life, as do contexts such as the typical nineteenth-century 'gothic' graveyard.

CREATING PRESENCE

This dynamic tension contributes to the ambivalence of allure, and fuels its capacity to excite. It is not only a concept closely aligned with that of the

---

[35] Ingold (2011: 145).   [36] Otto ([1917] 1924: 12–23).
[37] Lindsay Jones (2000).   [38] Otto ([1917] 1924: 123).
[39] Malinowski ([1948] 1974: 51).

uncanny, but also bears conceptual resemblance to individuals' relationships with their apparently 'dead' kin. I say 'apparently' because death is, again, such a slippery concept that even the fact that a body is obviously dead, whether buried or cremated, does not remove the potential 'sense' or influence of the deceased. Whether in terms of powerful memories, dreams, inherited items, or a personal likeness, the deceased come to mind. Anniversaries as moments in cyclical time; graves and memorial sites in geographical locations—all provide opportunity for the dead to endure and be encountered, particularly at moments of crisis in a person's life.

The Triadic Appearance

While one example of such an encounter lies in Christine Valentine's use of the notions of absence and presence to reflect on the continuing nature of grief, it is to her reflection on how her interviews sometimes 'created space for the deceased person', and how her conversation partners were 'introducing me to that person', that I draw attention. The interview context gave her 'a feeling of his or her presence between us'. Valentine sees the dynamics of this kind of situation, where a stranger is introduced to a deceased relative of the bereaved person, as unlike Walter's 'conversational remembering' of a deceased person in talk between friends.[40] Valentine speaks of how the informant was given to producing 'a detailed recollection' and how it generated a 'presence between us'. In this she identifies a social fact seldom explored in sociological analysis, viz. how an interpersonal relationship of *two* people may become the occasion for a sensed *triadic* moment. This resembles the phenomenon associated with some traditionally religious events as when individuals in a pastoral context 'sense' an additional divine presence, or when a large number of people also 'sense' the presence of God amongst them—a well-known motif within the history of religion, not least from theologian Robertson Smith's seminal work on Semitic sacrifice that radically influenced Durkheim's classic study of religion.[41] Christian scriptures also furnish their own framing for such interpretations of social interaction in texts presenting Jesus, stating that where two or three people are gathered in his name he is there in the midst of them.[42] The very notion of otherness identifies this widespread human capacity to speak in terms of sensing the presence of an 'other' of various kinds.[43] It is not surprising, then, that periods of grief, with their intensified emotion, carry their own powerful, even uncanny, sense of presence. Here a double reference

---

[40] Valentine (2008: 86); Walter (1996 and 1999).
[41] William Robertson Smith (1889); Durkheim ([1912] 1976).   [42] Matthew 18: 20.
[43] Douglas J. Davies (2011: 228–32), including reference to van der Leeuw's ([1933] 1967) extensive account of 'power'.

to C. S. Lewis, one of the most influential popular Christian thinkers and children's novelists of the twentieth century, is apposite. The first relates to his suggestion that one of the key elements underlying much Christian theology was the fact that people 'feel the dead to be uncanny'.[44] The second comes from another 'establishment' figure of British Christianity, the New Testament translator J. B. Phillips. Though he had only known Lewis through correspondence, he nevertheless related how the post-mortem Lewis appeared to him twice, once when he was watching television and once when he was in bed. On both occasions Lewis spoke words of particular comfort to Phillips at a time of some personal difficulty. He who had spoken of the uncanny dead did not, however, become uncanny to Phillips, whose Christian sense of the resurrection of Jesus allowed this 'appearance' an intelligible theological interpretation.[45]

National and Local Churches

Over time such uncanny possibilities easily become associated with particular places, whether of local or national importance. One frequently taken-for-granted feature of British religion is its cathedrals, which unite diverse eras and locales, and express death's ubiquity and memory's perpetuity, as well as fostering aspects of the British 'Establishment'. Durham, Liverpool, and Coventry's Anglican Cathedrals, for example, bring together the tenth, nineteenth, and twentieth centuries as sites where individuals may engage in some personal fashion with death and memory. Today these are used more than ever for a diversity of religious, social, and cultural events, with their architecture and location pre-adapting them for a media age of celebrity.[46] Their relative accessibility for most hours of most days of the year, unlike local churches that are usually locked except for religious services, means that millions visit them each year. Just what these visitors do in their relatively quiet or even silent walking around, looking at, and sitting in these places lies beyond our knowledge, but we do know that many of them not only engage in thoughtful memory of those who are dear to them, but express their thoughts as written prayers, as chapter 4 will demonstrate.

RITUALS OF MEMORY: SOLDIERS, MINERS, AND CIVILIANS

Paralleling that personal domain, cathedrals also provide the means for recalling local, regional, and national cultural memory. Durham Cathedral,

---

[44] C. S. Lewis (1947: 154). The other key element being that people make coarse jokes!
[45] J. B. Phillips (1967: 89–90).   [46] David Brown (2015).

for example, does this for industrial life and death in at least two specific ways, for not only does it have a permanent Miners' Memorial, including a book of specific names of County Durham miners killed at work and a 'laid-up' banner of a local colliery lodge, but it also hosts an annual event on the afternoon of the day of the Durham's Miners' Gala in the summer. This attracts a full cathedral in the afternoon of a day that has filled the small city with marching bands with banners of former Miners' lodges, and with representative presence of and speeches from working-class and trade union movements. The cathedral service involves brass band accompaniment and includes the playing of the hymn tune Gresford, a highly emotive symbol of industrial death, marking the mining disaster at Gresford Colliery in North Wales in September 1934. In that disaster, 260 miners died—all barring eleven—and they are still entombed in that pit, a place now with its own actual as well as online virtual memorial. 'A wave of public sympathy arose throughout the land' in response to that underground explosion, of which 'there is no language in which to describe the inferno': so runs part of a House of Commons debate concerning the disaster and its subsequent formal inquiry. Its description of working conditions described 'men working almost stark naked' wearing 'clogs with holes bored through to let the sweat run out', and in 'air think with dust'.[47] It raised the theme of moral responsibility and not simply of the legal obligations of mine owners and operators, and of the desirability of strong trade unions.[48]

Certainly, in 2013, Gresford was played at the massed entry of banners into the cathedral. Just how this ceremonial event should be classified raises its own question of death and memory and pinpoints the classificatory conundrum of traditional religion, diverse spiritualities, the secular, and world views at large. Sociologically speaking, this particular ritual event, as repeated in 2013, as in most years, begins as hundreds of people, most in small family groups or with friends from their particular village or town and largely comprising middle aged and older people, over rather than under fifty years of age, take their seats amidst a low murmur of conversation. Then at the appointed time cathedral clergy welcome everyone and, with people silent, the brass band contingent, along with their very large banners, make their entry in less of a march than a slow walk, with each band and banner followed by members of its aligned community. They take their place around the crossing at the centre of the building. The many individuals comprising this ingress mark it as a community rather an elite group. This entry of band and people integrates elements of a traditional religious entry to a formal service by arriving down the central aisle, with the marching and walking of the same group through the streets of Durham having taken place earlier in the day. Historically speaking, the banners paraded are as likely to be inspired by biblical images fostered by

---

[47] *Hansard*, House of Commons, 1937. Vol. 320. Cc. 1858.
[48] *Hansard*, House of Commons, 1937. Vol. 320. Cc. 1890.

the Methodism once so strong in England's North East, as by any secular political ideology. They also cover many sorts of industry and occupation, but the key feature is that a banner is paraded by a group of people identified with its motif and social setting. Those actually paraded within the cathedral in any one year bring their particular concern within the validating architecture and communal rite of the region. The event is one of community cohesion and, in Durkheimian terms, displays the sacred things, normally set apart, and certainly not available for trite or profane purposes. Their 'revelation' adds significance and cultural power amidst an overall mood of communal remembrance of things past within a community identity of the present.

The Aberfan Disaster

Seldom has such a communal remembrance been as notable as in yet another mining disaster—that of Aberfan; a small mining community in the industrial valleys of South Wales.[49] This took place on Friday 21 October 1966 when a mass of black industrial waste some 40 feet deep, the outcome of generations of coal mining, rushed down upon the village, engulfing Pantglas school and killing 116 children, teachers, and others; a total of 144 people in all. While industrialists and politicians could, and were, blamed for this, it occurred in a country where the industrial revolution had, from their childhoods, familiarized thousands of working-class people with hardship, industrial accident, and disease. The subsequent report on the event spoke paradoxically of 'decent men led astray by foolishness or ignorance...of responsibilities'.[50] In that very society, however, most decent men tried hard to keep the culture of pitwork, including its swear-word language, separate from the life and language of the home. But in this tragedy the pit came to the 'home' in the form of children in school. This was, I suspect, one subconscious reason why the death of so many schoolchildren was so appalling. In Mary Douglas's anthropological terms it was an abomination where the boundary between two worlds had been breached; separate worlds met, and met in death. The emotional sense of shock, grief, and community feeling that came over that part of the country, with sympathy from across the world, was intense.

When this black avalanche covered the school, hundreds of miners immediately came from work at other mines to see who might be saved or to recover the dead. These men were used to hard industrial lives, accidents, and pitdeath, but this was different. My father was one of the miners who came from nearby Taff Merthyr Colliery to dig in that place. I was a student who had only recently left for university and could share only at a distance in what had

---

[49] I have referred to this episode in Day and Lövheim (2015).
[50] *Report of the Tribunal Appointed to Inquire into the Disaster at Aberfan* (1967).

happened. Soon afterwards, however, when I was home again and went to Aberfan, I stood with my father in one house: he pointed to finger-marks on an inside wall where someone had tried to escape the mud. Nothing was said, nothing could be said, nothing was ever said about it again: but the message was intense. Today a very large memorial stands above the village in Bryntaff cemetery, with arches linking each individual grave in a very long row. This powerful statement of corporate tragedy is also marked by what is, perhaps, one of the earliest cultural expressions in Britain of individualized grave-markers, with one boy's grave, for example, having a marble football on it. The building of that memorial followed the much-publicized funeral of October 27 1966 when some two thousand or more people came to that village, along with Glynn Simon, the Archbishop of the Church in Wales.

This particular disaster exemplifies in the most literal sense that slippery transition between vitality and mortality with which we began this chapter. It also marks something of the uncanny in the distinctive industrial history of a community within which a kind of cultural betrayal took place between industrialists and workers. War graves as memorials, and this massed memorial to industrial spillage, resonate with a certain element of the uncanny not only because they reveal the encounter between life and death and the cultural means by which cultural life is sustained against an enemy or by accessing energy to support society, but also because of the sheer geographical intensity of disaster and the way a site and a name become integral to cultural memory.

WARS, CONFLICTS, AND DISASTERS

Coal-mining produced a substantial amount of the raw energy needed to drive the Industrial Revolution and, as this muscularity of miners combined with military might, they both contributed to the emergent British Empire, and each was an arena in which life and death were common. Cultural vitality was impelled by physical energy-supplies. The daily attrition of industrial death matched the death of serving soldiers, whether from conflict or disease, not forgetting the continuous death from and surrounding childbirth that beset the women who often also had to carry the weight of widowhood. British history, resembling that of all nation states, is death-marked through wars and armed conflicts, and their aftermath.

Britain's political power struggles match those of most other European nations in terms of inter-state warfare, with the two major World Wars pervading the subsequent social worlds of the twentieth and twenty-first centuries. Internal conflicts, too, whether in the English Civil War of 1642–51 or the political–religious 'Troubles' of Northern Ireland in the later decades of the twentieth century, have exerted their own influence. Military death assumed its inevitable role in these contexts, as ideas of martyrdom and heroic death played their part in attempting to render suffering intelligible and furnish some kind of backdrop for the more problematic interpretation of civilian casualties.

One eminent voice, that of R. R. Marett, expressed something of the complex emotions underlying these harsh realities. A distinguished Oxford anthropologist, originally from Jersey and with numerous European links, he prefaced his autobiography in a way that catches the mood of deepest reflective sadness of a Briton and European once more witnessing the mutual destruction of great civilizations. Writing as the Rector of Exeter College, he ponders:

> A Great War once again devastating Europe. My splendid sailor-son killed in action. My native Island under the heel of the enemy. My College depleted and disorganized. Myself past seventy-four. What a moment to start on an autobiography![51]
>
> Marett (1941: v).

Here his sense of loss is palpable in 'sorrow for kith and kin, sorrow for the country, nay, sorrow for the better part of humanity'.[52] Here, too, we see an intensified expression of that loss that almost became invisible through normality amidst Britain's Industrial Revolution. This is not to say that work-related deaths were uncommon in Britain's long agricultural history, but the rise of industry with its massed workforces and the very nature of heavy-industrial production brought death into the workplace in ways that had not been seen before, just as it brought longer-term industrial diseases such as pneumoconiosis, and just as it could also spill over into the wider community as in the case of Aberfan.

Memorials

The architectural environment of Britain, most especially its extensive material culture, often includes memorials to the dead amidst its 'deathscape'.[53] Two of the most contrastingly and yet equally dramatic are, respectively, those to Prince Albert and to the Unknown Warrior, the former a response of grief-stricken Queen Victoria at the death of her soulmate husband in 1861, the latter of a grief-stricken nation to the carnage of millions of its men, many very young, in the War of 1914–18. Their location and character serve well as dramatic examples of ideal-type memorials that, divided by half a century, reflect something of the personal and national polarities of bereavement.

---

[51] *Report* (1967).   [52] Marett (1941: v).   [53] Maddrell and Sidaway (eds) (2010).

The public location of the Albert Memorial, situated in a park adjacent to London's Royal Albert Hall, itself a complementary memorial to the Prince, marks the dramatically public mourning adopted by Queen Victoria in response to her deep grief at the loss of the love of her early life. Much more than life-size, Albert's gilded figure, sculpted in bronze by John Henry Foley, commands the open space around it, attended by subsidiary statues of 'native' persons and indigenous animals of Africa, America, Asia, and Europe, as well as 'groups symbolizing Agriculture, Manufacture, Commerce and Engineering', and a 'frieze depicting 169 men who had excelled in the arts'.[54] Designed by the foremost exponent of the Gothic Revival style, Sir George Gilbert Scott, the Memorial commands its environment as completely as did Victoria's far-flung Empire. Apart from its statement of grief, this memorial opens its own window upon the then existing British Empire, itself a version of political, economic, and communicative globalization.

By sharp contrast to this open space and its symbolic interplay with the national–cultural edifice of the Royal Albert Hall lies the grave of the Unknown Warrior, or the Unknown Soldier as it is often popularly called, located inside the main entrance to Westminster Abbey. With it we pass from a famed identity to one unknown; but we will explore this more fully in chapter 7 and war memorials in general, including London's Cenotaph. Suffice it to note at this stage how both this very public grave for an unknown man, and the Cenotaph—or 'empty tomb'—exemplify the double process of concealment and disclosure. So it is that industry, warfare, illness, accident, and disaster possess dynamics of their own that accompany distinctive places that focus remembrance.

Obituaries: speaking of the dead

So it is, too, that the ways in which a culture speaks of its dead provide most telling access to its values and social intentions, with written memorials marking the intersection of private thought with public appreciation. Clergy have been known to criticize some sorts of memorial as being too personal or sentimental for the public place of the churchyard and, indeed, bishops of the Church of England may formally object to them if they wish.[55] One instructive historical case occurs in William Hazlitt's 1825 *Spirit of the Age* whose essay on Lord Byron—'a pampered egoist'—critically exposes Byron's poetry as consisting 'mostly of a tissue of superb commonplaces' but then pauses to tell us the following.

---

[54] Dixon and Muthesius (1978: 164).
[55] On the basis of the Cemeteries Clauses Act of 1977, Article 13 of the Local Authorities Order; though in practice they tend not to do so.

We had written thus far when news came of the death of Lord Byron, and put an end at once to a strain of somewhat peevish invective, which was intended to meet his eye, not insult his memory. Had we known that we were writing his epitaph, we must have done it with a different feeling.[56]

Hazlitt, critical essayist as he was, saw in death 'a sort of natural canonization. It makes the meanest of us sacred.' It also 'cancels everything but truth, and strips a man of everything but genius and virtue.' Accordingly, he decides to let stand what he had already written in criticism of Byron, for he cannot 'now turn undertakers' men to fix the glittering plate upon his coffin'. Nevertheless, Hazlitt's cultural world compels 'a different feeling' in the final page of his essayed assessment of Lord Byron.

The timeliness or untimeliness of deaths provide their own form of historical significance, as when Emily Dickinson, in her early 40s and in the cause of women's suffrage, ran in front of King George V's horse at the national sporting focus of the Epsom Derby in 1913 and died some four days later. She had already been imprisoned on numerous occasions for acts of suffragette protest and this event, whether or not it might have involved some element of suicide, was seen by some as a heroic, even martyr-like, sacrifice in the cause of women's rights in the politics of the nation. On 14 June her coffin was brought to London's Victoria Station and thence to a funeral service at St George's Bloomsbury before finally returning north by train to St Mary's Church, Morpeth, Northumberland, where her coffin was buried. The pall covering her coffin carried the words 'She died for women'. This London funeral, with horse-drawn carriages, procession including a woman cross-bearer, other women attendants, and insignia of suffragist movements, along with an 'estimated 6,000 marchers, some of them men (including some robed clergy)', presents a clear case of death being used as a vehicle for a political movement. Peter Street's account of these events, a century later, notes their centenary memorial at London's St Mary's Bloomsbury and, indirectly, offers an example of the anniversaries of many and various types in today's British society.[57]

The proliferation of memorials

A letter in *The Times* in July 2011 picked up some of that paper's current correspondence on the 'proliferation of memorials', a correspondence occurring just when Her Majesty the Queen had opened a memorial to those whose role in code-cracking at Bletchley Park during the Second World War had played a major part in an earlier end of the War than might otherwise have been the case.[58] Indeed, the early twenty-first century in Britain shows no

---

[56] Hazlitt ([1825] 1970: 117).   [57] Street (2013: 19–20).
[58] Heazell (2011: 26), referring to letters of 16 and 18 July 2011.

diminution of memorials but, if anything, an increase. Sunday 30 September 2012, for example, was marked as an Annual Police Memorial Day, focused upon police officers who have died in active service and their bereaved families. This large-scale event, with some forty or so chief constables from across the country present, was held in York Minster and was addressed by Dr John Sentamu, the Archbishop of York. It was, in fact, the ninth such annual event of this kind, something that speaks of its relative innovation. But such innovation, while it is able to recall those who have died over a long period of police history, is also able to highlight contemporary events, in this case the killing of two women police officers within the preceding fortnight and whose funerals were held on successive days in early October in Manchester Cathedral. The harnessing of the media to these events links what might otherwise be of sectional concern to the widest of public attention. In so doing the events prompt moments of intensification of public sentiment in and through the suffering and grief of individuals, families, and immediate workmates. This York service for the police and bereaved families adds yet another circuit to the wide net of social arousal and intensification of affect within the country.

Many other examples of media-led reflections on the past exist, on television channels such as the eponymous 'History Channel' or on radio programmes serving as obituaries. One prime example occurred on 11 January 2014 when a full three-hour slot was dedicated to Gilbert Harding (1907–60), described as one of the first social celebrities to emerge on the radio in the post-war period, with much made of his reputation as the 'rudest man in Britain'. One interesting feature on parts of this programme, and I mention it because of its ubiquity, lay in a certain tone of voice adopted by many on such programmes when dealing with the famous dead. This 'wise after the event' tonality gives a sense of competence and mastery of the speaker in relation to the dead and is in marked contrast to ways in which people speak of the living and also in slight contrast to those who had been really close to the person concerned. It is as though a relative degree of acquaintance confers authoritative tone while real acquaintance involves a degree of reserve, the social self and the intimate self seemingly prompting differential knowledge.

Lockerbie

One of the clearest examples of the power of the media in relation to memorialization occurred on 21 December 2013, the twenty-fifth anniversary of a plane crash over the village of Lockerbie in Scotland. This was widely believed to have been the outcome of a terrorist bomb, instigated by political sources in Libya. It occasioned extensive investigations that led to the imprisonment and subsequent release on health grounds of a Libyan citizen who subsequently died of cancer. The crash killed some 270 individuals, many of them American citizens. On the occasion of this quarter-century anniversary not only was a religious service held at Lockerbie, but also and concurrently at Westminster Abbey in London, and at America's National Arlington Cemetery where each name was read out, accompanied by the ringing of a hand-bell. While this was a clear example of the media globalization of memorialization, the fact that some thirty-six students from Syracuse University had been killed on the plane resulted in an annual scholarship of two Scottish students attending that university. What is more, the deep personal grief flowing from that event and which resulted in Lockerbie welcoming relatives of the deceased at various times shows how the potentially impersonal global communication of the media needs to be set alongside the personal stories of individuals caught up in events. The televised anniversary offered one direct example of a local–global dialectic of sympathy: Westminster Abbey, Arlington National Cemetery, and Lockerbie would not normally share a televised event.

Roadside memorials

One distinctive feature of memorials beginning from the closing decade of the twentieth century took the form of what many came to call roadside shrines. Whether as relatively ephemeral bunches of flowers or more permanent markers, these identified the site of fatal road accidents, and, by the first decade of the twenty-first century, came to assume customary significance. Although examples could be drawn from practically anywhere in the UK, I take one typical example from the front page of a local newspaper, the *Sunderland Echo*, of October 2012. This marked the death of a local seventeen-year-old cyclist, hit by a car. Photographs of the teenager and of the accident site included tributes 'tied to the bus stop' where he 'was in collision with a car'. These included a bunch of flowers and a baseball on which various messages were written: 'Love you mate'; 'RIP bro love Harry and Callum'; and the one taken as the headline for the story—'An angel in the sky'.[59] The motif of angels, whether here or in many other written memorial notes, offers what is, probably, the best cultural shorthand for popular ideas of transcendence that exists in contemporary British society. Unlike the notions of both 'spirit' and 'soul', that are essentially invisible and impersonal in the sense of not being embodied, 'angels' align with millennia of narrative and iconographic representation.

Such material tributes, and associated messages and idioms, bring significance to spots otherwise devoid of value. The depth of relationships that make kinship and friendship worthwhile demands recognition at times of loss, not least against the background of stretches of roadway that are amongst the most anonymous of spaces where few would wish those they love to die. Such

---

[59] Kevin Clark (2012: 1).

senseless spots can easily be described as a 'hopeless non-place'.[60] While some might be tempted to pursue this roadside phenomenon in terms of religion and secularization, glossing it with cases of roadside shrines in essentially Catholic countries, it is probably safer viewed in terms of Hans Mol's notion of sacralization, alluded to earlier and elaborated upon in the next section as a process of response to phenomena that help develop our sense of identity.

Both the identity of the otherwise nameless dead and of those who loved them come to the fore. The ascription of value to a place that triggered the transformation from life to death becomes perfectly intelligible. Alongside this relatively recently invented tradition of roadside tributes, which were possible catalysed by the public use of flowers at the funeral of Diana, Princess of Wales, is the similar act of placing flowers and other tributes such as toys or football-fan items outside the house where some kind of fatality has occurred, whether in a domestic fire or some other cause of bereavement. This public display of sympathy for loss is especially the case for neighbours or friends rather than for immediate kin, who have their own more intimate private as well as public and funeral means of expressing their grief. In chapters 9 and 10 we will see something both of this intimacy and of social memorials in terms of body-art and the national arboretum, while chapter 6 expresses the rather different cyber-world of online memorials.

VALUING MEMORIALS

In the UK, then, various memorials offer a means of symbolizing core cultural values, especially those of family membership, friendship, and their intersection with wider public life. Death affects every family in some way or other but, alongside the immediately bereaved, certain deaths come to hold high social profile and attract the emotional attention of wide circles of people, whose own, socially unknown, grief finds some resonance with and potential for expression through the high-profile case. In this sense we can understand how the death of an extremely high-social-profile person such as Princess Diana could allow for thousands of pockets of private grief to open within a public focus on her death, funeral, and commemoration. But it is not only in such a distinctive and relatively rare case that the flow of empathy and the triggering of emotional participation can occur, for the annual rites of war memorial in November each year also provide opportunity for a symbolic interaction between war memorials and family graves, or between national loss and family loss.

---

[60] Douglas J. Davies (2005: 170–1) develops the notion of non-place.

Moreover, family loss is now more frequently experienced as apart from war, yet the nature of emotion is such that it can be effective on a shared base and not only as a sentiment prompted by an identical experience in others. There is a sense in which the very public Cenotaph, and the one day of national focus upon it, is not symbolically and emotionally isolated from a single family grave or site where private ashes have been located. The opportunity for a medium through which different levels and even kinds of grief may be expressed is one that many may welcome.

The NHS and the Welfare State

Perhaps the most important cultural frame for understanding this social world of death in Britain from the mid-twentieth to the early decades of the twenty-first century lies in the NHS and, within it, the extensive role of local general practitioners, hospitals, and hospices. By the intersection of these centuries the hospital had become the locus of death for approximately 60% of the population, with hospices accounting for around 5%, and the remainder dying in old people's homes or at their own homes.

The significance of the hospital, in particular, is allied with its association with a variety of human emotions, and with family life, from birth, through pain and illness to death; all topics that underlie human identity and dignity and align with a sense of the sacred, in this sense hospitals are endowed as places of deep personal significance. Stirred through the joy of birth or the anguish of pain and bereavement hospitals are not emotionally neutral spots on our life-map, just as churches and other 'sacred' places attract that designation through the emotional effects felt by many at them. Here it is important to say that when the explicit ideas, narratives, and rites framing those experiences are clearly theological it is easy to speak of 'sacred places', but places framed by other narratives and actions aligned with depth of personal, family, and communal experience may also be 'sacred' in precisely the sense of possessing a quality of marked personal significance. I once demonstrated this for the 'sacred' nature of crematoria as a relatively new architectural feature that became common only from the mid-twentieth century within the UK as sites of death-related rites.[61] The hospital is, of course, not just a site of death but also a place of hope and encouragement, not least through its maternity wards, and its many thousands of successful operations and recoveries from serious illnesses and accidents, all of which contribute to people's sense of appreciation and to the way they view 'the hospital'.

---

[61] Douglas J. Davies (1996).

Hans Mol

To speak of these emotions of support is to speak, albeit in a slightly different language than usual, of human spirituality, integral to which is its own dialect of the sacred. One significant theoretical approach to the way people attribute such a quality to events, places, and individuals lies with Hans Mol.[62] Already mentioned in this and the previous chapter, his perspective can be read in terms of a graduated sense of personal response to identity-conferring phenomena on a scale from respect to awe or, even, worship. His theory is grounded in the dynamic quality of relationships underlying processes of identity formation. In its own way it is a form of attachment theory, though expressed in entirely different ways from how 'attachment' theories are normally construed in relation to loss and grief. Mol's 'sacralization' involves the ascription of strongly positive properties, to phenomena, whether in the form of persons, places, or things, that undergird our sense of identity. These are phenomena we are likely to cherish and to defend if attacked, for, in a sense, those phenomena comprise part of ourselves. In contemporary society such phenomena are extremely visible in terms of religious symbols that mark religious identity. So, for example, the Prophet Mohammed is so integral to Muslim identity that, given the widely assumed cultural ban on depicting him, any portrayal is deemed an offence against Islam at large. In Mol's terms it is the very identity of such an offended devotee that is threatened when the symbol conferring identity on that person is maligned. The variety of symbols that dominate or partially contribute to our identity is enormous, which is why, in an increasingly diverse society, the capacity to offend or take offence is great. Among the phenomena that help confer a sense of identity upon us are those that enshrine or embody our core cultural values. At the highest level this might involve, for some, the monarch; for others, their family, home, or job, or their hobby. For many, the very person of our mother or father, children, and spouse constitutes the profoundest source of identity, making them, and their memory when dead, such as to be described as 'sacred'. This aspect of meaning-making that is nothing less than identity-formation offers its own form of social force that parallels and embraces theories of grief, whether in terms of a severed loss of attachment to a beloved source of identity or of ongoing imaginative bonds with the dead. It is a theoretical perspective that also complements reciprocity theory, itself described above, especially in terms of those inalienable 'gifts' that link us with our dead, and which bring their own form of family-derived social force to frame the 'sentimental value' of inherited phenomena, be they objects, music, or even physical resemblance. I have discussed and applied Mol's thinking in previous studies,[63] and will

---

[62] Mol (1976).
[63] Douglas J. Davies (1984: 58–61), and (1996); also Davies and Powell (2015).

invoke it again in chapter 10, but I use him here to highlight the dynamic power of identity and, now, to suggest that the hospital has become its own form of sacralized phenomenon or 'sacred place', as a pivotal point in the emotional lives of millions of Britons.

Hospital care

This is attested by the fact that enormous numbers of people speak of the 'wonderful' treatment they have received in hospital; and of the 'angels' of nurses, and the almost 'godlike' capacity of doctors to change their lives, even though the early decades of the twenty-first century have often witnessed serious criticism of some (albeit a media-accentuated minority of) clinical staff and their deplorable behaviour, as we discuss in chapter 3. That behaviour is, however, deemed all the more deplorable precisely because of the high status hospitals had achieved in the later twentieth century. This balance of praise and blame, but especially of blame, is not entirely unlike experiences of some Christian churches over the same periods in relation to cases of sexual abuse. Mol's insight over entities that help confer identity upon us and of our responsive ascription of quality to those entities is, then, directly relevant to the hospital as a site of birth, healing, suffering, and death. With that in mind it is worth considering, albeit briefly, the emergence of the hospital in its NHS mode focusing on the 1942 hallmark Report of Sir William Beveridge. In so doing I suggest that the NHS has become its own manifestation of core cultural values, and in that sense stands as a potentially sacred institution to which we will return in chapter 5 when discussing the notion of spirituality as it has developed within this institution.

Beveridge

The Beveridge Report, emerging half-way through the Second World War, and entitled *Social Insurance and Allied Services*, assumed a real cooperation between the state and the individual, with the 'the restoration of a sick person to health' being 'a duty of the State and the sick person prior to any other consideration'.[64] Heralding the emergence of the Welfare State through an economic scheme of national insurance it highlighted the five 'giants' of Squalor, Ignorance, Want, Idleness, and Disease.[65] We can see in this the basis for what came to be an increased state-framing of life, whether in

---

[64] W. Beveridge ([1942] 1966: 159).
[65] Not all admired Beveridge. See, e.g. Barnett's most controversial book, which said that 'he thought a lot of himself, righteousness went hand in hand with authoritarian arrogance and skill at manipulating the press' (2001: 26).

education, social welfare, town planning, or, more particularly as far as this volume is concerned, in health—or vitality—and mortality. Certainly, Beveridge's emphasis lay on health rather than on sickness and death, with only a brief note on funerals observing that Britain would, unlike 'almost all countries . . . which have a scheme of compulsory social insurance' not provide 'a funeral benefit' when someone died.[66] The stress on the value of positive health and, indeed, on happiness, is evident in his concern that 'to attempt to force people to retire before their powers and desire for work fail . . . should be avoided by any system of social insurance designed to increase human happiness'.[67]

The ensuing emergence of the NHS in Britain, not least its further expansion from the 1970s and 1980s, meant the hospital not only gave the general practitioner a base from which to provide health care, but, whether unwittingly or no, also became the place where increasing numbers of Britons died. This cultural shift of the deathbed from home to hospital explains the tendency for many to speak of the hospitalization of death as the medicalization of death as well as of sickness and dying.

In theoretical terms, Beveridge's emphasis on the state–individual bond reflects that constant social-scientific consideration of the relationship of individual and society discussed in chapter 1's *Homo duplex* motif, but now expressed through its intrinsic ethic of duty on the part of the individual as well as the state. For a significant number of people this duty and personal responsibility has transmuted into a sense of right, if not of dependency, over the last half-century, placing enormous strain and economic burden on the NHS.[68] Lifestyle choices of excessive eating, drinking, and lack of exercise have added to this pressure, as have increased longevity and illnesses of older age. While Archbishop William Temple, who knew Beveridge personally,[69] may have thought that his Report was innovative in embodying 'the whole spirit of the Christian Ethic in an Act of Parliament',[70] it is unlikely that he would have anticipated the cultural shift that came to invest so many people's hopes and expectations in the NHS.[71] Moreover, the financial implications of cost and benefit resulting from longevity and medical advances in treatment of illness have added their own constraints to this social innovation.

---

[66] W. Beveridge ([1942] 1966: 292).   [67] W. Beveridge ([1942] 1966: 96).

[68] Barnett (2001: 241), between 1949 and 1950 the costs of the NHS doubled.

[69] Iremonger (1963: 258). W. Beveridge describes Temple after his death as 'greater than his great office', and 'the greatest evil of war' as being 'spiritual even more than material, in rousing evil passions and sanctifying them under the name of patriotism, in breeding materialism, cynicism, and disillusion'.

[70] Barnett (2001: 29), quoting Janet Beveridge (1954: 135).

[71] William Temple (1881–1944), Archbishop of York (1929–42), Canterbury (1942–6).

CONCLUSION

While there is no empirical proof that the increased significance of the NHS is causally linked to the relative decline in 'religious' beliefs, these two cultural domains need to be considered alongside each other as this volume proceeds since values associated with each carry considerable potential to compete or complement each other in terms of life and death. That slippery transition between vitality and mortality which challenges the nature of human identity and society in the face of industrial, militaristic, and nationalist contexts of death will also be carried forward in this volume.

There now remains one domain of death and remembrance that merits consideration as we move to the next chapter on ritual and body disposal; that which invokes the ultimate frame of God and divine activity. This is a significant perspective given Britain's Christian heritage on one hand and secular questioning of many traditional religious ideas, not least that of afterlife and resurrection, on the other. For, as our empirical evidence has shown, there exists today something of a problematic interface between traditionalist believers who firmly adhere to traditional ideas of bodily resurrection and others who wish to espouse some other view of human destiny.

John Inge, in his *Christian Theology of Place*, is one theologian so committed to the theological idea of embodiment, and to resurrection as embodiment's rider, that he ends his book with more than a speculative commitment to the idea of a post-death transformation of each individual in a divinely created domain.[72] In obvious acknowledgement of the difficulty of belief in a 'place' for people after death, given a popular understanding of the universe as something that will ultimately come to an end, he joins his thought with the speculation of John Polkinhorne, the latter being both a 'distinguished scientist', indeed a Fellow of the Royal Society, and also an ordained Anglican priest. He is one of a group of Christians whose scientific training, especially in physics, provides them with theoretical models or images for expression of their faith, including a 'belief in destiny beyond death' grounded in the notion that 'God will remember the pattern that is me and recreate it in a new environment of his choosing', with the 'matter' of that new environment coming from 'the transformed matter of this present world'.[73]

Here the nature of remembrance passes from the domain of memorials as human constructs giving shape to the past and to its deceased human inhabitants, to an elaborated idea of remembrance as a divine process. From a theological view grounded in faith, and reinforced by contemporary ideas of

---

[72] John Inge (2003).   [73] Polkinhorne (1995: 90–3), in John Inge (2003: 141–3).

'information' stored and processed by computers, God is seen as the ultimate basis for all knowledge about an individual. Such information can then, in due course, be used in recreating any particular individual in alignment with, or in the very stuff of, 'the transformed matter of the present world'. From a non-theological perspective, this image of divine memory can be aligned with the numerous examples of imagination-driven memorials within a broad category of identity-preserving processes that foster human community.

3

Ritual and Body Disposal

Nowhere does the interface of lifestyle and death-style become more intense than in the pivotal nature of the funeral, where the preceding period of dying passes into ensuing memory and memorials of the person who once was. Here the body 'speaks' in past, present, and future tenses within a funeral that serves as a transitional moment of social visibility and domestic relevance. To refer to 'the disposal' of the human corpse, as in this chapter's title, is to use an odd word that makes sense for descriptive and analytical purposes but which finds little resonance in the lexicon of the bereaved or service providers. Even so, 'disposal' needs some qualification to add a dynamic charge to its somewhat static property. For the dead are relatively highly mobile, and behind the scenes of everyday life corpses are removed from hospital beds, where the majority die, as from their homes, care homes, and hospices. They pass to hospital morgues, to the premises of funeral directors, and thence to crematoria, churches, or woodland burials. For a great many their journey does not even end at the crematorium as cremated remains are taken home, to a cemetery or natural burial site, or to some place of deep personal and family significance.

Just how each of these movements might constitute a ritual act poses an interesting theoretical question that will be addressed in different ways in this and the following chapter, but they do highlight the varied social contexts—staging posts—of the dead, and are a reminder that preparatory activity as well as formal ceremonial carries an economic charge: ritual costs money. Ritual also involves its own emotional costs and benefits, as human beings shift in their relationships with each other and depend both upon ritual specialists and wider circles of support to enter into and complete behaviours deemed necessary in their social world and in their own driving psychology.

Another background factor providing its own dynamic for British lifestyle and death-style is that of custom and convention informing social life; something often thought to be much more static than it actually is. Death rites have been assumed to be 'very traditional' and, under certain circumstances there is truth in that, but funerals, as pivotal points in a dead person's social existence can also become markers of social change, as has been the case in Great Britain in the decades before and after 2000. Not least significant in such changes to custom and convention within the British context is the nature of social class and the Establishment; and the media that reflects society to itself and plays its own part in lifestyle shifts.

TRADITION AND SENSE

From a baby's earliest days, the way human beings 'make sense of things' in life depends upon the degree to which they participate in the social institutions of family, friends, employment, recreation, or, indeed, in 'religious' activities. As for funerals, these often include people engaged in many of these circles of activity, beginning from the most intimate, and offer their own means of 'making sense' of their dead within all of those contexts.

Within any society, this process of making sense of things and people is located within a 'tradition', an inclusive concept expressing familiarity with and a degree of sharing in overlapping world views and ways of life. As for British 'tradition', the very idea depends upon one's initial perspective on many layers of life that could, theoretically speaking, begin at either the individual or national level. A bottom-up view would start with 'family traditions' of how daily life and household are organized, including the special events of birthdays, anniversaries, Christmases, or funerals. A top-down perspective might begin with state ceremonial or national festivals, including major sporting and entertainment events. As far as death is concerned there might be occasions when both intersect as when, for example, a soldier dies in battle and is given a funeral with military honours. At that point the larger stage is invoked, even if there is a 'private' or 'family only' event aligned with it.

In this volume I am specifically not pursuing the topic of 'tradition' in terms of, for example, nineteenth-century modernism or twentieth- and twenty-first-century postmodernism; the former with its differentiation of social life into discrete institutions and the latter with its 'dedifferentiation' of life into eclectic bundles of individual relevance.[1] This is partly because enough has been said by many on this topic and partly because it often derives more from relatively elite intellectual groups and less from the mass of society at large. But, more than this, I am far from sure that widespread experiences of death and grief easily fall into these categories. Despite social diversities and the ways cultures manage emotions there remains a sense in which human identity often mirrors existential experience of loss across time and place in ways that do not easily bespeak dramatic and qualitative human

---

[1] Heelas (1998: 2–18).

differences.[2] Furthermore, there is an emphasis upon individuality in the postmodern category that, issues of urban loneliness aside, belies the complex interpersonal networks frequently surrounding and activated by death. So, I prefer to remain with complexity, even if this means abandoning the relative security of marking identity and self-society bonds by current categories and adopting a general notion of 'tradition'.

Accordingly, I approach British death rites as embedded within a tradition constituted through an interplay of parliamentary democracy, monarchy, the military, and legal–judicial, educational, and health and social-welfare systems, set alongside local government, and the whole commercial world that frames family and individual life and the realm of employment, sport, and leisure. The London-based Olympic Games of 2012, for example, was a national phenomenon that engaged and expressed most of these, and, in the clearest way, also highlighted the enormously significant part played by sport as both leisure and entertainment for many millions in Great Britain and around the world. They also illustrated the extensive influence of the media. In having mentioned the legal–judicial system it is also important to note the criminal world and criminal acts that result in death and create an attitude of mind that opposes such things as bribery and corruption and assumes that a certain transparency of conduct should underlie social life. In recent years this has also come to include terrorism and its results. Through this networked complexity, a system of checks and balances sustain 'tradition' and also influence social changes.

THE ESTABLISHMENT

In Great Britain tradition is also fostered and enhanced through geographical, architectural, and historical factors that provide not only an ongoing repository of cultural memory, often including the famous dead, but also a stage for contemporary expressions of current life. Another telling aspect of 'tradition', one that also raises the issue of social class, is captured in the notion of the Establishment.[3] This is manifested in practically every aspect of life, from the tonality, accent, and pattern of speech and dress, through the diversity of sporting and cultural events, the military and judiciary, to the availability of school and university places. Moreover social class and 'establishment' also affect the ritual symbolism of death. In reality no sociology of British religion

---

[2] See Rogerson (1995: 158–62) for 'tradition of commitment' regarding William Robertson Smith's intellectualism and spirituality embedded in ancient Hebrew scripture ongoing in Christianity.

[3] For one approach to traditional elites via Roman Catholic thought see Oliveira (1993).

nor of death rites would be complete without some account of the Establishment's influence and the social force it exerts on British life in general.

What is relatively distinctive about Britain when compared with many other European societies is its long-term cohesion as an identifiably evolving polity amongst a very large population that has been sustained throughout religious Reformation, Civil War, Industrial Revolution, world wars, world Empire and post-colonial realignment, and now through the dynamic adjustments necessitated by its European Union and multicultural contexts.[4] Elsewhere, some recent analysis of the idea of establishment in the USA, Canada, and beyond, has sought 'to destabilize the notion' while also being crucial to the notion of 'dis-establishment' in order to 'open space for questions about how establishments are both shifting and being maintained'.[5] However, to limit establishment and disestablishment ideas simply to formal church–state relationships in a denominational sense tends to ignore the distinctive English case, where many more factors of social organization and culture cohere as the twenty-first century has got underway. In all of these discussions, however, death often plays a significant role in expressing cultural values, whether in terms of martyrdom, industrial deaths, military mortality, terrorist assault, or 'establishment' and celebrity deaths, as well as in the ordinary deaths occurring every day in thousands of families across the country.

Many of these cultural shifts are marked by the social force-field of history evident in the buildings that house the nation's dead and, periodically, provide for the funerals of major personalities who enshrine aspects of national concern. They create a stage for memorial events for millions of the war dead and make tradition tangible, as in the cases of the funerals of Princess Diana and of former Prime Minister Margaret Thatcher. In respect of such events, and in much wider contexts, Britain is noted for its ritual–ceremonial expression of national identity and cultural values; a phenomenon of some significance as far as death and memorialization are concerned and which is intimately allied with the notion of the Establishment. Essential to this capacity lie the nation's military forces, who are widely recognized in their competence in combining military–ceremonial and military warfare.

Numerous aspects of that ceremonial often include collaboration with the Church of England, its clergy, and buildings, all involving a ritual–symbolic expression of the British force-field of history. When acting quite apart from the military, the Church of England has been one major means by which national and local levels of 'tradition' have been mediated. There is, for example, a certain correspondence between Archbishop and local vicar at their respective levels of social engagement. A diocesan bishop and the local Member of Parliament also play complementary roles, not least at times of

---

[4] See Davie (2000) on European religion.   [5] Beaman and Sullivan (2013: 6–7).

local disaster and death. Moreover, if we applied the idea of handshake distance between an 'ordinary' person and persons of intense social significance, anyone meeting a local Anglican priest is likely to be no more than one further handshake away from the Queen since the priest will have shaken hands with his bishop and the bishop with the Queen, all as part of the Church of England as by law established. Indeed one of the interesting resistances to this part of the British Establishment concerns the issue of the potential disestablishment of the Church of England, a separation that occurred in Wales in the second decade of the twentieth century, and in some other similar countries marked by the sixteenth-century Protestant Reformation, as in the case of the Sweden Lutheran Church in 2000.

The Church of England is, however, only part of the British Establishment; interwoven with its more senior clergy is the social-class system of networked families, private schools, some church schools in the public sector, and those universities that are, quite unselfconsciously, described by the media as 'elite'. In 1990 it was said that it would be 'hard to overstate' the influence of the private (paradoxically called 'public') schools, 'upon the institutions of power in Britain', and that opinion of key media presenter Jeremy Paxman would be as strong nearly twenty-five years later. He noted how former Prime Minister Margaret Thatcher was a grammar school girl and her husband a minor public schoolboy, but their son Mark was sent to Harrow and, in the process they became 'trapped by the spider's web' as the Headmaster of Westminster School is reported as saying.[6]

Pierre Bourdieu has analysed 'top academic nobility' in the French system, with its 'relationship between the academic title and the great state bureaucracy', and something similar would certainly be possible for Great Britain.[7] So, too, is the case with the networks pervading the professions, especially the law, medicine, the military, and commercial company board rooms. A certain upper-middle-class culture embedded in these domains frequently furnishes a stratum of people who serve as High Sheriff or Lord Lieutenant within local counties—individuals who represent the monarch and meet royalty when visiting their areas, and others who help direct many charitable organizations. The place of church and clergy in all of these should not be forgotten, not least as they represent one stream of familiarity and engagement that offsets the notion of secularization in some social class contexts. Indeed, no account of secularization could be complete without an account of the secularization of the Establishment, and that is notably absent in scholarly studies.

Social class also deeply influences the calendar as the right sort of people ensure they attend the right sporting and cultural events, and are seen to do so. In this sense the Establishment classifies its own sense of time. As for

---

[6] Paxman (1990: 157).   [7] Bourdieu ([1989] 1996: 375).

recording the status of persons, Britain possesses its own, aptly titled, *Who's Who*, a volume in which those selected for inclusion are, annually, invited to update their credentials. When dead the 'right' people are given obituaries in the more serious newspapers and in the 'dead' version of *Who was Who*.[8] The death of film director Richard Attenborough—Lord Attenborough—was, for example, not only marked by a memorial service at Westminster Abbey on 17 March 2015, at which his brother, the equally famous naturalist Sir David Attenborough, spoke, but also by extensive coverage in *The Times*, with an appropriate photograph on the front page and an entire page-and-a-quarter of names of individuals 'expected to have attended'; around two thousand people in all.[9] Complementing such 'society' events are large numbers of guilds, professional associations, and trade unions whose sense of tradition can also be enormous even if some might see themselves as anti-establishment. It is against this background of social forces experienced through custom and convention that people live and, when dead, the vast majority then become subject to funeral directors who constitute their own form of tradition as we will see in due course. Before that, however, it is worth saying more about the complexity of British social life, tradition, and Establishment as the matrix of individual identity and the arena of funerals that mark the power of the dead.

Establishment Networks

The British Establishment is one form of elite social organization that has itself been the subject of some classical sociological and anthropological as well as political analysis.[10] Anthony Sampson's 1962 *Anatomy of Britain*, followed by his 1999 and 2004 revised analysis *Who Runs This Place?*, refer to the Establishment as always having been 'a hazy concept' but nevertheless consisting of a 'network of liberal-minded people who could counteract the excesses of autocratic and short-sighted governments'.[11] Sampson's account of Establishment brings together some two-dozen interlinked groups from Parliament, monarchy, the law, the media and broadcasters, and commercial and financial interests, as well as a subtext of private education and its resurgence following the demise of Grammar Schools in the 1960s. His revised analysis of 2004 reckons that the 'archbishops and the clergy have

---

[8] Originally copyright by A. & C. Black, it now carries the Bloomsbury imprint.

[9] *The Times*, 18 March, pp. 1–3.

[10] Cf. Bottomore (1964) for summary of early theories; Bourdieu ([1989]1996) for France and theoretical issues; Shore and Nugent (eds) (2002) and Savage and Williams (eds) (2008) for elite cultures; Rio and Smedal (eds) (2009) for a wider analysis of hierarchy; and Leonhard and Wieland (eds) (2011) for the notion of nobility.

[11] Sampson ([1999] 2004: 354).

almost vanished from the political scene' while bankers have higher profile, with 'the colour being the colour of money'.[12] But that was before key Islamist terrorist events (to be discussed in chapter 7) and the banking crash and world economic crisis of 2007–8 following which bankers came to be a byword for contemporary malpractice, if not of evil; and also before Justin Welby became Archbishop of Canterbury in 2012. This old Etonian and graduate of Trinity College Cambridge, whose mother is Baroness Williams of Elvel, not only possesses such establishment networks but was also, pre-ordination and theological training at Durham, involved in international commercial work. A not insignificant element in that clerical shift lay in the fact of the death of his very young daughter when he was some twenty-seven years of age and of his rethinking his faith surrounding that bereavement. His subsequent clerical career, itself part of the Anglican establishment, involved parochial and cathedral positions: he set up, amongst other things, parochial bereavement support teams. His former financial and commercial experience, while in his short stay as Bishop of Durham, led to his being invited to join the Parliamentary Commission on Banking Standards in 2012, a commission that directly engaged with bankers and their activities surrounding the economic crisis mentioned above. This case is important for our study of British religion and death because it involves numerous elements of life experience and lifestyle in national life, not least in a period where the Church of England has become increasingly alert to its loss of effectiveness for many people in the country to the growing number of secular and civic funeral officiants whose self-selection and semi-formal but self-validated qualification is not unlike the expansion of higher education and its resulting dilution of status.[13]

Integration and Differentiation in 'Honours'

Two of many possible contexts exploring Establishment in Britain will be cited here as cases where the largely implicit presence of establishment becomes sharply explicit and, because core cultural values are processed, are important for our study of religion. The first expressed a critical voice over a period in early July 2014 concerning who should head a government inquiry into child sex abuse, while the second, two years before, hardly attracted much popular interest but is just as telling on the Establishment, albeit in a rather different way.

---

[12] Sampson ([1999] 2004: 360).
[13] See Sampson ([1999] 2004: 199) for higher education expansion.

Abuse of the Young

The July 2014 case concerned Baroness Butler-Sloss, a most distinguished high court judge. Though now retired and in her early 80s, she had just been appointed to head a wide-ranging inquiry into allegations of child sex abuse that would explore how 'state and other public bodies, including the BBC, churches, and political parties, dealt with allegations of paedophilia'. Child sex abuse that had first appeared in recent decades through child abuse by Catholic priests then gained enormous publicity in 2013–14 through the once-feted music celebrity Jimmy Savile who, after his death in 2011, became the focus of a great deal of accusation of sex abuse of young people. Similar accusations were raised for other musical celebrities, with a major trail, and conviction and imprisonment, of Australian Rolf Harris, musician and artist, in July 2014. The appointment of Lady Butler-Sloss to this investigation followed these cases that had triggered social concern over paedophilia. However, some protest followed her appointment that, despite clear assertions of her full integrity and wide experience in such matters, reckoned her unsuitable precisely because her late brother, Lord Havers, had been Lord Chancellor and part of the Establishment at large at a time when some other members of that sector of society might have been involved in questionable behaviour regarding sex and children. Though Butler-Sloss's immediate response to calls for her to stand down was not to do so, within days she had done so.[14] One lawyer representing some clients alleging sex abuse spoke of Butler-Sloss as being 'too close to the establishment' at this very time when there is a 'deep and well-founded distrust of authority figures'.[15] Just after this, an even more popular newspaper ran front-page headlines and a four-page account involving accusations of sexual impropriety with under-aged youths on the part of senior and almost all deceased Conservative Party politicians at a Party Conference. The one disclosing this, who had been a teenager and young Party activist in the 1980s, and, in retrospect, saw that he was 'manipulated' and 'groomed', was now said to be disclosing these things 'because he fears an Establishment cover-up'.[16]

---

[14] In terms of 'establishment', Butler-Sloss was to serve as Deputy Coroner of the Queen's Household, and Assistant Deputy Coroner for Surrey in respect of the Inquest into the deaths of the Princess of Wales and Mr Dodi Fayed, but stood down when it was decided that a jury would be required and she was unused to that jury process.

[15] Little (2014: 7).

[16] Drake (2014: 4–7). This newspaper item published a photograph of former Attorney General Lord Havers along with three politicians alleged to have been involved He was described as 'socialising' with MPs.

Rejecting Honours

A quite different example of Establishment has already been discussed in the Introduction in terms of 'the honours system', as a ritual–symbolic expression of notability and public recognition of people, albeit in terms of those who had refused such awards. There we identified two directions of flow in those responses; one integrating and the other differentiating the individual and their 'preferred' group. In contrast to the life-enhancing aspect of the humility response lies the opposite phenomenon, identified as the 'hubris syndrome'[17] and elaborated for some former Prime Ministers, such as Tony Blair and Margaret Thatcher (but not, for example, John Major), whose use of language tended to over-use the personal 'I' and 'me' in what is seen as an exaggerated sense of self, not least in terms of being answerable to 'history' or to 'God'.[18] Self-aggrandisement is not, however, typical of the honours system, just as it tends to be absent in relation to death when all are seen to be mortal—whether in the face of history or God.

Death has itself been integrated into the honours system precisely when self-aggrandisement is not a typifying characteristic of someone, as when, for example, fifteen-year-old Stephen Sutton, who died in May 2014, was post-humously awarded an MBE in June of that year. He had gained considerable publicity as a courageous teenager dying of cancer who had supported the Teenage Cancer Trust and attracted support from several well-known media personalities. He had received the letter concerning the award before his death and had, as his mother reported, thought it 'awesome'. He had, she said, 'touched and inspired a huge number of people' and the award would 'help promote the legacy of his Facebook page which is named "Stephen's Story"'. One popular newspaper used his name to head their listing of honours, saying that he was 'recognised along with a wealth of A-list celebrities in today's Queen's Birthday Honours—just weeks after losing his life to cancer.'[19] This is a good example of social integration, with death adding its own force to that of the royal–social honour.

The differentiation model, including the context where an honour is re-fused, marks individuals whose lifestyle is frequently highly 'individualized', almost as a necessity of and for their activity. Writers, artists, and critics, for example, often see themselves as 'individualists', often spending a great deal of their time not as 'team players', as do soldiers or entertainers, but in isolated work. Their 'creative' task is to write, sculpt, think, or bring to being entities different from prevailing patterns. Their pleasure is self-generated and their

---

[17] Owen (2008).   [18] Garrard, Rentoumi, Lambert, and Owen (2013).
[19] Reynolds (2014: 4).

'work' its own reward. These are people who would not wish to have 'their voices muffled by ermine'.

Honours and Vitality Depletion and Enhancement

This excursus into establishment, honours and their rejection and revocation, and the humility response not only highlights the existence of a social background factor to many public events concerning death and cultural memory but also identifies the double process through which a social force either enhances or depletes the vitality underlying cultural life. One dramatic example highlights honours and, linking with the previous sex-abuse allegations, followed the burial of Sir Jimmy Savile. The honours that had been accorded him by a variety of forms of British Establishment and that were technically revocable were revoked posthumously. These included an honorary degree, honorary 'green beret' by the Royal Marines, and the removal of his name as a Freeman of the Borough of Scarborough. His British knighthood and papal award could not be revoked, simply because there is no means to do so in those institutions. Moreover, the enormous gravestone over the previously concrete grave in which he was buried at a fort-five-degree angle so that he might see the sea was removed by his family: its large inscription had been 'It was good while it lasted'—and it lasted nearly eighty-five years. There were calls for his exhumation and cremation, but this never materialized.

This individual came close to receiving the accolade of being a 'national treasure' and had been associated by millions of young television viewers, during what was the first major flush of the television age for children and teenagers, as a life-enhancing figure. Here was a kind of embodiment of vitality that expanded itself from the world of entertainment into the domain of charity and the support of hospitals. At an implicit level he was one of the first celebrities to link children and teenager television, the NHS, and charitable work. He developed relationships with politicians and with some members of the Royal Family, and his media position ensured that he was photographed with them.

His charity-grounded relationships with both Stoke Mandeville Hospital for Spinal injuries and Broadmoor, the high-security psychiatric hospital, gave him wide access to young people, to prisoners, and even to the hospital morgue. The post-mortem shift in his cultural status was from one of enhancement of identity to one that resulted in its radical depletion in all these areas. His wish-fulfilment programme 'Jim'll Fix It' ran from 1974 to 1995 and its general impact was one of joy and pleasure, yet, after his death and the new turn of events which saw adults revealing their childhood experiences of abuse now triggered accounts of radical life depletion: of their childhoods being spoiled and innocence shattered. And this is a crucial feature for this volume where core cultural values of care and, within care at large, the care of children and the sick—values that have often been aligned with religious institutions—came to be strongly bonded to the NHS. Savile becomes a crucial symbolic figure as one who seemingly embodied care and interest in children and the sick and who brought both his media celebrity and his establishment status to it. In this sense his posthumous shaming highlights the significance of the NHS as a medium of core cultural values and of the vitality aspect of identity enhancement.

Here we have seen something of how tradition and establishment carry with them a complex social force that provides a cultural gravitas to society at large and to distinctive subsections within it, and how the advent of celebrity society within a media-driven world extended this arena which is best symbolized when members of the British Royal Family engage in public events. Even phrases such as 'film-star' or 'sports royalty' catch up on the idea, albeit with a cautious and fuzzy boundary line, as with the much-admired footballer David Beckham, of whom it was said that 'a gasp went round the room' when his name was mentioned as a potential candidate for *Country Life* magazine's Gentleman of the Year Award, for, after all, despite having 'wealth, a famous wife, and a recently acquired Notting Hill townhouse . . . when it comes to his place in society some think money can't buy one class'.[20] Still, it is this diverse social gravity that can help people at times of crisis and provides its own framing for various kinds of grief. Beckham's presence to memorialize a popular social disaster would have considerably more significance for more people than one of the landed and titled men well-known amongst the county set. It is unlikely that a gasp emerged when Roger Bannister, from a middle-class background, and who when an Oxford medical student was the first to break the four-minute mile, was knighted. From his sporting interests he, too, could speak, for example, of the 'powerful establishment body' of the flagship Marylebone Cricket Club 'that all-powerful governing body of cricket', as a force in the sporting world.[21] Both with that body, as with a hundred others in the United Kingdom, a special tie could mark a man as a person of significance, and that long before we move down the social ladder to blue-collar and other workers.

TREATING CORPSES

While our body and its dress provide the basis of both opportunity and constraint during our life, our corpse presents society with the universal

---

[20] 'Mr Beckham a gentleman? It's just not cricket.' *The London Evening Standard* Wednesday 28 April 2014, p.16.
[21] Bannister (2014: 198).

constraint of death, and it is here that the cultural creativity of societies emerges in the ways they treat it. Shifts in funerary forms then afford some expression of social change and of transformations in the very idea of what a person and what their social network signifies, including the degree to which they are 'establishment' figures or much more ordinary members of society. In this, one society and era differs from others to marked degrees so that, for example, the fifteenth-century Korean practice of burying the placenta of a royal baby in a wonderfully produced white porcelain urn at a site deemed auspicious through geomancy would make as little sense to a contemporary Briton as would today's cryogenic freezing of a corpse in the hope of a future medical cure of a terminal illness to a fifteenth-century Korean.[22]

Here 'culture' makes a significant re-appearance and we are reminded again of Raymond Williams and his concern with nurturing 'culture', a reminder that 'culture' is a broader notion than simply the social traditions of a group and also includes the dynamics of the natural world, its resources, and what is made of them. Already, in 1958, he presciently described human survival by setting society and its political forces within its 'natural' environment. In retrospect his comments on 'the creative capacities of life', on 'channels of growth', as on the 'seeds of life' and 'the seeds of general death', all reinforce notions of biological environment in a more literal sense, and do not serve only to highlight the importance he accorded to the forms of language that we use in daily life and which inform our thinking and make our 'culture'. He emphasized the importance of attending to 'our environment as a whole' and of not exploiting it in ways that would soon 'bring long waste'.[23] These thoughts, coming towards the very close of his comprehensive work on *Culture and Society*, indicate a theme that subsequently grew into the notion of 'ecology' and which, for example, reached a wide population in the eco-logical advocacy of James Lovelock and his 'Gaia hypothesis'.[24] In the scope of this chapter these environmental and ecological themes became important as the closing decades of the twentieth century began to be influenced by people's sense of different environmental locations for human remains.

Inventive Possibilities

One notable example of an innovatory process often described in terms of its 'carbon footprint' is that of Resomation. The invention of Scottish engineer Sandy Sullivan, it is a process already introduced as 'green cremation' in the USA but not, as at the time of writing, in the UK. Resomation, itself a copyright trademark, is a process of dissolving bodies under pressure in

---

[22] Jaeyeol Kim (2003: 25); Shi-Dug Kim (2012).
[23] Raymond Williams ([1958] 1961: 322–3).   [24] Lovelock (1995).

alkaline solutions, to leave a white residue that can be disposed of much as with cremated remains.[25] Even by 2010 some British crematoria had already begun to consider the possibility of this technology.[26] Though at the time of writing there is no legislation either validating or forbidding this technique for use in the UK, one way forward might simply be implementation followed by public response, legal challenge, test cases, and its potential acceptance; a pattern that would reflect the earlier history of cremation in Britain. This highly controlled process—one whose technology pairs it with cremation rather than with any type of burial—might well find a place within the buildings we now call crematoria; for the incinerator or oven, and the reso-mator or dissolving chamber, are potentially similar in that a body is taken and rendered into powder. Though these processes differ from traditional and natural burial, their ash or sediment outputs could be returned to relatives in what have now become familiar containers to many British families. Their contents could then be placed in traditional or natural graves or some other spot of private significance. Just what elective affinities will arise here remain to be seen: might the symbolism of white powder foster ideas unlike the generally more grey granularity of cremated remains?

Whether or not a suitable name-change for crematoria would emerge if and when they double their function by incorporating resomators would pose its own issue of cultural innovation. The Resomation option is interesting for while it resembles cremation in being an 'industrial process', one in tune, perhaps, with the later industrial revolution, the twenty-first century's appetite for such a process of body-disposal remains to be tested. At the cultural level, just how water and the dissolution of a corpse might find emotional–symbolic acceptance when compared with fire and its ensuing ashes remains to be seen. What is obvious is that contemporary society and the commercial interests that operate and profit from it now extend their politically favoured notion of 'choice' to funerals, with every increase in funerary options offering scope for the emotion-driven hopes and fears of individuals. As they consider their own mortality and desire for lifestyle and death-style coherence, each available choice makes death more 'thinkable', and for increasing numbers of people it is 'good to think'.

Happy Places

One literary imagination that exemplified funerary innovation was that of Samuel Butler's imaginative anthropology of the 'good to think' customs of

---

[25] Rumble et al. (2014).

[26] Some 12% of UK crematoria surveyed in 2010 were 'considering' Resomation. Douglas Davies, unpublished paper delivered to Cremation Society Conference, Bristol, 2011.

*Erewhon—nowhere—*a satirized reflection on his own Victorian society. There, people constructed their own funerary monuments while alive and, once dead, were cremated and had their ashes located at places of personal choice. What is more, the living were obliged to host this deposition for, 'no one is permitted to refuse this hospitality to the dead'. He conceived of people as selecting such a place in 'some garden or orchard which they have known and been fond of when they were young', or some 'locality where they have once been happy'. This imaginative account of memorials, cremated remains, and places of personal choice was highly prophetic, appearing more than a decade before modern cremation was practised in Britain. These 'superstitious' practices, as he imagined and derided them, would, almost exactly a century later, become socially normative, with cremated remains in Britain being taken to places where people had once 'been happy'.[27]

Bodies: biological, social, and spiritual

So it is that the body, alive, dead, and situated within its social world, is the pivotal phenomenon of this chapter as we seek to understand religion and spirituality in contemporary life. Chapter 1 presented some crucial aspects of the body as both a physical and as a social entity which now require further analysis. In its muted position following a life where it has housed a human brain, the most complex organ in the known universe with its embodied nature engendering individual and social identities in complex interaction with the environment, including the environmental factor of death, the corpse becomes problematic. For, having been the dynamic centre that helped create relationships, ideas, and aspects of material culture, it now falls silent, leaving both material and memory traces. This fall into silence has been one factor, perhaps even the major factor, in the attraction presented by the major world religions to death-beset human beings.

What is more, those religions tend to be successful in popular terms to the degree that they focus basic and ultimate human concerns on recognizable individual persons including Abraham, Confucius, Gautama, Jesus, Krishna, Nanak, and numerous allied disciples and revivifying followers. All bear titles that describe a variety of attributes and qualities, whether those of being specially chosen, inspired, enlightened, or even as participating in deity in some way. But the key attribute of all is the belief in their existence as identifiable bodies. Each had a body and, in that sense, provides devotees with some degree of likeness and affinity. Each provides a focus for the cultural intensification of beliefs. Even when the ultimate deity is reckoned to be beyond any bodily form or any imaginable likeness, that ultimacy is rendered

---

[27] Samuel Butler ([1872] 1939: 112–13). See also Douglas J. Davies (2011: 113).

proximate in a body. Such a body is deemed to be faithful and wise, often engaging in miraculous acts that mark their attraction. For the most part these bodies are sufficiently 'like' us so as to make sense to us, but are also sufficiently unlike us so as to attract us by transcending our own sense of incapacity. One of the absolutely prime incapacities addressed in these traditions—and here they are frequently joined by the majority of local traditions with their ancestors and spirit worlds—concerns death. Given that this volume is also concerned with the secular, with mixed religious–secular traditions, and with varieties of self-defined spiritualities, it will also be important to address them, and that we will do in chapters 4, 5, and 9, though even some of these self-define in relation to the formal religious traditions.

THE RITUAL IN BODY DISPOSAL

The nature of ritual has long held a prime place in the anthropology of religion, not least in the seminal work of William Robertson Smith who gave precedence to 'conduct' and to rite rather than to formal belief. The anthropologist A. R. Radcliffe-Brown, who described him as 'that great pioneer of the science of religion' followed the emphasis that 'in attempting to understand a religion it is on the rites rather than on beliefs that we should first concentrate our attention', fully alert to the fact that, in European countries, especially since the Reformation, 'religion has come to be considered as primarily a matter of belief'. Radcliffe-Brown's approach, often described as structural–functionalist, is interesting in wanting to redress this 'false psychology' by emphasizing the nature of ritual or, rather, of the way in which 'rites and the justifying or rationalising beliefs develop together as parts of a coherent whole'.[28] For him 'rites can be seen to be the regulated symbolic expressions of certain sentiments, which control the behaviour of the individual in his relation to others', and which help transmit sentiments 'on which the constitution of society depends' from generation to generation.[29] In this his view resembles the classic expression of Durkheim, whom he cites and also links to Robertson Smith, but, interestingly, he first aligns it with the cultural wisdom of ancient China and the third-century-BCE *Book of Rites,* in that in connection with further Confucian texts he is able to give due place to the way 'rites serve to "regulate" and "refine" human feelings'.[30] Moreover, this tradition also brings him to issues of death and funerary rites and to the importance of ancestor cults in demonstrating, as he saw it, the social function of religion as integrative of ongoing society. At the very end of his special lecture

[28] Radcliffe-Brown (1952: 155).   [29] Radcliffe-Brown (1952: 157).
[30] Radcliffe-Brown (1952: 159).

on 'Religion and Society'[31] Radcliffe-Brown acknowledges that in complex societies in which a 'separate independent religious structure' emerges with its 'churches or sects or cult groups . . . the relation of religion to the total social structure is in many respects indirect and not always easy to trace'.[32]

It is, indeed, a complex if not ultimately impossible task to trace the webs of significance between sentiments or values that help transmit a culture from generation to generation, not least in a multi-layered society of diverse religions and other ideologies.[33] It is precisely because of this complexity that it may help to begin by focusing on death rites as one set of windows upon social worlds that cohere within a single geographical domain of Britain, even if we discover that some death rites may serve to divide the society rather than integrate it, as in the case of some terrorist acts.

In following Robertson Smith and Radcliffe-Brown's general preference for beginning with ritual performance and with an emphasis upon death we can move forward a scholarly generation to note the intellectually bold yet socially prophetic stance taken by d'Aquili and Laughlin in arguing that ritual provides one of humanity's very few means of resolving the 'ultimate problems and paradoxes of human life'.[34] While they were not referring in any specific way to death, it is in connection with death that their assertion assumes a highly significant proportion in contemporary life. In discussing 'ritual' it is wise to extend the phrase to ritual symbolism to acknowledge the radical combination of formally acknowledged patterns of behaviour with symbolic material, be it verbal or musical, or in the form of objects, times, and places. Works completed since d'Aquili and Laughlin's pronouncement on ritual make it even more persuasive that people benefit simply from acting together in an organized and formal fashion. The abstract idea of human sociability takes pragmatic form in shared behaviour that has expectation built into it, and from which some form of uncertainty is removed. Just as Durkheim spoke of the sense of transcendence in the ritual context so, here, we may speak of the performative sense of transcendence. The role of silence at some point marks communal recognition of what has happened, followed soon, perhaps, by applause as the only serious possibility of unified audible response. Here we can think of the pleasure of being social and the fact that communal experiences carry their own reward. The positive emotion of being at one with many others is intensely rewarding to many people and is probably the reason why millions engage as football and other sports fans, and as the many followers of performance arts. It is worth attending many 'ordinary' performances just for the one that outstrips the rest in its pleasurable feedback. Similarly with those

---

[31] The Henry Myers Lecture 1945 (1952: 153–77).   [32] Radcliffe-Brown (1952: 177).
[33] See Lawrence ([1915] 1949: 345–6) for trenchant interplay of 'human aspiration . . . fear and love', and 'national taste and need'.
[34] D'Aquili and Laughlin (1979: 179).

following sport, their team may lose many matches but the one they occasionally win makes the endurance of being a supporter all the more pleasurable.

The Pleasure of Sociability

So, too, the experience of social support gained from joint action has its complement for those who perform in public, whether singer or actor; occasionally they also enjoy the experience of a communal unity.[35] After a particular performance there is silence amongst a large number of people. People may speak of an atmosphere felt by all in a kind of transcendence of the ordinary nature of things: it becomes a moment to remember and is very special, a fact compounded by its only occasional occurrence. Such a performative silence may come in only one performance amongst a whole string. Just how might we interpret this kind of event? It would seem to reflect a distinctive social dynamic in a moment of shared unity occasioned by music or drama, by the act of representatives. One or a small group of us has or have brought the rest of us to a certain sense of unity. In some respects this reflects a sense of *communitas*, to use Victor Turner's term; a shared oneness. Turner, of course, following Van Gennep, uses *communitas* to describe the experience of the state of liminality in the overall process of rites of transition or rites of passage, and we are far from that social process in this case of performance. But the case of theatrical or musical performance is not entirely alien to the dynamic process of removing people from their everyday lives and bringing them into a set-apart arena where they gain a physical–social unity as 'audience'. If they then so share in the performance as to become 'one with it' then they can be said to enter into the performative flow of events. Here the notion of 'flow' has its own provenance in the psychology of the unified sense of engagement of a person, such as that of a sportsman in the sporting act itself.[36] It resembles the Zen Buddhist notion of unified action devoid of distinction between thought and action.

Ritual symbolism is, in a sense, the cultural opposite of a vacuum, for as with the popular idea of 'nature' abhorring a vacuum so, too, with 'culture'. And this is precisely because 'culture' is the meaning-packed quality of social life. Deploying symbolic material which, within its background society, makes sense to those sharing in it, ritual–symbolic action activates, performs, and makes real the often implicit ideas and expectations of a group. The very fact of utilizing symbolic material ensures that emotional dynamics of life are

---

[35] Personal conversation with Sir Thomas Allan, famous baritone, and Chancellor of Durham University, 13 December 2011.
[36] Csikszentmihalyi (2002 revised edn).

triggered and, in the sense sketched in the Introduction, this transforms ideas into values. As and when these enacted values frame our sense of identity, indeed even of our sense of destiny, they emerge as beliefs and religious beliefs.

In terms of human emotions, ritual creates activity alert to and capable of managing emotions, not least those of uncertainty, anxiety, and fear. This view of ritual has a long history in anthropology as, for example, in Malinowski and van Gennep, who appreciated how individuals benefited from being taken in hand by 'society' at times of crisis.[37] But ritual symbolism is a dynamic process and should not be thought of as some static repetition of strictly prescribed behaviour even if, for example, some cases of liturgy in highly literate church cultures have remained unchanged, formally at least, for centuries. Periods of social change, occasioned by a wide variety of circumstances, can and do result in shifts in ritual–symbolic practice as this chapter demonstrates for cremation, the use of cremated remains, and woodland burial.

Ritual Art

Within these changes it is not inappropriate to consider ritual symbolism as an art form revealing an imaginative creativity that pleases those engaged with it as emotions are schooled in traditional forms and appreciate re-engagement with familiar words and actions. Cézanne (1839–1906), one of the greatest nineteenth-century painters, not only spoke of 'the ability to renew one's emotions in daily experience', as the very nature of 'genius', but also said that 'art is religion', because 'its aim is the elevation of thought'.[38] It is precisely this combination of emotional renewal and elevation of thought that emerges in effective ritual symbolism and which allows some to align aesthetic awareness with a kind of spirituality akin to religion.

These are important issues as far as funerary rites are concerned, most especially when involving innovation, for the capacity to create new ritual cannot be ensured or guaranteed. It requires a degree of artistry, not least if and when intended for a large variety of people. For over four hundred years this was the case, for example, in the primary form of funeral used in the Anglican Book of Common Prayer, whose major influence was Archbishop Thomas Cranmer,[39] once described as 'above all, a supreme liturgical artist, transfigured by that strange sub-conscious intuition of the artist to do things as they had to be done in his medium, whether the results were or were not according to the theories he was at other times pushed or pulled to take up'.[40] Without idealizing the Book of Common Prayer's funeral services, they

---

[37] Malinowski ([1948] 1974); Van Gennep ([1908] 1960).
[38] Kendall (2001: 297). Paul Cézanne, 1839–1906.
[39] Thomas Cranmer, 1489–1556.   [40] Hebert (1935: 171).

probably achieved a degree of match with the hard realities of both life and death for centuries of British life, while including all in a unified sense of loss and grief that comes to all sooner or later. From 1980, with its Anglican *Alternative Service Book*, and *Common Worship* of 2000, funeral rites were increasingly adapted for a wider variety of forms of death that reflected lifestyle and death-style shifts from the later twentieth century.

Disclosure and Concealment

Chapter 1 alluded to the significance of disclosure and concealment as conceptual tools for approaching issues of death. This is something we can now take up directly in terms of ritual symbolism in association with death in general and with its prime symbol of the corpse in particular. To align concealment–disclosure with the corpse as a symbol of death is valuable as a technical understanding of symbols as phenomena that both reveal and hide specific meanings in a complex duality that relates both to the intricate nature of our emotional engagement with ritual and to levels of analysis accessed by ritual specialists and those they serve. Certainly it is the case that people bring different levels of understanding, ignorance, and desire for knowledge and emotional satisfaction to ritual–symbolic events. Their levels of historical knowledge of ideas associated with a particular symbol and their psychological responses associated with engagement with a symbol vary a great deal. If we follow a broad definition of a symbol as formally practised and socially recognized behaviour involving gestures, words, and objects participating in that which they represent, we can see yet again the complexity of symbolic revelation and concealment in terms of the human corpse and its management as the prime symbol of death.

For the corpse both reveals and conceals the nature of 'death', as it also does the nature of life: mortality and vitality begin to differentiate themselves from each other. In this the corpse involves both the known and the unknown, at the level of both cognition and affect. In all this a corpse is both familiar and strange. It reflects one we have known and yet one who is absent or non-existent. The very fact that in English we speak of a corpse as 'it' rather than he or she partly reflects this ambiguity. This is dramatically obvious when a relative might say something like, 'it's not my mother . . . she's not there'. In such a case the corpse no longer reveals the relationship between the living and the dead, for that relationship is now set at a different level of awareness, whether in memory or by believing the dead parent to be in an afterlife context.

Yet another aspect of this disclosure–concealment pairing lies in the fact of the unknown. In contemporary society death creates an odd and unusual, indeed one might well say an abnormal, situation. Theological shifts and secular trends mean that relatively few hold shared beliefs over death and, especially, over an afterlife as its resource of significance. The churches are relatively silent on matters of detail in their theology of death and afterlife, while secular speakers advocate a this-worldly celebration of life and not some afterlife process of salvation.[41]

Dressing the Dead

The interface of religious institutions with other service providers and with the public at large has become increasingly complicated in Britain as secular trends have increased. One telling point that reflects this relates to dressing the dead, itself part of the ritual field of funerals and which reveals something of the power exercised by different agents within the funeral service. Certainly, the mainstream Christian churches are largely silent on the topic of dressing the corpse, reflecting the division of labour between priest and funeral direct-or. More theoretically speaking, this also offers an example of the double view of mortality–vitality, as Margaret Gibson's observation on the 'Western pre-occupation with concealing mortal flesh' makes clear. In terms of what we might call corpse costume, there is much in her interpretation of dress as a 'visual defence against seeing the deadness of the subject'. She interprets the 'clothing the dead' as offering 'symbolic armour against the loss of identity and the corruption and metamorphosis of the body into flesh'.[42] Even though the British do not employ brick-lined graves of the more usual American form—a structure that is relatively easily interpreted as some form of insulation against death coherent with cosmetically prepared bodies and hermetically sealed caskets—they do still dress their dead, either leaving it for the funeral director to use trade-made shrouds or, less frequently, providing clothes that were once used by the deceased when alive. As far as available evidence suggests this dressing also remains true in the context of 'natural burial' where the dead are not placed naked in their ecologically friendly container of bamboo, willow, or wool, but are dressed in ways the family feel appropriate.

So it is that the corpse of another simultaneously reveals and conceals aspects of our own life. It marks deep relationships that now pass into memory, dreams, and into some sense of embodied connection with the dead—especially when the living person has a sense of looking like or behav-ing like the dead person. The 'family resemblance' between the living and the dead presents a likeness whose curiosity both reveals and conceals, for there is a deep sense of both revelation and concealment in every life whose intrinsic narrative reveals what is otherwise always concealed by the future. What is more, it is precisely the nature of formal religious traditions to provide some

---

[41] Sumegi (2014).   [42] Gibson (2008: 107).

frame for this life past and life future, not least in fostering ideas of acceptance, forgiveness, faith, and hope. In all of this, the body—its management, dying, death, and disposal, set as it is within the broad cultural tradition of society— remains the prime arena of concern; but just which meaning-making narratives are available to frame it and provide an emotionally intensified sense of identity remains a key question. And it is a question present at the national level of political–ethical policy as well as for individuals and their families. Some of these issues will become apparent as we discuss key forms of body disposal in this chapter. But, in advance of that, it is important to consider the role of funeral directors as they undertake the care of the corpse and symbolize both concealment and disclosure in most distinctive ways.

FUNERAL DIRECTORS AND RITUAL LEADERSHIP

Although funeral directors are easily taken for granted in contemporary Britain, their status and future are far from secure and they exist on a cusp of cultural change—an issue that can be approached through the question of whether funeral directors are tradespeople or professionals. How do they, for example, fit or not fit into the Establishment? This is a valuable question for the sociology of religion in Britain in the context of secularization, for funeral directing is an unregulated trade or business activity and anyone can arrange a funeral and handle bodies as long as all necessary certificates and formal procedures are properly processed with those managing crematoria and cemeteries. However, though associations of funeral directors and managers have established codes of conduct and some institutional self-certification of training, they do not constitute statutory regulations.[43] These individuals, and the companies that manage large numbers of them, have as their broad task: collecting the body from the hospital, where most people currently die; taking it to their premises; treating it in a variety of ways by washing and dressing it, keeping it cool, and in some cases also embalming the body; and placing it in a coffin and room where family members may come to visit it; all prior to placing it in a hearse for taking to a funeral service or ceremony, and its final cremation or burial. They may, subsequently, also collect and deliver or otherwise deal with cremated remains, and manage some form of material memorial, whether in the traditional headstone for burial or in a great variety of other means of marking a person's identity after cremation. And all this involves the invoicing of fees for services rendered; fees that remind us that in death, as in life, we pay for space and time. In this case we pay for the funeral

---

[43] Parsons (1999);Valentine, Woodthorpe, and Easthope (2013).

director's time, for his vehicles, and for the space in which to store and prepare the body, and to allow it to be viewed.

Amidst these activities, three of the funeral directors' duties attract comment in terms of the concealment–disclosure theme, viz. their managing decision-making over ritual leadership, embalming, and social presence on the day of the funeral; and all three touch the theme of secularization. Secularization, though, is also a strange or difficult word because, framing the funeral director's work, we find a certain mystique as far as the public are concerned. One way of pondering this, albeit indirectly, is through de Certeau and Giard's approach to ancient buildings amidst modern town architecture, which they saw not only as creating exotic effects that prompt a certain kind of uncanniness but also as a context that some forms of economic situation can turn to its own advantage. Something similar can be said about the role of funeral directors in developed societies. For not only can the dead body generate its own form of uncanniness, as we will discuss in chapter 6, but, like some ancient buildings subject to renovation, 'it is also made the object of fruitful operations'.[44] In other words, the nature of funeral directing is, itself, aligned with the uncanny (a notion already introduced in chapter 1) as part of the overall emotional experience embedded in grief and bereavement. But, rather like ancient buildings in modern townscapes, the dead and their uncanny quality become embraced and shaped by economic forces, in this case the economics of funeral directing and memory shaping.

Concealed–Revealed Management, Embalming, and Leading

In terms of decision-making, funeral directors are the most likely to be contacted first after a death has been certified by a medical practitioner. They come and remove the body to their premises from the hospital, home, or other place of death. Subsequently funeral directors visit the family home, or meet family members at their funeral premises or 'funeral home' and discuss what is to be done in terms of the body, the choice of clothing and coffin, and the form of service. It is at this point that the issue of whether to engage a priest or some other form of non-clerical ritual leader is broached along with the decision on form of funeral and place of ceremony. And it is here that the funeral director can wield considerable power, especially in the way he or she may ask whether the family is religious or not or whether they want a priest or not. At the present time in British life, where the role of the churches in relation to people's practice is very mixed and often a distant experience, the fact that a priest or minister of religion is optional may come as a surprise and, potentially, as a welcome one.

[44] Giard ([1994] 1998).

Upwardly Secular

It is in such contexts that ideas and decisions take place that not only influence the ensuing ritual but also what, sociologically, some would describe as secularization. This is the roots-up direction of secularization in which the decision-making catalyst of the funeral director rather than the parish priest can play an enormous part. Questions such as 'Was your father very religious?' or 'Was he a churchgoer?' can easily lead to a conversation in which the funeral director can explain that a priest is not necessary and that he knows other people who are very good at conducting funerals and who can give the family just what suits them and matches the lifestyle of their deceased relative. In some respects it is easier for the funeral director to 'employ' a funeral celebrant than to negotiate with a priest since the latter often assumes that he or she is 'in charge' of a funeral, most especially if it involves a service in church. But that church-based event is relatively rare, since the crematorium is far more likely to be the site of the public ceremony. And the crematorium is a challenging space since it 'belongs' to a local authority or to a private company and not to 'the church'. It is in this sense a borrowed place, and one that is as open for Christian, Hindu, Sikh, or Buddhist usage as for specifically humanist or general secular or mixed use.[45] There is, then, a sense in which the management decisions over the form of service involve a slight degree of concealment and disclosure, for it is the time when a family has to be explicit about numerous implicit aspects of its values, beliefs, and preferences.

Embalming involves a much more obvious expression of the concealment–disclosure theme, for while it is seldom medically necessary, especially given the refrigeration facilities so readily available to the funeral managers, it is a procedure that symbolizes their expertise. It is, in a powerful sense, part of a claim to professionalism. As a practice concealed from the family for obvious reasons of emotional sensitivity it might also be interpreted as a prelude to the deceased being 'revealed' to them if they wish to visit and 'see' their dead; an act often socially framed as 'paying respects to' the dead.

Finally, the social presence of the funeral director at the funeral itself marks his or her public focus. It is, if anything, an increasingly popular practice for the funeral director to walk in a ritual fashion in front of the hearse for some part of the journey to the funeral site. For this he is likely to wear, and if it is a woman she is likely to imitate, the male morning-dress of top hat, tails, and silver-topped walking cane. The person who is symbolic of the funeral directing process, which has involved the private domestic decisions, and the even more secluded preparation of the body, now becomes a very public figure leading the

---

[45] Very occasional cremations for Jews and Muslims reflect individual circumstance, often of 'mixed marriages' or the like, but are not culturally preferred funeral traditions. See Schofield (2005: 428–9) for Zoroastrian cremation in the UK.

mourning party, showing family to their seats, and indicating when and how to leave the crematorium or church. The shift from concealment to disclosure has taken place. Other aspects of the funeral director's lifestyle and death-style coherence will be explored in chapter 9, but now we consider the major forms of funeral in which funeral directors play their significant role alongside clergy, other forms of celebrant, and funeral facility staff.

TRACKING FUNERAL CHANGES

Until the closing decade of the nineteenth century, burial was the sole means of funeral in modern Britain. Then, with the innovation and rapid development of cremation, a major change took place so that by the mid 1960s cremation had overtaken burial in Great Britain. Then, almost a century after cremation's initial appearance, woodland burial made its appearance, with burial sites rapidly emerging across the country. Though we approach these diverse forms of funeral under their own sections in what follows (with the exception of woodland burial which is discussed separately in chapter 10), there will also be a considerable overlap of topics as theoretical issues necessitate their own forms of comparison and contrast.

Burial

Earth burial, with its cultural alignment with Christianity and the death, burial, and resurrection of Jesus, has a long tradition within British life, not least through the rites of the Church of England and the words of the Book of Common Prayer from the sixteenth-century period of the English Reformation. While the importance of Jesus and Christian tradition will be detailed in chapter 4, here it is sufficient to say that Christian assumptions concerning Jesus, his body, death, and resurrection have brought a symbolic potency for funerals, not least in association with the nature of the British Establishment as a cultural force. Here the theological–mythical domain has long interplayed with 'established' cultural practice and its framing social forces.

Historical rationale

One of the clearest rationales for the practice of English burial was formulated by Richard Hooker in his comprehensive sixteenth-century theology of the new Anglicanism where, contrary to the 'dumb funerals' of Puritan practice in which the avoidance of prayer or homily ensured that nothing untoward might be said about the destiny of the deceased person since that was, as

Puritan leaders believed, known only to God, he allowed for an official form of service and funeral sermon, as well as the use of 'mourning apparel'.[46] Four themes underlay his account of funerals, viz. love, honour, comfort, and hope, and, together, these reflected his general theological combination of sense of the naturalness of religion with its divinely revealed scriptural warrant. First, then, 'funeral duties' 'which nature requireth' express a love towards the dead, and take on local customary expression, as in the wearing of funeral dress. Hooker shows a marked appreciation of the nature of the social individual, i.e. of the individual embedded within society. He disagrees with the theological perspective that would laud only the sincere intention of a particular individual and that saw only hypocrisy in pretending to some sorrow. For Hooker, it is right to express a sorrow that is genuinely felt, but even if such a feeling is absent 'the signs are meet to shew what should be'. This makes it clear that his theological focus is not lodged deep in some personal heart nor yet only at the public level of behaviour but at the complex interface of individual and society, with which any 'laws of ecclesiastical polity' must inevitably deal. The second task of funeral rites is to honour the dead in appropriate ways. In today's terms his approach reflects ideas of dignity, not only in death but also in life. Working from the rationale that 'the life and the death of the saints is precious in God's sight' he urges that this be brought to the fore at a time when people may be especially open to embracing this idea. Once again, however, he strikes the personal–social chord by suggesting that mourners may be prompted 'both to live and to die well' if they think that their lives will, one day, also be subject to public comment, and as they hear how God dealt mercifully with the dying person they now mourn. His third theme, that of comfort, includes both supportive words and also such things as 'funeral banquets', which may help the 'pensive...natural affection' of the bereaved. Finally, and beyond these factors, the greatest 'duty of Christian burial is an outward testification of the hope which we have touching the resurrection of the dead'. It is to ensure a grasp of this that an appropriate form of service should be used. The fact that no form of service is evident in scripture should not detract from a proper sense of 'judgement' that God gives to the Church to see the benefit of such a thing and to deploy it 'to strengthen true religion'. In all of this Hooker also adheres to the notion of an immortal soul, noting it as an ultimate truth even when appearing in the mistaken view that 'the souls of men departing this life do flit out of one body into some other'.

The image of the local vicar in his white surplice with black cassock and scarf standing at the head of a grave, reading the fixed funeral service and surrounded by a relatively small group of family and more intimate friends, expressed this theology in a practical way. In many a film the immediate

---

[46] Hooker (1965: 444).

context was that of a churchyard, even though for the great majority of urban churches the graveyard, if it existed at all, would be full, with the burial actually taking place in the local civic cemetery. These are cemeteries that came into existence following burial law reform in the mid nineteenth century in answer to the rise of urban populations following the Industrial Revolution.

The funeral director became an increasingly natural partner within this scene as the twentieth century advanced so that, by today, it is almost certain that the four or so 'bearers' of the coffin will be employed staff who will have placed the coffin into the hearse earlier, attend it during any church service, carry it to the grave, and let it down with straps at the beginning of the rite.[47] They then retire, though the funeral director himself, and now increasingly herself, will remain at the grave-side and have some soil ready to throw into the grave and onto the coffin when the priest speaks the words 'earth to earth, ashes to ashes, dust to dust in sure and certain hope of resurrection to eternal life through Jesus Christ our Lord'. Members of the family may also throw in some soil, either at that point or slightly later as the rite draws to a close. It is often the case that this act is limited to close kin, and to those with a sense of close relation to the dead. In many respects this is the one ritual act that marks a complexity of relationships and emotions that different individuals may feel towards the dead. It is a moment of parting, for after it the burial party leaves the grave for whatever kind of reception has been organized, and it is at this point that cemetery employees emerge to fill in the grave. The family members then leave the scene, often driven in the same formal limousines provided by the funeral director to drive them to the cemetery. This act of being driven singles out the immediate family as those who are relatively passive in the process of the funeral from wider circles of mourners who usually drive their own cars to the event.

The reception, often described as a 'wake', now takes place in a wide variety of venues, from the family home to a public house, hotel, or hall of some kind. Food of the finger-buffet kind is laid on and it is customary for alcohol to be consumed. For the great majority of funerals of those with 'normal' death in older age, the shift in emotional tone from the quiet solemnity and grief-framed behaviour in the cemetery frequently to a more positive and socially supportive atmosphere is normal. In analytical terms there is a shift to life affirmation. Stories, anecdotes, and memories of the dead are common and, in their own way, speak of the 'life' of the deceased rather than of their dead state. At this moment they are still 'alive' in common memory and shared experience. The nature of this event, its venue, and its food and drink expresses the lifestyle of the family concerned.

---

[47] In parts of Scotland kinship hierarchy dictated who held particular straps.

Though, for the great majority of people, this event brings the burial–funeral to its formal end, for a relatively small number it will be followed by a memorial service of a more public and celebratory kind. And this is precisely where the nature of the British 'Establishment' makes its presence felt, whether at a national or much more local level; for such a memorial is its own statement that the deceased held a position of social significance whether in the professions, politics, the media, or in entertainment and sport. One variant of this pattern of burial service, reception, and memorial event is sometimes evident where a funeral service, often in a large church building, and attended by the family and a wide variety of other people, is followed by a 'private' or 'family only' burial or cremation. This pattern, too, can involve a subsequent reception when the family returns and rejoins the larger gathering in the appointed venue.

Though the body is now interred, some members of the core kin retain a relationship with it by visiting the grave, often at anniversaries or other significant dates. This becomes all the more significant once the headstone is placed on the grave after it has settled, perhaps up to a year after the funeral itself. At this point the dead person's body is socially replaced by the basic facts of his or her life in terms of name, birth and death dates, and primary kinship relationships. This newly located social identity of the dead serves to qualify the term 'disposal' of the dead because they are now given a clear public identity amidst the mortal identity of all others in the cemetery. The grave becomes an identifiable site and focus for visiting and for the placing of flowers or other tokens of memory-relationships, while technological developments, implemented from approximately 1990, now allow for photographs of the dead person to be worked into the headstone, allowing the deceased to be depicted at any age or appearance chosen by the family.[48] In some respects this has increased the personal nature of memorial markers by adding the pictorial face to the otherwise straight text mentioned above.

One major feature in the early twenty-first century touches on the death of infants and children and consists of what almost counts as a nursery area of memory in some cemeteries. There the small graves of children are frequently covered in toys, and messages of love, affection, and regret. Some cemeteries have also instituted a common memorial for such infants whose names appear together on a pillar or tablet, again often with soft-toy objects. For a significant group of parents, the choice of burial over cremation for very young children offers this form of concrete memory when, in a chronological sense, they have but very short actual memories of their child. This innovation in childhood memorials offers a clear example of the interplay of lifestyle and death-style. The importance of a child to is central to very many contemporary British

---

[48] Douglas J. Davies (2002a: 49–51).

families, especially when people plan to have a child, or to have another child; this addition to their family is seen as integral to their parental identity as a couple, whether formally married or not. The very fact that pre-natal scans can result in photograph-like images of the foetus and a knowledge of its gender makes for a highly personalized relationship with the child that was not possible in previous generations. The pre-natal child becomes an integral part of a lifestyle involving considerable planning and consumerist involvement, not to mention pre-natal classes and the social connections made with other potential mothers and even fathers. This networked pregnancy lifestyle makes neonatal loss all the more acute, and makes an active memorializing of the baby all the more significant. Here pregnancy lifestyle and neonatal or infant death-style cohere; and cohere much more, for example, than in the loss of a very aged parent to a middle-aged person, when that elderly parent has ceased to play a dominant role in their adult child's pattern of life.

Cremation

For the great majority of the British public of, say, 1880, the thought that by 1980 nearly 65% of the dead would be cremated would have been incredible. Yet, the emergence of cremation as a dominant mode of dealing with corpses in the UK has been one of the most remarkable pieces in the jigsaw of social change over the last century. Initial growth in the area was slow, with the first cremations of 1885 numbering 3 persons, and subsequent years being easily counted as 10 (1886), 13 (1887), 28 (1888), 46 (1889), 54 (1890), and only making 99 by 1891. The numbers remain easily countable, passing from 840 in 1910 to reaching 1,023 by 1911. The cremation rate does not reach 1% of the total figures for method of body disposal until 1932 (1.14%). It then progresses as Table 3.1 indicates, where I have selected moments of key shifts and rounded up or down the rates to whole numbers.

This early trajectory not only highlights the point of intersection between social process and key individuals who embody ideals and through whom change is effected, but also presents a challenge to symbolic analysis and ritual process, pinpointing professional changes in society at large. It also raises issues of architecture and crematoria, as well as of columbaria and other means of ash deposition.

Table 3.1. Early cremation rates in the United Kingdom

Year	1943	1944	1946	1949	1953	1956	1958	1963
%	6	7	9	14	20	26	30	41

Note: values are percentages of total figures for method of body disposal.

Dr William Price

As for individual influence, one crucial case comes in the person of Dr William Price, whose life, itself stranger than fiction, practically spanned the nineteenth century. Born in March 1800 and dying in January 1893, Dr William Price was cremated in South Wales, with tickets having been issued for his open-air cremation and, it is reckoned, with perhaps 20,000 people in attendance.[49] This surprising man, a Welsh-born son of an impoverished Oxford-educated clergyman, became one of the youngest members of London's Royal College of Surgeons and, as such, a firm candidate for the British Establishment. However, as a self-styled Druid, an active Chartist who once had a reward on his head, and an advocate of free love, he probably falls into a qualified anti-establishment identity. This position is reinforced by his non-conformist life in Nonconformist Wales where he fathered his first son when eighty-three years old and not only named him in Welsh *Iesu Grist*—Jesus Christ—but, when the boy died aged five months, his father began to cremate him on a mountain above Llantrisant in January 1884. Public outcry led to his arrest, but at the Glamorganshire assizes he was discharged. The presiding judge, Mr Justice Stephens, declared the act not illegal. The extensive judgment included a synopsis of cremation in antiquity and differentiates between burial and cremation in terms of the speed of destruction of the body rather than anything else. It was, perhaps, fortunate that this judge had also served in India where, of course, cremation was normative. Dr Price went on to complete the cremation of his son in March 1884.

This judgment strengthened the resolve of the British Cremation Society, which had been established a decade earlier in 1874 as the Cremation Society of England by Sir Henry Thompson, a result of his having been inspired at the great Vienna World's Fair of 1873 by potential models of crematoria engineering. In January 1874, along with a group of like-minded friends, a declaration was signed expressing disapproval of burial and preferring cremation, at least until some better method was discovered that would 'rapidly resolve the body into its component elements' without 'offending the living'.[50] Thompson became a surgeon to Queen Victoria and his fellow signatories were relatively well-known medical professionals and literary figures; as such they reflected part of the British Establishment, as did, in his own inimitable fashion, Dr William Price. As Stephen White has shown in his legally focused history of the nineteenth- and twentieth-century pathway of cremation into legitimacy, the Cremation Society had decided to buy land and purchase a cremator, and this they did at Woking, having been frustrated by the Bishop of Rochester when seeking land for this use at the Great Northern Cemetery in London.

[49] See Dean Powell (2007: 27) for much of this account.
[50] Jupp in Davies and Mates (2005: 135–43).

The episcopal objection was that the land was consecrated. The fact that one Captain Hanham had cremated two of his own family on his own private land in 1882 primed the Cremation Society for action since the Home Office did not take action against him, and the judge ruling, when Dr Price's case came before the Cardiff Assizes, that cremation was not illegal as long as no public nuisance ensued, furthered their cause. Despite a private member's bill aimed at regulating cremation being defeated in the House of Commons in April 1884, the Cremation Society decided to press on with cremation at Woking and this occurred on 26 March 1885.[51] After a variety of legal and institutional ventures, the Cremation Act was passed in 1902 with regulations following in 1903, and this opened the way for cremation to be developed across the UK, not least as local authorities could see the saving of land as burials were replaced by cremations. Still, in 1903 the cremation rate in Britain was still less than one per cent of the dead (0.8%), and would not pass that level until 1932 (1.14%). Then, by very steady increments, it had reached 6.04% by 1943, and then, at an increase of between one and two per cent a year, it reached nearly a fifth of the dead by 1953 (19.86%).

During the 1960s the rate increases by approximately 2% each year until in 1968 it strikes 51% for the UK as a whole, thus overtaking burial as the newly normal British form of dealing with the human body. The rate then continues at approximately one to two per cent a year, with 1975 showing 61% being cremated. The rate then either increases at around one per cent or remains static (in the 69% range from 1987) until 1993 when the 70% mark is reached and heralds a new plateau of between 70 and 73% in the decades before and after 2000 AD, with over 74% sustained in 2011 and 2012. Table 3.2 displays some of the most recent rates, with actual percentage of the UK population being cremated given.

This overview confirms that cremation has become the dominant form of funeral—from a handful of cases in the 1880s to nearly three-quarters of the population over approximately a 130 years. In its earliest days, as Peter Jupp has ably demonstrated, the protagonists who spearheaded the Cremation Society of Great Britain belonged to what we described earlier as the Establishment.[52] Only with time did cremation become democratized and as such the normal form of funeral for working-class people. For the greater

Table 3.2. Some recent cremation rates in the United Kingdom

Year	2008	2009	2010	2011	2012
%	72.45	73.41	73.13	74.37	74.28

Note: values are percentages of total figures for method of body disposal.

[51] Stephen White (2005: 131–2).   [52] Jupp (2006).

part of this history social scientists, philosophers, theologians, and historians alike paid scant attention to this major form of social change in death practice. It was not until the 1980s that a young generation of scholars, largely motivated by sociological, theological, and existential reasons, spearheaded an academic turn towards death that prompted a rise in what has come to be called death studies within the UK.

Crematoria and cremated remains

The fact that crematoria emerged as the technical basis for this increasingly dominant funeral form might have prompted its own architectural critique, but this did not take place until the pivoting of the twentieth and twenty-first centuries. Yet, just as factories and railways marked the Industrial Revolution, so did crematoria mark the funeral revolution, and in their own way also emphasized engineering in the control of fire. The crematorium was, in effect, a factory for processing the dead. But this was not simply a speeding-up of the process of bodily dissolution as stated in the judgment passed on Dr Price, for the entailment of cremation was cremated remains. The human body was rendered into ash, and this begged the question of what to do with it.

From the late nineteenth and into the early decades of the twentieth century, ashes were either buried, sometimes in miniature graves, or were placed in urns that were, themselves, located in columbaria—specially architected halls with many shelves for containing ashes. These locations did not, however, retain their appeal for long, with examples such as the Golders Green Crematorium columbaria being notable for their rarity. Had the columbarium approach to ashes established itself it would not only, in a pragmatic sense, have required a considerable amount of storage space, but it would also have introduced into Britain a symbolic innovation that might well have been an innovation too far. This can be explained in terms of symbolic concealment and disclosure. For burial as practised in Britain largely concealed the process and outcome of burial. Unlike the traditional world of Greek Orthodoxy in the Mediterranean where graves were until very recently exhumed fairly soon after death with the bones cleaned and place in an ossuary, the British dead received no such treatment. Though gravediggers would unearth bones as they dug 'new' graves, they would treat the bones as local custom implicitly directed, but there was no formal rite or social expectation of formal ceremony. Death and burial were, essentially, concealing processes, all awaiting the final judgement and the resurrection for the dead which would be its own glorious form of disclosure.

Urns in a columbarium displayed human mortality in a cultured fashion. They reified the dead and marked a shift in symbolic distance from earth-bound ashes awaiting the divine miracle of resurrection. But columbaria did not establish themselves; they separated people both from the earth, kin, and memory in far too stark a fashion. Columbaria contradicted British symbolic patterns of death. Soon ashes were increasingly buried or scattered in crematoria grounds or elsewhere in family graves.[53]

Ritual Negotiation

However, in a quiet way and by popular activity, largely from the mid 1970s, the British took cremated remains away from crematoria to use them in ways they decided upon for themselves. To most Britons this did not seem strange, but to most other Europeans at that time it did, not least because this individual declaration of funerary independence was inconceivable in most European countries, where laws controlled the destiny of cremated remains.

Britons were, in increasing numbers, simply acting as they saw fit. It is possible to see their behaviour in terms of secularization and argue that they were dispensing with the services of the church. But there was nothing simple or direct about this change, for many will have had a clergyman take the crematorium service dealing with the corpse but, once that service was over it would be very likely that crematorium staff would scatter or bury the ashes within the crematorium grounds in a fashion that, while 'proper', was not ritualized. In essence, then, the cremation rite was split into two parts; one in the crematorium with the coffined corpse and clergyman, the other with the cremated remains dealt with by a crematorium official who scattered or buried them in the crematorium grounds. It was possible, though, for a priest to be involved with the ashes, especially if they were interred in a churchyard or cemetery. Indeed, in the Church in Wales, interment of remains was prescribed. But in England at large families increasingly took possession of remains, took them away, and dealt with them as they saw fit, removing even the crematorium staff from the circle of disposal. What is more, the fact that death affects all, including people involved in the media, means that, occasionally, they find their own life experience worth reporting for the world to hear about, and in the process make innovative practice more 'normal'. Jan Etherington, for example, writing in the *Daily Express*, tells how she, along with three sisters, took their mother's ashes to the beach at Weston-super-Mare and deposited them there whilst having a champagne toast to their deceased mother; '"To mum. You always loved Weston and wanted to come back. Now you have, so we hope you can rest in peace".'[54] She continued her article with reference to a recent Co-operative Funeral Society report describing how some three-quarters of those cremated have their ashes taken home

---

[53] Jan Etherington (2011). 'Scattering ashes on a beautiful sunny day', *Daily Express*, 13 September.
[54] Jan Etherington (2011: 14).

by relatives before they decide what to do with them. But she extends her half-page article by citing the great variety of contexts in which ashes seem to be placed in contemporary Britain. Her overall tone could be echoed in what many say about such experiences, speaking with an emotion-tinged positivity, complemented by a degree of humour and a sense of doing what the deceased would have wanted. One feature of many such accounts concerns the wind and the way the ashes are blown, especially if some of them come back onto the relatives present.

Having sketched the rise of cremation and what has been done with the ensuing remains we have identified the decreasing level of ecclesiastical ritual conducted in relation to them. The gap between church and popular ideas and practice reveals its own form of secularization and, with it, something of the ritual dissonance between clergy and people. Even when clergy now take funeral services, the event frequently involves a degree of negotiation over what will be said and who will say it, what music and readings will be used, and what special effects or acts may take place. Such ritual negotiation creates a distinctively different ethos of status, hierarchy, and service as far as clergy are concerned; one that differs significantly from the past where the priest was and felt himself to be in control. This is, however, precisely the context in which secular and civil ritual leaders find their strength in meeting and talking at some length with bereaved families so that in a direct sense their ritual performance is, essentially, mimetically narrative. In other words, the funeral leader, frequently termed the celebrant, repeats in a person and family-focused narrative what he or she has gathered in information about the deceased. This is very different from the traditionally ecclesiastical funeral in which the minister's task is to frame the event in the Christian grand narrative of Christ's death and resurrection. To a certain degree representatives of the British Humanist Association also have something of an informing grand narrative of humanism that they need to correlate with personal family accounts of the deceased. Against this background we see that the notion of ritual negotiation involves some complex processes rooted in the degree of understanding required between the ritual leader, the family and friendship network of the dead, and any professional theological or ideological frames at work.

In a sense, even family members often had to 'negotiate' amongst themselves just what to do with the remains, and sometimes even with the container that had once held remains. They were, in effect, taking from the churches what many religious leaders would have seen as an ecclesial function. The practice even entered the literary world when, for example, P. D. James has her insightfully ascetic detective, Commander Adam Dalgliesh of New Scotland Yard, dispose of his aunt's ashes in a corner of a specific East Anglian churchyard: 'She had left with her will a request that her ashes should be strewn in the churchyard there without ceremony and by him on his own.' She had not been 'a religious woman', and the request surprised him. But, 'in recent weeks he had been visited by the nagging guilt of a duty unfulfilled, almost a spirit unpropitiated.' This had prompted him to think of 'man's insistent need for ritual'. P. D. James catches something of the paradox of ashes when contrasting the aunt's 'secretive but powerful personality' with the 'plastic package, curiously heavy, of white grit'. In a corner of the churchyard, aware though glad that he had not sought permission for this act, he 'tipped out the ground bones like a libation. There was a flash of silver and all that remained of Jane Dalgliesh sparkled among the brittle autumn stalks and the tall grasses.'[55] Though being familiar with the words of the Church of England funeral service, James has Dalgliesh recall not its 'ashes to ashes' motif but what can only be described as an enigmatic text he had recently seen cited on an old cottage. 'That which hath been is now; and that which is to be hath already been; and God requireth that which is past.'[56]

One appropriate literary complement to P. D. James can be found in John Betjeman, whose poetic account of the ordinariness of English life is legendary, and who has even been described as 'the greatest poet of the Church of England in the Twentieth Century' because of his doubting reflections on faith. His handful of poems on death and its haunting near-futility capture both the faith of some and the doubts of others. In his 'House of Rest', for example, he visits an old vicar's wife, husband long dead, and sons too, 'so motor-bike mad then'; her daughters 'far away'. In her simple room with its old wedding photographs and his tobacco jar, now with 'Dried lavender inside', she is still able to see beyond the present. What is more, 'when the bells for Eucharist / Sound in the market Square . . . the veil between her and her dead / Dissolves and shows them clear / The Consecration Prayer is said / And all of them are near.'[57] Her piety is such that Betjeman felt quite unable to ask to which Church party her husband might have belonged, 'Lest such a question seem to be / A mockery of Our Lord.' Here, Betjeman creates his own poetic version of a sociological ideal type. And he does exactly the same in his 'Aldershot Crematorium', albeit with a different type, as he captures a certain English *habitus* that often still emerges around some funeral rituals.[58] This poem exists in earlier and later versions and probably belongs to the period 1970–4. It captures a time when cremation was becoming established in England. Its lines move between earth and heaven; they aspire only to be deflated. It sets the crematorium scene almost prosaically, 'Between the swimming-pool and cricket-ground / How straight the crematorium driveway lies!' But then our eyes are directed upwards, 'And little puffs of smoke without a sound / Show what we loved dissolving in the skies.' Smoke that takes with it, 'Dear hands and feet and laughter-lighted face'. Immediately, however, we return to earth amongst others who do not 'know quite what to

---

[55] P. D. James (1989: 142–3).   [56] Ecclesiastes 3: 15.
[57] Gardner (2005: 40–1).   [58] Gardner (2005: 26).

say', not least because, as he places in parentheses, 'Friends are so altered by the passing years'. In typically English style they take recourse to the weather, 'Well, anyhow, it's not so cold today'. 'And thus', he says, 'we dissipate our fears.' At this very point he inserts the opening sentence that would have been used at such a cremation service, a sentence used indiscriminately from the Church of England's Funeral Service in its Book of Common Prayer, and taken directly from the Gospel of John: '*I am the Resurrection and the Life*'. But the poem does not end with this aspirational sacred text, for, after a colon, the final line reads, 'Strong, deep and painful, doubt inserts the knife'.

In 'House of Rest' and 'Aldershot Crematorium' we find apt expressions of differing cultural perspectives on religion providing powerful depictions of social worlds, much as descriptive statistics provide in their own way else-where in this book. They show ritual contexts in which faith soars or quivers in doubt or disbelief. For the vicar's widow the Eucharist brings her dead and absent ones close to her; at the crematorium even the chimney's 'little puffs of smoke' that dissolve 'in the skies' contrast implicitly with potential beliefs in a soul passing on to eternity. For the nurse bringing tea for her patient and finding her already dead, Betjeman's 'Death in Leamington' moves from the 'Chintzy, chintzy cheeriness / Half dead and half alive', to rhetorically ask his reader 'Do you know that the stucco is Peeling? / Do you know that the heart will stop? / From the yellow Italianate arches / Do you hear the plaster drop?'[59]

Many other literary allusions to cremation, crematoria, and cremated remains emerged and grew after the 1970s.[60] By the time of such well-known novels as Iain Banks's *The Crow Road* of 1992, themes such as the coffin sliding away into the wall or purple curtains descending, or even a formal leaving of the chapel under the tutelage of funeral directors are all normal. His dramatic first line echoes urban myths and some real technical worries with its famous, 'It was the day my grandmother exploded' (because the local doctor had not removed her heart-pacemaker; a doctor who then dies of heart failure himself as he tries to run and stop the cremation before the explosion occurs).

Demystification and Disenchantment of Corpse and Ashes

This shift to 'ashes' seems to have been a degree of demystification of death, itself often an experience surrounded by questions of cause and reason. While the nineteenth-century advocacy of cremation was, for example, firmly driven by science and social welfare concerns, the image of unhealthy vapours

---

[59] Betjeman (2003: 1–2).   [60] Douglas J. Davies. (2005: 301–5).

associated with overfull city cemeteries carried its own echo of accounts of the 'matter of mini-miasmic clouds breathed in and out' associated with formal medical accounts of the plague in the sixteenth century.[61]

In Britain today, the corpse may also be viewed as something unusual and distinctive, and while it may be too extreme to speak of it as holding a degree of awe or mystery it certainly remains far from neutral as far as emotions are concerned. This cannot be said to apply to the ashes of a corpse to anything like the same extent. At its absolute simplest, a corpse needs several people to move it; ashes need one. Tales abound of people taking a casket of ashes from place to place, posting them, or otherwise dealing with them in private ways. The very nature of cremated remains in terms of portability rendered the dead symbolic in new ways. In one sense, of course, ashes are also 'cheaper' than corpses in terms of their mobility, but they also allow for issues of identity to be played out in ways that satisfy individuals. So, for example, the front-page news in a popular newspaper of Sunday 7 July 2013 carried the headline, 'Bernie to be buried with baby's ashes'.[62] Bernie, aged fifty-two, had died three days earlier surrounded by her family. She had been one of the once-celebrated 1970s singing group, the Nolan Sisters. The headline referred to Bernie's wish to be cremated and have her ashes buried next to those of Kate, her stillborn daughter. She had, in fact, already planned her own funeral to a marked extent, to be held in Blackpool's Grand Theatre, the site of many of the Sisters' concert appearances. This double-page spread detailed the family's presence with and around their sister when she died peacefully, and also the party-frame for the funeral. In this example we draw close to one version of a 'good death' in contemporary Britain where the dying person is surrounded by family and knows that her identity will be complemented both by the venue of her previous stardom and the location of her remains with her stillborn daughter.

Although ashes were not the subject at hand, when Max Weber spoke of rationalization of life as involving disenchantment, he could well have been speaking of ashes. For Weber, urbanization and industrialization were key factors in world demystification, and these two factors were also crucial in the rise first of cremation itself, and then of the issue of dealing with ashes. When cremation was first introduced in the 1890s remains were buried in miniature graves or placed in specially built columbaria and, as such, ashes retained some element of mystification, inheriting the seriousness previously allied with the corpse. With the dramatic rise of cremation into social normality from the mid 1960s the scene was set for a shift in that stance. And part of this very probably resides in the nature of their treatment. As long as clergy were involved, and used some form of liturgical ceremony, the symbolic objects

---

[61] Healey (1993: 21), cited by Rohan Elizabeth Brown (2012: 114–15).
[62] O'Boyle (2013: 1, 4–5).

were framed to some degree in a sacred fashion. Once people took it upon themselves to scatter, bury, or keep their relatives' remains, the loss of hierarchy transformed the action. Something similar has occurred with some woodland burials, as will be discussed in chapter 10.

Displaced–misplaced bodies

Not all bodies receive any of the above forms of disposal, and, when they do not, some considerable problems may ensue; problems that exhibit their own windows upon mortality in a culture. The case of body parts retained after post-mortems in Great Britain, for example, came to a head in the later 1990s with the knowledge that many hundreds of body parts, especially of babies and children, had been retained without parental knowledge, not least at hospitals in Bristol and Liverpool. This led, for example, to the formation of the Bristol Heart Children Action Group and, in 1999, to a public inquiry. This, among other things, led to the Human Tissues Act of 2004 which forbade such organ or tissue retention without appropriate permission and introduced the new offence of 'DNA theft'. Later, the Redfern Report of 2010 explored an increased sense of concern with human bodies and their treatment within the NHS as an existing social context that originated with a basic concern for the relationship between individual and society, or the 'state' as it was originally framed, and as we have already discussed in chapter 2 in association with 1942's Beveridge Report.

NHS BONDS

However, Redfern, even more than Beveridge, emphasized the institution–individual bond and not simply the state–individual bond. Here the acceptance of responsibility at the hospital level and by individual doctors develops the earlier sense of responsibility by the state. Above all, perhaps, concern with babies and body parts marks that symbolic nature and relationship between the human body and 'society' that was more germinal in the 1940s. It also highlights the pivotal role of the hospital as an arena within which symbolic material of core cultural worth is handled. The all-pervasive influence of the NHS was dramatically evident in the 2012 Olympic Games when 'Danny Boyle, the impresario, waltzed a worldwide audience through Britain's socio-economic history', notably included in it 'our celebration of the National Health Service'.[63] This iceberg tip in the Olympic showcasing of Britain to

---

[63] Bannister (2014: 335).

the world reveals its own condensed symbol of the NHS as part of the very fabric of social life, but it also prompts awareness of the NHS as its own force within the British Establishment. With the construction of major hospitals, and with previously existing hospitals and medical schools, senior medical consultants and professors had long constituted a medical elite that sat naturally within the British class system and the 'establishment' at large with its Royal Colleges of Surgeons and other senior professionals. This has made the rise of health-service managerial staff and their political managers a source of debate and, occasionally, of conflict.

Moreover, the generic political dictum that 'the health service is safe with us' reflects the core significance of this aspect of British cultural life, with political parties engaging with the NHS with a sense of caution, alert to its significance within the lives of millions, and to the role of those millions as voters. More even than the education system, the NHS affects the vast majority of the population at some time in their lives, and in ways that directly influence health, wellbeing, and death. In ways that could not have been fully envisaged at its inception, these NHS activities create a nexus between the people and the state, one that was catalysed by the pre-existing cultural sense of the importance of medicine and that has only been intensified through advances in medical science (to this we return in chapter 5). Meanwhile, we highlight the bond between individuals and the state played out for the great majority of people in terms of their relationship with the health services through the local General Practitioner, ante-natal classes and care of the child during its early development, during adult illnesses and bodily conditions, and onwards to end-of-life care. The rituals of medical consultations and care do in some respects echo religious equivalents.[64] While medical and clerical ritual specialists provide distinctive forms of support for changing populations, with the former now eclipsing the latter, each has suffered from public criticism, with blame levelled at those who abuse patients or parishioners. Bad medical and bad ecclesial practice not only raises issues of ethics but of the ritual power of practitioners, whether in the clinic, hospital, or church. As the media and law courts disclose aberrant behaviour—its own form of desecration—so the ritual capacity of and ritual arenas for welfare are potentially decreased. This is because trust, the foundational social emotion, is weakened. At the same time, however, alternative forms of medicine and health care on one hand, and alternative spiritualities and ritual practice on the other, raise wider issues of the relationship between traditional and innovative practice.

---

[64] Douglas J. Davies (2012a).

CONCLUSION

We have seen that, until the mid-twentieth century, one other major context of social bonding relevant to this volume lay with the Church, especially the Church of England, through hosting marriages, baptisms, and funeral rites. But the closing decades of the twentieth century witnessed a decrease in utilization of these rites as some individuals and family groups took it upon themselves to organize events matching their personal preference, encouraged by personnel who set themselves up as lay ritual leaders. While this re-allocation of rites dealing with the disposal of the dead presents its own form of secularization in terms of the churches and their public provision of services, one might also describe it, almost paradoxically, as its own creation of the sacred. This is no mere playing with words but is an understanding that 'the sacred' can quite properly be identified in terms of the depth of life's meaning held within personal and family values. In terms of both the sociology and history of religion 'the sacred' need not be aligned only with the doctrinal and liturgical schemes of one church or religion. It *is* of interest, however, when a society that has capitalized on having many popular rites performed in some degree of association with its 'establishment' clergy, thereby supporting the social force of 'establishment' in general, passes into a more commercial ritual world of negotiated choice.

The journey of self-identity, described at the outset of this chapter in terms of a series of staging posts, is now shared by those informed by formal religion, by secular and other world views, and with proximate and more ultimate health-care provision provided by the state. Still, as is often the case in history, the funeral remains a platform for expressing contemporary life values, whether or not they include afterlife beliefs. The lifestyle and death-style interplay that frames the meaning of contemporary life is revealed within the wider framework of a ritualized Britain in which marriage, same-sex union, partnership, and the naming of children may be conducted in a wide variety of licensed premises and in many ways. This increasing diversity of ritual forms available for one's life-course is both a mark of social change and one means of advancing it, as the following chapter's concern with the sacred and secular will make clear.

4

Christian and Secular Death Rites

Though 'religious' and 'secular' categories present too crude a distinction for understanding contemporary British life, these abstract terms do capture something of the diverse world views many experience today compared with the past. Moreover, many experience change in their own life views as they age, for times change within biographical as well as social history.

That 'the early-modern period English mind' possessed 'no neat division . . . between culture, religion and politics' is a view with some resonance for twenty-first-century Britain, where a Christian-grounded historical culture influences society at large, albeit lightly, while some religious groups express a distinctively intensified commitment to the faith tradition.[1] Mirroring aspects of traditional Christian organization, Jewish, Muslim, and Indian-originating traditions, as well as minority 'new age' or Pagan perspectives, voice their own competing identities in today's media-sensitive world, as do some atheist and agnostic parties. All such stances become more obviously visible through funerary rites as death-styles surface in reflection of diverse lifestyles.

In effect, a large number of regional, local, and choice-led groups continue to speak the main language and some dialects of Christian culture, often within Christian architectural contexts and through words and music of essentially Christian form. Large numbers of the populace engage in Christian-related festivals, notably at Christmas, while many city and town centres are framed by churches great and small. Their allied historical cemeteries also mark the past as a Christian present. Areas within civic cemeteries may also include a small section devoted to the Jewish dead as well as to the Christian subsets of Anglican, Catholic, and Orthodox persuasion. Increasingly, Islam also offers its own mortuary territory as well as its minaret-presence in key cities of the land. Set against these, the language of secular world views has also become more formally ritualized over recent decades. Moving out from long-established philosophical circles into the media and

---

[1] Larkin (2014: 293).

public debate, these often engender their own celebrity embodiment in figures such as Richard Dawkins while also taking their place in the ritualized arena of funerals. It is precisely this diversity of historical and contemporary ritualized forms of funeral that occupies this chapter.

BELIEFS AND ACTIONS

While such sharp distinctions between belief and unbelief, or between religion and secularism, are relatively easy to pursue philosophically and through social surveys of belief and attendance at religious institutions, they oversimplify life. To 'believe' or 'not to believe' is far from a distinctive mode of human being and, while it may suit the needs of some thinkers and their research methods, it overlooks the interwoven nature of human thought and its emotional dynamics as life circumstances change over time (as chapter 5 shows for the Sea of Faith Network). It has been far too easy for sociologists to use questionnaires to ascertain what people 'believe', just as religious leaders can far too readily speak of what church members 'believe'. By contrast, there are few social scientists who would study an exotic society and separate its 'religion' from its 'culture', or its 'religious beliefs' from wider 'cultural' acceptances in as easy a fashion as with British 'beliefs'.

The influence of elites within society, especially in theological, philosoph-ical, and sociological groups, may help transform a culture through such interpretations, but their assumptions are not necessarily shared by non-elite majorities. This is especially important in Britain with its history of religious reformation and free thought and is a reminder that there will have been many 'secular' devotees within the churches and many 'religious' opponents of religious belief. It also hints at the emotional commitments of some explicitly atheist individuals whose emotional zeal and commitment echoes that of strong religious sectarians. All of these belong to and only make sense within a shared historical culture pervaded by Christian imagery, narrative, and ethics, and contested arguments over each of these domains. The depth of Christianity's making and sustaining of British society is so significant here that the majority of this chapter will be devoted to it.

The Christian Foundation

The fact that a first-century Mediterranean Jewish sect should have been transformed into a distinctive Christian movement, one including a contem-porary British monarchy whose coronation rites are symbolically rooted in ancient Israel, is one of the wonders of the cultural world.[2] Christianity's largely European transformation into Orthodox, Catholic, and Protestant variants, and their subsequent universal missionary programmes and growth of sects, transformed the world. That wonder increases when we consider the Eucharist historically as an extremely durable ritual in which lifestyle and death-style factors exist in a creative correlation. If we follow the argument that today's Christian Eucharist—albeit in its many denominational variants—is a transformation of the early Jewish Passover feast, we can appreciate that its core lies in a sacrificial, blood-related deliverance rite of salvation. Theologically speaking, Jesus replaces the Passover lamb of Egypt, and the faithful are now delivered from sin as their forebears were from political captivity. Since Judaism did not become a proselytizing movement, something left for its Christianized metamorphosis to adopt, this move to Eucharist—circling as it does around Jesus' suffering, death, and resurrection—increasingly developed an impact upon the masses due to deep affinities felt between its symbolic resources and human needs aligned with suffering, dying, death, and destiny. While the major traditions of Hinduism, Buddhism, Sikhism, and Islam, along with Christianity's parent, Judaism, all have death as a prime concern, Christianity is distinctive in focusing mortality upon the human figure of Jesus. In him, the forces of mortality and vitality are carried into the domain of destiny.

This is evident, for example, in Adam Smith's dramatically pragmatic *Wealth of Nations*, which described religious instruction as having the goal not so much of fostering 'good citizens of this world, as to prepare them for another and better world in the life to come'.[3] These social and eternal dynamics were embodied and personalized through the figure of Jesus in a way that answers humanity's sense of self as eternal. The gospel narrative and its ritualized form in ecclesial liturgy resonate with this desire for a meaning that transcends death. This was interpreted theologically in Augustine's sense that God made humanity for himself; sociologically in Hertz's notion of society conceiving itself as immortal; and in cognitive science as an over-plus of meaning-making in human thought processes. Though there are some who are content to die apart from ideas of immortality, it is likely to be the case that for very many the idea of immortality is, itself, a symbol of the massive complexity and incomprehensibility of this life, let alone that of the availability of a future environment of being. These complexities are, to some degree, simplified when encountered as a flowing narrative and ritual practice.[4]

---

[2] The use of the well-known Anthem 'Zadok the Priest and Nathan the Prophet anointed Samuel King', one of G. F. Handel's Coronation Anthems of 1727 for King George II manifests the musical framing of this fact.

[3] Adam Smith ([1776] 1860: 330).

[4] A few would prefer a 'demythologized' form of Christianity.

The meaning-making narrative of Jesus is not only told within the frame of the wider Jewish accounts of deliverance but achieves an ecclesiastical cultural intensification in the symbol of Jesus within the Eucharist. There symbols of bread and wine express his sacrificed body and blood while eternal life is vouchsafed to their participants. Here we are presented with prime ritual symbolism of mortality and vitality. The affinity between Jesus—defined over the early Christian centuries as possessing both human and divine natures—and millions of ordinary people lies in the ready emotional base of sympathy associated with illness and healing, controversy with official power bases, and most especially with suffering, death, and death transcendence. What is more, other figures surround Jesus to create a web of mortal concerns over pain, suffering, and death, as in the central case of his mother Mary who witnesses and suffers the loss of her son. Her iconographic depiction spans the emotional spectrum, from the time of conception (the annunciation) through the mother-and-child image of the Nativity, to the crucifixion of Jesus where she becomes a central agent in his 'descent from the cross', depicted as the mother holding the corpse of her son. In due course, especially in traditional Catholic belief, she is said to have been subject to an assumption into heaven, body and soul, and not to have endured the mortal decay to which the rest of humanity is subject.[5] Statues and other images of Mary, as well as of lesser saints whose lives also embraced suffering, have played significant roles in both the public and private devotions of people and, doubtless, helped many focus their pain and grief in a context which promised some intercessory help from these most significant religious 'others'.

For our purposes, it is the treatment of his body in death and resurrection that marks the mortality–vitality theme within historically Christian cultures. Their complex symbolism has frequently been reflected in the form of the crucifix, a preferred form of Catholic piety; and the empty cross, the preferred form of Protestant worship. While the latter more easily symbolizes 'absence' or the resurrection of the corpse into a transcendent heavenly domain, the former powerfully evokes human sympathy. Condensed within these symbols lie a swathe of theological and devotional elements related to ideas of salvation, a concept that, above all, speaks of the affinity between a devotee and Jesus within an overall divine plan. For the idea that his death was a sacrifice for sin, fully intended by God, whilst also being an unjust death imposed by Roman authority under the connivance of priestly Jewish authorities also underlies the overall theological narrative.

The artistic treatment of Christ's dead body frequently demarcates church traditions from each other, whether in Catholic crucifixes, the preferred empty cross of Protestants, or Orthodox icons. Moreover, the essentially simple

---

[5] Idea originating around the fourth century, formally defined in the Roman Catholic Church in 1950.

shape of the cross appears in many forms, whether as an object affixed to churches, worn around people's necks, standing as war memorials, or in the very cruciform shape of many historical Christian churches. At its most basic the cross is also the shape of the human body with arms extended. It is a 'natural symbol' endued with an enormity of theological–cultural significance. Within churchyards and graveyards the cross marks a multitude of graves. As the means by which Jesus died it underlies gospel and other biblical narratives that frame the Eucharist. Then, as a calendrical manifestation of those narratives, Good Friday, even in publicly secular Britain, marks his death-day with marches of witness and relatively lengthy church services. In many of these church-related events we encounter hymns that do not simply engage with the actual death of Jesus on the cross but take up the motif of the cross itself as a focus of concern. While the Roman Catholic tradition frequently depicts a suffering or a dead Jesus on a cross, now defined as a crucifix, and some parts of the Catholic world even re-enact his crucifixion with actual devotees in Christ's role, Protestants have preferred a bare and empty cross, albeit one framed with hymns depicting his suffering and death.[6] This distinction reflects the ritual foci of each tradition, with the Catholic Mass being, essentially, a re-enactment of Christ's death, with his body and blood appearing in and through the sacramental elements of bread and wine, traditionally interpreted through the miracle of transubstantiation. Protestants moved away from this liturgical dynamic even though Lutherans and some Anglicans retained a good deal of the ritual actual and the piety that such ritual and theology engenders. The symbolic structuring of essentially Protestant ritual advocates an active memory of Christ's death without explaining just how that memory operates. In practice it works very significantly through hymns, public preaching, and the theological expectation that devotees will, in some way, gain an experience described in terms of the forgiveness of sins grounded in Christ's sacrificial death operating as an expiation for sin, and also of a regeneration of life rooted in Christ's resurrection. What happens here is a developing affinity between a devotee's sense of self and of his sense of Christ's passion and death. This lies at the heart of what is often called 'spiritual formation' or even simply the spirituality of a tradition, a notion that reappears in chapter 5.[7]

From a non-theological perspective what happens is that a person comes to live in their tradition; its rites, narratives and guiding myth.[8] Not least

---

[6] Wake (1889: 40), citing Forbes (1870: 228), rehearses how the Aymaras of Peru may engage in sexual excesses on Good Friday with restraints of authority being removed because 'God was then dead'.

[7] Note Paul Badham's (2013: 77) ultimate basis for 'offsetting the forces of death' as lying not in formal theological or philosophical rationales, but on what he acknowledges as the 'exceedingly frail foundation' of a 'strong, living relationship with God'.

[8] It is this embodied participation that makes any simple intellectual process of 'demythologizing' the essential Christian message problematic: it is not a simple rational task of classifying textual genres.

important are the paradigmatic scenes that enshrine these doctrinal myths and the liturgical contexts that enact them. The sacred texts of all traditions contain such narrative myths, and generate hymns and devotional songs. One Christian hymn of Victorian origin illustrates the dynamics of these processes when the devotee sings a prayer through the words:

> Jesus, keep me near the cross,
> There a precious fountain,
> Flows for all,
> A cleansing flood
> Flows from Calvary's mountain.[9]

While the dense theological symbolism structuring this verse spoke to millions within nineteenth to-twentieth-century Protestantism, influenced by what was traditionally called the theology of the cross that had been intensified through the Protestant Reformation, similar blood motifs have spoken to many Catholics through the theology of the Mass and its associated symbols such as the Sacred Heart of Jesus, and the Sacred Heart of Mary, originating in select circles in the Middle Ages but much popularized and formally recognized in the nineteenth century. It is notable that E. P. Thompson's extensive historical account of the English working class should have devoted an entire chapter to 'The Transforming Power of the Cross', largely in connection with the impact of Methodism upon social life in England.[10] He not only highlighted the place of blood and Christ's wounds in the 'strange imagery . . . perpetuated during the years of the Industrial Revolution' in the poetry and hymnody of Methodist and allied forms of religious dissent, but also its 'sublimation' into death motifs by the end of the eighteenth century.[11] This, along with wider Protestant and Catholic perspectives, reveals the wide cultural attractiveness of heart and blood symbolism within Christianity and pinpoints the idea of elective affinity explored at length in chapter 9.

There remains one crucial aspect of Eucharistic theology, liturgy, and piety that flows from Eucharistic action and bears upon funerary rites; it is best summed up in the paradox of divine presence and absence. Christian funeral rites possess a human corpse and promise a resurrected body in something paralleling the New Testament account of the corpse-grounded crucifixion of Jesus and his resurrection and ascension into heaven that results in his physical absence. One response to this in Catholic practice has been in the ritual creation, through divine miracle, of the 'real presence' of Jesus in and through the Mass; another has been to focus on the Holy Spirit as a 'replacement' phenomenon. Either way, the paradox of absence and presence highlights the

---

[9] Words Frances Jane van Alstyne, 1820–1915.
[10] E. P. Thompson ([1963] 1991: 385–440).
[11] E. P. Thompson ([1963] 1991: 409).

nature of faith, of that intangible orientation of believers that makes it so, that makes the absent present.

One intriguing entailment of these dynamics with regard to death concerns the paradox of the post-funeral absent corpse of the loved one and its 'presence' in memory. What I think is the case is that many people find an affinity between the dynamics of an absent/present Christ and an absent/present loved one. The world of the 'spirit', as the environment of the Eucharist, is not far removed from the environment of memory-recall of the dead. It is the emotional power ever potent in the one that is also echoed in the other. What is more, we should not restrict this 'absent presence' to Eucharistic liturgy, but see it as capable of extension to many allied Christian rites, not least to funeral rites, and, as we see in chapter 6, also to the spirituality of 'presence'.

Martyrdom and Victimhood

Before considering funeral rites, however, there remains another deep-seated element of Jewish–Christian–Islamic culture to consider; that of martyrdom.[12] Its significance is coterminous with Christianity's own theological culture of sacrifice, originating in the centuries immediately preceding and succeeding the lifetime of Jesus, where history was transformed through the experience of martyrdom developed theologically in the Books of Maccabees. These diverse books furnish influential material on death, suffering, and martyrs.[13] One idea driving these texts was that the death of martyrs would not pass unrequited by God whose righteous nature would vindicate their being resurrected. This extremely important point shows the intrinsic integration of death and moral values. The biblical case of Adam and Eve in the Book of Genesis revealed a similar alliance, albeit in its negative form, when death is introduced as a consequence of the pair's disobedience to divine commandment.[14]

Martyrs, in general, raise the crucial question of moral order and the meaning of existence itself, especially when they are portrayed as those obedient to God despite being oppressed by the wicked. Since the human drive for meaning integrates rational and emotional factors in a 'sense of things' it is understandable that a hope should emerge in disorder being ultimately righted by the deity as the ultimate source of moral order. In Christianity, the late Jewish notion of resurrection as God's ultimate vindication of the improperly lost life of the faithful came into its own when focused

---

[12] See Flanagan and Jupp (2014).
[13] The major themes concern immortality (2 Macc. 7: 9, 23, 37, and 4 Macc.); expiation (2. Macc. 7: 37ff.); and prayers for the dead (2 Macc. 12: 43–5).
[14] Genesis 3: 19.

in the individual person of Jesus. We might say that it is in the theological, liturgical, and ethical portrayal of Jesus that congruence emerged between lifestyle and death-style in ways that gave substance to a Christianly informed culture.

Other rather different though still martyr-like narratives informed this emergence, as in the ancient Jewish cameo of Abraham called upon to sacrifice his son, Isaac, to God.[15] Often interpreted as a test of faith and obedience to the divine, this agonizing narrative has frequently been seen to prefigure the actual death of Jesus as the son of the divine father. The Abraham event has reverberated across the millennia, not least as Jews, in various ways, sought to understand the Nazi holocaust.[16] British cultural history in its ecclesiastical turns has added new layers to the meaning of martyrdom both in the early evangelization of Britain and its first martyr, St Alban; in the later period of the Protestant Reformation with its Protestant and Catholic martyrs; and in Britain's Civil War. Each era provided opportunity for faith-related militarism and death, centuries before the inter-state wars of the nineteenth and twentieth century's Imperial period. At its best, the quest for political power combined with doctrinal idealism, while at its worst its affinity was with economics.

Another concept, that of victimhood, is also reminiscent of martyrdom in that the death of 'good people' for a cause, or the death of relatively helpless people at the hands of those deemed 'wicked', are events that cannot be easily ignored for they also challenge society's moral order. Here, too, slavery and diverse forms of emancipation shift the centre of gravity of life and oppose ideas of meaninglessness, for whenever death appears arbitrary its randomness frequently proves to be problematic, as the next chapter shows through the theoretical idea of dual sovereignty.

HOLY WORDS AGAINST DEATH

At the beginning of this chapter I raised the theme of historical change and notions of religion and secularity within British cultural history, and it is now time to illustrate the depth of this culture and exemplify something of its shifts over time by drawing from two representative voices, one from the seventeenth and one from the twentieth century, and from one contemporary popular re-reading of the latter that has generated its own form of popular spirituality concerning the dead.

---

[15] Genesis 22: 1–18.   [16] Paul Middleton (2011: 120–56).

Jeremy Taylor (1613–67)

In 1651 Jeremy Taylor published *The Rule and Exercise of Holy Dying* which followed *The Rule and Exercise of Holy Living* of 1650. Its Preface, dedicated to the Earl of Carbery, describes the work as 'the first entire body of directions for sick and dying people' that the author remembers being 'published in the church of England' (sic). He notes the many Catholic books on the subject but sees himself as being 'almost forced to walk alone' as he draws from scripture, the primitive church, and from his own 'experience in the cure of souls'.[17] Here, as a thirty-seven or so year-old man, he writes for those who are well and who ought to ponder their ultimate death, and not—it should be stressed—for those on their deathbed. As time shows, he will have another seventeen years of his own life left before his own death, aged 54. Writing at a time of dramatic social–cultural changes as the state expressed its own form of rejection of Catholicism and implementation of its own form of Protestantism, Taylor stands at a pivotal point between a medieval view of life–death and afterlife that was actively ritualized by sacraments of transition and the emergent view of life and death that repositioned priest and people in terms of what could be anticipated in the afterlife. This was a complex period of new theological and ecclesial elites, of old commitments retained in some localities and mind-sets, and also of eager acceptance of reformed belief and practice. Here were real lifestyle and death-style shifts embedded in longstanding custom and in zealously accepted innovation. Indeed, by the very time Taylor's twin studies were published, the English are said to have 'developed a powerful narrative about themselves'.[18]

And to this narrative Taylor brings his own addition in terms of the interplay of life and afterlife. The dynamics of ritual power were changing, dynamics that would alter the power possibilities of church and priest and of individual identity and responsibility in the face of ultimate destiny, not least in terms of merit and its manipulation by a church. Taylor approaches the dead not in terms of 'banks of good works, but a huge treasure of wrath'. While there were also many philosophical and theological debates, not least on the nature of the soul and afterlife flowing around him,[19] Taylor remained focused on pastoral issues in this volume. He sees no point in the former long-established Catholic practice of anointing the dead, nor yet of prayers for them since the prime means of preparing for death lies in the midst of life. 'The fearing man is the safest', as a person who has reflected upon 'the terrors of death' during life, and who is alert to the fact that 'death is the *king of terrors*'.[20] If a person has not benefited from such thoughts and from forty

---

[17] Jeremy Taylor ([1651] 1830: xviii).   [18] Larkin (2014: 300).
[19] See Ann Thomson (2008).   [20] Jeremy Taylor ([1651] 1830: 221, original emphasis).

or fifty years of the church's ministry, some last resort will be of no benefit: 'Can extreme unction at last cure what the holy sacrament of the eucharist all his lifetime could not do?'[21] Here, in the most obvious way, we find a classic example of the interplay of lifestyle and death-style, not simply in the very complementary nature of the titles of his two books, but in the way the *Holy Dying* volume works on the life–death motif. Since very few are now familiar with this landmark of English spirituality within the Anglican religious trad-ition I will outline some of its incisive perspectives, always bearing in mind how many clergy, as pastors of the people, would have been familiar with it across several centuries as it contributed to British culture as such.

Taking us into his pastoral world, Taylor reminds us that no special increase of imagination is needed to depict ordinary human life in a deeply negative mode since 'death meets us everywhere'.[22] We are reminded that 'the time we live is worth the money we pay for it', that death is, in fact, 'the king of terrors', making time ' . . . the most precious thing we have'.[23] Even our daily life offers clear examples of death's framing of life with sleep being its own 'image of death', and with bodily existence, as in 'baldness', being 'but a dressing for our funerals', since we are 'the heritage of worms'.[24] But that earthy and negatively valued heritage is far from the whole story, since a key motif underpinning Taylor's fundamental outlook falls to the soul: 'the soul [is] . . . the better part of man that never dies', with death itself taken to be 'a separation of soul and body'.[25] 'Two differing substances are joined together with the breath of God, and when that breath is taken away they part asunder, and return to their several principles; the soul to God our Father, the body to earth our mother.'[26]

Taylor's Christian identity naturally conducts this wider interpretation of death through biblical narratives including the Genesis accounts of Adam and Eve and their disobedience to divine command. Though here, too, Taylor adds some thoughts of his own. Had Adam not sinned, for example, he would have left this world for another because the Earth could not accommodate the growth in numbers. 'It is therefore certain, man should have changed his abode', as will all at the day of judgement. Death then 'is not the going out of this world, but the manner of going'.[27] This sense of the possibility of 'other worlds' for a potentially unfallen humanity appears curious to modern ears but makes perfect sense to Taylor, given that the future resurrection will necessitate new environments for all concerned. Still, as far as Adam was concerned, 'death is not an action, but a whole state and condition': 'the same

---

[21] Jeremy Taylor ([1651] 1830: xiv).   [22] Jeremy Taylor ([1651] 1830: 7).
[23] Jeremy Taylor ([1651] 1830: 23, 38, 40).   [24] Jeremy Taylor ([1651] 1830: 9).
[25] Jeremy Taylor ([1651] 1830: 52, 59). As with many Reformation thinkers, classical authors are often influential in background reference, and this is true for Taylor, as in his allusion to Seneca ([1651] 1830: 54).
[26] Jeremy Taylor ([1651] 1830: 101).   [27] Jeremy Taylor ([1651] 1830: 60).

day death began' for him, so too began 'a state of change and affliction'.[28] This state had both its physical dimension in the generations following Adam, whose own sins had also weakened the race and reduced lifetimes, and had also taken a toll in terms of 'despair': while 'no affliction is greater than despair', hope was the reality to be set against it.[29]

'*A coffin is a coffin*'

In terms of our concern with the interplay of lifestyle and death-style, Taylor has them as intimates that become visibly aligned at numerous points as in a prose text that approximates to poetry, where he describes the 'Advantages of Sickness', and embraces almost the entirety of human emotions, which, typical of seventeenth-century usage, he naturally addresses as 'passions'.[30] At other times he speaks of ageing and describes how his contemporaries are 'impatient of the thoughts of death; hence come those arts of protraction and delaying the significations of old age: thinking to deceive the world, men cozen themselves and by representing themselves youthful, they certainly continue their vanity . . . We cannot deceive God and nature, for a coffin is a coffin.'[31]

The realistic lifestyle view of death-style captured in 'a coffin is a coffin' is far removed from that self-deception that takes many forms, not only in what we today would describe as the cult of youth and its practice in cosmetic surgery—something with which he is obviously familiar in the cozening of his contemporaries as he so comprehensively describes in the previous quotation—but also in attitudes to religious culture. So, for example, he calls into question some popular ideas such as that embedded in the 'huge folly . . . that confession of his sins will kill him, or receiving the holy sacrament will hasten his agony', or that the priest might 'undo all the hopeful language . . . of the physician'.[32] Picking up what he had seen as popular cultural images he objects to the 'very great evil' evident in those who 'fear the priest as they fear the embalmer or the sexton's spade'.[33] This kind of association with death-focused things is not far removed from early twenty-first-century notions of people disliking the idea of making a will, lest it somehow provoke death. As for the dead, we should certainly not speak evil of them; indeed, 'it is an office of humanity and charge of humanity to speak no evil of the dead'.[34]

Taylor understands the self-concern of human beings, not least at times of bereavement. He understands that mourners may weep for a variety of reasons, from that of custom to those of need or fear, but he is also alert to

---

[28] Jeremy Taylor ([1651] 1830: 60–1). [29] Jeremey Taylor ([1651] 1830: 61, 65).
[30] Jeremy Taylor ([1651] 1830: 81). [31] Jeremy Taylor ([1651] 1830: 98).
[32] Jeremy Taylor ([1651] 1830: 119). [33] Jeremy Taylor ([1651] 1830: 190).
[34] Jeremy Taylor ([1651] 1830: 258).

the 'immoderate sorrows of those who too earnestly mourn for their dead, when, in the last resolution of their inquiry, it is their own evil and present or feared inconveniences they deplore: the best that can be said of such grief is, that these mourners love themselves too well'.[35]

Ultimately, however, death is not to be distanced from life but incorporated into it, precisely because of the role of death and life in the person of Jesus as Christianity's foundation. Death is its own kind of benefit—a point he makes through the analogy of angels; creatures that have a lively identity in his thinking. Though God sends angels 'to attend upon every of his servants, and to be their guard and their guide in all their dangers and hostilities', God has given to human beings 'a gift that the angels never did receive', and that gift lies in an understanding of death—'for they cannot die in conformity to and imitation of their Lord and ours'.[36] Death now appears in the gift of not standing alone, and not as a phenomenon in itself but as an imitation of Christ. The theologically pervaded death of Jesus yields an integrated approach to living and dying rooted in the belief that, 'God . . . hath made no new covenant with dying persons distinct from the covenant of the living', and because of that, God has 'appointed no distinct sacraments for them'.[37] Following his 'a coffin is a coffin' realism, this brings Taylor to the view that, 'a repentance upon our death-bed is like washing the corpse; it is cleanly and civil, but makes no change deeper than the skin'.[38] That there are potential changes that go far further than skin-deep is certain, but these come through a lifetime of faithful activity. Such individuals 'may receive into their dying bodies the symbols and great consignations of the resurrection, and into their souls the pledges of immortality; and may appear before God their father in the union and with the impresses and likeness of their elder brother.'[39] Here Taylor's theological anthropology makes itself clear as the body–soul division is marked by a paralleling of body with resurrection and soul with immortality, both in a summation with 'their elder brother'. This description of spiritual kinship—elder brother, rather than its alternative forms of Jesus, Christ, Lord, etc.—is interesting in conducing to a more intimate sense of relationship and family likeness.

A life lived apart from such spiritual entailments can only portend additional anguish, not least 'if sin thrust in that sickness . . . and hell stand at the door', for then

> patience turns to fury . . . rolls up and down with a circular and infinite revolution, making its motion not from, but upon, its own centre; it doubles the pain, and increases the sorrow. Till by its weight it breaks the spirit, and bursts into the agonies of infinite and eternal ages.[40]

---

[35] Jeremy Taylor ([1651] 1830: 56, 256).   [36] Jeremey Taylor ([1651] 1830: 155, 136).
[37] Jeremy Taylor ([1651] 1830: 187).   [38] Jeremy Taylor ([1651] 1830: 146–7).
[39] Jeremy Taylor ([1651] 1830: 216).   [40] Jeremy Taylor ([1651] 1830: 112).

The turbulence captured in these words reflects Taylor's theological anthropology of the dynamic energy of life when left to itself in self-prompting individualism. This dynamism is also to be anticipated in more creative and outwardly engaged activity in the afterlife. Certainly, Taylor follows New Testament cues in seeing it as containing 'great degrees and differences of glory', but he takes this further in his own speculation, couched in terms of gambling, that, 'it is ten to one but when we die we shall find the state of affairs wholly differing from all our opinions here, and that no man or sect hath guessed anything at all of what it is'.[41] Its basis lies in divine provision in resurrection and transformation, and we ought not to be worried how any form of death might influence that eventful future. While St Ignatius might have been eaten by lions and in that sense 'was buried in the bodies of lions', and St Polycarp 'burnt to ashes', that would not affect their future when they would 'have their bones and their flesh again'.[42] His own certainty is of an actively dynamic realm whose denizens 'are not dead' but 'know more things better' and whose patterns of engagement might best be interpreted in terms of our knowledge of ourselves when asleep, in the sense that it is 'a state of life so separate from communication with the body'.[43]

Henry Scott Holland's 'King of Terrors'

From this seventeenth-century Anglican pastoral Reformation re-orientation concern with dying and the dead we now jump two-and-a-half centuries into the pulpit of St Paul's Cathedral as the core of establishment Anglicanism, itself at the heart of the modern period. However, this leap in time still leaves us with the common humanity of death and its influence, not least in the motif of death as the 'king of terrors', already evidenced in Jeremy Taylor's seventeenth-century *Holy Dying*,[44] This designation originated in a part of the biblical book of Job that had much influenced Taylor.[45] The phrase appears in a passage focused on life's sufferings, where even God appears as Job's enemy as he ponders the worm-fed darkness of bodily corruption, and the grave for a home.[46] Despite his acknowledgement that God had 'overthrown' him, Job longs that his words might be 'written . . . printed in a book . . . graven with an iron pen and lead in the rock for ever'. Indeed, it is 'despite' these deeply dark recognitions that Job goes on to assert that he will, in and of himself, 'see God', even against the fact of his bodily decay.[47] The King James

---

[41] Jeremy Taylor ([1651] 1830: 222, 260).   [42] Jeremy Taylor ([1651] 1830: 258).
[43] Jeremy Taylor ([1651] 1830: 260).   [44] Jeremy Taylor [1651] 1830: 38, 221).
[45] Job 18: 14, King James Version.   [46] Job 17: 14–15.
[47] See Douglas J. Davies (2008: 104–7) for the 'despite' or '*trotz*' factor in Christian theology of death (*trotz* being German for 'despite').

Version of these texts had become highly influential in modern culture from the mid-eighteenth century through their use in Handel's *Messiah* and its soprano solo 'I know that my Redeemer liveth', and its enunciated paradox: 'and though worms destroy this body, yet in my flesh shall I see God'.[48]

So it was that the Job text appeared in a significant cultural fashion through what might be regarded as one of the most prominent sermons on death ever preached in England; that of Henry Scott Holland at St Paul's Cathedral on Sunday 15 May 1910. I cite it here for its original context, the intrinsic value of its content, and for one of its elements that has, famously, been radically decontextualized and redeployed in early twenty-first-century funerals. The sermon was preached at St Paul's, where Holland was a canon, and very shortly before he was appointed as Regius Professor of Divinity at Oxford. The ecclesiastical season was that of Pentecost, and each of these combined in significance for what he said and how he said it.

The fifteenth of May was significant as the Sunday immediately preceding the lying in state of the coffin of King Edward VII, who had died on 6 May after his relatively short reign following the socially and historically pivotal death of Queen Victoria and her funeral in February 1901. Perhaps as many as 250,000 people paid their respects to the dead monarch in Westminster Hall during his lying in state. There is a sense in which British society at that time of the monarch's death might be described as socially liminal, though some caution is needed since liminality as an anthropological idea specifically refers to the indeterminate phase during a process of ritual change of status of a person. From the Latin *limen*, or threshold, liminality denotes that transitional location or social status of persons undergoing a shift of status within their society. This organizational aspect of status dominated Arnold Van Gennep's original idea, while Victor Turner developed the emotional tone of the status of liminality as *communitas*, thus capturing the emotions associated with shared unity under duress, under the anxiety aligned with change.[49] Here I am applying this notion to the wide canvas of a nation at the time of its monarch's death.

So, Holland preached his sermon at a time of social liminality, a threshold period when the King was dead but not yet buried, and before the coronation of his successor George V in June 1911. Even the previous sentence involves a certain liminal paradox in that George V was, technically, said to assume the monarchy at the very time of his predecessor's death, and before his own coronation, 'The King is dead, long live the King!' being a cultural utterance of some power. Such a situation might be said to typify a state of social liminality—'the King is dead, to lie in state and be buried, while the King is also alive but yet to be crowned'. The social rituals of burial and of coronation serve as

---

[48] George Friderik Handel, *The Messiah*, 1741.
[49] Van Gennep ([1908] 1960); Victor Turner (1969).

axes for the basic nature of prime cultural time that frames the process of social life.

Amidst this liminality Henry Scott Holland mounts the high pulpit of St Paul's and addresses himself to a paradox of emotions surrounding death in general, prompted by this death in particular. Before describing these we must also recall that this was Whitsuntide, that period more properly called Pentecost, some fifty days after Eastertide. In terms of biblical narrative this is when the Christian Church celebrates the coming of the Holy Spirit as the animating force of the first Christian community. Its charter text in *The Acts of the Apostles* speaks of 'a rushing mighty wind' filling the house where the disciples of Jesus were gathered together; 'tongues as of fire' seemed to play around their heads, and they 'began to speak with other tongues': to outsiders they seemed to be drunk.[50] To gloss this theological text in an anthropological fashion is to see it carrying the hallmark of a liminal state and *communitas*-fired empathy, with believers drawing upon shared resources as they lived together, albeit with fear pervading them as miracles were performed through the newly energized apostles.[51] Theologically speaking, Jesus' departure was complemented by the Holy Spirit's arrival.

Henry Scott Holland, mentally agile as he was, reflected these social and theological, cultural and ecclesiological, drivers in what emerged as his King of Terrors Sermon. In almost triptych form, it offers 'two ways of regarding death', followed by a conclusive exhortation of dedication to an ensuing Christian life. The 'two ways' are typified in 'two moods'; 'the mood of violent recoil', and 'the mood of quiet continuity'. The former speaks of 'irrevocable disaster', an 'incredible thing' for which no preparation is possible. It is a 'cruel ambush . . . snare . . . destruction', and 'inexorable fate'; darkness surrounds it, and evokes 'protest' and 'bitter anguish'. By sharp contrast, the second mood evoked by the corpse is entirely different and 'as we stand there, death seems a very little thing'. We are persuaded simply that the deceased is not there but has passed beyond this life into another. 'That which we loved is not here. That is all. It has dropped out. It has slid away.' Holland alludes to this sense of certainty at the time of immediate bereavement as allowing us to 'be content . . . quiet . . . and calm', but is quick to observe that such a 'high mood' soon passes as the bereaved sink back from that insightful light into 'the twilight of the valleys'.

In the integrative third part of his sermon—let us call it the 'Sons of God' section—Holland develops a Christian perspective of the afterlife driven by the sermon's text.

> Beloved we are the sons of God, and it doth not yet appear what we shall be: but we know that when he shall appear we shall be like him, for we shall see him as he is. And every man that hath this hope in him purifieth himself as he is pure.[52]

---

[50] Acts (2: 2–4, 13).   [51] Acts (2: 43–6).   [52] 1 John 3: 2–3.

His rationale begins in a notion of a 'process, of growth', with a Christian's development into the afterlife being an 'outgrowth from what we are'. This is all to be an adventure, albeit one involving anxiety over taking our essential selves into a future reality. 'We go out stripped of all that has made us intelligible to ourselves'; this itself allows death to 'retain its terror of loss, the terror of finality to what has been hitherto the movement of our very life'. The confidence that is possible when anticipating this journey into the unknown country lies in being 'true to ourselves' within our identity as 'sons of God'. But Holland is not content to remain even with this identity of sonship, but now brings to it 'the white light of Pentecost' which grants knowledge to the sons of their possession 'of the first fruits of the Spirit'.

And it is at this point in the sermon that the monarch's death makes its appearance, for that 'white light breaks itself against the blackness of the closed coffin ... to embody the irreparable disaster of a death which has touched the very heart of our national life'. He reminds his congregation that they will 'creep around it in dismay as it lies in Westminster Hall', with the very 'pomp of state' making 'its silence more sinister'. However, even the blackness of that coffin is enlightened by 'the light of Whitsuntide'. Once more he invokes the biblical images of Spirit as a mighty wind and fire and ventures to assert that Spirit's presence as already existing in his congregation: 'the Spirit which we now possess is itself the Life of all Life, the Life of the Life beyond death.' Despite all his previous conversation of the future, of growth, and of a journey 'over the silent frontier into the secret land', he now switches to asserting that 'in the power of the Spirit we are already passed from death to life. Death is behind us, not in front.' 'We have passed over to the other side.'

At this very point in his sermon Holland aligns the dead King awaiting his burial with the religious status of congregation members. Their 'old sinful self ... is dead. It must be buried.' The chronology of the monarch in death and burial must be the time of critical process of believers. The old nature 'must be buried. We can commit it to the worm of destruction, to the avenging fire, without a shudder, without a fear.'

In a wise rhetorical move he deploys in the closing minute of his sermon the words of Jesus as presented in John's Gospel—'I am the resurrection and the life'—and passes immediately to exhort his hearers to 'stand on the strong Word. In its strength you can even now use your remaining days to bury that which is already dead.' They can 'strip off the clinging garments of decay, the deceits of the world, the flesh and the devil'. Indeed, the Spirit will assist as they let their sin go, as they 'uproot it. Bury it. Burn it out. Die to it. Kill it.' The wisdom of this closing rhetorical turn lies in utilizing the very opening words of the Book of Common Prayer funeral service—'I am the resurrection and the life'—words of familiarity to his entire congregation, and in immediately linking them with the closing ideas of that Prayer Book service, with its prayer that the living might rise from their death in sin. In ritual terms he brings to this particular day and to the flow of his argument sentiments that would have been well known to his congregation. His two-word and three-word sentences punch home the moral necessity of repentance motivated by a pre-existing spiritual status. The end comes with a final and intriguing allusion to an 'infinite amazement' and 'ever-growing surprise' inherent in how they 'will somehow become aware of what it might mean to become more and more alike to the Lord Jesus Whom you adore'.

Henry Scott Holland reduced—'Death is nothing at all'

Earlier, I indicated that this sermon is included here not only as an example of a funeral sermon at a critical time in British cultural history as the Victorian Age passed into the Edwardian and would soon experience the crushing force of the Great War, but also for its contemporary use in its own form of spirituality that frames the dead. In this contemporary mode it has been radically ruptured as the first element of Holland's triptych has been isolated into stand-alone prose that functions poetically and, over the closing decades of the twentieth and the opening of the twenty-first century, has become widely popular, not least in secular funerals. Its current use in funerals involves a section beginning, 'Death is nothing at all. It does not count', and goes on to rehearse the words, as it were, of the deceased: 'I have only slipped away into the next room.' The bereaved are encouraged to call the dead by their 'old familiar name' and not to force any sense of 'solemnity or sorrow'. The dead is waiting for the living 'somewhere very near, just round the corner'. And so it goes on, highlighting only the 'mood of quiet continuity', entirely avoiding both the 'King of Terrors' and what we might call the 'Sons of God' section of Holland's sermon. Its use in numerous contemporary funerals marks a shift into that qualified secular spirituality that typifies the early twenty-first century; one that gives voice to the importance of interpersonal relationships. Its popular familiarity carries with it a kind of secular religious tone that is not, however, devoid of resonance with traditional Christian affirmation of the ongoing identity of the dead 'in another place'.

SECULARITY AND SECULARIZATIONS

It is through ritual performances surrounding death that individual or family values take expression. In terms of contemporary Britain these can be rooted in traditional religious forms or in metamorphosing versions of tradition in opposition to such forms, or, indeed, in terms of innovative world views. Such dynamic cultural resources invite an approach to secularization as a continuum from strong to weak versions with its strongest expression an active philosophical secularism contesting and replacing religious belief as the dynamic agent governing public and private life, as in Communist-inspired eras. Its medium-strength version reveals the sociologically driven idea of a process of decreasing influence of religious beliefs over social life even if they retain significance in the private domain. Its weak version presents secularization as a mixed economy of value motivation that may draw certain elements from religious, philosophical, aesthetic, or other traditions in an ad hoc fashion, but without any of the more systematic understandings upheld by formal religious institutions.

One key problem with 'secularization' that has bedevilled discussion lies in the sociological, and sometimes theological, assumption that people are rational agents driven by crisp ideas and systematized doctrines. The use of rational choice theory in some American sociology of religion is one case in point.[53] Human nature is, however, seldom driven by rational choice, and much the same can be said for some major social institutions, including major banks, where it might be easier to assume rational control of bureaucratic processes. This perspective has the tendency to misunderstand social change and the enormous complexity of how ideas capture emotions, and emotions capture ideas, within a culture. Behind many of the debates on secularization it is possible to detect subtle forms of value competition. In the new decades of twenty-first-century Britain, for example, numerically small but vocally militant atheism and theism have contested each other over values and beliefs, all against a wider British culture relatively amused or bemused by this. The biologist Richard Dawkins presented the hard face of atheism, mobilized through the ideological world of biological evolution, and popularized through the media that often set him against hardline creationists. By sharp contrast, the physicist Brian Cox, who is happy with an occasional aside dismissing non-scientific explanations of the world and cosmos, has become increasingly influential as a media celebrity who describes the nature of things in a way that appreciatively frames them in wonder. Here the visual complexity of the natural order is contextualized and descriptively explained. His television work, in particular, offers an aesthetically pleasing perspective that touches emotional responses. In stylistic terms he smiles, whilst Dawkins invariable holds a serious public face. In terms of yet another public figure, Cox takes to a higher theoretical point what the long-serving film and television presenter David Attenborough offers as an old-style naturalist. He, too, smiles, is intrigued by nature's variation, and is much concerned about the future of declining species. And it is this very concern for the future of Planet Earth and its species that brings me to include these individuals here—when Attenborough and Cox raise the theme of ecology as the dynamic of our human

---

[53] Malcolm Hamilton (1995: 214–28); Bruce (1999); Alan Aldridge (2000: 94–122).

environment; when it has become timely; when the cultural sensitivity of an increasing number finds it easy to link these concerns with the notion of spirituality.

As for this notion of 'spirituality', it began to gain non-ecclesial currency from the 1970s in association with New Age movements; while it was largely restricted to small groups of people, it marked an enfranchisement of a rising margin of middle-class individuals, most especially women. Their concern was often rooted in personal development through agencies other than mainstream churches. The wider adoption of 'spirituality' running roughly in parallel with an increased sense of secularization in Britain might be seen as paradoxical but, in effect, simply reflects many people's concern with the significance and deeper meaning of their own life that cannot be ignored even if their involvement with religious denominations that have been the customary vehicles of meaningful significance has declined or ceased.

In 2013, for example, some attempt was made to establish 'an alternative Remembrance Sunday for atheists' that would utilize the already existing Sunday Assembly movement's secular gathering that ritualizes the gathering of people where 'a "host" leads a congregation through songs, poems, moments of contemplation and a secular talk'.[54] This innovative venture was to be hosted by 'the TV historian Dan Snow', a significant fact for this volume in that he, too, can be considered a media-cum-academic establishment figure.

Indifference, Irrelevance, and Death

While any volume touching the sociology of religion must, then, address the issue of secularization, I largely agree with Christian Parker that sociologists of religion have, or should have, 'moved beyond the theory of secularisation'.[55] He is right in criticizing the overly church- or denominationally focused interest of many scholars (albeit an interest that is understandable since those sources often generate statistical data that make a sociologist's life easier). He wishes to refocus attention not on denominational groups but on varieties of ordinary activity. While I largely concur with his emphasis upon 'the creativity of ordinary people', his influencing context being that of America, and mine the UK demands that I retain some significant interest in the formal activity of an organized religion, in this case the Church of England, for the USA and UK are in many respects quite different social worlds which their mutual use of the English language easily hides. Of fundamental difference, for example, is the place of the civil rights movement in the USA that runs alongside its racial divisions which, together, have no

---

[54] Summers and Grimston (2013: 7).   [55] Christian Parker (2006: 72).

direct equivalence in the UK; likewise the UK's NHS as a symbol of post-war social transformation has no equivalent in the USA. The presence of a state Church accompanied by a generally relaxed attitude to religion in Britain and the absence of a state religion in the USA accompanied by something of a preoccupation with this fact offer their own differences. The other major distinction that is often also ignored is the fact that the United States of America is precisely that; a group of united states and not a single country in the way that, for example, the United Kingdom, devolution factors included, is a single entity. The very size of the two landmasses and population also adds its own distinction. These are all significant factors as far as the sociology of religion is concerned in each domain, not least in terms of the very meaning of secularization.

Many studies in the sociology of religion have devoted considerable time to the topic of secularization, focused on the decrease of influence of the Church as a social institution in the public life of people at large. This focus on the public realm was happy to think that religious motivations might well influence individuals in their private domains. Because of this public–private divide much debate follows social surveys and censuses as they record how individuals may self-define their religious allegiance on one hand and yet actually participate or not participate in congregational attendance on the other. While I have deployed some statistical material in this book it has not, primarily, been to force an argument on secularization but simply to seek additional material for a descriptive account of meaning-making in the UK and to draw attention to issues of death; issues that have largely been ignored by mainstream sociologists of religion.

For me, as for Parker, it is precisely 'the creativity of ordinary people', itself captured in the general notion of 'spirituality', that must not be ignored, especially since in my approach it influences the social force-field of their wider society and, in the process, prompts responses from formal organizations such as the Church of England. One issue that is difficult to handle in this connection lies in social-survey material on 'beliefs' in an afterlife on the one hand, and in the actual performance of funeral rites on the other. While I cite some empirical findings on afterlife 'beliefs', my emphasis will lie on the nature of ritual performance in funerals. The overall impact of this, particularly in the period 1970–2010, is to suggest an increase in the active irrelevance, or only partial significance, of ecclesiastical force upon a growing majority of 'ordinary' people.

One valuable discussion of secularization that admits the theme of religious relevance lies in Eric Hobsbawm's brief account of religion as part of the total scene of the 'Age of Revolution' between 1789 and 1848.[56] There he pinpoints

---

[56] Hobsbawn ([1962] 1973: 266–84); a celebrated sociologist, Marxist intellectual, he died in 2012.

a valuable variety of concepts that contemporary and later sociologists would elaborate upon with some gusto and often no small partisanship. He, quite naturally, discusses the 'unprecedented . . . secularization of the masses', and the way the 'working class as a group was undoubtedly less touched by organized religion than any previous body of the poor in world history', noting that by the time of the British religious Census of 1851 there were, in any event, church places available for between 29% and 34% of the populations of Sheffield, Manchester, Liverpool, and Birmingham. As he rightly pointed out, the problems of pastoral care in former rural parishes 'were no guide to the cure of souls in an industrial town or urban slum'.[57] And, certainly, there were repercussions of that shift in the mid-nineteenth-century rise of civic cemeteries that might contain the architectural mimicry of parish and dissenting churches and chapels but were, in fact, divorced from the heart of parish communities.

As significant a point for our argument is his view that even though organized religion might, for a period, grow stronger in numerical terms, it was no longer 'dominant' but 'recessive': terms he explicitly took from genetics, and which capture the image of a factor that is present but only manifest under particular conditions.[58] To this dominant–recessive aspect of formal religion we need to add his highlighting of 'gentlemanly religious indifference', an attitude that might seldom appear as atheist, but which was part of a 'widespread dechristianization of males in the polite and educated classes' that had roots even in the late seventeenth century.[59] More recently, of course, Callum Brown would argue that secularization needs close identification with his version of the decrease of religious participation of women in the mid-1960s.[60]

Indifference

Hobsbawm's notion of 'religious indifference', applied to males, females, the young, middle aged, or old, and to different contexts, is well worth pondering. Indeed, what might be called the phenomenology of indifference in respect of religion is a profoundly useful concept, and one worth developing as part of an approach to death. Such a phenomenology might centre on the tension of consciousness of individuals whose drive for meaning finds early limits. Though the sociology of knowledge works on the general assumption of such a drive for meaning as the normative case for human attention in and to life, this needs some caution in that many social groups, and perhaps the great majority within any population, have limits to their curiosity. Their everyday life-world achieves an early level of satisfaction matched by many

---

[57] Hobsbawn ([1962] 1973: 271).   [58] Hobsbawn ([1962] 1973: 269).
[59] Hobsbawn ([1962] 1973: 267).   [60] Callum Brown (2009).

others. When, for very many people, life reaches a satisfactory level of explanation there is no need to push boundaries further. An indifference to further speculation arises, or a sense that 'others' can deal with those complex issues. In emotional terms there is safety within the realm of the known and shared; to venture further is to prompt anxiety, even though it might be perfused with excitement. The 'contented' life is not a contested life. This scheme of ordinariness and security applies to broad swathes of the population and is tellingly reflected, for example, in the case of those whose ordinary life becomes potentially extraordinary when they win their country's Lottery. The potential disruption that great wealth might bring is feared and caution is strongly advocated, as the deeply embedded sense of natural reciprocity seems to have been altered.[61] Similarly, the speculative and experimental interests that motivate elite groups of theologians, philosophers, and scientists are notable for their rarity. And there is little reason to see any difference between theological, philosophical, and scientific domains as far as this is concerned, and much the same might be said for politics. There may well be periods in a society's life when serious attention is paid to one of these domains by large numbers of individuals, but, equally, there are times when interest drops off and indifference ensues. This would seem to be the case for many in Britain today in all the above domains. Indifference involves lack of perceived need to ponder and act unless some specific issue triggers response. So it is that though some Islamic and atheist groups in England are far from indifferent to the liberal majority and its easy acquiescence in general notions of religion, for that majority, though they experience some economic and personal family difficulties, not least through 'ordinary' bereavement, life retains a satisfactory level of making sense of things. Moments of disillusionment may come and go but a grip upon reality is maintained.

In terms of secularization, Hobsbawm bypasses the notion of the disenchantment of the world as emphasized by Max Weber, for whom this disenchantment motif was driven by industrialization. In this respect Hobsbawm's 'Age of Revolution' roughly equates with the industrializing age of Weber's disenchantment. While we might slightly caricature Weber and say that nature lost its mystery as manufacturing gained its mastery, this would still ignore the important issue of death. Manufacture and modes of rational control of production and management are one thing—and might well differ from the rural world of growth, harvest, pest, and hunger, all being under the vicissitude of the elements—but death is another. And it is distinctive because the issue of mystery, in this specific context of mortality, is not so easily mastered by technology.

---

[61] Falk and Mäenpää (1999: 158–63).

Irrelevance

Another perspective, mirroring Hobsbawn's 'indifference', occurs in A. G. Hebert's concern with 'irrelevance'. Gabriel Hebert (1886–1963), an Anglican Kelham Father, was much in contact with continental Catholicism as well as Swedish Lutheranism, in the first half of the twentieth century, and was fully alert to 'the movement of contemporary society away from God'.[62] His influential study *Liturgy and Society* clearly identified the fact that 'theology simply fails to make contact', and that 'it is set aside as irrelevant'.[63] Other scholars of religion have said much the same, as with Dupré: 'We may call the prevailing climate a-theistic, not because faith has disappeared in our time, but because the question whether we believe in God or not, retains little or no practical bearing upon our lives. . . . Even to the believer the flame of faith has become secret, since it no longer enlightens his whole life.'[64] While this is especially true as far as afterlife beliefs are concerned and it is, for example, almost an understatement for one Protestant author writing on *The Christian Art of Dying, Learning from Jesus* to say, 'we must be careful, of course, about claiming to know more than we do',[65] it is even more evident in terms of ritual practice. The ritual leader chosen for contemporary funerals is one significant factor expressing the 'practical bearing' of our lifestyle in death-style, not least in respect of ecclesial engagement.

Hebert's response to what he saw as a failure of contact between the Church of England and English people lay in a hope that ritual might exercise influence, viz. in the paradigmatic scene of people coming together at a suitable time and with an appropriate sense of community to a parish communion. Allured by the attractive liturgical words of the Church of England's worship, they would be eager to draw other people into this way of life. In many respects this hope, fired by Hebert's own monastically liturgical life and by some successful experiments in European contexts, was also reflected in the subsequent revisions of the Church of England's *Book of Common Prayer* throughout the 1960s, culminating in the *Alternative Service Book* of 1980 and *Common Worship* of 2000.

Changes in church scenes

Popular, and often caricatured, images of clergy playing guitars and singing 'modern' hymns and songs, for example, accompanied these hopes in the 1960s and 1970s, but they were not realized in any growth in ordinary congregations. However, through the charismatic movement's emergence in the late

---

[62] Arthur Middleton (2007: 19). Kelham, Nottinghamshire, was an Anglican theological college run by a monastic order.
[63] Hebert (1935: 135).   [64] L. K. Dupré (1981: 14).   [65] Verhey (2011: 203).

1960s amongst largely middle-class groups, some congregations did grow quite considerably, but this was not because of liturgical reform, but because of the degree of emotional freedom in what appeared to be a more spontaneous form of worship amongst people who had tended, hitherto, to be more emotionally confined. It also produced social intimacy amongst people who were probably experiencing a degree of isolation, not least because of their professional style of life.[66] The charismatic movement did, however, exert practical influence on liturgical reform in terms of an openness to a variety of prayers and opportunity for congregational participation. Tellingly, however, relatively little attention was paid to revision of funerary rites, largely perhaps because the great majority of people still called upon Church of England clergy to conduct funerals and there was no apparently pressing need for change. What is more, in its earlier years those participating in focused charismatic events tended to be younger or middle aged and, in a sense, fewer of these died at that time than amongst older and more mainstream congregational members and members of the public at large. Because of that, and apart from a few deaths of celebrity charismatics, this innovative stream of British church life engaged but little in issues of mortality and very much more on vitality, on the power of the Holy Spirit to engender a sense of dynamic spirituality and communal flourishing. However, this vitality–mortality dynamic became dramatically focused in the case of the Revd David Watson, perhaps the most famous of evangelical and charismatic Anglicans in the UK in the 1970s and 1980s, who was diagnosed with cancer and died in 1984, aged 51.[67] A considerable part of his work had involved healing, and numerous well-known healing-focused leaders, not least from the USA, sought to help and heal him. This was a remarkably high-profile case of illness and death amidst a life-focused religious group, and brought the reality of death home to what was probably the most flourishing religious context in the Britain of the 1980s, one that continues in a variety of forms today.

Returning to the general population, people die, and in their families' task of responding to death their funerals offer their own window upon British cultural values. Here, again, we encounter secularization in a focused fashion as secularist groups such as the British Humanist Association and the National Secular Society become involved in death rites. Indeed, death and death rites have come to be one focused arena of debate and competition between these and traditional religious groups. The ritual option of a secular funeral stands at the heart of this question and is a fundamental element for analysing secularization in terms of a reduced role for the traditional Christian clergy and innovative opportunities for secular officiants and for non-aligned individuals who self-train or put themselves forward as aspiring funeral celebrants in

[66] Douglas J. Davies (1976).
[67] Mathew Guest describes him as 'often being idolized, especially after his death' (2007: 218).

entrepreneurial training schemes. This variety of ritual practice suggests that funerary rites may well serve as a potential index of secularization. This suggestion is unusual since, as already said and with but a very few exceptions, sociological studies of British life, even of British religion, have largely ignored the theme of death or relegated it to a remarkably subsidiary place. Tony Walter is the clear exception, for his work has, for decades, brought changes in social attitudes towards death and practice of funerals to centre stage. Bauman has also addressed life and death issues as part of wider social change.[68]

SECULARIZATION AND THE FUNERAL CELEBRANT

In early twenty-first-century Britain there is a growing social awareness that a funeral does not have to be taken by an official ecclesiastical functionary but that clearly secular agents, whether aligned with the British Humanist Association or as independent individuals who may or may not claim religious personal adherence but who are eager in their professional service, are also able offer their client an entirely secular, a religious, or some mixed ritual–symbolic event. The key to the service provided is that it is client focused. In practice this means that the agents discuss the deceased individual with the relatives and arrive at a form of service that expresses the survivors' wishes combined with an acknowledged sense of the identity of the dead person. Typically, this involves the use of readings and music favoured by the dead person, along with some well-composed thoughts on the life lived, delivered as a eulogy by the hired officiant, and/or by members of the family or friends. In terms of material culture, photographs of the dead or even a combination of photographs and a video montage may be used if the event is in a suitably equipped modern crematorium. The secularization factor in such cases lies in the absence of ecclesiastical leader or liturgy or in their greatly marginalized position. Even when clergy service such funerals the keynote lies in the negotiation between them and the family in terms of what is said and who will say it; so too for the music used. This issue will recur in chapter 6 in connection with the funeral of Diana, Princess of Wales.

In terms of ritual symbolism the prime focus is on the deceased and, in this context, ritual purity can be conceived as set in the identity of the dead memorialized by the ritual celebrants and participants. This often involves a degree of retrospective fulfillment of their identity as life-cameos depict their interests and activities, something that may be further ritualized if their cremated remains are placed in sites aligned with those interests.

[68] Bauman (1992); Walter (1994, 1996).

Status and Ritual Leadership

As far as independent ritual celebrants are concerned, much can be said in terms of their social status. One feature links back to chapter 3 concerning tradition and 'the Establishment' in Great Britain in that funeral directing is a largely unregulated activity. Practically anyone can set up as a funeral director without any prior training or formal qualification and this makes the activity difficult to describe as a 'profession'.

When it comes to death and funerals we encounter the intriguing social arena of status interplay. For while a sick person, typically in hospital, is under the care of the trained, qualified, and formally employed in terms of recognized standards of practice and behaviour, once the patient becomes a corpse and passes through the morgue into the hands of the funeral director he or she enters non-regulated practice. Apart from the next of kin gaining death certificates and the funeral director also acquiring necessary certification when cremation is the mode of funeral, the rest of what takes place is wide open to choice. There is legislation over crematoria and cremation, as also over formal cemeteries and the burials taking place in them, but the actual mode of preparation of the bodies and the forms of rites associated with their deposition is left open to custom and practice. Funeral directors and local authority providers of death services have, in recent years, formed associations for themselves that have included the creation of service-based training qualifications. Institutions like the British Cremation Society have been influential in advocating codes of practice that seek to provide an ethical base for business.

Similarly, one independent person set up a company to train 'civil celebrants'.[69] This has been an interesting example of the institutional growth of a self-validating group that has, in part, incorporated methods of business management with the use of established 'professionals' from academic and other circles in its training events. The use of a certain self-certification and the growth of numbers so trained and so placed on contact lists provided by this agency, combined with the cumulative experience of its members, has generated a valuable source of personnel. The role of the internet is important in giving this group a public presence, as it is for individuals who simply set themselves up as funeral celebrants without any formal training.

Reasons why people engage in this self-directed activity are numerous but certainly include two factors related to prior personal and, or, work experience. Prior experience is often of a funeral deemed unsatisfactory, usually

---

[69] Ann Barbour and 'Civil Ceremonies'.

because a priest failed to please, leaving the individual with a sense that they could have done better themselves. If they then find themselves retired or with appropriate time on their hands it may seem appropriate for them to enter the funeral market. Some others have been involved with people at times of crisis and feel that their prior occupation, say as a nurse or as a civil registrar, could be taken further in terms of engaging with bereaved families and dealing with the dead. What such individuals often find, and it includes something that has been long familiar to professional clergy, is that a certain kind of emotional satisfaction follows the performance of ritual and reinforces them in their decision to take on this kind of work.

What is more, practically speaking, the performance of a funeral cere-mony depends a great deal more on an individual's emotional competence, social alertness, and capacity to perform in public than it does upon theological training, especially as practically all that is to be said and done has already been drawn from the family concerned. In other words, this kind of funeral functionary, unless closely aligned with a clear secular agency such as the British Humanist Association, does not have the responsibility of bringing an established theological–symbolic world to bear upon the life and wishes of the family of the deceased. Here there is carte blanche and no official liturgy.

There are of course both potential advantages and disadvantages to this open-ended ritual symbolism. Advantages include a greater coherence be-tween the content of the event and the one whose death it marks, as contrasted with a formal ecclesial liturgy into which the life details are incorporated. Since a significant minority of Britons do not, for example, accept ideas of resurrection, it is likely that formal church rites speak in a language that means little or grates with many at the event. Disadvantages of the more ad hoc scheme is that of the potential absence of familiar and comforting words, phrases, and ideas rooted in customary church rites and which may well have accompanied experience of previous funerals.

All this means that the typical hearse on its way to a funeral is, in itself, a multi-symbolic object, not simply in the sense of carrying the corpse and allied floral symbols, issues we have already discussed, but in terms of the priest or the funeral officiant plus the funeral director. The priest will almost certainly be a trained and ecclesiastically ordained person and, as such, a representative of an established profession that is also party to the British Establishment to some degree, while a civil celebrant, with a wide variety of life experience but with no formal qualification, is less 'establishment', leaving the funeral director—whose competence is essentially lodged in custom and convention and who knows the necessary forms that need compliance—in a distinctive category between 'establishment' and self-defined professionalism. In this sense both the hearse and the crematorium are places of potential contestation of social status and cultural significance.

CONCLUSION

This chapter's eclectic combination of historical and contemporary material has accounted for some of the complexity associated with overly easy accounts of British life as religious, secular, or spiritual. In describing some influential Christian theological ideas embedded in the figure of Jesus, his body, death, and symbolic presence in the Eucharist, as well the symbolism of the cross, of martyrs, and the theological writings and sermons of striking figures of Britain's cultural heritage, we have acknowledged resources and resistances marking the ever-changing nature of British world views. Religious reformation and industrial revolution have been seen to play a part in creating a spectrum of those perspectives, not least evident in terms of cultural deathstyles. The professional clergy, along with the 'traditional' emergent profession of funeral director and aspiring professionalism of civil celebrants, have all been considered within the dynamic world of the British 'Establishment' while not ignoring the creativity of ordinary people, and it is to that creativity that the next chapter will be devoted through the notions of salvation, folk wisdom, and spiritualty.

5

Soteriologies

Spirituality, understood as the combined attitudes and behaviours that express the way people value and give a sense of depth to their existence, is set alongside the abstract notions of salvation and folk wisdom in this chapter to complete a threefold perspective for assessing life views in relation to death. Albeit somewhat arbitrary, this triangulation allows for interplay between traditional religion's concern with salvation as an established category in religious studies, folk wisdom as a generic default position of popular meaning-making, and the more recent culturally fashioned notion of spirituality. We begin with the longstanding but easily ignored theme of salvation and allied aspects of traditional British Christianity before considering folk wisdom and then the chameleon-like notion of spirituality, including its place in the UK NHS. Having charted these domains we will be in a position to consider some of the dynamic outcomes of their interrelationships in terms of death.

SALVATION

Salvation has almost disappeared as a concept within recent sociology of religion. This is unfortunate, not simply because of its longstanding academic significance in the history of religion and its extensive theological significance in the ongoing practice of major religious traditions—frequently described as salvation religions—but also because of its sociological possibilities when analysing moral meaning-making.

Salvation has, in the worldwide 'salvation religions', involved ideas of being delivered from some form of evil. In traditional Christian terms it has meant being delivered from sin, death, and hell—a threefold negativity that has, however, undergone significant transformation within British forms of Christianity in recent centuries. In theological terms theories of atonement developed to describe how disrupted relations between deity and humanity could be restored and provided ritual practice through which emotional awareness of 'salvation' could be experienced. One of the more distinctive features of twentieth-century Christianity, or perhaps we should say Christianities, involved increased diversity of interpretation of the sin or evil in and from which people need deliverance, on a spectrum from exorcism of people possessed of evil spirits in some versions of Pentecostalism to the interpretation of corrupt political–social organization in Liberation Theology. Behind these lie traditional engagements with human sin approached through the sacraments, and the regular ongoing church life experienced by large numbers of 'ordinary' believers. Within Christianity at large, especially outside Western European contexts, millions adhere to ideas of heaven, sometimes but not always partnered by ideas of hell. Still others interpret evil in more psychological ways and see salvation in terms of divine and self-acceptance. Such divergence not only makes 'salvation' utterly specific for some and almost indefinable for others but also prepared the way for even more varieties of 'salvation' advocated by non-traditional individuals and groups often described as 'spiritual'.

Such changes help foster the relative incapacity of one generation to understand the world view of previous ones, something that is, ironically, enhanced by the speed of communication now sustaining early twenty-first-century life. Nowhere is this more evident than in the case of death, as even a brief reference to one of the many cases that could be taken from British culture history shows. The influential historian E. P. Thompson, for example, described English Methodism at the turning of the eighteenth into the nineteenth century as undergoing a 'desolate change' in which 'the negation or sublimation of love was tending towards the cult of the opposite: death'. As a reflection on this he cited one of Charles Wesley's hymn verses, 'Ah! Lovely appearance of Death! / No Sight upon earth is so fair. / Not all the gay Pageants that *breathe* / Can with a dead body compare.'[1] This contrast between love and death, highly reminiscent of Freud's *eros* and *thanatos* motifs, echoes this volume's concern with vitality and mortality and signposts that polarity for the nineteenth century. It also underscores the fear of death that Thompson aligns with developments during this period, when 'Methodist preachers perfected techniques to arouse paroxysms of fear of death and of the unlimited pains of Hell', something that also applied to inducing fear in children lest they misbehave. He even cites William Lecky's earlier historical notion of 'religious terrorism' to describe this approach at the close of the nineteenth century.[2] In parallel, Thompson also describes the rites of initiation into trade union and allied fraternities that not only involved oaths but also the used of the figure of death itself as something the initiate had to face; a

---

[1] E. P. Thompson ([1963] 1991: 410), original emphasis.
[2] E. P. Thompson ([1963] 1991: 411). See Purcell (1998) for 'spiritual terrorism' in twentieth-century American Christianity.

phenomenon with close parallels in Freemasonic initiation.[3] Such references demonstrate death's relatively recent cultural role across a swathe of British society in ways that early twenty-first-century Britons might find hard to imagine. To compare a dead body today with a joyous pageant would attract ridicule not pious sentiment showing just how the dynamics of salvation in popular religion, spirituality, and folk wisdom shift over time.[4]

Death and Merit

Whether presented in terms of eighteenth-century 'religious terrorism' or the anxious anticipation of demise in an old people's home in the twenty-first, death remains a constraint to life's meaning-making, evident in the millennia-long success of religions and their afterlife ideologies ritualized in funerary rites. One of the most extensive notions framing these doctrines, myths, and rituals of salvation has been that of reciprocity, a theoretical notion describing the ongoing interaction between people that helps create society itself and which takes a markedly powerful form in its distinctive mode of merit-making. By observing social rules and, where they exist, underlying divine commandments, members of society generate a kind of 'merit capital' that not only enhances social status in the here and now but can benefit post-mortal status: afterlife worlds thus reflected the reciprocal nature of lifetime cultural realities.[5] In the Jewish–Christian–Islamic domain this merit is generated by a saviour figure, saints, and martyrs, or by ordinary individuals who have followed legal codes expressed as divine commandments. In traditions of Indian origin with their notion of cosmic order, 'karma' has directed the interplay of worthy and unworthy acts and their outcome for the transmigrating 'self'. In many local traditions beyond those 'world religions' obedience to the ancestors has occupied a very similar role in fostering wellbeing or incurring wrath.

Christianity's own concept of grace also generated its own discourse around daily life and destiny in which ideas of divine goodwill towards errant human beings has played a dominant role. The interplay of grace with merit has, in the past, afforded the major means of dealing with death in both ritualized and emotional ways. If merit is understood as a kind of commodity that influences human destiny beyond death then grace can be viewed as its nemesis, and that in at least two ways. First, grace describes a quality of relationship between divine and human agents in which the over-abundance of divine goodwill

---

[3] E. P. Thompson ([1963] 1991: 556–9).

[4] See Llewellyn (1991: 19–27) for a sixteenth-century 'Dance of Death'.

[5] See Douglas J. Davies (2004), and also (2011: 164) for 'salvation capital', and Robert A. Yelle's later and independent account of 'notion of Spiritual Economy' (2013: 27).

eliminates the inadequacy of human merit. The notion of love is often invoked to account for such an imbalanced relationship in which, paradoxically, inadequacy soon recedes as devotional responsive love grows towards the source of grace. Second, following a more mathematical path of accounting for sin, grace becomes the moral capital base accumulated by a divine or divinely influenced figure from whose treasury of merit the impoverished sinner's account may be fully credited. In Catholic Christianity the treasury of merit was accumulated on the basis of Christ's obedient life and death, along with those, albeit in relatively subsidiary roles, of his Virgin Mother, martyrs, and saints, and could be dispensed through a variety of ritual processes including the granting of indulgences through formal masses and informal prayers and acts of intention by the living for the dead. Protestant Christianity took deep exception to those ritual paths and focused entirely on the relationship between the divine Father and Son and the way Jesus, as Son, fulfilled his Father's commandments in such a way that those allied to Jesus by faith had merit-flooded grace showered upon them. While certainly not ignoring love, this approach frequently stressed the legal model of an offended, injured, or sinned-against God and the need for restitution and satisfaction that had been achieved through the sacrificial death of the divine Son.

Valuing Life

These dynamics of salvation have been played out in many contexts as in our previous references to Methodism where 'being saved' can also be seen as one means of thinking about and revaluing a person's life. E. P. Taylor, for example, could account historically for Methodism's popular success through the three factors of 'direct indoctrination, the Methodist community-sense, and the psychic consequences of the counter-revolution', including the 'enthusiasm' that embraced 'swooning, groaning, crying out, weeping and falling into paroxysms', and the 'revivalist pulsation' involving 'an oscillation between periods of hope and periods of despair'.[6] Amidst such emotional accounts through which individuals might revalue themselves we ought not to ignore the place of how some people love the idea of 'truth' and of engaging with it, not only through learning—even if this is experienced at some point as indoctrination—but also through ritual experience, not least when in the form of revivalist 'frenzy'.[7] To engage with truth is to offer a powerful medium for revaluing personal life. Whatever the emotional dynamics, it is not improper to assume that it is the value of a person's life that is important to them,

---

[6] E. P. Thompson ([1963] 1991: 412, 418, 427).

[7] E. P. Thompson ([1963] 1991: 427). He uses 'frenzy' for the followers of Joanna Southcott.

especially if set amidst 'the chiliasm of despair'.[8] Despair might include a sense of both social and personal constraint with the idea of sin as a prominent driver of personal identity. Christianity's capacity to tap negative emotions and turn them into positive social forces owes much to the notion of salvation in Christ, especially when this process is framed more in terms of psychological experience than of sacramental ritual action. The capacity of a new religious movement like Methodism to generate its own kind of social force depended a great deal on mobilizing and directing the sense of salvation evoked within its large membership. This kind of salvation involves the harnessing of personal transformation of individual life into a corporate effect, with death playing a profound part in the motivation. Ideas of sin and salvation afford their own model of and for the relationship between an individual and society at large, driven by a particular preference for patterning and managing human emotion. 'To be saved' meant something in that context and still does for many millions in the world where the evangelical form of conversionist spirituality predominates.[9]

I emphasize this Methodist scenario for its historical importance on salvation as a core Christian theme, and because it raises the question of the significance of salvation in Britain today, especially in terms of folk wisdom, spirituality, and death. What wider currency is afforded to salvation which has been, and remains, a core theological idea of mainstream churches and is even intensified in the more sectarian groups such as those of the Jehovah's Witnesses and Mormons? Certainly, for many evangelical Christians, and for some of more traditional convictions within mainstream churches, the idea and experience of salvation, or of active participation in the sacramental life of faith, remains significant in terms of death and an afterlife with God. Even so, the notion of salvation has become a more generalized perspective in the ongoing life of many churches, with the idea of a hell to punish the wicked after death giving way to a more inclusive 'other world' for those still adhering to that hope.[10] Even by 1912 George Bernard Shaw's scathing criticism of traditional Christianity not only spoke of the 'perils of salvation' but also of the way beliefs in hell were 'fast vanishing': 'all the leaders of thought have lost it; and even for the rank and file it has fled to those parts of Ireland and Scotland which are still in the seventeenth century. Even there, it is tacitly reserved for the other fellow.'[11] Be that as it may for hell, there still remains more to say on salvation as a sociologically understood idea, not least in terms of the world views of secular and mixed spiritualities.

---

[8] E. P. Thompson ([1963] 1991: 411).   [9] B. R. Wilson (1970).
[10] But see David Powys (1997: 415–16) for biblical considerations.
[11] Shaw (1946: 98–100). George Bernard Shaw (1856–1950), despite being a Nobel Laureate for literature, refused a knighthood, thus indicating something of a paradoxically contradictory status in 'establishment' terms.

Good-person 'salvation'

In theoretical terms salvation can be understood sociologically in terms of meaning-making and the way individuals and groups construct a sense of plausibility for their lives. Though I have previously argued that case for the purpose of aligning 'world religions' or 'salvation religions' with local–traditional 'religions',[12] it remains as potent for British contexts of secular or mixed spirituality where people still generate and maintain plausibility in the interplay of emotional and rational aspects of life.

One idiom that provides immediate access to this creative moral process lies in the phrase 'good person', which is not uncommonly heard in expressions such as 'I'm a good person' or in its double-negative form, 'I'm not a bad person'. This is an extremely telling expression against the historical Christian background of a Britain whose liturgical forms and general theological outlook regarded human beings as—albeit saved—sinners. For practically five hundred years churchgoing Anglicans described themselves as 'lost sheep' that had 'erred and strayed' and who had 'no health' in them.[13] Most other mainstream Christian denominations followed suit on the 'miserable sinners' programme of salvation through faith in Christ as the divine sacrifice for sin, and the church with its message of salvation and means of grace. Despite the salvation motif this might still engender a sense of shame that could overshadow an individual's life.[14] Later twentieth-century liturgies retained the general doctrine of human sinfulness while often moderating or reducing the incidence of self-deprecating language. At one early morning Pagan-led ritual conducted at an annual conference of the Sea of Faith Movement, for example, the specially invited leader organized the fifteen or so 'non-Pagan' participants in a circle and, after invoking the deities of the place, expressed the thought that most of those present had Christian backgrounds and were used to saying 'how bad they are' at the beginning of a religious event.[15] He would now, by sharp contrast, invite individuals to step forward and make a brief statement on something they were very good at. This was a telling moment in both senses of the word, not least because instead of marking an entire group as 'sinners' in general it depicted individuals possessing distinctive, good, capacities. It was fairly remarkable to hear the variety of statements made and it offered an interesting category of religious testimony, itself a phenomenon that opens windows on the world view of a group as, for example, with Mormonism whose strong positive affirmation of the self in the total process of death-conquest avoids the normal Protestant self appraisal of being a sinner.[16]

---

[12] Douglas J. Davies (1984).
[13] *Book of Common Prayer* (1662), Evening Prayer and Holy Communion Services.
[14] S. Pattison (2000).   [15] Davies and Northam-Jones (2012).
[16] Douglas J. Davies (2000: 128–30).

One of the major dynamic foci in contemporary secularized shifts lies precisely with the handling of the moral sense as taken up in what follows in respect of 'ethics committees'; but another lies with individual life, where there are no such committees sitting over family or friendship networks (while there are, increasingly, over professional contexts). Here the individual is left as a free agent but within a social field that still exerts a moral force in terms of expected reciprocities of behaviour. In such a context selfishness, for example, may lead to avoidance by friends or associates and 'being a good person' can become a desired category for the relatively 'free agent' controlled by traditionally religious mores.[17] Yet it is a category that can also be used by traditionally religious people who may or may not have an explicit moral–religious checklist underlying their self-appraisal. One way of identifying this question-begging notion is considered in the 'Spirituality' section of this chapter, in line with Rappaport's use of the notion of 'deutero-truth'.

A concrete and illuminating example of the 'good person' motif is found in the Ipsos MORI poll conducted in 2011–12 for the Richard Dawkins Foundation for Reason and Science already encountered in chapter 2. There, in a section asking self-defined Christians what contributed to their sense of identity, the largest response (some 58% of total respondents) thought that being a Christian meant trying 'to be a good person'. Forty per cent thought that identity lay in how they had been brought up as a Christian; 22% focused on 'the teachings of Jesus', with another 22% 'accepting Jesus as my Lord and Saviour'; and 14% said their Christian identity gave them 'hope in an afterlife'.[18] It is likely that professional Christian leaders would not take that largest group with its 'trying to be a good person' as their criterion for Christian identity, but would see the acceptance of Christ or, perhaps, following Christ's teachings as more normative. This variation indicates something of the way in which the resources of traditional religion, of wider folk wisdom, and of emergent forms of explicitly claimed 'spirituality' may be marshalled to make sense of life.

FOLK WISDOM

The term folk wisdom may well seem odd or out of place in a volume such as this but I deploy it here as a working category describing how a society makes its own meaning of the world. This reflects a previous sociologically driven study of wisdom that focused on Church of England leaders,[19] though

---

[17] See Owen Jones ([2014] 2015: xvii–xviii) for good and bad people and 'Establishment' institutions.
[18] Question 50.   [19] Douglas J. Davies (2003).

here I take folk wisdom as a default position on world views. Existing relatively independent of historical religious traditions and their formal theologies, folk wisdom can develop, when conditions are right, into new conceptions of life, such as some describe in terms of spirituality. In other words, this is a generic category that allows for wide cultural expression of life values that may be related to but not entirely dependent upon formal theologies, and which also provides a basis for innovation in world views when required. I do not equate it with such ideas as 'folk religion', 'implicit religion', 'subterranean theology', or the like because such categories seem too dependent upon 'religion' in some way.[20] Daniel Miller's approach to the anthropology of everyday life expresses much of what I have in mind here, especially when he speaks of the aesthetic of people's lives focused on the 'centrality of relationships to modern life', on 'the centrality of material culture to relationships', on the fact that 'people make up customs as they go along', and also on the fact that 'there is no evidence of people becoming "fully formed" at some point in their lives'.[21] In this way folk wisdom or an aesthetic of everyday life captures something of the way values are enshrined and occasionally expressed, as some examples will make clear.

I take an opening English example from R. R. Marett, the first holder of an official university post in Anthropology at Oxford University.[22] His youthful theoretical speculations had been amongst the first to argue for a kind of pre-animistic source of human inspiration and for the force of ritual in driving or even creating belief. Much later, when he came to end his autobiography with a brief apologia for his life and world view, these same insightful ideas still drove him when he spoke of believing 'in goodness . . . in an active sense, as the creative and directive principle that is manifested in the development of the life force, and especially in the moral evolution of Man'. Defining himself as 'a member of the Church of England, though possibly a flying buttress rather than a pillar of the Anglican establishment', he is especially content to be able to 'read into its ritual forms' the meanings that suited him, and to see great advantage in the ability of the Church 'to tolerate a considerable latitude' regarding both theory and practice. 'In plain English, I have trusted in life, and it has not betrayed me.' From a seventy-four–year-old scholar writing amidst the Second World War and having suffered the loss of his 'splendid sailor-son' these are telling observations of what we might call folk wisdom.[23] In saying

---

[20] See Towler (1984) for discussion of terms and for his five types of 'very conventional religion' (1984: 1) in UK religiosity, viz. exemplarism, conversionism, theism, gnosticism, and traditionalism. Cf. chapter 9 for cognitive styles of these types of UK religion. See also Davies (1983) for pastoral theology and folk religion.

[21] Daniel Miller (2008: 287, 289, 291).   [22] Robert Ranulph Marett 1866–1943.

[23] R. R. Marett (1941: 329). Marett tells how Charles Gore had tried to persuade him 'to enter the Church' but that he never entertained the idea because his ancestry had no such engagement and 'ecclesiastical superiors' might not have 'appreciated a man who was inclined to preach the Gospel according to his own version of it' (1941: 326).

this, I do, of course, appreciate that his outlook might equally be described in terms of 'spirituality', showing just how difficult it is to use these terms. What is of special interest is the ease with which he locates his deeply human issues alongside the state church. His commitment to intellectual freedom, social responsibility, and cultural tradition easily combine. We take this example up again in chapter 9.

Another folk wisdom example also draws from kinship bonds, this time of a present-day mother and small daughter set in April 2011 at the Welcome Trust Medical Museum in London. One object in its small yet selective collection was a text-bearing and dated earthenware plate, made as a decorative domestic wall-decoration. It read, 'You and I are Earth 1661'. While moving slowly from this simple piece to the next exhibit I lingered, caught by the manner in which a mother pointed out this plate to her small daughter, a child who had, it seemed, not long learned to read. Having helped her little one complete this text—for 'earth' is not the easiest of words—she then in the calmest, most gentle, and matter-of-fact way explained how we all live, die, and then are buried in the earth. So it is that 'You and I are Earth'. Such was her practical expression of folk wisdom. In historical terms, just one year after the production of that plate the 1662 *Book of Common Prayer* would be published, giving shape to its 1549 and 1552 predecessors, and bringing the expression 'earth to earth, ashes to ashes, and dust to dust' into normal use for the Church of England for the ensuing centuries. The domestic wall-text and the liturgical utterances at funerals would become echoing partners for the many families for which bereavement was not an infrequent experience. What our very middle-class English mother did not include in her simple lesson on life was the affirmation with which the English prayer book complemented its 'earth to earth' phrasing, viz. 'in sure and certain hope of resurrection.... Through Jesus Christ Our Lord'. From her tone and apparent intention this was probably not part of her own belief.

This vignette offers but one entry into a world of popular belief. Did the plate-maker intend those who saw the educative decoration to complete the text with the resurrection complement, or was the text itself the final message? There is no obvious answer. But what the moment of the mother and daughter presented was a case of folk wisdom whose primacy lies in the sharing of a human self-understanding in a context of a serious relationship. Such a sharing of understanding lies at the core of all understandings of life and comes close to a working definition of 'wisdom'. The fact that it was in a museum context and neither that of a home or, indeed, of a church with wall-bearing texts, reveals something of the multi-dimensional nature of human self-understanding and of contexts of seeing, understanding, and sharing of insightful knowledge framed by an emotion of trust. Trust is not, in this case, nor in any that really bears upon folk wisdom, a secondary theme but underlies the emotional matrix of whatever is said or done in sharing human understanding. Trust is one of the most deep-seated of human feelings and marks the manner in which we relate to each other both in life and death. Trust is integral to forms of reciprocity, whether of the alienable or inalienable types we describe in what follows. It also pervades many closer kinship and friendship links, while its negation in betrayal instigates one of the most destructive forms of human self-awareness. Within the contemporary social world associated with death in Britain, trust becomes an important feature of the way bereaved people relate to funeral directors, to the care of the corpse, and to funeral management. The funeral director is, in a very pragmatic way, one embodiment of cultural wisdom concerning death. This was and is especially the case when the funeral director complements the work of the priest and vice versa. It is because of the dynamics of trust over funerals that issues of betrayal of that trust in care of the dead or in fees charged for funeral services often lurks in the social margins, ever ready to be pinpointed by the media in some occasional malpractice.

Wisdom and Mysticality

Although I described in chapter 1 what 'mystical' means in terms of dual sovereignty, I now take 'mystery' in a different direction as a phenomenon deeply embedded in the natural meaning-making life of human beings. One significant dimension of 'mystery' worth pinpointing here concerns the double complexity over the meaning of the 'self' lying in individual psychology and cultural relativity. The degree to which any single individual 'knows himself' is highly questionable not only for reasons of inaccessibility to the multitudinous motivating forces of the 'self' but also because of the views of others that influence the social identity of a person which, in turn, influences the sense of self. To this we may add the culturally relative fact that social groups differ over their preferred models of 'self' pursued in and through socialization. Still, there is something about the sense of 'self', its property of consciousness, that draws upon the mystical. To be speculative about this, one might even say that it has generated both the idea of a soul and of some post-mortal destiny.[24] Such a sense of life, in itself, bears the mystical quality which is, perhaps, best thought of in terms of vitality. Even the human capacity to judge the difference between things that are alive and dead reflects this mystical capacity. To speak in this way does not, of course, invoke the popular ideas of 'magical' or 'religious' beliefs, though it is likely that such notions are also derivative of this dimension of personal identity. As we saw in chapter 2, another perspective upon the 'self' has been offered by Hans Mol's notion of the sacralization

---

[24] Including ideas of ghosts, see Finucane (1982), and McCorristine (2010).

of things that confer a sense of identity upon us, whether individual or communal and probably both.[25] We might even expand on his idea to say that very close kin, especially when they have just died, also partake in this phenomenon of sacralization and, because of that, make funeral behaviour distinctively special.

Still, within ordinary life, various swings of mood under different circumstances—notably when associated with grief—all help accentuate this 'mystery' surrounding the very existence of individuals. In chapter 1 this was highlighted in George Herbert's poem 'Giddiness'; that literary insight could be complemented by psychoanalysis and its notion of the unconscious. In other words, human existence entails an awareness of mystery that is grounded in the very existential nature of life, long before ideas of mystery may come to be couched in terms of supernatural forces. What this suggests is that the category of mystery comes into its own when the drive for meaning encounters constraint. This is something that some contemporary cognitive scientists see as one influence on the original emergence of religion. That is to say, the enormously powerful drive for meaning—itself both cognitive and emotional—is no respecter of limitation but engages in imaginative creativity to generate a sense of satisfaction.

This is something that is very evident in a classic of the history of religions and of the theology of religious experience—Rudolph Otto's *Idea of the Holy*. There, as he surveys the philosophical–theological work of others, he identifies the 'sheer overplus' that comes when engagement with 'empirical reality' seems to generate 'intuitions' and 'feelings' that there is more there than meets the eye, and this is intuited in consciousness. Though these are 'groping intimations of meanings figuratively apprehended' they are nevertheless 'true as far as they go'.[26] Such intimations are enormously important within religious traditions, often leading to extensive theological development; something that would hardly occur were it not for the interplay of ritual and intimation. The feedback loops between ritual, doctrine, and intimations of 'mystery' lie at the heart of religious success or demise. To emphasize this significance I will sketch aspects of classic works by Otto and one of his contemporaries—Friedrich Heiler, on, respectively, the *Holy* and *Prayer*.

Heiler and Otto

Religious traditions focus on such supernatural domains and generate their own theologies and mythologies to explain this dimension of human awareness. Near canonical forms of such awareness are found, for example, in Friedrich Heiler's analysis of prayer and Otto's elaboration of the 'holy'. For

---

[25] Mol (1976).   [26] Otto ([1917] 1924: 150–1).

Heiler, 'the central phenomenon of religion', consists in 'a living communion of the religious man with God, conceived as personal and present in experience, a union which reflects the forms of the social relations with humanity'.[27] He speaks of 'the mystery of the human spirit', and of certain 'secular' endeavours such as 'scientific investigation' that parallel the 'mystical devotional life'.[28] An interestingly similar use of natural or secular aspects of life and of distinctively religious phenomena recurs in Rudolph Otto's renowned *Idea of the Holy*, published just a year before Heiler's *Prayer*. Otto devoted himself to identifying a distinctive and irreducible element of human awareness for which he coined the term the *numinous,* and famously developed it as the source attracting a person to a powerful mystery or wonder, summarized in his Latin expression *mysterium tremendum et fascinans.* In this an 'element of awefulness' attracted and thrilled a person in a way that might resemble fear rooted not in ordinary fears of the material world,[29] but in an ultimate awareness of mystery arising from a sense of something that is 'wholly other'.[30] Though much debated but now somewhat marginalized as a historical classic, I include Otto here for the way he invests this 'numinous' awareness with an 'energy', 'urgency', indeed with a 'vitality' of its own and, thereby, reinforces my own stress on 'vitality';[31] and the conviction that it is difficult to give any cultural account of human emotion without discussing 'power', and this is just what Otto does, not least in his brief account of the dead where he reckons that the basic fear of a dead person arises from disgust at the 'putrefaction, stench, revoltingness' of a corpse, and from the 'startled fright' occasioned by sight of a corpse, when one's own 'will to life' is 'disturbed'. Otto thought that both disgust and startled fright existed amongst animals, his own horse, Diana, having once been startled when coming across a dead horse! In his view even these responses required cultural development in and through the experience, and reflection upon experience, of particular 'founders'.[32] Otto's work took place when sociological and psychological disciplines were beginning to develop firmer lineaments of their own and this seems to have given Otto some ideas to use in his own study of the history and phenomenology of religion influenced both by philosophy and theology. His task was one in which essentially 'social feelings' were different from 'the feeling of the numinous', itself 'a primal element of our psychical nature that needs to be grasped purely in its uniqueness and cannot itself be explained from anything else'.[33] Ultimately, Otto's is a confessional study rooted in his theological ideas of God and of a divine presence that some people experience at different times

---

[27] Heiler ([1918] 1932: xiii, 358).   [28] Heiler ([1918] 1932: 361).
[29] Otto ([1917] 1924: 7, 12–17).   [30] Otto ([1917] 1924: 28).
[31] Otto ([1917]1924: 23).   [32] Otto ([1917] 1924: 123–4). I assume he did not wish the 'will to life' to be included in the equine response; it is unclear in the text.
[33] Otto ([1917] 1924: 128–9).

and places, and not necessarily limited to ecclesiastical sacraments.[34] Theological purpose is not the perspective of this present volume, but Otto serves well as a type case of those whose explanation of some sense of 'otherness', of thrill and excitement in life, speaks of a mystery that is persuasive. He can also be read as giving some account of a generic folk wisdom regarding life's dynamic sense of mystery.

Mystical authority does not, however, only exist in this 'pure' form, but may also be found as a kind of mystical–jural authority allied with reciprocity when divine commandments take the form of a legal code operative after death. The claims of medieval Christendom, and of Christianity at some other times and places, have involved a balancing of heavenly rewards or hellish punishments, or purgatorial suffering, all as a result of divine commandments of a religious–legal kind. Obedience or disobedience to such commandment, much as in obedience or disobedience to civic law, incurs the reward of a good name and afterlife status—or of its opposite. Here blessing has its shadow-side of curse. While 'folk wisdom' may, indeed, have seemed an odd phrase to use in a contemporary study, I have indicated that its general default position of shared meaning-making can become more formally structured whether in traditional religions, in explicitly secular life-orientations, or in the emergent notion of spirituality, found in a variety of contexts, to which we now turn.

SPIRITUALITY

As many authors have made clear, 'spirituality' is a term of many applications, colouring a spectrum from extremely traditional religious 'formation' of a dedicated priest, through the 'self-religion' often associated with New Age phenomena, to contemporary ideas of possessing a certain aesthetic towards values and cultural products of art and music within life.[35] There is a considerable comparative literature on those who might self-define as both 'spiritual' and 'religious'.[36] Indeed, a 'spirituality debate' has almost superseded the long-standing debate of secularization; certainly it shows something of the overly simplistic divide between sacred and secular domains. This becomes obvious within medical worlds where 'spirituality' has, for decades, been used to discuss clinical attitudes towards patients, most especially in terms

---

[34] Otto ([1917] 1924: 176–7, 220).

[35] One description of 'some of the most human qualities' cited in a text from a relatively conservative Christian publisher furnished the cluster, 'creativity, empathy, reverence, spirituality, aesthetic appreciation, abstract thought, and problem solving (rationality)', Brooks (2011: 256).

[36] Possamai (2009: 62–5).

of end-of-life care.[37] In this last case, ideological or theological contents of 'spirituality' become relatively irrelevant when balanced against generalized values of patient and family 'care'. Whilst 'care' will be taken to ensure that appropriate chaplaincy services of different Christian denominations or other religious traditions are available for people of those persuasions, that will be as part of the wider field of medical, nursing, and social welfare provision. In these contexts, there is an assumption that human relationships, their embedding in family and personal history, and the interplay of medical and social welfare staff all carry a depth of significance as far as the emotional lives of patients and families are concerned, and that this depth is allowed to play its part in the closing phase of human life. This shows how spirituality, in its broadest embrace, concerns life-meaning and in the hospice and end-of-life care contexts, where it appears in the question, 'what is important for you?'

Theoretically speaking, it is worth highlighting the fact that the many accounts, definitions, and debates over 'spirituality' in recent years have used it as a symbol of the religious–secular frontline. Groups compete over 'spirituality': it is a positively charged term; one worth owning as part of self- or group validation. It also offers its own way of relocating debates over religion and religious authority. In an interesting way as far as religious studies is concerned, Robertson Smith, whose influential anthropologically informed studies of Semitic ritual have already been discussed, and who was taken in by Cambridge University after he was tried for heresy in his native, Presbyterian, Scotland, made his own observation on spirituality as a quality of individual life.

> Intellectual culture say some is apt to make a man less spiritual. This supposes the spiritual part of the mind to be a peculiar faculty. In fact the emotional is meant. But a man may as readily err by trusting his own emotions as by trusting his own intellect. Spirituality is not the development of one part of the mind but the development of the whole mind *in a special direction.*[38]

As for the Church of England, following the English Reformation, it emerged to assume religious precedence over the Roman Catholic Church, with various emergent Protestant denominations being rendered marginal for several centuries. Its position as the state church ensured a high profile, with its dioceses and bishoprics being roughly coterminous with major counties and their Members of Parliament. Indeed, after disasters, especially when they involved death of distinctive severity, the local Anglican bishop was very likely to be one key player whose voice was heard, even before the local Member of Parliament, reflecting the folk wisdom domain. From the second half of the twentieth century, however, the Church of England found itself in an increasing

---

[37] E.g. Burnard (1987); Burkhardt (1989); Oldnall (1996); Hanley (2005: 51–81).
[38] Black and Chrystal (1912: 64, original emphasis).

co-presence not only with other Christian denominations but also with other religious traditions and with both more passive agnosticism and more active secularism. No longer would doctrinal formulae, ritual practice, or social status constitute 'tradition' in such a way as to guarantee primacy of place in a great majority of people's lives. But, at the same time, various clusters of people, and some notable individuals not party to religious groups of any sort, were not prepared to abandon language of life-significance just because they did not wish to speak through traditional religious formulae. It was precisely at this interface that the language of spirituality came into its own. Those not party to the established religion of Anglicanism and its ecumenical Christian partners, nor to other major world religions, did not need to be disenfranchised from life-meaning language. It is not surprising that 'spirituality' emerged as an existential *lingua franca*, nor that its 'meaning' should have blurred edges. In many respects 'spirituality' exemplified the notion of 'deutero-truth', a term alluded to previously and developed by anthropologist Roy Rappaport to describe terms used in an easy fashion on the assumption that everyone knows what they mean, but whose 'meaning' may fragment once precise definition is sought. Derived from the Greek *deuteros* or second, 'deutero-truth' indicates a second-order or meta level of understanding that facilitates conversation on complex topics without having to be neatly precise in the process.[39] Words such as love, hope, and trust are, often, of a similar status within particular speech communities, as also is God. And this is a crucial factor, for such terms foster discourse within a group but can hinder discussion between groups if they are not alert to potentially crucial differences of significance. The evaporation of strict defined meaning under critical pressure is perfectly understandable for words relating to complex, non-technical, aspects of life.[40] Moreover, the rise of 'spirituality language' seems to have paralleled in social institutions at large the emergence of a wide-spread concern with 'ethics' and the creation of ethics committees. It is as though the secularization of the church resulted in the need for explicitly identified forms of spirituality and ethics.[41]

Spirituality Spectrum

More within our concern lie issues of spirituality and the interplay in matters of lifestyle and death-style, not least with how different groups approach terminal illness and dying. One example of this dramatically increased area

---

[39] Rappaport (1999) derived this term from Gregory Bateson's earlier work and developed this idea alongside the notion of 'ultimate sacred postulates' of each tradition.

[40] Rappaport (1999).

[41] Cf. Douglas J. Davies (2011: 280–1).

of health, wellbeing and care is exemplified in Sheila Hollins and Irene
Tuffrey-Wijne's 'books beyond words', intended for people who have a 'learn-
ing/intellectual disability' and for whom a picture-book might 'help them
understand more about their illness and about dying'.[42] The book offers
some forty-one almost cartoon-like events in a young or middle-aged man's
life, from a visit of a doctor to the house through to his death-bed. It was based
upon the 'Veronica Project' which drew on the experience of terminally ill
people with learning difficulties. The intent of the book is that the pictures can
be shared with terminally ill people who can provide their own words as a
commentary on the pictures, though a final few pages offer a 'ready-made
story rather than tell their own'. This simple and direct book includes a
concluding few pages on guidance for supporters of the dying as well as for
health-care professionals. This includes an incisive paragraph on 'spiritual
needs' that notes different ideas on 'spirituality', focused on 'those aspects of
our lives that give life meaning', whether in 'their religion', expressed in the
wish to talk to a 'priest . . . or somebody familiar with the traditions of their
own community', or shown in that the person might only 'like to spend more
time listening . . . to some music which has a special meaning for them'. To
music we return in a moment, followed by a consideration of mindfulness, but
first we pursue two examples of this motif in popular spirituality and in an
additional, more philosophical, outcome of one of these.

Weekend spirituality

First we consider one 'Weekend Magazine' section of the *Financial Times*.
Though this context may seem a far cry from spirituality, here, once more, we
encounter 'the need to be spiritual'. In one of its combined articles by a
philosopher and psychotherapist we have the former disliking the 'slippery
concept' of 'spirituality' whilst acknowledging the need for 'morals to live by'
and also for some means of framing the profundity of 'experiential life' evident
in 'beauty, love, wonder, and awe'. The psychotherapist, by contrast, takes up
the spirituality theme more readily and in terms of 'what is most conducive to
our overall flourishing as human beings'.[43] Her concern lies with a 'rich inner
life' and yet, along with her philosopher partner, no reference is made to death.
While it could, of course, be argued that a relatively entertaining article
responding to the question, 'Do we need to be spiritual?', even in what is
amongst the more serious of weekend newspapers, need not include death in
its response, I highlight it precisely because it reflects a great deal of early
twenty-first-century material that ignores death as a framework for life. This
particular article emphasizes the bodily integrity of human beings and notes

---

[42] Hollins and Tuffrey-Wijne (2009: back cover).
[43] Baggini and Macaro (2011: 51).

the error of any sort of dualism that adds a soul to a body. Yet, even when arguing that 'We are flesh and blood' whose 'animal nature' and 'material needs' require satisfaction, the article still turns to 'the life of the mind', to 'thought and imagination', for its final resolution.[44] Given that death is a final constraint of flesh, blood, animal nature, and material needs, it is interesting that death and any emotional reflections on it are absent. Once more the functional fiction of life eclipses mortality. One reason for this probably lies in that popular-philosophical notion that not only pinpoints life as, rationally speaking, meaningless, but also frames this depiction as absurd. From that perspective death, funerals, memorials, and the like would hardly attract particular attention.

Habitual existence

A second insightful account of contemporary British life comes when Michael Foley not only argues that 'no one mentions finitude', and that, 'now, in the city, death is invisible', but also when he picks up the pragmatically valuable sense that 'living is itself habit-forming...we get terribly used to being around'.[45] This aphorism catches the spirit of 'the age of old-age', not simply for the elderly but for their adult children and grandchildren who are used to having them around. Opportunities for the learning experience that bereavement brings become less frequent than was once the case in Britain and still is the case in many developing-world countries where infant mortality rates are high and mortality for adults occurs at younger ages than in the UK today. There are many events in life for which no-one can prepare or learn in special classes, and grief is one of them, as many a doctor, funeral director, and priest has found. For even a professional life where engagement with the death of others may be immediately direct offers no impunity by familiarity for the time when bereavement hits at the closest of human relationships, and a personal sense of grief emerges. This form of 'learning' appears in Foley's reflections, doubtless in the light of his youthful Irish experience where death was much more socially visible, as he comes to the conclusion that many have found over the years that 'to learn to die is to learn to live'.[46]

High-information existence

A third point, prompted by Foley's simple expression that 'living is habit forming...we get terribly used to being around', is worth developing in terms

---

[44] Cf. Bowker (1973) and (1978).
[45] Foley (2010: 209–10). Significantly, he sees Camus, unlike Sartre, as linking happiness and absurdity (2010: 47–8).
[46] Foley (2010: 211).

of an individual sense of self and its grounding in 'reality'. This individual focus differs from the notion of cultural intensification of meaning that has, earlier, been applied to the ritualizing of cultural values and to intensification of cultural wisdom. Though a speculative idea, the point I want to make here is that many in contemporary British society, most especially in younger generations, experience an increasingly multi-faceted and plural-channelled network of information that embraces both the tellingly named 'social media' linking an individual to others, and the information-based sources that allow practically instant access to many people and myriad facts. *Facebook* and *Wikipedia* exemplify these dimensions on a continuum from information about the public image of a person to information about the world at large.[47] One consequence of this double domain of 'friends' and 'facts' is that a person's everyday life-world is intensified. Their multiple links with, and access to, people and phenomena, when coupled with the way they are targeted by consumerist agencies, confers an intensified field of relevance.

If, indeed, there is any truth in this argument, it would influence personal dynamics to a marked degree and lead us to reappraise T. S. Eliot's poetic version of that wider idea that 'humanity cannot bear very much reality'.[48] While the mystical inclination of this expression carries its own appeal to many, allowing 'death' to be part of the reality that many cannot bear, that is not the symbolic point that I wish to signpost. My focus lies, rather, on the immensity of 'reality', in the form of potential 'knowledge', amidst which the self becomes located and which, in principle at least, lies in the control of an individual. 'Reality' is, in this sense, tamed by technology: it is caged and accessible online, and it is not a mystical domain. But it remains a deeply personal and interpersonal domain within which my 'friends' can easily become my enemies given the way the online world is fraught with potential fear of cyber-bullying, identity-theft, or other harms to the self. The increasingly conditioned and socially expected need to be in touch with many others and to be able to communicate by voice and by visual messages brings to a person a sense of being part of a dynamic and extensive world in which their own sense of relevance has become deeply enhanced and expectation of relational stimulus increased. And all this takes place in a wider social world where, especially in terms of entertainment, celebrity, stardom, and fandom, there is much going on around them. There are now relatively few television or radio programmes—except for the serious news spots on central media—that do not encourage some instant feedback by twitter or email, with the announcement that 'Alice from Bedford says ...'. This welter of opinion presumably gives three seconds of fame to Alice from Bedford, an identity

---

[47] Blakely (2014: 29), citing advertising company Sparks and Honey, describes the 'screen-agers' of 'Generation Z' in the USA, born after 1995.
[48] T. S. Eliot ([1935] 1944) 'Burnt Norton', 1: 44–5.

usually presented without surname, whilst also giving the impression of the outgoing programme being alert to its widespread audience. In this, electronics has, to some degree, changed the world of identity and spirituality by stimulating and engaging people's responses and shifting their reflective centre of gravity to a somewhat unstable location in cyberspace.

It is into this maelstrom of real and apparent communicative relevance that death so easily strikes its blow, as though the electronic environment and death belong to entirely different logical types of experience. In terms of this volume, the communicatively dense world reveals a species of vitality, while the striking of grief marks mortality. Moreover, the notion of tragedy easily becomes enhanced in this existentially intensified milieu, especially over the death of younger people, not least at a time when youthful death is relatively rare. Here I do not include issues of older people (already discussed in chapter 2) except to say that time alone will tell how electronically intensified generations will cope in older old age, if and when their networks decrease through the death of others and factors of which we are, at present, unaware. What are involved in this wide process of intense interaction and the possibility of its demise are the profound issues of attachment and loss in the more psychological–sociological sense of networked identity rather than in terms of grief theory, though applications to that sphere might also be deeply relevant.[49]

Musical spirituality

One dimension of experience that would be very widely recognized as belonging to a category of 'spirituality' is that of music. Not only has music often been associated with death and grief, whether in the laments of many traditional societies or in the worldwide culture of requiem masses, but it has found a welcome home in Western societies as an expression of grief that fits well with many musical genres. One example will suffice; one that produced an enormously popular song, 'Tears in Heaven', by the doyen of modern popular guitarists Eric Clapton following the death of his son Connor.[50] Reflecting on his loss he has spoken of writing the song as part of 'sharing grief and pain', and of 'channelling it into music'. He saw himself as covering an 'experience people couldn't verbalize' and, perhaps like many others, he spoke paradoxically of having a 'fairly strong faith about something or other', and yet describing it as 'not strong'. The outcome was that he was 'not bitter or sad', despite all this loss. The appearance of this 'poignant new material', including 'Tears in Heaven' on his 1992 album, 'Eric Clapton unplugged', led to sales of

---

[49] Castells (2010: 9–10). See chapter 1 for Castells' notion of networked identity.
[50] Eric Clapton's interview with Paul Gambaccini on his 'For one night only' series: Radio 4, 6 October 2012.

many millions and contributed a popular classic to musical spirituality, not least that of grief. In an age of celebrity, the fact that grief strikes the famous allows for fan-fondness to benefit from that grief experienced and expressed by people such as Eric Clapton. Here a deep popular spirituality benefits from the pathos of lyrics facilitated by the whole culture of musical media.

Mindfulness

If music is its own resource for spirituality so is a wider appeal to the body and its processes evident in another and increasingly influential discourse ground-ed in the notion of mindfulness, where 'mindfulness' serves as the applied and practical expression of the more theoretical idea of embodiment. At one recent NHS-related conference dealing with caring for the bereaved before and after death a medical practitioner gave a presentation on Mindfulness and Grief.[51] While identifying the notion of mindfulness with its Buddhist origin, she framed it for therapeutic use as a non-religious phenomenon and proceeded to lead the entire group of more than a hundred death-care professionals in a guided exercise of mindfulness centred around posture, breathing, and the observation of one's own sense of one's body and direction of thoughts. Her description of this practice as a secular technique derived from Buddhism also included a passing comment on the Buddhist notion of 'loving kindness', presented in terms of being non-judgemental of oneself when one's thoughts might seem to wander whilst engaged in mindfulness exercise. I cite this case at which I was present not as something exceptional but to exemplify the way 'mindfulness' has become moderately normative within therapeutic con-texts.[52] Though there was no reference to the term 'spirituality' in association with mindfulness and grief at the conference itself, this kind of meditative practice does offer a clear example of a practical level of spirituality within a health-care context. In some ways this mindfulness-based cognitive therapy (MBCT) is a more recent development of what emerged in psychological studies of 'the relaxation response' in the 1970s.[53]

One book on 'Mindfulness', published as a 'practical guide to finding peace in a frantic world',[54] was reprinted eight times in its year of publication (2011), then seven times in 2012, five times in 2013, and five times in 2014. This says a great deal about what its foreword describes as people 'sorely lacking, if not starving for some elusive but necessary element in our lives'.[55] Echoing the theme of celebrity, it is worth noting how the paperback cover of the 2014 publication carries messages from media personality, humourist, and

---

[51] Susan Hennessey (2011).
[52] Kabat-Zinn (1990); Segal, Williams, and Teesdale (2002); Williams and Kabat-Zinn (2012).
[53] Benson (1977).   [54] Williams and Penman ([2011] 2014).
[55] J. Kabat-Zinn, Foreword to Williams and Penman ([2011] 2014: ix).

comedienne Ruby Wax, and famed Hollywood star Goldie Hawn. The former aligns this 'life-changing bestseller', with freedom from anxiety and stress, and the latter with finding inner peace. Interestingly, the theme of death as an ultimate challenge to life occurs but a couple of times in the book in the context of our 'vulnerabilities', for the volume is intrinsically concerned with the development of a mindfulness lifestyle as such.[56] This is reminiscent of Terry Eagleton's broad brushstroke treatment of *Culture and the Death of God* where he typifies the 'modern age' through Feuerbach's conversion of theology into anthropology, with human identity 'marked by boundless strength' and where, in echo of Charles Taylor's recent work, he refers to 'modern human-ism' and a notion of 'flourishing' devoid of awareness of death.[57] There would seem to be some truth here, in that the longish tradition of self-help books is reflected once more in this mindfulness text and its eight-week programme of what is, essentially, a ritualized scheme of embodied attention. Though fo-cused on the reader as individual its entire ethos is collective: we are all in this together. Its grounding or, we might say, its 'truth' lies in discoveries of how the brain and its embodied processes work; there is an almost entire avoidance of reference to religion of any sort or to 'spirituality'. Indeed, it is clearly stated that 'meditation', the basic process of the mindfulness advocated in the volume, 'is not a religion. Mindfulness is simply a method of mental training. Many people who practise meditation are themselves religious, but then again, many atheists and agnostics are keen meditators too.'[58]

NHS Spirituality

Such 'mindfulness' in the context of the UK's NHS has, in the new decades of the twenty-first century, itself become concerned with the notion of spiritual-ity developed as part of patient care, especially in the context of end-of-life care. I would like to speak of this in terms of a 'new spirituality' partnering a 'new secularization', in that it has been driven by this, the largest social institution, and not by the churches as such.[59] In some theoretical respects this approach renders redundant a great deal of sociology of religion's 'secu-larization' debate that revolved around ideas of the decrease of influence of the churches in the public life of society, by dealing instead with the NHS as a national institution of an essentially non-religious or a-religious nature

---

[56] Williams and Penman ([2011] 2014: 117, 162).

[57] Eagleton (2014: 142–3), his recent mirroring of Christian orthodoxy alludes to 'an executed body' with 'death at the centre of its vision' and to a 'faith' where there can be 'no flourishing without confronting it'.

[58] Williams and Penman ([2011] 2014: 6).

[59] From unpublished paper 'The New Secularization' given at historian Hugh McLeod's retirement Seminar, Birmingham University, 2010.

initiating the issue focused on life-meaning in critical contexts of birth, health, illness, and death.

This new secularization is, then, driven neither by secularist ideology or religious drift into unconcern with religious ideas nor on topics of church attendance, alignment with religious beliefs, or the reduction of religious influence to the private rather than the public sphere. It is driven by a broad existential care for patients' needs. These needs may involve traditional religious desires and the role of hospital chaplains acting in 'role' as Anglicans, Catholics, Methodists, Muslims, or some other group, but they may also involve such chaplains playing a more generic existential role for patients not carrying a formal religious identity. What we might, then, call the new secularization is evident in welfare-provision spirituality, a phrase denatured of its ecclesial meaning, and in search of a new meaning, definition, and application in end-of-life care situations. This is an extremely important situation as far as both religion in Britain and death are concerned if we take the NHS to be a focus of British cultural values and, in this sense, one that in its emphasis upon spirituality may well be assuming something of an erstwhile religious quality as the ritual–symbolic focus of core cultural values. We touch on this later in this chapter and again in chapter 8, in connection with suicide which becomes highly problematic for an institution dedicated to vitality rather than mortality and which, as far as mortality is concerned, seeks to foster end-of-life care and not the instigating of death in, for example, assisted suicide or doctor-assisted death.

On the positive front, the NHS has, through a variety of means—including the work of the National Council for Palliative Care in setting up of the Dying Matters Coalition in 2009, and a major national conference entitled 'Finding the Missing Piece' in London in 2010—sought to explore the meaning of spirituality within a health-care context. The 'piece' here was an intentional play on 'peace', in acknowledgement of the need for some element that would complement the NHS's medical work with care that found what might be missing as far as the individual patient's need of peace was concerned. A complementary conference a year later spoke of 'Finding a Common Language', again marking the difficulties of possessing an appropriate mode of discourse for a wide variety of traditionally religious, secular, or mixed clientele at critical times in their lives and the lives of their families. I was fortunate in being part of both these conferences and also of a 'good death' group in north-east England which led the way in the UK in researching popular attitudes to thinking and talking about death and allied matters that, in fact, feed into these issues of care and a spirituality appropriate to it.[60] More or less concurrent with those NHS ventures was the emergence of a Royal

---

[60] NHS North East 2010 *A Good Death*.

College of Psychiatrists interest group and its first publication *Spirituality and Psychiatry* with its working definition of spirituality as grounded in human creativity that fosters reflexive or transcendent awareness in relation to meaning, purpose, and ultimate values.[61] Amongst the many other engagements with spirituality we might, for example, pinpoint John Cottingham's philosophical approach in his *The Spiritual Dimension* with its focus on 'certain kinds of intensely focused moral and aesthetic response, or on the search for deeper reflective awareness of the meaning of our lives and our relationship to others and to the nature of the world'.[62]

From an expressly secularist perspective André Comte-Sponville has argued well for the way secular individuals also possess the need for existential satisfaction, though still feels that non-religious funerals leave something untouched in his perception.[63] An interesting example of an outline of possible transformations in spirituality is given in Alain de Botton's *Religion for Atheists* which seeks to take back from religions aspects of life that are still needed by secular society; things whose beauty or psychological value could help console contemporary sceptics. He sees this as a process of 'reversing' or 'expropriating for the secular realm' what Christianity colonized for itself from other ideologies and practices across the centuries.[64] Interestingly, the book is quite weak on issues of death and funerals despite the fact that humanists are much engaged in the conducting of funerals. In contrast to de Botton, whose upbringing was in a firmly atheist family, Geoff Heath speaks as someone keen to rethink his life-outlook having given up intellectual belief in God in finding that he no longer felt an emotional 'need to believe in God'.[65] In what amounts to a personal confession of someone who is not content with 'vague drifts' nor those who simply drift 'out of belief in the traditional God but perhaps retain a vague sense of a "power greater than ourselves" or, as is becoming popular, a vague sense of "spirituality"', he works towards a clearer philosophical opposition, rather than de Botton's aesthetic sense of appropriating helpful phenomena. As is, perhaps, appropriate for a philosophical exercise, his focus on death is largely restricted to some eight lines in over a hundred pages of apologia where he asserts how he values his mortality; it is 'not a burden' to him, and his death is 'uniquely the experience from which' he 'cannot learn by reflecting on my experience of it'.[66]

---

[61] Cook, Powell, and Sims (2009: 4). Cf. Lawrence and Head's chapter with its allusion the 'the quest for meaning' (Lawrence and Head 2009: 284).

[62] Cottingham (2005: 3).

[63] Comte-Sponville (2007: 10): 'a non-religious funeral almost always seems flat, artificial and impoverished.'

[64] De Botton (2012: 15).   [65] Heath (2003: 2, 3).

[66] Heath (2003: 109–10).

Sea of Faith

De Botton's more convivial secularism and Heath's more aggressive atheism
form a natural transition to another version of contemporary spirituality that
can be more immediately related to death than it can in those authors. It
appears in the Sea of Faith movement which furnishes yet another window on
British religion. This movement takes the form of a network of individuals
that emerged from the work and influence of Cambridge theologian Don
Cupitt, which included a television programme of 1984, along with a volume
entitled *The Sea of Faith*. These words echo Matthew Arnold's poem 'On
Dover Beach' to indicate something of the direction of Cupitt's theological
work that moved from relative theological orthodoxy into a non-realist theology grounded in the notion that both the idea of God and the phenomenon
of religion were human constructs.[67] By 1988 a conference was organized, and
after a couple of these events the actual Sea of Faith Network was established
through a meeting of some sixteen people who wished to promote the theme
of religion and faith as human products. The network grew, and now holds an
annual conference, and has some regional groups, and a magazine and some
other publications. All of this is accessible through the Network's website. This
position brings its own style of philosophy of religion into alignment with the
essentially sociological notion of knowledge as the product of human imagination formulated within social groups.[68] Through a number of books Cupitt
advocated what has been called a non-realist theology which, essentially, states
that there is no independent being—God—but that religion is, essentially, a
human construct. In 2008, after some seventy years in the Church of England,
he formally ceased to be a communicant member, 'making this symbolic
gesture' since the church goes 'to almost any lengths to keep fundamentalists
within the fold, but will not do anything to retain the allegiance of modern,
doubting people'.[69]

At the request of the committee of the Sea of Faith Network in the UK I was
asked to undertake a brief research assessment of their current situation, which
I did between 2005 and 2009, when I presented some preliminary results to
the Network's conference at Leicester followed later by a publication that
included material on death.[70] The empirical material cited here is based on
some fifty-five individuals (62% male and 38% female) who responded to a
questionnaire sent out by the Network to its members.[71] Of the respondents
who were not single 67% were married, 19% widows/widowers, 10% divorced,
2% cohabiting, and 2% in civil partnerships. Practically all were university

---

[67] Wain (1987: 166–7). 'Dover Beach' first published in 1867, probably written 1850s.
[68] Rue (2007) affords a classic and more popular example of this perspective.
[69] Cupitt (2009: 7).   [70] Davies and Northam-Jones (2012).
[71] We cannot be sure how many actually received the questionnaires.

educated and most were professional. In employment terms approximately 58% were retired, 11% semi-retired, and 30% working. In terms of attending the annual conference 35% had never done so, 31% had attended many, and some 34% one or some. In line with the overall theological assumption of the Network, the great majority (94%) agreed that God was a construct of human imagination: practically all (94%) thought that the church misleads people. Despite this theological stance on God, human imagination, and church misleading people, actual church attendance of these people was interesting with 66% reckoning to attend church once or more each week, 9% once a month, 19% occasionally, and only 6% never attending. Some 43% reckoned to have had some difficulties with church leaders, some of this being related to there being some clergy among the respondents. This small piece of evidence may well help give the lie to the widely popular phrase of 'believing and belonging' in popular sociology of British religion, for these belong very much but believe very little, at least in recognizable theological terms.

What then of death? With that background in mind we can now consider their responses to issues of death and afterlife explored through a question-naire that had been well tried and tested in a previous and very much larger and well-sampled British population.[72] As a measure of afterlife beliefs we asked the Sea of Faith respondents whether the 'soul passes on' after death: 85% said no, but 15% did not know. Given that, for example, our national survey had some 63% of women agreeing with this passing on (see chapter 2) the Sea of Faith women show a marked difference. Then, in terms of trad-itional resurrection beliefs concerning 'the body awaiting resurrection', a clear 94% (men and women together) did not agree with that, with some 6% 'not knowing'. Addressing the issue of what some might call reincarnation, but which we approached in terms of 'coming back as someone or something else', 83% disagreed with 17% not knowing. In our previous (and much earlier) survey of some 1,603 individuals across the UK we also used a broad question about trust in God and leaving all in God's hands as far as the afterlife was concerned. In terms of the Sea of Faith people 67% disagreed with that, but 15% said yes, and a further 10% 'yes with qualification'; a final 8% did not know about trusting God and leaving everything in God's hands. Their choice of funeral has already been covered in chapter 3 alongside the choices of the wider population.

These Sea of Faith results are interesting even if they reflect a distinct group and a very small and far from perfect sample from which I would certainly not want to extrapolate. What is particularly telling, however, is that even for people who almost unanimously agree that 'God' is a product of human imagination there remain degrees of uncertainty over the 'soul passing on',

---

[72] Davies and Shaw (1995).

or 'coming back', or 'trusting in God'. This uncertainty is, I think, to a large degree due to some questing individuals who are not prepared to be dogmatic in areas of simple uncertainty but who do find general support for their beliefs within a network of this kind; at least some 83% said they did, with some 71% also thinking that the group helped them articulate their beliefs. As for Don Cupitt as its founder and ongoing charismatic presence, many did find him influential, either 'somewhat' 35%, or 'a great deal' (49%), or 'hardly at all' (16%). Likewise with his books, these influenced respondents 'a great deal' (53%), 'somewhat' (33%), or 'hardly at all' (15%).

This cameo of a small group of Christians who had changed their minds during the course of their lives offers its own evidence for the way religious beliefs and church attendance may relate in complex ways yet where, never-theless, a distinctive ideological lifestyle and death-style assumes a high degree of congruence, with a non-realist notion of God paralleling no expectation of personal afterlife.[73] But, it is a case that does pose the complex question of whether these individuals are engaged with religion, cultural wisdom, or spirituality. Each might be used in different contexts and could help draw out different issues.

Secularization of thought

What the Sea of Faith exemplifies is a certain secularization of thought in the sense that traditional Christian theological ideas give way to or are trans-formed into quite different expressions of the way things are within specific individuals. This brings the issue of secularization down to the individual level and reveals the sheer complexity of ideological change as far as individual identity is or identities are concerned. And I use both the singular and the plural here for the same person because identity shifts, drifts, or transform-ations are complex and often related to context. Tanya Luhrmann's notion of 'interpretative drift' is one useful model for thinking how people seem to 'drift from one way of making sense of the world into another through the process of becoming experts in magical practice'.[74] Though not quite 'magic practice', the Sea of Faith does offer its own form of sense-making through a kind of expertise in philosophical analysis of belief combined with group or network interaction. This is exemplified in this case where it seems that people attend-ing the conference do so in their 'Sea of Faith' identity, but that, at other times and in their own local church context, that identity may, by some, be con-cealed or kept in low profile.

This generation, one aged in its twenties when the theological options of secularized theology were booming in the 1960s and 1970s, was much influenced

---

[73] See chapter 9 for Towler's notion of exemplarism.   [74] Luhrmann (2002: 121).

by experiences of church life. Their identity has a marked ecclesial-community rooting, but, also being intellectual, it has, with time and increasing age, sought different interpretations of faith. For these, the Sea of Faith Network has allowed that intellectual dimension to flourish whilst also providing a degree of community as its frame. While books, study, and the media and internet, as well as local and national conferences have all played their part in facilitating reflexivity of belief and self identity for church-rooted identities, it has been the role of a clerical academic as a guru of atheistic faith that has been serendipitous. Just what prompted critically reflexive belief has varied greatly and has included life contexts of bereavement and illness, and disagreements with church leaders, but with educational experiences and the challenge of new ideas also much cited. What we have here is the sense of intelligent minds challenged by life contexts and framed by traditional religiosity.[75] What we find in this group is a reflexive transformation in belief sustained to a degree by a continuation of ecclesial practice. Indeed, the nature of these beliefs is especially important in a way sometimes ignored in sociological studies.

One way of making this point is to distinguish between three ideal types of operative beliefs to explain something of their mode of action; so implicit, explicit, and critically reflexive beliefs give us some purchase on religious beliefs. *Implicit beliefs* are the stuff of cultural convention and accompany many religious devotees of ethnically rooted traditions. In most respects we might align these with our notion of cultural wisdom. *Explicit beliefs* occur when individuals or groups possess an elite hierarchy that devotes time to formal study of its tradition that frequently involves different schools of interpretation. Explicit beliefs, by definition, play a significant role in conversion from one group to another or, within an individual, moving from an implicit position to one of a greater degree of awareness of the significance of ideas previously held in a relatively unthinking fashion. *Critically reflexive beliefs* take the explicit type a degree further, subjecting ideas to critical judgement, often deploying some extra-religious hermeneutical tool in the process. In theological contexts, for example, the nineteenth-century notion of 'higher criticism', used to discuss the literary methods and sources of biblical authors and editors, furnished one example of reflexive belief that had some effect upon aspects of faith for new generations of believers. Don Cupitt's emergent non-realist theology has done much the same for these individuals.

Liberal testimonies

In speaking of beliefs it is important not to ignore the emotional charge often embedded in them, in the contexts of earlier acquisition, and in periods of

---

[75] See Livingstone (n.d.) for collected poetry of group members.

change. In this case we are dealing with highly educated individuals who are old enough to look back across a lifetime of religious engagement; moreover this very variable of age is fundamentally important to the perspective held by most of the fifty-five persons from whom we have data. In explicitly asking them to look back over their lives and describe any changes in outlook they have experienced we fostered a narrative of biography that is, itself, deeply influenced by the group to which they belong—that is, itself, rooted in a critical analysis of traditional forms of belief that have driven many people's religious practice. In other words, we have canvassed a reflexive biography from people already immersed in a reflexive and highly critical and apologetic movement. Within this self-aware group there already existed a form of what might be described as 'testimony', albeit a personal account of a shift from traditional and conservative forms of Christianity to what may be called liberal views. Unlike classical evangelical Protestant testimonies that typically speak of life as being relatively meaningless and lost in some sort of sin prior to hearing and personally appropriating the gospel message of salvation, these personal narratives—and they are not called or even, I think, conceived as 'testimonies'—often begin within some kind of firm traditional Christianity and then tell how they moved to a different kind of awareness of belief. These testimonies to the loss of traditional forms of faith often move to describing the appropriation of another perspective. We can express something of this change in both empirical and narrative versions; a complementarity that adds its own caution to overly simplistic accounts of people's lives. We know that the self-description of this group has changed in terms that are culturally familiar within many British churches. The shift has been from demarcations indicative of relatively exclusive identity to those of a broader and more inclusive sense of life's meaning so that, for example the twenty-nine who described their former alliance as Anglo-Catholic now appear as sixteen. The five evangelical markers dropped to none; so too with the three charismatics. The twenty-three who described their earlier identity as 'liberal' now rose to thirty-three.[76]

The following two abbreviated and anonymized autobiographies express something of the intimate complexities of religious habit and ideological change that simple numerical descriptions cannot capture.

> About ten years later . . . listening to a lecture by Richard Holloway (then still a bishop, I think) it suddenly became clear to me that I was, in the terms understood by most church people, an atheist. This was near to being a Road to Damascus experience. It was also a great relief. . . . I disengaged myself at church, which was not difficult as all the church did was hold masses. I gave myself

---

[76] It was, of course, possible for someone to self-identify in more than one way, e.g. as both Anglo-Catholic and charismatic, or also as liberal.

permission to meditate or daydream during mass, and not to say the creed. But I was unable to go off and be a happy non-churchgoer because I cannot convince myself to abandon the Christian way of life, the inner life of the spirit, the pattern of the liturgical year, the Bible, the English Hymnal, or my Christian heritage and culture. I joined the Sea of Faith Network with fairly high hopes of finding kindred spirits, but found I was not sufficiently intellectually sophisticated to fit in. I had not read the right books and did not really want to. The bits I enjoyed at the one conference I attended were: (a) a talk by [well-known novelist] whose books I loved; (b) circle dancing; and (c) the amusing spectacle of a lot of serious sceptics listening politely to a pagan describing how to humour the local weather gods. I have since found a nice [county named] . . . group that meets about once a year for a meal and uses email a lot in between. In recent years, I have become less worried about my contradictory position as a churchgoer—and one with a private prayer life too—with no belief in the supernatural elements of the faith, wholly lacking a personal relationship with Jesus, and with no story to tell as to why I feel totally compelled to remain within the fold. I don't know if it is of interest to your survey, but other long-running themes in my spiritual development have been to place value on the importance of ecumenism and inter-faith understanding, a strong inbuilt tendency towards nature worship and a compulsion to visit sacred sites from the prehistoric to the present-day.

Or again,

When I moved to my present community I was drawn into the life of the church as a way of becoming involved in the wider community, and I was a PCC member etc., but I was becoming steadily less accepting of a simplistic message. A turning point came when I was 47 and had established myself on a career plateau. The Sea of Faith TV series grabbed my attention and I read the book. Its approach appealed to me and I began to read more widely people like Lloyd Geering and Karen Armstrong. Other than my wife there was no one else in my community who was interested in discussing religion as a human creation but I had some very stimulating discussions about religion, politics and society whilst at summer schools and weekend workshops. It was only about five years ago after I had retired that I became involved in S of F meetings; first as a member of a local group and then attending two annual conferences. I did not go this year as I have become disenchanted with them. It is clear that there is an 'in group' who all know each other and have been going for at least ten years and I have found them, perhaps not surprisingly, not very welcoming of newcomers. Where am I now? I see religion as a human creation with a fascinating history. I have a great interest in the role of organised religion in past societies. I have an interest in church architecture. . . . For me having been brought up in a Western European country I see the Christian ethic as the major ethical influence within this society. Aesthetically and emotionally I treasure the legacy of church music from Bach onwards. Today if I go to church I do not say huge chunks of the creed. I am a detached observer of the church, despairing of the illiberal stance on gay priests and women bishops. I am grateful to the S of F influence but I think that I now need its input less than I did five years ago.

These accounts reflect the interplay of personal reflections and group membership; a dynamic also reflected in the fact that while some 72% thought that the Sea of Faith group does 'have a message',[77] only 35% thought that it 'had a future'.[78] As for the group's having a future, one insightful individual caught some of the internal dynamics of the group quite well, when saying:

> I find that hard to answer. I have always felt there were two distinct constituencies within SOF, one comprising people like me who are seeking ways to remain within our existing religious communities while reinterpreting the language of doctrine and worship, the other being those who seek to develop new forms of religious expression. For a short-hand (and with a twinkle in my eye) I call these two groups 'Godless Vicars' and 'Tree-huggers', and I think the future will depend on which group gains the upper hand.

This dual image depicts something of lifestyle and lifestyle changes that have been important aspects of this very small segment of the British public that may, perhaps, be a tip of a much larger iceberg whose mass is reflected in the more numerical profiles of people self-designating as Christian but whose thoughts are as diverse or even more disparate than those represented above. This largely middle-class group happened to come across in this Network and in Cupitt a voice and writings dealing with religious beliefs in a theological way that expressed their own situations; for a period at least, the group fostered a sense of being with like-minded people.

But religious shifts are, of course, nothing new, and influence more people than we may at first imagine, not least bishops in the Church of England, as a study of retired bishops by my colleague Mathew Guest and myself showed. One question within the study concerned the disestablishment of the church, with some 22% being strongly against the idea at the time of their ordination but only 10% against it after a lifetime serving within it.[79] In that study we also looked at differences between bishops' views and those of their adult children, and devised the notion of 'transformed retention . . . to describe the critically creative process of adaptive change by which beliefs and values pass from parents to children, or from mentors to those they influence'.[80]

However, this term might also serve well to describe the critically creative process of adaptive change of beliefs and values within a single individual during the course of life. In terms of our bishops the changes were also from more to less conservative, with them coming to embrace aspects of church life different from their early experience, which is what we would anticipate in a rising managerially and pastorally inclined group; it is also a shift entirely

---

[77] 'Have a message?' 72% 'Yes'; 20% 'No'; 7% 'Don't know'; 2% 'Hope so'.
[78] 'Have a future?' 35% 'Yes'; 28% 'No'; 23% 'Don't know'; 14% 'Hope so'.
[79] Davies and Guest (2007: 65).   [80] Davies and Guest (2007: 170).

acceptable within the wide church institution. The SoF is, in some ways, similar, despite its theological perspective going beyond the bounds of normal acceptability, for a person's ideological change need not always be expressed or become a pragmatic problem—as this individual made clear who was of '…traditional C. of E. home and Public School upbringing. Increasingly disillusioned gradually since age of 19–21. Now an atheist, though very much a part of my local church still (where I have attended for thirty-five years) as I still see it as a force for social good.' Such is the diversity of opinion within this broad-based institution within which 'salvation' may also come to mean a personal narrative of change.

DYNAMIC OUTCOMES

The final part of this chapter brings back the themes of reciprocity and dual sovereignty from chapter 1 to engage with salvation, folk wisdom, and spirituality in human relationships surrounding death and in the NHS. Outside the narrower doctrinal views of traditional Christianity salvation carries little weight except insofar as a significant minority are prepared to think that God will, in some way, care for their dead, as motifs of the dead going to heaven or being in heaven indicate; much as our later case study reveals. Still, the generic folk wisdom of 'living a good life' continues to carry considerable weight, while the relatively common idiom—'what goes around comes around'—reflects a loose ethical reciprocity not far removed from more formal ideas of karma in the Indian traditions. This suggests that, despite an increasingly widespread disregard for ideas of a divine, commandment-based, and judgement-directed afterlife, people still sense the pull of reciprocity-embedded entities, not least as they seek to do their best for their dead and give them a 'good send off'. In more recent convention, priest and funeral director join forces to ensure that sense of what is right and proper. Their bond became established and powerful for much of the later nineteenth and practically all of the twentieth century in Britain and offers a clear vantage point for considering British religion, folk wisdom, and developing spiritualities through Needham's dual sovereignty and Mauss's reciprocity theory.

For the corpse has to be handled and, as the often unfeeling expression puts it, 'disposed of'; and someone needs to be paid for doing this on some market basis of cost. In this sense, the funeral director holds a market position dealing with a commodity and service-provision, albeit one saved from being a mere monetary transaction through the ritual of the funeral service and its ceremonial officer, whether a minister of religion or a humanist or civic celebrant who deals with the inalienable, the 'real worth', of the corpse as a person in the face of ultimate destiny and in the more proximate life of family and friends.[81] The fact that he or she will be paid for their services becomes a hidden factor in the transaction of ritual management, reflecting the hidden–revealed theme recurrent in this present volume. If the deceased is a regular member of a church and known to that minister it is perfectly possible that no 'fee' would be charged; itself an expression of the multiple factors underlying value, worth, and death. In such a context the mystical factors and inalienability come to cohere in a fundamental fashion and can be seen as the symbolic opposite of what was once the case in Britain in the 1960s, for example, when a duty priest would literally carry out a whole line-up of funeral services at a single crematorium and be paid for his service to people he did not know at all. Many found this an unsatisfactory scheme which, in technical terms, we can see as an example of the corpse being processed as an alienable commodity in a largely jural fashion.

To speak of 'disposal' adds its own dimension to this discussion because it implies low worth or worthlessness to something that is, actually, cherished. For we normally speak of disposing of stuff no longer needed or valued. However, some people do refer to their future corpse as something that will not be of any 'worth' because 'they' will be 'gone'—referring either to belief in a departed soul or else that they will simply be dead and beyond caring. For bereaved relatives, however, the corpse is still the symbol of one they cared for and loved; of one for whom they still carry a sense of responsibility. And, in that sense, it is of great worth; it is inalienable. This issue of worth versus value then comes to the fore in the choice of coffin and style of funeral and this is an arena that has witnessed considerable change in British deaths since approximately the 1990s. Once it would have been seen as a joke for someone to say that they would like to be taken away in a cardboard box when they were dead. Now it has passed from a joke to a simple commercial option since cardboard coffins have become available. But, and this is a crucial factor, such a container tends only to be used at the explicit and prior request of the deceased person. For it to be someone's wish for this to happen would be an expression of their values, and for it to be enacted an expression of the family's respect for those values. This is radically different from a family deciding on a cardboard coffin as an economic decision. In other words the relationship between the inalienable worth placed upon the dead person exists in dynamic tension with the economic cost of 'disposal'; moreover it is the funeral director who constitutes the pivotal point of these negotiations. Getting the balance right is no easy matter, for it also involves the social class and context of death and family life.

It is here that the jural–mystical and reciprocity-based dynamics of the relationships between the living and the dead and between the living and the

---

[81] See chapter 9 for an account of inalienability within reciprocity theory.

ceremonial officers fuse so closely, for we can see how jural and mystical types of authority cohere within the complementarity of funeral directors and priests, as the former, along with medical doctors and crematorium managers, have primacy in dealing with legal aspects of death certification and the identity of the deceased, most especially in relation to cremation. Funeral directors also handle the financial transactions of a funeral so that, for example, actual money does not pass directly from the bereaved family to the priest, but is passed on as fees. The funeral celebrant in complementary contrast touches more the mystical authority of ultimate 'meanings' of life and of the powers that cause people to flourish in their relationships with each other and with any supernatural forces in which they may believe. In this and other societies, priests, shamans, or other authorities frequently manage these forces inherent in deities, ancestors, sacred texts, one's dead, or in forces of nature.[82] In contemporary Britain, as we saw in chapter 3, the family also plays a powerful role in the mystical dimension of relating to the dead in ritually performing the deceased's wishes or expressing his life values in and through the funeral.

Refraction: Religion as Spirituality and Ethics

So, whereas traditional religions framed cultural wisdom and ethical codes within a narrative-embedded form of worship, the process of secularization largely removes this integrative worship factor, allowing the erstwhile complementary phenomena of spirituality and ethics to separate. In relation to this, we can argue that the rise in usage of the word 'spirituality' has paralleled that of 'ethics' as more or less free-standing areas of concern.[83] In other words, secularization involves a process of fragmenting religion into its complementary elements of ethics and spirituality, but with the loss of worship in the process. Within the United Kingdom 'ethics' has increasingly become a focus of concern within most social-welfare, work-based, and leisure institutions, with 'spirituality' slowly emerging alongside as a concern over the quality of life of the members of those institutions. Following from what we have already discussed, the NHS stands at the head of this ethics-coupled-with-spirituality social project. One valuable way of differentiating between this ethics–spirituality pairing lies in Rodney Needham's notion of dual sovereignty which distinguished between jural and mystical forms of authority. The jural element concerns the formal control of social groups through legal procedures, while the mystical has to do with the sense of their wellbeing and

---

[82] See Crossley (2014: 280) for the 'raw power' of the Bible as deployed by politicians.
[83] This currently awaits empirical demonstration.

flourishing associated with ritual blessing and festive occasions of goodwill. The negative forms of jural and mystical authority lie, respectively, in the criminal verdict of guilt and the ritual form of curse.[84] This is, of course, but one way of interpreting human identity and its social milieu, but it is particularly appropriate for this volume in that it deals with the complex interplay of social forces with human emotions. Needham was interested in how jural and mystical forces complemented each other in social life.[85] At the level of 'the establishment' examples include the Lords Temporal and Spiritual in Parliament's Upper House, or of the police and doctors or the police and clergy. Examples at the domestic level would include sources of discipline and encouragement within families and between generations, while work-based cases would relate line managers and mentors. This theoretical perspective guarantees that the emotional dynamics of individual life, with all that means for a person's identity, are foregrounded in relation to social forces and to the variety of establishment or establishment-like contexts in which people flourish or are diminished. These are the very dynamics that 'spirituality' entails and which ethics embrace.

Worship, secularization, and significant others

As already intimated, one element lost in this assumed secularization process of transformation of religion into ethics and spirituality is that of worship; behaviour that relates a group to a most significant other, usually a deity figure, ancestor, or personified principle. In this category we might also include contexts of meditation on the nature of the self, though even this often involves a strong relational grounding in monastic communities or guru–disciple relationships. Most such worship contexts express or intensify the mystical dimension of authority. In terms of ethics, the 'significant other' takes a jural form, often focused upon the ethics committees of medical, educational, commercial, industrial, and leisure institutions. Indeed, the rise of such committees may well represent one of the most significant indices of the secularization of religion. Moreover, the demand that religious institutions create their own ethical codes, as with dealing with adult–child contact, marks the incursion of wider ethics-marked society into the religious establishment whose own canon law once sufficed. In terms of spirituality, the mystical domain predominates. In its para-religious mode this retains the form of some significant Other as in nature spirituality where Gaia, the Earth, or cosmos, stands as an arena within which worship occurs. Or it may be more radically

---

[84] Needham (1980: 63).

[85] This balance would, for example, help Charles Taylor with the straining of the 'juridical' and 'redemption' metaphors at the heart of Christianity (2007: 652).

self-referential and seek self-development quite apart from transcendent others, the mystical component arising from the inner resources of the self. The use of meditative or other body-techniques allows access to these resources.[86] Doubtless, the role of the counsellor, life-guide, or psychiatrist as a significant other or as a facilitator of such processes of access to mystical resource and personal flourishing is germane because it is often difficult for one role to include both forms of control. This can be a paradoxical issue in, for example, the doctor-psychiatrist and patient relationship when issues of sectioning under the Mental Health Act arise.[87]

Having considered these issues it now makes sense to return to the NHS and appreciate that the values underlying its advocacy of spirituality are, essentially, inalienable values. Rooted in life as a precious possession, this institution deals with the foundational values of health and wellbeing as well as having to handle some fundamental aspects of dying and death. However—and this is a crucial fact—the NHS has to operate financially in a market-based economy of an alienable kind. The distinction between the inalienable and the alienable is a distinction between value and cost and highlights the government's problem in handling this particular part of national life.[88] The emphasis upon the NHS in this volume circles around the inalienable aspects of health care and wellbeing that people long to experience as embracing their personal worth as individuals. As and when a person experiences hospital care as something rendered to them in an impersonal way, they complain; and if their experience is even more negative, so that, for example, even a medical doctor suffering from cancer can speak publicly of the NHS as dehumanizing her, the situation is worse still. This doctor emphasized her sense of how death is part of life and how it should be framed by dignity and not regarded as a failure as some 'senior consultants' seemed to do.[89] We explore this dignity motif more fully in chapter 8, just as in the Introduction we considered the Shipman murders as an example of cultural betrayal played out through his NHS general practice. It is as these emotion-laden ideas of care or betrayal become prime cultural values that we see how hope or despair encircle this social provision and, especially in terms of hope, this indicates something of the NHS's resemblance to religious institutions.

---

[86] As Mauss ([1936] 1979) once called such aspects of embodiment.

[87] I am indebted to a discussion at the 20th Spirituality and Psychiatry Special Interest Group of the Royal College of Psychiatrists for this observation.

[88] See Owen Jones ([2014] 2015: 120–1) for government cuts to the NHS depicted as 'sanitized savings' by the BBC.

[89] Borland (2014: 29), citing Dr Kate Granger 'addressing managers at the NHS Confederation Conference', 6 June 2014. See Kirkpatrick (1967) for criticism of some bad nursing care.

FORCE AND FUNERALS

Getting funeral dynamics right for all concerned is not easy, given the experiences of grief in the immediately bereaved, the social response of wider social circles, and the role of assisting professionals. It is here that both the jural and mystical forms of authority combine with practicalities of reciprocity in terms of 'social force' and the nature of tradition, expectation, and innovation. In the history of anthropology, for example, some have long pinpointed certain types of 'force or power' as distinctive drivers of particular kinds of behaviour. These include 'magic', and religion; indeed, the 'power' theme applies to most aspects of life.[90] In chapter 6 we will see something of the negation of such pressure when grief-stricken people speak of a feeling of unreality and sense no obligation to engage with others. For the moment, however, we remain within the positive domain and the sense of empowerment that can be approached theoretically as a kind of blessing; a notion that might seem out of place in accounts of modern spirituality, and yet nothing could be further from the case. For, just as 'mystical' comes with its own ecclesial-linked meanings, so too does the word 'blessing', yet the latter offers considerable opportunity for understanding mystical forms of authority that arise within semi- or totally secular contexts. 'Blessing', as I have discussed elsewhere and in relation to a number of other scholars, involves a sense of abundance, 'superabundance', or plenitude.[91] It concerns life enhancement and wholeness, and plays a role in what we have already identified in chapters 1 and 2 as the 'moral–somatic' dimension of life.[92] Such blessing may come from a variety of sources; from a parent to a child, or from relatives or friends. It represents a relationship of goodwill and of that enhancement of the self that runs contrary to what I have also detailed elsewhere as 'identity depletion'.[93] Blessing plays a period role during the life-course from birthdays through times of success, marriage and partnerships, graduations and so on, for the time-lines of life are also emotion-lines of life, and these also embrace periods of bereavement when grief benefits from social support. Such nurture brings blessing, encouragement, and enhancement of hope for the future; its absence fosters despair. The major religious traditions, not least Christianity, expend a great deal of energy in theological, pastoral, and liturgical action directed towards death. Here we often find a focus of mystical authority and scope for blessing through inalienable inheritances. Traditionally, of course, many formal ecclesial rites include a 'blessing' given by senior priests on the basis of their priestly status; its liturgical ubiquity denotes its significance. Indeed, its widespread use by the

---

[90] Mauss ([1902] 2002: 151) 'force or power...presents the magical idea, gives it being, reality, truth'.
[91] Douglas J. Davies (2011: 175).   [92] Douglas J. Davies (2011: 186–91).
[93] Douglas J. Davies (2011: 68–94).

laity as part of everyday language should also not be overlooked. 'God be with you', 'God-speed', 'Adieu', or the widespread 'God bless' uttered by millions of parents to children at bedtime—all bespeak the goodwill of person to person amidst life's unknown future. In the erstwhile secular or simply lay world of families wishing to engage in much of the preparatory work of a funeral as well as its execution, their activities express their own form of 'blessing' of the dead in 'doing their best' for them. While this may well also be a time when family politics work themselves out in difficult ways, the goal is to achieve a positive ritual outcome and not some expression of negativity. Finally, at a national level there is in the national honours system, already described in chapter 3, offering its own form of 'blessing', an expression of goodwill from the monarch, who is not simply a symbolic Head of State but a physical person in whose actual or representative presence the 'ordinary' or even 'celebrity' person receives their award.

Candles: Tradition, Folk Wisdom, or Spirituality?

In tying down some of these ideas in a concrete example we now offer some evidence of relationships with or attitudes towards the dead, focused on one of the most extensive popular symbols now used in association with the memorialization of death, though much less with actual funeral services as such—that of the candle.[94] One of the most focused accounts of what candles currently symbolize for people at large spoke of hope, the human spirit, joy, opposition to darkness, and of them as an international symbol in a world of different cultures and of culture clashes. Here we have an 'easy-living symbol' that expresses the 'human soul itself', one that is so 'pliable a symbol' that 'it can mean anything'. Some spoke of 'faith against all odds', another of the 'flickering light keeping back the darkness' and, in reminiscence of biblical imagery, of 'sharing an act of creation'. The Revd Garth Hewitt, an Anglican minister of a London church and whose personal background did not lie in traditions that made much of candles in ritual, spoke of the way candles had become increasingly significant to him as he pondered the 'hurts of the world' and the 'fragility of hope', not least when he thought of the contemporary problems over Palestine and Israel and of friends living in those places. He was alert to the fact that a candle can always 'go out', and was not sure 'that the fragility of hope will survive'. At another personal level one woman spoke of having undergone several sets of IVF treatment, all unsuccessful, and of then attending a Candlemas service where people were invited to light candles of their own while a minister quietly read various categories of people who could be

---

[94] 'Candlelight, The Living Flame', Radio 4 Extra, 20 December 2013.

remembered. This included abused children and those who had died in famine and war, as well as those who had been conceived but died. The resonance that arose in this particular woman came while lighting her candle; she became oblivious to all others there as she felt a sense of being allowed to let an unknown and unborn child 'come to be' and also allowed 'to let go'. Yet another contributor, a former political prisoner released through the work of Amnesty International, spoke of the fortieth anniversary of that organization involving people carrying forty candles, some symbolizing individuals who had died or had been 'eliminated' by certain regimes. He noted how Amnesty International had as its motif a candle surrounded by barbed wire: few compound symbols could speak more clearly of the interplay of hope and repression.

A tone of deep seriousness underlay this entire radio programme and its personal accounts of life experience. As such it differed from the 'entertain-ment', 'factual-reporting', and 'inquisitorial' forms of tonality underlying the great majority of programmes. This 'existential' tone of life-seriousness is highly significant on radio, television, and other media where matters of life and death are concerned, and often provides its own framing of material concerning death.

Following Victor Turner's anthropological terminology, candle symbolism, and in this case its allied tonal seriousness, offers an excellent example not only of the multivocality of a symbol, in which many potential meanings cohere or run in parallel, but also of both the sensory and ideological poles of the candle as a symbol.[95] As an object the candle is a simple structure, often white in colour, with its single flame. It is, in itself, an active process in which one substance comes to appear as another: wax becomes flame. In sensory terms it has to be handled, taken, and lit—then its light and warmth are obvious. Just what meaning is brought to its illumination then depends on the ritual context. For most people in British societies candles are first, experi-enced on birthday cakes. They are lit and blown out whilst 'making a wish', and are accompanied by the singing of 'Happy Birthday to You'. Such cakes and candles run through children's lives and we all experience them many times for ourselves and for others. This means that candles engender an emotional 'birthday' or anniversary celebratory resource that can, with appro-priate contextual shifts in music, silence, joy, or seriousness, be combined with a great variety of other resources, not least those of remembrance.

Christian culture offers a wide liturgical frame for candle symbolism. The Candlemas rite, which traces a fifth–sixth-century origin in a Christian cele-bration of Jesus Christ as the light of the world, served as a background cultural resource whose ritual frame allowed this woman to experience her

---

[95] Victor Turner (1969). See Frederick Turner (1990) for account of his father, Victor Turner's, imaginatively constructed funeral.

own sorrow in not having a hoped-for child, and to do so in a way that allowed her to begin to live with that experience and develop in a more positive fashion. This ritual resource, which usually takes place in February, has an equivalent Christianly networked symbolic power in Advent candles lit during the four Sundays of Advent leading up to Christmas, where interpretations of the four candles often involve ideas of hope, peace, joy, and love.[96] The more recent Christingle services, largely focused on children and parents, use candles mounted on oranges as symbols of the world at large. All this is set against the background of daily and weekly use of candles in many Christian traditions as well as in birthday celebrations in many homes. The rise of scented candles as a commercial venture for use in the home at special family or personal moments is another part of candles' growing use. The powerful use of candles occurs in a wide variety of places at times of accidental or other tragic death events.

This background now allows us to consider one such implementation in the case of a very particular use of candles by visitors to Durham Cathedral, people who also write what might best be described as prayer requests on pieces of paper that are left behind in a box. Approximately fifty are left each day. These are, anonymously, used by cathedral clergy within the context of ordinary worship services. By my own arrangement with Cathedral authorities prayers were retained for general analysis of the topics covered by visitors over the period of Armistice Day (11 November 2010), Remembrance Sunday (14 November 2010), Christmas Eve (24 December 2010), Christmas Day (25 December 2010), and New Year's Day (1 January 2011). Some other days surrounding these events were also included for purposes of comparison.

This research is still underway at the time of writing with subsequent years and other institutions also being considered. However, in provisional terms it is worth sketching the fact that, of the 948 items studied so far in terms of the general themes presented, the largest general category, approximately 42% of all items, concerned the dead.[97] These memorial prayers can be subdivided into two groups of 24% and 18% respectively. The first consisted of messages *to* the dead, written in direct speech; relatives 'spoke to' their dead grandparent, mother, father, child, or friend. The second consisted of messages *about* the dead, as though written to a third party, as to the priest or to some other person who might read the prayer. Of the other prayers as part of all those collected, approximately 16% were prayers for family and friends on other topics; 12% sought good luck and health; 11% took the form of mini letters of a 'Dear God', or 'Dear Lord' form having many diverse requests; 9%

---

[96] Simmel (1959: 42) described 'the Christian festival of Christmas' primarily as 'a universalistic expression of the communion of peace'.

[97] This approach, like Towler's (1984: 14–18) involves a cumulative characterization of responses.

specifically mentioned sick individuals and asked for their health and comfort; 5% concerned 'world peace'; 5% were not in English and reflect the variety of visitors to the Cathedral, not least from Eastern Europe and East Asia; while 1% invoked the aid of angels. Some of the prayers not listed here as about death did in fact include some reference to bereavement and loss but as one theme amongst others. I have kept these apart from the very specific 42% focused on the dead in direct or indirect speech so as not to over-emphasize death in an artificial way.

Many of the 42% referred to heaven and tended to assume the deceased individual was 'somewhere'; indeed the direct-speech versions seemed to indicate an ongoing relationship with the dead in active memory. They struck a note of love and continued memory and of not forgetting. The specific context of prayers did influence their content. On Armistice Day, for example, roughly 70% of the prayers either directly addressed the dead (41%) or addressed them indirectly (29%). Interestingly, on Remembrance Sunday itself, when the Cathedral was packed with people at the formal remembrance service, the direct and indirect address to and of the dead was as much as on ordinary days (22% and 16% respectively) with general prayers for family and other interests (40%) much higher than on ordinary days (which tended to be between 13% and 20%). It may well be that many of those who had already been at the Remembrance service had, as it were, already addressed the dead in a corporate rite and were left 'free' to address other concerns.

Another special day worth considering is that of Christmas Day, in this case Christmas 2010. Here, again, the dead were evident with some 37% encountered, but of these the direct address was evident in 32% and the indirect only in 5%. In fact this indirect reference to the dead had the lowest incidence of all the days studied. The general 'pray for' group of prayers, at 20% of all prayers, was relatively high, with the family standing out as a reference point. Perhaps it should also be noted that of the prayers directly addressing the dead (noted above as 32%) some 15% of that group were written in terms of 'Christmas Greetings'. The family context of prayers for and to the dead is obviously important in the above, and went along with the lighting of votive candles for placement in large candelabra provided by the cathedral.

CONCLUSION

Beginning from its tripartite concern with salvation, folk wisdom, and spirituality, this chapter has considered dynamic aspects of moral behaviour conducing to meritorious status and to such popular idioms as that of being a 'good person'. Its scope has, quite intentionally, been wide enough to accommodate the ritual–symbolic contexts of death, whether in terms of more religious, more secular, or more mixed world views, including the case study of the Sea of Faith movement as a firm reminder of how social change is actually reflected in lifestyle shifts of belief within individuals. In terms of the celebration of life, we have found the social force-field rebounding from the resistance of post-mortality to the life already lived and have stressed the role of the British NHS as one medium in and through which important cultural values of both life and care have increasingly come to be expressed. We have also complemented accounts of established scholars of the sacred with the immediate relevance of the 'high-information existence' generated around individual lives by social media. It is extremely telling that in an age when online memorials flourish many people also light candles and speak with their dead, and it is with that kind of diversity of emotion in mind that we move to the next chapter and its more focused account of grief, media, and social emotions.

6

Grief, the Media, and Social Emotions

The previous chapter's depiction of salvation, folk wisdom, and spirituality paved the way for this chapter's exploration of the intimately personal experiences of grief and the socially marked behaviour of mourning that together make bereavement one of the clearest windows upon the relationship between individual and society. Yet, while grief presents us once more with the theme of social force at this intersection of individual and society, the question of what counts as 'social' in Britain today is complicated, given death's impact upon the immediately bereaved family, on closer and more distant kin, networks of friends, work and leisure colleagues, neighbours and often beyond them on 'friends' in the virtual domain of social media.

Bearing in mind these complex emotional interfaces between self and society, this chapter will begin with a reflection on how we 'learn grief', before considering some selected theoretical approaches to grief evident in a variety of sources from the past and present. This brings more technical notions of identity and sense of 'presence' alongside ancient, medieval, and modern literary resources to show the importance of narrative in our emotional sense of self. This interplay of individual and social 'forces' lies at the core of social science whether at the level of international politics and economics where financial markets easily fluctuate depending on the mood of dealers, through ordinary social life in family, school, employment, and leisure, to the realms of religion and the multiplicity of fluctuations in 'the magician's mind' where 'force or power' brings its own sense of 'reality' and 'truth'.[1] These dynamics, in turn, provide the basis for the media, who flourish through a creative management of the public's emotional response, not least to death. The previous chapters' discussion of the social 'establishment' in Britain also comes to a focus and transformation here in the death, funeral, and memorializing of Diana Princess of Wales. In considering this cultural watershed and numerous supporting concepts, this chapter will, once more, reflect this

---

[1] Mauss ([1902] 2001: 150–1).

volume's eclectic approach in which academic disciplines often partner material from the popular press and media at large.

LEARNING GRIEF

In approaching grief we draw, once more, on our earlier theoretical approach to emotions that pervade ideas to generate values that may, in turn, transform into beliefs if they help create a sense of destiny. We can apply this to grief by seeing how the 'bare' word becomes clothed by personal emotional experience to create a cultural value of considerable force. If we think of both 'grief' and 'death' as a child might 'normally' experience these words over a lifetime, we begin with simple words amongst other words acquired and spoken in society at large, having a distant, even abstract, significance, devoid of any particular personally grounded emotion. Over time, however, children learn that some-one they hardly know, or some celebrity, has died, and they pick up a general emotion in association with that circumstance. Children, and ourselves when adult, learn that death comes with an emotional mood and that we should empathize with a bereaved relative, friend, or neighbour. Even so, there remains a degree of distance until, one day, a close relative or friend dies; then, in what is often experienced as strange or uncanny—but certainly as a novel experience—we come to feel grief and know death in ways that reach deep levels of identity.

As this experience touches the core of who we are as a person the sense of the ordinariness of the everyday life-world is disrupted: the sense of time shifts, as do mundane priorities, and, at its strongest, the effect may cause a person to say that their world seems to collapse around them. 'Grief' and 'death', as abstract ideas, zoom in from their distant pole to a near point of intimacy. Colin Murray Parkes, from his extensive experience of bereaved people, not least in pathological contexts, described grief as a loss resulting in a 'reaction of intense pain or yearning for the lost object' without which 'a person cannot truly be said to be grieving'.[2] In more technically symbolic terms we might say that both 'grief' and 'death' become terms that participate in what they represent; they move from being indicative signs to deeply moving symbols, and, in so doing, individual experience echoes and partici-pates in the shared experience that underlies public life. This complex process of emotions pervading ideas is but one expression of the combined social and individual force-fields of mutual relationships and personal identity.

[2] Parkes (2006: 29).

Background to Grief

A great deal of material exists on emotional patterns of grief, with preferences for stage theories competing with mapping of variously recurring patterns of feelings.[3] The twentieth-century dominance of attachment-based theories related to the experience of loss has been assailed by advocates of continuing bonds with the dead, as memory and personal narrative coupled with studies of the enduringly material culture of death have gained popularity.[4] Despite the detailed consideration merited by these complex accounts of the psychological and social forces influencing individuals in society this chapter will be highly selective in using sources that align individuality and publicity within some past and present cultural highlights, beginning with Charles Darwin and Geoffrey Gorer.

Charles Darwin

Darwin's own experience of grief has been described historically in terms of his Victorian era and the absence of Christian comfort in notions of eternal life, as well as more psychologically for his tendency to repress personal loss.[5] As with many of his day, his personal loss was extensive, embracing the death of his mother when aged eight, his father when aged forty, as well as three of his own young children, notably that of his cherished ten-year-old Annie when he was forty-two. Against that background, his later work on emotions stands as a veritable lighthouse in the British history of human feeling, not least of grief. Alert to the social conventions, habits, and contexts that influence emotion he noted that 'Englishmen rarely cry, except under the pressure of acutest grief; whereas in some parts of the Continent the men shed tears much more readily and freely.' Traveller-scholar that he was, he also tells how, in Tierra del Fuego, he saw a man recently bereaved of a brother, 'who alternately cried with hysterical violence, and laughed heartily at anything which amused him'.[6] In this Darwin, with his pre-Freudian peers, clearly understood ideas of energy or power influencing human beings in terms of their psychological dynamics.[7] Their biological preoccupation took British empirical interests away from the abstract philosophical engagements as drivers of human life and civilization that held dominance elsewhere through Kant and Hegel.[8] In terms of our study it is this engagement of psychological

---

[3] Cleiren (1991: 13–86).

[4] Parkes, Stevenson-Hinde, and Marris (eds) (1991); Valentine (2008).

[5] Jalland (1996: 343–50), including references to Bowlby's psychological analysis.

[6] Darwin (1872: 155–7).

[7] Darwin (1872: 200) acknowledges Herbert Spencer (1863) on 'nervous energy'.

[8] Darwin's outlook is, however, quite distinct from the European tradition of Hegel (1770–1831) on the developmental outworking of 'Geist', or Spirit. One might, however,

energy with social force that is of interest, depicting as it does the overall dynamics of an individual's social world in a way that encourages a socio-logical rather than a philosophical approach to life. This view is especially germane in that most religious and secular spiritualities and ritual[9] events concern degrees of emotional experience and should not overemphasize historical, social, philosophical, or theological factors that marginalize their intrinsic emotional forces.

Geoffrey Gorer

Just as Darwin emphasized 'man' as one animal amongst others, as did Sir Thomas Browne two centuries before him, so did Geoffrey Gorer a whole generation later as he set a sociological–anthropological dimension to emotion that presaged numerous 'death, grief, and mourning' studies.[10] Gorer's 1965 *Death, Grief, and Mourning* captured interests that would soon be expressed by many others across a spectrum of disciplines. He was already known for his 1955 essay on 'The Pornography of Death', which argued that while obscenity is known worldwide, pornography is probably restricted to literate societies; and that while obscenity is a social behaviour, pornography is more likely to be a private behaviour largely concerned with sex. He argued that during the twentieth century death 'as a natural process' was becoming unmentionable just as sexual material was increasingly mentionable, inverting the nineteenth-century context of sex's unmentionables but death's public celebration. 'The natural processes of corruption and decay have become disgusting, as disgust-ing as the natural processes of birth and copulation were a century ago.' His wish was that death should be mentioned and discussed, while his focus on grief spoke of a 'long-lasting psychological process with physiological over-tones and symptoms', especially 'disturbances of sleep and weight loss'.[11] He notes the dreams of about a third of those he studied, and provides a sketch of 'styles of mourning', some nine in all. These include 'mourning before death' in cases of known incurable illness when 'a great deal of mourning may take place during this period so that the eventual death is felt emotionally, as well as intellectually, to be a release'.[12] Another is of 'mummification', when a relative keeps a kind of shrine for the deceased person. However, much of Gorer's concern lay with the relative lack of funerary ritual in British society and, in that sense, with the presence or absence of contact with social force, that

---

speculate on the appeal Darwin's vision would have held for Immanuel Kant's (1724–1804) interest in nature's contribution to understanding.

[9] One Arabic-speaking postgraduate whose English is also excellent unconsciously spoke of 'ritualities' when referring to ritual complements of diverse 'spiritualities': a pleasing neologism, I think.

[10] Hertz's highly seminal work ([1907] 1960) on double burial had not yet become influential.

[11] Gorer (1965: 53).   [12] Gorer (1965: 68).

vitality-infused engagement with others. Gorer's anthropological, empirical, and qualitative approach to death, grief, and mourning in Britain in the mid-twentieth century is valuable, as is its brief summary of preceding grief theories including Peter Marris's 1956 study *Widows and Their Families* that focused on seventy-two working-class widows in the East End of London; and Bowlby's work. He notes how Marris continues Freud's concern over a bereaved person's 'loss of contact with reality', as well as offering his own 'three stages' moving from an 'initial period of shock', followed by 'violent grief and disorganization' (of about six to twelve weeks in Britain), and a final 'longer period of reorganization'.[13] He firmly notes the importance of ritual, emphasizing the importance of other people during the first two phases and of potential problems if no help is forthcoming. In all this Gorer is influenced by his own experiences of grief, not least, one assumes, by the loss of his father, drowned when the *Lusitania* sank in 1915, when the young Geoffrey was ten years old. These biographical elements, alongside Gorer's substantial comments, made some impact on Philippe Ariès in his monumental work on death, though his excessive historical rather than empirical emphasis seemed to find some evidence quaint. 'It is rather remarkable that in 1963, in Gorer's investigation, and only among the old, one encounters the anthropomorphic eschatology of the nineteenth century.'[14] By this he refers to people 'seeing' their dead and talking to them after death; phenomena that are, today, no longer 'rather remarkable' as we become more familiar with wider patterns of memory and grief experiences.

NARRATIVE AND DEATH

Whether in historical narratives with Ariès, ethnographic studies with Gorer, or the life stories shared with others, we are attuned to narratives as integral aspects of both individual and group identity discerned through the emotions they portray and imply. Turning our linguistic competence into such accounts of daily activities not only allows our sense of individual identity and community evaluation to develop but also provides opportunity for moral judgement to be expressed and social control maintained. The status of such social–moral narratives varies a great deal, from secretive gossip to established histories of nations, with humanity's myths, theological dogma, and political

---

[13] Note that he speaks of mourning and not of grief, even though stage theories of grief were already emerging as formulaic ways of trying to understand responses to death.

[14] Ariès ([1977] 1981: 575–9).

scenarios also playing their part in weaving accounts of life's origin, meaning, and destiny. And this is why science has come to be problematic over the centuries, especially in Western thought; for science, too, presents its own form of narrative accounts of life, including the significance of death. The major difference between the former and the latter being that myth, religious doctrine, and even political ideologies possess ritual forms to express their narrative, while science has but few ritual expressions for people at large, even though some practising scientists are likely to experience their laboratory work as a kind of ritual.

Whether in scientific or mythical form, narratives provide a primary means of organizing ideas of life and influencing experience of social force, not least of the nature of the individual in relation to personal and impersonal others. Previous chapters have already shown how funerals deploy narratives, whether in the liturgical narrative of Christian thought or in the life-focused narrative created by civic, secular, or humanist funeral celebrants. We have also seen how individuals provide distinctive narratives of changes in their own religious opinions. Narrative is inescapable since it is the medium in and through which identity is created and maintained, from the practically constant daily general inner dialogue of us all[15] to the way many talk to their dead at graves or in the privacy of their own thoughtful inner dialogues.

Literary Narratives

In the most obvious sense, 'literature' is entirely replete with narratives expressing local culture seminally applicable to a worldwide readership and valuable for analytical consideration by academic disciplines. Of the worldwide possibilities, three are pinpointed here, each a different genre and from a different era, viz. the Synoptic Gospels of the first century, the poetic fable *The Pearl* of the fourteenth, and one of D. H. Lawrence's twentieth-century stories. These exemplify deep human emotions pervading relationships surrounding suffering and death, and though we might be tempted to avoid reducing poems and formal texts to any pragmatic literalness, it will do no harm in this context to observe the strange weariness of grief that brings rest to overcharged senses.[16] A fourth example, from a novel by Carson McCullers, will be added later when exploring the theoretical notion of crisis of 'presence'.

---

[15] Douglas J. Davies (2006).
[16] Prinz's account of emotions includes the importance of 'attention' in his psychological 'AIR theory of consciousness' involving *'attended intermediate-level representations'* (2004: 209–12, original emphasis). Though he does not discuss grief, this could be one model applicable to grief's weariness and sensed detachment.

Biblical

One familiar challenge concerning text and emotion lies in the Christian Gospels and has challenged biblical interpreters in telling ways, viz. the paradigmatic scene presented in the Synoptic Gospels of Matthew, Mark, and Luke and set in the Garden of Gethsemane prior to Jesus being arrested, tried, and crucified to produce what is probably the most influentially famous death in the history of the world. Jesus takes three disciples, Peter, James, and John there as companions for his period of prayer, anticipating possible arrest and trial and, who knows, also perhaps death. In Mark's Gospel, Jesus, being 'exceedingly sorrowful', bids them watch with him while he prays that perhaps events might fall out more positively than anticipated, asking God that he 'take away this cup from me: nevertheless, not what I will, but what thou wilt'. Jesus returns to find his disciples asleep. He chides each of them in turn for not watching with him, before delivering the famous words, which have entered the English language in their own right, 'The spirit truly is ready, but the flesh is weak'.[17] In Matthew's Gospel, sleep is allied with temptation still: 'their eyes were heavy' or weighed down, for the spirit was also willing but the flesh weak,[18] but in Luke's Gospel there is something of a parallel between Christ's anguish, involving his sweating as it were great clots of blood, with his chosen disciples 'sleeping for sorrow'.[19] One New Testament commentator glosses this verse by arguing that Luke's is an 'unskilful attempt to adapt the Marcan story so as to spare the reputation of the Apostles', noting that Luke 'spares them the shame of being found asleep three times'. His own attempt at incisive criticism is that 'Grief keeps [one] awake'.[20] But it is not necessarily so and, to return to our ordinary world, there will be many in contemporary Britain who have watched at the bedside of a dying relative until they are practically overcome by a deep weariness created by a combination of physical, psychological, and existential exhaustion.

The Pearl

As with the gospels, our next story is also one with which some bereaved people will have found some affinity because of their own experience of death and crisis-linked tiredness. It comes from the fourteenth-century *Pearl* poem that gives an account of grief at the death of a child whose parent falls asleep with grief. There follows a dream of travelling into the heavenly realms where the child appears as a bride of Christ—she is the pearl without a spot.

> My saddened soul still showed its sore;
> I fell upon that grassy floor

---

[17] Mark 14: 33–8.   [18] Matthew 26: 41–3.
[19] Luke 22: 44–5.   [20] Leaney (1958: 273).

> Asleep, my ravaged senses shot,
> And dreams a swooning dream before
> My precious pearl without a spot.[21]

The longing to be in that place with the deceased becomes as intense as was the intensity of longing after her loss on Earth.[22] The dream reveals the heavenly Jerusalem whose allure is enormous, but the desire to pass into it 'did not my true Prince please' and, just as the boundary river is reached, 'my steps He stayed / My walk was wondrously delayed'. Then 'My dream did flit away and fade! / I woke just where I first did fall asleep.'[23] This poem expresses the depth of grief for the loss of one so much loved, and engages with a belief in a blessed afterlife before ending with an affirmation that the Earth-life of the bereaved parent must be satisfied with the presence of Christ in and through the Mass. The very fact of dreams as a medium of ongoing relation with the dead would still resonate with many today, for dreams of the dead offer their own means of emotional relationship and have long provided a basis for their distinctive kind of ongoing bonds with the dead, as has a sense of the dead's presence, as we discuss below. Even Freud rehearses a dream of an exhausted father falling asleep after the death of his daughter who then 'appears' to him in a dream.[24]

D. H. Lawrence

Our example from Lawrence, that most astute interpretative author of English emotion, comes in his short story 'The Horse Dealer's Daughter'. This typifies the complexity of personal relationships and self-understanding surrounding an individual lifestyle and chosen death-style.[25] Here we meet Mabel, who had kept house for years for her uncouth brothers until, when poverty befell the household, this woman, who had gone 'regularly to church . . . and lived in the memory of her mother, who had died when she was fourteen', seems to have decided to commit suicide—though the phrase is entirely absent. For her, 'the end had come . . . she would follow her own way . . . she would always hold the keys of her own situation'. Then 'in a sort of ecstasy', she seemed to 'be coming nearer to her fulfilment, her own glorification, approaching her dead mother, who was glorified'. Mabel took a small bag containing shears, sponge, and scrubbing brush and went to her mother's grave in the local churchyard. 'There she always felt secure . . . immune from the world, reserved within the

---

[21] *The Pearl.* Lines 56–60.

[22] *The Pearl.* Lines 245–6: 'Since losing you a lasting blight / Of care has come—it cuts, unkind!'

[23] *The Pearl.* Lines 1165–71.

[24] Freud ([1900] 1976: 652–5). Despite such data he still considered grief as detachment of links and the reinvestment of psychological energy elsewhere.

[25] Lawrence ([1922] 1968: 164–70).

thick churchyard wall as in another country', and there she clipped grass from the grave, arranged flowers, and scrubbed the headstone. Lawrence creates an image of a woman who gained 'sincere satisfaction' from this tending when, 'She felt in immediate contact with the world of her mother . . . as if in performing this task she came into a subtle, intimate connexion with her mother.' Lawrence is interesting here, as he juxtaposes 'the world of her mother' and that 'subtle, intimate connection with her mother'. Lawrence gives no hint of Mabel speaking with her dead mother; her 'intimate connexion' has more to do with his overarching grasp of her situation, viz. that 'the life she followed here in the world was far less real than the world of death she inherited from her mother'. From tending her mother's grave Mabel walked directly to a local pond and, having 'stood on the bank for a moment . . . waded slowly into the water . . . deliberately towards the centre of the pond'. This defiant act of self-resolution, of what some would now identify as taking control of her destiny—'it was the right thing to do, *I* knew best then'. However, the young local doctor—who could not swim, 'was afraid' but, already intrigued by this young woman, sees her act from a distance, wades and tumbles into the 'foul, earthy water' with its 'cold, rotten clay' and saves her: she recovers and they declare their newly discovered yet almost ambivalent love. The use of water to clean the grave contrasts with the dirty water of her near-drowning and entry into 'the world of death' inherited from her long-dead mother. But when the doctor carries her to safety, he removes her 'earthy-smelling clothing' and, as he rubs her dry and wraps her 'naked in blankets', we are presented with a kind of typical rural birth, albeit of an adult as good as dead. His role as a doctor interplays with that of a new-found lover—'this introduction of the personal element was very distasteful to him, a violation of his professional honour'. So it is that, within this single story, Lawrence evokes a spectrum of emotions pervading personal autonomy versus negative family commitments and positive filial longing for another place, first evinced in attempted suicide then in nascent man–woman love.

PERSONHOOD AND 'SITUATED MOMENTS' OF PRESENCE

Lawrence's sympathetic creativity in that story offers a natural progression to the many accounts of bereavement that now exist, with but two cited here, one by Christine Valentine and another by Jenny Hockey.

Valentine's sensitive account of *Bereavement Narratives* demonstrated the sheer complexity of death-related narrative, achieved through descriptions of how individuals talked to her about their deceased relatives in such a way as to prompt her distinctive theoretical call for 'a more flexible and nuanced understanding of personhood'.[26] One consequence of her work is to under-mine the ease with which scholars sometimes characterize the nature of persons by carving 'history' into named periods that typify people in terms of their adhering to 'Modernist values . . . postmodern perspectives', 'roman-ticism', or the like. This has almost become a neologistic industry in contem-porary sociology where, for example, 'Generation X' follows on from the 'Baby Boomers' or 'Baby Busters' . . . born between 1946 and 1964 or 'Generation X' or 'Xers . . . between 1965 and 1980', to be followed, inexorably it would seem, 'by the Y generation between 1981 and 2000'. Following these come the 'dot. coms, the millennials, the Net Generation or the Thumb Generation [because of the use of remote controls or mobile phones]'.[27] Almost in completion of the alphabet a USA advertising company has added to that classification by designating a rather similar group, born after 1995, one that is 'brimming with prudent, if rather puritanically, socially-aware, self-starting entrepre-neurs. They have been called the "first tribe of true digital natives" or "screen-agers".'[28] Apparently, 'smarter than the Baby Boomers born in the wake of the Second World War' and 'quite distinct from the slackers of Generation X' who are 'stuck in terminal cynicism', they plan 'to change the world for the better'. Interestingly, given that the 'Baby Boomers' were born in the shadow of the Second World War, this group is described as having been 'brought up in the shadow of 9/11'—referring to the terrorist destruction of New York's Twin Towers on 11 September 2001.[29]

While such categorization has some partial value for advertising and sales, its application to the deep emotions of love, loss, and grief will occupy a different territory or emotional formation and has yet to be demonstrated. Still, in cultural terms such designation of generational types is but a natural progression from the way historians have long named eras after patterns of attitudes, and, before them, how biblical scholars schematized various 'dis-pensations' of divine engagement with humanity.[30] Indeed, intellectually, one might almost ponder secularization in terms of the classificatory shift from theological 'dispensationalist' eras to the sociological and cultural-studies proclivity for concepts such as modern, postmodern, late-modern, high-modern, and so on; for the way scholars classify time says much about their world view and religious–ideological convictions.

Whatever one's view, such classification of time and eras merits caution, not least in relation to death, and, for example, Philippe Ariès' extensive historical

---

[26] Valentine (2008: 174).   [27] Possamai (2009: 2).
[28] Sparks and Honey (2014).   [29] Blakely (2014: 29).
[30] Douglas J. Davies (2010: 42, 60). See Newport's (2006: 163) case for Branch Davidian movement.

analysis of European mortality.[31] For it is easy to see in both ancient and modern sources emotional responses to bereavement that closely resemble each other and cut across time in a way that seems to hallmark the family likeness of grief. This could be exemplified from Babylon's Gilgamesh through early Christianity's St Augustine to the texts presented here. Certainly, it is worth noting the caution with which the distinguished intellectual Arnold Hauser when considering the Renaissance approached the issue of individual and individualism; an issue of distinctive importance for both religion and death. He agrees with many that its 'cultural transformation' concerned 'the change that came over the concept of individualism', but he is clear that individualism is 'a phenomenon . . . to which no historical beginning can be attributed' since there have always been 'leading personalities . . . individuals in the truest sense of the word', but he sees in that era one in which some 'deliberately cultivated or sought to cultivate it'.[32]

It is just such carefulness of expression over the scholarly era-defining propensity that merits caution for, as Valentine notes, many apparently characteristic features may be juxtaposed as in a certain 'spirituality that encompassed traditional religion, new age beliefs and supernaturalism'.[33] Similarly, grief-related behaviours can all too easily be interpreted under all-embracing headings, whether of 'attachment and loss' or more recently of 'continuing bonds'—some explanatory subtlety is always commendable and this is certainly evident in Hockey's critical consideration of interviews between researchers and the bereaved. She describes 'situated moments' where, 'in the moment of the one-to-one interview, not only the past but the dead are also present', and in that she sees the 'often unacknowledged intimacies of the research interview'.[34] This is something that would seem to lie beyond Ariès' scope, for here the 'research interview' is less some kind of neutral acquisition of information from an informant or a historical text than it is a creative relationship that involves the dwelt-upon and, in a deep sense, a newly created sense of the dead person who lives again in this remembered form. That research context itself belongs to a wider continuum that embraces widespread human experiences associated with religious behaviours in which a 'situated' sense of otherness arises, as the following four brief examples indicate.

Exemplifying 'Presence'

First, in the most formal context, sacramental forms of the Christian Eucharist—its own form of 'situated moment'—have spoken for millennia of *anamnesis* or memorial in which believers recall and enter into events in the

---

[31] Ariès ([1977] 1981).   [32] Hauser (1965: 33).
[33] Valentine (2008: 172).   [34] Hockey (2002: 214, 219).

life of Christ. It is no psychological accident that the notion of the 'real presence' of Christ has also developed in the context of the eucharistic elements of the sacramental bread and wine, for devotees do speak of a sense of divine presence, a phenomenon reflected biblically in the text that where 'two or three are gathered together in my name there I am in the midst of them'.[35] The sense of a presence other than that of the worshippers is far from strange in contexts of Christian worship, whether reflected in demonstrative emotional behaviours believed to be inspired by the Holy Spirit or in conservative silences of undemonstrative believers. Previous empirical research, for example, showed members of the Church of England describing their experience at the Eucharist as having a 'sense of being at one with God' (87%), and having 'the sense of presence of dead loved ones' (37%). To this sense of an 'other' can be added their 'sense of unity within the self' (74%), and of 'unity with others' (68%). Framing these experiences was 'a realisation of what Jesus did for the believer on the Cross' (85%), itself adding a practical dimension to the formal theological notion of *anamnesis*: in other words, experience paralleled the historical theological formulation.[36] Such phenomena offer one example of how religious experiences along with their interpretation offer suggestive subject matter for sociological study, not least when the living and the dead become 'entangled'.[37]

A second example, quite unlike the well-planned and well-conducted interview programme just mentioned, took an entirely unscripted form in a chance meeting captured in a minuscule cameo of 2011, the year in which many British churches celebrated the 400-year anniversary of the publication of the King James Version of the Bible, often by a kind of relay-reading of the entire text. It so happened that I was at a conference literally next door to a small but ancient city church in Bristol and went in while such a reading was taking place. The peacefully impressive atmosphere amongst the handful of people sitting there was focused on the verses being read; individuals came and went at will, and I happened to leave at just the same time as an elderly gentleman who turned to me in the church porch and in a reserved voice expressed in an entirely unselfconscious way the thought that 'if only we had eyes to see the angels!' His intention was clear: he assumed that I, too, had sensed the invisible heavenly host in attendance. Such apparently idiosyncratic moments are far from uncommon in the ongoing life of major churches, even if they seldom find their way into sociological or even anthropological accounts of 'religion in Britain'.

---

[35] Matthew 18: 20.
[36] Davies, Watkins, and Winter (1991: 260), based on some 489 interviews with parishioners in rural England in 1990 (there were slight numerical differences between men and women on these factors, but they were not statistically significant).
[37] Straight (2006: 101–10).

A third example would take us to practically any spiritualist church where in many towns every week a medium will reckon to link for a moment an erstwhile dead relative with their bereaved survivor. The atmosphere is expectant and excited as a bereaved wife or mother longs to know that things are 'all right' with their dead kin. The sense of there being 'another world' or of there being loved ones on 'the other side' or 'in spirit' all reflects the human capacity for a sense of otherness. That sense reflects a certain 'common-sense' attitude to human experience, one that Jenny Hazelgrove highlights when accounting for spiritualism's appeal, one complemented by the way a séance can mix 'the familiar with the uncanny'.[38]

A fourth and rather different example, not itself formally religious, but also participating in the power of memory is found in the 'Memory of the Flesh' as Katherine Young described the experience, often in older adults, of people who now see in themselves a feature of behaviour, posture, or utterance once so familiar in their now-dead parent.[39] A very similar phenomenon has been identified by Margaret Gibson as 'spectral histories'.[40] All these cases, whether in formal liturgical or personal domestic contexts, bespeak the power of human imagination to enter into sensed relationships with significant 'others'.

In theoretical terms these observations reflect the complex nature of individual life in societies and the occurrence of different levels of cultural engagement that attract distinctive identification. What appears to be the case at the level of international or national life described in terms of industrial, post-industrial, service-focused economies can easily differ from the nature of interaction within communities of diverse origin within a single city, school, workplace, family, or church. And all that complexity itself frames the personal, inter- and intra-personal dynamics of self-awareness and behaviour. This is, precisely what gives the academic disciplines of, for example, anthropology, psychology, sociology, economics, politics, and history their particular lens upon life, even if they do not always engage with death as frequently as they might.

GRIEF: IMPLICIT AND EXPLICIT

The imaginative biblical, medieval, and modern narratives sketched above exemplify their own contexts and forms of conventional wisdom in how societies deploy narrative means of responding to death. It is often tempting to think that 'traditional' societies work in implicit, taken-for-granted ways of coping, while more modern societies are driven by more explicit, medically,

---

[38] Hazelgrove (2000: 21–2). See also Georgina Byrne (2010).
[39] Young (2002: 25–48).   [40] Gibson (2008: 135).

psychologically, or professionally informed approaches. While there is some truth in this, and bearing in mind our earlier caution over categorizing types of social era, it is important for 'modern' or even 'postmodern' people in developed societies to understand that their own medically or psychologically driven theories also become, to some extent, implicit, taken for granted, and 'traditional'. This happened throughout the 1980s and 1990s when Elisabeth Kübler-Ross's work on how people responded to being told that they were terminally ill progressed into a widely held public sense that bereaved people could be understood as having stages of grief through which they needed to pass, viz. denial and isolation, anger, bargaining, depression, and acceptance.[41] The fact that this stance came to attract criticism and was showed to have very little empirical support gained nothing like the public awareness of 'stage-theory' itself.[42] These issues manifest themselves in numerous contexts, as, for example, when modern historian Adrian Gregory's powerful account of the First World War suggests that even the powerful public memorialization of the military dead had 'not led unproblematically to the supposed final stage of mourners in the classic account, which is acceptance'.[43]

Such background factors make it all the wiser to think of contemporary theories of grief as indigenous to particular groups; of being a species of the folk wisdom described in chapter 5, even if they do possess a scientific–medical background. This caution is important because thinking people often face the double task not only of acting in a natural fashion as ordinary members of their society but also of reflecting critically upon their society's normal assumptions. This echoes a key point of chapter 1 concerning the distinction between the taken-for-granted versus the critical attitude towards the customary world of our everyday lives.

Uniqueness of Grief

One contemporary taken-for-granted view that seems to hold the status of an obvious truth amongst many middle-class Britons is the idea that grief is unique to each individual. This, I want to suggest, is a strange idea. Given that society operates on the basis of shared experiences and behaviours, it is worth pondering this voiced sense of uniqueness because it highlights the process by which we both accept social sentiments and subject them to critical analysis. In considering this I fully acknowledge the speculative nature of my discussion, for I suggest that grief-uniqueness is a cipher for groups that prize individuality but rarely experience bereavement. It is a way of framing the deeply moving experiences of one person whose social networks have relatively little

---

[41] Kübler-Ross ([1969] 1989).   [42] Flatt (1987: 143–8); Corr (1993); Parkes (2013).
[43] Gregory (2008: 275).

similar experience. It calls attention to this person's distress, to the plight this one person is undergoing. If, indeed, it does mark inexperience in others it may even provide some basis for excusing their inability to sympathize. Much has been made of the way friends and associates avoid the bereaved or do not know what to say to them. Another frequent expression is that 'no one knows' or that 'no one can understand' what a bereaved person is 'going through'. From one philosophical perspective this is clearly true, in that no one individual is identical to another. One might say, for example, that no one knows what *I* am 'going through' when I have to visit the dentist, or that 'no one understands' what particular joy *I* gain when eating a russet apple. Life-scenes on which most of us could write pages of intimate description lie within this immense territory of human privacy surrounding much of our lives. However, despite or alongside this domain of unique individual experience lies the other world of society in which we live through shared assumptions, values, and the names we give to many aspects of life.

In stressing this social context of grief I do not want to ignore the sense of disturbed inner meaning, or even chaos, that a life-history of relationship, health and sickness, wellbeing or distress, creates in a person now bereaved. The quirks of family history, of individual perception, and of physical–mental constitution all underlie the social constraints and resources activated in bereavement. When, for example, two years before his own death, the great Roman orator Cicero lost his daughter in 45 BC, he 'became inconsolable. He had read many books of comfort for mourners, but they were of no use to him. He would spend all day in a thick wood with nothing but a book for company, but he could not keep the tears in check.'[44] At home he tried writing 'a *Consolation to Himself*, and would go on writing through the night, for he could not get much sleep'. Indeed, writing seemed to be the only thing that could 'take his mind off his grief . . . and so he began his series of philosophical books'. It appears that this experience of grief led Cicero to a form of religious experience grounded in a sense that pure souls, such as that of his daughter, 'went straight to the gods to share in their nature and glory, while the others went into darkness waiting for a reincarnation in another human body'.[45] It is understandable how such a literary and self-reflective person should engage in a literary response to a deeply felt grief, for literature allows deep expressions of self to emerge as a very particular form of engagement with the social world of readers and their response.[46] So, too, with George Herbert, whose sense of human dividedness we encountered in chapter 1 and whose poem on grief not

---

[44] I know of two well-known authors of 'death books' who said to recently bereaved individuals who have also 'studied' death that such learning is of little help at the actual time of grief; but also know students who found their 'death studies' helpful during family bereavement.

[45] Ross (1972: 19–20).

[46] Cf. chapter 2 and the pathos of Marett's introduction to his autobiography amidst the Second World War.

only sought to 'suck up a river to supply mine eyes / My weary weeping eyes, too dry for me', but also doubted the capacity of both music and verse to answer his 'rough sorrows'.[47] A great deal hangs on the manner in which such private and public elements of life influence individual identity and the manner in which people relate to each other socially. Certainly, social class and the assumptions and resources groups bring to bereavement and grief are foundationally important and are revealed as much in literary forms as in empirical studies, though there is relatively little current research evidence of the latter.

Coding Grief

One entry point for considering death and social class in Britain is that of Basil Bernstein's dated, much debated, and yet enduringly valuable theory of linguistic coding.[48] Communities operating on what he terms a 'restricted code' base will assume that we do share a sense of what grief is, and can engage with each other accordingly. By contrast, those operating on the 'elaborate code' base espouse ideas of individual difference, will favour grief-uniqueness, and are likely to constitute that minority in Britain today who wish for a more hands-on approach to funerals in order to accentuate the individuality of the deceased and of their relationship with them. What is significant is that many speaking publicly or engaged in bereavement support may well be over-represented by this elaborate code type.

From a more philosophical–literary direction, Roland Barthes addressed much the same issue in his distinction between 'classical' and 'modern' forms of language: the former marking relations between things in 'a superficial chain of intentions', and the latter 'an explosion of words . . . devoid of background'.[49] Finch described these distinctions as, respectively, 'horizontal' and 'vertical' forms of language, depicting a distinction between the networked relatedness of people on one hand and the isolated individual in verbal display on the other.[50] This faithfully reflects Barthes' depiction of an 'explosion' of words in writers whose joy lies in word-play and whose linguistic juggling and sub-textuality, at least from a sociological perspective, highlights their individuality as a polar type of Bernstein's elaborate code user; in intellectual terms they can be described as seeing themselves as part of postmodern thinking and living.

---

[47] Herbert (1994: 144).

[48] Bernstein (1971) as an educational sociologist significantly influenced anthropologist Mary Douglas and her work on social control and forms of bodily behaviour.

[49] Barthes (1967: 44–6).　　[50] Finch (1993: 15–17).

One empirical example that suggests how socio-economic groups who probably would reflect the elaborated–restricted code spectrum differ can be drawn from my own research on people's choice in where they would prefer their cremated remains to be placed. These data, drawn from interviews with 1,603 individuals, reflect Britain in the mid 1990s, revealed that the higher the occupational group, the greater the desire to have their future cremated remains located in a place of personal significance. The linear relation showed socio-economic or employment groups AB (26%), C1 (20%), C2 (15%), DE (12%).[51] Similarly, when asked about the issue of their family using a grave that had once been occupied by another family, for that research project was focused on the 'reuse of old graves', it was found that employment groups AB had a 69% support for reuse, compared with C1 at 59%, C2 at 53%, and DE at 50%.[52]

Presence and Grief

The multi-disciplined underpinning of studies of death evident in a small way in the literary as well as empirical material in this chapter so far reflects something of the growth in discipline-specific studies of grief and death, from palliative and end-of-life care of a nursing or psychiatric kind, through to archaeological, historical, and literary endeavours, as well as in social-scientific pursuits. As a further example of this I again take up the notion of 'presence' to depict a distinctive form of interplay between social force and individual identity already mentioned in the Introduction and chapter 1. It is a concept analogous to a more sociological–phenomenological depiction captured in the motif of the 'life-world'.[53] Here 'presence' and 'sense of presence' describe an approach to human identity within a challenging environment.[54] It is a topic related to the 'self', its emergence, and development amidst potential hazards; and in chapter 8 it will reappear when discussing the notion of 'dignity'. We should also emphasize that, here, 'presence' does not refer to the sense of the presence of the dead, though as I will indicate, it cannot be entirely separated from that given the interrelational nature of human identity.

Primarily speaking, then, I am approaching the notion through de Martino's engagement with a 'sense of presence', referring to a personal awareness of our 'being-here', and of the 'regulating function of the "being-here"'.[55] This form of discourse is extremely useful for reflecting upon the complex issue of

---

[51] Davies and Shaw (1995: 72).   [52] Davies and Shaw (1995: 57).

[53] Schutz (Natanson, 1973), developed the notion of the life-world (German—*lebenswelt*) from Husserl's more philosophical foundation of phenomenology.

[54] De Martino ([1972] 1988: 147). 'Presence' is 'the united being-within-the-world of the person'. White ([1972] 1988).

[55] De Martino ([1972] 1988: 76, 86).

'my death', given his assumption that 'the presence cannot accept death'.[56] This non-acceptance is grounded in the dynamics of 'being-here', and of all that generates and sustains this distinctive human sense. But, with bereavement, we face the apparently obvious fact that some other 'self' is no longer in a state of 'being-here'. This is where the notion of 'presence' becomes valuable as a means of discussing grief at the death of another in and through the issues of the dynamics of identity as something open to 'risk and redemption'.[57] In doing this I take what de Martino says largely about shamanic initiation and apply it to grief, for both initiation and bereavement have to do with self-survival and self-transformations at 'critical moments of the "being-here"' that include loneliness and fatigue. The very words we use to discuss grief become significant here, and highlight de Martino's concern to make us aware of our taken-for-granted 'socio-cultural attitude', and of our *preference* for' certain world views.[58] So, for example, to speak of an 'experience' of grief rather than a 'sense of grief' is, itself, subtly telling; to 'experience' grief distances the person from 'grief' slightly more than does a 'sense' of grief. The distinction is, doubtless, slight and nuanced but remains important, especially if one wants to think of grief less as a medicalized and more as a natural human 'condition'.

Here we see grief, whether profound or slight, in terms of contexts when and where a crisis frames our sense of presence. The profounder pole may often involve a 'disintegrating' sense of 'being-here', when we are 'incomplete' and only 'vaguely here', such a person being 'divided interiorly between himself and the spirits that have not yet been mastered', all as 'the disintegrating "being-here" tends to form itself into a new equilibrium'.[59] De Martino's use of language of rebirth, physical transformation, and a new sense of presence that has emerged through the hardships of initiation may, at first sight, seem far removed from modern life, bereavement, and grief, but further consideration shows it to depict a dynamic self aimed not simply at surviving life's hardships but at being transformed in the process. In chapter 1 we spoke of the religion–spirituality/ideology continuum as an emotional–rational meaning-making process that undergoes times of cultural intensification dispersed amongst periods of ordinariness and low arousal. Here we see how 'grief' is just such an event in which our 'being-here' may be shaken in a crisis of presence generating issues of whether life is worthwhile, or whether anything really means anything at all.[60] While de Martino speaks of shamanic initiation and its 'restoration of presence' as proceeding 'in stages', I am cautious of the 'stage' element given the overly concrete application of 'stage' theories' in popular use. What do need accentuation are the 'existential drama'

---

[56] De Martino ([1972] 1988: 75).   [57] De Martino ([1972] 1988: 92).
[58] De Martino ([1972] 1988: 45, original emphasis).   [59] De Martino ([1972] 1988: 93).
[60] Toulis (1997). This study of migrant Jamaican women in Britain is a good example; their disturbed sense of 'presence' being accommodated through Pentecostal religion.

assailing a person's sense of presence and ways of engaging with it that may enhance the sense of presence—of 'being-here'.[61]

A good example, one that adds to the literary cases used above as narrative framing issues of identity and death, occurs in an American novel of the early 1960s concerning one J. T. Malone, an elderly pharmacist in small-town, southern-state USA. 'Death is always the same, but each man dies in his own way'—so begins the account of Malone's response to the unexpected news that he has terminal leukaemia.[62] He now begins to see things in a different way to how he did before hearing the diagnosis.

> The lamp post, the wall, the tree would exist when he was dead and the thought was loathsome to Malone. There was a further confusion—he was unable to acknowledge the reality of approaching death, and the conflict led to a sense of ubiquitous unreality. Sometimes and dimly, Malone felt he blundered among a world of incongruities in which there was no order or conceivable design.[63]

Malone seeks 'comfort in the church'. Indeed, when tormented by the unreality of both death and life, it helped him to know that the First Baptist Church was 'real enough'. After all, many local pillars of society were devoted members and, surely, such influential people, rich from commercial, political, legal, and real-estate businesses, could hardly be wrong about the church-taught views on the afterlife. Still, even after a sermon on salvation by their well-qualified minister, 'death remained a mystery, and after the first elation he felt a little cheated when he left the church'. He comes to wonder at the 'alien emotions' he now comes to feel over certain people, even making him 'cold with loathing and hatred'. He appreciates that being 'split by love and hatred' was due to 'a terror that choked him'; a terror not lying in the fact he was to die but in 'some mysterious drama that was going on—although what the drama was about Malone did not know'. The author, however, lets us in on its nature: 'He was a man watching a clock without hands.'[64] This incisive cameo of experience reveals its own grasp of human life at times of crisis, portraying that 'mysterious drama' going on around fictional pharmacist Malone, a drama whose theme was unknown to him and yet induced his own crisis of presence. Induced by the diagnosis of terminal illness this 'crisis of presence' marks its own form of what, later, would be designated as 'anticipatory grief'.[65] It similarly predates Kübler-Ross's stages of grief, a pattern widely accepted by the public and yet much subject to criticism by influential professionals.[66]

---

[61] De Martino ([1972] 1988: 95, 153).   [62] McCullers ([1961] 1965: 7).
[63] McCullers ([1961] 1965: 14–15).   [64] McCullers ([1961] 1965: 27).
[65] See Singh (2009: 538–42) for types of grief.
[66] E.g. Cleiren (1991: 22–37) and Parkes (2013).

Wayfaring

Yet another way of approaching self-identity and grief can be developed from Tim Ingold's anthropological notion of 'wayfaring', offered as an 'integrated, practical understanding of the life world', and which has strong connections with de Martino's approach and with the phenomenology of the life-world that has influenced sociology for some time.[67] This mode of analysis creates a theoretical scheme out of what numerous mythical and theological traditions have long exemplified in their pondering of life as a journey.[68] Ingold comes up with the neologism 'alongly' to describe how we acquire knowledge as we move along in the world, this helps him think of life experience as accumulated in and through the 'meshworked' events that constitute our life experience as a 'knot of stories'.[69] This could find resonance in other thinkers, as, for example, in Dan Sperber's discussion of symbolic thought as the ongoing acquisition of a type of knowledge that influences previous experience just as it is influenced by that previous 'symbolic' knowledge. Indeed, Sperber distinguished between symbolic knowledge that is thus 'acquired' from the more formal encyclopaedic knowledge of 'facts' that is formally 'learned'.[70]

Still, Ingold is valuable for his stress upon this dynamic idiom of wayfaring because it brings out the transitional aspect of grief and bereavement amongst individuals, families, friends, and others. For these the dying of others and its consequences in their own grief occur 'alongly', meshworked with the grief of some but not with others. Underlying Ingold's analysis of knowledge and the life-world is a desire to clarify the problematic fact that some people—and he sees this as typically occurring in much scientific classification of the world— tend to take ideas from daily events and systematize them in abstract classifications of things and, in that process, do some injustice to the complexity of life as lived. While we can see the value of such a process for scientific and other theoretical work it is always wise to appreciate that this is a formal process that transforms 'knowledge'.

The relevance of this for grief is obvious in that it not only warns us against the abstraction of 'knowledge' of grief in such things as stage theories, or any other 'theory' of grief for that matter, but also encourages us to see 'the epitome of alongly integrated knowledge' in 'the story'.[71] In other words it makes a positive issue both of post-bereavement's ongoing way of life and of the life that preceded it. His inclusion of 'the story' within life-interpretation complements what has already been said about narrative. Within each society this can also mean that personal narratives can be influenced by available

---

[67] Husserl, Schutz, Berger, etc.   [68] E.g. Chaucer (1951).   [69] Ingold (2011: 154).
[70] Sperber (1975: 88).   [71] Ingold (2011: 160).

cultural narratives whose enduring existence depends upon them having proved valuable to bereaved people in the past.

Dreams, Graves, and Presence

Cultural narratives do not, however, always exist as such, especially during periods of cultural change. Contemporary Britain, for example, is not overly filled with public accounts of the dead and their kin, which is one reason why accounts of terminal illness, dying, death, and funerals of celebrities provide their own medium of death narrative, as we see in the following chapter for several high-profile individuals.

The need for such media narrative of death may, perhaps, be illustrated by empirical research depicting the dynamic but relatively silent and publicly unnoticed relationships that people have with their dead. This will exemplify the emotional complexity of individual identity and power of memory in recreating the dead as 'living' agents, whether in dreams or in a sense of the deceased's presence when awake. One major UK-based empirical research project of the 1990s, already cited above, and which I conducted with Alister Shaw, found approximately 35% of a national sample of over 1,600 individuals reporting a sense of the presence of the dead. Of this group of 554 individuals approximately 9% reckoned to have the experience often, and 14% occasionally, while 6% said it happened 'rarely', and 7% just once. As for the relationship to the 'presence', this took the pattern of the presence as parent (15.4%), grandparent (10.3%), spouse (5%), sibling (2.2%), friend (1.7%), child (1.1%), other kin (3.6%), and other non-kin (0.7%). In terms of location of the experience, the majority said it was in their own house (46%) or at a relative or friend's house (9%). Small numbers reported the sensed presence at spiritualist meetings (2%), at graveside (1.7%), and for some eight individuals (1.4%) while driving their car.[72] As for this kind of sensed presence only 4% of this sample said that it had taken place in a dream, but the question had not been about dreams of the dead but asked 'have you ever felt a sense of the presence of someone you know after they have died?'[73]

In that survey, one of the most extensive of its kind in Great Britain, it is worth noting that while under 2% reckoned to have had a sense of the presence of the dead at the graveside we know that, for example, as far as partners were concerned a majority of the total sample, approximately 52%, visited a grave every six months; another 22% visited once a year or less often, with some 25% reckoning never to visit. As for visiting parents' graves, we found approximately 25% visiting every six months, another 30% visiting once

---

[72] Davies and Shaw (1995: 96–8).   [73] Davies and Shaw (1995: 123).

a year or less often, and some 44% reckoning never to visit. Finally, regarding visiting grandparents' graves, some 70% never visited them, with approximately 10% visiting once a year.[74]

This suggests that many grave visits, whatever takes place at them in terms of tidying graves and speaking to the dead, did not result in the more direct sensed presence. What is more, this notion of feeling a sense of presence did seem to make real sense to those interviewed because, in addition to the 'positive' responses mentioned above, a clear 63% of the total sample of 1,603 said they had not had such an experience; only twenty-three individuals said they did not know if they had gained such an experience or not, and only three individuals did not answer the question.[75] It would seem that experiencing the presence of the dead is a notion possessing some cultural clarity in the UK, with people not being in doubt over their own position in regard to it, even if it is a topic not widely discussed as such.

Mutual support groups

The lack of widespread discussion of death is problematic for some who are left with unfinished narratives but no attentive listener. One response to this has been in the growth of mutual support groups in relatively open society—where family contexts may be absent or unfriendly to grief, the role of mutual support groups certainly comes to be of considerable value, not least in terms of health and wellbeing. The relationship between grief and health is a significant element within health regimes, even in, or perhaps especially in, societies where adults may not lose their parents until these adult children are over fifty years of age. What is more, bereavement extends itself beyond the familiar 'widowhood or bereavement effect' to other kinship links with Cleiren, for example, showing how sisters can easily become one forgotten group when other members of a family seem to attract primary attention as the key bereaved people.[76] Though his work was in Holland, it is unlikely to be different in the UK. Similarly, some Swedish research has explored the consequences of parental death on various age groups of surviving adult children, not ignoring the gender of the deceased parent and surviving 'child'. These are areas of great complexity because of the many social, psychological, and pre-existing health factors affecting bereaved individuals that must be taken into account. But their complexity ought not to marginalize these issues, especially when, in this national case, the evidence suggests that, for example, 'men who have lost their mothers appear to be particularly vulnerable'. Even so, the death of an aged parent may also 'bring relief from worries and release the

---

[74] Davies and Shaw (1995: 77).   [75] Davies and Shaw (1995: 96).
[76] Cleiren (1991).

adult offspring from other burdens, such as the provision of informal care'.[77]
The existence of support groups in which others sympathize is one example of
adaptation to bereavement in complex societies and reveals the capacity of
people to create a supportive domain within the wider field of social force, one
in which themes of 'presence', sense of self, and existential dramas in contexts
of grief are not deemed strange.

Speculative possibilities: mirror neurons and androids

As we have seen, psychiatrists, medical practitioners, clergy, and grief coun-
sellors have developed and espoused theories of grief encompassing such
experience but it should be said that further light may yet be thrown on
grief by more recent cognitive-science studies including work on 'mirror
neurons' and android robotics. I mention these in a speculative and exploratory fashion and almost as an interdisciplinary interlude in this chapter
because a great deal of further research needs to be conducted on grief in
these areas to ensure that grief theories do not remain too cabined and
confined. Moreover, it is work that could enhance the sociology of religion
by understanding the way death relates to the embodiment of those cultural
values that are often framed as sacred.

'Mirror neurons', for example, were discovered by Giacomo Rizzolatti and
his colleagues only in the 1990s and concern neural networks activated in such
a way that when one person sees another person in a particular state or
engaged in a particular kind of behaviour the first person gains a sense of
experiencing what the second person is doing.[78] It is as though to watch
another person play tennis is to be aroused in such a way as to sense oneself
as also playing. Malcolm Jeeves cites the distinguished scientist V. S. Rama-
chandran's prediction that 'mirror neurons will do for psychology what DNA
did for biology: they will provide a unifying framework and help explain a host
of mental abilities that have hitherto remained mysterious and inaccessible to
experiment'. That was reported for the year 2000, and included Ramachan-
dran's comment that he regarded Rizzolatti's 'discovery as the most important
unreported story of the last decade'.[79] Exactly what this means for grief
remains to be seen in terms of empirical experiment, though, even at this
stage, it would seem reasonable to think that such a system underlies the
sense of sympathy evoked by seeing a person distressed by bereavement.
Some have already identified this possibility in the context of literature, as in

---

[77] Rostila and Saarela (2011: 236–49). 'Already after a few years, their death rates
exceed that of same-aged men with living mothers, and after 5 years, they have a mortality
rate that is approximately 18% greater than that of men in the comparison group' (p. 233).

[78] Giacomo Rizzolatti et al. (1996), cited in Malcolm Jeeves (2011: 199, n. 55).

[79] Jeeves (2011: 199).

Shakespeare's *King Lear*. This perspective hints at a deep level of human mutuality of reaction to loss in a way that demands a revaluation of the nature of learned cultural response to a social context of bereavement. Even if someone adopted a strong culturally learned stance on mourning behaviour the role of mental mirroring could still play a significant part in mutual response.

But there is another aspect of mirror neurons that merits some consideration; that occurs when one is looking at a dead person. The question that arises here as far as mirror neurons are concerned is 'how might they operate?' If mirror-neuronal activity involves a dynamic system of 'imagining' and, in a sense, actually 'performing' in one's own mind a behaviour witnessed in somebody else, how might this work with a dead person? Might this not be the mental basis for the often-repeated philosophical dictum that we cannot imagine ourselves as dead, that proposition being based on the assumption that the imagination is, by definition, a living process? Perhaps there is a form of dissonance experienced by the process of neural-mirroring when a situation—an encounter with a corpse—is not capable of being 'mirrored': an experience of non-reflection. Such a speculation may be partly substantiated by another line of research allied with the technological development of androids.

Androids, as human-like robots, offer a distinctive avenue of research that bears on the human experience of death, given that some robotics workers have observed their own human reactions to these objects under particular situations, not least contexts in which normal robotic functioning ceases. These observations can be said to have stemmed from a sense of the uncanny, which was developed in the notion of the 'uncanny valley' by Masahiro Mori in 1970 when it was argued that human-like robots that possessed something that detracted from looking human engendered an unease in people that amounted to an eeriness, taking the situation into an 'uncanny valley'.[80] This notion of the uncanny echoes something of the concern already alluded to in chapter 1 but which now can be taken up again in direct alignment with grief and which sees the uncanny as possessing roots in our human awareness of our environment, not least environments of mortality.[81] Mori has suggested that 'when we die, we fall into the trough of the uncanny valley. Our body becomes cold, our colour changes, and movement ceases.' His suggestion is that the 'still valley of the corpse' may be something that is a necessity within

---

[80] In Spring 2014 Durham University hosted an exhibition of robots including one non-functioning human-like robot 'lying down' in a glass case. This I did find 'odd' in something of the 'uncanny valley' sense, but being already familiar with the topic found myself in something of a double-take situation.

[81] Otto ([1917] 1924: 133) aligns a type of 'shuddering' when in an empty house. Cf. Hazelgrove (2000: 22) for the 'uncanny' in spiritualist séances.

human response, albeit something awaiting future study.[82] MacDorman and Ishiguro's subsequent research explores the idea that 'an uncanny robot elicits an innate fear of death and culturally supported defences for coping with death's inevitability'. They see human-looking robots as a valuable means of exploring 'heightened sensitivity to any deviations from human looks', which is what a corpse presents, especially when it is recalled that stillness is problematic for humans given that 'it is nearly impossible for a human actor to hold a static pose', since 'human bodies are constantly moving, however slightly', and because 'the normal functioning of our visual system depends on this movement'.[83] Their deployment of other ideas on trauma research and people's responses to death-related cues brings them to the decision that 'the eerie sensation identified with the uncanny valley may be characterized as affective, although it seems difficult to identify it with one or more primary emotions like disgust.'[84] While the 'affective' or emotional dimension is obvious, it might be useful for them to extend their range of reference from that of psychological testing to embrace some of the traditional philosophical–theological debate on awe represented in our previous chapter's concern with Otto and Heiler. Certainly, the relevance of android-focused emotion is significant given the question of 'reality' posed by science-fiction literature and film.[85]

CELEBRITY–ESTABLISHMENT: DIANA, PRINCESS OF WALES

From androids as models for potentially expanding our sociological and psychological understanding of grief, we move to the historical case of the death of Diana, Princess of Wales in 1997; to a person whose face and life millions in Britain and elsewhere felt they knew almost personally—a know-ledge that merits some caution. For, while it would be easy to criticize their sensed familiarity as misplaced fandom (though some element of that prob-ably existed for many), there remains a type of knowing grounded in an affinity rooted in such shared experiences as personal betrayal, family loyalties, disruptions and personal affairs, and concerns over self-image and fashion, as well as sympathy for suffering children through wars or for adults suffering from AIDS or other conditions, or whose sexuality might be critically judged by some conservative members of society. In a media-fuelled age of celebrity

[82] Mori (1970) cited in MacDorman and Ishiguro (2006: 312).
[83] MacDorman and Ishiguro (2006: 313–14).
[84] MacDorman and Ishiguro (2006: 336).
[85] E.g. the film 'I, Robot' directed by Alex Proya.

and glamour there would also be some ordinary members of the public who wished they were like one who possessed such attributes. In anthropologist Claude Lévi-Strauss's famous aphorism, Diana was 'good to think', presenting an image that could somehow capture the way a person felt about themselves.[86] In what are complex processes, probably involving the mirroring behaviour described above as well as that of 'projection' that psychologists and philosophers have been discussing for centuries, human beings 'see' themselves in others, aligning themselves with a public figure who speaks of things they feel themselves, as has often been the case with the religious followers of a charismatic leader. In all these ways this princess was a potential empathy-bond for the emotional identities of millions, for whom her death was far from a neutral experience. Similarly, thousands who had no such affinity often expressed amazed wonderment at best, and cynicism at worst, over all these people crying, lighting candles, and depositing flowers in public. Whichever was the case this event was important in British cultural history in terms of religion, death, media-related aspects of grief, and the themes of celebrity and the British Establishment. In approaching its complexity we first pinpoint some key media moments on the death before approaching it in a broader interpretative fashion.

Media-wise, the dramatic nature of this totally unexpected death on 31 August 1997, followed by a set of paradigmatic scenes surrounding the Princess's funeral cortege to, the funeral service at, and her departure from Westminster Abbey, was such as to exceed any that might have been scripted for a British version of a Hollywood blockbuster movie. All was conducted before cameras that took it to billions across the world—to more than had viewed any formal cinema-set film. Here were 'seven days that shook our nation' as the very popular *Daily Mail* newspaper put it as part of its 112-page tribute that covered practically all parts of Diana's earlier life and royal relationships and conflicts, and her extensive charitable endeavours.[87] Other newspapers and media did the same, with extensive reports complemented by vignettes revealing much of British cultural life at the intersection point of individual and society. On the day of the funeral service, for example, 'pregnant Lisa Downey, 29, gave cups of tea and chocolate bars to mourners camping at Westminster Abbey . . . . she said she did it because Diana helped her brother when he was dying of AIDS three years ago'. The Great Western train the *Red Cross*, that had been named by Diana, 'remained on Platform one at Paddington Station' to allow some 490 passengers somewhere to sleep for the night. Again, as part of the *Daily Mail* coverage, details were given on how to 'make your own symbol of sympathy', since 'no one is manufacturing black ribbons'.[88] Or, again, the Vicar of St Mary Abbot's, a high-visibility church in

---

[86] Lévi-Strauss (1962: 89).   [87] *Daily Mail* (1997) Saturday, 6 September.
[88] *Daily Mail* (1997) Saturday, 6 September, p. 33.

London's Kensington and technically Diana's parish church, was astonished at hearing of her death on radio on the Sunday morning. From first thinking it might have been a hoax, he soon found himself at his early morning church service where the clergy decided to wear black vestments 'appropriate for a requiem mass' and afterwards set up a 'special black candle near the altar which has become a focal point for constant devotion'. The following Friday they held a memorial Mass with over a thousand attending and many turned away. The vicar also tells of 'a mysterious looking lady dressed all in black, wearing a long black scarf over her head' who paid him a cheque to say a 'special Mass for the soul of Princess Diana'. She gave him a cheque, thanked him, and left. She said that 'the Princess had been her "saviour"' but without elaborating.[89] Of the many other episodes that could be given, one from experienced broadcaster Martyn Lewis will suffice. He tells of being awakened at home around 4 a.m. when it looked as though the Princess was, indeed, dead. His daughters had tears in their eyes, and when taking his BBC car for the studio he could see the driver's hands 'shaking on the wheel'. Lewis was then on air until 1 p.m., with the two major BBC channels uniting for this work. When he finally went home, having already been broadcasting some fifteen hours the previous day, he tells how he 'finally let out all the feelings I'd been bottling up. I fell into my wife Liz's arms and cried.' He had been vice-president of Help the Hospices, of which Diana was president, and had meet her several times. He spoke of 'two Princesses', one seen in an 'air of sadness about her', her other in 'that wonderful smile': 'it was as if there were two Princesses. I'll miss them both.'[90]

These scenes speak of strong feelings evoked by one woman's death and of emotions now pervading ideas of relationship, love, betrayal, royalty, monarchy, and stardom and celebrity. They also highlight the family bonds of grandparents, divorced parents, and children. Powerful elective affinities were at work and continued on the day of the funeral, prompting massed ritual action of millions of people both at the local level in signing memorial books, and at the national and world levels through the multi-media of television, press, and the emergent online world.

The social structure making all this possible was provided by the Establishment of government, military, police, and church, all framed—once more—by the media. It could all have been a blockbuster movie, but it was social fact pervaded by social shock. Seldom, if ever, had a news event come as such a jolt to a world population as well as to media journalists; it deeply influenced the tone and the visual presentation of news announcers and commentators throughout the first day and some following days of this 'story'. Moreover, these events seemed to be less media-led than media-followed in 'real' time, or

---

[89] Gelli (1997: 26). Such payment for masses is neither usual nor normal, then or now.
[90] Martyn Lewis (1997: 26).

at least in that peculiar sense of emotionally distanced time that often frames bereavement. Still, this was the all-too-real world of time and place where the tolling of Westminster Abbey's muffled bells fell once per minute and where the military precision of the cortege to the Abbey—already practised the night before—took one hour and forty-seven minutes.[91] Such detail reflected the cultural value of military ritual that would pass seamlessly into the liturgical world of the Anglican funeral in which tradition was negotiated with innovation, creating new possibilities and models for future attitudes to death and funerals.

The news story became a media narrative put together on air as news broke and new information emerged. It came, unscripted, 'out of the night' in a quite literal sense and told of the already world-famous and divorced Princess being in Paris with Dodi Al-Fayed, the rich son of the owner of London's famed Harrod's department store. They appeared to be in a serious mutual relationship and he was a Muslim. Together they died in a car crash in a tunnel while, apparently, fleeing a pack of news reporters whose immediate status attracted highly charged negative judgement—the very name, *paparazzi,* became strongly negative. Here was a dramatic media event in which the media are portrayed as influencing if not causing the car crash while seeking a story, and while now having to report a different one. Never had grief, media, and social emotions been so intimately combined. Following the dawning reality, Prince Charles, Diana's erstwhile husband, goes to meet the body and it is returned to England by Royal Air Force plane with all appropriate military support in place. World television is practically taken over by these scenes.

At the time, a kind of historical amnesia combined with the distinctive cultural shock amongst many media commentators who presented the popular response as unique. This it was not, as the account of the *Titanic* memorial in the next chapter will show, but, of course, it was unique within their life experience.[92] There was further novelty in the immediacy of television and its worldwide linkage in an age of celebrity. Here, the disclosure and concealment theme (already raised in chapters 2 and 3) was now appearing alongside conspiracy theories surrounding her death.[93] The image of paparazzi photographers actually giving chase to the Princess and her potential fiancé highlights issues of privacy and publicity, a pairing that reflects the concealment–disclosure motifs aligned with death at large.

From hearing of her death early on a Sunday morning there followed a week of intensive media engagement that brought entire sets of core cultural

---

[91] Alan Hamilton (1997: 3) gives detailed notes, e.g. 'At 10.26 the gun carriage will be joined by 533 representatives of some of the Princess's favourite charities'.
[92] See Wolffe (1999 and 2000) for historical accounts of famous deaths and popular responses.
[93] Qualtrough and Brown (1997).

values into play with traditional religion and diverse forms of spirituality, dynamically interacting with celebrity, monarchy, domesticity, and freedom of the press; with charities, health, wellbeing, and death. The widespread British notion of giving the dead a 'good send-off' was, ironically, turned on its head in giving Diana's corpse a poor welcome-back, at least at the very outset. For her body was brought home to Britain by her former husband, Charles, Prince of Wales, who had previously left her. As for the Queen, then in Scotland, she was deemed by the media to be slow in responding to the death and coming to London. When finally returning she walked amongst the people in a relatively informal fashion and shared in what was becoming an extensive national period of *communitas*; of shared emotional bonding under adversity with flowers carrying much of the symbolic weight of feeling. Flags as symbol carriers also became focal points, and through popular pressure the Royal Standard, which normally only flies over Buckingham Palace when the Queen is in residence, was raised on her return but was, uniquely, replaced by the Union Flag—and that flown at half mast—when she left for the funeral at Westminster Abbey. Here our concern with social force and the way it often moves from the Establishment, not least from royalty, to the people was, if anything, reversed. And here 'force' has to be allied not only with 'emotion' but with explicit reference to emotion as an expression of the will of the people. The more conservative newspaper, the *Daily Telegraph*, ran the head-line 'Queen bows to her people: Address to nation and Palace Flag to fly at half-mast'.[94] Another journalist expressed the social force well in his headline, 'It isn't what you see, it's what you feel'. He wrote of 'a united nations of people' at Kensington Palace, where bunches of flowers were arriving at the rate of 100 bunches a minute, and where people were 'united by sorrow'.[95]

At the Abbey service her brother, the ninth earl Spencer, spoke movingly of her life, concerns, and of her boys. At one point he seemingly speaks 'to' her in the second person singular—you—thus initiating or at least validating a new cultural trend in Protestant and secular-Protestant Britain of engaging with the dead at their funeral in a novel way. He speaks boldly and many see him as distancing his family and sister, and to a degree his nephews, from the Royal Family as such: and all this in the presence of the Queen herself, with the Royal Family playing no speaking part in the event. His address was applauded, reflecting the use of applause in celebrity events at large and marking the need of massed people to employ such methods as they can to respond. And celebrity there was, not least the celebrity of the entertainment world, focused in the very person of a knighted pop star, Sir Elton John, singing a revised version of the song 'Candle in the Wind', playing his own shipped-in grand piano in

---

[94] Hardman (1997: 1). Extensive comment on 'criticism that has caused profound distress to the Royal Family' regarding 'disrespect to the Princess'.
[95] Edwards (1997: 33).

Westminster Abbey. *The Times* newspaper had an internal headline: 'Service will blend liturgy with pop'.[96] The Establishment, headed by monarchy and aristocracy, conjoined celebrity stardom on a liturgical–ceremonial stage of ritualizing Anglicanism.

Following what was, to all practical intents and purposes, though not 'officially', a state funeral, soldier pall-bearers placed the coffin in a hearse, one not unlike the hearses used by all families in the land, which then drove slowly away, being increasingly covered with flowers thrown by crowd members. In what were frequently described as 'outpourings of grief' thousands of individuals showed signs of grief in tears, mutual support, and applause. Indeed, applause as ritual interspersed much of the day. The *communitas* element framed the hearse bearing her body away from the Abbey in quite a different way from the gun-carriage which had brought it there; the hearse was followed by some male members of the Royal Family, including the boy princes, their father, and grandfather. The hearse finally left for an entirely private ceremony when the Princess was buried in a grave on a small island in a lake on her brother's family estate at Althorp. It was widely thought that she was not buried in the local parish church of St Mary the Virgin, alongside generations of her ancestors, lest the church become overwhelmed by visitors.

Behind this entire episode in national history lies an apparently romantic union of a prince and a beautiful young woman in a televised religious marriage ceremony of traditional form at Westminster Abbey, conducted by the Archbishop of Canterbury, which brought the nation and many millions across the world to an entire viewing 'experience' in July 1981. The material culture of commemorative mementos of Prince Charles and Princess Diana's wedding had flooded London and beyond. There followed the birth of two royal princes, with apparent intrigues within the Royal Family concerning Diana and gossip of affairs by both partners, finally resulting in a divorce in August 1996, a year before her accidental death. Meanwhile, Diana had gained additional fame in charitable ventures both in terms of the AIDS epidemic of the 1980s and of casualties of scatter-bombs used in conflict zones. In other words, the sick, dying, and injured—all rooted in core cultural values of care; the same essential values as those of the NHS—gained alliance from the Princess who, in some ways, came to embody them. Illness and death played an enormously important role in this, with the role of care and concern rising in significance and symbolized in the Princess meeting and touching AIDS patients. The embodiment of care generated a highly potent symbol of national concern at large as AIDS emerged as a fearful danger. But she had also become a celebrity on the world stage as one known to and having met large numbers of 'stars', including John Travolta, Liza Minnelli, Michael Jackson,

---

[96] Hamilton and Webster (1997: 2).

Paul McCartney, Roger Moore, Richard Attenborough, Luciano Pavarotti, and, of course Elton John. All of these meetings were reproduced as photographic memorials after her death, including one in which she sits next to and comforts Elton John at the memorial service for none other than Gianni Versace, the world-famous clothes designer who was, himself, shot dead in July 1997 in the USA.[97]

Vitality and Mortality

This extensive series of events in the life of Charles and Diana affords a narrative open to many interpretations. The events exemplify aspects of the British Establishment at work as well as the complex dynamics of social force that, in terms of social hierarchy and class, can work bottom up as well as top down given appropriate circumstance. In these, and many other aspects of these events, we also see the double relationship of hidden and disclosed issues, not least in the flow of events just described from Diana's death in a road tunnel in Paris (reckoned to have involved photo-journalists in pursuit of the Princess's car), through a post-mortem, high-profile funeral processions and Abbey Service, through to an extremely private burial on an island. In terms of social symbolism, the themes of publicity and secrecy, of revelation and disclosure, which have periodically surfaced in this volume, are very obvious, and they all pivot on dynamic themes of vitality and mortality.

In definitional terms, it is practically impossible to divide between traditional Christianity and spiritualities of cherished values embodied in Diana as one now dead. What is radically significant, and it pinpoints a key theme of this volume, is that one known to be full of life, embodying notions of vitality in a complex way by bringing together establishment and celebrity powers, motherhood, and care for those whose sickness, notably in AIDS, was dead. In other words, she confronted mortality in and through her vitality and, we might argue, through her death provided a form of rebounding conquest of the tragedy of her death in her two sons, the royal princes, who participated in her mortality through their private grief but also in their very public long walk behind her coffin at the funeral. Then, in due course, and having become men, they now engage in very life-affirming activities, both in the military and, for example in the marriage of Prince William and Kate Middleton on 29 April 2011. Once again we are in Westminster Abbey in full panoply of the Church of England and with the Prince and his brother in military dress uniform. The

---

[97] *Daily Mail*, Saturday 6 September 1997: xxvi–xxvii.

couple leave the Abbey which, this time, has no half-muffled bells, but all are in full voice, pealing for three hours.

Such is the nature of ritual in the UK, where it is sometimes necessary not to see the end of a ritual event such as the monumental funeral of Princess Diana as an end in itself but as part of a ritual series in which the dynamics of social force extend over time. In this we also see the cultural effect of death and life as new generations take a society forward. What is more, such events are hard to quantify in terms of traditional religion and secularization. The hearse, as it drove from universal publicity to familial privacy, expressed the ritual–symbolic shift from disclosure to concealment in the most dramatic form, reflecting the wider public–private experience of death, bereavement, and memorialization in Britain.

The social stage of this funeral had as a backdrop cultural stage-sets of music, film, and sport stars that from the 1960s increasingly existed in an unusual tension with the celebrity of royalty. In Great Britain, rather unlike the USA, these domains had to contend with the influential constraints of social class and what we have been discussing in earlier chapters as the Establishment. Indeed, over time it has been interesting to see increasing reference being made to 'film royalty', or 'Hollywood royalty', with 'royalty' being the dominant model. The radically germane point about such celebrity culture, whether royalty, entertainment, or sports based is that it has to be performed. Performance lies at the heart of celebrity culture, and the media are crucial in depicting such performance. While the monarchy exists, as it were, in its own constitutional right, it too requires performance, and the death of Diana heralded a period in which that 'performance' was extended beyond its normal bounds of familiar encounter between the monarch and her people. Moreover, as anthropological theory has argued, grief also involves social performance, almost irrespective of whatever private emotional experience of grief may take place.

These very dynamics of celebrity performance and grief performance came into sharp focus in the Diana death complex when the A-list celebrity entertainer, Elton John, played and sung a version of a popular song first written with actress Marilyn Monroe in mind, but now echoing within the liturgical setting of the Westminster Abbey funeral. That performance, as well as many other elements in that service, provided the means for a popular expression of affinity with Diana and, especially, with her surviving sons who were still but boys. What is also not to be forgotten in this complex scenario is the presence of ruptured relationships. When Diana's brother's eulogy indicated something of a rift between the Royal Family and 'his' family, including his nephews, he was not speaking of a unique situation, for by the close of the twentieth century millions of other Britons were divorced, remarried, or in complex and often problematic relationships, including those of mixed religious commitments. Family politics frequently come to a head at funerals and find their own form of expression, and the Royal Family was no different. The issue of acceptance of rejected individuals also played its part in the public dynamics of the funeral, not least at a time when AIDS and HIV affected significant minorities and had their own death–bereavement focus in Britain at the time, especially amongst gay people whose rejection by family left its psychological mark. The fact that Diana had close links with HIV–AIDS individuals and brought a kind of acceptance to a rejected group allowed for an intense expression of appreciative grief in significant segments of mourners.

One interpretation of this funerary episode in British life emerges from a conversation John Inge cites with the Anglican theologian and bishop Stephen Sykes, suggesting that the widespread popular reaction to the death of Princess Diana lay in the fact that the

> . . . contemporary generation had invested huge hopes in this life in a way that had never happened before, and that this life simply could not hold those hopes. Consequently when the life of an individual who held within her own person many of those hopes, being, as she was, young, rich, beautiful, elegant, famous— and a princess—was cruelly cut short, those hopes were symbolically dashed.

Inge, along with Sykes and the Christian tradition, reckons on the fact 'that this life cannot hold all those hopes. They are for the future, for God's future.'[98] This is an interesting theological interpretation of events and, whatever its appropriateness, it highlights the social arena as one in which individual emotional responses find ready expression. Certainly, the impact of this death and funeral had numerous consequences. It probably helped foster a growing trend of people to choose elements of their funeral service in a freer way, bringing popular songs and music into liturgical settings, especially in crematorium chapels where the greatest number of funerary rites occur. What is more, the popular face of Diana's memory did not entirely disappear into the Althorp island grave. Many interesting yet quite different factors continue to serve as their own form of ongoing memorial as, for example, the memorial fountain in London's Hyde Park and the memorial to both Diana and Dodi Al-Fayed in the basement of Harrod's store, at its Egyptian escalator. The Egyptian motifs of that part of the store, photographs of the two individuals, along with candles and flowers constitute a kind of shrine evoking easy association with ancient Egypt and the tombs of the famous dead. Quite another 'memorial' is embodied and living in her sons, not least Prince William with his partial facial resemblance to her. His adult life, marriage, and fatherhood develops a narrative of his mother's for all with a long enough memory to recall the days of her death and funeral.

---

[98] John Inge (2003: 138), citing personal conversation with Sykes.

SOCIAL EMOTIONS AND GRIEF

This whole extensive narrative of the death, funeral, and memorializing of Diana, Princess of Wales has shown something of the complex interface between individual emotions of grief and their rippling effect into society at large, and of the reverse flow from society to individuals. While all emotions are 'social' to some degree this case reveals the power of 'large-scale togetherness', a phrase that accentuates the interpersonal dimension of large group activity more than does the almost impersonal implication of 'crowd'. Durkheim's long-established concern with the power of group activity to change the level of awareness of individuals and to intensify social cohesion is not irrelevant here.[99] His language spoke of a kind of transcendence over self in a feeling of heightened excitement generated by group ritual activity, and while it is easy to associate such an experience with group events of a celebratory kind this should not lead us to ignore gatherings that have a more sombre timbre as in many British funerals. However, there has also been something of a shift in emphasis in some British funerals that does emphasize the 'celebration' of a life, a shift marked in many respects in the highly influential 1994 film 'Four Weddings and a Funeral'.[100] This cultural drift into positive affect can even complement funerals that are often and understandably described as tragedies, when they seek to draw out the potential positive outcomes of untimely deaths. In secular contexts, in particular, the desire to find a meaning in someone's death is all the more urgent when survivors have no sense of a person's existence continuing in some supernatural afterlife.

Emotional Juxtaposition

The death of Diana, Princess of Wales, with its extended period of emotional presence sustained by the media, and the periods of grief experienced by many families and friends over much longer periods, offer a certain timing of emotions over relatively long periods of weeks, months, and over years in terms of recurrent emotional-memory moments. But there is another kind of emotional duration of quite a different order that the media in particular make possible and even create in relation to death through what might be called emotional juxtaposition. For example, on Monday 13 January 2014 at approximately 7.30 a.m., on *Today*, BBC Radio 4's flagship morning news programme, two immediately adjacent news items concerned an act of

---

[99] Durkheim was intellectually 'converted' through reading Robertson Smith's *Religion of the Semites* (1889), as the transition from his *Suicide* to *The Elementary Forms of the Religious Life* makes clear.

[100] Richard Curtis as screenwriter and Mike Newell as director.

cannibalism in Africa and the Golden Globe Awards in the USA. The former gave a report on Christian–Islamic conflict in the Central African Republic with an account of a Christian young man who ate part of the leg of a Muslim who had been pulled from a bus and killed by a 'mob'. The young man, dressed in 'designer T-shirt, skinny jeans, with a machete tucked in', was personally interviewed and was reported to accept the name of 'Mad Dog' quite happily. He explained that it was an act of revenge for a Muslim attack that resulted in the death of his wife, sister, and sister's baby, and because his sister's breast had been cut off. Having sworn revenge, he had now taken it. The programme announcer explicitly made the point that this news item might well be regarded as disturbing and unsuitable for children to hear and there was a momentary pause before the item began, presumably to allow parents to switch off. Immediately after this account the programme flowed into a report of the media-celebrity world of Los Angeles and awards for best films.

Another such example, on Thursday 24 July 2014 and at roughly the same time on the same programme, set a gruesome killing alongside an international festivity. The killing had taken place the previous day in Arizona, USA, in the form of a legal execution of Joseph Rudolph Wood, a double murderer convicted in 1989. Its prime newsworthiness lay in the time of some two hours or so that it took him to die, with a second feature in the problem of concocting an appropriate drug mixture for the lethal injection, given that the UK and EU sources once supplying these components no longer did so for humanitarian reasons opposing capital punishment. This death-scene was partnered by the festivity of the opening of the 2014 Commonwealth Games in Glasgow, where the Scots had laid on a full entertainment of music and performance, all following the Queen's formal opening of the Games.

This kind of juxtaposition of news is only slightly more morally and emotionally incongruous than many others encountered daily in every medium of contemporary communication. What is more, it is a direct product of media that are not immediately interpersonal, having no opportunity for person to empathize with person and giving no chance of non-verbal emotional interplay. Perhaps both the immoral depths and the celebratory heights of these two stories have their tails trimmed when imported into kitchens across the land. Too little time exists even for some cognitive dissonance to emerge between our ordinary and relatively safe, non-cannibalistic and non-celebrity lives and those reported to us from some 'other' place in the world. The point of this situation for our present study lies in the way death, albeit through mob killings, revenge cannibalism, and religious oppositions fringed by 'magic' beliefs, is framed by the media with items deemed far more positive.[101] It is difficult to say whether or not this involves the compassion

---

[101] Sometimes disasters are reported in real time, making juxtaposition a different complement, e.g. the Libyan Embassy siege in London, 1984, and the Hillsborough football disaster of 1989.

fatigue sometimes thought to beset excessive charity-based advertisements following catastrophes or disasters.

Online Presence

Though such events are immediately transient in airtime they are very often accessible in an ongoing form through the internet which has, itself, become a resource initiating considerable opportunities and difficulties as far as death is concerned. The simple shift of traditional advertising into online formats has been an obvious and simple move but one that has allowed funeral directors, insurance companies, and, for example, the innovation of woodland burial sites to gain immense publicity. It is now increasingly the case, for example, that modern British crematoria offer the possibility of having the cremation service streamed online to relatives or others not able to be present in the crematorium itself. This suggests an interesting development of ritual participation at a distance.

For those with an online presence in social media settings, people whose immediate concerns are with life and not death, their public identity does become problematic when they die if family are unfamiliar with their online identity, or web-page managers are ignorant of their death. In other words a person may have an online life long after they are dead, and this can become a problem for those left grieving if they find themselves in difficulty in getting the deceased person out of online circulation. This problem is slightly analogous to the material cultural objects that we inherit from the dead and which Daniel Miller, for example, has pinpointed in the 'process of divestment' when considering how the living deal with objects once belonging to their dead and in processes by which 'biological death' moves into 'social death'.[102] While this creative thought plays well into the theme of embodiment and the way our sense of identity is dressed by objects and surrounded by the 'stuff' once owned by others, it also highlights the difficulty of 'divestment' when 'stuff' is digital and no longer involves objects in our physical possession. This is a reminder of how physical objects tend to follow a 'slow' form of communication as they are passed from person to person, often following processes of reciprocity discussed elsewhere in this volume. By contrast, digital media belong essentially to 'fast' forms of communication, which explains their appeal at the death of national or international celebrities. Things become a little more complicated, however, when digital media offer platforms for memorialization of uncertain and potentially extremely long duration.

---

[102] Daniel Miller (2010: 146, 152).

Traditionally formatted sympathy cards passed amongst friends are rather unlike online messages of condolence or of a fan's feelings at the death of a celebrity, because online material leaves us unsure as to just what 'grief' means in that wide context. Digital media have, in turn, prompted an interest in death online both in the sense of being used by sick people to communicate with both their actual and online friends and by others who express their emotions in online memorials to those who have died. Tim Hutchings, for example, has outlined a large number of death-related functions conducted online, some leading to a resurgence of older forms of memorialization such as photography, whilst also allowing millions access to such events as the death of entertainer Michael Jackson.[103] He has pinpointed how 'many forms of digital mourning raise issues around ownership and disenfranchisement' and how such media allow the living to speak to the dead through the form of 'direct address' messaging that are normal within such media. Hutchings also notes, for example, how Elizabeth Drescher ponders in a Christian context: what is happening to the 'concepts of "eternity" and "salvation" that are subject to radical restructuring in postmodern, digitally integrated culture'?[104] What is obvious is that digital media dealing with death bring new questions to the sociology of religion, not least to the theme of the potentially distinctive social force-field created online whether addressing the dead, supporting the bereaved, or even mocking the dead.

The ubiquity of media information also means that a sharing of sympathy amongst millions can also occur in rapid fashion when citizens of many countries die together, as in the case of a plane crash on Wednesday 18 July 2014 in an event that remains something of a mystery at the time of writing. On 23 July news media reported how bells were rung across the Netherlands as bodies of the many Dutch citizens killed in that Malaysian aircraft shot down over the Ukraine en route from the Netherlands to Kuala Lumpur were repatriated.[105] This case of loss of 298 passengers and crew included some 192 from the Netherlands, 44 Malaysians, 27 Australians, 12 Indonesians, 10 Britons, 4 Germans, 4 Belgians, and 3 Filipinos. This disaster, at least in the days following the event, fell into an odd category of death. For it seems as though pro-Russian partisans in armed opposition to the Ukrainian government might well have used a ground-to-air missile to destroy the aircraft by mistake, taking it for an 'enemy' plane. If that turns out to be the case, it will have been a stupid act of semi-professionals using missiles that were, apparently, gained from Russian sources. Given the extant political situation, some Western politicians were quick to blame Russia's President Putin for,

---

[103] Hutchings (2013) and (2012).
[104] Hutchings (2013: 206), citing Drescher (2012).
[105] See, e.g. BBC Radio 4, news at 6 p.m.

assumingly, providing the missiles for the political rebels. At the time of writing, considerable uncertainty surrounds this disaster, leaving it in something of an unusual category of death in the modern world. Its apparently anomalous status left the news media in something of a quandary and highlighted the fact that major cultural agencies prefer to be able to identify and 'cause' and in so doing attain some kind of mastery of the situation. What ensued in the ritual ringing of bells and repatriation of bodies was, however, an available cultural response that played its own part in this particularly extensively covered media event.

CONCLUSION

Whether on- or offline, ongoing life is framed by narratives taking the forms of personal memory, reminiscence of our dead kin and friends, grave markers, property, photography, or the dead's physical offspring. All have tales to tell and hear. The media, whether in the more impersonal public forms of television, film, radio, and the press, or the more personal social media, all thrive on narrative. The former pitch their narrative at a more general audience while the latter deal with much more personal engagement, yet it is the human individual who creates and consumes narrative as an intrinsic aspect of existence. While the former may engage in libel, it is the latter that can become the insidious vehicle for cyber-bullying, as will be evident in chapter 8. What is obvious is that emotions pervade narratives and are elicited by them. Moreover, narratives are frequently complemented by gestures that are powerful when manipulating, displacing, and modifying objects,[106] not least the objects left behind by the dead. Indeed, the value in combining narrative and gesture in our consideration of grief lies precisely in the fact that the dead become complex entities in the ongoing life of descendants and the way the living acknowledge the dead. Death frames every life in different ways. For the recently bereaved, it often carries a heavy frame; for the young it is generally much lighter, marginalized by intense life activities. For many, death's frame intensifies or reduces as one's life-course brings bereavement, post-bereavement, old age, or serious illness. Within any individual there exist level upon level of untellable sensations, untold feelings, dream and waking experiences of the dead, and anticipations of the future, on a spectrum of hope or despair. For some, these states interplay with religious experiences that

---

[106] De Certeau, Giard, and Mayol ([1994] 1998: 141) focus on gestures and narrative 'in the lexicon of things' relating to remaking urban landscape.

reinforce acknowledgement of an afterlife, while for others the terminal end of life is precisely that. Just how to cope with these emotional complexities remains a question for everyone, whether or not we are up to matching the great artist Paul Cézanne's definition of genius as 'the ability to renew one's emotions in daily experience'.[107]

---

[107] Richard Kendall (2001: 297).

7

Military, Sporting, and Celebrity Deaths

The media, as we have seen, engender a social force in relation to human grief, creating emotion in the very act of reporting it. The pivotal funeral of Diana, Princess of Wales, made that evident enough, but, as this chapter reveals, the complex affinities between key historical events and core cultural values also surface through military, sporting, and entertainment worlds as well as through the death of high-profile individuals. Though particularly obvious with military personnel—who predominate in this chapter—the death of sports and entertainment figures also opens cultural windows on an inter-linked nexus of the British 'Establishment' with its own alignment of celebrity and religion.[1] To help describe and interpret the interplay of lifestyle and death-style in these social worlds this chapter will continue to use and develop theoretical ideas concerning symbolic concealment–revelation, dual sover-eignty, and the uncanny.[2]

MILITARY FACTORS

The military, in particular, bring death to sharp focus as contexts of war and terrorism intensify basic cultural values. Thinking only from the twentieth century this has been true for Britain with the First and Second World Wars, the Cold War with Communism, active military ventures in Israel–Palestine, Cypress, Egypt, Ireland and Northern Ireland, the Falklands, the Middle East, and in Iran, Iraq, and Afghanistan. For many churchgoing people born after 1945 the regular worship of many mainstream denominations has seldom been devoid of prayers for peace, both for those lost and injured in action, and for the leaders of the world who have to try and resolve these conflicts. Death has haunted liturgy and, especially from the late 1960s, the prayers of the

---

[1] Graeme Turner (2004: 25).
[2] Described, respectively, in chapters 2, 5, and 6.

Church of England have involved a constant stream of war-related concerns, with the Northern Ireland 'Troubles' being the closest to home. In Britain, events occurred such as the bombing in Manchester in June 1996 (itself a highly visible image); this was believed to have been the work of the Irish Republican Army. Along with hundreds of incidents in Ireland itself, this served to highlight the complex interplay of political and religious motivating factors. The goal of home rule for an Irish Republic combined with a long Catholic tradition to oppose the Unionist and Loyalist Protestantism of those firmly committed to a bond with the rest of the United Kingdom. Many commentators have plied their trade, arguing variously for this being essentially a 'religious' or a 'political' 'war'. Indeed, the formal commitment to the word 'troubles' rather than 'war' played its own political role in the mainland interpretation of events. Much the same could be said for the 1982 Falklands 'conflict', 'crisis', which was, in effect, a 'war', between the United Kingdom and Argentina triggered by Argentina's claim over these British-held territories off its South Atlantic coast, to which we return in chapter 10 to consider its 'establishment' memorial.

The Troubles in Northern Ireland, which, despite the Good Friday Agreement of 1998, still rumble on in sporadic attacks and radical disagreements on both sides, disclose the power of symbolic activity and death to focus community, political, and religious values. As 2013 closed yet another new commission was proposed to discuss such issues as the flying of flags and the right of groups to march in places deemed sensitive to others. For many on mainland Britain there is a degree of incomprehension if not of the absurd in these issues of pipe-bands, flags, and the like—though the previous chapter's case of flag-flying following the death of Princess Diana alerts us to the social force pervading appropriate flag and other ritual behaviour, which brings meaning and vitality to some people's lives regarding those they see as heroes and martyrs even though others may view them as terrorists. Though criminality is very likely to play a background part in the ongoing aggression of very small numbers of people, so is the focused religious commitment of many more. During 'the Troubles' there were numerous occasions when those killed during what their fellows regarded as the line of duty were, illegally, given something of a military funeral. Some kind of face-off with the police or military was not unknown. The sense of heroic death of a soldier, albeit a provisional or someone deemed a terrorist by the other side, pervaded these events. In all of this, the death of many young men, and some older men too, was death for a cause. One even wonders whether the strange proposition argued by historian Mark Schantz over the American Civil War of 1861–5, with its 620,000 dead, might not have some bearing on the Northern Ireland situation. He proposed that Americans fought their Civil War prompted by a 'death-embracing culture' containing 'messages about death that made it easier to kill and be killed'. And that message was grounded in a hope of 'the heavenly country'.[3] Here, almost in parenthesis, one wonders whether secularization's influence, involving a far from extensive commitment to afterlife beliefs in early twenty-first-century Britain, will carry its own constraint on the readiness to go to war today, a factor that might differentiate between the USA and UK.

In terms of our main argument, however, the death of millions, most especially of Jews in Nazi-controlled prisoner of war camps, was in no way related to anything like a shared 'death-embracing culture'. While the British have their own long and chequered history of engagement with Jews, as indeed with Germans, the issue of the Second World War holocaust influenced cultural values a very great deal. For there was no possible way of understanding the tortuous and bestial killing, burning, and slave labour in the concentration camps as anything like conventional warfare. Indeed, the popular awareness of those events influenced an entire generation of Britons in their broad views of Germans, with war films reinforcing latent antagonism in new generations.[4] Indeed, the historical episode of the 'death camps', along with their sense of Hitler's dictatorial drive for his Third Reich, has probably helped create a category of 'death' that has influenced a British, if not a German, sense of national identity. British Jews, along with other Britons regardless of religious affiliation, see just how powerful death can be as a vehicle of and for political will and dominance. The death camps exposed one of the elementary forms of death—population destruction or genocide—which the human animal is capable of exacting upon its own species. Though not limited to Nazi operations, concentration-camp existence, like many other forms of torture, can be understood as a process intended to overwhelm prisoners, 'reducing feelings of vitality and aliveness. Jewish prisoners were typically left numb, helpless, and impotent in the face of this bizarre reality.'[5] Of the many outcomes of this attempted genocide was the post-war growth in the state of Israel, itself an expression of the importance of Jews, their persecution, forced migrations, and their new state option as far as emergent European identity was concerned. Further consequences of that would involve the dynamics of Middle Eastern politics, not least the conflicts between Israel and Palestine, that, in their own way, involved the wider political antagonisms of supporting countries.

Military force as an expression of intensified social force played its own part in all of these events and left both Germany and the UK with their own sense of the place of the military and military death in their respective societies. The 1939–45 War, in particular, left sediments of intra- and inter-cultural

---

[3] Schantz (2008: 4, 11, 47).

[4] Perhaps even international football should be included as a factor in sustaining certain oppositional mentalities in some.

[5] Moller (1996: 221).

Table 7.1. Cremation rates for Germany and United Kingdom for selected years.

Year	1930	1935	1936	1937	1951	1953	1957	1964	1968	1999
Germany	7.5	8.6	9.6	10.1	8.2	8.9	10.0	11.2	12.5	40.0
UK	0.8	1.7	2.0	2.4	17.4	19.8	28.3	43.2	51.2	69.8

Note: Approximate percentage of the dead. This source covers most countries.
Source: Davies and Mates (2005: 444-7).

embarrassment in numerous European countries where collaboration with enemies and other political shadows still fall upon today's more liberal elites, and where the role of the military is strongly circumscribed. In microcosm, it remains the case, for example, that a contemporary German student living in Britain can experience a degree of dissonance when seeing soldiers in military uniform present in a Christian church during Remembrance Day services.[6]

As for the particular phenomenon of the post-war cremation of the civic dead we can see that while Germany was one of the leading early twentieth-century proponents of cremation practice, far in advance of the UK, despite the fact of parts of non-Lutheran Germany being traditionally Catholic, this changed dramatically post-war. The Holocaust had thrown one of its dark shadows on cremation, exemplified by the fact that Germany's significantly higher cremation rates than the UK in the 1930s declined dramatically after 1939–45. For example, it took until 1957 for the cremation rate to reach 10%, a figure equivalent to its 1937 value, compared with the same period for the UK where rates had grown from roughly 2% in 1937 to 28% by 1957. This is one strong example of the influence of military action deploying cremation to destroy selected bodies in an industrial fashion rather than ritually cremating or burying them, and of its subsequent consequences for its own civilian population. Table 7.1 presents a comparison the figures between the two countries.

Sacred Soil

Quite a different example of historical militarism touching later eras was heralded by a popular UK newspaper report on 'Sacred soil for war memorial'. This reported how some seventy bags of 'sacred soil' were brought to the UK from First World War battlefields in Flanders. Having arrived on HMS Belfast these were reported as having been 'blessed and scattered in a memorial garden' that was created for the 2014 centenary anniversary of the

---

[6] This was a German student studying at Durham University in 2013–14 who was astonished to see uniformed soldiers taking part in the Remembrance Sunday service *inside* Durham Cathedral.

commencement of the Great War. The symbolism of this event was complemented by the bags of soil being brought by gun-carriage to London's
Wellington Barracks for the 'Flanders Fields 1914–2014 Memorial Garden'
which was designed by a Belgian architect, Piet Blanckeart. An eight-year-old
boy from London, Patrick Casey, helped place some of the soil into its new
place. 'It made me proud and excited', said the lad, while the Defence Minister,
Lord Astor, found it 'very moving'; the fallen should be remembered: 'they
were killed for our freedom, they paid a very high price for that, and we are
enjoying the freedom now'.[7] The accompanying photograph of sacks being
unloaded from a horse-drawn gun-carriage in a highly ritualized fashion by
uniformed soldiers would leave readers in no doubt of the significant solemnity of the event. Moreover, the additional photograph of the boy and architect
emptying a box of soil, whose dust-like appearance was obvious, would almost
certainly have reminded many of the act of scattering cremated remains, a
process that millions of British families have now experienced for themselves.[8]
Just what it means to take soil from battlefields where many bodies were lost
raises its own paradox and certainly displays the symbolic power of things
both hidden and disclosed.[9]

The cultural symbolism of this relatively simple event is enhanced through
the haunting background of Rupert Brooke's extensively known poem 'The
Soldier' with its reference to 'some corner of a foreign field' that would be
'forever England' in hosting the First World War soldier's corpse as a 'richer
dust concealed'.[10] However, while the importing of such 'sacred soil' is
redolent of these images, it also seems to denature them precisely in the act
of its importation, for the power of Brooke's poem lies precisely in 'some
corner of a foreign field' rather than a Memorial Garden not far from
London's Buckingham Palace, despite the poem's almost liturgical form in
closing, ironically or not, with 'hearts at peace under an English heaven'. The
overall poem presents an almost dualist distinction between the body's dust
and its heart that becomes 'a pulse in the eternal mind, no less'; one that 'gives
somewhere back the thoughts by England given'. This allusion to an inalienable reciprocity prompts a strange comparison with chapter 3's account of
contemporary woodland burial, and of chapter 9's account of the way some
people speak of wanting to 'give something back' to the soil in their option for
natural burial, albeit without a corresponding emphasis upon any pulsing in
the eternal mind.

---

[7] *Sunday Express*, 1 December 2013, p. 13, 'Sacred soil for war memorial' (no author given).
[8] (Photographs by Mark Kehoe and Adrian Harlem.)
[9] Soil samples collected from significant venues were placed in the coffin of King Richard III
when buried in Leicester Cathedral in March 2015.
[10] Rupert Brooke died in 1915, aged 28.

Sacred Sensation

Chapter 1's allusion to the influence of the First World War and the idea of
the sacred now requires some elaboration given the twentieth century's
nature as the most murderous in recorded history.[11] The sacred has long
been a widely prevalent notion in technical writings as also in liturgical rites
of worship as a description of things symbolizing deity. This intensified as the
lives and deaths of hundreds of thousands of soldiers touched the lives of
families across Europe and beyond. Rudolph Otto's notable study *Das Hei-
lige*, translated as *The Idea of the Holy*, was highly influential in capturing
philosophical and theological accounts of awesomely thrilling experiences of
the divine.[12] Then, in 1918, Friedrich Heiler aligned a variety of sources,
including William James's pre-war classic, *Variety of Religious Experience*, in
an extensive account of prayer as 'an incompressible wonder, a miracle of
miracles which is daily brought to pass in the devout soul'.[13] That same year
witnessed the publication of Karl Barth's commentary on the biblical Epistle
to the Romans, in which, from his own distinctive position as a Lutheran
pastor reacting against Liberal Theology and the fact of war, spoke of 'the
Word of God' emerging 'only when the miracle takes place'. And for him this
'miracle' was not to be easily aligned with 'religious experience', which,
paradoxically to many outside his way of thinking, 'is not the same thing
as faith or righteousness', but is 'our human and, consequently, our very
questionable relation to God'.[14] This is not the place to explore Barth's
theology, nor the outworking of these other studies, but it is important to
note the shared genre of theological *cum* history of religion's interest in the
topic of deep human experience and the question of how it relates to what
some say is or is not an experience of God: and to see that genre framing the
European anguish of the First World War and its shaking the location and
quality of the 'sacred'.

WAR MEMORIALS, THE UNCANNY, AND
THE GREATER LOVE MOTIF

The sacred is, however, but one concept that captures human emotions in the
face of social conflicts and periods of historical change. Another is that of the
uncanny, mentioned in chapter 1 in relation to aspects of urban landscape that
make their presence felt in ways that are not easy to describe but which carry

---

[11] Hobsbawm (2002: 16).   [12] Otto ([1917] 1924: 363).
[13] Heiler ([1918] 1932).   [14] Barth ([1918] 1968: 366).

the past into the present in ways that give people an experiential pause for thought.[15] One distinctive genre of this type of uncanny structure is found in war memorials, which, in the UK, occupy extremely public as well as more private or group-specific spaces. In fact memorials to the dead of the First World War (1914–18), as well as of the Second World War (1939–45), constitute the most extensive constructions of public architecture focused on a single theme, and include the National Memorial Arboretum discussed in chapter 10. Though hard to think of them in terms of 'public art', such monuments do exemplify the process of image construction created both in response to public need and as a means of evoking widespread public response. Much more significant than their static artistic nature is the fact that many if not most of these symbolic artefacts are also the focus of ritual activity, being, in the fullest sense, ritual symbols.

Here Jon Davies has made an important contribution regarding British war memorials, working from the widespread prevalence of memorial inscriptions in citing the biblical text 'Greater love has no man than this, that a man lay down his life for his friends'.[16] He developed the notion of 'Euro-Christianity', whose symbolism embraced the image of dead soldiers in symbolic association with Jesus.[17] To European societies that were in the early and mid twentieth century much more biblically literate and aesthetically aware than is probably the case today, the death of Jesus Christ through crucifixion was understood to have been the basis of Christianity's belief in humanity's salvation from sin. Suffering and death were not only united but were implacably set against evil. The iconography of the suffering, dying, and dead Christ had become universal through both the artistry of Roman Catholic religion and through the texts, hymnody, and preaching of Protestantism. Protestantism had on the whole avoided the use of the crucifix, largely as a mark of identity-divide from Catholicism, and this often extended to there being no representations of the cross at all, either in or on religious buildings. The Church of England, though formally Protestant, very largely retained a widespread use of the bare cross and, within its more Catholically persuaded constituency, also of the crucifix. It was against this symbolic background that war memorials emerged. And it is here that a certain cultural creativity engaged with cultural restraint to generate this new form of public construction, albeit one of some considerable diversity. At its starkest it was a bare list of names whose appearance as a text reflected Protestantism's favoured medium. These may be found in many contexts, including such places as post offices, or one at London's Paddington Station recalling staff who died in wartime. More elaborately,

---

[15] Drawing from de Certeau, Giard, and Mayol ([1994] 1998: 133–43).
[16] Gospel of John 15: 13.   [17] Jon Davies (1995).

yet still conforming to a Protestant reserve, major public memorials could express civic pride in large-scale statues, often depicting uniformed soldiers in battle, in death, or in postures of remembrance. Indications of an earthly–heavenly link were frequently provided through the motif of angels, those winged agents that allow the varied religious imaginations of Protestant, Catholic, and those uncertain of any fixed allegiance to find satisfactory significance. These visual cues for moral and emotional meaning were frequently glossed by formal inscription, often with the 'greater love' motif. What is radically important in this symbolic arena of eclectic textual and visual material is the expression of emotion. The human response to war and the loss of millions of husbands, sons, lovers, nephews, cousins, and grandchildren generated what can be seen as a form of culturally shared grief, whose weight, pressure, and psychological power demanded some social expression; and the war memorial became a foundational means for this.

Here the idea of social force surfaces again, frequently sanctioned by representatives of the Establishment when calling citizens to war, and later focused on grief through memorials and their unveiling.[18] This outcome in 'public art', if that term is not too anaemic for this context, generated a shareable element of public space that binds together the suffering and death of human beings, the fact of the evil of war, and the case of the death of Jesus. Indeed, Jon Davies has done a great deal to highlight the significance of these sites and I can, albeit modestly, align that aspect of their ritual–symbolic power with the notion of the uncanny, drawing inspiration yet again from de Certeau and Girard's treatment of uncanny architecture in structures that 'function as history, which consists in opening a certain depth within the present'; these are things that are not simply 'pedagogical; they are not "pacified", nor colonized by semantics'. They are, rather, 'wild objects' and are the 'equivalent of what the gods of antiquity were, the "spirits" of the place'.[19] However, unlike de Certeau and Giard's sense of a building simply standing there from one stylistic cultural age to another, war memorials are energized and brought alive in the UK through the ritual events surrounding Armistice Day and Remembrance Sunday in November each year. Within the British context these memorials as symbols both conceal and reveal, the most profound case being that of the grave of the Unknown Warrior in Westminster Abbey, already alluded to in chapter 2, and a good example of an invented tradition, a notion previously described in chapter 1.

---

[18] Gregory (2008: 275) describes how some women's letters expressed a sense of 'sacredness' surrounding London's cenotaph. See also Gregory (1994: 215): 'the need to stress the sacrifice of women . . . was far less in 1945 than in 1919.'
[19] De Certeau, and Giard, and Mayol ([1994] 1998: 135).

The Unknown Warrior

This venture in Westminster Abbey was first proposed by the Revd David Railton, a young front-line army chaplain who, after the War, as Vicar of Margate wrote to the indefatigable Dean Ryle of Westminster Abbey suggesting that an unknown soldier's body be repatriated and buried with appropriate recognition. This was an outcome of a memory Railton had carried with him from one calm evening when he saw a grave near Armentieres with 'a rough cross of white wood', on which 'was written in deep black-pencilled letters, "An Unknown British Soldier . . . of the Black Watch"'. He had wanted to write to Sir Douglas Hague to suggest such a memorial in the homeland, but he did not get around to acting on his thought until returning home. It appears that the Dean, personally warming to the idea, approached Lloyd George and Sir Henry Wilson, whose immediate enthusiasm won over the King who had, initially 'shrunk from the idea' since it was 'novel . . . emotional, and . . . poised most precariously on the tightrope of taste'. That notwithstanding, plans moved fast and a blindfolded officer was led into a hut containing six coffined bodies retrieved from major battle areas. The 'chosen' pine box was placed within a large coffin of oak obtained from Hampton Court, returned to England and interred with considerable state ritual on 11 November 1920. Written decades before the funeral of Diana, Princess of Wales, Ronald Blythe's insightful study rehearses how on this 'gentle and fair' day things were 'curiously quiet everywhere', and that London's West End, 'packed with a vast multitude', observed 'this most stately public show . . . with an intensely private emotion'. The authorities, he says, had known the event would be well-planned and 'dignified' but 'they never dreamt it would be overwhelming'. For here 'a perfect catharsis' had been achieved. 'The formal programme broke down into a great act of compassion and love.'[20] The service was even recorded—for the first time in the Abbey's history—and sold as records. Over a million people visited the grave over the next five days and some hundred thousand wreaths were also laid at the Cenotaph in Whitehall, itself the more bureaucratically organized memorial to the massed dead of the War, as of subsequent wars, and at which the coffin of the unknown soldier had stopped on its progression to Westminster Abbey. Blythe's stylish account captures the power of emotion surrounding these events and shows how a nation of bereaved families, whose dead were largely in battlefield graves abroad, could be given a sensed unity in grief. Here we have a dramatic example of the power of ritual symbolism, allied with the invention of a tradition, to conceal and reveal at one and the same time; the paradox lying in an unknown soldier who could have been everyone's son, brother, or lover, being located in

---

[20] Blythe ([1963] 1964: 19).

arguably the most sacred public space in the United Kingdom. This also exemplifies a focused expression of controlled social force, where values marshal strong emotional dynamics within a cultural narrative.

The Cenotaph

In terms of ritual symbolism, the tomb of the unknown warrior is mirrored in the national ritual space of London by the Cenotaph, set firmly in the middle of a major thoroughfare in Whitehall, between Trafalgar Square to the north and the Palace of Westminster with its Houses of Parliament to the south, and practically adjacent to Downing Street with its prime minister's residence. Trafalgar Square, as it came to be called in reference to Lord Nelson's naval victory, where Nelson is set upon his near-two-hundred-feet-tall column, also possesses other state leaders on three plinths, while a fourth is now used for an ever-changing series of sculpture pieces as is perhaps appropriate since the Square has the National Gallery of artistic works as its northern boundary.[21] Trafalgar Square—at Christmas, when it boasts the 'national' Christmas Tree, itself a standing gift from Norway, and also at New Year's Eve—is typically a place of intense and dynamic life, whether festive or part of its central-London location. Similarly, the Palace of Westminster is also a location of intense national debate and policy-making. Together these reflect something of the social dynamic and cultural force of British life—of the Establishment—in its capital city. Whitehall, linking the two, is also, for most days of the year, a linking point, with the Cenotaph being a relatively unnoticed structure. That relative concealment, if the term is allowable in this case, is radically transformed on Remembrance Sunday, the Sunday nearest to 11 November each year, the date of the original Armistice agreement signalling the end of the First World War, when Whitehall becomes a national arena of ritual symbolic activity.[22] Led by the monarch, there is a laying of memorial wreaths at the foot of the Cenotaph, a brief religious service, then a military march-past. Death interpreted as military sacrifice undergirds this event as mortality emerges amidst the spatial continuum from the vitality of both Trafalgar Square and the Palace of Westminster. In historical terms Adrian Gregory has accomplished a great deal, not only in mapping the sacrificial and blood-based sentiments of military loss in the First World War, but also in engaging with the complex

---

[21] August 2013, for example, hosted an enormous, blue metalworked farmyard cockerel, while March 2014 presented a contorted skeletal horse.
[22] See Gregory (1994: 184–212) for discussions surrounding choice of Armistice Day and Remembrance Sunday.

and often competing class, gender, and traditional and popular religious interests surrounding the portrayals of this particular war.[23]

Notably, the Cenotaph became a powerful symbol of social force and national sentiment in that it was, originally a temporary construction set to mark the Armistice after the Great War, but as people left wreaths and flowers at it there was a decision taken, by the War Cabinet, to have it replaced by a permanent structure. The architect Sir Edward Lutyens achieved this in Portland stone, replicating his temporary wood and plaster format. As the name Cenotaph indicates, it is, in fact, an 'empty tomb', a tomb that completes the top of the edifice. In many respects it reflects a kind of altar for that tomb. Here, then, we have a national memorial that was, quite literally, solidified through national sentiment. Here, again, we encounter the double process of symbolic concealing and revealing; the tomb conceals death by the emptiness of the stone coffin whilst revealing it for all to see atop a large rectangular plinth. It also shows clearly how a ritual event transforms what is there for all passers-by to see daily into a focal point for regimented people to pass by. The transformation of passers-by into people attentively passing the monument marks the power of ritual, as behaviour brings emotion to ideas to create cultural values that are framed by religiously ritualized beliefs and sacred references. In this sense the Portland stone edifice becomes uncanny amidst the halted daily traffic, as ordinary time passes into sacred time, and as silence and then military music create a soundscape of memory. The social innovation of London's Cenotaph has not been an isolated event as, for example, Belshaw and Purvey have demonstrated for British Columbia and its 'cenotaph movement'.[24]

Titanic

Another British example will reinforce this uncanny nature of the unknown warrior and empty tomb. It came in the symbolically contradictory phenomenon of 19 April 1912, in a service at St Paul's Cathedral held in memory of those who died in the sinking of the Titanic. Here the paradox lay not only in the 'unsinkable' ship that sank, but also in its disappearance at sea being balanced with this highly visible national rite. This symbol of British engineering, pride in sea-going, and of the bond linking Britain and America vanished. So much was, as the saying goes, 'lost at sea', through the devastation wrought by an iceberg, itself one of the most obvious natural symbols of concealment and revelation, characterized as having the majority of its bulk hidden beneath the sea's surface. The ship itself furnished a condensed symbol

---

[23] Gregory (2008).   [24] Belshaw and Purvey (2009: 51).

of industrialization, engineering, and great wealth, as well as social status and national pride. Its loss was inevitably great, with the emotional themes of bravery and cowardice highlighted in the 'women and children first' motif. The fragility of life, even within the apparently indestructible vessel, included the potent severing of bonds of mother, father, and children. The British response was enormous, with the famous Dean Inge of St Paul's recording that 'thousands were unable to get in'.[25] Three generations later, the entertainment industry ensured that many thousands, indeed millions, did 'get in' to their own engagement with this catastrophe through James Cameron's 1997 film, *Titanic*, starring Leonardo DiCaprio and Kate Winslet. As winner of innumerable awards, *Titanic*, offers an interesting example of the interplay of history, celebrity, death, and human emotion through the world of mass entertainment.[26]

Studdert Kennedy

Returning to the First World War, however, we find a time of concealment and disclosure grounded in the suffering and death of innumerable friends and comrades. As often with life-shattering events, many did not talk about their experiences when returning from the battlefield.[27] A few, whether in the turmoil of war or its aftermath, gave literary expression to what had impressed itself upon them. While the 'war poets' remain well known, others have been forgotten. One such, the Revd Geoffrey Studdert Kennedy (1883–1929), is worth recalling here because of his interpretation of Christian faith in warfare. His theme circled the Cross and the passion of Christ, and what these implied for God's own suffering in relation to death. William Temple (1881–1944), Headmaster of Repton, Archbishop of York and then of Canterbury, and one of the landmark social-theological thinkers of his day, described this priest as 'one of God's greatest gifts to our generation'.[28] Born in Leeds to an Irish clerical family he, too, was ordained, and gained a degree of famed admiration as a military chaplain whose sobriquet—'Woodbine Willy'—reflected his direct contact with ordinary soldiers with whom he shared cigarettes and who frequently found his direct speech about life and Christianity attractive.

---

[25] W. R. Inge (n.d., p. 15).

[26] Few now recall the 1953 version of *Titanic* produced by Jean Negulesco.

[27] Typical of certain forms of traumatic group experience and developed by Whitehouse (2004) in his 'two-mode' theory of religion.

[28] Temple (1929: 237). Cf. William Purcell, who noted how the much-respected F. R. Barry, Vicar of St Mary's Oxford and later Bishop of Southwell, thought that Studdert Kennedy along with Tubby Clayton and Dick Shepherd were the only clergy known by the man in the street in the 1920s, a period of 'an all pervading cynicism'. Some wanted him buried in Westminster Abbey. Purcell (1962: 154–5, 178).

Following the suggestion that he turn his arresting ideas into verse, Studdert Kennedy produced many Kipling-like poems with 'The Unutterable Beauty' being one of his most telling.[29] It disowns the idea of a high and mighty God ruling the earth from some 'heavenly-hellish throne' in strong preference for the God who suffers in and through Christ; for him, 'life demands a Cross as its meaning'.[30] Following the War, he spoke of the 'trouble' that pervaded men's minds following the loss of their sons in the War. The wife, too, in her status as 'the mother', 'has never been quite the same since the War; she keeps on trying new religions, and she used to be a standby in religion'.[31] This is, itself, a telling comment in terms of secularization and the role of women in mainstream churches.

As for his poems, Studdert Kennedy is revealed as both troubled and comforted by the Christian idea of the passion of Jesus in his pre-death and crucifixion anguish. This is, for example, very unlike Wilfred Owen's sober anxiety as expressed in his poem *Dulce et Decorum Est*[32] whose Latin title asserting the sweetness and propriety of dying for one's country is rendered as 'the old lie'. He ends with one dying man's 'hanging face' after a poison gas attack being described as being 'like a devil's sick of sin'. Here there is no alliance with some significant other, let alone a divine 'other', but only a futility and the poignancy of a highly self-conscious self-witnessing inhumanity. This is one of those moments in which the bond between individual and society is strained and establishment challenged when submitted to social analysis.

From a rather different cultural, institutional, emotional, and ethical perspective comes a brief speech given by Prime Minister Stanley Baldwin on 19 December 1923 when unveiling a war memorial for the British Board of Trade, of whose civil service 'only a limited number could go and fight'.[33] This not only speaks of a 'disenchantment' over the years since the ending of the 1914–18 War but also of 'some of the controversies, and sordid things, the selfishness and the greed' aligned with the War and its aftermath. He speaks of these as arising 'among the good deeds like poisonous fungi'. Noting the rise of memorials across Britain 'in stone and bronze', he heralds them as aids to recollection of his generation and of their power 'to tell the world and the unborn generations of the magnitude of the sacrifice by which we attained our victory'. Indeed, he hopes that it will be this magnitude that 'will be revealed' while the 'sordid' things 'will be hidden'. This interplay of the hidden and the revealed is poignant, coming as it did from a leading politician of the day.

---

[29] Carey (1929: 132).   [30] Studdert Kennedy (1925: 54)
[31] Studdert Kennedy (1923: 27). This suggests a kind of secularism a generation or so before Brown (2009) pinpointed the secularization of women in the 1960s.
[32] The expression comes from one of Horace's Odes (111.2.13). Owen's poem was written in 1917 and published post-war in 1920. Born in 1883, he died on 4 November 1918, one week before the War ended.
[33] Baldwin (1923: 243–6).

Furthermore, he not only notes the 'seven millions' who 'perished in Europe', and that deaths touched most lives of living relatives, but also that, as far as civil servants were concerned, 'many lives sacrificed in the war, sacrificed under the strain of continuous overwork as truly and in the same spirit as those who gave their lives in battle'. For him it was highly germane that 'in our country, almost alone in Europe' the 'strength and the moderation of character of our people' resulted in 'freedom from unconstitutional rebellion'. This was one element of a 'silver lining' of the war's dark cloud. Still, it would now take 'super-human' effort in each person's 'vocation to the service of our common humanity' to 'maintain our civilization at the level to which it has been raised'. That is to be the response to 'those who gave their lives for us', so that we might say, as he says in closing his address, '" They have not died in vain"'.

BRIMMING VITALITY

Here, then, military deaths raise the topic of the value of life aligned with the notion of social force and expressed in terms of vitality. The idea of the homeland or of Queen and Country becomes pervaded by emotions allied with protection of the family and of freedom to create a powerful value for this life.[34] Even more than that, issues of national, family, and individual identity, even of destiny, cluster around military life and death and raise these phenomena to the level of belief. This remains especially important for volunteer and, during war, for conscripted soldiers, but not for mercenary soldiers. One classic example of duty and embeddedness within a cultural tradition was that of Japanese soldiers in the Second World War. Coming from the intensely hierarchical and integrated realm of Japan, where the Emperor was still identified as a living deity, and where there was a tradition of honourable suicide typified by samurai warriors, the war dead have been described as those 'brimming with vitality, which may have strong power to negate their death and pollution'.[35] This 'brimming with vitality' is a very telling description as far as this volume is concerned because it can be identified as a major resource available for social direction.

As we now argue, some might categorize 'vitality' in terms of some form of 'capital', and there are contexts in which that will make sense, but one might also approach vitality as natural energy culturally directed. In terms of

[34] See Reimers (2012) for a high-profile funeral of a murdered woman in Sweden.

[35] The self-cutting of the stomach after ritual bathing, dressing, and eating, in the act of *seppuku*, often known outside Japan as *hara-kiri* acknowledged shame or defeat. It involved a helper who rapidly beheaded the samurai to minimize suffering. Though technically outlawed in 1873 it persists. Hyunchul Kim (2011: 99–100).

historical sociology we might think in terms of Durkheim's *Homo duplex* and the combination of an individual or personal life force bonded to a public–social identity, with the interplay of these two 'forces' generating the 'social person', a concept I explored in a previous study when seeking to integrate numerous theories of self and society.[36] To identify the soldier as one distinctive embodiment of such a social person, brimming with vitality, then poses particular problems when a soldier dies. And something similar occurs with some celebrities from sporting, entertainment, or other national contexts.

Vitality as an energy or life force is a highly social phenomenon being something that one person perceives in another, with each social group having its own scheme of identifying, fostering, or constraining 'vitality'. It is, in this sense, a more individual form of 'social force'. Cultural motifs such as extraversion or introversion bring their own framework to it, as do popular notions such as an 'active' or 'dynamic' person, while notions such as 'restless' or 'lethargic' typify an opposite view. Vitality takes shape when it is sensed by individuals as the energy enabling them to pursue meaningful activities. It is the sensed energy that helps constitute a clear sense of identity in and through socially available goals. And that phrase, 'sense of identity' is crucial, for identity is 'sensed', albeit in a multitude of ways. Moreover, there are times in the life of an individual or group when existence feels purposeful and folk are able to attempt and endure many things, but there are also times when existence appears pointless as in periods of devastating grief when, as I have described elsewhere, a form of identity depletion occurs.[37]

Sacrificial Vitality

In seeking to analyse this vitality, especially in a military context, we now turn to a variety of thinkers whose differing theoretical perspectives contribute to our understanding of sacrificial death.

Hertz

Hertz's classical approach, like that of his Durkheimian circle, tended to reify society, allowing him to speak of society and death in this way.

> Society imparts its own character of permanence to the individuals who compose it: because it feels itself immortal and wants to be so, it cannot truly believe that its members . . . in whom it incarnates itself should die.[38]

---

[36] Douglas J. Davies (1984: 155–64).
[37] Douglas. J. Davies (2011: 68–94). See also (2000a).
[38] Hertz ([1905–6] 1960: 77).

Though Hertz focused on materials derived from very traditional and small-scale societies and not from nation states with armies, there is much of use in his abstract depiction of 'society', for, in terms of the sociology of knowledge, societies do stand above the fragile temporality of individual members. Hertz is well known for his notion of 'double burial' describing cultural settings where the corpse receives a primary burial or containment until its flesh and organs decay (this he called the 'wet' phase of funerary ritual), followed by the secondary burial or treatment of skeletal material (described as the 'dry' phase). He also saw the passage of time taken by these phases as being mirrored in the processes of grief amongst living kin. Cremation, for him, simply speeded up this process, such that he could describe it as 'far from destroying the body of the deceased, it recreates it and makes it capable of entering into new life'.[39]

If we accept that this kind of sociological abstraction reflects its own form of philosophical reflection upon human beings such that sociology and philosophy, and one might also add psychology, come to share much in common, then a notion such as a 'character of permanence' expresses a powerful property. When Hertz speaks of 'society' he is, in effect, depicting the general outlook of many individual people and saying that in collective terms people have a sense of the permanence of things; a sense that would be contradicted by the fact of individual death unless some ritual forms went on to provide an identity for the dead amongst the living. This is precisely where the issue of memory and its expression in ritual symbolism come to the fore. The sentiment that the memory of those who die *pro patria* will live forever not only discloses that desire for permanence but also the value of life as such. Accordingly, the sentiment that 'their name liveth evermore' is strongly evident on many a war memorial. Moreover, if we identify 'brimming vitality' with the socially formed soldier, then society cannot 'truly believe' that his death was pointless, for soldiers are 'more social' than civilians; their life focuses social force in a more direct fashion, and behind the military stands the social 'establishment' that validates life's values and formal religious or ideological beliefs. In Hertz, then, we get much more than a strictly anthropological–sociological interpretation; we are also offered a social-scientific existentialism and one expressing a clear social force.

Weber

In terms of the sociology of knowledge and human depictions of life Max Weber, foremost of sociologists, developed an approach characterized by people's orientation to the world that was, in itself, an expression of a drive

---

[39] Hertz ([1905–6] 1960: 42). Davies ([1997] 2007: 27–34) developed these ideas for twentieth-century cremation and cremated remains in the UK.

for meaning.[40] Such meaning varied from the affective 'meaning' of ecstasy and mysticism to doctrinal forms of a rational, intellectualist meaning.[41] Through the concept of elective affinity[42] Weber saw considerable significance in the preference certain groups might possess not only for particular formulations of 'meaning' but also for different types of salvation.[43] What is more, this idea of correspondence reappeared in his important though brief discussion of death amongst soldiers and his judgement that 'war does something to the warrior which . . . is unique: it makes him experience a consecrated meaning of death which is characteristic only of death in war'. Weber contrasts this 'community unto death', with its sense that an 'individual can believe that he knows he is dying "for" something', with 'ordinary death' that comes to everyone and which does not attract a distinctive rationale.[44] Moreover, such ordinary death is likely to be subject to that 'disenchantment of the world'[45] that Weber associated with shifts in religious explanation of the world that subsequent generations have described as secularization. He discusses this in relation to Tolstoy's ruminations on whether death is meaningful or not and seems to concur with Tolstoy in the view that 'for civilized man death has no meaning'. This is because civilized man may simply become 'tired of life' with all its new challenges and progressiveness, whereas 'Abraham or some peasant of the past' might die 'old and satiated with life' having been rooted in a more 'organic cycle of life', with life having given him all it had to offer.[46] However, beyond the military, Weber is keen to observe that there is, also, a 'brotherliness of religion' driven by a sense of 'vocation' that can also produce a sense of meaning in death: 'only those who perish "in their callings" are in the same situation as the soldier who faces death on the battlefield.'[47] The idea of 'vocation' was important to Weber, much as it had been centuries before in the theology of Martin Luther, and reflected the idea that a Protestant laity could possess a strong sense of serving God in and through one's work much as monks had done through their monastic 'religious' life.

As for warfare, a contemporary of Weber, A. R. Radcliffe Brown, reckoned that one of 'the social functions of religion is in connection with war'. What he had in mind was the 'faith and confidence and devotion' that religion could give to those going into battle. Having the all-too-recent World War in mind, he saw this religious influence as affecting all parties, since 'the German people

---

[40] Weber ([1919] 1991: 143).   [41] Weber ([1915a] 1991: 351).
[42] Weber ([1915a] 1991: 285). See chapter 9 for elective affinity, and chapter 4 for its application to ecological burials.
[43] Weber's contrast between 'sorcerers' and 'priests', and their different tasks in awakening 'heroic ecstasy' and 'conserving tradition' among the young resembles Whitehouse's later 'two modes' theory of religion. Weber ([1915a] 1991: 351); Whitehouse (2004).
[44] Weber ([1915a] 1991: 335). The quotations come from a lecture delivered in 1945.
[45] Weber ([1919] 1991: 155).   [46] Weber ([1919] 1991: 140).
[47] Weber ([1915a] 1991: 335).

seem to have prayed to God for victory no less fervently than the people of the
allied nations'.[48]

While such an approach highlights the issue of life's meaning and purpose
at times of crisis it also poses the question of just what the 'meaning of life' is
for increasing numbers of people living in a secularized culture during times of
relative peace. While family and work offer two ready arenas of meaning, even
these may become problematic in societies undergoing shifts in family patterns, reductions in some long-term commitments, and experiencing increasing short-term employment and unemployment. Similarly, retirement and an
isolated old age after a relatively nondescript job set their own question mark
against the value of a life lived. However, military life often cuts across such
uncertainties when, for example, families of young soldiers killed in recent and
contemporary conflicts speak of them dying doing something they loved, and
gaining some emotional recompense in that. There is, then, much in Weber's
approach cautioning us not to see all deaths as alike, and identifying military
lifestyle and death-style as something distinctive.

One of Weber's other concepts, that of charisma, is also valuable for our
discussion of vitality and intensification of social force. If one takes its form in
the 'magic' or charisma of office then one aspect of that lies in the difference
between the charisma 'of a British Prime Minister' that is 'always less with us
than the magic of an American president in the USA. This is because the
magical component of authority in Britain is taken away from those who have
the power and invested in the Monarch.'[49] Though this was something that
C. P. Snow argued in the late 1960s, the fact that it seems to me to remain
largely true half a century later suggests a certain durability of the idea, not
least as exemplifying the sustained influence of the British 'Establishment'
headed by the monarch. It says much about the general cultural intensification
of values and their embodied personification in designated individuals and
their charisma of office. But there is also a more personal form of charisma,
one well known in some religious groups, that attracts followers and is
important as far as 'vitality' and the natural 'force' of an individual are
concerned, for it allows followers to see a path by which their vitality may
be enhanced and directed. These two types of charisma carry their own
consequences for popular response when the charismatic person dies: the
death of a monarch is not the same as the death of a unique social celebrity.

Marvin and Ingle

We now move from Weber to a more essentially Durkheimian stance, and one
that, because it is focused very specifically on the military in the USA, needs

---

[48] Radcliffe-Brown (1952: 161).   [49] Snow (1969: 126–7).

considerable caution given our main attention is with the UK. I include it here as an example where the motif of sacrifice embraces the importance of military death in a cognate culture, albeit one that has, traditionally, sought to repatriate its military dead, something that was rare in the UK until recent military ventures yielded relatively small yet highly newsworthy numbers of soldiers killed in action.

This work of Marvin and Ingle argues that warfare was foundational in forging an essential American identity symbolized in and through the President and the flag. For them sacrifice lies at the heart of the USA as a culture in general in which 'the bloody slaughter of our own children lies at its heart'.[50] Behind the flag symbolism, itself a prime symbol of the USA's civil religion, lies a kind of secret, viz. that 'society depends upon the death of its members at the hand of the group'.[51] This is a system of 'willing victims' operating around the cult of the flag whose omnipresence is, for example, quite unlike the relative absence of the Union flag in the United Kingdom, where, one might argue, the monarch embraces both the roles of the US President and US flag. Marvin and Ingle speak of the military as 'death touchers' and go so far as to see the military ring of Westpoint Academy for elite military leaders as its own form of wedding ring, war wounds as their own form of medals, and the boot camp as generating its own 'band of brothers': moreover, 'since violence is contagious death-touching soldiers must be set apart'.[52] The Durkheimian approach to the sacred defined as things 'set apart and forbidden' makes considerable sense in this context. What is, perhaps, less obvious is the way they interpret the dramatic importance of funerals with military honours as a rite in which the flag taken from the funeral casket is ceremoniously folded and handed back to the blood kin as a kind of baby. Here their intent is to highlight the general anthropological idea that death rites often include some episode of symbolized fertility and the ongoing nature of life despite death. Their work can, usefully, be complemented by that of Mark Schantz on the American Civil War,[53] and seen as a compound cultural integration of ideas of sacrifice for society and of an afterlife for the dead.

Baudrillard

From a more philosophical approach to sociological matters, Baudrillard highlights the significance of military deaths as a kind of cultural capital invested in soldiers, taking the state to be a form of 'bureaucracy of death'.[54] Nothing should escape the state's power, or if it does then it is subversive as in the case of terrorists,[55] murderers, and suicides, all of whom are problematic

---

[50] Marvin and Ingle (1999: 312).
[51] Marvin and Ingle (1999: 2).
[52] Marvin and Ingle (1999: 100).
[53] Schantz (2008).
[54] Baudrillard ([1976] 1993: 175).
[55] Baudrillard ([1976] 1993: 37).

for society.[56] By sharp contrast, soldiers—who also kill—die 'for the father-land', upholding the state's authority against the enemy. Because of this socially supportive nature of military death he interprets the war dead as being 'exchanged as values in accordance with a general equivalence', or, in other words, 'we might say that they can be converted into gold, the world has not lost them altogether'.[57] The war dead become precious in having main-tained society's authority. Baudrillard is highly reminiscent of Hertz here, though there is no reference to him in this connection. His theoretical debt to the reciprocity theory of Marcel Mauss is, however, quite obvious, though we would do well to think of those who do die for their country as reflecting more of Mauss's fourth obligation in their expression and transmission of inalienable values rather than the simple reciprocity of market exchange. While Baudrillard's approach, grounded in ideas of state power and control and expressed in terms of value exchange, provides one insightful approach to military and 'subversive' deaths, it does not quite capture or allow for the sense of vitality or the language of sacrifice invited by it.

Bloch

A better model of vitality can be drawn from Maurice Bloch's influential anthropological work on ritual, enshrined in his synonymous notions of 'rebounding vitality' or 'rebounding violence'. In his anthropological study of particular initiation rites he argues that the ritual processes by which boys are culturally metamorphosed into men involve acts of symbolic death and rebirth, with the 'new men' setting out to display their new vitality by hunting down symbolic expressions of their 'boyhood' identity. Though it is seldom possible to apply models derived for and from traditional, small-scale societies to complex modern societies without serious qualification, such models are often suggestive of forms of cultural analysis and interpretation. This has been the case for early anthropological ideas of rites of passage and van Gennep, reciprocity and Mauss, and double burial and Hertz, all discussed in this present volume. Bloch's rebounding conquest deals with the issue of power or force in a society and the way members conceive of it and manipulate it in symbolic fashion and through ritual activity, and in relation to human birth, development, and maturation. In other words the life course is itself a force-field of cultural opportunity, giving young people the chance to develop adult identities and contribute to their social world. Bloch's driving idea is that human beings do not simply take life on its biological terms of birth, life, and death, but, rather invert those terms or culturally transform them so that biological life becomes cultural life, or 'natural' life becomes 'social' life.

---

[56] Baudrillard ([1976] 1993: 175).   [57] Baudrillard ([1976] 1993: 175).

Flesh–Spirit transformations

This, at least, is one way of approaching ritual death and ritual rebirth motifs found in numerous world contexts, and is well known, for example, in Christianity in the complexly linked forms of water baptism and Spirit baptism.[58] The first speaks of a person brought for baptism as one who now 'dies' to the 'flesh' and is born through the Holy Spirit of God. Water's multi-voiced symbolism speaks of this as cleansing from sin and as a grave out of which the newly baptized rises. An intensified and theologically enhanced version of this is typical of Pentecostal and charismatic Christianities when asserting that 'new life' comes to a sinner when the Holy Spirit of God comes to a person and they become 'born again'. The biological facts of birth and death are reversed: the person, already biologically born, now dies to sin and is reborn in the Spirit. The language of 'flesh' and 'Spirit' often stands symbolically for the 'old' and 'new' identities. The dominant model driving this cluster of ideas lies in the death and resurrection of Jesus. The initiate 'dies with Christ' in order to be reborn through the power of the Holy Spirit who or which is, in effect, the equivalent creative force that emerged in early Christianity to 'replace' the resurrected and heavenly ascended Jesus.

These theological ideas of ritually transformed identities which Christian traditions assume will also involve moral transformations through ongoing participation in the sacramental life of churches are not far removed from the discussions of military existence mentioned above. Soldiers are initiated in order to transform youths or civilians into fighting men. Formal initiation lies in training and 'passing out' as military personnel while there may also be informal initiations to establish bonding of individuals into a group. The image of dedication, service, and protection of country, and, perhaps, of ideals such as human rights or democracy or the like, is an image that might also be seen able to carry a religious notion of salvation. The military are trained for the proper use of the force-field of society vested in them by the political 'establishment' to defend, protect, or 'save' their society. Numerous theological motifs of salvation used to interpret the work of Jesus as the divine saviour are also couched in martial motifs, from early Christianity's notion of the harrowing of Hell through to the historical restatement of this by the Swedish scholar-bishop Gustav Aulén.[59] The title of his most famous book was *Christus Victor*; in this his perspective moves from God's being and the divine movement towards human beings, most especially in the Incarnation and in Jesus, and the 'conflict of God with the dark, hostile forces of evil, and His victory over them by the Divine self-sacrifice: above all, we shall hear again the note of triumph'.[60]

---

[58] Douglas J. Davies ([1997] 2002: 19–20).   [59] Gustav Aulén (1879–1977).
[60] Gustav Aulén ([1930] 1970: 158). Original title *Den kristna forsoningstanken* (English: *The Christian Idea of the Atonement*).

British Christianity in the 1930s, the very decade leading up the Second World War, and for decades afterwards, had *Christus Victor* as a book; even as a phrase this was 'established as a technical term in its own right', whether 'in Swedish, German or English'.[61] In this very motif of the victor we may, perhaps, see an affinity between Christian thought and military life that could validate the sense of conquest for those seeking some validation from their wider religious culture.

Dual sovereignty: ritualizing jural–mystical factors in remembrance

The complexity of death is such that while we gain considerable, albeit partial, insight from the thinkers just discussed there are many other possibilities of interpretation, one being that of dual sovereignty, an idea discussed in previous chapters but now particularly germane in terms of military deaths.[62] For, from what we have already discussed, we see how a 'soldier' is explicable in terms of jural authority framed by mystical authority, much as a religious martyr might be described in terms of mystical authority framed by jural authority. While it is tempting, in the military case, to speak of the 'mystical self' and the 'jural self', it is wiser to resist in order to avoid a certain reification and to retain the emphasis upon kinds of authority. In a similar way, one could refer to the way a state engages with both jural and mystical forms of authority, accentuating one or the other as occasion requires.

One recurring example of such an interplay is associated in the UK with the annual period of Remembrance surrounding Armistice Day, 11 November, and which brings us once more to the ritualized aspect of war memorials. For example, on the nearest Sunday there is a military parade allied with a religious service replete with a robed Anglican choir and appropriate bishops and clergy. Moreover, on the preceding Saturday night, a major memorial event takes place at London's Royal Albert Hall, itself an immense structure commemorating Queen Victoria's beloved husband, Prince Albert, whose early death led to decades of formal mourning by his bereaved Queen. Today's Remembrance event combines many forms of military display and accounts of bravery and of the loss to families, as well as the involvement of young children in a form of peace-pledge. The extensive activity and movement of the displays along with much music comes to be ritually allied with two minutes of memorial silence set amidst a specifically religious service, led by an Anglican bishop but also involving military chaplains of other denominations. All ends with the National Anthem and three 'military' cheers for the Queen, who is present with numerous members of the Royal Family. The very

---

[61] Pelikan (1970: xix).
[62] This concept would enhance Christian theology of the atonement.

structure and process of this event, which is broadcast on prime-time main television, fully express jural authority on one hand, in and through the military activities, and mystical authority on the other, expressed in the religious service. All takes place before the very eyes of the monarch, who, in the UK context, unites jural and mystical domains in being the head of the judiciary and of the Church of England.[63]

The entire ritual event is sustained through the interplay of music and silence and also by the use of thousands of symbolic red 'poppy' petals that are released high in the dome of the building during the two-minute silence and fall upon the heads of those below. Each is said to represent one who gave their lives in war. The descent 'from above' offers another linking of domains of a more mystical than jural kind, and, just as much, this silent moment of descending petals evokes its own form of the uncanny. The military and ecclesiastical personnel present, not least military chaplains, along with be-reaved relatives and representatives of many segments of British society, and the monarchy, come together because of death in war.

In a democracy devoid of capital punishment, war is not only the most pronounced example of the implementation of jural–legal authority, when Parliament sends the military to fight and with the full expectation of some ensuing death, but is also, in a complex way, a demonstration of the mystical authority of the state when its *raison d'être*, its intrinsic sense of self-value, is challenged.

Popular participation

Mystical authority is also evident in society through a host of charities devoted to the wellbeing and flourishing of people, these very often being run by volunteers in a way reminiscent of Mauss's fourth obligation of passing on values of more than market value. In their way such voluntary organizations help constitute the complex nexus of weights and balances that helps sustain the political–cultural dynamics of the British form of national democracy and local government. Some of these have emerged in direct response to death and issues of memory, as in the case of hospices, Cruse Bereavement Care and many targeted grief-support groups.

One organization of particular relevance here is the Royal British Legion, established in 1921 and receiving its Royal charter on its fiftieth anniversary in 1971. As a major charity, the British Legion not only helps support injured military personnel and their families but also organizes the Festival of

---

[63] At local levels the Cenotaph event on the Sunday is mirrored in hundreds of church services across the UK, where the monarch is 'present' through the Lord Lieutenant, alongside the clergy and the military.

Remembrance in the Royal Albert Hall just described. This widely televised event complements the following Sunday's remembrance services and events held across the country in which the Legion plays a major part. Its poppy campaign each year raises considerable sums of money in support of its charitable aims. In 2013, for example, the organization contacted millions of households with a package in the red, white, and blue colours and pattern of the Union flag, including a small wooden cross holding a poppy; it also contained a leaflet telling 'The story of the Unknown Warrior'. The request was for financial support to the charity to 'plant' the cross in a regional 'Field of Remembrance' along with any message or 'Remembrance Tribute' that the supporter wished to provide. Other information reminded readers that some 300,000 British soldiers had 'unknown graves'.

To include the military in this account of British death is of fundamental importance because it introduces a dynamic interplay of vitality, power, and excitement that is different from the dynamics of death in urban society. One might even argue that the sociology of British religion requires an understanding of the interplay of the deaths of soldiers and resident householders. The battlefield and the suburb, the war zone and the market town, the trenches and the rural village; all provide appropriate complementary settings for the wider British experience of death. Sometimes these scenes have been geographically separate and sometimes united, and those very spatial differences carry distinctions of their own as both the London Blitz and the more recent terrorist bombings on London transport make all too evident. But the military in their more domestic and ceremonial role are also of fundamental importance to the highest-profile ritual events of the UK, as we saw in the previous chapter in the death of Diana, Princess of Wales.

One echo of Diana's funeral as a public performance of grief recurred in 2010–11 amongst the villagers of Wootton Bassett in Wiltshire, who began to turn out in numbers to line the street in honour of repatriated dead soldiers. Initiated in a relatively impromptu fashion by members of the Royal British Legion, these former soldiers, seamen, and airmen and women served as a nucleus for other villagers and, as things developed, for the families and friends of the dead. The local parish church bell was tolled and added its traditional voice to what was, in effect, less an invented tradition than a local performance of respect-driven grief and an act of solidarity with the dead and their bereaved kin. Once again the media, once they appreciated what was occurring, added a yet more public and national dimension to this village whose proximity to the airbase into which the dead were flown had occasioned a deeply human ritual response. When it was decided to repatriate the dead through a different airbase, Colonel Richard Kemp, former Commander of British Forces in Afghanistan, argued that 'another Wootton Bassett is needed to honour our dead', since there was some suggestion that local responses should be discouraged at the town of Carterton lest it disrupt trade. Kemp

argued that 'this is not a matter of efficiency but of symbolism'.[64] Wootton
Bassett was, in fact, granted the title 'Royal' by the Queen in recognition of its
innovative mode of respect for the war dead. It might be said that the town's
action reflected a certain uncanniness of the personnel in the liminal process
of repatriation.

Celebrity and mourning's diversity

Death has, indeed, often stirred the British public to react in number and
forceful fashion, as, for example, when George Muller died in Bristol in 1898
and occasioned a very large following of his cortege to Bristol's Arnos Vale
Cemetery, not least of children. For he had initiated the Bristol Muller
Orphanage for children who had been disinherited or abandoned. By contrast,
it has been said, that when Lord Kitchener died during the period of the First
World War, he whose military efforts were not all crowned with success, the
public's mourning for him 'did not entirely conceal the long thankful sigh of
official relief at his passing'. From a quite different perspective, when Steve
Jobs, founder of the Apple corporation died of cancer aged 56 in October 2011
his high profile as the charismatic leader of the high-tech company ensured
that his thoughts on life and death gained coverage across many media. One
much-cited reference was drawn from his commencement address at Harvard
that included the idea that death was a most valuable phenomenon because it
cleared the past and opened the way for new things. While the social creation
of celebrity depended upon the rise of television and other media with their
increasing numbers of viewers/users, the case of Steve Jobs was doubly
complex in that millions used his Apple computing and phone products as
the very means of accessing mass media. The media enhanced the kind of
interrogative celebrity that took politics and popular opinion into the world at
large, and while this differed from musical and sporting celebrity, these in turn
depended on television and the new record industry of the 1950s onwards.

These developments were significant as the boundaries of deference around
the social class system of elite rule gave way to, or began to run in parallel with,
the novel complementary 'Establishment' of media celebrities. One such is
worth highlighting here, a man who once said 'The first time I walked into
a television studio I thought "I'm home".'[65] This was Sir David Frost
(1939–2013), to whom a quarter-page photograph was devoted on the front
page of *The Times* on Monday 2 September 2013 following his death two days
previously. This was followed by part of the leading article of the day, a two-
page obituary, and a further two pages relating to his life, including his famous

---

[64] Kemp (2011: 10).
[65] *The Times*, 'Register', Sir David Frost, 2 September 2013 p. 47.

interview with former US President Nixon, who, in relation to the Watergate Affair admitted that 'he had let the American people down' and would have 'to carry that burden' for the rest of his life.[66] Commenting on the 1960s, his obituary observes: 'Frost was now a celebrity', as well as noting that it was on Frost's television show that the Beatles 'gave the world premiere of "Hey Jude"'.[67] The more popular press also gave extensive coverage to Frost's death, with the *Daily Mirror*, for example, presenting half the front page along with two sets of double-page articles and photographs of famous interviews including Muhammad Ali, Margaret Thatcher, John Lennon and Yoko Ono, and the Shah of Iran.[68]

Frost was made on OBE in 1970 and was knighted in 1983, aged 44. Perhaps it was appropriate that such a celebrity, described as having 'repeatedly redefined the possibilities of television', should have died of a heart attack aboard the Queen Elizabeth cruise liner hours after departing from Southampton docks. He had been due to give a lecture as part of series for the news agency Al-Jazeera. Over his lifetime he had interviewed eight British Prime Ministers and seven US Presidents. Frost had been the son of a Methodist minister and had 'spent a year as a lay preacher before going to Cambridge'.[69] Frost, as with many sons and daughters of British ministers of religion, seemed to have demonstrated what my colleague Mathew Guest and I have described as 'transformed retention'—a 'critically creative process of adaptive change' as beliefs and values pass from parents to children.[70] From preaching he moves into a kind of exhortation grounded in interrogative interviews; meanwhile he exemplifies the emergent notion of media celebrity whose interviews with leading world politicians extended that celebrity into more obvious 'establishment' domains.[71]

THE MEDIA AND TERRORISM

As with the death of Diana described in the previous chapter, the media are responsible for presenting news across the world and in an instant become the apparently innocent agents of terrorism in televising threats and atrocities, and political responses to them. Populations untouched by trouble or anxiety have terrorist news brought into their homes whether they like it or not: nothing could serve terrorists' goals more directly. The rise of militant Islam, now often described as Islamism, presents a clear example in British

---

[66] Billen (2013: 5).   [67] *The Times*, 'Register', Sir David Frost, 2 September 2013, p. 48.
[68] Palmer (2013: 4–5).   [69] David Brown (2013: 4).
[70] Davies and Guest (2007: 170–6).   [71] Graeme Turner (2004).

and much Western life in the decades following the turn of the twenty-first century. Its importance lies squarely in portraying death in a fashion that is both simple yet dissonant to most British ears, because it advocates ideas of warfare, identity, and destiny familiar to the British, but in an unrecognizable pattern.

In this chapter we have already considered the idea of military death *pro patria*, for the Fatherland, and, in that sense, can understand why people might want to die for a high ideal against some obvious enemy. But we considered that motivation in relation to the 'greater love' motif that takes its significance from the Christian understanding of the sacrificial death of Christ. We have seen how thousands of British war memorials portray this integrative scheme of self-sacrifice for monarch, country, freedom, family, and fellow soldiers. But then we encounter individuals who proclaim their own identity in terms of Islam and its worldwide community even though they are legal British citizens, and it is here that two sets of emotion-pervaded value systems come into conflict; that of traditional British values of 'Queen and Country', and that of a version of Islam as God and Islamic community— Allah and Ummah. For the relevant communities the former carries images of military death, even heroic death, while the latter carries the sense of martyr-dom. While death, or 'the ultimate price', typifies the former, a martyr's entry to Paradise typifies the latter. Indeed, one of the affirmations—perhaps it might even be described as a taunt—that some terrorists have made is that unlike ordinary British people who fear death they, as dedicated Muslims, do not fear it but believe they will be welcomed into Paradise as martyrs. Here, death itself becomes not only a touchstone of value and motivation but also a paradoxical point of debate, since people on both sides value sacrificial death in defence of an imperilled community: the problem comes in one 'side' understanding 'the other' in an emotional as well as a rational sense.

Again, a single case will illustrate this aspect of British social life. On 22 May 2013 two men, claiming Islamic motivation, used a car to run down a man they identified as a British soldier in the Woolwich Barracks area of London. At the time this man, fusilier Lee Rigby, was wearing a 'Help for Heroes' T-shirt, an advertisement for a charity supporting injured soldiers. The two assailants then tried to hack off the fallen man's head. A photograph of one of these men, with blood-red hands and a meat cleaver, has been widely pub-lished in the press. He spoke to numerous people while waiting for the police to arrive, and did so further in the ensuing court case for murder. His general argument was that he operated on an 'eye-for-an-eye' principle, because the British government was involved in 'the affairs of the Muslims', especially in Afghanistan. In court, the counsel for the prosecution, Richard Whittam QC, argued that 'killing to make a political point or to frighten the public to put pressure on the Government or as an expression of anger is murder and remains murder whether the Government in question is a good one, a bad one, or a dreadful one'.[72] This case highlights the role of death, in this case socially defined as murder, as a vehicle for a political message, but it also highlights the perceived community—an international Islamic community— within which the perpetrator located himself. He saw himself as a 'soldier of Allah'. Both men were convicted of murder and imprisoned. One feature of this murder lies in its extensive media and online coverage, including reporting interviews with the police as one of the convicted individuals speaks calmly and rationally of their choice of a soldier as an appropriate person to kill. What was telling was the expressed desire of both individuals to be killed by armed police responding to an episode where the perpetrators had a gun and made as though to use it—they wanted to be Islamic martyrs. But, as part of the dramatic spectacle of death in a very public place, they were only injured and disarmed by police shots. Moreover, they were then rendered first aid by the armed police, before being taken into custody, whereupon they were even hospitalized to aid recovery.

In this and other contexts of military life and death it was no accident that in the year 2000 a UK Ministry of Defence booklet, *Soldiering—The Military Covenant*, highlighted the very idea of a military covenant understood as a mutual obligation and unbreakable bond between nation, army, and individual soldiers involving notions of identity, loyalty, and responsibility.[73] This very notion was taken up by politicians who obviously sensed appropriate affinity with it, not least because it echoed so positively the general-public-sensed need for the military and sympathy with the death and injury soldiers suffer. This covenant reflects the political–military and social-class dynamics of the British Establishment at large and, in its own way, acknowledges the importance of how the military focuses and intensifies the social force-field of national life and of its extension into times and places of military action.

THEORY OF OFFENDING DEATH: HILLSBOROUGH

The fact that death is an inevitable component of warfare does not carry over easily into civilian life where death as manslaughter or murder attracts high judicial penalty. Indeed, death and justice stand close together in the human understanding of life's values, much in accordance with our preceding discussion of dual sovereignty, most especially in a parliamentary democracy where the interwoven strands of jural and mystical authority create a pattern of satisfying meaning. Contexts in which death challenges such meaning and disrupts the social force-field trigger cultural dynamics in distinctive ways, one

---

[72] O'Neill (2013: 5).
[73] United Kingdom Ministry of Defence (2000) *Soldiering—The Military Covenant.*

of which will now be analysed through a single individual, her family, and a very large number of ordinary people and their commitment to football.[74] This case, in its own fashion, mirrors the previous chapter's focus on the death of Diana, Princess of Wales, but has as its focus not a particular celebrity but a very large number of 'ordinary' people. It embraces family-focused mutual support groups, the deceased as victims, and the media and the power of online public activity, as well as high-level politics.

We begin with the political dimension and the UK's House of Commons on Monday 18 October 2011 in a debate on the events framing the death of ninety-six individuals in what appeared to be crowd surging within the Hillsborough football stadium at Sheffield on 15 April 1989 in a national football cup semi-final game between the Liverpool and Nottingham Forest teams. Despite the fact that this had been a televised event in which millions had participated it had long been felt that official accounts of that day had covered up crucial issues of mismanagement and responsibility, not least involving the police. One outcome of the deaths was the creation of the Hillsborough Family Support Group, itself a reflection of the numerous mutual support groups that emerged in Britain in the second half of the twentieth century. Its chairperson in 2011, Margaret Aspinall, whose 18 year-old son died at Hillsborough, spoke of this 'massacre of innocent people', and of a 'complete blanket' having been 'put over Hillsborough the very minute it happened'. She hoped that this parliamentary debate—which promised through the Home Secretary Theresa May that all documents relating to the event would be made publicly available, not least through the Hillsborough Independent Panel chaired by James Jones, the Bishop of Liverpool—would allow 'families and their survivors to get some sort of closure': 'closure would happen when the real truth of Hillsborough—a truthful truth—is published'.[75]

The nature of the parliamentary debate behind this hoped-for truthfulness is of particular significance for several reasons. In the first instance it was occasioned by the government's innovatory idea of parliamentary time being given to issues raised by large-scale support through online petition: in this case of 140,000 people. This affords one of the clearest examples of the ever-increasing significance of social networking sites serving issues of bereavement and grief as well as of political protest. Second, this debate illustrated the way in which matters of death can bring social situations, and the modes of discourse sustaining them, into distinctively serious communicative tones. Within the debate, for example, Steve Rotherham, a Labour Member of Parliament and former Lord Mayor of Liverpool, solemnly read the names

---

[74] See Heller (1993) for a republished account of an off-duty doctor's recollection of the event.

[75] *The Daily Telegraph*, Tuesday 18 October, *Sport* section, pp. 10–11. See Douglas J. Davies (2015) for offending deaths in Finland and Wales.

of each person who had died at Hillsborough. As the ninety-six names were read, the silence in the Chamber was deep. This matrix of silence also sustained the emotional nature of this and other speakers, whose voices strained to hold back tears. In popular terms, the event was 'emotional'. Notably, there was applause; applause that is conventionally censured and markedly absent in the House rang out in affirmative support, marking this debate and its subject matter as distinctive. For, in the third place, this debate combined the issue of death with that of legality and of responsibility for those deaths, and did so in the central social arena of the nation.[76] In so doing it serves as a valuable example of the notion of 'offending death'.

I first developed the 'theory of offending death' to explain phenomena in which there was some kind of massed public response to the death of people deemed to be innocent victims of injustice perpetrated by or concealed by some authority figure identified as culpable and now called into question.[77] Diverse cases that both furnished examples and invited interpretation included British responses to the sinking of the *Titanic*, the death of Diana, Princess of Wales, or the Belgium White March of 1996 that responded to paedophile murders.[78] Though the details of individual examples vary, this type of 'offending death' highlights the way in which the legal dimension framing notions of justice–injustice is embodied in and affects people's emotional lives. To foreground the deep significance of such interplay between law and feeling I introduced the notion of 'moral–somatic' relationships. We have already encountered this important idea in chapters 1, 2, and 5; it accounts for the bonding of the social world of laws, conventions, and familiar habits with the emotions, moods, and sensory dynamics of embodied life. It describes the significance of people saying they 'feel sick' or 'disgusted' at certain actions of others when those actions contravene social convention, law, or, where appropriate, divine edict. It describes the very fact of embodiment, with its complex development of biocultural emotions and moods, which requires an appropriate public response—a response that becomes a form of ritualized behaviour all of its own. Moral–somatic relationships also become significant for ritual as the medium of embodied social values, and not least for beliefs accounting for life and death.

It is against that theoretical background that the Chamber of the House of Commons shifted from its normal debating-chamber status—one that despite

---

[76] For personal memory of a doctor attending the catastrophe, see Heller (1989: 300–4).

[77] Douglas J. Davies (2001). This is not the same as, for example, C. P. Snow's account of the death of American President Franklin D. Roosevelt in April 1945, when there were 'people in tears all over London that morning, going to work in their buses and underground trains'. Snow added: 'I have never seen such a flow of feeling in the town. It didn't happen when Churchill died' (1969: 127).

[78] *New York Times*, 21 October 1996. '275,000 in Belgium Protest Handling of Child Sex Scandal.'

or perhaps even because of its distinctive form of democratic legislative function is often marked by its own ritualized noisy opposition—into a commemorative ritual space open to the sensitivity of offending deaths. As such it deployed symbolic elements of British commemoration in presenting lists of the 'ordinary' dead, so common in Britain since the major World Wars; group silence, and terms redolent of deep significance such as 'truth' and 'justice'. The Home Secretary spoke of doing everything that was in her power 'to ensure that families and the public get the truth': full 'disclosure' would ensure that 'no stone would be left unturned'. But, not only were 'justice' and 'truth' much in evidence, so too was 'closure'. This is a very significant addition, for 'truth' and 'justice' on one hand, and 'closure' on the other fully complement each other in reflecting the theoretical import of the concept of offending death in exemplifying moral–somatic relationships. For 'closure' has become a widely popular concept used in terms of bereavement, not in terms of ordinary grief and the loss that befalls us all in society, but for problematic deaths; for deaths in which unusual circumstances, blame, responsibility, and guilt are involved. 'Closure' intimates a hoped-for positive emotional outcome to a bereavement involving some problematic social situation. One journalist reporting this parliamentary debate captured the dynamics of these issues very well, not only in explicitly pinpointing the theme of a potential 'establishment cover-up' over 'whether any former politicians and policemen were culpable', but also noting that, 'For the families of the 96 Liverpool fans who went to a football match on April 15th 1989, and never returned home, some form of closure will come only with full disclosure'.[79] At the time of writing a new inquest is continuing to hear evidence with, for example, the chief police officer on duty at the time of the tragedy finally acknowledging 'that he had made grave errors', with *The Times* newspaper heading its report: 'Hillsborough police chief admits he caused 96 deaths'.[80] With this inquest and its high-profile participants, as with the House of Commons event, elements of the British Establishment once more come to the fore in terms of mortality and experience their own kind of negative social force.

CONCLUSION

This chapter has, then, taken the theme of social force into the domains of lifestyle and death-style associated with the police, the military, the church, and celebrities from sport and entertainment. It has shown the media to be

[79] Bascombe, *The Daily Telegraph, Sport*: 10–11.
[80] *The Times*, Wednesday 18 March 2015, p. 7, reporting on the previous day's hearing.

highly significant in documenting key events framing high-profile 'establishment' deaths and in fostering public emotions. We have seen how the British
military are, one might say, civically consecrated to deal with social forces in
explicit knowledge that they might die in the path of duty, and how, accordingly, they have been ceremonially memorialized. Through the theories of dual
sovereignty and offending death, as also of the uncanny and of the power of
symbols to conceal and reveal, we have been able to align legal and emotional
factors for military and celebrity death and for tragedies befalling ordinary
citizens. In accounting for paths of dutiful military sacrifice and of appropriate
memorialization for establishment and ordinary citizens alike, this chapter
strongly complemented chapter 6 and now prepares the way for chapter 8 and
its focus on some very popular literary texts.

8

Wayfaring Mortality, Fear, and
the Good Death

Medieval, Victorian, and modern texts begin this chapter. Each in its own mythical form portrays the negotiation of life through core values and leads into a brief consideration of justice and death, before moving to the increasingly poignant themes of 'bad' and 'good' death manifest in suicide and assisted dying. In this, the relationship between individual and society takes the particular form of conflict between individual lifestyle choice of personal control and the social constraints of the 'Establishment' in its medical–clerical–political social forces. Pervading these relationships we will encounter fear, a deep emotion that neither social-scientific nor humanities-based reflections should ignore, as well as the much-desired sense of respect in life and dignity in death.

LIFE NEGOTIATION

Negotiation, both as navigating a journey and resolving difficulties, is characteristic of human life and has been expressed in many ways by most cultures. Poetically and musically this has been magnificently captured by Ian Bostridge in his literary and musical engagement with Schubert's *Winterreise,* whose musical tonality frames Mayrhofer's poem, presenting cameos of our journey through life and its kaleidoscopic emotions: 'How do we live in the world and relate to others? Where is God? What can we know of the divine?'[1] He plays on the fact that while 'death draws nearer' as the song cycle concludes, it does so 'equivocally', as the music of the hurdy-gurdy man 'allows us the freedom to choose our own ending'.[2] Bostridge ends his reflection on Schubert's musical negotiation of life, loneliness, and impending death with an intriguing few pages that are not entitled anything like 'conclusion', or even 'postscript',

---

[1] Bostridge (2015: 272–3).   [2] Bostridge (2015: 480, 484).

but as 'aftermath'. This not only captures the existential, emotional, historical, and cultural epic through which he has taken us but also glosses his comment, 'What happens after a performance of *Winterreise* is a little mysterious but usually follows a pattern', viz., 'an extended silence . . . a mute, stunned applause . . . which can swell into noisier acclaim'; there is a 'sense of seriousness, of having encountered something above and beyond, something ineffable and untouchable . . . there can be a sense of embarrassment or awkwardness between audience and performers, which the applause does its best, eventually, to eradicate.'[3]

Two elements that echo our wider discussion strike me from his sensitive account—that of spirituality and of the form of a British funeral. Despite our many accounts of 'spirituality' in this volume it is, perhaps, this 'sense of seriousness' that best reveals the tip of the existential iceberg carrying a person's reflective meaning of the depths of life. And it is no accident that music is its medium, given its capacity to integrate symbolic with more rational dynamics. It may be that *Winterreise* as performance is experienced by a small minority of Britons, but musical preference frequently underlies the sentiments of relationship and self-understanding affecting all classes, as musical choices at funerals clearly display. As for 'aftermath' and the form of many British funerals, we see in each a seriousness of performance prompting a silence that leads into embarrassment or awkwardness as the ritual theatre is left for that kind of social 'applause' lying not in clapping but in greeting and meeting in the post-funeral world abutting the ordinariness into which mourners pass.

Though a great deal more comparative comment could be made between such a musical reflection and funerary ritual at large,[4] we now move to a more expressly social-scientific engagement with life negotiation in anthropologist Tim Ingold's idiom of 'the wayfarer', a motif already encountered in chapter 6. His concern with the 'task of the wayfarer', not in acting 'out a script received from predecessors but literally' in being able 'to negotiate a path through the world', helps identify the sharp divide that often exists between literary–liturgical traditions that seek to enact sacred scripts and 'wayfaring' traditions that seek innovative negotiation.[5] The former take 'tradition' as the very notion of receiving and transmitting information from predecessors to successors, while the latter generate knowledge through action and, perhaps, represent it in new stories. Sharp dichotomies, however, seldom reflect real life, where these rather ideal modes of action engage each other in complex ways, sometimes engendering conflict between old and new—a phenomenon well known in the sociology of fundamentalism, or emerging as liberal forms

---

[3] Bostridge (2015: 486–7).

[4] Simon Mills (2012). For discussion in terms of social class see Conway (2013).

[5] Ingold (2011: 162).

of understanding achieved through negotiation. For traditionalists, often represented in clergy of an established church, this may involve a double negotiation; one involving interpretation of tradition and another an active engagement in the life choices that laypeople undertake as they make their way in the world, not least in the context of death and bereavement.

TEXTUAL TRADITIONS—OLD AND NEW

Three texts that present different literary accounts of emotional schemes for coping with death have been selected from the hundreds of possible candidates offering insight into this negotiation of lifestyle amidst 'establishment' ideas framing potential emotional pathways. One is medieval, one Victorian, and one contemporary. For today's readers the first is likely to be unknown, the second familiar as a title but probably unread, and the third one of the most read books in history, especially by children and younger people. In terms of the history and sociology of religion, these texts conduct us from medieval through Victorian to contemporary life and offer their own depiction of transfer from an uncanny magical Christianity, through a muscular individualistic Christian piety, to a contemporary networked secular-like spirituality.

Saint Erkenwald

One English literary–historical example of the dynamics of death as framed by the interplay of theological and popular belief exists in the late medieval poem *Saint Erkenwald*. This tale describes London workers finding a remarkable tomb beneath what had been a pagan temple now in process of transformation into the Christian St Paul's Cathedral. The grey marble tomb, with its grimacing and crouching gargoyles has unreadable gilded lettering. Its discovery quickly attracted townsfolk and, when the lid was laboriously removed, they witnessed a gold-lined interior housing a magnificently attired and entirely uncorrupted corpse. Though crowned and sceptred, none could identify the deceased. All this was reported to Bishop Erkenwald, who returns rapidly to his palace from visiting an Essex abbey and spends the night in fervent prayer seeking the divine will to deal properly with this event. The next scene opens with Bishop Erkenwald already in the cathedral, vested for Mass, after which he describes the Lord's power and then 'talks to the corpse'. He reminds the corpse of Jesus' crucifixion and calls the dead man to tell of his life. It turns out that he lived before the days of Christ and was a lawyer or judge of such moral probity that he was dressed as a king by an appreciative public when he died, while 'the Ruler of rights' kept his body from decay, for he had not been embalmed. The corpse then prays to God, addressed as the 'maker of men', telling how he had died without knowledge of God's plan, love, or mercy. Even when Christ harrowed hell and even took souls from Limbo this individual was left there. And that is where we are told his soul remains to this day, even as his body now talks to those who hear him on Earth. He asks what good all his own honesty had brought him given the location of his soul.

> Here my soul can but sigh in her sorrow and pine
> In a dark, chilly death where the dawn never comes,
> Pine in hell, ever hungry for heaven's great feast
> Before seeing the supper the saved all enjoy.[6]

Bishop Erkenwald, moved by these words, weeps as he invokes God and wishes for Holy water to baptize this person in the name of the divine Father, Son, and Holy Ghost. As his tears flow one falls on the corpse's face, transforming the situation, for the tearful water and the words spoken are perceived by the corpse to constitute baptism. He now tells that his soul has immediately been admitted to the heavenly feast and, with his gratitude to God and the bishop fully expressed, he slips into silence and his appearance totally changes from ruddy healthiness to black decay and dust. Here we find expression of a widespread European belief that the destiny of the soul and the integrity of its body are mutually related, with its rider that non-corruption symbolizes either distinctive sanctity or immorality. In this case a pagan sanctity is recognized and by a most unusual means is baptized into Christianity. All who see this mix mourning with mirth as they give praise to God; all the borough bells ring out at once, with all this being rooted in the place that once was a pagan temple and had now become a Christian church.

The cultural motif of the life-like face of a corpse becoming instantaneously disfigured through decay into dust, albeit due to the salvation of the corpse's attendant soul, is as close as any analogy could be to today's innumerable cinematic representations of the effects of good and evil upon heroes and villains. Whether for depictions of Dracula as a vampire, zombies, or the many other forms of living dead, the figure of the face as the arena of moral destiny has, in this case, changed very little in more than half a millennium. And this is to be expected, since the face condenses the symbolization of life and death, whether in sighted or sightless eyes or in breathing or breathless lips.

In contemporary British society it is likely that a considerable majority of people do not think of death as entry into some form of judgement with punishments attached. Though hell had begun to vanish as a socially shared idea in the late nineteenth century, a minority will still respond positively

---

[6] Finch (1993: 325). *Saint Erkenwald*, lines 305–8.

to the idea as survey data in chapter 2 showed.[7] Even so, the expressions 'to burn in hell' or, interestingly, 'to rot in hell', remain powerful curse-like formulae vented against criminals who have been cruel, molested children, or otherwise tortured or harmed those deemed least able to defend themselves. It is this sense of social disregard that provokes ideas of the impurity of such criminals, and it is likely to be the same disregard for social unity, albeit expressed as a divine command, that traditionally made suicide a culpable legal offence or a sin of considerable proportion in ecclesiastical judgement. Today's hell is, if anything, more metaphorical, anticipating old old age lived in senility or decrepitude with a this-worldly shift intrinsic to its secular setting.

Tom Brown's Grief

From St Erkenwald's magical–miraculous piety we now move to a telling form of nineteenth-century Christianity where piety remains strong, not least in the forging of character in alliance with the birth, or at least the burgeoning, of the Establishment through public schools. This system of private residential education and its alliances developed through elite universities, social networks of families, the professions, and the military allowed the influence of the Church of England considerable power for a century and more, an issue seldom considered in the sociology of religion. These links are still influential in contemporary Britain and are, for example, frequently expressed through newspaper obituaries and memorial services following after funerals. For while the great majority of the working and middle classes simply have a funeral service, members of 'the Establishment' frequently have a subsequent memorial service at some later date to that of the funeral itself.

One classic expression of the character sought through public school education lies in *Tom Brown's Schooldays*, published in 1858.[8] It had gone through five editions by November of that year and had sold some eleven thousands copies by January 1859,[9] and remains in print today. Pre-Freudian and pre-Darwinian, it offers a cultural marker on one form of grief in Britain, that of a 19-year-old for his mentor and practical Christian apologist,

---

[7] Ariès ([1981] 1991: 610) thinks that the belief in hell as an explanation of evil that linked death and spiritual punishment waned from 'the eighteenth—perhaps as early as the seventeenth century', with belief in it being 'over' by the beginning of the nineteenth century 'in Catholic and Puritan cultures'.

[8] Thomas Hughes ([1858] n.d., p. 67). Character in the form of being a 'brave, helpful, truth-telling Englishman, gentleman, and a Christian'.

[9] Briggs ([1955] 1965: 156).

the famous Dr Arnold of Rugby.[10] Its youthful hero, Tom, learns emotional control once his father handshakes him farewell to school; kissing must cease as must the hug which Tom would have preferred.[11] And what we see in Tom we can see in wider echelons of nineteenth- and earlier twentieth-century British life where grief is profound, understood by others, and yet 'mastered' in public.

At school, death plays a significant part. Tom experiences the way another pupil, Thompson, dies of a fever. We read how 'a feeling of seriousness and awe at the actual presence of death amongst them came over the whole school'.[12] When the headmaster speaks to the school about this he tells how, when coming from the deathbed, at a time when the school did not know of the death and were playing and enjoying their amusements, he 'felt there was nothing painful in viewing that', indeed, 'the unsuitableness in point of natural feeling between scenes of mourning and scenes of liveliness did not at all present itself'. But he did sense that if at that moment some serious misdemeanour of 'falsehood or drunkenness' had been reported to him, then the combination of mourning and liveliness would have been 'most intensely painful', because it is at 'such a moment that the eyes are opened really to know good and evil'.[13] This entry, as it were, into Tom Brown's emotional experience of mortality was reinforced at Thompson's 'burial service' which was 'so soothing and grand always, but beyond all words solemn when read over a boy's grave to his companions'. It brought Tom 'much comfort, and many strange new thoughts and longings'.

Only a week later, Tom learns how typhus had killed the devoted parish clergyman and father of his friend, Arthur. Arthur also, becomes seriously ill at school and, when pondering his own death, accuses God of injustice in denying him a life of fulfilled work. Then, when pondering his deceased father, 'a heavy numbing throb seemed to take hold of' his 'heart, and say, dead—dead—dead'. He sensed that, when lying in a dark tomb, its 'black dead wall was cleft in two', he was 'caught up and borne through into the light by some great power, some living mighty spirit' to a place where he 'saw men and women and children rising up pure and bright', and his dead father was there too, alongside familiar people from his own childhood, people who were in their day 'called Atheist and infidel'.[14] Young Arthur's experience with its vision of light and a fixed boundary between this world and another which he was not allowed to pass would, a century later, probably have been described

---

[10] Thomas Arnold (1795–1842), Headmaster of Rugby (1828–41). Regius Professor Modern History, Oxford University, (1841–2), social reformer, and advocate of education in generating a Christian character of duty, service, and unity of people beyond mere ecclesiasticism. He opposed the Oxford Movement and attitudes of divisiveness, e.g. 'Sectarianism: Its Evil and Origins' (n.d.).

[11] Thomas Hughes ([1858] n.d., pp. 65–6).   [12] Thomas Hughes ([1858] n.d., p. 259).
[13] Thomas Hughes ([1858] n.d., p. 260).   [14] Thomas Hughes ([1858] n.d., pp. 270–1).

as a 'near-death experience'. Certainly it took away from him any fear of death, but the main reason for that was his conviction that the 'dead' and the living were all engaged in a special divine work, even though he could not discern exactly what it was.

But this is not the end of Tom's experience of death and grief. For the author brings the book to a conclusion—'Finis'—with the death of Tom's old headmaster, only just appointed to an Oxford professorship. Shortly after Tom has completed his own first year at Oxford, specifically dated as 1842, the actual year of the historical Thomas Arnold's death, Tom goes fishing with friends on the Isle of Skye. There, from an outdated newspaper, and amidst bits of news on politics, racing, and cricket, he is told of Arnold's death. Tom is actually fishing at the time, his response, though unnoticed by his friends, is described.[15]

> You might have knocked him over with a feather . . . he felt completely carried off his moral and intellectual legs, as if he had lost his standing-point in the invisible world . . . the deep loving loyalty which he felt for his old leader made the shock intensely painful. It was the first great wrench of his life, the first gap which the angel Death had made in his circle, and he felt numbed, and beaten down, and spiritless.

Tom searches the paper, at first thinking its report untrue. He leaves his friends to go for a walk, 'to be alone, and master his grief if possible'. His friends 'sympathizing' and 'wondering', don't understand that he 'should be so fond of his old master'. They wait an hour and a half for his return but, at supper 'he could not join their cheerful talk'. He follows his 'irresistible longing to get to Rugby', meets the school's 'little matron' who was 'deeply mourning'; he 'tried to talk, moved nervously about . . . but couldn't begin talking'. He goes and finds the 'old Verger', also called Thomas, 'seized his hand and wrung it': he recognizes why Tom is there, and sits and tells his tale, wipes his spectacles, 'and fairly flowed over with quaint, homely, honest, sorrow'. After this 'Tom felt much better', and is directed to where Arnold is buried 'under the altar in the chapel, sir'. The old man appreciates that young Tom would prefer to go to the chapel by himself. On the way he looks at his once familiar surroundings and appreciates their futility—an old order is gone; another will soon arrive. Still, he unlocks the chapel and goes in: 'fancying himself the only mourner in the broad land, and feeding on his own selfish sorrow'. Memories danced through his brain while his heart throbbed 'with the dull sense of loss that could never be made up to him'. He groans aloud, gets up, moves back to the seat he first occupied as a little boy. Old memories rush back, 'but softened and subdued, and soothing him'; he sees the name of a lad he recalls scratched into the oak panelling, he thinks of other boys, then of

---

[15] Thomas Hughes ([1858] n.d., p. 313).

his own family, 'then the grief which he began to share with others became gentle and holy'. He gets up, moves to the altar and while 'tears flowed freely down his cheeks', he kneels down 'humbly and hopefully'. There we are encouraged to leave him, as he lays down 'his share of a burden too heavy for him to bear in his own strength', where he had felt before and now needs to feel again, 'the drawing of the bond which links all living souls together in one brotherhood'. The book ends with what is, perhaps, the first literary expression of a 'stage theory' of grief, drawing together all that has been described above, as its author, full of his Christianizing mission, writes:

> And let us not be hard on him, if at that moment his soul is fuller of the tomb and him who lies there, than of the altar and Him of whom it speaks. Such stages have to be gone through, I believe, by all young and brave souls, who must win their way through hero-worship, to the worship of Him who is the King and Lord of heroes.[16]

I have dwelt on Tom Brown because it is a cultural classic highlighting the handling of death in this essentially Victorian tale while also exemplifying 'wayfaring' in the process of becoming more adult through grief. The bereaved young man 'had to learn by that loss, that the soul of man cannot stand or lean upon any human prop, however strong and wise, and good', but only upon God—'upon whom alone a sure foundation for every soul of man is laid'.[17]

Here, almost in parenthesis, it is worth observing that some 130 years after *Tom Brown*'s publication a self-selected but very large group of some 100,000 very active churchgoers of major denominations in Great Britain responded to a survey that included a question on the identity of Jesus by offering a series of statements that people might choose on a five-point scale from 'very helpful' to 'incomprehensible'. Despite the fact that we might criticize the crucial question on 'what God has achieved for us through the life, death and resurrection of Jesus Christ' for bringing several factors—'life, death, and resurrection'— into the frame, the largest response of 75% on the 'very helpful' point went to 'Christ, our teacher, pattern, and example', with some 63% also opting for 'Christ has won the victory over evil and death'.[18] This might well be read as echoing something of the *Tom Brown* 'Lord of heroes' motif.

Certainly, *Tom Brown* was written to win boys' hearts for Christian discipleship and for service to society through the growth of character. It might well be that such a desire for character-building on a distinctively English form of Victorian Christianity can be seen in a transformed version set on a more secular spirituality base in what rapidly became cultural classics for young people in J. K. Rowling's *Harry Potter* series. In moving from Tom to Harry we

---

[16] Thomas Hughes ([1858] n.d., pp. 318–19).
[17] Thomas Hughes ([1858] n.d., pp. 313–14).
[18] *Views from the Pews* (1986: 14–15).

move from a traditional form of Christianity to a late twentieth-century perspective on life's meaning that is deeply humane, perhaps even better described as humanist, and which depicts its own form of spirituality grounded in friendship, love, mixed motivations, and a psychological sense of self-awareness.

Harry Potter, Death, and Grief

Harry Potter, a boy of 'mixed' ancestry (part wizard, part 'ordinary' human), suffered the death of his parents in a wizarding attack from the evil figure of Voldemort, with his mother sacrificing her life as she saves Harry. Harry's miserable life with his 'human' relatives is transformed when he is whisked away to Hogwarts, a school for wizards, where he forges deep friendships with a small group of peers symbolized at one point by 'what appeared to be fine gold chains' woven around and linking pictures of friends: 'Harry realised that the chains were actually one word, repeated a thousand times in golden ink: friends . . . friends . . . friends . . .'[19] Harry is also deeply bonded to the elite headmaster–wizard Dumbledore. Through a series of seven books Harry's education involves a deep undercurrent of preparation to destroy Voldemort, the 'Evil Lord'. This venture involves nothing less than death conquest. Many die as friendships are forged and betrayals beguile, all amidst overarching themes of good and evil, and selfish pride and selfless sacrifice. While the books are, primarily, for children, many thousands (perhaps millions) of adults have also read them, with translations running to some seventy or more languages. These facts alone call for some brief analysis of the Harry Potter character and of the way its author's approach to death reveals some key attitudes of a later twentieth-century British 'death-driven spirituality' of a non-traditional or Christian nature.

   It has been widely reported that Potter's creator, J. K. Rowling's mother's death, aged forty-five, when Rowling was twenty-five, made an enormous impact on her life and on the fact that death, parental bonds, and friendship run in parallel throughout her works, while the theme of good versus evil also stands in sharp parallel.[20] Magazine and newspaper articles, based on interviews with the author, reflect on the original text for Harry Potter being written as her mother was dying, with the loss of parents, involving sacrificial

---

   [19] Rowling (2007: 461).
   [20] Rowling (2007: 7) prefaces the final Potter volume with quotations from Aeschylus' *The Libation Bearers* on 'the grinding scream of death . . . the grief, the curse no man can bear'. And from William Penn's *More Fruits of Solitude* where '[D]eath is but crossing the world, as friends do the seas; they live in one another still . . . This is the comfort of friends, that though they may be said to die, yet their friendship and society are . . . ever present because immortal.' See ([Hoggart ([1957] 1958).

love on the part of the mother, laying the foundations for the early volume.[21]
The theme of Harry's ongoing experiences with his deceased parents reflects
something of the psycho-sociological motif of the 'continuing bonds' theory of
grief already discussed in chapter 6. The hero-worship link between Harry and
his headmaster Professor Dumbledore is really quite close to that of Tom and
Dr Arnold. The theme of death conquest, typified in the evil of Voldemort—
the one who is not named by others, though fearlessly identified by Harry
Potter—is contradicted by the self-sacrifice of Harry's parents in dying at
Voldemort's hands while saving their son, and engendering the motif of love
that also pervades the books. Individual deaths increase as the series develops,
from the relative innocence of the younger children at Hogwarts (the school
for magicians), to the young adulthood of Harry in his more immediate
conflict with Voldemort as his life force grows. As the Potter series flowed
out from 1997 so the number and nature of individual deaths, and their
motivation in good and evil desire, varied from eight in the first, and three
each in the second and third, to eleven, thirteen, and fifteen in the fourth to
sixth, respectively, reaching to more than forty in the constantly embattled
final *Deathly Hallows Part II*. That final volume, for example, circles around
'The Tale of the Three Brothers' who were granted an apparent boon by the
figure of Death who is 'cunning'.[22] The 'combative' brother gained a 'wand
worthy of a wizard who had conquered Death', the 'arrogant' brother sought a
stone with 'the power to bring back the dead', while the 'humblest' and 'wisest'
brother was, grudgingly granted his own 'invisibility cloak' that allowed him to
leave the scene without being followed by Death. This was a story of the fear of
death.[23] It ended with the first brother murdered. The second, 'driven mad by
hopeless longing', commits suicide[24] once he realizes he cannot resurrect his
former girlfriend into full human life. The final brother, however, survived to
pass his cloak on to his son and 'then greeted Death as an old friend, and went
with him gladly, and as equals'.[25] In this single pivotal 'story' we have murder,
suicide, and a 'good death'.

   As for Harry, he faces many deaths; of parents, Dumbledore, and friends.
One poignant summarizing case comes with Dobby, 'the little elf' with the
large shining eyes who saves Harry in one of his final battles with evil. Harry
catches Dobby as he dies—'Dobby, no, don't die, don't die'—and the elf's last
words are those of his friend's name—'Harry ... Potter ...'.[26] This experience
is described as 'like sinking into an old nightmare', as Harry sees himself once
more kneeling at Dumbledore's body. Harry calls after Dobby though he

---

[21] Greig (2006).   [22] Rowling (2007: 450–1). See p. 783 for the story as 'a sort of legend'.
[23] Rowling (2007: 470).
[24] Rowling (2007: 518). For a murderous suicide see the silver hand given by evil Voldemort
'to his most cowardly servant' which finally chokes its owner.
[25] Rowling (2007: 452).   [26] Rowling (2007: 524).

knows the elf has 'gone where he could not call him back'. In his 'grief for Dobby' he can 'take no interest' in what others arre discussing; he is 'so consumed with grief' that it even seems to drive 'Voldemort out'. At that very point the author adds that the old headmaster would have said it 'was love' not grief that did it. Here the interplay of grief and love for friends becomes unified. 'Understanding' now 'blossomed in the darkness' as Harry dug a grave for Dobby. He did it 'properly', by sweated labour and 'not by magic'. His immediate friends understood and joined in the realistic task. As he dug, so 'loss and fear' drove out his 'obsessive longing' to destroy Voldemort's power base. The dead elf is dressed in Harry's jacket; they place shoes and socks on the naturally bare elvin feet, and a woollen hat over his 'bat-like ears'. And Luna, the friend who had the gold ink- and love-entwined photographs of her friends, wearing a friend's coat, 'tenderly' closes the dead elf's eyes. '"There" she said softly. "Now he could be sleeping".' Harry placed the body in the grave; he 'forced himself not to break down as he remembered Dumbeldore's funeral'. Luna then says she thinks they 'ought to say something': she goes first, and in a typical contemporary fashion—perhaps first fostered by Princess Diana's funeral by her brother—she addresses the one who is dead. '"Thank you so much, Dobby, for rescuing me from that cellar. It's so unfair that you had to die, when you were so good and brave. I'll always remember what you did for us. I hope you're happy now".' The others manage a single word or two of agreement. Harry stays behind a moment on his own, much as did Tom Brown at the Doctor's tomb, and he places a single white stone from a nearby flower-bed on Dobby's grave, 'over the place where Dobby's head now rested'. He then takes his magic wand, inscribes 'Here lies Dobby, A Free Elf' on it, and walks away, 'his mind full of those things that had come to him in the grave, ideas that had taken shape in the darkness, ideas both fascinating and terrible'.[27] These ideas would undergird his final conquest of Voldemort and, in that sense, of death in the magic world.

So, by its closing episodes, the epic circles around dying, death, and sacrifice in the personal and cosmic worlds of wizards. Harry's already dead parents and other significant figures appear to him and say they will always be near. Prior to his voluntary engagement with Voldemort, Harry overhears a conversation that explains that he would have to die as and when Voldemort dies because, by some rebound of an original spell, part of the evil one is part of himself: he is one of the 'horcruxes' in which part of the vital identity of the evil one is hidden and which Harry is out to destroy. So it is that Harry, in his own self-understanding, will allow himself to be killed by Voldemort. He does so with his parents and some other close friends with him; they are 'part of' him. He has already asked them whether death hurts. '"Not at all"' is the

---

[27] Rowling (2007: 526–30).

answer. '"Quicker and easier than falling asleep".' His mother smiles at him, 'his father nodded encouragement'.[28] After letting himself be 'killed' Harry, in an unexpected and mystical event, finds himself alone, naked, in a white place full of light. He wishes for and immediately finds new robes and, amazingly, meets the already deceased Dumbledore in what seems like a light-infused mystic King's Cross Station, reminiscent of popular images of near-death experiences along with their tunnel of light. Harry learns that he is now dead but that his 'soul is whole' and completely his own. He learns from Dumbledore that the old wizard had also, when young, 'sought a way to conquer death', and even to bring back his own dead parents; 'to drag back those who are at peace': power was his weakness and he had sought it; he might even have killed his own sister. He tells Harry that he, Harry, is 'the true master of death because the true master does not seek to run away from death. He accepts that he must die and that there are far, far worse things in the living world than dying.' This contrasts so sharply with Voldemort who 'fears the dead. He does not love' them and would not wish to bring anyone back from the dead.[29] Amidst his conversation with Dumbledore and its ever-increasing explanation of his life, Harry recognizes that he has 'to go back' from this warm, light, and peaceful place. He has a choice, but he chooses to return to the fray. Here the modern idiom of 'going back' from the 'near-death experience' plays itself out quite naturally. His final exchange with Dumbledore is to ask if all this 'is real . . . or happening inside my head?' The response is 'inside your head' but glossed with 'why on earth should that mean that it is not real?'[30] As things turn out, Voldemort and Harry meet in final combat and Voldemort is 'killed by his own rebounding curse'; he hits 'the floor with a mundane finality'.[31] Harry survives, the ultimate magic wand is abandoned, and he and his remaining close friends move into the ordinary world, marry, and have children who, in their turn, set off for their wizarding education at Hogwarts.

I cite this material—and volumes more would be feasible, including website material that, for example, lists deaths and their causes and perpetrators, as well as last words or sounds[32]—to reflect a narrative venture that has engaged millions and must have entered the psychological and moral awareness of death of an entire generation of young people. Some have taken this material with considerable academic seriousness for this very reason.[33] 'The students of the illustrious Sciences Po University in Paris, for example, are reported as being offered a course by François Comba on Harry Potter books as 'an

---

[28] Rowling (2007: 766–7).   [29] Rowling (2007: 782, 785, 789, 790).
[30] Rowling (2007: 792).   [31] Rowling (2007: 815).
[32] Derived 30 Dec. 2013 from, <http://harrypotter.wikia.com/wiki/List_of_deaths>.
[33] One of the largest seminar groups at the Death, Dying and Disposal International Conference, held at Durham University, 2009, focused on 'Death in Harry Potter'.

extremely rich and complex work that has not been properly appreciated by critics'.[34]

The themes of vitality and mortality and of the social force-field within which they interact also run in many ways throughout the *Potter* series as through *Tom Brown's Schooldays*. Hogwarts may not be Rugby, Dumbledore not Arnold, nor Harry a Tom, nor even muscular Christianity a magical world, but death still plays vehicle for core cultural values in the emotional arena of self, family, friends, and death in both domains. Given the cultural impact of the *Potter* series, and of the complete identification of actor Daniel Radcliffe with the Harry Potter character, it is telling that when one of his fellow actors, Richard Griffiths, actually died in April 2013, aged 65, Radcliffe was shown in the popular press attending the funeral, with comments on the fact that he 'did not hold back the tears'.[35]

JUSTICE AND DEATH

The values inculcated in the St Erkenwald myth, in *Tom Brown* and in *Harry Potter*, express the deep concerns of good and evil depicted in terms of moral virtue, whether pre-Christian now validated by a Christian bishop, the Christian ethics of Victorian muscular piety, or the codes of a 'magical world' abutting that of ordinary life. Bishop and headmaster as establishment figures mediate the social force of their respective societies and, in theoretical terms, they embody it in ways that reflect our earlier discussion of dual sovereignty. For headmasters Arnold and Dumbledore are much concerned with the legality of virtue as well as its mystical capacity to bless and cause to flourish. In Potter, as in many films and books of the closing decades of the twentieth century, good and evil take the form of magical powers set against each other and often embodied in figures of zombies or vampires as the mutated dead, while in *Brown* the moral oppositions appear in the character and behaviour of individual human beings. As for the St Erkenwald myth, a good pagan is allowed to pass into a positive post-mortal world through the offices of Christianity itself. Whatever the figured image of death, however, it serves as a vehicle for the espoused core values of the world at hand. Tom and Harry, both caught up in the schoolboy's ideas of fair play, are, in effect, reflecting the more abstract theoretical concern with reciprocity which becomes most pointed in terms of life and death and which underlies the very contracted bond between individual and society.

---

[34] Sage (2013: 33).
[35] *Daily Star* (Wednesday 23 April 2013), 'Tears for Richard', p. 2.

It was just this human commitment to reciprocity, already alluded to in the previous chapter's comment on the radical denial of Jewish death in concentration camps that subsequently engendered a sense of horror. The human proclivity for degrees of justice in life has even been described as arising from human experience of reciprocity, with some psychologists suggesting that human evolution has involved a selection of genetic patterns favouring reciprocal behaviour.[36] Whether that is or no, there remains, as I have shown elsewhere, ample evidence of patterns of reciprocity underlying swathes of human behaviour extending from legal judgments to the sense of wellbeing or the prompting of sickness.[37]

Today, in Britain, it is common to hear people reflect on death in reciprocity-related ways; sometimes this assumes a divine give and take, sometimes a secular equivalent. For example, 'God only takes the best', is one such expression, not least when younger people die, as are 'it's not fair', or 'it's so unfair' when a person dies before what is regarded as a proper time in older old age. It is as though life is viewed as a commodity whose 'capital' has its proper place in existence's exchange. Similarly, in cases of murder or unlawful killing relatives are frequently reported as expressing a similar variation, whether thinking that 'justice has been done'—even though it 'won't bring back' their killed relative—or that a verdict 'is not enough' when what is perceived as a short prison sentence is matched by relatives against the extent of their loss.

In terms of capital punishment there remains an ongoing sense that a national census might well attract a popular majority even though no majority in Parliament would be likely or feasible, given its parliamentary abolition from 1965. Events such as the effective slaughter of the off-duty solder Lee Rigby in 2013 evoked a number of popular responses to the effect that capital punishment would be the only right response to a desire for proper balance in a kind of 'eye-for-an-eye' ethic. Images in the popular press of one of the two culprits photographed with bloodstained hands and meat cleaver, asserting that he supported 'holy war' and considered himself a Muslim warrior, would not carry weight with the vast majority of a popular readership.[38]

Against that kind of background, as extreme as it is, or even against the background of the numerous domestic murders that occur each year in Britain, what sense does it make to discuss such murderous slaughter alongside suicide? While the obvious answer in the above case of Lee Rigby is that his assailants probably wished to be killed and not merely disabled at the arrival of armed police, in order that they might be held up as Paradise-gaining

---

[36] Some psychologists propose that human evolution has selected for behaviour of a reciprocal kind (Rolls 2005: 446).

[37] Douglas J. Davies (2011: 165–85).   [38] Cheston (2013: 1).

martyrs, the less obvious response is to see suicide as another form of society being deprived of one of its members by a disapproved of, if not actually detested, means. But there is another dimension to suicide that aligns it with the Rigby murder in that ordinary citizens, caught up in their everyday lives, see such deaths as unintelligible. This is what gives rise to the idea that 'no-one in their right mind' could do such a thing, and it is why notions of being a martyr, driven by authentic religious dogma, make little rational–emotional sense to a modern British majority. There may also be a sense in which the mass killings of both World Wars between essentially Christian cultures, as well as subsequent war and terrorist deaths in relation to Islam-aligned groups in the Middle East, have rendered the notion of martyr or sacrificial deaths things of the past. This unintelligibility factor also surfaces in terms of the popular notion of 'cults' where the notion of 'brainwashing' falls easily to hand for members of a society whose broad participation in, or familiarity with, traditional religion, whether at funerals, marriage, Christmas, other festivities, or through religious leaders in typical Church of England bishops or local clergy is entirely benign.

Deaths—Good and Bad

Historically speaking, religious traditions tend to make a distinction between good and bad forms of death on the basis of how the mode of dying will affect the person's identity and experience in their afterlife. Many advocate that words of sacred texts be recited to the dying, especially if they are unable to recite them themselves. This is to help focus the mind on eternal matters and the journey about to be undertaken. Catholic Christianity has long practised praying for the dying and the deceased precisely to aid their onward spiritual journey, with extensive popular belief in prayerful assistance of the dead in purgatory. Much the same happens in significant segments of Islam. The concept of a 'good death' in such contexts is, then, one that is believed to confer benefit upon the dying person. Doubtless, the relatives are also advantaged since the more contented the dead are in their lot, the less likely they are to trouble the living.

Once more, in traditional terms, a bad death tends to be ascribed to someone dying outside the influence of their religious tradition or in ways that seem to contradict its core values. In practical terms 'bad deaths' are frequently those that disrupt normal expectations of a society. Death in childbirth, when away from home, in accident, murder, at an inappropriate time of life, and especially in suicide, is frequently deemed a 'bad death'. The emergent souls or spirits may be deemed restless, lacking successful transition to the next stage of their journey, and may disrupt the living, hindering ordinary life until appropriate restitution is made on their behalf.

Bad deaths are often spoken of as if they have left a kind of pollution behind them. Whilst such talk often seems to refer to some kind of literal infection, a kind of invisible miasma, it does allow us to gain some access to the way societies prefer to operate. In theoretical terms such idioms speak of the actual rupture or dislocation that has occurred in social relationships and the world around them. The core value of the meaning and worth of life has been assailed. A bad death is a socially disruptive death; one in which the social force-field is disrupted.

SUICIDE

Against that background it is also understandable how suicide came to carry with it the notion that the balance of a suicide's mind might well be, or must have been, disturbed, since no 'normal' person would do it. One way of beginning to engage with this complex issue is through the interplay of the notion of the uncanny and the life-process of meaning-making, concepts already raised. For suicide, in the British context, is not only highly relational but is also a complex phenomenon that mystifies and clarifies life at one and the same time, its mixed complexity making suicide such a problematic aspect of contemporary life. The popular desire for clarification lies in wanting to know 'why' he did it—and in the UK it is much more likely to be a man than a woman. And this 'why?' is perfectly understandable, for 'to know'—were such knowledge certain—would be to gain that kind of conceptual comfort that pays its own debt to embodied unease or unhappiness over the loss of someone. Philosophically speaking, the world retains meaning as long as the veil of culture adorning Earth's surfaces lies untorn, but suicide is one action that tears it apart, with even obvious social–psychological 'reasons' leaving untied ends that bind clarification to mystification. Still, suicide also provides opportunity for deeply personal forms of memorial that help retain some of the ties that bind the dead with their kin.[39]

Mystification

For mystification has to do with many aspects of lived experience that are sensed as not succumbing to the explanations proffered by our social worlds. Myths, doctrines, and theories often entail domains of the untold, untellable, and uncertain that thrill, engender awe, or stimulate further research. These

---

[39] E.g. Maple et al. (2013).

run in opposition to that demystified or, as Max Weber would have it, disenchanted world ensuing from an increased rational control of modes of production and of the bureaucratic organization of social life, a process many others discuss in terms of secularization.

This is precisely why suicide is problematic, for it affords its own form of 'natural symbol' of life's complexity against the relatively simple systems that social organization wishes to create. Yet it is the complexity that tends to prevail and in this we all share, from it death is the only exit, passage, or termination. In terms of this volume at large, and its undercurrent motif of symbolic disclosure and concealment, suicide stands as a distinctive phenomenon. It probably stands at the highest level of concealment, in the sense that many relatives and friends are left 'not knowing' why he 'did it', and yet, at the same time suicide is typically associated with a 'suicide note' or 'suicide letter'. Paradoxically, however, such communications often serve more as an indication that the death was suicidal than as an explicit explanation of the reasons for death. In this sense, suicide's concealing power reflects something of the wider and often unpalatable fact of life—that each of us knows much less about others, and they of us—than our society likes to admit. This echoes the words of George Herbert's 'Giddiness' poem of chapter 1 with its incisive reminder: 'Surely if each one saw another's heart / There would be no commerce / No sale or bargain pass: all would disperse / And live apart'— and the issue of suicide would be so much clearer than it is now, when each has to guess, seek to intuit, or otherwise clear or condemn ourselves of the motivating cause.[40]

From a slightly different perspective, however, suicide presents a specific example of the general truth that death possesses a great capacity as a social message carrier.[41] Death is seldom a simple event in which a body dies, but a social and psychological event entailing other things. In a classic expression of Christian tradition, not only is death an unnatural phenomenon, being a divine punishment on the mythical Adam and Eve for human disobedience to divine commands, but the death of Christ is also unnatural, being a divinely intended sacrifice responding to that human sin. This interpretation, which itself entails extensive theological and ritual thought from ancient Israel through to the liturgy of the Eucharist, ensures that any death over two millennia of Christian cultural history is painted on a theologically primed canvas. The New Testament's overwhelming concern with the death of Christ ensured that subsequent Christian thought would devote serious attention to death in human experience. As for suicide, it is rare in the biblical text, with the case of Judas who betrayed Jesus being notorious.[42]

---

[40] Herbert (1994: 110).   [41] Mäkinen and Wasserman (2001).

[42] See Moo (1983: 299) for Judas and the Old Testament figure of Ahithophel, the only two suicides in the Bible.

Augustine's Christian View

St Augustine's *City of God*, for example, a text of the early fifth century,[43] takes as axiomatic the commandment, 'Thou shalt not kill' as far as human beings are concerned. Though he does note in passing that plants, too, have life in them, the divine law applies to humans and to oneself; the only exception is if God commands a killing, or indeed if a magistrate does so![44] Augustine argues that murder produces guilt and that suicide is its own form of murder. The case of Judas Iscariot is offered as one in which he is guilty not only of betraying Christ but of adding to his own guilt by killing himself: in so doing he reveals a 'despair of God's mercy'.[45] Augustine then argues against the idea that a Christian virgin, for example, should wish to kill herself rather than be raped. For him sanctity lies in the mind, her virtue is left untouched if her mental resolve is retained, no matter what happens to her body. In his chapter 25, however, he cites some women who drowned themselves in a river to flee from their persecutors: these have been 'honoured with religious memorials'. His response to this is interesting: 'Well, of these I dare not judge rashly in anything.' Perhaps they did this not through 'mortal fear' but through 'heavenly instinct'? What if it was 'holy love' that caused it? Augustine acknowledges that his own judgement cannot 'penetrate into the secrets of the heart'. Still his general view is clear: voluntary death is wrong. And as for anyone who suggests voluntary death straight after baptism so as to avoid sin, 'he is plain mad'.[46] It is interesting that Augustine does not seem to invoke the idea that God is the giver of life in these chapters; presumably he takes that for granted. It is a sense of law that he stresses. Many later Christian views on suicide have stressed the idea that God gives life and should be the only one to take it—whether by war or capital punishment or by other 'natural' means.

In following centuries we see Christian attitudes to suicide develop. At the Council of Braga (AD 561) suicides are denied normal burial and prayers. Later, from his magisterial position in the thirteenth century, Thomas Aquinas argued that, because it was natural for a person to love himself, it was contrary to natural law and charity to kill oneself; moreover, life belonged to God whose gift it was to humanity. To commit suicide was thus to act contrary to the divine order of things, for it belonged to God to make alive and to render dead.[47]

Shakespeare reflects this general Christian understanding of the normal prohibition of a Christian burial to suicides in his *Hamlet*, where it takes the Coroner to allow Christian burial to Ophelia who had been utterly mentally disturbed by her father's death and had apparently taken her own life by

---

[43] St Augustine, *City of God*. Book 1. Chapters 16–27.
[44] Ibid., 19, 20.   [45] Ibid., 16.   [46] Ibid., 26.
[47] Aquinas, *Summa Theologica*, 11–11.64.5.

drowning,[48] though a clear implication is that the legal decision was swayed by her being 'a gentlewoman' for otherwise 'she should have been buried out o' Christian burial'.[49] Still, the condition had been tellingly described as the outcome of 'the poison of deep grief',[50] and this in the same Act where actual deadly poison is intended for use in murder.[51] The priest, explicitly described as a 'Doctor of Divinity', who buries her expresses many cautions because 'her death was doubtful', and had it not been for superior order 'she should in ground unsanctified have lodged'. With his doubts he wants only the bare minimum of ritual, for

> We should not profane the service of the dead
> To sing a requiem and such rest to her
> As to peace-parted souls[52]

Her brother, Laertes, anguished at her death entirely disagrees and depicts his sister's destiny as that of 'a minist'ring angel' by contrast with the 'churlish priest' whose destiny is to 'lie howling'. Then in a fascinating turn of events Hamlet arrives and declares his love for the dead woman whose brother has already jumped into the grave to hold her 'once more in mine arms'. In misplaced competitive grief Hamlet addresses Laertes, 'Dost come here to whine? To outface me with leaping in her grave?'[53] The background intrigues of treachery progress until both die in a fencing duel involving a poisoned weapon, but not before treacherous misunderstandings are resolved, and they 'exchange forgiveness'.[54]

It is some distance from Shakespeare's literary culture of the late sixteenth century, embodied and played out as it was on stage, to David Hume's philosophical Scotland in the mid-eighteenth century with its tracts and treatises. Yet each of them engages with death, suicide, and the significance of life amidst one's loves and social duties. Certainly, Hume's philosophy of experience and reason sketches its own version of reciprocity, presaging some of the reciprocity theory discussed in anthropological terms in this present volume. As he says, 'All our obligations to do good to society seem to imply something reciprocal. I receive the benefits of society, and therefore ought to promote its interests.' But he also conceives it reasonable that an individual might also withdraw himself 'altogether from society' and then be bound no longer. That decision might follow one's self-understanding of no longer promoting 'the interest of the public', or being 'a burden to it'. Moreover, even if a person believes that God appoints his place in the world, that does not mean that if 'pain or sorrow so far overcome my patience, as to make me tired

---

[48] Hamlet (Act V. Scene i. line 4).
[49] Hamlet (V. i. 23).
[50] Hamlet (IV. v. 76).
[51] Hamlet (IV. vii. 38).
[52] Hamlet (V. i. 25).
[53] Hamlet (V. i. 268).
[54] Hamlet (V. ii. 312).

of life' that I should not think of myself 'as recalled from my station in the clearest and most express of terms'. Hume is clear that 'when the horror of pain prevails over the love of life; when a voluntary action anticipates the effects of blind causes' then suicide not only seems reasonable but the individual can even be said to be lawfully employing 'the power with which nature has endowed him'. Simply to let events take their own course under all circumstances would mean that 'it would be equally criminal to act for the preservation of life as for its destruction'.[55] Personal judgement acting under the constraints of emotional circumstances drives his argument, but it was not one that attracted much support, and his essay on the subject was not properly published until decades after being written and Christian antipathy to suicide prevailed.

Over the centuries many countries added criminal status to the act as did the UK; it remained a crime until 1961. Roman Catholic Canons (1184) of 1983 allow Christian burial for suicides, but those who have attempted suicide are not subsequently allowed to be ordained. In pastoral practice a softer approach has often been taken especially under the legally influential notion that, as already mentioned above, a suicide's balance of mind has been disturbed. These and many other theological and ecclesiastical views ensured that suicide became established as one polar form of death, with martyrdom and sacrifice occupying the other extreme.[56] Here this chapter's reference to suicide not only complements chapter 7's account of military death counted as sacrifice, but also raises the deeply paradoxical fact of the suicide of soldiers.

Soldiers' Suicide

The number of soldiers returning from active service in the decades surrounding the turn of the twenty-first century and who, subsequently, commit suicide in their civilian status is not simply a profound loss for their relatives and friends but also a cultural conundrum. For such a death sets strongly pro-social values against anti-social values. Symbolic parallels tempt one to say it sets hero against coward, though even the thought of using the word 'coward' presents its own unease. Still, an unease there is, even though the form it takes is one of sadness rather than blame; sadness that one who served society now withdraws from it. Soldiers whose bodies are returned and given a funeral with military honours, and the funeral of an ex-military individual, sit uneasily together, both culturally and psychologically.

---

[55] David Hume (n.d., [c.1755, 1783] 4–9).
[56] Kant, for example, describes a suicide as a 'rebel of God'. See Mappes and Degrazia (2001: 398–402).

Still, as secular and more widely spiritual frames have come to characterize British life, albeit retaining a certain social positive value for sacrificial death, suicide has lost much of the negative connotation rooted in sin or crime. It is within the greater intimacy of family and friendship that suicide continues to pose dilemmas. For it is far from unusual for families, friends, and associates to wonder what they might, could, or should have done that would have prevented the suicide, even when literal suicide notes may be left as their own form of testimony explaining a sense of impossibility of going on with life. Suicide is frequently framed by an attempt to disclose whatever the suicide had concealed prior to the final act, despite the fact that suicide brings the concrete nature of human individuality into the limelight of the social stage. For social life, most especially the intimate life of spouses, partners, and families, requires some degree of knowledge of the other in order that social communication may proceed and life be lived in a successful fashion. Such issues undergird the key motifs of this volume especially as encoded in the notions of meaning-making and narrative, cultural intensification and identity, and embodiment and sense of presence. We make meaning in our lives through the biographical narratives created within family and other networks, through the identities we develop in relationships with others, and through our developing awareness of embodiment and sense of presence of self amidst others. Our dreams, too, both of the living and the dead, play into this self-awareness, even if it is ignored in much social-scientific discourse. In all of these, dynamic vitality is played out in relation to mortality and under an awareness of the jural–mystical dynamics of dual sovereignty. Suicide is, however, an unwelcome narrative that flows uneasily if at all within a family or friend's sense of understanding.

Durkheim

So it is that suicide highlights the contrast between the inwardly knowing self and a person's presentation of a version of self to society. This very idea of the 'self' is, of course, deeply problematic and is understood in many different ways from society to society, not least in Western European thought where we could easily oppose a Freudian psychoanalytic dynamic of conscious and unconscious realms pervaded by his *eros* and *thanatos* drives for life and death against Durkheim's deeply sociological conception of a person described as *Homo duplex* in which the organic entity of an individual person is as set against the social dimension of the social person. While many other defin-itions of self could also be listed we will stay with Durkheim, not only because his *Homo duplex* motif bears repeated consideration but also because he is the thinker who 'taught the modern world how to think about suicide', as Richard Sennett, one of today's leading social scientists, affirmed in the first line of his

Introduction to the 2006 Penguin Edition of Durkheim's *Suicide*, a volume first published in 1897. Sennett, in an essay that is important in its own right, clearly makes the point in this way. 'Durkheim saw that suicide has a social dimension. People from different religions, classes and religious backgrounds destroy themselves in different proportions. Durkheim asked why this should be' (2006: xi). Sennett notes the wide cultural background against which Durkheim wrote, a European background informed by 'virtual suicide', as in Socrates' self-administered poison cup, by Christianity's rejection of virtuous suicide, and by an eighteenth-century acknowledgement of the 'romantic suicide' of sensitive individuals. By pitching his study not in the psychic depths of individual dynamics but in 'social facts', where statistics could reveal the incidence of suicide amongst different populations, he could invite interpretation of these very demographic profiles. But no scholar is devoid of personal influences and motivation for his or her work, even if that actual work turns solidly on statistical data; and so it was for this young Jew from a long line of rabbis, who formally abandons his faith when aged twenty-one, who perhaps found it hard to be accepted into non-Jewish French society. Then, as a young man of twenty-eight his friend Victor Hommay committed suicide in 1886. Some thirty or so years later, in 1915, the fifty-seven-year-old scholar would also lose his son André in the First World War; Durkheim died but two years later. Marcel Mauss, his nephew and the scholar who gave us so much in his thinking on reciprocity, reckoned this was a main cause of Durkheim's death.

As for Durkheim's theory, he posited three main types of suicide, each depending on the qualitative nature of the relationship between an individual and society. Accordingly, *egoistic suicide* is the outcome of people not being enmeshed in appropriate networks of support at a time of serious difficulty; the self or ego left to itself is unable to cope. He reckoned that Catholics, for example, were less likely to commit suicide than Protestants, and wondered if this was due to a Protestant overemphasis upon the self as a sole religious entity before God. Second, *altruistic suicide* involves what might be seen as too great a group involvement, such that suicide might be the best way out from an interminable situation; the only way out of a shameful or socially intolerable situation seemingly being that of suicide, which then becomes a kind of sacrifice for the good of the group, even if the group might not see it like that. Third, *anomic suicide* occurs when people find themselves in a world without rules, or where rules seem to shift as social change occurs. Questions of meaning and meaninglessness arise here, not least in relation to upward mobility and economic shifts. A fourth, albeit rare, kind of suicide would be *fatalistic*, where an individual possesses little or no sense of freedom and meaning in life. Following his broad theoretical sense of people being socially integrated or not Durkheim found that married people generally have the lowest suicide rates, and divorced and widowed people have rates that are two or three times higher. In comparative terms other factors become important, as in the high rate of suicide among unmarried young women in rural China and the problem of arranged marriages there. In other countries the unemployed offer a higher risk group than the employed.[57] But, certainly, suicide has been identified as a 'major health-care issue' especially where increasing numbers of women, adolescents, and elderly women are concerned.[58]

Among other theorists Thomas Joiner has reduced types of suicide to the two broad categories of a need for 'belongingness' and a 'need for effectiveness or sense of competence'. On the first count he sees suicide in terms of 'thwarted belongingness' (i.e. thwarted love, ruptured relationships) and on the second a 'perceived burdensomeness' (assaulted self-image, fractures control, anger related to frustrated dominance).[59] His reference to a 'sense of competence' closely resembles Ernesto de Martino's notion of 'sense of presence', already discussed in chapter 6.

These clustered ideas of a sensed social uselessness and burdensomeness reflect a perceived disconnect with the field of social force and demand scrutiny as we now move from the theme of suicide as such to that of assisted death because, if anything, this recent concern highlights a positive sense of competence, affirming a 'sense of presence' rather than 'a crisis of presence' in de Martino's terminology. For here we are dealing with individuals taking a positive and socially engaged stance over their identity and desire for death. Because this stance seeks a degree of control over dying while in a strong relationship with appropriately significant 'others' it seems to involve a degree of demystification of death and in this sense it reinforces secularization. This reflects Max Weber's long-established sociological view on the increase of rational control in society over time, a process in which 'the world's processes become disenchanted, lose their magical significance, and henceforth simply "are" and "happen" but no longer signify anything'.[60] While he rooted this world view in intellectualism it has become increasingly democratized in Western European countries. This may be one reason why most religious traditions, albeit institutionally implicitly, find it unacceptable because it trespasses upon their sacred ground, though there are exceptions to this as we see in the following section.

Assisting dying

Just as words may fail people in explaining suicides that touch their own lives, so do words become increasingly important over what we are now about to

---

[57] See Wasserman (ed.) (2001), and Honkasala and Tuominen (2014) for insightful resources on modern suicide.

[58] David Aldridge (1998: 7).

[59] Joiner (2005: 96–7). Joiner (2005: 30) also tells of his own father's suicide, reflecting perhaps our earlier comments on Durkheim's experience of suicide.

[60] Weber ([1922] 1966: 125).

discuss in that such expressions as 'assisted dying' and 'assisted suicide', and 'doctor-assisted death' and 'doctor-assisted suicide' each carry assumptions arising from a person or group's moral position. To reiterate, here words are important, and this is understandable given the religious and legal histories of suicide just sketched and the fact of social change that encourages Britons to think of their life in terms of choices amongst options. This consumerist-style model of life has been forwarded by the UK government not only for educational policies of change in terms of parental choice of school for children but also for health-care policies in terms choice of hospital and doctors for particular operations. This choice-based political platform has been underpinned by performance tables of schools and hospitals that, in turn, have been related to funding and managerial control. In other words, a great deal of political activity with high social profile has engendered a sense of responsibility and personal agency in the UK over the latter decades of the twentieth and start of the twenty-first centuries, all after the establishment of post-war reforms of education and institution of the welfare state.

However, a deep paradox then arises when the choice model in national health care stops at the point of death. This paradox picks up that stream of thought in this volume which considers the NHS as its own form of religious–spiritual institution, in the sense of its hosting and implementing certain core cultural values. In this case the paradox emerges from the political desire to have the NHS both as an economically efficient service of health care and as an opportunity for individual choice of service.[61] At the same time, however, the NHS is the place where thousands of medical and health-care workers live their professional lives, often motivated by their personal ideological–cultural–religious values. In other words the hospital, general practitioner health centre, and other related venues become sites of contesting values and desires.

It seems that increasing numbers of citizens seem to want the option of ending their own lives if and when they are terminally ill or suffering from illness that they see as totally debilitating and rendering any 'quality' as negligible. The cultural lifestyle of 'choice' encounters considerable problems in terms of a death-style of choice because the law intrudes to remove choice. And while the Director of Public Prosecutions has acknowledged something of the shift in popular opinion in a tacit understanding that persons who help a person to commit suicide would not be prosecuted if motivated by compassion and not some murderous intent, the law does not allow that assistance to come

---

[61] A survey by Ipsos MORI for Richard Dawkins Foundation for Reason and Science (UK) (2014) asked a church aligned sample if they supported hospital chaplains being paid for by NHS budget and not by the chaplains' religious organization (question 35). Ten per cent strongly supported the idea, 22% tended to support, 22% were neither/nor, 20% tended to oppose, 19% strongly opposed, 6% didn't know, and 1% preferred not to say.

from the medical profession. A week before the Lords' debate, the Rt. Revd Lord Harries of Pentregarth, a former Bishop of Oxford, published an article in the *Church Times*, a well-read newspaper of the Anglican establishment, supporting that 'present legal set-up', viz. that for 'a person motivated only by compassion' who helps 'another person to die . . . there should be no prosecution'. He feared that any change might lead to 'a slippery slope' taking assistance beyond the proposed scheme of a person having a terminal illness, no more than six months to live, and an opinion of two doctors. He reckoned that if 'voluntary assisted dying' was introduced now it would not be long before 'euthanasia' would emerge 'in which people not able to make a decision for themselves would be killed on the decision of doctors'. Another criticism was against 'the fear of loss of control' that people seemed to express, for this he considered to be 'a false individualism'. In what could be read as a classic expression of much sociological thought, and certainly of the Durkheimian view, he asserts; 'We are not just a series of isolated individuals, but persons in relationship to each other.'[62] That edition of the *Church Times* also carried an article on the need to improve palliative care at the end of life, and another, entitled 'Meanwhile, further down the slippery slope', adopted a comparative stance on other European countries.[63] A further article, on 'The dubious morality of choice', cited the popular Anglican priest Giles Fraser both in identifying 'choice' as 'a sort of cuckoo in the nest, driving out all other values', and as 'the final triumph of market capitalism: we have become consumers in everything, even when it comes to life and death'.[64] This point echoes our earlier discussion of 'choice' as a political litany over recent decades. These contributions summarize many that are currently heard expressed by those opposing assisted dying and offered their church-grounded readers a brief introduction to the debate in the House of Lords on 18 July 2014 dealing with Lord Falconer's 'Assisted Dying Bill', one at which Lord Harries also spoke and made similar points as above.

The debate itself was notable in that no fewer than 133 members of the House of Lords spoke, with a near unanimous outcome that it should go into a Committee stage of consideration. The debate reflected the various dimensions of the British Establishment, not least those of medicine and the Church of England. Some of the contributions were of considerable significance as far as a sociological understanding of cultural values of life and death in the UK are concerned. Baroness Emerton, a distinguished nurse, highlighted the importance of words, noting that this second Bill referred to 'assisted dying' whereas its predecessor referred to 'assisted suicide', a change that was, she

---

[62] Harries (2014: 14).
[63] Respectively by Willmott (2014: 15), Bishop of Dover; and freelance writer Jonathan Luxmore (2014: 15).
[64] Andrew Brown (2014: 43).

suggested, a 'much more attractive term to the public'. Her deepest concern, however, lay in the natural support and care for patients as they die for this, she considered to be 'real assisted dying'.[65] This sense of social concern also underlay one of the Church of England voices, that of the Rt. Revd James Newcome, Bishop of Carlisle, who spoke of the 'true dignity' of human beings lying in their 'interdependence' and 'willingness to be served by others'.[66] Another supportive religious voice, this time from the well-known Sikh, Lord Singh of Wimbledon, also pinpointed the social nature of persons as a key factor. For him, an overly 'narrow view of autonomy is little more than an unhealthy obsession with self which is condemned as one of the five deadly sins in Sikh scripture'. For him 'the reality is that all of us are part of a wider society'.[67] With an eye to actual events, Baroness Young of Old Scone, an individual much experienced in health management, reckoned that 'an estimated 300' people were 'helped to die each year by friends and family' with another 1,000 being 'assisted to die by medical practitioners'.[68] That bare description, aimed at giving a sense of the way things are, can be contrasted with the contribution of Lord Ribeiro, former President of the Royal College of Surgeons, who contrasted his College's 2004 and 2011 comments on assisted dying; the former saw the matter as something as 'a matter for the individual' doctor while the latter argued that the law as it stands ought not to be changed because 'no system should be introduced to allow people to be assisted to die'.[69]

Intersection

Despite the progress of this Bill into its next parliamentary phase, time alone will tell whether this concern will be validated and implemented. But, for the immediate future, this option looks unlikely given that, despite widespread popular opinion, the House of Commons, voted 330 against and 118 for assisted dying, in a party-free private member's bill vote on 11 September 2015.

The key issue as far as this volume is concerned turns on the way the British Establishment intersects with the population at large through the theme of death, and here the NHS becomes the focal point where the medical, legal, and political establishments meet, and where the churches and religious institutions also take their stance. In line with the arguments of this book, it is perfectly understandable that the majority of medical professionals would

---

65 *Hansard*, House of Lords, 18 July 2012, column 892.
66 *Hansard*, House of Lords, 18 July 2012, column 909.
67 *Hansard*, House of Lords, 18 July 2012, column 869.
68 *Hansard*, House of Lords, 18 July 2012, column 870.
69 *Hansard*, House of Lords, 18 July 2012, column 910.

object to a change in the law, even if the personal choice of doctors to engage in assistance was firmly preserved. For doctors are symbols of life: their work offers hope, and they reflect the vitality dimension of this present volume. In other terms they reflect a sense of ritual purity in being those who preserve the cultural value of a valued life.[70] This is reflected in the medical professions' general sense that the ancient Greek Hippocratic Oath has considerable force in emphasizing patient care, not doing any harm, and in generally declaring 'the core values of the profession', even if it is not the practice of all medical schools to administer the 'oath' as such.[71] Reference to this Oath and its numerous variants, especially following the Second World War and recognition that Nazi doctors had abused medical practice, reflects an increase in concern with ethics in a world where religious tradition no longer guarantees good behaviour. Against that background, and in the light of the quite different contemporary British interest in assisted dying, it is quite understandable that the notion of human dignity should come to assume a high profile alongside core cultural values of human wellbeing during life, towards life's end, and after death.

Dignity

'Dignity' is, however, difficult to define given its antecedent meanings of self-respect or formal demeanour in high office, contexts bearing affinity with 'Establishment' as such, and because 'dignity' has also attracted new significance for human identity surrounding dying and death. Still, one classic description of dignity that holds value for its succinctness and enduring relevance is that of Hobbes. Hobbes describes dignity as 'the public worth of a man, which is the value set on him by the commonwealth', an attribution to be distinguished from simple 'worth'—where 'the buyer determines the price' of the 'use of his power'.[72]

To think of dignity as the value set upon someone by 'the commonwealth' or, as we might now say, by society at large, is to highlight the social context out of which identity emerges and is sustained. Following earlier chapters we can see not only how this sense of value is reflected in Mauss's inalienable identity of things or persons but also how such worth is a prime cultural expression of vitality taken in the direction of ethics. This is a contested notion in that some would wish to apply it to life and a natural death while others would apply it to an assisted death, though we see 'worth' as the frame of each context.

---

[70] Duschinsky and Lampitt (2012: 1195–207).
[71] Hurwitz and Richardson (1997: 1671–4) reported around half of UK medical schools using some oath at that time.
[72] Hobbes ([1651] n.d., pp. 57–8.)

In terms of social theory this is a significant issue because it differs from theological arguments that would establish the 'dignity' of human beings from some combination of our status as created or redeemed creatures. This would include the idea that in the incarnation God becomes human in the figure of Jesus and therefore marks humanity with a distinctive dignity. From a broad philosophical standpoint it may not matter whether one derives 'dignity' from the domain of society or of divinity; it is the outcome that matters. And this is why many, whether secular social philosophers or religious theologians, find an affinity with 'dignity' as a shared basis for discussing human rights, not least in relation to death and dying. So, for example, in instances of individuals seeking doctor-assisted death or even doctor-administered death, 'dignity' has frequently been invoked as a word covering the worth of individuals and the degree to which their wishes should be heeded. Its centrality within the Bill of Human Rights is pivotal in a spectrum of subsequent usage such that 'dignity' has become a self-evident principle when considering human behaviour.

One British example may suffice in highlighting 'dignity' and the common-wealth as it is paradoxically present in early twenty-first-century Britain. It is the case of Mr Tony Nicklinson, a man who had been so severely affected by a stroke that he became paralysed from the neck down, in what is loosely described as 'locked-in syndrome', able to communicate with others only through blinking. Mr Nicklinson had sought a High Court judgment allowing him to die through active intervention of doctors, for he is too incapacitated even to avail himself of doctor-assisted death. The judgment in August 2012 went against him on the basis that it was not a legal decision that was required but a change in the law enacted by Parliament since what he currently sought would be accounted as murder. A leading article in *The Times* newspaper responded to this judgment by saying that 'the reluctance of the courts and Parliament to act even in such rare and specific cases means that regard is being paid to the sanctity of life but too little to its dignity'.[73] This stubborn issue in British culture was taken up and taken a step further two years later by Tony Nicklinson's widow, Jane, along with a paralysed former builder Paul Lamb. They approached the UK's Supreme Court asking for a judgement on 'whether the ban on assisted suicide was incompatible with article eight of the European Convention on Human Rights'. The outcome, on 25 June 2014, by seven judges to two,

> did not uphold the appeal against the 1961 Suicide Act. But a majority of them concluded that the court did have the constitutional authority to make the decision. However, despite concluding that the case for the current law was 'by no means overwhelming' the court made it plain that this was now a matter that should be considered in parliament.

[73] *The Times*, 18 August 2012: 2.

The judges thought that a judge or independent assessor ought to be involved in each case as well as two doctors but they also reckoned that 'no physician should be involved in administering the fatal poison'.[74] However, The Assisted Dying Bill 2014 precisely designated a 'health professional' whether the 'attending doctor' involved in the decision-making of the patient from the outset, or another doctor or registered nurse designated by that original doctor, to administer the fatal medicine. As for the death certificate, it would carry the cause of death as 'assisted death'.[75]

Certainly, opinions run high over this particular lifestyle–death-style inter-section as a final comment will both exemplify, yet again illustrating the importance of words whether in clarifying or taking hostage key cultural values. This one, from the journalist Melanie Phillips, preceded the Lords' debate which she reckoned 'ushers in a new dark age'. It is an important point because it is a good public expression of the more technical sociological theme of cultural classification.

> In a stroke of propaganda genius, the Voluntary Euthanasia Society renamed itself Dignity in Dying. Instantly, killing was transformed into dying. Killing is bad, but dying is inevitable. And people are frightened of dying in pain or distress. The unconscionable was thus turned into the unstoppable. The seedy and sinister became enlightened and compassionate.

Consonant with this she also argues that any future acceptance of the Bill 'would turn doctors into executioners, brutalising society in the process'.[76] In her argument, as in a significant number of speeches in the debate, the issue of dying framed by the potential of medicine, by the traditional role of doctors in wellbeing, by the fear of pain, and by a desire for autonomous control, reveals a period of social change. This is, in many respects, a key topic for issues of secularization. It is also a point at which the dynamics and tension of trad-itional religion and the mixed complexity of religious, humanistic, and secular spiritualities enter a pragmatic arena of social opinion, and it is one that we can still interpret as driven by Durkheim's *Homo duplex*. For when Phillips ends her article by advocating a 'proper balance between compassion for individuals and protection for society' she is, in theoretical terms, expressing the dynamic interaction of an ethics concerning the self and legislation for society.

The fear of dying, and the right to die: statistical profiles

The themes of pain, fear of pain, and attitudes to one's death are interesting given that contemporary British society is, relatively speaking, pain-free

---

[74] *The Times*, leading article, Thursday 26 June 2014, p. 28.
[75] Assisted Dying Bill 2014. Sections 4 (10) and (10. 2b), and 7 (2.2).
[76] Melanie Phillips (2014: 26).

compared with past eras and with many other less-developed countries. A Theos-commissioned survey of April 2009 (cited in chapter 2 for different purposes) contacted over 1,000 people, in which some 50% reckoned to fear the process of dying.[77] Looked at in more detail this involved 20% fearing both the way they might die and the fact of death itself. The other 30% also feared how they might die but not death as such. A further 25% reckoned to have neither a fear of dying nor of death. In terms of age, it was the 18–24-year-olds who most feared both the way they might die and death itself (26% compared with a national average of 20%).

Another survey (also cited in chapter 2) asked people who reckoned some degree of Christian identity and alliance with a Christian church whether 'it should be legal to assist the suicide of a terminally ill patient who has clearly and consistently expressed the wish to die and is considered by doctors to be mentally and emotionally competent to make the decision'.[78] On a seven-point scale the percentage results showed: 'Strongly agree' (29), 'Tend to agree' (30), "Neither agree nor disagree' (15), 'Tend to disagree' (8), 'Strongly disagree' (12), 'Don't Know' (2), and 'Prefer not to say' (2). These are interesting results, not only in that the 'don't know' and 'not saying' only make 4% between the two of them, but with under a quarter (20%) tending towards disagreement or strongly disagreeing. It is interesting to see that the results over the 'abortion' of an 'unwanted pregnancy within the legal time limit' revealed a very similar response.[79] For ease of comparison these two lifestyle choices are compared in Table 8.1.

The similarity of profile suggests an affinity between abortion and assisted dying. The former, once intensely problematic in Britain, is still, of course, contested by pro-life groups, especially within the Roman Catholic Church. In England and Wales in 2013, for example 185,331 abortions were carried out and of these some 5,469 were for women not normally resident in the United

Table 8.1. Attitudes to assisted suicide and abortion (approximate percentages)

	Strongly agree	Tend to agree	Neither agree nor disagree	Tend to disagree	Strongly disagree	Don't know	Prefer not to say
Assist Suicide	29	30	15	8	12	2	2
Abortion	30	33	13	11	9	2	3

Source: Richard Dawkins Foundation.

[77] ComRes interviewed 1,018 adults online between 24 and 26 April 2009.
[78] Ipsos MORI for Richard Dawkins Foundation for Reason and Science (UK) (2014: Question 39).
[79] Ipsos MORI for Richard Dawkins Foundation for Reason and Science (UK) (2014: Question 38).

Kingdom. Significantly, 67% of that group were normally resident in the Republic of Ireland and 15% in Northern Ireland, statistics that almost certainly represent a continuing cultural Catholic opposition to abortion as such, and reflect an ongoing debate in the Republic over this religious stricture in terms of a woman's essential human rights. A cognate statistic, germane for this volume, lies in the fact that of the 1,201 abortions of foetuses over twenty-two weeks' gestation 68% were subject to what the official documentation of the Department of Health categorizes as feticide. This procedure, advocated by the Royal College of Obstetricians and Gynaecologists, involves the foetus' heart being stopped medically before the foetus is removed. For a further 26%, the heart was described as stopping of its own accord 'prior to evacuation of the uterus'.[80]

In terms of this present volume it is worth noting that feticide is a term practically unheard of in public discourse; it belongs to the concealed element in the concealed–revealed motif of death in many lifestyle and death-style interfaces that has been noted in earlier chapters. While there are, indeed, serious medical conditions affecting a relatively small percentage of foetuses, and while the medical rationale for a great number of abortions lies with opinions on the mental and physical health of the mother, the fact of abortion, very largely conducted through the NHS, reflects the fact of social control over reproduction and, to a degree, of a desire of control of a woman over her personal life, often expressed in the cultural idiom of 'it's my body'. This control element, whether or not embedded in medical welfare, reflects the control over one's life, symbolized in 'my body', that reappears in the phenomenon of assisted dying. The parallel significance of abortion and assisted dying, a parallel that might be depicted as 'assisted non-birth' and 'assisted death', is strong. It is not far removed from the way in which the idea of 'natural birth' was a stimulating idiom in promoting the notion of 'natural death' espoused by the Natural Death Centre established in 1991 as a charity fostering bereaved persons' choices over forms of funeral and a natural attitude towards death.

CONCLUSION

If abortion offers one constraint in negotiating one's way through life, and assisted dying another form of 'wayfaring', they certainly highlight that dialectic between lifestyle and death-style underlying this entire volume. Not only do they reflect different modes of interaction between individuals and the

---

[80] *Abortion Statistics for England and Wales, 2013* (Department of Health) p. 15.

'establishment' framing of social force in British life, but they also symbolize social change. Symbolically and ethically speaking, the antipathy of the church 'establishment' towards assisted dying presents a reversal of the St Erkenwald myth in which an emergent ecclesial establishment of social power validates preceding paganism. As for *Tom Brown* and *Harry Potter*, they speak of and from rooted establishments, one rooted in Victorian Christianity, and the other the fictional domain of 'magic'.[81] Finally, suicide and assisted dying bring us to the all-too-real world where social change and conflicting political messages set some individuals against the medical–legal–ecclesial–political establishment. This world of pragmatic necessity is also one where pain plays a constant and almost invisible emotional role shadowing life, indicating the challenge of 'wayfaring' for a society that increasingly prizes respect, individualism, and the absence of pain while depending for this on the competent provision of professional services that are still pervaded by 'establishment' forces.

---

[81] Recalling that the *Potter* world has its own division between magicians and 'muggles', the latter being 'ordinary' people devoid of magical natures.

9

Death-Styles and Lifestyles

The idioms of lifestyle and death-style now focus on selected cases exemplifying the social forces influencing death in Britain. We begin with a brief consideration of the notion of style, the cognitive aspect of which is pursued through a 1960s analysis of British religion, followed by a consideration of the emotional dynamics of aesthetic style of selected death-related art work. The theme of the British Establishment and death is then directed to the funeral of Baroness Thatcher and the re-interment of the bones of King Richard III. The role of funeral directors is then re-examined, followed by a consideration of the media, specifically digital media, and death. Amidst these institutional discussions we will neither forget the creative role of the bereaved individual in a case of personal grief and the reburial of cremated remains, nor of wider social interest in relatively anonymous roadside memorials. As for the innovative practice of woodland burial we retain that distinctive lifestyle shift for chapter 10.

STYLE

Societies and their religious phenomena differ in the way power is vested in persons and institutions and this makes it difficult, for example, to compare the sociology of death and religion in the USA and in the UK, and also gives pause for thought within the different cases analysed in this chapter. Our preoccupation with style in the idioms of 'life-' and 'death-' styles has been intentionally informed by this power-based context.

Although Max Weber drew on the notion of habitus as shown in chapter 1, it is Bourdieu's engagement with it as a 'generative formula' underlying any lifestyle that attracts most attention. In a passage singled out for critical comment by Luce Giard, Bourdieu spoke of social behaviours revealing preferences in food, clothing, or cosmetics as being 'organised according to the same fundamental structure, that of the social space determined by volume and composition of capital'. This criticism focuses on the sense of stasis, of an unchanging passing of custom from generation to generation, notably on features received from one's mother. With Giard, I prefer to give full allowance for change in custom and habitus shift, accepting 'the inventiveness of the group or the individual' that may result from broadened tastes derived from 'chance discovery' or simply from encounters with new cultural practices.[1] In previous chapters we have seen just such changes in death rites that have frequently been assumed, often incorrectly, to be conservative within societies.

Styles change. So, utilizing 'style' for death not only catches the power of 'style' when widely used and accepted in the motif of 'lifestyle' but, by extending it to death, it helps create the parallel focus on these two modes of behaviour. Furthermore, 'style' is a valuable bridging concept between more abstract and more concrete forms of dealing with behaviour. It is telling, for example, that while one of the most prestigious of Japanese fashion designers of the twentieth century, Yohji Yamamoto, can have his approach described by others in highly abstract terms, he can, himself, pinpoint its impact in the most directly pragmatic of terms. Accordingly, his 'distinct design philoso-phy', typified as focusing on 'the negative space between the body and the garment', can be set against his own view that 'fashion is only complete when it is worn by ordinary people who exist now, managing their lives, loving and grieving'.[2] This brief excerpt from the multi-million-pound domain of fashion design exemplifies a problem that easily arises when philosophy-like abstrac-tion confronts pragmatic bodies and their emotions. Yamamoto's 'loving and grieving' as part of the ongoing management of our lives has a tone about it that sits uneasily with the formally proposed abstraction of a 'distinct design philosophy' that somehow concerns 'the negative space between the body and the garment'. For Yamamoto, to speak of loving and grieving is to speak easily of the clothes appropriate for each sort of event by lovers and the bereaved. Still, the critical abstraction of 'the negative space' should not be ignored as fanciful conceptual play but kept in mind as offering a potential insight to the styles in question.

Force Expanded

The distance between different interpretations of style and the practicalities to which they refer is just as important for the clothing of death as for life. The dead, like the living, are dressed, temporarily accommodated, and transported to a 'final' resting place, and each of these domains carries stylistic options. How should a corpse be dressed? Which coffin is appropriate? What of the hearse-limousine or horse, or hand-drawn carriage that will be paid for in the

---

[1] Giard ([1994] 1998: 182).
[2] Hywel Davies (2009: 202), citing Yamamoto (n.d.) *Talking to Myself.*

funeral? And what of the burial site or of the cremated remains? Just how the lifestyle of a person comes to be reflected in these aspects of death-style has been one underlying issue of this whole volume and comes to focus now as we think of these 'styles' as expressing aspects of social force in the power of custom, tradition, or, indeed, of innovation.

That force is experienced by individuals both as an emotional response to the behaviour of others and as an individual appropriation of cultural values as such. In the Introduction we spoke of this appropriation in terms of 'emotional transformers' that influence individual perception; we can now also see such transformers as influencing an individual's expression of emotion in terms of 'style' that can be recognized and perhaps even appreciated by others. The influence of force on style cannot always be predicted, especially when a society allows for a considerable latitude in choice and, in effect, for a relatively wide spectrum of expressed emotions.

As indicated in the Introduction, nearly fifty years ago Anton Zijderveld discussed the relationship between social institutions and human emotions in the modern world in terms of 'force'. He saw that the Church as well as the hospital, the army as well as the university apply bureaucratic principles of organization, and noted the 'impersonal bureaucratic attitude' encountered in them. Following Max Weber in terms of societies that become complex and in which one institutional provision is differentiated from others, he saw that 'bureaucrats who perform their role appropriately do not hate, nor do they love: they do their job'.[3] He goes on to argue that bureaucracy, unlike religion, 'cannot care about a meaningful existence for the individual. Its main interest is efficiency.'[4]

Much influenced by the early phenomenological sociology of Peter Berger and Thomas Luckmann on the segmentation of life manifest in differentiated institutions within pluralistic society, Zijderveld saw a gap between the formal provision of institutions and the private lives of individuals in which 'private meanings escape the control and rationality of the rest of the social structure and are experienced as the subjective and inalienable foundation of human existence'. While the individual may sense this privacy as 'freedom', it actually remains 'largely illusory'.[5] Though he wrote in the 1960s and early 1970s, appropriately expressing his analysis in terms of modern industrial society (in echo of Max Weber), much of Zijderveld's analysis is as applicable to early twenty-first-century Britain as a post-industrial, service-based society. However, one proviso to this depiction concerns minorities within some conservative Christian and Muslim groups whose sense of identity lodges not simply in a privatized self that many sociologists would categorize as postmodern but

---

[3] Zijderveld ([1970] 1972: 133).   [4] Zijderveld ([1970] 1972: 134).
[5] Zijderveld ([1970] 1972: 135).

in their identifiable traditions often reflecting forms of religious conversion or a history of recent immigration. The way each of these social streams experience the wider current of society's force varies to a considerable degree. Alert to this, I am, nevertheless, seeking to take my concern with 'force' and its specific focus within social institutions into the individual's sense of presence as far as welfare, dying, and death are concerned. While the large-scale institutions of Church and NHS have already been discussed, it remains to explore their engagement with social force at different levels of and in different modes of life. To that end, this chapter follows a rough timeline from the 1960s to the present.

COGNITIVE STYLE OF RELIGION

Beginning with the 1960s, one most insightful case study of religion in Britain lies in Robert Towler's analysis of the extensive data of self-selected letters written to the once controversial Anglican Bishop of Woolwich, Dr John Robinson, briefly described in the Introduction. This account of conventional and ordinary religiosity in the UK in the 1960s presents a point of transformation from the Victorian and World War periods, as Britain reset its social compass to an as-yet uncertain future through the 1950s and beyond.

Towler not only discerned five 'types' of ordinary religiosity in the UK, derived from 'four thousand or so' self-selected reactions to Robinson's 'Honest to God' debates of the 1960s,[6] but also insisted on the need to describe what he called the 'cognitive style' aligned with these types. These styles were one explicit response to Rodney Needham's insistence that much more research needed to be done on 'modes of experience' that frame forms of 'belief'. Needham, writing as an anthropologist in the later 1960s and early 1970s on the specific question of how forms of feeling might or might not be embedded in statement of belief, was touching on an issue that Anton Zijderveld, the Dutch sociologist, highlighted at the same time when arguing that 'a sound sociological theory of emotions does not yet exist'.[7] These were reflecting an intellectual awareness that would take a variety of shapes and intensify over the next few decades in theories of embodiment,[8] of the need for sociology to embrace psychology rather than follow the historical commitment to Durkheim's 'social facts' interpreted in social ways,[9] of ethnographic accounts of emotion,[10] of one attempt at an explicit sociology of emotions,[11] of

---

[6] Towler (1984: 15).   [7] Needham (1972); Zijderveld (([1970] 1972: 141).
[8] MacLachlan (2004).   [9] Serge Moscovici (1993).
[10] E.g. Hardman (2000).   [11] Riis and Woodhead (2010).

emotions in psychiatry and philosophy,[12] of emotions in religion in general,[13] and in alliance with identity and religious groups in particular.[14]

Despite these various developments on emotion in religion, Towler's early stress on cognitive style remains valuable not only as a theoretical way of describing this 'distinctive part of religiousness' but also in terms of attitudes towards death.[15] In Table 9.1 I sketch his types and styles in tabular form and then note how he saw them related to death.

Table 9.1. Towler's types and styles

Type	Style
Exemplarism	Hope (this worldly)
Conversionism	Assurance
Theism	Trust
Gnosticism	Scientific
Traditionalism	Unquestioning acceptance

In terms of death, Towler saw exemplarists, those who focus on Jesus as an example for life rather than a resurrected being, as having no 'expectation of a life beyond the grave . . . life is here and now or not at all' with people looking forward to a better life on Earth as the example of Jesus expands. This exemplifies the potential available to human beings in 'an age which finds it difficult to accept concepts of the supernatural'.[16] This stance also depicts Jesus as something of a moral hero, echoing the Victorian Christianity evident in *Tom Brown's Schooldays* examined in chapter 8, and which Towler saw for his day as the 'unchurched working class'.[17] This category also relates to our discussion of the Sea of Faith group in chapter 5 which adds the insight on how people may change in their beliefs over their lifetimes and move into such a type.

It is not sufficient for Towler that Conversionism be described in terms of cognitive style simply by the word 'belief', nor even by 'faith', but, rather, by a 'certainty' that is even more perfectly expressed as 'assurance'.[18] This is an assurance of having been saved from sin. Interestingly, Towler does not deal with the afterlife beliefs of this group; perhaps they was taken for granted since the experience of conversion is closely aligned with the evangelicalism that frames this type and for which a heavenly afterlife is entirely assumed.

Theism, grounded in belief in a creator God and an essentially good Earth, presents a form of natural religion for which Towler adopts the idiom of 'earth-mother' who 'gives comfort' rather than the 'sky-father' who 'excites ambition and inspires great deeds'.[19] Here the cognitive style is that of 'trust';

---

[12] Ratcliffe (2008).   [13] Corrigan (2004; 2008).
[14] Douglas J. Davies (2011); Davies with Warne (2013).
[15] Towler (1984: 31). Cf. Needham (1972: 188).   [16] Towler (1984: 33–4).
[17] Towler (1984: 37).   [18] Towler (1984: 46–7)   [19] Towler (1984: 56–7).

Towler places great stress on this position as 'the norm for the West' in a general 'world-affirming monotheism' adopting a stance that does not concern 'belief that' but 'belief in'. The sense in which he sees it as a 'norm' is slightly problematic in that he speaks of it more as a kind of background stance and does 'not for a moment claim that it is the commonest religious attitude'.[20] We can expand this perspective in that his brief allusion to death in this type and style is aligned with a citation from Richard Hoggart[21] concerning people seeing 'Heaven as Home' as part of a 'a larger plan'[22] and reinforced by the Davies and Shaw survey of 1995 which used as one afterlife option 'Trust in God: everything is in God's hands' and which found a 22% response rate amongst the 1,603 respondents across the UK.[23] In chapter 5 we have seen this style reflected in Marett's—'I have trusted in life and it has not betrayed me'—despite that author's personal grief and institutional sorrow. Moreover we saw him, as Rector of Oxford's Exeter College describe himself more as a 'flying buttress' than as a 'pillar of the Anglican establishment'.[24]

Gnosticism is a term Towler uses to depict people with a sense that the material world is not the most basic of realities but that beyond it lies a more ultimate spiritual plane echoing something of the spiritualist church and of Christian science. He identifies the associated cognitive style of this stance in two words, viz. 'knowledge' and 'scientific', to stress the need for a real sense of understanding the way things are, often expressed in language that mirrors scientific objectivity. Thus its style 'includes a belief in personal survival after death' where the problems, pains, and contradictions of this life are transcended.[25]

Traditionalism constituted Towler's final type along with its cognitive style of 'unquestioning acceptance' that might be expressed as 'I cherish and hold dear'.[26] This style can, however, manifest itself 'in more moods than one' as in 'distress, disgust, dismay' if the traditional way of things is assailed, just as at other times the cherishing factor predominates. Towler interprets this cultural outlook as fostering a stable social situation, for it has no answer to any 'question in particular, but in its own special way it is able to prevent any troubling question from being asked at all'.[27] The issue of death falls under the sense that religion has the answer for this especially as expressed in appropriate 'rites of passage' which, in themselves, 'provide the clearest examples of this mechanism at work'.[28] Towler gives a brief account of how the wider British 'tradition' of which this traditionalist religious type is an intensified form works in the national church institution with its bishops in the House of

---

[20] Towler (1984: 66).   [21] Hoggart (1958: 164).   [22] Towler (1984: 65).
[23] Davies and Shaw (1995: 92–3). For Christian groups—Church of England (17%), Roman Catholics (32%), Church of Scotland (31%), Methodists (30%).
[24] Marett (1941: 326).   [25] Towler (1984: 75).
[26] Towler (1984: 83).   [27] Towler (1984: 85).
[28] Towler (1984: 86). The 'mechanism' being the traditionalist type and style.

Lords: 'concerned with matters of state "as their subordinates are at the civic and rural levels".... The clergy are not only guardians of religion but are themselves religious symbols every bit as palpably as are cathedrals and parish churches.'[29] In this Towler glosses one aspect of the British Establishment and of those who sustain it as such, not least with a deep 'concern with morality' and the need for a 'fixed set of rules'.[30]

While Towler certainly acknowledges that other 'types' of religion existed, he sees his five following Weber's approach to ideal type description of something that 'exaggerates certain aspects of a phenomenon' whilst also presenting 'an analytically coherent account' of them. He went so far as to see his types or exaggerations as showing 'orthodox, conventional religion' as 'composed of heresies'. His analysis allowed themes to 'become visible, instead of being intertwined and therefore not apparent'.[31] His overall sociological sense revealed the dynamics of 'the agony of doubt and the thirst for certainty' in many of the letters he read, across the spectrum of types and styles. This 'need for certainty results from the desire for order', one existing in a British context of those 'used to living in an orderly world' with many 'things under our control or under the control of someone we can trust'. Still, he cites economic inflation, redundancy, examination failure, and bereavement amongst the things that 'profoundly distress people every day', with working-class people being more subject to them than others.[32] Amongst the adaptive resources able to deal with such things he cites human perspectives on 'the supernatural' (this is an easily used word in Towler, as is 'Providence') which 'can encompass everything', but, it is important since 'one of the most striking features of the supernatural is that it introduces more order than there would be without it'.[33] He ends his study not simply by describing the security rather than insecurity that both meaning and order bring but also noting how tradition and innovation interplay in developing society. In this he identifies 'faith' as a significant aspect of religiosity that bears more of a family resemblance to doubt than to certainty, with faith of this sort being 'the cognitive style of conventional religion' overall. Towler then explicitly goes beyond his proper sociological boundary to express his personal opinion that such faith 'is superior to certitude', with doubt being 'an intrinsic part of faith'. He clearly does go beyond normal sociological bounds by describing certain 'sectarian' outlooks as 'degenerate' but his real intention is to highlight the need for a sociological concern with 'conventional religion', rather than with groups that appear to be 'more interesting'.[34] At his time of writing those 'interesting' topics often concerned the religious sects of Christianity.

---

[29] Towler (1984: 87).   [30] Towler (1984: 92).   [31] Towler (1984: 99).
[32] Towler (1984: 100–2).   [33] Towler (1984: 103).   [34] Towler (1984: 107–9).

AESTHETIC STYLE

Though Towler's study precedes explicit disciplinary concerns with emotions in the sociology of religion we can, in retrospect, see that his focus on 'style' carried a similarity of intention. Following that trajectory I pursue here the impact of emotions through the cultural creativity of art in providing responses to bereavement and death, for art discloses the bonds between lifestyle and death-style as culturally creative individuals produce objects that are 'good to think' and 'good to feel'.[35]

Whether broadly conceived as the invention of painting, poetry, or music encountered in galleries and concert halls, or more narrowly as favoured music, domestic poetry, and keepsakes evident in many a modern funeral, all of these present material of considerable value for analysis in the human and social sciences. The following death-focused examples embrace a variety of social worlds that invoke their own forms of 'establishment' and 'celebrity' within the UK class system.

Tattoos

The body art of tattooing has become one intimate means of remembering the dead, setting memorials on the bereaved in a most direct way.[36] Body art, a widespread and ancient human practice, as such, developed extensively from the 1990s with older people and with social class groups 'having a tattoo' who once would have seen the practice as firmly not for them but more typical of those in military service. The post-2000 growth of tattoo parlours across the UK followed in the wake of numerous other 'body-focused' outlets such as tanning parlours, mini spas, and nail-care shops, albeit inviting much greater participation for men. Designs, patterns, and symbols adopted vary a great deal with the skill and reputation of 'artists' being of particular concern to potential clients.

What is significant for this volume is that the availability of tattoos has allowed some mourners to affirm their relationship with their deceased kin or partner. The 'continuing-bonds' psycho-sociological theory of grief has great scope for implementation through tattoos, and does so in terms of an intentional embodiment of the 'other' in the body of the self as two recent examples from County Durham show. The first concerns the case of parents whose nine-year-old son was killed by a speeding moped ridden by a nineteen-year-old man delivering pizza in July of 2011. The bereaved mother spoke of herself as a mother who would 'go to the grave a broken woman', while her husband

---

[35] Lévi-Strauss (1962: 89), concepts already introduced in chapter 1.
[36] Schiffmacher (ed.) ([1996] 2005: 15, 336–7).

had 'teardrops tattooed on his face to show his grief'.[37] The second case comes from a tragic case of multiple murder perpetrated on New Year's Day 2012 when a taxi driver shot and killed three women who were, respectively, the mother, sister, and aunt, of a young twenty-three-year-old man. This man's grief responses included the design of an extensive tattoo that took some eight months to be inscribed on his back with his three relatives depicted as angels along with 'a lily and a yellow rose—his mum and aunty's favourite flowers', as well as a butterfly for his sister.[38] Inscribed below these images is a text taken from their funeral headstone. 'Too Well-Loved to Ever Be Forgotten.' The man is reported as saying: 'These were my three angels and now I have them on my back . . . Everyday I can look in the mirror and I see the tattoo and it will remind me of them.'[39] While this expression of grief linking the dead with their gravestone and the young man's image of them is remarkable in its extent, many lesser examples exist, followed by many people whose practice is known more through personal encounter and anecdote than from social survey. Only in terms of those known to the author, for example, there is one mature woman in her fifties who had a relatively unnoticeable name-tattoo placed on her lower arm recalling a miscarriage experienced decades before. Her own adult daughters have their own tattoos of other things and her own growing familiarity with their easy acceptance of the culture of tattoos facilitated her own small inscription that expresses thoughtful emotions that had long been present but otherwise unmarked. Another young woman, this time in the USA, memorialized her dead grandmother by having a tattoo of a photograph of her grandmother as a young woman placed unobtrusively on her arm. More generally speaking, body decoration as tattoos is moderately well known from archaeological and anthropological research, and its original significance generally assessed in terms of the relatively high social status of the deceased. Important examples come from the Altai Mountains within parts of China, Mongolia, and the former Soviet Union. Excavations of the 1930s to 1950s of material already 2,500 years old revealed some bodies that had been well preserved in the permafrost of their burial-mound tombs. On them were found arm, torso, and leg tattoos marked with fantastical animals such as 'strange deer with eagles' beaks' and 'winged lions'. In one sense such body markings resemble the incised marking on stone, whether associated with graves or not, in that such markings assert a human presence.[40] More recent discoveries of, for example, fifteenth-century bodies preserved by cold conditions in Greenland also show tattoo line marks on the forehead.[41] From

---

[37] Hunter (2012: 3). Mr and Mrs Maggs lost their son Brandon on July 2011 at Ingelby Barwick, near Stockton.

[38] Involving both the 'Lucky 777' and 'Gecko Images' tattoo parlours, respectively of Seaham and Easington.

[39] Marissa Carruthers (2012: 7).   [40] Joussaume ([1985] 1987: 74, 160 illustration 6).

[41] Chamberlain and Pearson (2001: 126, 133–40).

Egypt too, at least one Christian burial of the seventh to eighth centuries shows a woman with a tattooed monogram of the Archangel Michael on her thigh. He was a patron saint in the Sudan at that time.[42] Academically speaking, it is worth observing that *Primitive Culture*, E. B. Tylor's classic work and one of the very first to present anthropology as an academic discipline in Great Britain, includes the domain of tattoo, not least for the New Zealand Maori.[43] Such body art offers an example of the theoretical notion of embodiment understood less in its implicit sense of the *habitus* of life, where people acquire behavioural characteristics typical of their group, than in the more explicit sense of using the body as a canvas-like medium for group communication. The National Portrait Gallery's BP Portrait Award 2013 included an excellent example in 'The Rose and the Bee', a full tattoo of the lower left arm in a portrait by Mark Farmington (born 1957) of his nephew Pádraig's tattoo dedicated to his maternal grandmother, Rose, and grandfather, a beekeeper.[44] This artwork allowed a very public expression of what otherwise would have been a memorial known only to a small family circle.

Pottery, Gallery, Museum, and Church

The next artistic engagement with death takes one exhibition that moved between an art gallery, museum, and church. I specify these three locations because the work I have chosen for analysis is the *Quietus* exhibition of Julian Stair, staged, chronologically, at Middlesbrough's Institute of Modern art (mima),[45] the National Museum of Wales at Cardiff, and Winchester Cathedral,[46] all before a final exhibition with allied symposium 'Matters of Life and Death'[47] at London's Somerset House, where the exhibits were housed in a subterranean, crypt-like cellar. Stair is a potter and his clay and ceramic objects in *Quietus* vary from six-foot vertical jars and horizontal sarcophagi to twelve-inch or so diameter pots.

Much could be said about the symbolic significance of these objects when manifested in each of the exhibition's venues, from the stark focus of each exhibit at Middlesbrough, through the addition of Bronze Age and other pots already in Cardiff's collection and presented amidst Stair's modern work, through to the juxtaposition of his sarcophagi alongside pre-existing ancient tombs in Winchester Cathedral and, finally, to the 'Dead House' in London's Somerset House. In each of these contexts we can understand how exhibits in relation to context could be both 'good to think' and 'good to feel'.

---

[42] Taylor and Antoine (2014: 182–5).   [43] Tylor (1871).
[44] BP Portrait Award 2013, London: National Portrait Gallery, p. 40.
[45] See Tooby (2013).   [46] Tooby (2013).
[47] Tuesday 10 December 2013. Exhibition, *Quietus: Death, the Vessel and the Human Body*.

The Middlesbrough venue, with its dramatically high entrance hall, presented the visitor with a full-frontal prospect of some 130 cinerary urns, presented on a grid of twenty-six vertical and five horizontal shelves.[48] This is probably the tallest, albeit temporary and erstwhile, symbolic columbarium ever constructed, while, in another room, the exhibit 'Reliquary for a Common Man, 2012' showed a single bone china reliquary into whose material Stair worked some of the cremated remains of Lesley James Fox, a relative. A spotlight illuminated this object in a dark room in which also ran a repeating film, photographic, and audio representation of the deceased person.[49] This element was not permitted at Winchester Cathedral, where one of the clergy, Roland Riem, described this decision as 'made by instinct, but for sound underlying reasons'. Fully alert to the fact that the 'Cathedral's foundation is tied up with human remains, the relics of St. Swithun', he nevertheless asserted that Christian theology argued that 'we cannot hold on to people beyond death'; something expressed in the liturgical act of committal at a funeral. He cites 'the modern tradition of retaining material' or ashes, whether 'on the mantelpiece' or transformed into jewellery, as contradicting that committal. Moreover, he invokes a doctrinal belief to indicate that 'out of the nothingness of death, God can bring new life-resurrection of the body'.[50] This is an excellent example of an ecclesiastical comment linking lifestyle and death-style, finding an apparently human desire to retain rather than commit the dead to the divine will inappropriate. In terms of time and social change, however, the collection of cinerary urns would not be alien to many Britons for whom cremated remains and their disposal has become a significant moment in family life.

In terms of popular engagement with this exhibition, Michael Tooby produced a record of the visitor figures, viz. Middlesbrough 32,665, National Museum of Wales 10,045, and Winchester 64,658.[51] Many of those at Middlesbrough, for example, included school visits, with one teacher describing the exhibition as a 'launch pad into a difficult area', almost a classic expression of the 'good to think' theme just mentioned. From the Cardiff case one person wrote of the objects, 'There is a simplicity in them which I admire, the wish to touch them, getting a sensual impression about something which is not possible to reach—death'; an excellent example of something being 'good to feel'.

The two catalogues associated with these exhibitions present highly informative entries dealing with historical, cultural, and artistic aspects of these

---

[48] Beighton (2013: 21–5) describes mima's near perfect ten-metre cube display area.
[49] Beighton and Stair (2012) (eds) pp. 43–5.   [50] Riem (2013: 43).
[51] Tooby (2013: 47–55) is explicit about problems of accuracy and comparability of figures, especially since Winchester includes worshippers at formal services who may or may not have engaged with the exhibition.

death-related objects and how they 'speak' to contemporary visitors.[52] In one of these Andrew Renton, following Julian Stair, draws from Philip Rawson's 'seminal book, *Ceramics*', which encourages the use of anthropomorphism in understanding '"transformative" or symbolic relationships between ceramic vessels and the human body'. The theme involves resemblance between our human bodies and ceramic pots, based on the sense of each involving containment.[53] There are, indeed, many examples of belief that the body is understood to be a container of the soul or of some life force and is, correspondingly, viewed as only an 'empty' container or shell once that vitality has departed. Such comments are common in contexts of cremating a 'body'.

However, there is also much more than a simple comparison of containers involved in this approach involving a complex affinity between people and their bodies; here we are back with the 'good to think' and 'good to feel' motifs of what we might see as popular 'totemism'. Some of the visitors to the exhibitions expressed a desire to touch and feel the texture of the sarcophagi pots, and Stair, for his part, supported that wish. There was, for example, a tacit understanding with the exhibition stewards at Middlesbrough that people would not be actively prevented from touching the pots even though the implicit understanding of such an exhibition space normally assumes a hands-off policy.[54]

Here we can see the emergence of art as ritual symbol, in the sense that touching offers its own nascent ritual form. Symbols cease to be simple signs indicative of some 'idea' when they participate in that which they represent and when that 'participation' involves the sensory domain. The fact that some of Stair's large freestanding pots are life-size and could easily hold an adult human body immediately allows for an affinity between them and 'us'. Our reference in chapter 4 to the biblical description of Adam as made from dust and returning to dust now becomes much more than a passing reference, for its mythological domain is one that understood 'wet' dust as living and dry dust as death.[55] So, too with the ancient Babylonian *Epic of Gilgamesh* whose hero mourns the death of his friend Enkidu and says in his grief, 'How can I stay silent, how be still. My friend whom I love has turned to clay, am I not like him?'[56] Whether in ancient myth and the cultures they reflect, or in today's Britain and its experience of burial and cremation, the 'earth to earth, ashes to ashes' motif still rings true. As we have already seen, especially in chapter 2,

---

[52] Tooby (2013: 49) also presents questionnaire survey results (only 185) for these venues and uses them to ponder word associations on 'what felt familiar' or 'surprised' visitors.

[53] Renton (2013: 29).

[54] Hacker (2013: 40) writes on touching exhibits and differences between gallery and sacred space.

[55] The biblical valley of dry bones, Ezekiel 37: 1–14, tells of sinews, flesh, and skin covering them, and the wind-breath finally animating them.

[56] Tablet 9.

the recent innovation of natural burial may be shifting the symbolic weight of this 'dust' motif, but in so doing it simply provides a new content for the same form: dust, earth, ashes, and even clay furnish an allied set of vehicles for expressing the vitality–mortality schema. One intriguing perspective for ancient Britain lies, for example, in an early Bronze Age beaker excavated in Glamorgan whose highly decorated surface contained inset calcined bone material which may well be human in origin.

> This use of white material, whether bone or something resembling it, incorporated into the blood-like red clay 'body' or 'flesh' of the pot and made invisible by a coating or 'skin' of red surface colorant seems to suggest a symbolic association with the human body.[57]

As with any archaeological find, interpretation is always provisional, but the fact of symbolic creativity by the potter goes without saying, irrespective of what it was he or she was seeking to say. The challenge to interpretation of dust, earth, and clay as funerary symbols evident in this early Bronze Age beaker is part of that wider symbolic world captured in biblical and other myth as also, for example, in Freud's *thanatos* principle.[58] It continues today in the many ceramic and other urns commercially created for wide popular use. The fact that a person can now have a relative's ashes worked into the substance of a container as well as their being contents placed within it reveals a dramatic link across some five-thousand years. Such a fact of comparative symbolics offers its own challenge to over-easy classifications of eras on the basis of differences of motivation and world view and hints at similarities evoked across millennia by elements as basic as clay. In the second of the two cases of 'Establishment Funerals' that we now consider, this is tellingly revealed in the cultural complexity of 'forces' that witnessed the archaeological excavation of the skeleton of King Richard III, as from 'clay', and his repositioning from under a car park into a relatively adjacent tomb in Leicester Cathedral; but first the funeral of Baroness Margaret Thatcher.

ESTABLISHMENT FUNERALS: BARONESS THATCHER

If simple artifacts of clay may evince cultural comparison, so too does ritual behaviour in which a lifestyle is mirrored in funerary death-style, as the case of one woman's funeral amongst the eight-hundred or so women's funerals

---

[57] Renton (2013: 31).

[58] *Thanatos* may be 'most captivating intellectually' but is 'more alive now in departments of literature than in the consulting room of therapists' (Breger, 2009: 2).

in Britain on Wednesday 17 April 2013 makes clear.[59] This centred on Mrs Margaret Thatcher, or Baroness as she was in titular terms of establishment. This eighty-seven-year-old woman had been three-times Prime Minister of the country, had led the nation into the Falklands War, and had created a style of politics and social economics given the name of Thatcherism. In one of the most popular of tabloid newspapers her funeral was given seventeen pages of pictorial and textual coverage, offering its own ideal window upon aspects of British cultural values, on the Establishment, and on the celebrity underpinning of contemporary British life. The special edition of *The Sun* carried an extra cover-page whose full outer spread depicted her coffin being carried by 'heroes from key Falkland units' and a brief lower headline 'R.I.P. Mrs T', along with a quotation from her friend and a key establishment figure, Richard Chartres, the Bishop of London, who preached the funeral sermon in his calm, commanding, and resonant voice.

> After the storm of life lived in the heat of political controversy, there is a great calm. Today, the remains of the real Margaret Hilda Thatcher are here at her funeral service. Lying here, she is one of us, subject to the common destiny of all human beings.[60]

The inside cover gave a map and timing of her journey by hearse from the Palace of Westminster (10.00), past Downing Street—home of the Prime Minister (10.01), to St Clement Danes Church in the Strand (10.17), which served as the transition point from hearse to horse-drawn gun-carriage which then proceeded along Fleet Street (10.44), to St Paul's Cathedral (10.53), where her funeral procession is led by her two adult grandchildren bearing the insignia of honours bestowed upon her (11.03). After the service, her body arrives at Mortlake Crematorium for a private service of cremation (16.46). Each of these cameo movements is presented on a timeline to indicate the minute detail that would have gone into the planning of this ceremonial event, as of many formal events involving the British military, and is its own marker of 'the Establishment' in its ceremonial mode. So too with the paradigmatic scene of the liturgical clothing of the Anglican clergy at St Clement Danes and at St Paul's, and of the formal morning wear of laymen officially involved at the former church. Complementing this highly formal, public, and establishment dimension of tradition, the main front page of the paper cites Mrs Thatcher's former bodyguard, Barry Stevens, as he refers to her daughter at the subsequent cremation. 'As the curtains closed, Carol wept. I wept . . . it was the hardest goodbye'. Trevor Kavanagh, well-known political commentator and associate editor, covered the event under the heading, 'A victory for decency'. He praises the Bishop of London's 'perfectly pitched speech', noting

---

[59] Very approximate statistic for the UK.
[60] *The Sun*, special edition, Thursday 18 April 2013, special full cover.

that he had once written a sermon delivered by Archbishop Runcie, then Archbishop of Canterbury, at a service following the 1982 Falklands War and which has been much discussed in terms of dissonance between Runcie and Thatcher. The reference to 'decency' followed days in which many in the media had reported on individuals and parts of the country, including in online contexts, that had expressed delight in her death, including controversy over whether the BBC should play the popular song 'The Witch is Dead' which opponents had rapidly catalysed into prominence. The very few who came to London to protest in some way at the funeral were vastly outnumbered and out-voiced by tens of thousands of supporters.

Celebrity Presence

This same newspaper went on to give two pages with photographs of some sixteen political leaders, and a further two pages of celebrities including a 'cast of famous faces from the world of showbiz and politics', including Joan Collins, Dame Shirley Bassey, Sir Terry Wogan, and 'opera star Catherine Jenkins'. Yet another two-page spread gave a picture from the dome of St Paul's down onto the centrally located coffin surrounded by the family, famous politicians, and other celebrities. The accompanying article is by Jeremy Clarkson, a journalist and popular entertainer known for his laddish outspoken views on cars and many other topics on which he felt able to offer comment. Nearly two years later a moment of physically and verbally aggressive behaviour led to his being sacked from the BBC in March 2015. At Thatcher's service his wandering thoughts included surprise that there was no noticeable public protest; he spoke of 'the toffs' and the trade unions who were reasonably happy before Mrs Thatcher was appointed as Prime Minister and before she changed many aspects of the social order. He wondered why her funeral was so full of 'pomp and nonsense' since she seemed to him not to like such things. Addressing his car-loving audience he positively described the variety of cars and, negatively, the final horse-drawn gun-carriage that took part in transporting the coffin across London. A final page offered a pair of articles dealing, respectively with well-wishers—'Tears, Cheers, . . . Just a Few Jeers',[61] and 'a mob of placard-waving protesters . . . gleefully chanting "Maggie, Maggie, Maggie—dead, dead, dead"'.[62] While much could be said about this funeral as ceremonial it suffices to locate it as a ritualized expression of the Establishment in which the military, politicians, and church combined activities in a paradigmatic scene of social force enhanced by extensive media coverage.

---

[61] France, Syson, and Sabey (2013: 12).   [62] Harvey (2013: 13).

ESTABLISHMENT FUNERALS: KING RICHARD III

While the media, as well as the political, military, and clerical worlds would already have planned for Margaret Thatcher's funeral, with much protocol in mind, no one would have anticipated the discovery in September 2012 of the skeleton of King Richard III, who had died in 1485 at the Battle of Bosworth Field in the English Midlands, nor would the spectrum of national establishment figures have had anything like a funeral planned for him. This is what makes the discovery of the skeleton under what was, by then, a car park in Leicester so intriguing, being so unlike Baroness Thatcher's funeral, and yet, in terms of the activation of the social forces of the British Establishment, so like it.

Detailed accounts were given of the numerous phases embracing the historical sense of his likely location, the archaeological find itself, the identification of living ancestors and the DNA comparison that indicated a significant likeness, the civic claims over the body for its ultimate resting place whether in York Minster or Leicester Cathedral, the coffining and transporting of the bones to sites of historical significance before they were entombed in Leicester, not to mention the final liturgical rites and the ecclesial and popular coverage by the media. Here we can but allude to how archaeologists of the University of Leicester undertook this venture, with all the necessary legal and ethical rules in hand, and, hope beyond all hope, found the last of the Plantagenet Kings of England. Few bones have ever triggered as much scientific, literary, political, and media attention as these, prompting questions as to whether the king, whose skeleton did indicate an abnormality of the spine, justified Shakespeare's depiction as a hunchback—one 'rudely stamped . . . Cheated of feature by dissembling nature. Deformed, unfinished, sent before my time into this breathing world, scarce half made up, and that so lamely and unfashionably.'[63] He could also speak in moral self-evaluation:

> But then I sigh, and with a piece of Scripture,
> Tell them that God bids us do good for evil.
> And thus I clothe my naked villainy
> With odd old ends stolen forth of holy writ,
> And seem a saint, when most I play the devil.[64]

There are times when fact is stranger than fiction, and this idiom is fully applicable to this case. The king's identified descendant turns out to be a carpenter from Canada who becomes responsible for making the outer rectangular coffin whose inner lead-lining would hold the bones, as well as a small box containing earth drawn from key sites of the king's action. Individuals

---

[63] Shakespeare, *King Richard the Third*, I. i. 22 (Sisson, 1954: 686).
[64] Shakespeare, *King Richard the Third*, I. iii. 330–4 (Sisson, 1954: 694).

from historical re-enactment societies help frame some of the visits made by the short cortege; these even include two horsebacked 'knights' in shining armour who escort it through Leicester's streets to the Cathedral. The horse-drawn cart on which the coffin rested was not a formal military gun-carriage. Still, members of the current armed forces were in attendance and served as pall-bearers for the heavy, lead-lined coffin that was, after considerable ritual, entombed at a focal point in the Cathedral. In what some would inevitably identify as an imitation of Princess Diana's cortege, a relatively small number of people threw flowers onto the coffin.

Time alone will tell how these much-televised events will be evaluated. In terms of this volume, we draw attention to the role of the Establishment in its several divisions in framing and staging the ceremonial. The Church of England furnished a Cathedral, Bishop, Archbishop, and choir. Academically robed scholars gave their account of events including the University of Leicester's Public Orator and, of course, university-based scholars provided the bones and their identification with a descendant, and a liturgical pattern for the re-interment of the king derived from an erstwhile forgotten medieval liturgy. The Poet Laureate wrote a poem that was read by Benedict Cumber-batch, one of the highest-profile of international actors; the Cardinal Arch-bishop of Westminster, Vincent Nichols, delivered a sermon; the Archbishop of Canterbury, in cope and mitre, conducted the entombing with incense and holy water—something far removed from his native heath as an Evangelical; and the choir sang well-chosen music from King Richard's era and from today. The current Duke of Gloucester took part in the events and read a lesson, while Sophie, the Countess of Wessex, represented the Queen. The various congregations included a variety of establishment figures, with Leicester's multi-faith population being evident. Sir Julian Fellowes, himself a likeable establishment figure and author of novels and the extremely well-known *Downton Abbey* television series was but one whose opinion was canvassed on the full supporting programme aspect of television coverage.

This literally unique window upon contemporary Britain depicts scenes that invite analyses directly related to this present volume of lifestyle and death-style, and to that complex social force of which we have made much in previous chapters and which touches mortality-aligned emotions. Here was, essentially, a test case for the nature of emotions experienced and performed. In many respects it was a funeral without grief. Certainly, it would be hard to speak of it as an event grounded in bereavement, even for the five–hundred-year time lapse for Richard's Canadian descendant. Yet emotion there was. That individual described himself on television as largely 'speechless' after the entombing: his solemnity was palpable. Scholars who had invested a great deal in the excavation and subsequent detective work involving DNA analysis had their own emotional excitement, and many thousands of citizens queued to pass by the pre-interment lying in state of the king and coffin.

In much of this we can, I think, see an example of the scheme, alluded to earlier in this volume, of how an idea may become pervaded by an emotion to create a value. Here we have the idea of a king's bones, those of one of the few medieval kings holding something of a resonance for thousands who know nothing of the history as such, and know it through Shakespeare—himself a key literary pillar of the English Establishment. To have the bones found under a car park was to elicit the contemporary desire for respect and dignity—two of the commonest idioms used of death and the dead in Britain today. In other words, it is the contemporary emotion of dignity for the dead, combined with the sense of 'history' and monarchy, that generated the emotion that could pervade the bare-boned idea of a long-lost king. Emotion is always an experience of the moment, but it can easily be evoked by symbols from the past. The fact that there already existed a King Richard III Society, people with a commitment to his memory and place in British culture history, also provided a base with its own emotion.

One way of summarizing this unique 'establishment funeral' is to distinguish between 'comment' and 'ritual'. The comment provided in a swathe of newspaper columns varied from the *Daily Mail*'s full-page spread entitled, 'It's mad to make this child killer a national hero'. There Michael Thornton assumed he was not the only person thinking that 'the world had gone stark staring bonkers' as he viewed 'with mounting stupefaction the grotesque televised travesty . . . involving the remains of the usurper-king Richard III— without question one of the most evil, detestable tyrants ever to walk this earth'. He questions the sanity of key players; did the Cardinal Archbishop's 'preposterous eulogy' indicate that he had 'temporarily lost his marbles?' As for the role of today's Duke of Gloucester, himself Patron 'of the absurd Richard III Society', he could well 'blink in a bemused way' at 'this distasteful jamboree' that included a twenty-one-gun salute. Even a much more moderate leading article in *The Times* asked a series of quite appropriate questions:[65] 'Is all this knowingly absurd, or not absurd at all? Is it ancient history or very modern sentimentalism? Is it all for the tourists, or done for the national soul?' Its response was that, 'In every case the answer is "both".' The article's heading, 'A Hearse. A Hearse'—in imitation of Shakespeare's 'A horse, a horse, my kingdom for a horse' in the penultimate scene, in which King Richard dies,[66] enables the author to nimbly balance his opinion. 'Only in Britain can the tightrope between pomp and parody be so carefully trodden.' In terms of this volume we might take this 'tightrope' as the kind of multivocal symbol that both conceals and reveals social dynamics or, better perhaps, as a cautionary stance slightly unsure of the status of a unique cultural event within a complex social world.

---

[65] *The Times*, Tuesday 24 March 2015, p. 29.
[66] Shakespeare, *King Richard the Third*, V. iv. 13 (Sisson, 1954: 726).

FUNERAL DIRECTING STYLE

One figure relatively absent from the event just described was the funeral director. Given that the bones were the preserve of university archaeologists who 'handed them over' to ecclesiastical functionaries, and since military personnel engaged in the complex burial of the heavy casket, with specialist engineers closing the tomb, there was little scope for funeral directors as such in this most unusual venture.

In chapter 3 we considered the funeral director's more evident role, albeit in terms of its dichotomous, concealed–disclosed, function. It is, however, now time to take this further in terms of the lifestyle and death-style motif approached in terms of selected dynamics of funeral directing. For funeral directors, or appropriate staff within their organization, experience a set of differing yet interlinked face-to-face engagements with their immediate clients and wider circle around them. They move from moments of potentially considerable privacy both with the bereaved family and with the corpse, through to the public stage of the funeral itself. This exemplifies Irving Goffman's sociological notion of the 'presentation of self' in social arenas, and in chapter 3 we noted an increased formality of dress, of public precedence-walking, and of hearses, all marking the director's expression of or claim to professionalism.

Framing all those actions is the financial nature of the services provided, as well as the notions of 'tradition', 'establishment', and perhaps even 'celebrity'. For funeral directors have increasingly developed a sense of themselves as sustaining 'tradition', while their public performance frames them as a kind of 'establishment' of their own. Moreover, to a limited extent it is also hard not to think of them as some kind of silent yet highly visible celebrity with their increased use of formal dress with accoutrements of top hat and silver-mounted cane, of bowing to or acknowledging the coffin at moments in the ceremonial; such activities being being of particular ritual significance in a period of ritual change within funeral practice.

When funeral directors are actively managing the family and guests at a church, crematorium, or cemetery funeral conducted by clergy of most Christian churches, they experience a degree of formal consonance with the priest, with their respective roles reflected in the 'special' nature of their clothes when compared with the great majority of middle- and working-class people at British funerals. Priest and funeral director tend to move and act in generally prescribed ways, expressing something of that ritual purity described in previous chapters.

However, with the advent of increased numbers of secular or humanist celebrants, who include numerous women amongst their leaders, an intriguing question arises in terms of style of dress for the funeral as a ritual event and for the status of the leaders. For while the fully costumed funeral director easily

mirrors the clerically attired priest or minister, while also standing apart from
the other functionaries, this can now become an issue of discord in respect of
an 'ordinarily', albeit smartly, dressed funeral celebrant. Secular, or even
'spiritual', funeral celebrants are not easily differentiated from the congregation of the bereaved, family, and friends. Nor are they all set within a
'traditional' framework of expectation of religious hymns, prayers, and sacred
texts. The focal differentiation of the ritual event now becomes complex
through the presence of the coffin, sometimes with a photograph of the
deceased alongside it; through preferential music and readings; and through
the words of the celebrant. Typically, the rite is described as a 'celebration of
the life of' the dead person, and the words use a combination of themes
gleaned from conversation and other communication with the family, and
perhaps with the help of resource material and books available to some secular
or civic celebrants.

The role of words uttered now becomes more pronounced than ever it was
in the standardized ecclesiastical-based services. In the absence of any 'traditional' framework that could 'carry' the event along almost irrespective of
individual contribution by priest or anyone else—factors that become increasingly unacceptable to many, especially the many who are relatively unfamiliar
with church language or rite—words uttered now become increasingly powerful. Aggregated anecdote now becomes the performative utterance of the rite
and what is said about the person assumes enormous importance, creating a
situation that is easily contrasted with some that may have been overseen by
traditional priests who 'did not know' the deceased and who might even have
used an inappropriate name for them.

Words do, indeed, carry a considerable weight, not only in the newly
emergent rites but even in their description and analysis, as is apparent in
comparing the generic 'officiant' (notably a person in a professionally designated clerical–priestly office) with a celebrant. While 'celebrant' did come to
be used in the Church of England for the person leading the Eucharist towards
the close of the twentieth century it was 'minister' that characterized the role in
the *Book of Common Prayer*; 'minister' was retained in the *Alternative Service
Book* of 2000, but with the addition of 'President' for the Eucharist. As
'celebrant' evolved in the twenty-first century it came to be adopted within
ecclesiastical, secular, and civic contexts. These verbal variations serve as ritual
signatures for the form and content of ceremonies: the noun 'minister' is
determined by the fact that he—and it was usually a male—ministered the
word of God: the noun was determined by the verb; the office by its function.
Likewise with the 'President' who presided over the action of the Eucharistic
rite. 'Priest', by contrast, was determined by official ordination. As for 'celebrant', this demarcated a person engaged in a celebration, and it would be the
celebration of the life *of* someone. As such the celebrant could be a minister or
priest or lay-person, as with most civic or secular individuals, but the celebrant

did not 'preside'. It is precisely this celebration of an individual life that typifies the modern role. And it is this that serves to express its own form of secularization. In other words, the personalized and individualized form of death rite easily facilitates a secularization of religious influence in which the social force one vested in the priest, especially in the clergy of the established Church of England, is now dissipated. The ascribed status of ordination now becomes an achieved status gained through conducting funerals in such a way as pleases the bereaved families, creating a reputation that supports future employment as a funeral celebrant. In all of this, funeral directors are, essentially, silent. Their role on the day of the funeral is to direct the moving of the body and the movement of mourners; they direct action. As chapter 10 will show for the innovation of woodland burial, this can involve some shift in preferred convention.

Still, ethos and professionalism extend in many circles around those who undertake death duties and funerals, whether advertising in local newspapers, on television, or online; and keeping their business free of any criticism or potential criticism is of the essence. This can sometimes misfire, as in the case of a gravedigger who, it is reported, was 'dismissed by the funeral directors who use his services, after being photographed stripped to the waist and grinning, in the grave he was digging'. He had, apparently been asked to pose by a passing 'news photographer', and the resulting photograph in the *Shepton Mallet Journal* attracted negative comment from some members of the public which, in turn, gained the attention of the editor of the popular *Sunday Express* who viewed it as a 'national tragedy', exemplifying a nation 'that has turned toxic from political correctness' and whose middle-managers in business possess 'inflated expenses and lifestyle' compared with those who 'actually do stuff. Like digging holes, in mud, to bury people.'[67] What appeared as a genuine cameo of basic human activity conducted by a realistic workman enjoying a moment's rest and potential publicity, not least in a culture where photographing practically anything that moves, is common was apparently taken by others as somehow degrading the dignity of the dead, or at least of their graves. Little could be further removed from traditional Britain, whose gravediggers have frequently been understood to share more in a degree of gallows humour than in careful qualities of middle-management. Shakespeare dwelt on this very issue long ago in his use of a clown as a gravedigger whose singing as he digs prompts Hamlet to ask his companion Horatio whether the man 'has no feeling of his business' because he 'sings in gravemaking'? Horatio responds pragmatically that 'Custom hath made in him a property of easiness'—one of the most direct links between lifestyle and death-style that one might imagine.[68]

---

[67] Townsend (2013: 31).   [68] Shakespeare, *Hamlet*, V. i. 61–3 (Sisson, 1954: 1035).

DIGITAL MEDIA

Still, this case illustrates the power of the media as such, irrespective of how their output is received by different sectors of the public. We have already seen the impossibility of considering the relationship between lifestyle and death-style factors in contemporary Britain separately from the media, given their role in publicizing tragic, terrorist, and celebrity death. Beyond those news-related items, the media frequently find 'death' a compelling basis for gaining an audience, as the following example indicates.

In September 2012 the BBC 2 television channel ran a brief series entitled *A Dead Good Job*.[69] Focused on a series of funeral directors, these prime-time documentaries combined accounts of their professional lives and of both ordinary and rather distinctive aspects of changing funerary practice in the UK. The programmes are worth sketching in the context of our discussion of lifestyle and death-style for their attempt at embracing almost as many innovatory options as were currently available in Britain at the time. This included a Hindu funeral with the family both witnessing the entry of the coffin into the cremator and later distributing the cremated remains in the river Thames from a specially deployed riverboat. Another specialist firm of father and daughter covered Muslim funerals helping to fill a gap in Islamic funeral provision; while sketching the male-only role and presence at the graveside and the relative unhappiness with this by a relatively non-practising westernized adult daughter, it ended with her sensing a firmer bond with her Islamic identity having followed the otherwise accepted convention. Another Islamic funeral, of a man without relatives, showed how local Muslims, including his former employer's family, collected money for the funeral from members of the Mosque and some non-Muslims in the locality, resulting in a large funeral. That programme, the final one, ended with a well-instructed Muslim describing how, when the men depart the filled-in grave, the two angelic visitors would come to question the dead man as to his faith. He cited the established Islamic tradition of the 'corpse' sitting up in his grave at their coming to question the 'deceased', and of how that was 'the beginning' rather than the end of the story of that person's destiny. Yet another case concerned the innovative practice of woodland burial, which in this case involved a man's body being kept at home in a wicker coffin before being transported to church in his familiar van and then on to the natural burial site. The wife fully acknowledged the importance of her faith as a Latter-day Saint or Mormon, which includes extensive belief in the reuniting of family members in the afterlife. As one would expect in a Mormon context, her large and supportive family and others sustained her throughout this intense level of

---

[69] Final BBC 2 programme aired Thursday 26 September 2012 between 9 and 10 p.m.

family and church–community activity. Two other women, both in relatively closing phases of life with terminal illnesses, though still mobile, were shown preparing for their funerals. One was choosing a crematorium in association with an innovative funeral director who has established a *Go As You Please* funeral service at Newcastle upon Tyne in response to his mother's funeral that he deemed ordinary; served by the professionals, but lacking personal quality and, because of that, lacking a certain sense of love. He expressed numerous dissatisfactions with funeral directors and their more prescriptive ways; including their dress, such as the carrying of gloves that they do not wear. Reflecting our earlier comments on dress, tradition, and establishment, his open-necked shirt, jacket, and jeans, contrasted with the woman funeral director at the Mormon event whose formality included a top-hat with trailing black veil, that was incongruous even against the typically dark-suited Latter-day Saint family. The other terminally ill woman's event was that of a pre-funeral 'wake' or party taking the form of some hundred friends and family crowded into what seemed to be a Catholic church hall for a celebration of her life in her presence. She was keen to have many photographs of the event and of herself with her infant grandson so that she might be remembered in the future. Another woman, also with her box of letters for her family members after her days, explicitly described her funeral preparations as a form of establishing control over events in the light of the fact that she had no control over her terminal illness. There may be no better example of lifestyle control passing into an innovative death-style, with the fact that such an event was broadcast to millions allowing others to gain ideas for themselves. The invention of tradition can no longer be considered separately from media exercises like this.

These cases also exemplify the theme of vitality and of individuals and family engaging in acts that were deemed personal and meaningful to them. The Hindu and Muslim cases, as also with Anthony—a Nottingham man who died alone—revealed remarkably diverse activity of community involvement, from total community action through to almost total individual action. The case of Anthony was interesting in that the officiating priest engaged extensively in what we have already identified as an address in the second person singular. Reflective of Buber's famous 'I–Thou' relationship, this priest spoke to the deceased in a speculative way about his being a 'loner' who seemed to love animals, with a vibrant recording of the hymn 'All things bright and beautiful, all creatures great and small', being played as the coffin was taken into the very traditional Wilford Hill Crematorium at Nottingham. The priest spoke of not knowing which school the deceased might have attended, but wondered about other possible aspects of his life so as to create a life-narrative for a man whose identity, in terms of relatives, the local authority had, despite rigorous effort, been entirely unable to ascertain.

In a style typical of contemporary documentary-making the BBC had garnered interestingly distinct examples of contemporary attitudes to funerals and, in some sense, to death, yet, apart from a hand and a foot, what was almost completely absent was any view of a corpse as such. While this is entirely understandable in terms of family and community custom and respect, as well as of broadcasting ethics and public sensitivity, it reflected something of the second-hand engagement with death with which the media are particularly susceptible. In one sense there is an inevitability to this partial sighting since the television, computer, or any other screen is precisely what its name implies, viz. it screens in the sense of displays and screens in the sense of hides. In this the 'screen' acts as does many a symbol—disclosing and hiding at the same time.

Cyber Worlds, Digital Death

As a more specific dimension of the media the enormous rise of online resources through the internet cannot be ignored given its natural place in contemporary lifestyle practice. The mass adoption of internet use amongst the general public has witnessed the emergence of significant advantages and some potential unintended and negative consequences for individuals and families in terms of death. We will comment in chapter 10 on the role of the internet for woodland burial but here I pinpoint two other influences, one on suicide and the other pornography.

One aspect of suicide that significantly marks changes in lifestyle witnessed during the first decades of the twenty-first century has derived from what, in a most telling phrase, came to be called the social media. Driven by computer, miniaturization, and satellite developments of electronic technology, millions of individuals have gained personal access to highly populated networks of people who might be known to them locally or even quite unknown to them on a more global front. In terms of one set of complementary opposites used throughout this volume, 'cyberspace' became an arena for concealment and disclosure, especially in written texts sent between individuals. This has a tremendous capacity to influence aspects of individual and corporate identity, allowing individuals not only to express themselves and their life concerns to wide audiences but also to invent fictional identities through which to relate to others, not always knowing whether they are linking with 'real' or equally fictive identities. This is particularly significant for children and young people, whose own personal identity is still in process of development and can be easily influenced, indeed manipulated, by older people, by advertising pressures, and by the malevolent.[70]

---

[70] Jonathan Brown (2013).

The nature of most innovation is to find that its explicit purpose soon triggers unintended and, perhaps, even unforeseen consequences. What is more, it can be argued that certain long-embedded aspects of human life now find new opportunity for expression. This not only applies to benevolent but also to malevolent streams of human intention. The fact that human sexuality as well as profit motive have driven a vast volume of cyberspace devoted to many aspects of sexuality including pornography is well known. It has also become apparent that the human capacity for bullying, a behaviour so readily rooted in relatively close interpersonal relationships of individuals and groups, has also taken to cyberspace with considerable ease. The apparent anonymity of a message sender still allows the potential viciousness of individual spite and malice to be addressed to others, whether known or unknown. One case attracted considerable media and political attention in August 2013 when one fourteen-year-old girl hanged herself, as was thought, because of online bullying. Even an online website set up in tribute of the girl had to be taken down because 'it was bombarded by cruel and repulsive messages'.[71] The girl's sixteen-year-old sister, who found the body at home was, herself, the subject of further online bullying. It seems unwise even to repeat here some of these messages because of their capacity to stain a reader's imagination when aligned with a young woman's death. Numerous other young people have killed themselves due, as those close to them and others have thought, to internet media. Here the very concept of social media seems to merit description as anti-social.

Yet another case takes cyber-bullying and death in another direction. It concerned a seventeen-year-old youth in Scotland who 'killed himself after threats that his webcam chats would be shown to his family'. He was buried on 16 August 2013. His uncle spoke of the '"sickening" Skype-based scam' which is believed to have led to his nephew's death, while another person who had been responsible for an agency concerning online child exploitation and protection has spoken of young people's fear of the 'threat of being exposed for private sexual behaviour' and of how that has 'massively increased the power that tormentors' threats had over vulnerable young people'.[72] Here the internet is shown not only to have taken its own place in the long-enduring social force-field of criticism and identity but also to play its role in the phenomenon of concealment–disclosure which may be an art that young people, and not only young people, may not yet comprehend.

No matter how innocuous some young people's ventures into the cyber world may be, not least in terms of their emergent sexuality, the wider web-world of sexuality and pornography raises other issues, not in terms of suicide, but in terms of deeply personal activities that many would not wish their

---

[71] Lay (2013: 1).   [72] Jonathan Brown (2013: 4).

relatives to know about during their lifetime but which might well become problematic in contents of unexpected death. But one example of this was an article by Bob Smyth in a popular Sunday newspaper in February 2011 entitled 'Why you should make plans for digital death'. Citing a postgraduate research-er, Wendy Moncur, Smyth's message was that since 'not everybody has led a life beyond reproach' it might be wise for people to arrange with their soli-citor to destroy specific online accounts on a client's death. To achieve this a person should leave their username and password with such a professional.[73] Deploying the notion of 'digital inheritance' Smyth was prompted by the fact that millions now participate in online social networks such as Facebook, where much personal information is carried and would probably need to be taken down after a person's death. His article alluded to the complex issue of more secret sites and to the silent life that some might lead. Here death takes on its own significance for the identity of the deceased as might become apparent to relatives having to deal with these sites. Whilst similar issues have always existed to some small extent in the papers left after a person's death, the nature of online material can be of quite a significantly different order.

This context raises the distinction between physical and social death in a compelling fashion, for dead people may still appear to be alive if their web pages are not removed, and removal is not always easy, even if their relatives are sufficiently web-savvy to know of those pages' existence. There is a certain haunting quality attached to an online reminder of some anniversary for which one should congratulate a person one knows to have died, especially if bonds of friendship are involved.

PAYING RESPECTS TO THE DEAD

This social nature of human identity, constituted as it is through relationships, is naturally intensified through interactive support and depleted without its sustaining social force. Once more, the general concept of 'power' not only describes the dynamic force sustaining people by converting ideas into values that give direction to life but also the sense of bonding that makes that direction liveable despite the constraints of grief. Moreover, the changes brought by bereavement involve shifts within the intimacy of the self and in its public expression, a tension captured in the expression 'paying respects to the dead'. That phrase bridges the private–public domain and brings us again not only to issues of obligation but also to forms of authority attaching to the dead where, once more, theories of reciprocity and dual sovereignty help

---

[73] Smyth (2011: 51).

interpret the interplay of a person's lifestyle and death-style, as the following case makes clear.

This example concerns a long-married couple where the husband is taken seriously ill and dies very quickly in hospital. Indeed, there were issues of potential medical neglect in diagnosis associated with his intense pain prior to death, and the wife, an intelligent woman familiar with local medical proced- ures, engaged in ongoing formal complaint over the lack of appropriate emergency treatment. But the factor relevant to this chapter concerns their relationship and of memory as a dynamic part of her ongoing identity. The husband dies in his mid seventies, and is cremated at a relatively new and rurally located crematorium with his remains interred in a lawned area whose small allocated spaces are identifiable by a grid system. A nearby stone memorial is also available on which the names of the deceased can be inscribed for approximately £500. Not long after the funeral the bereaved wife, who describes her relationship with her husband as having been very close, decided that it was not easy to identify precisely where her husband's remains were located, despite the letter:number grid system. She therefore requested the crematorium authorities to remove the remains from that spot and have them interred in a prime site located at the edge of a pond in the crematorium grounds. This was not an easy task in bureaucratic and procedural terms but it was accomplished. The new site is one of a relatively small number in this privileged spot and cost several thousand pounds. The new site carries an inscribed stone memorial of its own which takes the form of a small two-paged 'book' with her husband's details on the left-hand page and with the right- hand page blank, awaiting her own inscription after her death. She has already planned and paid for her own funeral and inscription on the blank page, whose essence will mark the fact that they are together again, just the two of them, as they had always been. In conversation she was eager to say that, as a couple, they had had no children; indeed, they were happy just as a pair together, and this had also applied to their holidays. They were happier to be on holiday, just themselves, and not in some larger group. During a conver- sation at the site, on a day when she was there tending the spot and replacing fresh flowers in a flower holder flush with the soil, she referred directly to her husband, looking at the memorial location and 'speaking to him' much as she spoke to me.

The relocation of his remains served to constitute a place whose nature was congruent with her sense of him and of the quality and nature of their relationship. Their close, couple-companionate life together could not be matched by the small rectangle of turf set amidst hundreds of similar spots in a single lawned area. The task of matching a letter and a number on a grid reference system to pinpoint her husband's spot would never be easy and, moreover, would probably not be an exercise that reflected her emotional tone in coming to 'visit him'. The new location, with its focal-point rose, flower vase, individual marble name, and expression of grief, all set in a circular area covered by white marble chips, could hardly symbolize an individual focus in any clearer way. What is more, the 'blank' page that awaits her own memorial adds her own 'presence' through absence in a most powerful fashion. Here, once more, we encounter a clear example of symbolic disclosure and concealment, a clear disclosure not only of her husband's identity and funerary location but also in a degree of public concealment of their intimacy that awaits a future consummation when her ashes join his. This case exemplifies our earlier concern with the direct relationship between money, space, and time in the lifestyle and death-style complex. For her increased expenditure quite literally bought a better place for her ongoing relationship with her husband; it showed how she valued him. In terms of reciprocity theory this 'value', although clearly transacted through a commercial payment, transcended its mere alienable nature, for its real meaning lay in their inalienable relationship, signified most dramatically in the page–name memorial stone that still awaited her posthumous inscription. For many others it is cremated remains as such that present a powerful inalienable 'gift' to spouses and family. If we add to that interpretation another drawn from our previous discussions of dual sovereignty we see this woman concerned with both jural and mystical aspects of her relationship, the former consisting in her pursuit of the propriety of medical treatment and the formalities in exhuming and relocating her husband's remains, while the mystical dimension lies embedded in the love shared with her husband in the past and still experienced both in memory and in the pragmatic visiting and caring for his memorial spot; one that is also hers for the future.

Other ways in which individuals relate to their dead include possessions, the items inherited from our families and even friends. When we speak of 'something to remember her by' we speak also of ourselves and of the items that help comprise our own identity, present and past. Such processes of remembrance can become far more than some reference to the past; they evoke pasts and make them present, as Therese Richardson, for example, demonstrated for the retained clothing of dead relatives that often fosters positive emotions of comfort but can also take on 'an "unhomely" or uncanny quality'.[74] Dan Miller, in his excellent treatment of 'the comfort of things' makes the incisive point that 'jewellery does not seem to be amenable to the same sense of gradual incorporation as clothing'; it seems to 'resist humanity', while retained clothing is more open to 'gradual assimilation of one person to another'.[75] As for the location of inherited objects, often within the home, this frequently sets the scene for sporadic recall and frames the current theoretical

---

[74] Richardson (2014: 72).
[75] Miller (2008: 39–44). See Wallman for 'stuffication', a critique of 'stuff' as 'today's most acute . . . affliction', albeit with a marked absence of reference to death (2015: 7).

interest in material culture and the dead. Margaret Gibson, for example, has done much to describe the way objects that have belonged to others may influence our memory, but she has also argued the case for bodies as 'encrypting machines of the living and the dead', not only in showing how positive emotions may rise from a sense of our being like a deceased parent in some behaviour or look, but also how some negative emotions or constraints may also arise from such phenomena.[76] The well-known Christian apologist C. S. Lewis, for example, reflected, on visiting his terminally ill father, that, 'My father and I are physical counterparts: and during these days more than ever I notice his resemblance to me'.[77] That observation is, itself, interesting for the way it is the father who is said to resemble the son and not the son the father as is, perhaps, more common in such retrospection.[78] Certainly this sensed likeness of ourselves to an elderly or, say a dead parent, has been recorded by others in a more analytical context, not least by Katherine Young, and is a clear reminder of the nature of embodiment and of how we can be a cameo of an other to ourselves.[79]

Roadside Memorials

That visit home by Lewis exemplified the power of place to capture and express some of the emotional entailments of bereavement and offers an appropriate link to roadside memorials. For when someone we love is rapidly removed from our lives, as in the case of a road accident, the need for some bridging of the intimate loss with its social recognition can become urgent given a death that offers its own challenge to meaning. Even though 'accidents' may be entirely 'natural', in the sense of being the outcome of a collision of vehicles, the ensuing death is seldom accepted as such; its very potential as randomness implies an essential meaninglessness that human beings are ill-disposed to accept. Accordingly, roadside memorials would seem to be an attempt to bring significance to an otherwise insignificant space. Indeed, such memorials, in the form of bunches of flowers, messages on cards, candles, and sometimes stones or more permanent markers, have proliferated in Britain, as in many other coutries, in recent decades.[80] One way of interpreting these is to see the intrinsically insignificant stretch of road on which someone died being transformed into a significant place. The idea that a person with a deeply meaningful life should die in a meaningless place strikes its own chord of

---

[76] Gibson (2008: 151).   [77] A. N. Wilson (1991: 112).

[78] Is this an example of what A. N. Wilson (1991: 110) pinpointed as that 'sublime egoism' generated from the experience of 'a man alone with God', now driving that individual's own sense of self in relation to others?

[79] Young (2002).   [80] Nešporová and Stahl (2014).

absurdity making the sight of flowers or other markers at a roadside intelligible in transforming a 'non-place' into a significant 'somewhere' emblazoned on the mind of bereaved kith and kin.[81]

The development of this practice in Britain, far removed from the idea of wayside shrines evident in some European Catholic countries, is an invented tradition grounded in the symbolic nature of floral tributes that accompany many different kinds of British celebration. It is, in fact, a good candidate for inclusion as a lifestyle extended to a particular form of accidental death such that not to mark an accident-spot in this way might well be regarded as remiss. It is an example not only of how an invented behaviour provides a focused expression of social force but also of cultural adaptation to felt needs.

CONCLUSION

This chapter has, then, considered some key dynamics of social force exhibited in the complementary elements of cognitive framing of religious perspectives as well as in artistic–aesthetic elements of human sensitivity to death, grief, and mourning, whether in the concrete world of memorials or in the rapidly pervading cyber world. Selected examples of lifestyle and death-style coherence and incoherence have shown how social forces related to grief are shaped by convention and innovation. Moreover, a degree of eclecticism of method in deploying a variety of approaches and theories has been deemed wise when approaching the complexity of death and its framing in a variety of world views. However, one cultural practice, whose innovation not only exemplifies the pairing of lifestyle and death-style idioms but also expresses shifts in the expression of social convention in establishment ways, is that of woodland burial, and to this we devote the next chapter.

---

[81] Douglas Davies (2005a: 170–1) for 'hopeless non-places', developing Augé on de Certeau's idea of 'non-place'. Cf. Marc Augé (1992: 70).

10

Natural Burial and Cultural Memory

While trees largely frame this chapter, both in terms of the twin-like development of woodland burial and the National Memorial Arboretum in the 1990s, the strongly militaristic nature of the latter is furnished with an architecturally contemporaneous complement in a school chapel created as a memorial to those who died in the Falklands campaign of April–June 1982.

In world-view terms of lifestyles ensuing in death-styles, the woodland sites speak of personal wishes fulfilled in a more private place, the Arboretum creates communal sentiment in a public meeting place, while the Falklands memorial offers its own example of the creative capacity of the British Establishment's social capital. All three cases demonstrate the dynamic capacity generated when an individual becomes motivated by an emotion-pervaded idea that attracts social support. In these accounts we see some clear perspectives of British social life through the windows of cultural practice that are both innovative and yet catalysed by pre-existing tradition.

In one, private life moves into a visually unidentifiable spot; in the second, national life is monumentalized at large; while the third takes a national event into the heart of a distinctive form of educational community. Here we not only encounter the apparently natural symbols of trees, but also the way the incised lettering of names both conceals and reveals human emotion, memory, grief, and hope, as quite different effects of social force are played out in autobiography, and in national and in more community-embraced history. Privacy and 'Establishment' make their diverse effects felt, with natural burial being properly described as a 'bottom-up', and the National Memorial Arboretum, and to some degree the Falklands' Memorial Chapel, being 'top-down' cultural developments, but with each originating in an individual's imagination.

At the outset, and in terms of this volume's many uses of the lifestyle theme in relation to death, we can say that few practices are as personally immediate as that of natural burial, few as culturally explicit as that of the National Memorial Arboretum, and few as engendered by the integrated values of an educational community as the Falklands Chapel.

The potential intimacy of woodland burial contrasts with the local, or school-based, or national location of war memorials, all as part of the memorial mapping of the British dead at large. In chapter 7 we considered London's prime memorial triad of the Cenotaph, Westminster Abbey, and St Paul's Cathedral. Now we will see how this has been extended to include a single rural arboretum site where material monuments are vitalized more by the spiralling and ever-growing world of plants than by the cyclical process of annual civic ritual. Yet ritual remains of deep significance, as will become apparent, with even the nation's annual keeping of two minutes' silence becoming, quite literally, a daily event at the Arboretum.

There is an enormous complexity surrounding the way different British groups and individuals live in and through these historical and contemporary monuments, whether these are in civic, urban, institutional, or rural contexts, just as there is for individuals and their woodland graves. The emotional dynamics driving memory foster affinities with and hostilities towards church- yard, civic cemetery, woodland burial, and crematorium in ways that may gain public expression or forever remain unspoken. The social changes that fostered the nineteenth-century inauguration of modern cremation and its twentieth-century burgeoning; the shifts in the deposition of cremated remains from the later twentieth century and the roughly parallel emergence of woodland burial; all stand as caveats against interpretative certainty and caution us against over-easy assertions about the meaning of space, place, and the dead, and of their associated material culture.[1] Nevertheless, the cultural creativity of individuals and the affinity some sense with their insight chal- lenge us at least to describe their influence, even if our fuller interpretation must await a greater passage of time.

NATURAL BURIAL

That being the case, to speak of 'natural burial' immediately raises the question of names and their intended significance, since this practice is often also described as woodland, ecological, or green burial, each carrying distinctive cultural significance, though here we largely focus on the 'natural burial' option, returning to the 'woodland' theme later when considering the National Arboretum. Though this name diversity has already been explored by Davies and Rumble there are still more features to consider following the theoretical pointers of this present volume.[2]

At the outset this practice illustrates something of popular creativity and the social force it may generate. The most thorough study of Natural Burial in terms of its 'landscape, practice, and experience' that has been conducted to

---

[1] Cf. Hirsch and O'Hanlon (1995), for space and place in diverse societies.
[2] Davies and Rumble (2012).

date is that by an interdisciplinary team from the University of Sheffield whose expertise covers a much greater range than that of Davies and Rumble, especially in terms of forms of landscape and the design and making of sites.[3] Their concerns with landscape issues complemented by insightful ethnographic studies need to be studied in their own right and will not be rehearsed here.

Bottom-up Social Force

Natural burial arose almost accidentally under the innovative creativity of Mr Ken West when he was responsible for a major cemetery at Carlisle in the north-west of England. If ever there was a good example of bottom-up cultural innovation that would engender a social force of its own this was it. Though one might be tempted to think the same happened with the emergence of the hospice movement and the work of Dame Cecily Saunders,[4] it has been argued that 'key figures in the British establishment' played significant endorsing roles in its emergence.[5] As for natural burial, however, it began essentially in 1993–4 when the practice of adopting land in a non-traditional form of cemetery use rapidly led to there being over 260 or so sites by 2014. Spread widely across the UK these take a diversity of forms whether in areas adjacent to long-established civic cemeteries, in simple fields set aside as part of a farm, or occupying sites within long-established woodlands. Some others sit in rather specialized contexts as, for example, one near Morpeth established near an old airfield and popular with deceased flyers. Some sites are run by private companies and some by local authorities; most have a strong web-page presence and some belong to the informally based Natural Death Centre, itself an example of individual creativity as ongoing editions of the *Natural Death Handbook* show.

Given that natural burial began in 1994 and cremation in 1885 it is remarkable that by 2014 there was an approximately similar number of each in the UK. One pattern followed by both innovations was that their initial users were more middle class than working class, with cremation not becoming more fully democratized until the 1950s and 1960s. However, one key difference between cremation and natural burial lies in the 'establishment' base of their founders. The British Cremation Society was formed by Sir Henry Thompson, surgeon to Queen Victoria, in 1874 shortly after he had been inspired by potential models of crematoria at the 1873 Vienna World's Fair. Mr Ken West, by sharp contrast, had left school at a young age and, with no family or financial advantage behind him, worked his way through

---

[3] Clayden, Green, Hockey, and Powell (2014).   [4] Saunders (1996: 318).
[5] Clark (1998: 43).

horticultural work into cemetery management through his own hard work and high intelligence. He was definitely no 'establishment man', yet woodland burial can, very properly, be seen as due to his responsive nature and democratic motivation answering a local and popular request for 'simpler' forms of funeral. This was highly charged by his deep interest in nature at large. His knowledge of natural burial is unrivalled, as his writing shows.[6] His endeavours did not particularly meet with the plaudits of funeral directors at large or with their own informal 'establishment' but, nevertheless, he did, in due course became an MBE in the Queen's Honours List for his services to ecology, and in that sense woodland burial received a kind of indirect Establishment approval. That became more explicit, perhaps, when Durham University conferred their honorary degree of Master of Arts upon him for his innovatory work in woodland burial.[7] What is telling is that West's influence is reminiscent of Bottomore's insight into elite groups, viz. that 'creation is an individual act, but it is facilitated by a general enthusiasm and liveliness of society at large'.[8] This is precisely what now seems to be happening over natural burial.

SECULARIZED–SACRALIZED VALUES

To approach this innovation as a world-view perspective allows us a double insight, first into the relatively familiar secularization and sacralization debates of the sociology of religion and, second, into 'sacralization' understood in the more psychologically nuanced approach to the sociology of identity espoused by Hans Mol.

As a world-view topic, if we understand secularization to mean the decreasing influence of mainstream religious ideas upon society at large, then woodland burial does involve a degree of secularization when its ritual symbolism is conducted by a secular celebrant, and this is as likely to be the case if it is a rite conducted by a priest. For those desiring a Christian world view to frame 'natural' burial it is perfectly possible for a priest to bless a grave (which does not involve formal consecration) and to use an official liturgy. However, the location of a woodland grave and the use of a formal rite outside of a traditionally recognized church building, or even civic cemetery offering explicit religious symbols in surrounding headstones, inevitably create a symbolic arena possessing its own implications. One of these, viz. 'nature', offers a concept that can, if family and priest so wish, be given strong

---

[6] West (2010).
[7] Here the author declares an interest in that Durham University's Centre for Death and Life Studies of which he was Director at the time sponsored the conferring of that degree.
[8] Bottomore (1964: 147).

theological significance in terms of God's 'creation', in the sense of a created order of nature. However, contemporary Christian liturgies offer few theological resources in this direction.

As a more theoretical issue sacralization can, however, assume quite different significance, through Mol's notion that phenomena contributing to our sense of identity are ascribed with sacred-like attributes (as detailed in chapter 2). In this sense 'sacralization' can, and often will, refer to aspects of life that carry the core values of an individual or, more likely, of a group. These values need not be traditionally religious in the sense that they are rooted in a notion of God, of divine revelation, institutions, or priesthoods and the like, but can just as easily have their reference in other phenomena, including ideas, that have come to be invested with emotion so as to become values, and, to follow the rationale outlined in previous chapters, these may assume the status of beliefs as they help in developing a sense of identity in people. The locating of these beliefs in a woodland site adds its own frame of destiny or long-term future to individual identity. In a different kind of way we see later how an English public school became the context for sacralizing identity.

But here it is the idea of 'nature' that is invested with an emotional charge as something dynamic and ongoing in which an individual may find some value for their own existence. This value then helps confer a sense of identity and becomes something of a belief involving a longer-term context of destiny. No such process can, of course, operate in a cultural vacuum and here British cultural ideals of nature that are aligned with parks and gardens come into their own. A very large numbers of Britons keep or have kept gardens and see the countryside, not least in terms of woods and forests, in very positive terms. It would, for example, be easy to belittle as simplistic sentimentality the once popular poem 'God's Garden' by Dorothy Frances Gurney who set the Garden of Eden alongside Christ's suffering in the Garden of Gethsemane, and created a distinctive sentiment, much appreciated by many and still reproduced on garden ornaments to the effect that, 'One is nearer God's heart in a garden / than anywhere else on earth'.[9] Such sentiment is perfectly understandable since emotions of peace often accompany a gardener's engagement with growth and life, as well as with death, all as part of the cycle of nature. For such individuals, gardens and by extension, parks, woodlands, and the countryside at large, become places of life, fertility, and the dynamic power of 'nature'. For those with traditional religious beliefs, whether held in some doctrinal precision of a creator, or in a much wider popular view of there being some higher power responsible for the way things are, such natural places stand ready for interpretation.

---

[9] Dorothy Frances Guerney (1858–1932). 'The kiss of the sun for pardon / The song of the birds for mirth / One is nearer God's heart in a garden / Than anywhere else on earth.'

In line with this sense of 'nature' the rules and regulations of natural burial sites tend to argue for or insist upon there being no headstone markers of graves or long-lasting memorials of other types. Sometimes wooden plaques are used, knowing that they, too, will decay. Bodies are strongly preferred not to have been embalmed and to be in easily biodegradable containers. Similarly, there is a general dislike of floral tributes in their plastic wrappings or metal frameworks, even if a family member may, occasionally, subvert the rules by hiding some small personal memento near the grave. For future identification and reference the management of these sites, as would be expected, keep strict records of the precise location of each grave, both in terms of ground maps and satellite mapping.

Here, in pragmatic fashion, we can see something of the very dynamics of 'the sacred' at work, as people's sense of themselves and of their relation to their grave in 'nature' engenders an identity aligned with vitality. Their destiny is to be integrated with the ongoing nature of 'nature'. In Hannah Rumble's research and in our joint volume we explored such intimations through the anthropological models of reciprocity as people spoke of 'giving something back' to nature and of helping to contribute to the future of the place to which their relatives might come.[10] Moreover, some spoke of this dynamic place as quite unlike the more static and 'dry as dust' context of cemeteries. There are often several cultural and psychological levels underlying what people say, and here the 'dry as dust' motif—reminiscent of the biblical injunction to Adam and Eve that they were taken from the dust and would return to it again, and of the 'ashes to ashes, dust to dust'[11] phrasing of the traditional Church of England funeral service—differs from the living plants and creatures of the natural burial site. The whole nature of 'destiny' might also have some symbolic echoes in these motifs, for the Christian burial of 'earth to earth' lay in hope of a future resurrection; there would be stillness, rest, peace, or the like until that time. But this pattern of belief in resurrection has been shown to be very low, even amongst Christians for whom the passing of the immortal soul takes precedence over some lying in wait.[12] By contrast, the woodland burial leads to a more immediate participation of the corpse into life processes, whether or not the deceased person believed in an immortal soul and its ongoing journey.

The sacred thus becomes a means of speaking about the worth and signifi-cance of the dead person and of their location and, as such, the sacred shares in the allied concepts of 'dignity' of a person whether in life, when dying, or in death. Dignity speaks of the sacred quality of the self in relation to others. In traditional religious contexts that relationship is framed by God; in secular contexts it is sustained in self and family–friend relationships along with the

---

[10] Rumble (2010); Davies and Rumble (2012: 70–3, 97–119, 140–2).
[11] Genesis 3:19.   [12] Davies and Shaw (1995: 93–4).

frame of natural processes. This is all the more powerful given the role of 'nature', environment, and cosmos as already indicated.

Ashes and Natural Burial

Working from this sacred–secular framing of natural processes, woodland burial comes to reveal something of the complexity of identity in the British public in respect of the interplay of life and death, for it also involves issues of social class, gender differences, professionalism, commercialism, and ecclesial involvement. Here we find ourselves at the cultural interface between cremation, as a late nineteenth-century technological innovation, twentieth-century popular appropriation, and the even longer-term British ideal of nature, gardens, parkland, and nature at large, albeit with the latter cultural motif being further intensified by the newer issues of ecology and world survival.

Moreover, the later twentieth-century emergence of personal choice, consumerism, and commercialism became increasingly germane as far as funerals and location of remains were concerned, as we have seen in previous chapters for thousands of Britons engaging in private rites with cremated remains in a wide diversity of places. The British sense of freedom that developed largely from the 1970s to do what they want with cremated remains enabled people to think of themselves as not being constrained by law or regulation as to what they do with ashes. That freedom has, generally speaking, not been the case in most Western European countries, such as, for example, Sweden,[13] and one might suggest that its absence has not fostered a similar freedom to respond to the innovation of natural burial.

Refuse and Revaluation

When thinking of traditional religion, emergent forms of spirituality, or simply of innovative ritual practice, and the lifestyles aligned with these, we should not ignore some of the most basic aspects of life that, in their own way, engender world views for many individuals and their families. In terms of this chapter's focus on natural burial these involve ecological issues, not in the more abstract debates on global warming or the depletion of the ozone layer, but at the most basic level of refuse collection. For while it is one thing for a few, media-savvy scientists, politicians, or body-minded celebrities to engage with ecological concerns and frame them as some form of nature spirituality, it is quite another for entire populations to be required to sort their domestic

---

[13] Dahlgren and Hermanson (2005: 60–4).

refuse into different bins for recycling or disposal purposes. Pragmatic ecology emerged of necessity in the early twenty-first century as local authorities responded to targets set for recycling with which households needed to comply. Within the UK many householders were already predisposed to engage in turning some of their refuse into compost as part of a moderately widespread practice of gardening, and such ordinary interests and concerns should not be overlooked when considering much wider world views. People's views are often pragmatically grounded in how they live, not least when embedded in their family, work, friendship, and leisure networks. While these pragmatics of life generate their own level of abstraction, this is not likely to reach elaborately systematic versions unless a person is a member of an organization that intensifies belief and the management of human emotions through its ideological scheme, organizational implementation, and ritual practice.[14] For churches, this works out as theology as expressed in liturgy and ethics where the professionals, in particular, who have been trained in theology and earn their living from church work, have their outlook more directly forged than do the laity or wider public at large. Beyond the churches there are other ideas that, similarly, find differential impact; amongst these are nature, ecology, and the health and wellbeing of bodies, all of which can be expressed and 'ritualized' in ways that vary from compost heaps to the local gymnasium, and in the process come to constitute their own form of spirituality for those who might wish to think in such terms.

Sites

To what we have already seen of the diversity of natural burial sites we need to add the fact that no innovation exists in isolation, whether economic, political, or cultural, so that, for example, changes in attitudes towards land use in agricultural contexts of set-aside land used for natural burial sites need to be measured against the future need for much land for arable use. Here important questions surround the economics of farming in relation to individual choices of some landowners that may not be sustainable in the long term; all compared with traditional churchyards and cemetery sites, including civic cemeteries, which are actually consecrated by the Church of England and that, therefore, offer a long-term commitment.

Some owners of large estates have developed areas of their land for woodland burial as part of diversification of use and of income. Here, in its own way, the issue of the British Establishment and of allied ideas of land, estates, and heritage, play their own part in advertising and in evoking British ideas of

[14] Mitchell (1999).

tradition. This is extremely significant in terms of ritual innovation and economics where the commercial world of funerary provision which has arisen in response to what was, initially, a small, niche, popular demand has developed its own grammar of discourse of death-style that evokes a lifestyle associated with the great and the good. But the complexity here is quite considerable, for intermingled with 'heritage' are ideals of ecology and 'nature', issues already partly discussed in chapter 4 in relation to changing notions of spirituality, whose breadth of engagement increasingly brought the body into the picture, whether in special spa treatments first for women and then for men, or physical training of the body through active gymnasium membership where sharing with like-minded fitness enthusiasts often engendered a kind of community feeling not entirely unlike that gained by some in their churchgoing. The point is that heritage frames nature and ecology in a value set that can frame the worth and dignity of the dead individual in quite a different way than the heritage of the church framed the worth of the dead in terms of their eternal destiny. Some substance can be given to this shift if one contrasts the 'rest in peace' motif of traditional Christian burial, with its theological anticipation of the future resurrection when all would 'awake' to their eternity, with the notion of burying someone in a spot with a 'good view'. This latter idiom is far from rare, as will become apparent in the following case studies that are taken from filmed interviews produced in the documentary *Natural Burial and the Church of England*, made in association with an empirical study of the Barton Glebe Woodland Burial near Cambridge.[15]

CASE STUDY: BARTON GLEBE, CAMBRIDGE

Barton Glebe Woodland Burial site was established by the Church of England in 2000 and very unusually within the UK it consists of formally consecrated land, but with a Lodge for ceremonies or refreshments that is not consecrated. This is a distinctive example of where the 'establishment' nature of the Church of England has influenced funeral innovation and has given to users, whether religious or not, a sense of the long-term commitment of the site to the purpose in hand; something that cannot be easily assured for sites dependent upon a single family's future business plans. Moreover, it marks the top-down 'establishment' consecration of land for a purpose of woodland burial whose origin, as we have argued, as definitely 'bottom-up' and, if anything, clearly secular in origin, albeit a secularity driven by what might, in retrospect, be

---

[15] Film: Sarah Thomas (2011). Book: Davies and Rumble (2012).

354 of Mors Britannica

described as a nature-concerned spirituality.[16] Here we explore the significance of the place through three filmed interviews, the first of a bereaved
daughter, the second of a widow, and the third of a mother and daughter who
had signed up for their own future burial at the site.

First we have the daughter, who spoke of her father who had been a local
farmer. When she began to look after him towards the end of his life she
wondered about his funeral and prepared for it in advance using the services of
a local funeral director, choosing hymns for the service. Going online to seek
an appropriate location she discovered that there was a woodland site in her
area and decided it was absolutely 'the right place for him' to be buried for a
number of very specific reasons. One of these was that his grave could face in
the direction of an area in which he used to shoot, for if he had been buried in
a churchyard with its prescriptive eastern direction of graves, that would not
have been possible. Moreover, she had a choice of named areas in which his
body might lie, and one of these was 'clover'. This clinched the issue for her
since 'he used to sow clover in the paddock'. The association of ideas was an
argument in itself, with the film showing still photographs of her father
ploughing with a tractor to underline this fact. Other photographs allowed
us to see him growing his prize chrysanthemums, and with his gun, dog, and
ferret to reflect his hunting activities close to the burial ground. In the film we
see the daughter walking to the grave and saying 'Hello Dad', gently sighing,
and saying that she always said hello to him when visiting the grave. Moreover,
she sensed a 'warmth' and that he was 'with her' here. As for her choice of a
water-chestnut 'coffin', this had also given her a good feeling, not least because
they had been able to decorate it with flowers. The wooden plaque placed on
his grave gave his name and life dates with the inscription 'At home walking
the dogs'. This example captures at least some elements of her relationship
with her father and with what she thought this location would mean in terms
of his interests and character. Her account of him as 'being able to see' in the
direction of the area where he used to hunt, and of speaking to him in an
intimate way, revealed her connection with him and with this choice of
burial site.

The second person was the devoted wife of an Anglican priest who had died
suddenly and unexpectedly. Her extensive reflections on life and death contain
a wealth of material both on grief and on the nature of woodland burial. She
described how the grave and the woodland burial site became a kind of safe
place for her at a time of life when she had to move between residences and
was not in that sense settled in one place. She would visit there not so much
'to speak to' her husband but because she felt secure there. She tells how she
used to tend the grave with particular care for some time after the burial,

[16] For legal and some liturgical aspects of consecration of graveyards see Rugg (2013: 15–18,
39–41, 182).

'weeding out thistles' and trying to organize plants so that there would be something in season throughout the year. One day this activity reminded her that she had always been used to cutting her husband's hair and that what she was now doing with plants on his grave revealed a similar activity. Slowly, she came to realize that her attempt at controlling plant growth was unwise and that nature should be left to do as it would. On a yet wider plane this woman, who held a significant professional role in society, reflected on how, for much of her life, she was involved in things that were not part of 'the core' of who she was. Her husband's death gave her pause for thought and brought this home to her. Reflecting on her husband's current identity she says that she cannot imagine that he 'does not exist somewhere'. Referring to 'layer upon layer upon layer upon layer' of life and existence, she thought he would have some realistic basis somewhere. She appreciated just how the seasons come and go and how that was reflected in the plant and animal life of the woodland burial ground; it did not seem likely that a cemetery frame for her thinking would have made these reflections so easy.

The third case was that of an elderly mother and her middle-aged daughter who had, together, been thinking about what to do about funerals in the future. They had heard from friends about woodland burial and wondered what it was about, and, discovering this particular site, they decided to purchase graves in advance of their deaths. The elderly mother repeatedly spoke of the site as not looking like an ordinary cemetery but being more like a park or a 'garden centre'. Indeed, several references to 'garden centre' exemplify the lifestyle and death-style idiom of this present volume in that garden centres have become an interesting feature of British life for a significant minority of middle-aged and elderly people. There are probably very few towns in Britain, even small towns, that do not possess garden centres that not only sell plants and varied allied goods but also possess a café or restaurant. Indeed, these places that began as a market for garden plants have undergone a dramatic evolution into places for other kinds of sales, not least of food and drink. Sunday lunch at the local garden centre, itself made very convenient for elderly people with its easy provision of car parking, has become a growing business and it would seem that the garden-centre image was one that had impressed itself on this old woman as she pondered her future grave site. Her daughter, who was a nurse, had attended several woodland burial events of some of her former patients and she spoke in terms of her own grave as being there with her mother. She added that various friends were also planning burial there so they would all be there 'together'. As an aside to her mother's positive comments on such a pleasant, and apparently social, place to be, she added that this practice would grow—it would 'be the future'.

These examples, with relatives speaking of a spot with a 'good view', of plants and hair, and of sociability, might easily lead an unthinking stranger to assume that the British have a theory allowing the dead to 'see' or be in good company. In comparative terms, just as one Madagascar society expresses 'praise for good views' as a way of capturing the significance of clarity of vision and distanced perspective, so some Britons do indeed refer to good views in a grave location, albeit as a means of expressing a satisfactory location for their dead.[17]

Woodland burial sites, much more than cemeteries, offer the possibility of choosing a diversity of location that allows the emotions of the bereaved some scope for talking about the dead in a fashion that suggests they retain a degree of agency. In effect this allows for a period after immediate bereavement in which the imagination of the living seems to engage with the dead through a cultural sense of place as an active arena of individual perception. As Layton tellingly says of fieldwork contexts, 'It is only by participating in indigenous discourse that we can attempt an appropriate interpretation', and this applies as much to life in an English county as to his Australian Aboriginal region.[18]

The emergence of such woodland sites into public recognition has been relatively rapid in British life. One index of this can be found in media soap operas, not least that of *The Archers*, the longest-running series in the world. During the first week of February 2011 this idealized depiction of the everyday life of country-folk focused on the inauguration of a natural burial site at the fictional village of Ambridge.[19] Given the rural nature of this community's life, the creation of this woodland burial site carries the sense of lifestyle and death-style coherence. For *The Archers*, the woodland burial idea seemed to develop as a perfectly coherent death practice in relation to an agricultural and ecologically informed lifestyle. Previous years and episodes had witnessed stories embracing death and bereavement, always allied with Church of England pastoral ministry and funeral rites, and often reflecting notions of grief responses popularized from the work of Elisabeth Kübler-Ross.[20] Indeed, over the Christmas and New Year period of 2012–13 the oldest village resident 'dies' and, devoid of relatives, we find many villagers attending his funeral service in the parish church. One younger adult, a likeable milkman with something of a dubious moral reputation, chides a most respectable younger woman who shows little interest in being there, reminding her that a funeral is 'a rite of passage' and that she ought to be there as part of her community involvement. Rather like the invoking of what is 'natural' in grief reactions, this formal use of 'rite of passage' reflects something of an increased self-conscious framing of aspects of death in British life.

---

[17] Bloch (1995: 65).   [18] Layton (1995: 230).

[19] A further high-profile burial 'took place' there in late July 2014 when someone who had long left the village was returned for a 'green funeral'—the term preferred in that virtual village.

[20] Kübler-Ross (1968). Her 'stages of grief' model, though popularly accepted, attracts much professional criticism—Corr (1993: 69–83); Parkes (2013).

NATURAL CONSTRAINTS

Such changes surrounding the emergence of natural burial cannot be divorced from other cultural influences affecting lifestyle themes and their death-style consequences, not least in terms of dress and ritual. Many of the new woodland sites involve mourners and funeral directors having to negotiate rough grass, bushes, and trees as they access grave sites off any immediately beaten track. If it is a wet day those present do better in wellingtons or other rough footwear and not the patent leather or other formal black shoes usually associated with the funeral director and mourners. For essentially urban funeral directors, their normal ritual environment at crematoria provides paved approaches and the *porte-cochère* over the main entrance that keeps all dry.[21] Even at most civic cemeteries, paved or roughly surfaced drives service most grave sites. These rough constraints at natural burial sites provide a ritual arena carrying their own sensory base that certainly impinges upon people's awareness in a different way than is the case with well-managed crematoria and even with ordinary cemeteries that tend to have some degree of road and pathway access.

As for the ethos surrounding woodland burial, its increasing informality is consonant with 'natural' roughness and its often celebratory air prefers to dwell on the lifestyle of the deceased than on their eternal destiny. The absence of ecclesiastical symbols, even those of crosses or scriptural texts on the headstones in formal cemeteries, makes this approach easier by providing a more neutral symbolic stage on which to perform whatever is desired by the family.

The 'traditional–professional' stance of many funeral directors does not immediately offer a parallel ethos. Something similar happens when a family decides that the service for a dead child or young person should be a celebratory event, not least when a church service is involved. If family and friends decide to attend in informal and colourful clothing, to reflect something of the deceased person, the funeral director can appear as the odd one out, for even the clergy find it easy to adopt colourful and festive liturgical dress for the event.

Quite unlike the state-linked funeral of Baroness Thatcher in the previous chapter that symbolized social force in a demonstration of top-down formality honed by tradition, many woodland burials reflect the quite different domain of cultural innovation created in a bottom-up search for new forms of funerals matching new freedom of lifestyle.

Here ritual innovation plays an important role in relation to desired and preferred emotions, with the theoretical notion of elective affinity (already

---

[21] Grainger (2005: 343).

discussed in chapter one) suggesting itself as a valuable interpretative tool. One application of this notion for our purposes reveals the millennia-long Christian bonding of death with burial being broken with the emergence of cremation in the late nineteenth century, to be followed roughly a century later by another shift as some people now link death not with cremation but with natural burial. In saying this I am deeply aware of the simplicity of this sketch and of the complexity of grief that frames the alignment of ideas, beliefs, and emotions within customary practice and changes in practice. Still, the elective affinity of emotions of grief with traditional burial allowed the language of hope to be expressed in terms of resurrection and of a personalized afterlife. Emotions of parting could be tempered by the hope of being reunited, or of a continued existence of the deceased in the afterworld. The grave housed the corpse, with visiting and memorials serving as one means of bonding.

As we have already seen, cremated remains, unlike the corpse, are portable, and the British, quite unlike their legislation-bound European neighbours, began in the mid 1970s to take away ashes and do many sorts of things with them. And this allowed a switch of emotional affinity with the dead that was not restricted to graves. Domestic gardens, holiday venues, sporting sites, and other places of identity location have all been made more significant through cremated remains. I described such practices some years ago utilizing the shorthand of a shift from eschatological focus of essentially Christian identity to a retrospective fulfilment of largely secular identity.[22] With these I would now also align shifts in forms of emotional relationship.

Affinities Old and New

The innovation of natural burial now allows for former affinities to be broken and new ones formed. At this early stage in the emergence of natural burial three broad shifts may be taking place: one from traditional to natural burial—from cemetery to woodland; one from cremation to natural burial—from ashes scattered in preferred places to body buried in preferred place; and a third which is a variation in cremation practice—allowing ashes to be buried in natural burial sites. This co-presence of ashes with corpses already buried at a woodland site is a growing but originally an unintended consequence of the establishment of such sites.

In terms of affinity, it is worth rehearsing our earlier point on the diverse naming of woodland, natural, green, or ecological burials, and their ideological–emotional nuances. Woodlands carry long-term cultural associations in estate-managed Britain, with 'woodland' practically always preferred

---

[22] Douglas J. Davies ([1997: 3] 2002: 141), expanded in (2005: 117–27).

over 'forest': 'forest burial', where the associations would be more negative, is an alien concept in the UK. Although one might make a case for setting 'natural' in a perceived opposition to the 'unnatural' domain identified with cremation technology or the medical-professional and funeral-directing side of death, its centre of emotional gravity seems to be much more open: the 'natural' makes no oppressive demands. An allied issue concerns the desire for containers that are hand or craft made, replacing factory-made coffins. As for 'green' and 'ecological' funerals, these closely linked terms seem to move us further into an ideologically weighted perspective, acknowledging dangers to the environment and the potential failure of the Earth as a place for human life.

One feature of people's accounts of their desire for such burial lies in their desire to 'give something back'. Davies and Rumble explore this thoroughly in terms of gift-reciprocity theory and of the emotional reflexivity that pervades the way people come to think of their identity after death, when buried in their place of choice. In the British cultural context, especially under the influence of traditional Christianity, few ever speak of 'giving themselves' to the grave or, as was customary in Hindu cremation practice, of giving their body as a last gift to the deities upon the funeral pyre.[23] Indeed, the only widespread cultural preference for the verb lies in 'giving' one's body 'for medical research' or 'organ donation', an idiom that is redolent of ideas of social relationship and assumed worth. But, in 'giving something back' people indicate a spectrum of intention and emotional alliance, from giving back the physical body as compost valuable for the future of the earth, to providing a place where children and grandchildren may come and play, as in a park.

In all of this, individuals seem to anticipate their own death, as they view the deaths of their dead relatives, in terms of positive emotions of safety, peace, and an environment of life. They will be part of a dynamic place where life goes on around them in the plants, grasses, trees, insects, birds, and other wildlife; they anticipate themselves as participants and not as inert. Here the affinity of the dead with dry, cold, dusty, and socially burdensome graves contrasts with living nature. This is, perhaps, all the more relevant since, as we have already seen, increasing numbers of people no longer think in terms of a heavenly afterlife complementing an earthly lifestyle or serving as a place of reward. In the woodland burial context we tend not to encounter fear of decay as we did for ordinary cemetery burial—albeit for a small minority, in previous research of a large random sample of the population and which was conducted prior to the establishment of woodland burial.[24]

Emotional imagination works in terms of what is known and of what may be sought in relation to what is known, and one such desire is for security. In

---

[23] Parry (1994: 178).   [24] Davies and Shaw (1995: 26).

terms of death, that kind of longed-for security not only involves some kind of 'place' but a *relational* place; a place in which one has connections with others, not least family members. Traditional Christianity developed its own notion of a heavenly realm and, especially during the nineteenth century, fostered the idea of happy families finding fulfilment together 'in heaven' with innumerable gravestones announcing that deceased couples are 'reunited' or the like, despite the words of the church wedding service marking marriage as a state existing until separation by death.

As for the Barton Glebe site, it presents its own opportunities and constraints for thought, for, on one hand, it is a legally and ecclesiastically consecrated burial ground offering security of place that outstrips the great majority of similar settings that are not consecrated and could much more easily be given a new purpose in the future. On the other hand, however, the general absence of enduring memorial markers means that messages of heavenly unity inscribed on stone are absent and in that sense do not exist as imagination triggers for those visiting the graves.[25]

Place and Time

What natural burial sites do offer is a degree of openness for the imagination, whether for the living anticipating their own grave site or bereaved people thinking about their dead kin. This emotional potential, combined with a sense of the passage of time marked by the seasons and by a sense of sharing the place with others, yields a powerfully open-ended sense of the self in its future. Though many philosophers rightly speak of the unthinkability of death in the sense that one has to be alive and thinking to be aware at all, many ordinary people do not adopt that particular line of argument. They tend to anticipate the future, and, if suitable attractive symbols exist, imagine themselves in it. This is evident, for example, in the way people behave with the cremated remains of relatives or when expressing their own desire of where they would like their ashes to go after their cremation. This hope of having one's cremated remains located in sites of identity significance now takes on an even more dynamic possibility in the anticipation of having one's corpse placed in a symbolically and emotionally significant place.

In all of this the imagination plays with death and allows a relative to speak of how a dead person would be 'happy' in a spot where he can 'see' things in a particular direction, or where she may anticipate birdsong. Even notions of time—itself a most deeply embedded cultural category—are affected by

---

[25] As already indicated, all sites record each burial and its location, whether in paper, digital, or satellite location forms. It is the avoidance of enduring 'cemetery-like' headstones that typifies natural burial sites.

natural burial sites, where, for example, the notion of eternity that was pervasive in traditional churchyards and cemeteries through formal texts on headstones is replaced by the environmental signs of the seasons and the settling of the grave.[26] This may well be important as far as grief itself is concerned because grief is a word always covering a complex cluster of emotionally embodied memories and sometimes involving a sense of time and place. The churchyard and cemetery, especially when aligned with head-stone messages bearing ideas now 'written in stone', capture and perhaps even imprison emotions at that time of inscription. The natural burial site, by contrast, does not take so many hostages to fortune, not least in the way the one-off settling of the bare-earth grave mound created by the interment and the volume of the body-container to a more or less ground-level base, albeit one now irregularly covered by plant life, provides its own organic sense of time passing. This is complemented by a complex double action of 'natural time', first in the more ephemeral affinities afforded by the short-term flower-ing of plants, and, secondly, by the long-term growth of trees that both reflect the seasonality followed by the small plants and add their own trans-seasonal maturation.

SEMIOTIC ALLURE, SECULARITY, AND SACRALITY OF PLACE

Another way of speaking about these complexities is to think in terms both of semiotic allure and elective affinity, terms describing the attractive power and social force aligned with certain ideas, places, or persons. Indeed the image of affinities and, more particularly, of shifting bonds between persons reflects directly on Bergman's original scientific image of the physical forces driving chemical interactions (as depicted in chapter 1). Though crude, this hints at the field of social force that influences changing cultural patterns, not least in forms of funeral and ways of approaching death.

Any natural burial site, as a ritual–symbolic entity, carries with it consid-erable potential for bearing upon the notion of secularization precisely because of its cognate possibility of creating a sacralization of place. Such potent terms need clarification, not least because to speak of sacralization in this context does not mean a return to ecclesiastical control or to a theological interpret-ation of life but describes powerful human emotions being brought to bear upon ideas, and in particular upon the locations named by these ideas, and

---

[26] Research is wanting on people's experience of the settling of graves in cemeteries and their response to the time when the headstone is placed on it.

turning the ideas into value places that materialize the embodiment of a dead human being. Here we need to recall both Mol's notions of identity formation and ascription of 'sacred' status to identity generators, and my own suggestion that when an emotional charge is brought to an idea it becomes a value, and when that value is involved with a person or group's sense of identity it becomes a belief. This is particularly significant as far as the British innovation of woodland burial is concerned, for the 'idea' of natural burial shifts in significance when pervaded by emotions of grief and memory of a person buried there. Natural burial becomes a 'value' and, if allied commitments to themes of nature and ecology are also involved as frames for the identity of the dead we are soon in the domain of beliefs: whether they take a more traditionally religious form, are of a more mixed 'spirituality', or are avowedly secular makes little difference as far as the emotional dynamics of individuals are concerned.

Something of the public face of natural burial may, however, differ from this as we have already seen for Barton Glebe's consecrated land but unconsecrated ceremonial hall. We can exemplify something of the difference between the more traditionally religious and the more secularly spiritual tonality respecting death by comparing two events focused on the opening of two new woodland burial sites, at Durham in 2013 and at Liverpool in 2014, respectively in the north-east and north-west of England.

Durham

The Durham site was opened in a relatively low-key fashion with approximately fifty or so people present. Its wooden lodge was used as the focal point in which a few individuals spoke. One had been much involved in the planning of the project and expressed thanks to a variety of individuals and organizations that had played their part in the task. The more focused and formal act of opening the site and dedicating it for its purpose fell to the Rt. Revd Professor Stephen Sykes, now retired but who had been a leading light in theological circles of the Church of England as Professor of Theology at both Durham and Cambridge Universities, as Bishop of Ely, and as Principal of St John's College, Durham, and its associated theological college of Cranmer Hall that trains people for the Anglican Ministry. In a most direct sense he was a member of the British Establishment, having also served in the House of Lords when Bishop of Ely. At the time of this dedication, in 2013, bishop Sykes had been seriously ill and was in a wheelchair for this day. His presence at such a dedication was all the more significant in that, when Bishop of Ely, he had played a major role in establishing the Barton Glebe woodland burial site that, as we have already described, had been formally consecrated with all entailed by that act of church law. The Durham site, however, as with most others in the UK, was not to be consecrated, and in that sense was not part of a traditional religious frame, but was more 'open' in terms of allegiance or belief. What then of the performative utterance within the ritual of opening that 'made it so'? It was in a most distinctive fashion an utterance framed by our preceding description of the bishop, his previous influence, establishment status, and also his current existential status as a physically, but certainly not mentally, debilitated person. What he did was simply to read the liturgical text known as the *Benedicite* and which takes the form of praise to God from the lips of three young devotees thrown into a fiery furnace by their enemies. It was read in the form taken from the Anglican *Book of Common Prayer*, beginning with, 'O all ye works of the Lord, bless ye the Lord: praise him and magnify him for ever'. It then invites the angels, heavens, sun, moon and stars, showers, dew, frost, cold, ice and snow, winds, fire, heat, winter and summer, days and nights, lightening and clouds, wells, seas and floods, all to bless the Lord. It passes to the whales, fowl, beasts and cattle, before coming to the children of men, to Israel, to priests and servants of God, as well as to 'the spirits and souls of the righteous', and to the holy and humble hearted and to those three heroic young men in the fire; all are called to 'bless ye the Lord: praise him and magnify him for ever'. As the bishop recited this litany of praise that embraces the created order there was a deeply respectful silence in the group present and, reflecting on it as a participant observer, I suspect that for many it was a deeply moving moment, not simply because a bishop spoke liturgical words but because an obviously unwell man could sit at that boundary between life and death and speak these ancient words. There was no music or singing and, after the formalities just described, for which people had sat in chairs, there followed refreshments for all at the Lodge and a small marquee erected for the day. People then chatted and some went to view the burial site adjacent to the Lodge.

Liverpool Dedication

The Liverpool event was markedly different. It took place in the large, purpose-built and wooden, lodge-like structure comprised of some offices, a reception area, and one large ceremonial space with rows of chairs facing an immense window that occupies the whole of one wall facing onto a meadow-like area bounded by mature woodland. An hour-long programme comprised of some speeches from the company that had developed the site, including a brief speech from a young man who had been taken on as an apprentice and whose life had been bettered through this participation, as well as from its chief executive and more local manager. Because the site itself was being developed as part of long-established estates there was a brief speech from Lord Derby whose family had owned the site for many generations. This element of the proceedings was itself interesting in that having Lord Derby present—and he referred to some other local dignitaries who were also there— marked the presence of the British Establishment. This was a woodland burial site situated on ancient family lands, and came replete with a strong heritage motif. His embodiment of the 'Establishment' stood much higher than any civic, ecclesiastical, or other religious dignity; there was no bishop there, and the couple of clerically suited men present sat in the audience. A woman community chaplain whose denominational status was not entirely clear read a poem that had no essentially traditional religious format, while a dynamic and likeable community choir from the Liverpool area sang a variety of popularly arranged songs, none of which was hymn-like or 'sacred' in the traditional sense. What was especially obvious in terms of ritual analysis was that there was no moment of dedication—no performative utterance as such— the event started and ended, but, in technical ritual terms, there was no formula or intensified moment or action that launched the site or 'made it so'. Rather, the event was 'made' by a combination of a preceding reception, the many words of organizers and of the establishment 'patron', and by the choral pieces, followed by a walk around part of the burial site and an informal departure of guests.

NATIONAL MEMORIAL ARBORETUM

That walk around the wooded Lancashire landscape with its new-found significance for burial offers a ready conceptual shift to our consideration of the Staffordshire-sited arboretum that constitutes its own form of National Memorial, albeit devoid of dead bodies as such. This profoundly symbolic site of national memorial originated in the thought of David Childs of the Royal Navy and its birth is important for offering a rare example of the power of context, experience, individual creativity, and the invention of tradition in Britain. As part of his Royal Navy duties Childs was involved with the American military involving visits to Virginia. On one of these trips, going via Washington DC, a 'spare Saturday' produced the following events.

> It was a lovely day and I spent the morning walking through the Arlington Military Cemetery where the graves lie between wonderful lines of trees. In the afternoon I visited the National Arboretum and spent the rest of the day wandering around this 450 acre collection of beautiful and exotic trees. I returned to my hotel with my legs protesting at the miles they had covered that day.
>
> In the night I woke up with the last two places I had visited combined in my mind—a National Memorial Arboretum where tribute to those who had lost their

lives defending our country's future could be made by planting a tree, a living symbol of a future of hope.[27]

On the flight back to the UK he read in a newspaper that the government was launching an initiative for a new National Forest to be developed in Leicestershire, Derbyshire, and Staffordshire and this newspaper article serendipitously struck him as suggesting the opportunity and geographical area for a memorial arboretum.

Many ideas and meetings with individuals and groups flowed from this. One conversation was with Leonard Cheshire VC, OM, DSO—whose honours reflect his fame as an RAF hero of the Second World War, and who founded a charity providing support for disabled servicemen and women[28]—led to Childs' retirement from the Royal Navy in 1993 to set about what was an immense task. Its successful outcome resulted in the transformation of a 150-acre site at Alrewas near Lichfield into an enormous memorial site, opened in May 2001 with a dedication by the Archbishop of Canterbury in the presence of Her Majesty the Queen. The economic feasibility of this project was not always certain and, at times, hung very much in the balance, but was enhanced when the Millennium Commission supported it as a National Lottery Project; when, ultimately the Royal British Legion would assume ongoing responsibility for the site; and most significantly when the government decided in November 2000 that a new, focused, national memorial to the armed forces would be created and located in London. After much lobbying, by March 2002 the official mind had been changed, resulting in the parliamentary announcement that 'the Armed Forces Memorial will be sited at the National Memorial Arboretum in Staffordshire'.[29]

When compared with the rise of the woodland burial movement with its very clear 'bottom-up' motivation it would be slightly too easy to over-accentuate the Memorial Arboretum as having possessed a 'top-down' driver. Yet, as this shift in Cabinet-level decision-making, and as David Childs' account of the whole complex process, show, Childs' approaches to people and institutions did capture the support of a significant number of 'establishment' figures. However, Childs is very keen to note that it was the support and small-scale financial contributions of very ordinary folk that was evident at the outset.[30] Still, following a visit by the Duke of Kent in January 1998, as the site was in the process of development, Childs reflected that 'whatever maverick status we might have had, we were now "establishment". Our saplings had a future.'[31] So, though this new national institution was, in an almost literal

---

[27] Childs (2008: 10).   [28] Leonard Cheshire Disability is the charity's name.
[29] Childs (2008: 96–7). The Secretary of State for Defence had announced in Parliament in November 2000 that this would be in London. After much lobbying, March 2002 witnessed this further announcement.
[30] Personal communication, April 2015.   [31] Childs (2008: 29).

sense, grounded in one man's vision and his naval experience facilitated approaches to armed forces, government, civic, and other 'establishment' sources that cohered in ultimate success, the project was one that carried an affinity for individual women and men. In due course David Childs was awarded the honour of being a Commander of the British Empire in 2003.

This entire project merits much greater analysis than this chapter's cameo presents, for it captures that combination of personal networked contacts, personal difficulties,[32] serious economic support, wider difficulties and further planning, and the power of volunteers in Britain, as well as charismatic leadership that generated a national institution, albeit one still in its early stages of development within the national consciousness. However, we can touch on some symbolic and ritual elements that bring this National Memorial into some relation to the woodland burial movement and to some of the preceding themes of this present volume. Certainly, it shows how some dynamic aspects of lifestyles in Britain engage with styles of death that encompass memory and memorials within an optimistic view of the present and future.

Theoretical Reflections

In theoretical terms a variety of academic disciplines furnish approaches relevant to this memorial site. As in the many local sites of woodland burial across the UK, so in this hundred-and-fifty acres at Alrewas near Lichfield, trees are 'good to think'—an expression already explained in chapter 1 where I suggested that this anthropological motif of Lévi-Strauss might be extended to imply that some things can also be 'good to feel'. This extension explicitly adds an emotional dimension to a much earlier discussion on tree symbolism where I argued that 'the attractiveness of trees lies both in their physical nature and in the creative metaphorical capacity of the human mind'.[33] Working along similar lines, Stephen Daniels formed his geographical and culture-historical analysis when showing how 'trees and woodland have proved as rich a symbolic resource as a material one', echoing Keith Thomas's historical sense of trees as providing 'a visible symbol of human society'.[34] Later anthropological studies have offered similar case studies presented through more ethnographic detail.[35]

These notions of thinking, metaphor, and of symbolic resources play out in different ways at both the individual and society-wide level, allowing the multitude of personal memories to interact with institutional expressions of sentiment in the creation of a National Memorial. This innovative memorial

---

[32] Childs (2008: 140).   [33] Douglas Davies (1988: 33).
[34] Daniels (1988: 43); Keith Thomas (1983: 219).   [35] Rival (ed.) (1998).

site can be viewed in the context of at least three culturally germane phenomena: the hundreds of local war memorials in stone and bronze, the existence of woodlands and parks, and the emergent popularity of woodland burial sites. To these might well be added the British interest in personal gardens and plants that often carry their own weight of private memory. Indeed, drawing from the Barton Glebe woodland site research, it is worth noting that individuals reflecting on relatives' graves were, if anything, more concerned with the diverse wealth of small-plant life and animals than with the larger scale of trees. At the National Memorial Arboretum smaller plants certainly find a place, as in the War Widows' Rose Garden, the St Dunstan's Pathway with its scented plants for the benefit of the blind, and the Garden of the Innocents with its raised beds which symbolizes 'the confusion and bewilderment children suffer through war and violence': so, too, with the pre-existing Bronze Age burial mound, itself a remarkable site within the newly developed area. Still, the overarching botanical narrative lies with trees, whether planted in avenues, groves or woods.[36]

As a self-announced arboretum, this site sets itself alongside other distinguished British arboreta whose identifiable cultural category acknowledges a British commitment to trees, as recognized, for example, in the very naming of the site and tree collection at Westonbirt, Gloucestershire, as the National Arboretum. That Gloucestershire collection of trees, now managed by the Forestry Commission, originated in the 1850s as an estate of the Victorian landowner Robert Holford. Its advice and support to the National Memorial Arboretum have been considerable, including the donation of saplings derived from historically significant trees. Other historical and modern tree collections of botanical gardens and parks across the country also ensure popular familiarity of tree-themed landscapes, making the National Memorial Arboretum a newcomer that fits in easily. It has been easy to link memorial motifs to this cultural affinity with the heritage-like awareness of trees whose symbolic presence frequently marks a timeline longer than any single human generation.

As for the National Memorial Arboretum, it possesses over two-hundred memorials to an enormously wide variety of national groups, from the dominant symbol of the Armed Forces Memorial through key military memorials to those concerning neonatal deaths. The Armed Forces Memorial, already mentioned as a deeply influential support for the economic success of the Arboretum, was itself separately dedicated in the presence of the Queen on 12 October 2007. It is a most remarkable feature, constructed upon a six-metre-high mound reminiscent of 'ancient landscapes of prehistoric Britain', and containing historical bronze statuary reminiscent of 'the classical forms of

---

[36] *National Memorial Arboretum Guidebook*, edition 4 (n.d.) p. 34.

ancient Rome'. It echoes the thousands of urban war memorials across the United Kingdom with its partially encompassing walls naming some 16,000 personnel 'killed on duty in recent times'.[37] This is all so constructed that at the 11th hour of the 11th day of the 11th month—the date of the First World War Armistice—the sunlight passes through a space in the walls to fall upon the central, raised, wreath-memorial. Complementing this architectural–sculptural and natural–sun symbolism is the Millennium Chapel of Peace and Forgiveness set at some distance from this mound. Yet, here, every single day of the year the act of a two-minute silence is observed. Not only does a recording of the Royal Marines playing the Last Post and Reveille take place but at this very time a light shines on to the altar in such a way as repeats its natural beam on Armistice Day. So it is that this location focuses the invention of tradition in a variety of ways, some of which may be apparent to visitors and some not so apparent.

Described officially as the 'spiritual hub of the Arboretum' that 'welcomes all people from all faiths and all walks of life', this chapel's iconographic symbolism is, then, not only explicitly Christian and replete with calendrical elements of national memorial but also incorporates further symbolic webs that integrate Christian, military-memorial, and arboreal references in a uniquely powerful way.[38] High on the wall behind the alter hangs the Commowealth War Graves Sword of Sacrifice that, itself, echoes a symbolic cross, and bespeaks the symbol found worldwide in Commonwealth war grave cemeteries. Moreover, two large and rough-hewn crosses flank the altar and these are described as the 'crosses of the thieves' crucified alongside Jesus.[39] Not only do they carry that moral and theological significance of union in death with all the blame that might or might not inhere in those crucified with Jesus, but these crosses are described as made from 'elm trees destroyed by Dutch Elm disease', and taken from David Childs' garden.[40] This invites a remarkable symbolic analysis of trees, the very symbol of life throughout the Arboretum, which have now become a double symbol of death: the disease-ridden death of trees, as well as the capital punishment of Christ's criminal partners in death. Another Christ-related feature lies in the chapel being supported by twelve trunks of Douglas fir trees, marking His first twelve apostles, and being in memory of David Douglas after whom the tree was named and whose 200th birthday anniversary coincided with the first work on the chapel.

Even from what has just been described, this single geographical area reflects the social force underlying segments of society in ways that would be hard to match anywhere else. Its social inclusion of diverse groups is, for

---

[37] *National Memorial Arboretum Guidebook* (2011: 8–10).
[38] *National Memorial Arboretum Guidebook* (2011: 11).   [39] Luke 23: 32.
[40] *National Memorial Arboretum Guidebook* (2011: 13); Childs (2008: 34).

example, much wider in scope than the otherwise higher social and media profile of the military-focused London sites. This is very well symbolized by the Shrievalty Avenue on one hand and the Army Dog Unit (Northern Ireland) Association—Red Paw, on the other. The former takes the form of lime trees propagated from a 2,000-year-old tree of the famous Westonbirt Arboretum, and donated by High Sheriffs from across the UK; people we have also previously discussed in terms of the British Establishment and whose formal office extends to before the Norman Conquest of the eleventh century. The latter, Red Paw, memorial is a wedge-like piece of black granite with an engraved section and the 'Search and Secure' motto reflecting the dogs' work.[41] One final example is that of 'The Beat', consisting of a memorial avenue of trees dedicated to the memory of police officers. There is one tree for each Constabulary in the country, each aligned with a specific plaque and with some individual tree dedications. The selected tree-type is the chestnut on the basis that the original police 'peelers' or 'bobbies' were equipped with chestnut truncheons. This particular memorial was opened in 1996 by Jack Straw MP.[42]

These individual examples must suffice for giving some sense of the rationale underlying some of the Arboretum's symbols and tree formations. It would take an extensive venture in symbolic-ritual and cultural analysis lying beyond this volume's scope to account for the entire location. However, enough has been said to portray this place and how it marks 'memorial time' just as it marks memorial space, in a dramatically open, public, and ongoing fashion. In this the National Memorial Arboretum 'sounds' and reveals in a public memorial something of the silence and privacy of individuals and family inherent in woodland burial where 'nature' is set to envelop the dead.

THE FALKLANDS REMEMBERED

As a significant complement to the case of the Arboretum we now take up that of another armed-forces memorial which also came into being through the combination of a highly motivated individual, many procedural difficulties, and some significant establishment networking. The structure concerned is the memorial chapel for those who died in the Falklands War, built at Pangbourne College, an English public school with a naval-college background. Its conception followed a meeting between the headmaster and a parent of one of his schoolboys that triggered a link with Admiral Sir John 'Sandy' Woodward, who had been commander of the naval element of the

---

[41] *National Memorial Arboretum Guidebook* (2011: 112, 134).
[42] *National Memorial Arboretum Guidebook* (2011: 75).

Falklands conflict and who, along with other senior naval officers, was concerned that there was no substantial memorial to those who fought and died
there. Anthony Hudson, Pangbourne's headmaster from 1988 to 2000 and
himself a public schoolboy and graduate of Oxford University, had been
disappointed that this school lacked its own purpose-built chapel, and now
directed his energies to filling that gap, something enhanced by the establishment nature of his environment and the sense of absence of a needed focus of a
core cultural event of loss of life.

When two sets of plans were turned down, a national competition for an
appropriate design ensued, one that reckoned to reflect 'the lines of a ship' and
also the classical Italian *mandorla* or almond shape reminiscent of 'hands
clasped in prayer'. The inevitable multivocality of an inspired design meant
that the college boys also interpreted it as a rugby ball and the girls as 'an
egg'.[43]

In terms of this present volume's interest in cultural values and their
emergence, often through heated committee-based debates, it is worth recalling one key player in the later part of the Pangbourne Chapel's planning, viz.
Lord Fawsley, better known as the Conservative MP Norman St John Stevas,
who was at this time Chairman of the Royal Fine Art Commission.[44] Putting
his weight behind the project, he said that

> It must be at once subtle and powerful, stirring and calming; it must inspire
> reflection, and evoke memories, while instilling a sense of the numinous and a
> feeling of remembrance. These intangibles must be given play in the tangible
> product of an artist's imagination.[45]

That recipe-like formula could easily apply to a great many phenomena
otherwise described as 'spiritual'; it certainly captures much of what we have
said about symbols in terms of their concealing–revealing capacity in relation
to emotion-pervaded ideas.

As for the ensuing fundraising of over two-million pounds that would
provide the concrete tangibility of the building, this included two lunchtime
events at Mrs Margaret Thatcher's personal home in London, made possible
by Dennis, her businessman husband's prior involvement with the project. At
the first event of only some ten well-chosen individuals a sum of £200,000 was
promised. Not long after, a special lunch was held aboard the culture-history
rich HMS *Victory* in Portsmouth Harbour, with some £150,000 promised.
Later, Sir Jack Hayward, OBE, also Chairman of Wolverhampton Wanderers
Football Club, though normally resident in the Bahamas, made his gift of
£500,000—with Pangbourne College marching band reciprocating by playing
before an ensuing football match! The gift was prompted by an intentional

---

[43] Hudson (2002: 61).   [44] Chairman 1985–99.   [45] Hudson (2002: 58).

introduction of the Headmaster to Sir Jack at a previous, rained-out, football match. In all of these money-making ventures the networked social capital of key establishment players was engaged to good effect.

The chapel of memory was, after all this and other funding ventures, finally dedicated in November 1999 with Her Majesty the Queen coming on a major visit in March 2000. Anthony Hudson retired that same year and died in 2015.[46] His own account of the entire venture, often described in naval metaphor, reads as an unconscious essay on a major part of Britain's 'establishment' jigsaw, that of the public schools, charitable institutions, and their eminent trustees, of aesthetic–architectural resources, and especially of the military, big business, politics, and royalty.[47] Still, we should not forget the more intimate contexts of emotion provided by this chapel, not least for the families of those who died in the Falklands and for those who served alongside them. It is precisely here that the social force driving the symbolic power of material culture comes into its own, as with some relatives finger-tracing the names of their dead relatives inscribed on the interior of the chapel's walls. With an echo of Lord Fawsley's formula, 'on Dedication Day ... many traced the carvings with their fingers, receiving a tangible reminder of the one they had lost'; 'one woman proudly brought her two grandchildren to see—and touch—their father's name carved in stone and to hold the kneeler that bears his name'. These kneelers had been embroidered, each with the name of one lost individual.

> How important these kneelers were became clear on Dedication Day, when each bereaved family received their kneeler from the pupils of the College—taking it, looking at it, feeling it, hugging it, as though they were trying to touch physically the man who had been lost.[48]

One bereaved father—old, infirm, and whose finances only stretched for him but not also for his wife to come to the Dedication from Canada—hugged his kneeler 'to his chest and carried it around all day'. Indeed, he refused to be parted from it, so much so that one of the College officers found a bag for it, 'to conceal what was happening for fear that many others should wish to do the same'. This left 257 named kneelers in the chapel that marked their death and memory.[49] In anthropological terms we might, perhaps, note how this College, devoted to young people, their hopes for the future, and to the ethic of service to society at large, is its own arena of vitality and, as such, all the more potent as a site for memorial and acknowledgement of mortality. 'Death and the regeneration of life' immediately complement each other.[50]

---

[46] *The Times*, 20 March 2015: 55.   [47] Hudson (2002).
[48] Hudson (2002: 100–1).   [49] Hudson (2002: 101).
[50] Bloch and Parry (1982).

CONCLUSION

In this, as in much else, this chapter has been the most symbolically orientated part of this volume so far. We have seen how trees, both in woodland burial and in the National Memorial Arboretum, have been deployed not only to express the interplay of individual and family lifestyle in relation to death, but also to symbolize discrete institutions and their relation to cultural awareness and memory. The capacity of ritual symbolism to conceal and reveal aspects of life has been evident, as has the expression of social force in bottom-up and top-down forms of cultural creativity, while traditional cultural elements have been re-worked into novel forms of funerary and memorial behaviour, as in Pangbourne's Chapel. Such innovative contexts have generated outcomes achieving more than the sum of their parts. Here we have again witnessed the influence of the Establishment in British cultural and symbolic life.

At the core of the chapter we discussed the topic of secularization in its usual sociological terms but, not content with that, we went further in utilizing Hans Mol's sociologically innovative theory of how identity is 'sacralized' and, in turn, sacralizes the sources of identity generation. All this demonstrates the complexity of interplay of lifestyles and affinities with particular forms of death-style in contemporary Britain. The pragmatic basis of ritual and symbols covered in this chapter has served well as we move to the final chapter and some of its more abstract engagement with vitality and mortality.

Conclusion

Entailing Mortality

Vitality and mortality have balanced each other throughout this volume's focus on humanity's meaning-making expressed in lifestyle's intimacy with or distance from death. The driving assumption underlying previous chapters has been that religion cannot be appropriately understood separate from attitudes to dying, death, ritual symbolism, memory, memorial, and their associated forms of grief, whether for 'ordinary' people or for celebrities. This is especially important when definitional debates over traditional religion, self-religion, and spirituality as well as the often protracted discussion of secularization frequently ignore or marginalize death.

As a contribution to world-view studies, previous chapters have attempted to portray human destiny as diminished when death is largely ignored. This is especially important when the inevitably abstract categories of 'self' and 'modernity', with all their subtitled variety and potential pretense at classificatory vigour, ignore the profound emotional ties that bind and whose unbinding or stubborn knotting draw us into the near-universal domain of grief. Social theory should not ignore emotional theory: the biocultural nature of people, whether normally described as individual or 'dividual', demands an account of mortality.

Any analysis of contemporary religion also demands that the proclivities of social science- and humanities-based scholars should not overly dominate their views of what society at large thinks and feels. The academy, seminar, and conference do not constitute the world at large. In attempting to do some justice to the lived experience of a variety of British groups we have, of course, drawn from such scholarly theories that aid interpretation and help constitute the academic arena of debate, but always with an eye, ear, and awareness of contexts of popular practice. Accordingly, this volume has considered ideological and ritual factors evident in the cognitive domains of literary narratives, myth, and religious doctrines complemented by practical behaviour intensified through ritual symbolism.[1] Various theories, notably those of

---

[1] Cf. Seybold (2007).

reciprocity, dual sovereignty, embodiment, and of the uncanny, have been invoked to highlight the impact of social forces derived from mainstream cultural 'establishments' including churches and the NHS, while neither ignoring other impressive places and individual cultural creativity. These themes make their final appearance in this chapter to enhance some earlier ideas and to indicate their capacity for wider application beyond the scope of this volume.

RITUAL ADAPTATION

What has been obvious throughout previous chapters is that many enduring religious traditions have been remarkably adaptable as they have met, partially transformed, and have been transformed by the changing social circumstances of local cultures. Great Britain's Industrial Revolution with its urban population growth not only necessitated the creation of large, civic, non churchyard cemeteries, but also facilitated the industrial creativity of cremation. One of the unintended consequences of both of those developments was that the largely post-colonial arrival of thousands of Hindu, Sikh, Buddhist, and Muslim citizens throughout the twentieth century found a country pre-adapted for their preferred form of funeral. The Muslim death-style of burial was easily accommodated within appropriate portions of civic cemeteries while the cremation preference of Hindus, Sikhs, and Buddhists was met by existing crematoria, even if some changes in ritual form needed implementing.

The period of the 1960s–1970s, which as chapter 3 showed heralded the rapid growth in the building and use of crematoria, was a period in which many Protestant clergy, followed later by Catholics but not by the Orthodox, rapidly adapted to cremation and provided a valuable ritual buffer zone for the general public as it increasingly shifted popular practice from burial to cremation. That shift has, arguably, been its own index of secularization, closely associated with a decrease in afterlife belief. Such ritual relocation and partial innovation is not necessarily easy within a relatively stable society, but Britain had already experienced both the loss of many thousands of men in two World Wars that involved the absence of corpses to bury at home, and new modes of remembrance rites.

As for the role of the clergy, the crematorium setting allowed for a degree of their continuity as ritual leaders while the people were not confined to a building that was intrinsically a 'church'. It was not until the Church of England published its *Alternative Service Book* of 1980 and, more especially, its *Common Worship* in 2000 that a significant number of options in funeral form were provided. Moreover, it was not until the mid 1960s that the Catholic Church accepted cremation for its laity and for liturgical leadership by its priests. Then, by the turn of the century, the role of the clergy was becoming less certain, so that by approximately 2010 the Church of England was becoming concerned at its dramatically lowered ritual leadership of funerals. Lay leaders of many motivations were emerging as ritual functionaries. One ritual feature of the new decades of the twenty-first century in the UK has been this appropriation of funerary ritual by self-selected women and men, often prompted more by their own experience of 'poor funerals' led by clergy than by any avowed secularist ideology.

However, the 'new humanism', as a form of atheist humanism, that began to be asserted in the UK from about the 1990s partly in opposition to strong vocal expressions of conservative Christianity and Islam, also found a ready ritual base for itself within the adaptable and relatively ideology-free realms of crematoria and, latterly, of most natural burial sites. Moreover, such funerals offered humanist events ample scope for ritualization in the personalization of funerals, whether in the more philosophically explicit regime of the British Humanist Association or in the more family-negotiated ad hoc work of civil celebrants.

Crosses, flowers, and cards at roadside memorials; eco-coffins in woodland burial sites; poetry, music, and the body itself: all have reflected cultural adaptability involving ritual action. They have extended the range of sacred contexts where human identity and emotions of fear, grief, and loss find opportunity for some degree of transcendence. In this they have provided the basis for this volume's theoretical elaboration of a sociologically driven notion of salvation interpreted alongside issues of embodiment and the value-laden environments framing all human life.

LIFE'S VITALITY

Whatever the spectrum of life view existing as the twenty-first century now passes through its second decade, the leading question of the 'meaning' and value of life remains of sociological as of theological and general existential significance. This theme that, historically speaking, has been largely appropriated by religions has now become increasingly both more and less complex and also more democratized than in preceding eras. As for the key notions driving this volume—vitality and mortality, meaning-making and narrative, cultural intensification and identity, embodiment and sense of presence— these have all undergone significant shifts, even paradigmatic shifts, with the rise of scientific ideas of evolution, genetics, emotions, and the realignment of religious explanations of existence. What is more, death and dying have been and continue to be powerfully present at the intersection of religion and science as competitive meaning-making processes, with 'ethics' erupting as its own form of buffer zone.

In terms of British culture we have seen how, in relation to death rites, the crematorium came to be one symbol of science, or at least of technology, as did the rise of the hospital as a place to die. Inoculation, antibiotics, and scientific medicine at large, along with the very idea of 'research', have increased 'vitality' over 'mortality' in developed societies and, in terms of medical possibilities, they now also frame the option of assisted dying and euthanasia. Here 'medicine' becomes the double symbol of both life and death, with the issue of choice, ethics, and responsible use, becoming a prime arena of debate. Even the emergence of natural burial has allowed for science and ethics-like concerns with ecology to partner, if not to nudge to one side, traditional Christian ideas of a supernatural resurrection.

Digital Vitality

Moreover, many today, most especially younger generations fed through the personal communication system of social media, experience an intensity of life communication grounded in the electronic omnipresence of others and potentially available 'others'. It is not only an intensity that can foster both a sense of worth or provoke that of rejection but it also contrasts with the silence of death. I do not mean to say that this is a conscious awareness but, rather, a background presence ever capable of realization when circumstances dictate. If there is any force in the long-standing notion that 'the medium is the message', it lies in social media speaking a message of vitality not mortality.

The fuller phenomenology of this kind of life intensity, an issue quite unlike the 'intensive living' of those knowing they have but a short time to live,[2] has yet to be written as far as death is concerned, but some of its sharper profiles are well known in messages sent to kin from those about to die in catastrophes.[3] The promise of being 'in touch', itself the most embodied of phrases, is held out until the last. Similarly, relatives of 'lost' individuals ring their number, send them text messages, and hope for some response. It is this very emotional set of an anticipated answer, of a voice, or of written words, that helps engender such 'life intensity'. And it is all the more poignant when there is no answer, or when it becomes the last word from someone before they die 'out of touch'. The starkness of an intense message before the silence pinpoints the domain I have in mind. The use of jesting scenes in which a mobile phone has been inadvertently placed in a coffin and goes off during a funeral or when buried typifies the communicable power of life and its utter

---

[2] Glaser and Strauss (1965: 131–2).
[3] The South Korean ferry disaster of 16 April 2014 marked such tragic messages.

anomaly in death. The extensive density of sound, of the social noise of the living, makes the silence of death distinctly profound.

This is not to say that forms of grief are any greater than before, but that the silence of grief now has additional perspectives or 'auditions' to it. The relevance of life seems to be sustained in significant ways by voice and text messaging, and by online communication with actual and cyber-friends. Life is message-pervaded and communication-sustained. The coining and recognition of the acronym FOMO—fear of missing out—is indicative of a sense of identity sustained by a high degree of constant engagement in networks of perceived relevance. This new state of identity, for it transcends any life experience of previous human generations, poses some fundamental issues regarding death or thoughts of death.

It is, of course, a long-standing philosophical observation that death can be regarded as an irrelevance because I will not 'be there' when it happens; a view on which secular, spiritual, and some religious people might be able to agree, albeit for different reasons. That level of achieved irrelevance does not, however, weigh heavily on those whose health-framed sense of self is deeply rooted in highly networked and constant interaction. One example of cultural intensity of communication almost inevitably intrudes itself here, not so much in terms of the digital world but of the enduring presence of Christmas.

Christmas as Vitality Ritual

Almost in parenthesis, then, it is worth noting how vitality has, for recent centuries in many parts of Britain, been enshrined in the festivities of Christmas. Though its Christian cultural basis in the birth of Jesus Christ validates the celebrations, it should also be recalled that every member of society also enjoys a birthday of their own, and of related babies, which, in terms of the complex operations of the ritual symbols of cards, cakes, and candles, allows for many resonances of joy. However, whatever else Christmas may be, it is certainly a festivity of vitality, perhaps *the* cultural festivity of vitality. In anthropological terms, its core significance lies in the dynamics of the regeneration of life whose natural symbol lies in the birth of a baby, that of Jesus of Nazareth, while its theological significance (itself a distinctive form of its cultural significance) is conferred by the mother's dedicated nature and divine call. In the paradigmatic nativity scene, the baby-symbol forms part of a nuclear family of mother, child, and father while the supernatural frame brings miracles of virgin birth, deliverance, and vocation: wise men come to the scene while wicked men in positions of power seek to harm the family. Dreams, visions, and heavenly signs frame the erstwhile pragmatic narrative of journeying, census, and political hostility. The economic and commercial interests that pervade the social force of Christmas, along with the key 'establishment' moments of a broadcast royal Christmas Message and much media use of choral music from prime ecclesiastical sites, ensure an intensity of cultural vitality. And if the military play no role at this time the Salvation Army does so, while school nativity plays ensure their own version of communal pleasure aligned with traditional motifs. All this vitality, extensively expressed in numerous Christmas carols and popular songs, makes bereavement around Christmas highly problematic for many families when Christmas effectively becomes the anniversary of a death. This makes for a paradoxical link between festive and memorial dynamics of lifestyle.

INDIFFERENCE

The stark contrast between such active living and, notably, the death of children or young people, especially in an age when death falls in increasingly older age, raises this volume's key focus on strength of bond between lifestyle and death-style. For a minority whose own life experience or professional concerns involve bereavement it is understandable that they should wish for British lifestyle to have more resonance with death, and while there are active movements to try and get the nation talking about death, there remains a firm resistance to it.

The drive evident in the Dying Matters Consortium of the National Council of Palliative Care and such recent ventures as its annual Day of the Dead are notable but have not, as yet, attained a level of impetus that constitutes a widespread social force of its own. This may be, in part, because it has a disproportionately large gender balance towards women and may be less appealing to men. Something similar can be said of the 'death café' movement.

Still, this reflects a significant shift to a feminization of death in Britain, evident in the fact that increasing numbers of funeral directors and managers of crematoria are women; something that would have been rare even in the 1990s. This is an important theme for future research in that 'feminization' can, equally, be analysed in terms of increasing equality of opportunity in employment.

However, the one area in which silence is being loudly broken is, as we have seen, in terms of the political, legal, medical, religious, and secular ethics of assisted dying. Here we are witnessing a growing bond between lifestyle and death-style in that the population includes a growing proportion of increasingly old people who have vested interests in this matter. By sharp contrast, there is little evidence that young people and younger generations have anything like that interest; for them death is of marginal concern, even indifference. Britain is very far removed from, for example, Aldous Huxley's fictional *Brave New World* of 1932 with the sight of 'five bus-loads of boys and girls' returning 'from Slough Crematorium' prompting the account of how that Utopia's highly conditioned inhabitants were given 'death conditioning' from the age of eighteen months: 'Every tot spends two mornings a week in a Hospital for the Dying. All the best toys are kept there, and they get chocolate cream on death days. They learn to take dying as a matter of course.'[4] Today's children may have come to accept death as a matter of course in the many media and online worlds but not in any real-time world of sensed awareness, leaving death itself as something of an irrelevance.

So, despite the extensive presence of death through catastrophe, wars, and even celebrity funerals and suicide, a certain public indifference to death in general seems to prevail. Perhaps this is its own defensive stratagem for personal sanity or the result of encountering these phenomena through screens and not real life. Or, again, it may be that we should simply recall chapter 3 with Hebert on irrelevance and Hobsbawm on indifference. Yet, even since the latter's day there has been increased opportunity for choice and personal-family meaning-making in contexts devoid of assumptions that clergy must conduct funeral ritual. Certainly, there is no easily accessible language for discussing life and death such as was inherent in the religious sensibilities of the later nineteenth and early twentieth centuries in Western Europe. This shifting context is, certainly, describable as secular, given a service provision fired by a general cultural idiom of consumerist choice and facilitated by a widening resource of funeral directing and ritual leadership.

Youth and Popular Indifference

One influence hinting at this cultural shift and Hobsbawm-like indifference appeared in the teenage-generation matrix of the 1960s Beatles' songs. One classic—'Eleanor Rigby'—begins, 'Ah, look at all the lonely people', before describing how dutiful Eleanor gathers up the rice that has served as confetti at a church wedding.[5] With echoes of Goffman's presentation of self she has a fixed expression in public but 'who is it for?' The constant refrain 'all the lonely people', asks 'where do they all come from?'; 'where do they all belong?' The other pinpointed individual amidst these anonymous lonely people is Father McKenzie who writes 'the words of a sermon that no-one will hear', because 'no one comes near'. He darns his socks 'in the night when there's nobody there'. Eleanor dies 'in the church' and was 'buried along with her name. Nobody came': and Father McKenzie walks from the grave 'wiping the dirt from his hands': 'No-one was saved'. Weddings and funerals are not only united in futility as far as religion is concerned but there is also a hint at the

---

[4] Huxley ([1932] 2004: 142). [5] The Beatles ([1969] 1974: 80).

betrayal of wellbeing with the priest wiping 'the dirt' from his hands much as Pilate 'washed his hands' to attempt a symbolic distance from the death of Jesus.[6] The Beatles' emphatic 'nobody' and 'no-one' mirrors 'all' the lonely people, while Eleanor Rigby in her church activities 'lives in a dream'. This depiction of loneliness captures a sense of indifference to religion.[7] It can also be contrasted with many Beatles' songs focused on love, intimacies, and on the significance of inner mental states that might or might not be drug-aligned experiences.[8]

Still, it is problematic to generalize a view for an entire generation, for there are always individuals for whom death does strike a deeply personal chord. Just how disenchantment affects a person may seriously determine their outlook upon life whether by energizing them in new directions or simply dispiriting an individual. On the negative front, Michel de Certeau, for example, alludes to the *ennui de vivre* aligned with

> the general cult of youth and beauty, the fright inspired by old age and death ... the contradiction between the celebrated ideal of beauty ... and the reality of life-styles ... all this prevents the great number of people from feeling at ease with their body and accepting its imperfect image.

So, for example, he takes anorexia nervosa as being a 'question of hatred and death ... in a triumphant march towards death', as '"beauty capital"' plays an ignoble role in social exchange.[9] His allusion to reciprocity reinforces the way social force may take its effect at an individual level, evoking Durkheim's work on suicide.

On a more positive front, the classic psychological approach of Allport to religious meaning aligned 'the Bias of Intelligibility and the Bias of Optimism', with the 'Intelligibility' factor marking the rational domain of life while the 'Optimism' dimension achieves something similar for religion. His subtlety saw that these combined, not least at different times of life, as when he rehearsed George Bernard Shaw's observation that, 'no young man ever *really* believes he is going to die'.[10] That youthful stance being so different from that of some old or very sick people for whom assisted dying becomes profoundly significant and desired.

One of the major differences between rich and poor countries and between social classes in the UK as the twenty-first century settles into its teenage decade is that of variation in life expectancy. In an insightful article on the

---

[6] Matthew 27: 24.

[7] Just as 'Nowhere Man' mirrors the negatives of 'nowhere' and 'nobody', (Beatles ([1969] 1974: 33).

[8] E.g. 'All you Need is Love'; 'Love of the Loved'; 'All my Loving', Beatles ([1969] 1974: 87, 118, 123).

[9] De Certeau, Giard, and Mayol ([1994] 1998: 194).

[10] Allport ([1950] 1960: 20, 23; original emphasis), citing Malinowski.

desirability or distaste for a really long life, perhaps even into one's second century, John Walsh described a brief spectrum of literary opinion. He certainly showed some sympathy to Jonathan Swift's *Gulliver's Travels* where the mutant Struldbrugs lived for ages but at the cost of becoming 'morose and dejected', especially when seeing the joys of youth around them.[11] Walsh ponders this alongside aesthete-scholar's Walter Pater's pin-pointing of the nature of beauty when known to be short-lived. Certainly, the first two decades of the twenty-first century have disclosed case after case of maltreatment of aged people in some institutionalized contexts, something that had already been reported in terms of disgusting inhumanity for some in geriatric mental hospitals even in the 1960s where things could be terrifying. A 2014 Commission on Residential Care, chaired by Member of Parliament Paul Burstow, directly addressed these issues in a report tellingly entitled *A vision for care fit for the twenty-first century*, which revealed that a quarter of those polled would not consider leaving their home for a residential place, with 43% definitely not prepared to do so. One major reason, expressed by 54%, lay in fear of neglect or abuse, even though, as the Commission notes, such malpractice has only been reported for approximately 2% of the 450,000 people actually in care in the UK.[12] In terms of cultural values and the 'leap in lifestyle' perceived to be involved in leaving one's home for a care home, there was the expression of reluctance to endure 'illness, frailty, boredom, loneli-ness'; all of which in terms of our present volume reflect a depletion of vitality.[13]

MYSTERY OF MORTALITY

Such circumstances test the cultural notion of dignity in old age. They touch the deep concern of many as to their sense of 'presence' in their anticipated period at the end of life when personal control will no longer be feasible. Having drawn heavily from the dual-sovereignty model throughout this volume we do so yet again to see that the potential crisis of presence antici-pated in loss of personal control is mitigated by the hope of assistance in dying, a situation framed by both the legal and mystical dynamics of authority. And here we can interpret the mystical not only in our previous terms of things that cause people to flourish but also in terms of the unknown framing of circum-stances that death entails.

To allude to mystery as an entailment of mortality is also to embrace the uncanny factors of life, since death, whether anticipated or focused in grief,

---

[11] John Walsh (2010).   [12] Burstow (2014: 23–4).
[13] Burstow (2014: 22, 24). See Elsdon (1995) for critique of some nursing care.

creates a realm of mystery around the self and those who have, and in some ways still do, participate in that self. We might even say that the 'sociology of mystery' ought to be developed much more than it is as far as death is concerned. Certainly, significant numbers of bereaved people dream of the dead, sense their presence, and are prompted to ponder their own mortality. Within Great Britain such experiences are the stuff of mystery; of the mystery of the self, and of that self's destiny given that there is no publicly shared grammar of dream discourse. This mystery of mortality is left to forge its own variety of sympathies, and it does so with an increasing effect as dominant religious accounts of the afterlife decrease. Indeed, one area of dissonance within Britain may well lie between religious believers—notably Muslims—for whom the afterlife is part of their spirituality, and the rest of the population, including some religious believers, who hold no afterlife beliefs.

Just how these diverse sympathies and allied paradigmatic scenes are expressed in a mixed religious–secular economy requires ongoing analysis that will embrace theoretical issues of the elective affinity of people for particular ideas and practices, and of their preferred idioms of expression. While there is some truth in the rational-choice approach saying that people choose ideas when they are available, affordable, and attractive, the very nature of attraction takes us beyond the rational domain. For attraction possesses a variety of roots. Some are obvious and lie in growing social fashion, especially if espoused by celebrities or highlighted by media-covered events; some have specific psychological drivers; while others spring from an allure that may be hardly known or expressible only with difficulty. Indeed, that very difficulty is sometimes helped by cultural idioms that capture what cannot otherwise be easily expressed; one such is that of 'home'.

At Home?

'Home' in its many forms affords one of the prime security symbols of meaning in most societies, as evident in the earlier responses of how old people in the UK regarded care homes. Peter Berger, amongst many others, has written well of 'ways of being "at home"', and of the search for 'a redemptive community' to avoid that 'homelessness' that he associated with the 'discontents of modernity'.[14] It is interesting that in Britain the idea of a 'funeral home' developed at much the same time as families no longer keeping their dead 'at home' before the funeral. The alternative name of 'Chapel of Rest' also carried a positive resonance at a time of widespread religious adherence. The influence of secularization is evident in the preference for

---

[14] Berger (1974: 39).

these two names and their different loads of meaning. As already evident, the term 'old people's home' has also come to possess a certain ambiguity, including a negative connotation as a place of relative meaninglessness and social uselessness, as opposed to 'retirement home' or 'retirement living' that strives, commercially at least, to denote active people very largely in control of their lives. The emotions attached to these names underlie their social classification and are indicative of the more abstract ideas that help make sense of life.

In a period of social change in which both life expectation and expectations of life of and for different generations and social classes in Britain are in a considerable flux, the very concept of retirement, once so integral to the social welfare reforms allied with the birth of the NHS, is being transformed. In one sense the very category of 'time' or, better, 'lifetime' is itself undergoing change, one that the government is keen to impress upon people through the medium of money, by stressing the need for saving for the potential decades of post-work life. Time and money shift together as an index of duration, and both reach to the root of lifestyle in relation to what we have so insistently called death-style.

MEANING-MAKING AND SALVATION

In this, the very notion of 'the meaning of life' comes into sharp focus not in the sense of a question expecting a clear answer but as a concept in itself. What does it mean to speak of 'the meaning of life' in relation to longer life-span, shifting life-partners, divorce, and, increasingly, perhaps serial bereavement in older age? That question is especially germane given that this volume, as with the great majority of social-scientific exercises, works on the assumption that 'meaning-making' is integral to human life (as demonstrated in a previous monograph[15]). It becomes a telling question if used as a means of comparing traditional religions with secular and with mixed spiritualities. To reiterate, in terms of the study of religion, 'meaning-making' is notably poignant when aligned with the notion of salvation, yet 'salvation' seems to have become marginalized within the social-scientific study of religion. This is unfortunate given that a sense of transition in knowing and feeling from one state to another—whether in psychological terms of conversion and freedom from sin or of a movement on a path of enlightenment, or of rites that make an adult from a child—is widely prevalent in world cultures. Indeed, it is in

---

[15] Douglas J. Davies (1984).

acknowledgement of a need to have some insight into this state of being that the notion of spirituality has found its own constituency.

In comparative study we find that many societies have engaged with some such sense of metamorphosis from one level of knowing to another, often through actual trauma or the induced life crises of ritual initiation. And this applies not only to the major 'world' or 'salvation' religions, but to many local cultural traditions as, for example, in W. E. H. Stanner's classic work on the Murinbata. For these people, native to Australia, he depicted a cultural wisdom lying in an embodied appropriation of what he called the awareness of 'refuge and rottenness' in life, all as part of what he saw as an 'ontology of life'.[16] Initiates are reckoned to embody wisdom: they have 'seen' and 'know', and as people of 'depth' possess that allure that, in distinctive cases, appears as charisma. Stanner's work was but one earlier anthropological analysis of 'embodiment' before that concept became a popular topic in and of itself.

In the better-known Indian-derived traditions, notably in some schools of Hinduism, Buddhism, and Sikhism, the foundational notion of illusion, *maya*, drives entire schemes of religious thought and practice as devotees seek to move from evil in the sense of illusion's captive snare to a freedom from self or even a new attachment to a divine lover. Here cultural wisdom is fostered as a goal of a transitive 'seeing through' the way things appear to be in order to see them as they 'really' are. Such a philosophical programme of reflection runs alongside meditative practice controlling certain emotions and encouraging others. This mirrors Loyal Rue's 'formal definition of wisdom' as 'living in harmony with reality'.[17] A similar position emerges as a central theme in Comte-Sponville's atheist spirituality where it appears as 'tragic wisdom'.[18]

Compassion

Buddhism, in particular, has paid great attention to emotions; to naming them, and explaining the part they play in life's attachment to and longing for things and persons, as in their loss. Here longing has frequently been described as a negative aspect of that attachment, prompting an analysis of emotion and its lifestyle embedding, not least where 'longing' as a self-directed and negative desire may relate to compassion in an other-directed and positive sense. The pursuit of Buddhist living is exemplified in Peter Harvey's account of 'the development of heart-felt feelings of loving-kindness and compassion' intimately linked with 'one who has thoroughly seen through the delusion of the "I am" conceit'.[19] This Buddhist critique is not unlike the sociological analysis of the social construction of 'reality', of cultural relativism, and of

---

[16] Stanner (1960: 264, 245 respectively).   [17] Rue (2007: 135).
[18] Comte-Sponville (2007: 51).   [19] Peter Harvey (2000: 103–5).

seeing through 'the "I am" conceit'. But what Buddhism has developed, and what scholarly analysis lacks, is a life practice of emotional education to serve as the medium within which to come to terms with the intellectual insights over the provisional and fragile worlds of culture. That kind of integration of lifestyle with the ensuing approach of death may only be intensely practised by limited cohorts of devotees in Buddhism and other traditions but it stands apart from most contemporary British life where the emotions of loss aligned with bereavement come at best as a surprise, and at worst as a traumatic shock. For the majority, the realm of death and bereavement comes as a learning experience later in life and not, as in Huxley's Utopia, two mornings a week as a child.

These great themes, normally restricted to theological, philosophical, or religious studies, have a wide application to contemporary lifestyles and how people cope with grief, loss, and a positive sense of self in a complex world. We have seen something of this earlier, both in the form of advocacy of 'mindfulness' practice and in the notion of reverence for life. Indeed, the ethic of 'reverence for life', strongly advocated by Albert Schweitzer, constituted its own form of compassion, energizing his long-standing Christian spirituality, and bringing a new frame to his life narrative.[20]

ERAS AND GRIEF

Many such idealized life views, whether from traditional religion or other sources of informed embodiment practice, are current in the modern world; their diversity can be enormous and prompt attempts at labelling them. Michael Foley's much applauded *The Age of Absurdity*, for example, speaks of 'absurdity as the new sublime'. Amongst the many ways of coping with absurdity he includes the multi-millionaire who gains wealth by exporting Irish soil to rich Americans, including enough for one 'Galway born Manhattan lawyer to be buried in'; and Steven Friedman's 'Holy Land earth', where this man imports soil exported from the Holy Land under certain rabbinic approval.[21] While practices of this kind, as absurd as they may seem to some, can just as easily be framed by others in terms of spirituality, they are reminders of the social force that can be brought to bear through ritual action. Even when death may appear to be absurd, the human capacity to ritualize its necessity creates some degree of a positive outcome: action triumphs over reason.

---

[20] Schweitzer ([1931] 1948: 183–92), ([1919] 1974: 108–17).   [21] Foley (2010: 221–2).

This behavioural capacity, whether framed by thousands of years of theology, philosophy, and ceremony or by an immediate funeral innovation, speaks of the human animal's ritual capacity to cope with emotional disturbance. This ritual flow across centuries and cultures offers its own contribution and caveat to the way eras are seemingly controlled by academic classification. Life rolls on in societies while theoreticians create eras by chopping life experience into describable chunks, gaining academic or even cultural kudos from so doing. While there is no escape from this activity that has given us overly narrow-banded periods of Antiquity, the Dark Ages, the Middle Ages, the Renaissance, the Enlightenment, the Reformation, modernity, late modernity, postmodernity, and high modernity, not to mention mirroring concepts such as the post-evangelical or post-secular in the British religious scene, it is wise to view these with suspicion since some aspects of human experience may be far more enduringly comparable than abstract intellectualism might suppose.

To read of Gilgamesh and his grief at the loss of his intimate friend Enkidu is to encounter—some three to four thousand years later—descriptions that can be found today in accounts of bereavement.[22] The intervening millennia, from the time that eponymous hero announced 'I am afraid of death' yet came to acknowledge the inevitability of his own mortality, have created many cultural scenarios influencing emotional expression and patterns of mourning; yet the human depths of love, loss, memory, and hope stand taller than the nomenclature of eras. Even in today's families individuals acquire dispositions from grandparents and pass them to their grandchildren, straddling artificial divides in the process.[23] In reading many kinds of ancient texts similar intricacies of human entailment flourish.

As with historical periods so with contemporary comparative studies, human similarities are not to be ignored. Again, Stanner exemplifies this in his depiction of Murinbata life as being that of 'refuge and rottenness', a complementarity offering its own perspective on the motif of 'home', itself a concept whose overt stress on 'refuge' can easily overshadow its covert possibility of rottenness experienced by significant minorities today through family breakdown, divorce, or abuse. Yet, in its positive emphasis, 'home' reflects that aspect of human meaning-making enshrined in the experience of 'longing' and in the expression 'homesickness'. Many cultures have their own idiom for such a desire for place, one that has been so powerful that it has inspired numerous religious ideas of longing for a supernatural and post-mortal home as in British Victorian ideas of heaven as a place for reunited happy families or in the ongoing Mormon belief in eternal family life.

---

[22] George (1999). See Douglas J. Davies (2005: 2–5).
[23] Rugg (2013: 365) has, appropriately, questioned 'notions of modernity as they attach to changing burial practice'.

In terms of 'longing' at large, C. P. Snow, scientist, civil servant, and novelist, alluded to such human instinct in one embodied form when speaking of the Swede Dag Hammarskjöld,[24] once Secretary General of the United Nations, as a 'symbol . . . of a longing for reason in world politics—a longing felt by masses of people in small countries, and by many in great ones'.[25] That sentiment, published in 1967, has hardly decreased in a world whose international strife is just as great and where both political and religiously fundamentalist terrorism is even greater. By using 'symbol of longing for reason' of a particular human being Snow highlights the power of sensed affinity which, understood in its technical form of 'elective affinity', is a tool of the trade in symbolic ritual–symbolic studies, especially when 'reason' is complemented by emotional factors such as love or security. Taking this further, the dynamic aspect of emotions touching affinities in human relationships highlights the more philosophical and psychological interest in the 'theory of mind'—the understanding that others are somehow like me with thoughts, feelings, and an outlook on their world enabling them to engage with me in something like the way I can engage with them. Here empathy and sympathy are generated and, in terms of grief, foster condolence, with the force felt in bereavement support groups made intelligible precisely in terms of such 'theory of mind'. For grief in its many forms of affinity often overlaps emotions of longing and desire for the deceased persons that once constituted a feeling of 'home'.

CONCLUSION

Just how to cope with these loss-induced desires, with the longing for embodied forms of reason, love, and security, has long concerned religion, and is now shared by other voluntary and professional agencies. The social sciences and humanities tend to dwell upon meaning and the cultural attempts at stabilizing it amidst circumstances of potential chaos or through revolution-like paradigm shifts, and this volume has shared the same venture by considering the linked motifs of lifestyle and death-style. In final conclusion, however, it is worth raising the fact that any simple social dichotomy between life and death is rendered redundant not only by society's invention of funeral traditions to wrest some control over bodily mortality but also by biology's incessant activity. Human lifestyles of birth, maturation, and death—with their often

---

[24] Dag Hammarskjöld (1905–61) died in what some regarded as a suspicious air crash on United Nations' peace-making business to the African Congo. At the time of writing (April 2015) the United Nations is considering re-opening this case.

[25] Snow ([1967] 1969: 176).

ignored commitment to consumption and excretion—are ever complemented by the lifestyles of other organic entities, with which we cohabit the Earth during life, and which take responsibility for our bodies when we die. The soul may have invisible wings, and the creatures that devour our corpses may often fly far.

Bibliography

Adler, Jeremy and Richard Farndon (1999). 'The Life of Franz Baermann Steiner', in Jeremy Adler and Richard Farndon (eds), *Taboo, Truth, and Religion: Franz Baermann Steiner Selected Writings*. Oxford: Berghahn Books.

Aldridge, Alan (2000). *Religion in the Contemporary World*. Cambridge: Polity Press.

Aldridge, David (1998). *Suicide: The Tragedy of Hopelessness*. London: Jessica Kingsley Publishers.

Allport, Gordon W. ([1950] 1960). *The Individual and His Religion*. New York: The Macmillan Company.

Aquili, Eugene d' and Charles D. Laughlin, Jr (1979). 'The neurobiology of myth and ritual', in Eugene G. d'Aquili et al. (eds), *The Spectrum of Ritual: A Biogenetic Structural Analysis*. New York: Columbia University Press, 152–82.

Ariès, Philippe ([1977] 1981). *The Hour of Our Death*, translated by Helen Weaver. Oxford: Oxford University Press.

Ariès, Philippe ([1981] 1991). *The Hour of Our Death*. Oxford: Oxford University Press.

Aristotle (1963). *Ethics*, edited and translated by John Warrington. London: Dent, Everyman's Library.

Aquinas, *Summa Theologica*, 11–11.64.5. Notre Dame: Christian Classics. (1981). Translated by Fathers of English Dominicans.

Augé, Marc (1995). *Non-places: Introduction to an Anthropology of Supermodernity*. London: Verso.

Aulén, Gustav ([1930] 1970). *Christus Victor: A Historical Study of the Three Main Types of the Ideas of the Atonement*, translated by A. G. Hebert. London: SPCK.

Badham, Paul (2013). *Making Sense of Death and Immortality*. London: SPCK.

Baggini, Julian and Antonia Macaro (2011). 'The Shrink and the Sage: Do we need to be spiritual?' in *Weekend Magazine*. London: *Financial Times*, 16 April, p. 51.

Bailey, Tara (2012). *Going to Funerals in Contemporary Britain: The Individual, the Family and Meeting with Death*. Unpublished Doctoral Dissertation, University of Bath.

Baldwin, Stanley ([1923] 1939). 'A War Memorial', in Stanley Baldwin *On England, and Other Addresses*. Harmondsworth: Penguin Books, 243–6.

Bannister, Roger (2014). *Roger Bannister: Twin Tracks*. London: The Robson Press.

Barber, B. (1949). 'Place, symbol, and utilitarian function in war memorials', *Social Forces*, 28 (1).

Barnett, Correlli (2001). *The Audit of War: The Illusion and Reality of Britain as a Great Nation*. London: Macmillan.

Barth, Karl ([1918] 1968). *The Epistle to the Romans*. Oxford: Oxford University Press.

Barthes, Roland (1967). *Writing Degree Zero*, translated by Annette Lavers. New York: Hill and Wang.

Baudrillard, Jean ([1976] 1993). *Symbolic Exchange and Death*. London: Sage.

Bauman, Zygmunt (1992). *Mortality, Immortality*. London: Polity.

Bauman, Zygmunt (2011). *Culture in a Liquid Modern World*. Cambridge: Polity.

Beaman, Lori G. and Winnifred Fallers Sullivan (2013). 'Neighbo(u)rly misreadings and misconstruals: A cross-border conversation', in Winnifred Fallers Sullivan and

Lori G. Beaman (eds) *Varieties of Religious Establishment*. Farnham, Surrey: Ashgate, 1–11.

Beatles ([1969] 1974). *The Beatles Lyrics Complete*. Aylesbury, Bucks: Futura Publications Limited.

Beckford, James and John Walliss (2006). *Theorising Religion: Classical and Contemporary Debates*. Aldershot; Burlington,VT: Ashgate.

Beighton, James (2013). 'In other spaces: The sensitivity between ceramics and site', in Michael Tooby (ed.) *Julian Stair: Quietus Reviewed*. Bath: Wunderkammer Press, 21–5.

Beighton, James and Julian Stair (eds) (2012). *Julian Stair: Quietus, The Vessel, Death and the Human Body*. Middlesborough: mima.

Bell, Daniel ([1980] 1991). *The Winding Passage: Sociological Essays and Journeys*. London: Transaction Publishers.

Belshaw, John and Diane Purvey (2009). *Private Grief, Public Mourning: The Rise of the Roadside Shrine in British Columbia*. Vancouver: Anvil Press.

Benson, Herbert (1977). *The Relaxation Response*. London: Collins.

Berger, Peter L. ([1974] 1977). *Pyramids of Sacrifice: Political Ethics and Social Change*. New York: Penguin Books.

Bergmann, Torbern Olof (1785). *A Dissertation on Elective Affinities*. London: John Murray.

Berlin, Isaiah (1997). *The Proper Study of Mankind: An Anthology of Essays*. Henry Hardy and Roger Hausheer (eds). London: Chatto and Windus.

Bernstein, Basil (1971). *Class, Codes and Control*. London: Routledge.

Betjeman, John (2003). *Collected Poems*. London: John Murray.

Beveridge, Janet (1954). *Beveridge and his Plan*. London: Hodder and Staughton.

Beveridge, William ([1942] 1966). *The Report on the Inter-Departmental Committee on Social Insurance and Allied Services*. London: HMSO.

Beyer, Peter (2006). *Religions in Global Society*. London: Routledge.

Billen, Andrew (2013). 'A master of multiple TV talents and an unshakeable optimist', *The Times*, 3 September, p. 5.

Black, J. S. and G. W. Chrystal (1912). *The Life of William Robertson Smith*. London: Adam and Charles Black.

Blacker, Terence (2012). 'When a refusal is more noble than an honour', *The Independent*, 27 January, p. 25.

Blakely, Rhys (2014). 'Generation Z: smart, mature, prudent . . . and a bit dull? *The Times*, 31 July, p. 29.

Bloch, Maurice (1995). 'People into places', in Erich Hirsch and Michael O'Hanlon (eds), *The Anthropology of Landscape*. Oxford: Oxford University Press, 63–113.

Bloch, Maurice (1998). 'Why trees, too, are good to think with: Towards an anthropology of the meaning of life', in Laura Rival (ed.) *The Social Life of Trees*. Oxford: Berg, 39–55.

Bloch, Maurice and Jonathan Parry (1982). *Death and the Regeneration of Life*. Cambridge: Cambridge University Press.

Blythe, Ronald ([1963] 1964). *The Age of Illusion: England in the Twenties and Thirties, 1919–1940*. Harmondsworth: Penguin Books Ltd.

Bone, James (2011). 'The Times 2011 Person of the Year', *The Times*, 28 December, pp. 14–15.

Borland, Sophie (2014). 'How NHS dehumanises patients, by doctor, 32, who's dying of cancer', *Daily Mail*, 7 June, p. 29.

Bostridge, Ian (2015). *Schubert's Winter Journey, Anatomy of an Obsession*. London: Faber and Faber.

Bottomore, T. B. (1964). *Elites and Society*. Harmondsworth: Pelican Books.

Botton, Alain de (2012). *Religion for Atheists: A Non-believer's Guide to the Uses of Religion*. London: Hamish Hamilton.

Bourdieu, Pierre ([1972] 1977). *Outline of a Theory of Practice*. Cambridge: Cambridge University Press.

Bourdieu, Pierre ([1976] 1993). 'Some properties of fields', *Sociology in Question*. Cambridge: Cambridge University Press, 72–7.

Bourdieu, Pierre ([1989] 1996). *The State Nobility, Elite Schools in the Field of Power*. Oxford: Polity Press.

Bowker, John (1973). *The Sense of God*. Oxford: Oxford University Press.

Bowker, John (1978). *The Religious Imagination and the Sense of God*. Oxford: Oxford University Press.

BP Portrait Award 2013 (2013). London: National Portrait Gallery.

Breger, Louis (2009). *A Dream of Undying Fame, How Freud Betrayed his Mentor and Invented Psychoanalysis*. New York: Basic Books.

Briggs, Asa ([1955] 1965). *Victorian People*. Harmondsworth: Penguin Books.

Brooks, Alison S. (2011). 'What is a human?', in Malcolm Jeeves (ed.) *Rethinking Human Nature*. Grand Rapids, Michigan/Cambridge: William B. Eerdman's Publishing Company, 227–68.

Brown, Andrew (2014). 'The dubious morality of choice', *Church Times*, 11 July, p. 43.

Brown, Callum (2009). *The Death of Christian Britain*. Abingdon: Routledge.

Brown, David (2013). 'Inquisitor who extracted and apology from "tricky Dicky"', *The Times*, 3 September, pp. 4–5.

Brown, David (ed.) (2015). *Durham Cathedral, History, Fabric and Culture*. New Haven and London: Yale University Press in association with the Chapter of Durham Cathedral.

Brown, Jonathan (2013). 'Calls for decisive action on cyber-blackmail after teenager kills himself over web scam', *I on Saturday*—from the *Independent*, 17 August, p. 4.

Brown, Rohan Elizabeth (2012). *Timor Mortis Conturbat Me: Complicating Walter's Traditional Community-based Death Typology Using Popular Literature*. Ph.D. Thesis, University of Winchester.

Browne, Thomas ([1654] 1927). 'Religio Medici', in Charles Sayle (ed.) *The Works of Sir Thomas Browne*, vol. i. Edinburgh: John Grant, pp. xiv–lv.

Browne, Thomas ([1658] 1927). *The Works of Sir Thomas Browne*. Charles Sayle (ed.). Vols. I–III. Edinburgh: John Grant.

Bruce, Steve (1999). *Choice and Religion: A Critique of Rational Choice Theory*. Oxford: Oxford University Press.

Burkhardt, M. (1989). 'Spirituality: an analysis of the concept', *Holistic Nursing Practice*, 3 (3): 69–77.

Burnard, P. (1987). 'Spiritual distress and nursing response', *Journal of Advanced Nursing*, 12: 377–82.

Burstow, Paul (2014). *A Vision for Care in the Twenty-First Century*. London: Demos. <http://www.demos.co.uk>.

Butler, Samuel ([1872] 1939). *Erewhon*. London: Jonathan Cape.

Byrne, Georgina (2010). *Modern Spiritualism and the Church of England 1850–1939*. London: Boydell and Brewer.

Calder, Jenni (1979). 'Introduction', in Robert Louis Stevenson *Dr Jekyll and Mr Hyde And Other Stories*. Harmondsworth: Penguin Books, 7–21.

Carey, D. F. (1929). 'War Padre', in *G. A. Studdert Kennedy by His Friends*. London: Hodder & Stoughton, 115–64.

Carruthers, Marissa (2012). 'Angels tribute etched in ink on son's back', *Sunderland Echo*, 4 October, p. 7.

Castells, Manuel ([1997] 2010 2nd edn). *The Power of Identity*. Oxford: Wiley-Blackwell.

Certeau, Michel de, Luce Giard, and Pierre Mayol ([1994] 1998). *The Practice of Everyday Life*, vol. ii: *Living and Cooking*. Minneapolis: University of Minnesota Press.

Chamberlain, Andrew T. and Michael Parker Pearson (2001). *Earthly Remains: The History and Science of Preserved Human Bodies*. Oxford: Oxford University Press.

Chaucer, Geoffrey (1951). *The Canterbury Tales*, translated by Nevill Coghill. Harmondsworth: Penguin Books.

Cheal, David (1988). *The Gift Economy*. London: Routledge.

Cheston, Paul (2013) 'I love Al Qaeda . . . They are my brothers', *London Evening Standard*, 9 December, pp. 1, 5.

Childs, David (2008). *Growing Remembrance: The Story of the National Memorial Arboretum*. Barnsley, S. Yorkshire: Pen and Sword Military.

Cicero (1972). *The Nature of the Gods*, translated by Horace C. P. McGregor, with Introduction by J. M. Ross. Harmondsworth: Penguin Books.

Clapton, Eric (2012). Interview Radio 4, 9 October, on Paul Gambaccini's 'For one night only' series.

Clark, David (1998). 'Originating a movement: Cicely Saunders and the development of St Christopher's Hospice, 1957–1967', *Mortality*, 3 (1): 43–63.

Clark, Kevin (2012). 'An angel in the sky', *Sunderland Echo*, 4 October, p. 1.

Clayden, Andy, Trish Green, Jenny Hockey, and Mark Powell (2015). *Natural Burial, Landscape, Practice, and Experience*. London: Routledge.

Cleiren, M. P. H. D. (1991). *Adaptation After Bereavement*. Leiden: Leiden University Press.

Comte-Sponville, André ([2006] 2007). *The Book of Atheist Spirituality*, translated by Nancy Huston. London: Bantam Books.

Conway, Steve (2013). 'Representing dying, representing class? Social distinction, aestheticisation and the performing self', *Mortality*, 18 (4): 327–38.

Cook, Chris, Andrew Powell, and Andrew Sims (2009). *Spirituality and Psychiatry*, London: Royal College of Psychiatrists Publications.

Corr, C. A. (1993). 'Coping with dying: Lessons we should and should not learn from the work of Elisabeth Kübler-Ross', *Death Studies*, 17 (1).

Corrigan, John (2004). *Religion and Emotion: Approaches and Interpretations*. Oxford: Oxford University Press.

Corrigan, John (ed.) (2008). *Oxford Handbook of Religion and Emotion*. Oxford: Oxford University Press.

Coss, Denise (2012). *First World War Memorials, Commemoration and Community in North-East England, 1918–1939*. Doctoral Dissertation, University Of Durham.

Cottingham, John (2005). *The Spiritual Dimension, Religion, Philosophy and Human Values*. Cambridge: Cambridge University Press.

Crossley, James G. (2014). *Harnessing Chaos: The Bible in English Political Discourse Since 1968*. London: Bloomsbury.

Csiksentmihalyi, Mihaly (2002 revised edn). *Flow*. London: Rider.

Cupitt, Don, (2009). 'Changes and chances', in Dinah Livingstone (ed.) *This Life on Earth*. Newcastle-upon-Tyne: Sea of Faith (SOF) Network (UK), 5–8.

Dahlgren, Curt and Jan Hermanson (2005). 'Sweden—Ashes', in Douglas J. Davies and Lewis Mates (eds) *Encyclopedia of Cremation*. Aldershot: Ashgate, 60–4.

Daniels, Stephen (1988). 'The political iconography of woodland in later Georgian England', in Denis Cosgrove and Stephen Daniels (eds) *The Iconography of Landscape*. Cambridge: Cambridge University Press, 43–82.

Darwin, Charles (1872). *The Expression of the Emotions in Man and Animals*. London: John Murray.

Davie, Grace (2000). *Religion in Modern Europe*. Oxford: Oxford University Press.

Davies, Douglas J. (1976). 'Social groups, liturgy and glossolalia', *Churchman*, 90: 193–205.

Davies, Douglas J. (1983). 'Pastoral theology and "Folk-Religion" as a clerical category of self-absolution', *Research Bulletin, Birmingham Institute of Worship and Religious Architecture*.

Davies, Douglas J. (1984). *Meaning and Salvation in Religious Studies*. Leiden: Brill.

Davies, Douglas J. (1988). 'The evocative symbolism of trees', in Denis Cosgrove and Stephen Daniels (eds) *The Iconography of Landscape*. Cambridge: Cambridge University Press, 32–42

Davies, Douglas J. (1996). 'The sacred crematorium', *Mortality*, 1 (1), 83–94.

Davies, Douglas J. ([1997] 2002 2nd edn). *Death, Ritual and Belief*. London: Cassell.

Davies, Douglas J. (2000). *The Mormon Culture of Salvation*. Aldershot: Ashgate.

Davies, Douglas J. (2001). 'Health, morality and sacrifice: The sociology of disasters', in Richard Fenn (ed.) *Blackwell Companion to the Sociology of Religion*. Oxford: Blackwell, 404–17.

Davies, Douglas J. (2002). *Death, Ritual and Belief*. (2nd edn). London: Cassell.

Davies, Douglas J. (2002a). 'Portraying the Dead', *Source*, 32, Autumn, pp. 49–51: with pictures by David Trullo.

Davies, Douglas J. (2003). 'The sociology of wisdom', in James A. Beckford and James T. Richardson (eds) *Challenging Religion: Essays in Honour of Eileen Barker*. London: Routledge, 204–16.

Davies, Douglas J. (2004). 'Purity, spirit, and reciprocity in acts of Apostles', in Louise Lawrence and Mario Aguilar (eds) *Anthropology and Biblical Studies: Avenues of Approach.* Leiden: Deo Publishing, 259–80.

Davies, Douglas J. (2005). 'Literary cremation', in Douglas J. Davies and Lewis H. Mates (eds) *Encyclopedia of Cremation.* Aldershot: Ashgate.

Davies, Douglas J. (2005a). *A Brief History of Death.* Oxford: Blackwell.

Davies, Douglas J. (2006). 'Inner speech and religious traditions', in James A. Beckford and John Wallis (eds) *Theorizing Religion: Classical and Contemporary Debates.* Aldershot: Ashgate, 211–23.

Davies, Douglas J. (2008). *The Theology of Death.* London: T & T Clark.

Davies, Douglas J. (2008a). 'Cultural antensification: A theory for religion', in Abby Day (ed.) *Religion and the Individual.* Aldershot: Ashgate, 7–18.

Davies, Douglas J. (2010). *Jesus, Joseph Smith and Satanic Opposition.* Farnham, Surrey: Ashgate.

Davies, Douglas J. (2011). *Emotion, Identity, and Religion: Hope, Reciprocity, and Otherness.* Oxford: Oxford University Press.

Davies, Douglas J. (2012a). 'Ritual', in Mark Cobb, Christina M. Puchalski, and Bruce Rumbold (eds) *Oxford Textbook of Spirituality in Healthcare.* Oxford: Oxford University Press, 163–9.

Davies, Douglas J. (2015). 'Valuing emotion in tragedy', in Abby Day and Mia Lövheim (eds) *Modernities, Memory, Mutations: Grace Davie and Contemporary Religion.* Farnham: Ashgate.

Davies, Douglas J. and Mathew Guest (1999). 'Disposal of cremated remains', *Pharos*, Spring, 26–30.

Davies, Douglas J. with Lewis H. Mates (eds) (2005). *The Encyclopedia of Cremation.* Aldershot: Ashgate.

Davies, Douglas J. and Dan Northam-Jones (2012). 'The Sea of Faith: Exemplifying transformed retention', in Mathew Guest and Elisabeth Arweck (eds) *Religion and Knowledge: Sociological Perspectives.* London, Farnham: Ashgate, 227–46.

Davies, Douglas J. and Adam J. Powell (2015). *Sacred Selves, Sacred Settings, Reflecting Hans Mol.* Farnham: Ashgate.

Davies, Douglas and Hannah Rumble (2012). *Natural Burial, Traditional-Secular Spiritualities and Funeral Innovation.* London: Continuum.

Davies, Douglas and Alastair Shaw (1995). *Reusing Old Graves: A Report of Popular British Attitudes.* Crayford, Kent: Shaw & Sons.

Davies, Douglas J. with Nathaniel A. Warne (eds) (2013). *Emotions and Religious Dynamics.* Farnham, Surrey: Ashgate.

Davies, Douglas, Charles Watkins, and Michael Winter (1991). *Church and Religion in Rural England.* Edinburgh: Continuum.

Davies, Hywel (2009). *Modern Menswear.* London: Laurence King Publishing Ltd.

Davies, Jon (1995). *The Christian Warrior in the Twentieth Century.* Lewiston, NY: Mellen Press.

Day, Abby and Mia Lövheim (eds) (2015). *Modernities, Memory, Mutations: Grace Davie and Contemporary Religion.* Farnham: Ashgate.

Dico, Joy Lo (2015). 'Rebel with a cause', *London Evening Standard*, 4 March, pp. 32–3.

Dixon, Roger and Stefan Muthesius (1978). *Victorian Architecture*. London: Thames and Hudson.

Douglas, Mary (1966). *Purity and Danger*. London: Routledge and Kegan Paul.

Drake, Matthew (2014). 'Top Tories accused in rent boy parties', *Sunday Mirror*, 13 July, pp. 4–7.

Drescher, Elizabeth (2012). 'Pixels perpetually shine: The mediation of illness, dying and death in the digital age', *Cross Currents*, Vol. 62. No. 2, 204–18.

Droogers, André and Anton van Harskamp (eds) (2014). *Methods for the Study of Religious Change: From Religious Studies to Worldview Studies*. Sheffield: Equinox.

Dupré, L. K. (1981). *The Deeper Life: An Introduction to Christian Mysticism*. New York: Crossroad.

Dupré, Wilhelm (1975). *Religion in Primitive Culture: A Study in Ethnophilosophy*. The Hague: Mouton.

Durkheim, Emile ([1912] 1976). *The Elementary Forms of the Religious Life*. London: Allan Lane.

Duschinsky, Robbie and Sue Lampitt (2012). 'Managing the tensions of Essentialism: Purity and Impurity', *Sociology*, 46 (6): 1195–207.

Eagleton, Terry (2014). *Culture and the Death of God*. New Haven and London: Yale University Press.

Edwards, John (1997). 'It isn't what you see, it's what you feel', *Daily Mail*, 6 September, p. 33.

Eliade, Mircea (1978). *No Souvenirs*. London: Routledge and Kegan Paul.

Elsdon, R. (1995). 'Spiritual pain in dying people: The nurse's role', *Professional Nurse*, 10 (10): 641–3.

Etherington, Jan (2011). 'Scattering ashes on a beautiful sunny day', *Daily Express*, 13 September, at <http://www.express.co.uk/comment/expresscomment/270920/scat tering-ashes-on-a-beautiful-sunny-day>, accessed 14 June 2015.

Evans-Pritchard, E. E. (1962). *Essays in Social Anthropology*. London: Faber and Faber.

Falk, Pasi and Pasi Mäenpää (1999). *Hitting the Jackpot: Lives of Lottery Millionaires*. Oxford: Berg.

Finch, Casey (1993). 'Introduction', in *The Complete works of the Pearl Poet*, translated and with an Introduction by Casey Finch. Middle English Texts edited by Casey Finch, Malcolm Andrew, and Ronald Waldron. Berkeley: University of California Press, 1–42.

Finucane, R. C. (1982). *Appearances of the Dead: A Cultural History of Ghosts*. London: Junction Books.

Fischoff, Ephraim (1966). 'Translator's Preface', in Max Weber, *The Sociology of Religion*, translated by Ephraim Mischief, Introduction by Talcott Parsons. London: Methuen and Co., ix–xvii.

Fitzgerald, T. (2000). *The Ideology of Religious Studies*. New York: Oxford University Press.

Flanagan, Kieran and Peter C. Jupp (2014). *Mortality* (special edition: 'Mortality and Martyrdom'), 19 (2).

Flatt, Bill (1987). 'Stages of grief', *Journal of Religion and Health*, 26 (2): (Summer): 143–8.

Fletcher, Martin (2011). 'The Arab Spring has been astounding: Don't dismiss it', *The Times*, 28 December, p. 22.

Foley, Michael (2010). *The Age of Absurdity: Why Modern Life makes it Hard to be Happy*. London: Simon & Schuster.

Forbes, David (1870). 'On the Aymora Indians of Bolivia and Peru', *Journal of the Ethnological Society of London*, 21 June.

France, Anthony, Neil Syson, and Ryan Sabey (2013). *The Sun* (special edition), 18 April, p. 12.

Freud, Sigmund ([1900] 1976). *The Interpretation of Dreams*. Harmondsworth: Pelican Books.

Gardner, Kevin J. (ed.) (2005) *Faith and Doubt of John Betjeman*. London: Continuum.

Garrard, Peter, Vassiliki Rentoumi, Christian Lambert, and David Owen (2013). 'Linguistic Biomarkers of Hubris Syndrome', *Cortex*, 30: 1–15.

Gelli, Frank (1997). 'I set up a black candle near the altar which is a focal point of devotion', *Daily Mail*, 6 September, p. 26.

Gennep, Arnold van ([1908] 1960). *The Rites of Passage*, translated by M. K. Vizedom and G. Caffee. London: Routledge and Kegan Paul.

George, Andrew (1999). *The Epic of Gilgamesh*, translated and introduced by Andrew George. New York: Barnes and Noble.

Giard, Luce ([1994] 1998). 'Doing-Cooking', in Certeau, Michel de, Luce Giard, and Pierre Mayol (eds) *The Practice of Everyday Life,* vol. ii: *Living and Cooking*. Minneapolis: University of Minnesota Press, 149–248.

Gibson, Margaret (2008). *Objects of the Dead: Mourning and Memory in Everyday Life*. Melbourne: Melbourne University Press.

Glaser, Barney G. and Anselm L. Strauss (1965). *Awareness of Dying*. New York: Aldine Publishing Company.

Godbout, Jacques T. with Alain Caillé (1998). *The World of the Gift*. Montreal and Kingston: McGill-Queen's University Press.

Goethe, Johann Wolfgang ([1809] 1971). *Elective Affinities*. Harmondsworth: Penguin Books.

Gorer, Geoffrey (1955). *Exploring English Character*. London: Cresset Press.

Gorer, Geoffrey (1965). *Death, Grief and Mourning*. London: Cresset Press.

Grainger, Hilary (2005). 'Porte-cochère', in Douglas J. Davies and Lewis Mates (eds) *Encyclopedia of Cremation*. Aldershot: Ashgate, 343.

Gregory, Adrian (1994). *The Silence of Memory: Armistice Day 1919–1946*. Oxford: Berg.

Gregory, Adrian (2008). *The Last Great War: British Society and the First World War*. Cambridge: Cambridge University Press.

Greig, Geordie (2006). 'There would be so much to tell her', *Daily Telegraph*, 10 January.

Guénon, René ([1929] 2001). *Spiritual Authority and Temporal Power*. Hillsdale, NY: Sophia Perennis.

Guest, Mathew (2007). *Evangelical Identity and Contemporary Culture*. Milton Keynes: Paternoster.

Hacker, Sophie (2013). 'Quietus in Winchester: programme and process', in Michael Tooby (ed.) *Julian Stair: Quietus Reviewed*. Bath: Wunderkammer Press, 40–1.

Halsey, A. H. with Josephine Webb (2000). *British Social Trends*. Basingstoke: Macmillan.

Hamilton, Alan (1997). 'Silent procession through London will take two hours', *The Times,* 5 September, p. 3.

Hamilton, Alan and Philip Webster (1997). 'Service will blend liturgy with pop', *The Times*, 5 September, p. 3.

Hamilton, Malcolm (1995 2nd edn). *The Sociology of Religion*. London: Routledge.

Hanley, Elizabeth (2005). *Holistic Philosophy and Spiritual Wellbeing in People Facing Life-Threatening Illness*. M.Litt thesis, University of Durham.

Hardman, Robert (1997). 'Queen bows to her people', *The Daily Telegraph*, 5 September, p. 1.

Harries, Richard (2014). 'A greater compassion', *The Church Times*, 11 July, p. 14.

Hardman, Charlotte E. (2000). *Other Worlds: Notions of Self and Emotion among the Lohorung Rai*. Oxford: Berg.

Harvey, Oliver (2013). *The Sun* (special edition), 18 April, p. 13.

Harvey, Peter (2000). *An Introduction to Buddhist Ethics*. Cambridge: Cambridge University Press.

Hauser, Arnold (1965). *Mannerism: The Crisis of the Renaissance and the Origin of Modern Art*, vol. i. London: Routledge and Kegan Paul.

Hay, David (1990). *Religious Experience Today*. London: Mowbray.

Hazelgrove, Jenny (2000). *Spiritualism and British Society between the Wars*. Manchester: Manchester University Press.

Hazlitt, William ([1825] 1970). *The Spirit of the Age*. London: Oxford University Press.

Healey, M. (1993). 'Discourses of plague in early modern London', *Epidemic Disease in London*. Centre for Metropolitan History Working Papers, Series 1, 19–34.

Heath, Geoff (2003). *Believing in Nothing and Something*. Chesterfield: Bowland Press.

Heazell, Paddy (2011). 'Boffins memorial', *The Times,* 20 July, p. 26.

Hebert, A. G. (1935). *Liturgy and Society: The Function of the Church in the Modern World*. London: Faber and Faber.

Heelas, Paul (1996). *The New Age Movement*. Oxford: Blackwell Publishers.

Heelas, Paul (1998). 'Introduction: on differentiation and dedifferentiation', in Paul Heelas, with David Martin and Paul Morris *Religion, Modernity and Postmodernity*. Oxford: Blackwell, 1–18.

Heelas, Paul (2000). 'Expressive spirituality and humanistic expressivism: Sources of significance beyond church and chapel', in Steven Sutcliffe and Marion Bowman (eds) *Beyond New Age: Exploring Alternative Spirituality*. Edinburgh: Edinburgh University Press, 237–54.

Heiler, Friedrich ([1918] 1932). *Prayer: A Study in the History and Psychology of Religion*. Oxford: Oxford University Press.

Heller, Tom (1989). 'Personal and medical memories from Hillsborough', *British Medical Journal,* 23–30 Dec. 299(6715): 1596–8.

Heller, Tom (1993). 'Personal and medical memories from Hillsborough', in D. Dickenson and M. Johnson (eds) *Death, Dying and Bereavement*. London: Sage and Open University, 300–4.

Hennessey, Susan (2011). 'Mindfulness and grief, helping ourselves and others'. Unpublished address at 7th Annual Barts and London NHS Bereavement Conference. July.

Hensher, Philip (2012). 'Sergei Polunin and a lesson for Labour', the *I* newspaper, 27 Janurary, p. 15.

Herbert, George (1994). *George Herbert*. Louis L. Martz (ed.). Oxford: Oxford University Press.

Hertz, Robert ([1905–6] 1960). 'A contribution to the study of the collective representation of death', in R. Needham and C. Needham (eds) *Death and the Right Hand*. New York: Free Press. (First published in *L'Année sociologique*, 10, 1905–6.)

Hesse, Herman ([1905] 1973). *The Prodigy*, translated by W. J. Strachan. Harmondsworth: Penguin Books.

Hirsch, Eric and Michael O'Hanlon (eds) (1995). *The Anthropology of Landscape: Perspectives on Place and Space*. Oxford: Clarendon Press.

Hobbes, Thomas (n.d. [1651]) *Leviathan, or the Matter, Forme and Power of a Commonwealth Ecclesiastical and Civil*, edited and with an Introduction by Michael Oakeshott. Oxford: Basil Blackwell.

Hobsbawm, Eric ([1962] 1973). *The Age of Revolution, 1789–1848*. London: Abacus.

Hobsbawm, Eric (2002). 'War and peace in the 20th century', *London Review of Books*, 24 (4): 16.

Hobsbawm, E. and T. Ranger (eds) ([1983] 2005). *The Invention of Tradition*. Cambridge: Cambridge University Press.

Hocart, A. M. (1933). 'The purpose of ritual', in Lord Raglan (ed.) *The Life-Giving Myth and Other Essays*. London: Tavistock Publications with Methuen & Co. Ltd. 2nd edn 1952, with Introduction by Rodney Needham.

Hockey, Jenny (2002). 'Interviews as ethnography? Disembodied social interaction in Britain', in Nigel Rapport (ed.) *British Subjects: An Anthropology of Britian*. Oxford: Berg, 209–22.

Hoggart, Richard ([1957] 1958). *The Uses of Literacy: Aspects of Working Class Life*. London: Chatto and Windus.

Hollins, Sheila and Irene Tuffrey-Wijne, and illustrated by Lisa Kopper (2009). *Am I Going to Die?* London: RCPsych and St George's University of London.

Homer ([1946] 1991). *The Odyssey*, translated by E. V. Rieu; revised by D. C. H. Rieu with P. V. Jones. London: Penguin Books.

Homer (1987). *The Iliad*, translated and with an Introduction by Mark Hammond. London: Penguin Books.

Honkasala, Marja-Liisa and Miira Tuominen (2014). *Culture, Suicide, and the Human Condition*. London: Berghahn.

Hooker, Richard (1865). *The Works of Mr. Richard Hooker* (ed.) John Keble. Oxford: Clarendon Press.

Horlick-Jones, Tom (2012). 'Taking the bundle apart: Some reflections on the significance of Edward Thompson's work for the practice of sociology', *Sociology*, 46 (6): 1229–33.

Hudson, Anthony BE (2002). *Just to See His Name: A History of the Falklands Islands Memorial Chapel at Pangbourne College*. Pangbourne: Falklands Islands Memorial Chapel Trust.

Hughes, Thomas ([1858] n.d.). *Tom Brown's Schooldays*. London: Nelson.

Hume, David ([1783] n.d. 2005]). *On Suicide*. London: Penguin Books.

Hunter, Neil (2012). 'I was completely powerless to help him', *The Northern Echo*, 28 January, p. 3.

Hurwitz, B. and R. Richardson (1997). 'Swearing to care: The resurgence in medical school oaths', *British Medical Journal*, 315: 1671–4.

Hutchings, Tim (2012). 'Wiring death: Dying, grieving and remembering on the internet', in Douglas J. Davies and Chang-Won Park (eds) *Emotion, Identity and Death: Mortality Across Disciplines*. Farnham: Ashgate, 43–58.

Hutchings, Tim (2013). 'Death, emotion and digital media', in Douglas J. Davies with Nathaniel A. Warne (eds) *Emotions and Religious Dynamics*. Farnham: Ashgate, 191–212.

Huxley, Aldous ([1932] 2004). *Brave New World*. London: Random House, Vintage.

Inge, John (2003). *A Christian Theology of Place*. Aldershot: Ashgate.

Inge, W. R. (1934). *Vale*. London: Longman's Green and Co.

Inge, W. R. (1949). *Diary of a Dean, St Paul's 1911–1934*. London: Hutchinson & Co.

Ingold, Tim (2011). *Being Alive: Essays on Movement, Knowledge and Description*. London: Routledge.

Iremonger, F. A. (1963). *William Temple, Archbishop of Canterbury: His Life and Letters*, abridged edition by D. C. Somervell. London: Oxford University Press.

Jalland, Pat (1996). *Death in the Victorian Family*. Oxford: Oxford University Press.

James, P. D. (1989). *Devices and Desires*. London: Faber and Faber.

James, W. and N. J. Allan (1998). *Marcel Mauss and the Gift: A Centenary Tribute*. New York: Berghahn.

Jeeves, Malcolm (2011). 'The emergence of human distinctiveness: The story from neuropsychology and evolutionary psychology', in Malcolm Jeeves (ed.) *Rethinking Human Nature*. Grand Rapids, Michigan/Cambridge, UK: William B. Eerdman's Publishing Company, 176–205.

Jindra, Michael and Joël Noret (2011). 'African funerals and sociocultural change: A review of momentous transformations across the continent', in Michael Jindra and Joël Noret (eds), *Funerals in Africa: Explorations of a Social Phenomenon*. New York/Oxford: Berghahn Books, 16–40.

Joiner, Thomas (2005). *Why People Die by Suicide*. Cambridge, MA: Harvard University Press.

Jones, Lindsey (2000). *The Hermeneutics of Sacred Architecture: Experience, Interpretation, Comparison,* vol. i: *Reflections on the Eventfulness of Religious Architecture*. Cambridge, MA: Harvard University Press.

Jones, Owen ([2014] 2015). *The Establishment, and How They Get Away With It*. UK: Penguin Random House.

Joussaume, Roger ([1985] 1987). *Dolmens for the Dead: Megalithic Building throughout the World*, translated by Anne and Christopher Chippindale. London: Guild Publishing London.

Jupp, P. C. (2006). *From Dust to Ashes: Cremation and the British Way of Death*. Basingstoke: Palgrave MacMillan.

Jupp, P. C. (2005). 'Cremation Society of Great Britain', in Douglas J. Davies and Lewis Mates (eds) *Encyclopedia of Cremation*. Aldershot: Ashgate, 135–43.

Kabat-Zinn, J. (1990). *Full Catastrophe Living: Using the Wisdom of Your Body and Mind to Face Stress, Pain and Illness*. London: Piatkus.

Kant, Immanuel (2001). 'Suicide', in Thomas A. Mappes and David Degrazia (eds) *Biomedical Ethics* (5th edn). Boston: McGraw Hill, 398–402.

Kemp, Richard (2011). 'Another Wooton Bassett is needed to honour our dead', *The Times*, 4 July, p. 10.

Kendall, Richard (ed.) (2001). *Cézanne by Himself*. London: Little Brown and Company.

Kim, Hyunchul (2011). *Pollution and Vitality: The Process of Death in a Japanese Inaka (Rural) Town*. University of Edinburgh: Doctoral Dissertation.

Kim, Jaeyeol ([2002] 2003). *Handbook of Korean Art: White Porcelain and Punch'ong Ware*, translated by Moonjung Choi. London: Laurence King Publishing.

Kim, Shi-Dug (2012). 'Overview of Korea's funeral industry' in Natacha Aveline-Dubach (ed.) *Invisible Population: The Place of the Dead in East Asian Megacities*. Lanham: Lexington Books, 192–205.

Kirkpatrick, W. J. A. (1967). 'Conscience and commitment', in Barbara Robb (ed.) *Sans Everything*. London: Nelson, 48–57.

Kübler-Ross, Elisabeth ([1969] 1989). *On Death and Dying*. New York. Macmillan.

Larkin, Hillary (2014). *The Making of Englishmen: Debates on National Identity 1550–1650*. Leiden: Brill.

Lawrence, D. H. ([1915] 1949). *The Rainbow*. Harmondsworth: Penguin Books Ltd.

Lawrence, D. H. ([1922] 1968). 'The Horse Dealer's daughter', in D. H. Lawrence *England, My England*. Harmondsworth: Penguin, 157–74.

Lawrence, Robert M. and Julia H. Head (2009). 'Ageing', in Chris Cook, Andrew Powell, and Andrew Sims *Spirituality and Psychiatry*, London: Royal College of Psychiatrists Publications.

Lawson, E. Thomas and Robert N. McCauley (1990). *Rethinking Religion: Connecting Cognition and Culture*. Cambridge: Cambridge University Press.

Lay, Kate (2013). 'Troll death website offers to name girl's tormentors', *The Times*, 9 August, p. 1.

Layton, Robert (1995). 'Relating to the country', in Erich Hirsch and Michael O'Hanlon (eds) *The Anthropology of Landscape*. Oxford: Oxford University Press, 210–31.

Leaney, A. R. C. (1958). *A Commentary on The Gospel According to St Luke*. London: Adam and Charles Black.

Leeuw, Gerardus van der ([1933] 1967). *Religion in Essence and Manifestation*, translated by J. E. Turner (1938). Gloucester, MA: Peter Smith.

Leonhard, Jörn and Christian Wieland (2011). *What Makes the Nobility Noble? Comparative Perspectives from the Sixteenth to the Twentieth Century*. Göttingen: Vandenhoeck & Ruprecht.

Lévi-Strauss, Claude (1962). *Totemism*. London: Merlin Press.

Lewis, C. S. (1947). *Miracles*. London: Geoffrey Bles, The Centenary Press.

Lewis, Martyn (1997). 'The week that changed my life', *Daily Mail*, 6 September, p. 26.

Little, Alison (2014). 'Child abuse inquiry chief is backed . . . by nephew Nigel Havers', *Daily Express*, 10 July, p. 7.

Livingstone, Dinah (ed.) (2009). *This Life on Earth*. Newcastle-upon-Tyne: Sea of Faith (SOF) Network (UK).

Llewellyn, Nigel (1991). *The Art of Death*. London: Reaktion Books and the Victoria and Albert Museum.

Lovelock, James (1995). *The Ages of Gaia: A Biography of our Living Earth.* New York: Norton.

Luhrmann, Tanya (2002). 'Dissociation, social technology and the spiritual domain', in Nigel Rapport (ed.) *British Subjects: An Anthropology of Britian.* Oxford: Berg, 121–38.

Luxmore, Jonathan (2014). 'Meanwhile, further down the slippery slope', *Church Times,* 11 July, p. 15.

McCorristine, Shane (2010). *Thinking about Ghosts and Ghost-seeing in England 1750–1920.* Cambridge: Cambridge University Press.

McCullers, Carson ([1961] 1965). *Clock Without Hands.* Harmondsworth: Penguin Books.

McCutcheon, Russell T. (1997). *Manufacturing Religion: The Discourse on Sui Generis Religion and the Politics of Nostalgia.* New York: Oxford University Press.

MacDorman, Karl F. and Hiroshi Ishiguro (2006). 'The uncanny advantage of using androids in cognitive and social science research', *Interaction Studies,* 7 (3): 297–337.

McFarland, Ian A. (2011). 'Habitus', in Ian A. McFarland et al. (eds) *The Cambridge Dictionary of Christian Theology.* Cambridge: Cambridge University Press, 205.

MacLachlan, Malcolm (2004). *Embodiment, Clinical, Critical, and Cultural Perspectives on Health and Illness.* Maidenhead, Berkshire: Open University Press.

Maddrell, Avril and James D. Sidaway (2010). *Deathscapes, Spaces for Death, Dying, Mourning and Remembrance.* Farnham: Ashgate.

Mäkinen, Ilka Henrik and Danuta Wasserman. (2001). 'Some social dimensions of suicide', in Danuta Wasserman (ed.) *Suicide: An Unnecessary Death.* London: Martin Dunitz, 103–4.

Malinowski, Bronislaw ([1948] 1974). *Magic, Science, and Religion.* London: Souvenir Press.

Maple, Myfanwy et al. (2013). 'Still part of the family: the importance of physical, emotional, and spiritual memorial places and spaces for parents bereaved through the suicide death of their son or daughter', *Mortality,* 18 (1): 54–71.

Mappes, Thomas A. and David Degrazia (eds) (2001). *Biomedical Ethics* 5th edn. Boston: McGraw Hill, 398–402.

Marett, R. R. (1941). *A Jerseyman at Oxford.* London: Oxford University Press.

Martin, David. (2013). *The Education of David Martin.* London: SPCK.

Martino, Ernesto de ([1972] 1988). *Primitive Magic: The Psychic Powers of Shamans and Sorcerors.* Bridport, Dorset: Prism Press.

Marvin, C. and D. W. Ingle (1999). *Blood Sacrifice and the Nation.* Cambridge: Cambridge University Press.

Mauss, Marcel ([1902] 2001). *A General Theory of Magic.* Routledge: London and New York.

Mauss, Marcel ([1935] 1979). 'Techniques of the Body', in *Sociology and Psychology: Essays by Marcel Mauss,* translated by Ben Brewster. London: Routledge and Kegan Paul, 95–123.

Mayo, James M. (1988). 'War memorials as political memory', *Geographical Review,* 78 (1): 62–75.

Middleton, Arthur (2007). 'Heroes of Faith: Gabriel Hebert', *The Church Observer,* London: Church Union, pp. 17–21.

Middleton, Paul (2011). *Martyrdom: A Guide for the Perplexed.* London: T & T Clark.

Miller, Daniel (2008). *The Comfort of Things.* Cambridge: Polity Press.

Miller, Daniel (2010). *Stuff.* Cambridge: Polity Press.

Mills, Simon (2012). 'Introduction', *Mortality* (special edition: 'Music and Death'), 17 (2): 89–91.

Mitchell, Nathan D. (1999). *Liturgy and the Social Sciences.* Collegeville, Minnesota: The Liturgical Press.

Mol, Hans (1976). *Identity and the Sacred.* Oxford: Blackwell.

Moller, David Wendell (1996). *Confronting Death, Values, Institutions, and Human Mortality.* Oxford: Oxford University Press.

Moo, Douglas J. (1983). *The Old Testament in the Gospel Passion Narrative.* Sheffield: The Almond Press.

Mori, M. (1970). 'Bukimi no tani [the uncanny valley]', *Energy*, 7: 33–5.

Moscovici, Serge (1993). *The Invention of Society.* Cambridge, MA: Polity.

Myers, Russell (2014). 'Seven years on McCanns pray for their girl', *Sunday Mirror*, 4 May, p.15.

Natanson, M. (ed.) (1973). *Alfred Schutz: Collected Papers.* The Hague: Nijhoff.

National Memorial Arboretum (2011). *Guidebook* (4th edn).

Needham, Rodney (1972). *Belief, Language and Experience.* Oxford: Blackwell.

Needham, Rodney (1980). *Reconnaissances.* Toronto: University of Toronto Press.

Nešporová, Olga and Irina Stahl (2014). 'Roadside memorials in the Czech Republic and Romania: memory versus religion in two European post-communist countries', *Mortality*, 19 (2): 22–40.

Newport, Kenneth G. C. (2006). *The Branch Davidians of Waco: The History and Beliefs of an Apocalyptic Sect.* Oxford: Oxford University Press.

Niebuhr, H. R. (1951). *Christ and Culture.* New York: Harper and Row.

O'Boyle, Claire (2013). 'Bernie to be buried with baby's ashes', *Sunday Mirror*, 7 July, pp. 1, 4–5.

O'Collins, Gerald (2011). *Rethinking Fundamental Theology.* Oxford: Oxford University Press.

Oldnall, A. (1996). 'A critical analysis of nursing: Meeting the spiritual needs of patients', *Journal of Advanced Nursing*, 23: 138–44.

Oliveira, Plinion Corrêa de (1993). *Nobility and Analogous Traditional Elites in the Allocutions of Pius XII: A Theme Illuminating American Social History.* Rork, Pennsylvania: Hamilton Press.

O'Neill, Sean (2013). 'Eye-for-eye doctrine of "killer"', *The Times*, 30 November, p. 5.

Otto, Rudolph. ([1917] 1924). *The Idea of the Holy,* translated by John H. Harvey. Oxford, Oxford University Press.

Owen, D. (2008). 'Hubris syndrome', *Clinical Medicine*, 8: 428–32.

Palmer, Alun (2013). 'The Grand Inquisitor', *Daily Mirror*, 2 September, pp. 3–4.

Parker, Christian (2006). 'Towards a post-Western sociology of religion', in James A. Beckford and John Walliss (eds) *Theorising Religion: Classical and Contemporary Debates.* Aldershot: Ashgate, 60–74.

Parkes, Colin Murray (2006). *Love and Loss: The Roots of Grief and its Complications.* New York: Routledge.

Parkes, Colin Murray (2013). 'Elizabeth Kübler-Ross, On death and dying: a reappraisal', *Mortality,* 18 (1): 94–8.

Parkes, Colin Murray, Joan Stevenson-Hyde, and Peter Marris (1991). *Attachment Across the Life-cycle.* London: Routledge.

Parry, J. P. (1994). *Death in Banaras.* Cambridge: Cambridge University Press.

Parsons, Brian (1999). 'Yesterday, today and tomorrow: The lifecycle of the UK funeral industry', *Mortality*, 4 (2): 127–45.

Pattison, S. (2000). *Shame, Theory, Therapy, Theology.* Cambridge: Cambridge University Press.

Paxman, Jeremy (1990). *Friends in High Places: Who Runs Britain.* London: Michael Joseph.

Pearl Poet, The Complete Works ([14th century] 1993). Translated and with an Introduction by Casey Finch. Middle English Texts edited by Casey Finch, Malcolm Andrew, and Ronald Waldron. Berkeley: University of California Press.

Pei, Mario (1964). *Voices of Man.* London: George Allen and Unwin.

Pelikan, Jaroslav (1970). 'Foreword to 1970 edition'. Gustav Aulén ([1930] 1970). *Christus Victor: An Historical Study of the Three Main Types of the Ideas of the Atonement*, translated by A. G. Hebert. London: SPCK, xi–xix.

Phillips, J. B. (1967). *Ring of Truth.* London: Hodder.

Phillips, Melanie (2014). 'Assisted dying transforms doctors into killers', *The Times,* 7 July, p. 26.

Plato. *The Republic,* translated and with an Introduction by Desmond Lee (2nd edn, revised, 1974). Harmondsworth: Penguin.

Polkinhorne, John (1995). *Serious Talk: Science and Religion in Dialogue.* Valley Forge, Pennsylvania: Trinity Press International.

Possamai, Adam (2009). *Sociology of Religion for Generations X and Y.* London: Equinox.

Powell, Dean (2007). *Dr William Price.* Llandysul: Gomer Press.

Powys, David (1997). *'Hell': A Hard Look at a Hard Question, The Fate of the Unrighteous in New Testament Thought.* Carlisle: Paternoster Press.

Prinz, Jesse J. (2004). *Gut Reactions: A Perceptual Theory of Emotion.* Oxford: Oxford University Press.

Purcell, Boyd (1998). 'Spiritual terrorism', *The American Journal of Hospice and Palliative Care*, May–June: 167–73.

Purcell, William (1962). *Woodbine Willie.* London: Hodder & Stoughton.

Qualtrough, Stuart and David Brown (1997). 'Diana was murdered! The two vital questions', *The People,* 9 November, pp. 1, 6–7.

Radcliffe-Brown, A. R. (1952). *Structure and Function in Primitive Society.* London: Cohen and West.

Rappaport, Roy (1999). *Ritual and Religion in the Making of Humanity.* Cambridge: Cambridge University Press.

Ratcliffe, Matthew (2008). *Feelings of Being: Phenomenology, Psychiatry, and the Sense of Reality.* Oxford: Oxford University Press.

Riem, Roland (2013). 'Quietus in Winchester: conversation and reflection', in Michael Tooby (ed.) *Julian Stair: Quietus Reviewed.* Bath: Wunderkammer Press, 43–4.

Reimers, Eva (2012). 'Nationalization and mediatized ritualization: The broadcast farewell of Fadime Sahindal', in Douglas J. Davies and Chang-Won Park (eds) *Emotion, Identity, and Death: Mortality Across Disciplines*. Farnham, Surrey: Ashgate, 29–42.

Renton, Andrew (2013). 'Quietus in Cardiff: Post Scriptum', in Michael Tooby (ed.) *Julian Stair: Quietus Reviewed*. Bath: Wunderkammer Press, 29–36.

Report of the Tribunal Appointed to Inquire into the Disaster at Aberfan (1967). Led by Lord Justice Edmund Davies. London: Her Majesty's Stationery Office.

Reynolds, Mark (2014). 'How brave Stephen gave thumbs up to top honour', *Daily Express*, 14 June, pp. 4–5.

Richardson, Therese (2014). 'Spousal bereavement in later life: A material culture perspective', *Mortality*, 19 (1): 61–79.

Riem, Roland (1993). *Stronger than Death: A Study of Love for the Dying*. Foreword by Rowan Williams. London: Darton, Longman and Todd.

Riis, Ole and Linda Woodhead (2010). *A Sociology of Religious Emotion*. Oxford: Oxfod University Press.

Rio, Knut M. and Olaf H. Smedal (eds) (2009). *Hierarchy, Persistence and Transformation in Social Formations*. New York/Oxford: Berghahn Books.

Rival, Laura (ed.) (1998). *The Social Life of Trees: Anthropological Perspectives on Tree Symbolism*. Oxford: Berg.

Rizzolatti, Giacomo et al. (1996). 'Premotor cortex and the recognition of motor actions', *Cognition, Brain Research*, 3: 131–41.

Robinson, John (1963). *Honest to God*. London: SCM.

Rogerson, John (1995). *The Bible and Criticism in Victorian Britain*. Sheffield: Sheffield Academic Press.

Rolls, Edmund (2005). *Emotion Explained*. Oxford: Oxford University Press.

Ross, J. M. (1972). 'Introduction', to Cicero *The Nature of the Gods*, translated by Horace C. P. McGregor, with Introduction by J. M. Ross. Harmondsworth: Penguin Books.

Rostila, Mikael and Jan M. Saarela (2011). 'Time does not heal all wounds: Mortality following the death of a parent', *Journal of Marriage and Family*, 73 (1): 236–49.

Rowling, J. K. (2007). *Harry Potter and the Deathly Hallows*. London: Bloomsbury.

Rue, Loyal (2005). *Religion is Not About God*. New Brunswick, NJ, and London: Rutgers University Press.

Rugg, Julie (2013). *Churchyard and Cemetery: Tradition and Modernity in Rural North Yorkshire*. Manchester: Manchester University Press.

Rumble, Hannah (2010). *'Giving Something Back': A Case Study of Woodland Burial and Human Experience at Barton Glebe*. Doctoral Dissertation, Durham University.

Rumble, Hannah et al. (2014). 'Disposal or dispersal? Environmentalism and final treatment of the British dead', *Mortality*, 19 (3): 243–60.

Sage, Adam (2013). 'France's next political elite will have a spell with Potter', *The Times*, 6 September, p. 33.

Sampson, Mike ([1962] 2004). *Anatomy of Britain*. London: Hodder and Stoughton.

Saunders, Cecily (1996). 'Hospice', *Mortality*, 1 (3): 317–23.

Savage, Mike and Karel Williams (eds) (2008). *Remembering Elites*. Oxford: Blackwell/ The Sociological Review.

Schantz, Mark S. (2008). *Awaiting the Heavenly Country: The Civil War and America's Culture of Death*. Ithaca and London: Cornell University Press.

Schleiermacher, Friedrich ([1821–2] 1928). *The Christian Faith*. Edinburgh: T. and T. Clark. English translation of 2nd German edition, 12.

Schiffmacher, Henk (ed.) ([1996] 2005). *1000 Tattoos*. Köln, London: Taschen.

Schofield, Alan (2005). 'Zoroastrianism', in Douglas J. Davies and Lewis Mates (eds) *Encyclopedia of Cremation*. Aldershot: Ashgate, 428–9.

Schweitzer, Albert (1919). 'Reverence for life', in Albert Schweitzer, *Reverence for Life*, (1974) London: SPCK, 108–17.

Schweitzer, Albert ([1931] 1948). *Albert Schweitzer: My Life and Thought, An Autobiography*. London: George Allen and Unwin.

Segal, Z. V., J. M. G. Williams, and J. D. Teasdale (2002). *Mindfulness-Based Cognitive Therapy for Depression: A New Approach to Preventing Relapse*. Guildford: Guildford Press.

Seremetakis, Nadia (1991). *The Last Word: Women, Death, and Divination in Inner Mani*. Chicago: The University of Chicago Press.

Seybold, Kevin S. (2007). *Explorations in Neuroscience, Psychology and Religion*. Aldershot: Ashgate.

Shaw, George Bernard (1946). 'Preface', *Androcles and the Lion*. Harmondsworth: Penguin Books, 9–109.

Shaw, George Bernard [1928]. 'Personal Immortality', in Warren Sylvester Smith (ed.) (1967) *Shaw on Religion*. London: Constable, pp. 181–3.

Shore, Chris and Stephen Nugent (eds) (2002). *Elite Culture: Anthropological Perspectives*. London, New York: Routledge.

Simmel, Georg (1959). *Sociology of Religion*, translated by Curt Rosenthal. New York: Philosophical Library.

Singh, Sangeeta (2009). 'Grief, types of', in Clifton D. Bryant and Dennis L. Peck (eds) *Encyclopedia of Death and the Human Experience*. Los Angeles/London: Sage, 538–42.

Sisson, Charles Jasper (1954). *William Shakespeare: The Complete Works*. London: Odhams Press.

Smart, Ninian (1996). *Dimensions of the Sacred: An Anatomy of the World's Beliefs*. London: HarperCollins.

Smith, Adam ([1776] 1860). *An Inquiry into the Nature and Causes of the Wealth of Nations*. London: T. Nelson and Sons.

Smith, Wilfred, Cantwell (1963). *The Meaning and End of Religion*. New York: Macmillan.

Smith, William Robertson (1889). *Lectures on the Religion of the Semites*. London: Adam and Charles Black.

Smyth, Bob (2011). 'Why you should make plans for digital death', *The Sunday Post*, 12 February, p. 51.

Snow, C. P. ([1967] 1969). *Variety of Men*. Harmondsworth: Penguin Books.

Sparks and Honey (2014). *Forget everything you learned about Millennials*. www.slideshow.net/sparksandhoney/generation-z-final-june17. Accessed 1 August 2014.

Spencer, Nick and Holly Weldon (2012). *Post-religious Britain?: The Faith of the Faithless.* London: Theos.

Sperber, Dan (1975). *Rethinking Symbolism*, translated by Alice C. Morton. Cambridge: Cambridge University Press.

St Augustine, *City of God*, (1945). London: J. M. Dent and Sons Ltd.

Stanner, W. E. H. (1960). 'On Aboriginal religion. III, symbolism in the higher rites', *Oceania*, 31 (2): 100–21.

Stevenson, Robert Louis ([1886] 1979). *Dr Jekyll and Mr Hyde And Other Stories*, edited with an Introduction by Jenni Calder. Harmondsworth: Penguin Books.

Straight, Bilinda S. (2006). 'Becoming dead: The entangled agencies of the dearly departed', *Anthropology and Humanism*, 32 (2): 101–10.

Street, Peter (2013). 'Death on the path of suffrage', *Church Times*, London, 31 May, pp. 19–20.

Studdert Kennedy, G. A. (1923). *The Wicket Gate.* London: Hodder & Stoughton.

Studdert Kennedy, G. A. (1925). *The Word and the Work.* London: Longmans, Green, and Co.

Sumegi, Angela (2014). *Understanding Death: An Introduction to Ideas of the Self and the Afterlife in World Religions.* Oxford: Wiley-Blackwell.

Summers, Hannah and Jack Grimston (2013). 'God dismissed as atheists honour fallen', *The Sunday Times,* News Section, 27 October, p. 7.

Sunday Express (2013). 'Sacred soil for war memorial', 1 December, no author, pictures by Mark Kelloe and Adrian Harlem.

Sykes, Karen (2005). *Arguing with Anthropology: An Introduction to Critical Theories of the Gift.* London: Routledge.

Tarlow, Sarah (1999). *Bereavement and Commemoration.* Oxford: Blackwell.

Tavard, George H. (2000). *The Starting Point of Calvin's Theology.* Grand Rapids, Mich: L. William B. Eerdman's Publishing Co.

Taylor, Charles (2007). *The Secular Age.* Cambridge, Massachusetts and London: The Belknap Press of Harvard University.

Taylor, Jeremy ([1651] 1830). *Holy Dying.* London: Longman, Hurst, Rees, Orme, and Brown.

Taylor, John H. and Daniel Antoine (2014). *Ancient Lives, New Discoveries: Eight Mummies, Eight Stories.* London: The British Museum.

Temple, William (1929). 'The man and his message', in *G. A. Studdert Kennedy by His Friends.* London: Hodder & Stoughton, 205–40.

Thate, Michael J. (2013). *Remembrance of Things Past?* Tübingen: Mohr Siebeck.

Thomas, Keith (1983). *Man and the Natural World.* Harmondsworth: Penguin.

Thomas, Sarah (2011). *Natural Burial and the Church of England.* Film made in association with The Centre for Death and Life Studies, University of Durham.

Thomas, Terry (2004). '"The Sacred" as a viable concept in the contemporary study of religions', in Steven J. Sutcliffe (ed.) *Religion: Empirical Studies.* Aldershot: Ashgate, 48–66.

Thompson, E. P. ([1963] 1991). *The Making of the English Working Class.* London: Penguin Books.

Thomson, Ann (2008). *Bodies of Thought: Science, Religion and the Soul in the Early Enlightenment.* Oxford: Oxford University Press.

Times, The (2012). 'Locked out', 18 August, p. 2.

Times, The (2014). 'Moral law', leading article, 26 June, p. 28.

Times, The (2015). 'Anthony Hudson: Campaigner who enlisted Margaret Thatcher's help in raising funds to build a chapel in memory of those killed in the Falklands conflict', 20 March, p. 55.

Times, The (2015). 'A hearse, a hearse, look to Leicester to understand your nation', 24 March, p. 29.

Times, The (2015). 'Hillsborough police chief admits he caused 96 deaths', 18 March, p. 7.

Times, The (2015). 'Memorial service Lord Attenborough', 18 March pp. 2–3.

Tooby, Michael (2013) (ed.). *Julian Stair: Quietus Reviewed.* Bath: Wunderkammer Press.

Tooby, Michael (2013). 'Quietus: The visitor's voice', in Michael Tooby (ed.). *Julian Stair: Quietus Reviewed.* Bath: Wunderkammer Press, 47–55.

Toulis, Nicole Rodriguez (1997). *Believing Identity: Pentecostalism and the Mediation of Jamaican Ethnicity and Gender in England.* Oxford: Berg.

Towler, Robert (1984). *The Need for Certainty: A Sociological Study of Conventional Religion.* London: Routledge and Kegan Paul.

Townsend, Martin (2013). 'A word from the Editor', *Sunday Express*, 1 December, p. 31.

Trzebiatowska, Marta and Steve Bruce (2012). *Why are Women more Religious than Men?* Oxford: Oxford University Press.

Turner, Frederick (1990). 'Hyperion to a satyr: Criticism and anti-structure in the works of Victor Turner', in Kathleen Ashley (ed.) *Victor Turner and the Construction of Social Criticism.* Bloomington: University of Indiana Press, 155–6.

Turner, Graeme (2004). *Understanding Celebrity.* London: Sage.

Turner, Victor (1969). *The Ritual Process.* London: Routledge and Kegan Paul.

Turner, Victor (1975). *Revelation and Divination in Ndembu Ritual.* Ithaca and London: Cornell University Press.

Turner, Victor (1987). *The Anthropology of Performance.* New York: PAJ Publications.

Turner, Victor and Edith Turner (1978). *Image and Pilgrimage in Christian Culture.* Oxford: Basil Blackwell.

Tylor, E. B. ([1871] 2010). *Primitive Culture.* Cambridge: Cambridge University Press.

Valentine, Christine (2008). *Bereavement Narratives, Continuing Bonds in the Twentieth Century.* London and New York: Routledge.

Valentine, Christine, Kate Woodthorpe, and Lucy Easthope (2013). 'Opportunities and barriers to forming a professional identity: communities of practice within UK funeral directing', *Mortality*, 18 (4): 358–75.

Verhey, Allen (2011). *The Christian Art of Dying: Learning from Jesus.* Grand Rapids, MI: William B. Eerdmans Publishing Company.

Views from the Pews (1986). British Council of Churches and Catholic Truth Society: London.

Wacquant, Loïc J. D. (1996). 'Foreword', to Pierre Bourdieu ([1989] 1996). *The State Nobility, Elite Schools in the Field of Power.* Oxford: Polity Press, ix–xxii.

Wain, John (ed.) (1987). *The Oxford Library of English Poetry.* London: Guild Publishing.

Wainwright, Martin (2009). 'Student who urinated on war memorial spared jail', *The Guardian*, 26 November.

Wake, C. Staniland (1889). *The Development of Marriage and Kinship*. London: George Redway.

Wallman, James (2015, 2nd edn). *Stuffocation: Living More with Less*. UK: Penguin, Random House.

Walsh, John (2010). 'Never say die', *The Independent*, 'Viewspaper' section, 5 July, pp. 10–11.

Walter, Tony (1994). *The Revival of Death*. London: Routledge.

Walter, Tony (1996). 'A new model of grief: bereavement and biography', *Mortality*, 1 (1): 7–25.

Walter, Tony (2001). 'From cathedral to supermarket: Mourning, silence and solidarity', *Sociological Review*, 49 (4): 494–511.

Walter, Tony (1996). 'A new theory of grief', *Mortality*, 1 (1): 7–26.

Walter, Tony (1999). *On Bereavement: The Culture of Grief*. Oxford: Oxford University Press.

Walvin, James (1986). *Football and the Decline of Britain*. London: Macmillan.

Warrington, John (ed.) (1963). *Aristotle's Ethics*. London: Dent, Everyman's Library.

Wasserman, Danuta (ed.) (2001). *Suicide: An Unnecessary Death*. London: Martin Dunitz.

Weber, Max ([1915a] 1991). 'Religious rejections of the world and their directions', in *From Max Weber: Essays in Sociology*, translated, edited, and with an Introduction by H. H. Gerth and C. Wright Mills, and with a new Preface by Bryan S. Turner. London: Routledge, 323–59.

Weber, Max ([1915b] 1991). 'The social psychology of the world religions', in *From Max Weber: Essays in Sociology*, translated, edited, and with an Introduction by H. H. Gerth and C. Wright Mills, and with a new Preface by Bryan S. Turner. London: Routledge, 267–301.

Weber, Max ([1919] 1991). 'Science as a vocation', in *From Max Weber: Essays in Sociology*, translated, edited, and with an Introduction by H. H. Gerth and C. Wright Mills, and with a new Preface by Bryan S. Turner. London: Routledge, 129–56.

Weber, Max ([1922] 1966). *The Sociology of Religion*, translated by Ephraim Fischoff, Introduction by Talcott Parsons. London: Methuen & Co.

Weber, Max ([c.1910] 1991). 'Structures of power', in *From Max Weber: Essays in Sociology*, translated, edited, and with an Introduction by H. H. Gerth and C. Wright Mills, and with a new Preface by Bryan S. Turner. London: Routledge, 159–79.

West, Ken (2010). *A Guide to Natural Burial*. London: Sweet and Maxwell.

West, Ken (2013). *R. I. P. Off! Or the British Way of Death*. Leicester: Matador.

White, Paul Sayce ([1972] 1988). 'Preface', to Ernesto de Martino ([1972] 1988) *Primitive Magic: The Psychic Powers of Shamans and Sorcerers*. Bridport, Dorset: Prism Press.

White, S. (2005). 'Cremation acts and regulations', in Douglas J. Davies and Lewis Mates (eds) *Encyclopedia of Cremation*. Aldershot: Ashgate, 143.

Whitehouse, Harvey (2004). *Modes of Religiosity*. New York: Altamira Press.

Whittle, Brian and Jean Richie (2005). *Prescription for Murder: The True Story of Harold Shipman.* London: Sphere.

Williams, Mark and Danny Penman (2014). *Mindfulness: A Practical Guide in a Frantic World.* London: Piatkus.

Williams, Mark G. and Jon Kabat-Zinn (eds) (2012). *Mindfulness: Diverse Perspectives on its Meaning, Origins and Application.* London: Routledge.

Williams, R. and M. Oram (1954). *Preface to Film.* London: Film Drama.

Williams, Raymond ([1958] 1961). *Culture and Society 1780–1950.* Harmondsworth: Penguin Books in Association with Chatto and Windus.

Williams, Raymond (1961). *The Long Revolution.* London: Chatto and Windus.

Willmott, Trevor (2014). 'But what of terminal care?' *Church Times*, 11 July, p. 15.

Wilson, A. N. (1991). *C. S. Lewis: A Biography.* London: Flamingo, HarperCollins.

Wilson, B. R. (1970). *Religious Sects.* World University Library, London: Weidenfeld and Nicolson.

Wilson, Colin ([1956] 1963). *The Outsider.* London: Pan Books.

Wolffe, John (1999). 'Responding to national grief: British memorial sermons 1800–1914', *Mortality*, 1 (3): 283–96.

Wolffe, John (2000). *Great Deaths: Grieving, Religion, and Nationhood in Victorian and Edwardian Britain.* Oxford: British Academy and Oxford University Press.

Young, Katherine (2002). 'The memory of the flesh', *Body and Society*, 8 (3): 25–48.

Zijderveld, Anton C. ([1970] 1972). *The Abstract Society.* London: Allen Lane/Penguin Press.

Index

Index